THE FACE MAGAZINE
CULTURE SHIFT

THE FACE
CULTURE

MAGAZINE
SHIFT

NATIONAL PORTRAIT GALLERY, LONDON

CONTENTS

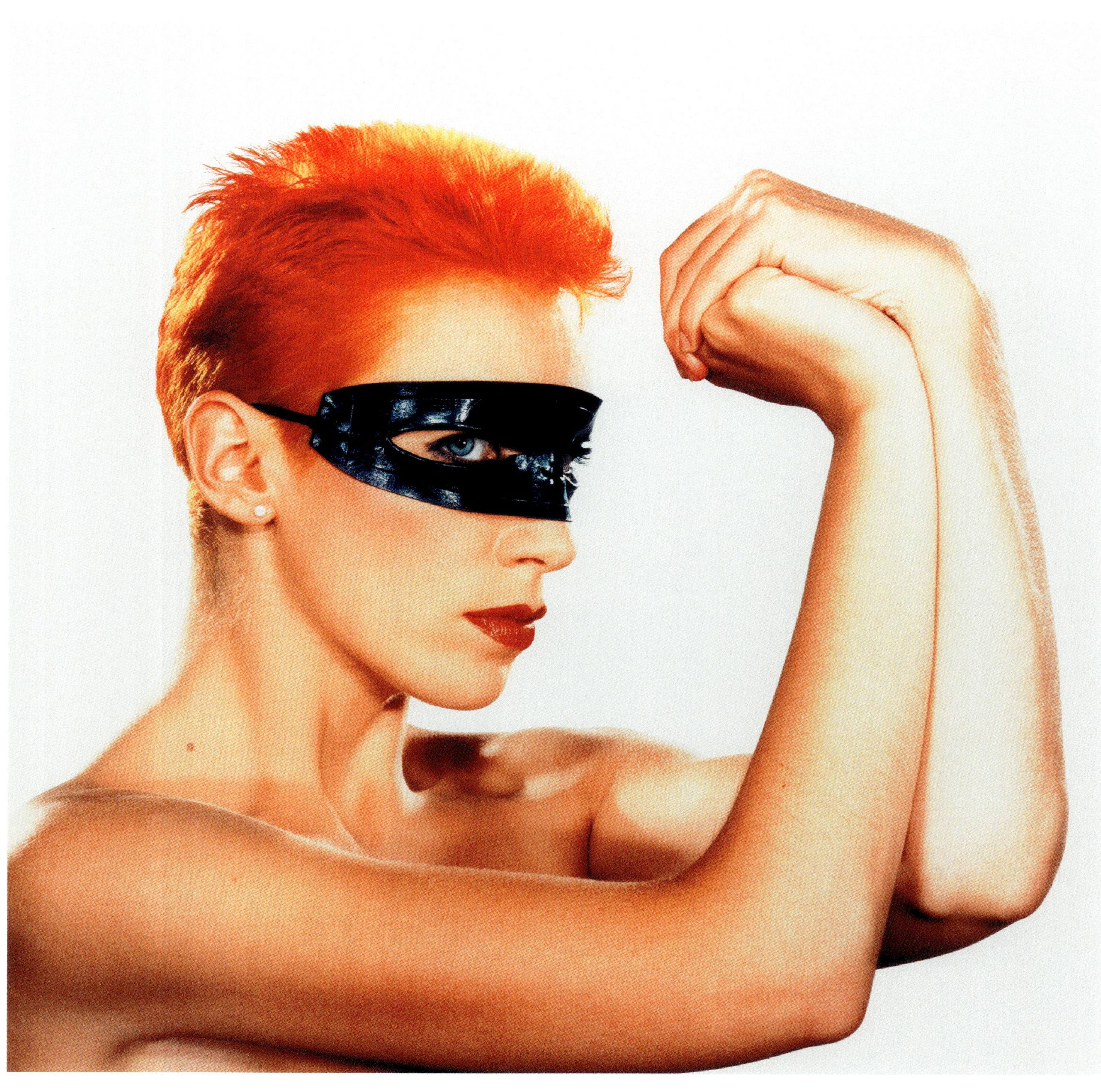

ANNIE LENNOX
By Peter Ashworth
October 1983

FOREWORD

VICTORIA SIDDALL, DIRECTOR, NATIONAL PORTRAIT GALLERY

The thousands of photographs that filled the pages of *The Face* magazine during its first 25 years reveal a publication that stood alone in its desire to empower image makers with the freedom to be truly innovative. These images revolutionised the language of fashion and portrait photography, and many feel as fresh and relevant today as they did back then. *The Face Magazine: Culture Shift* gives a new life to the photographs that appeared on the magazine's pages between 1980 and 2004. It celebrates the work of 83 photographers, depicting sitters ranging from musicians to fashion models, to movie stars, to unknown people on streets and in nightclubs. From its inception, *The Face* was known for usurping the usual hierarchies: if an image was powerful, it could be on the cover, regardless of the status of the sitter or photographer. The magazine's founder, Nick Logan, recalls in this book that: '*The Face* invited people to feel they could be different, be creative and do things that otherwise they couldn't. It opened a window and it encouraged diversity and tolerance.' This inclusive and boundary-pushing ethos, woven into every page of the magazine, is what makes the portraits so resonant now. *The Face* was a trailblazer, beginning a conversation about representation that is still ongoing. The magazine's open-minded attitude led to it launching the careers of countless photographers, models, designers, writers and stylists whose work can be seen here.

The National Portrait Gallery is delighted to be able to celebrate these inspiring images, which document and make visible key moments in culture and history. Alongside their cultural legacy is a technical one, as the photographers experimented with the latest innovations in their work, charting photography's evolution from analogue to digital, exploring and challenging the new possibilities of the medium.

In 2019, *The Face* was relaunched for a new generation, guided by the same principles of nurturing the best emerging talent, to shift culture in new ways. My first thanks are to the magazine's current team for their support and collaboration in enabling this exhibition and publication to reach an even wider audience.

I would like to thank the artists who have generously allowed us to share their photographs, many of which have not been viewed outside the context of the magazine's pages. Behind each image are the sitters, stylists, make-up and hair artists, art directors and designers who conceived, created and presented them. We are grateful to all those who have looked into their archives to retrieve negatives and prints, and to those who have taken the time to tell us their stories.

Finally, I wish to congratulate my colleague Sabina Jaskot-Gill, Senior Curator of Photographs at the National Portrait Gallery, and Curatorial Consultants, photographer Norbert Schoerner and *The Face*'s former Art Director Lee Swillingham, for their tireless work and dedication in sifting through a huge and diverse group of images and expertly shaping it into the exciting and thought-provoking selection we see in the pages of this book. ∎

IMAGES WITH ATTITUDE

PHOTOGRAPHY IN THE FACE

SABINA JASKOT-GILL

In May 1980 a new magazine arrived on British newsstands that would radically change the publishing landscape. *The Face* quickly became a cult magazine that operated outside of the mainstream but proved exceptionally influential in shaping the tastes of the nation's youth. The musicians featured achieved global success; the models it championed became the most famous faces of their time; and its pages launched the careers of many of today's leading names in photography and fashion styling. A trailblazing title, *The Face* didn't just document the contemporary cultural landscape; it played a vital role in creating it.

The Face was founded by Nick Logan, an unassuming titan of magazine publishing who had transformed the fortunes of the *New Musical Express* (*NME*) in the 1970s before successfully launching the teen music magazine, *Smash Hits*. Logan astutely

KIM WILDE
By Davies and Starr
March 1982

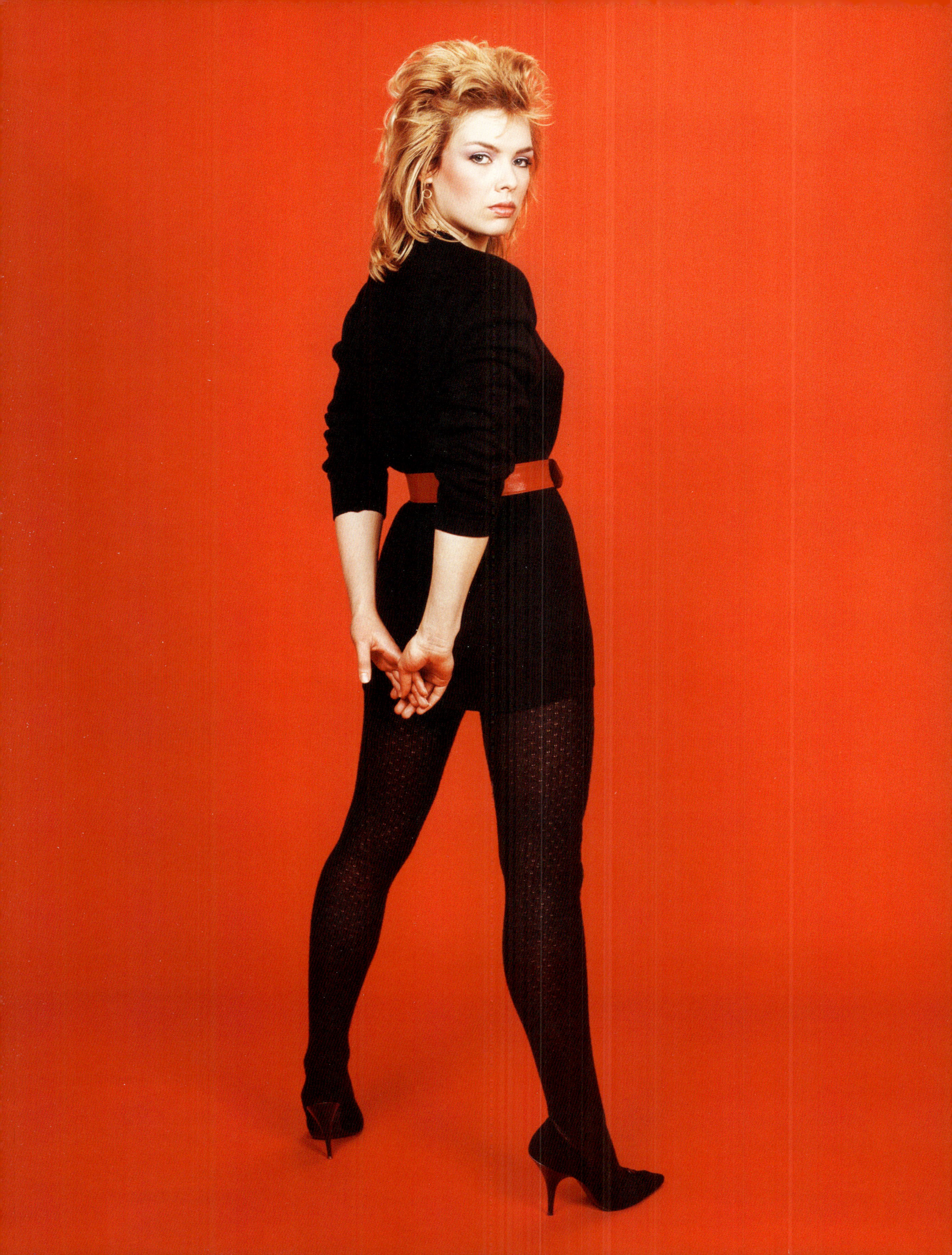

spotted a gap in the market for a monthly title aimed at a youth audience interested in a broad range of subjects — music, fashion, art, film, clubs, politics — that weren't being featured in glossy fashion publications, teen magazines or the music weeklies. In doing so, he invented a new genre of publishing: the style magazine.

The first issue of *The Face* was published the year after Margaret Thatcher was elected Prime Minister, presiding over a country riven with unemployment and social division. At the same time, London's punk movement had created an irrepressible do-it-yourself attitude — 'a mood of can-do optimism and will-do hedonism' that sparked 'a torrent of youth, energy and creativity'.[1] As Neville Brody, the first Art Director of *The Face*, later recalled, 'London was this thriving, humming, inspiring, exciting place to be at that time, where anything was possible.'[2]

Logan launched *The Face* with this punk spirit, using his own savings — a risky manoeuvre, but one that afforded him complete creative freedom. As he later explained, '*The Face* was to be my escape from a career where too often I struggled to explain myself to publishers or committees. No focus groups here: I was purely, wholeheartedly, following instinct.'[3] As an independent publication, with an editor promising creative autonomy, *The Face* attracted the most innovative writers, designers, stylists and photographers of its time.

ROCK'S FINAL FRONTIER

From the outset, Logan envisioned a magazine that celebrated the best of contemporary photography. 'The attraction of *The Face* is that it will be unique as a vehicle for the publication of outstanding photographs of popular rock and pop music artists', his original pitch announced.[4] To differentiate this new monthly magazine from the weekly music publications, Logan placed great emphasis on production values — choosing a larger format and prioritising good quality paper to showcase images to their full potential.

Logan reached out to young photographers he had commissioned at *Smash Hits* and *NME*, asking for colour photography and striking portraiture, rather than run-of-the-mill promotional shots that featured in the music weeklies, or 'inkies'. The list of contributors to the first issue reads as a who's who of the decade's most celebrated music photographers: Peter Ashworth, Janette Beckman, Adrian Boot, Anton Corbijn, Chalkie Davies, Jill Furmanovsky, Mike Laye, Keith Morris, Sheila Rock, Pennie Smith and Virginia Turbett. As Chalkie Davies recalled, 'I think all of us had kept stuff back which didn't fit into the narrow world of the inkies. Those were the photos that Nick was after. He opened a whole new world for us because, up until then, if you shot colour for the music press, which happened very occasionally, it reproduced very badly. Now we had a medium where we could start really working on the way we approached photography.'[5]

The Face's inaugural cover featured Davies's portrait of Jerry Dammers, founder of influential 2 Tone band The Specials, backstage at a gig in Paris. The ethos of The Specials spoke to the type of magazine Logan wanted to create, built around 'potent visual presence, social commentary and multicultural makeup'.[6] Logan acknowledged, 'I knew I could find something more current for a first cover than The Specials. But they embodied everything the magazine aspired to — they had a look, a passion, and great music — so there was never an alternative. In a sentimental way too, I owed 2 Tone a debt for the inspiration to pursue the idea.'[7]

Location shoots dominated in the first year but, from 1981, studios increasingly came to be the setting of choice for portraits. New territory for many of the young photographers, the studio fostered a spirit of unbounded creativity. Shoots were put together on a shoestring, which necessitated creative ingenuity.

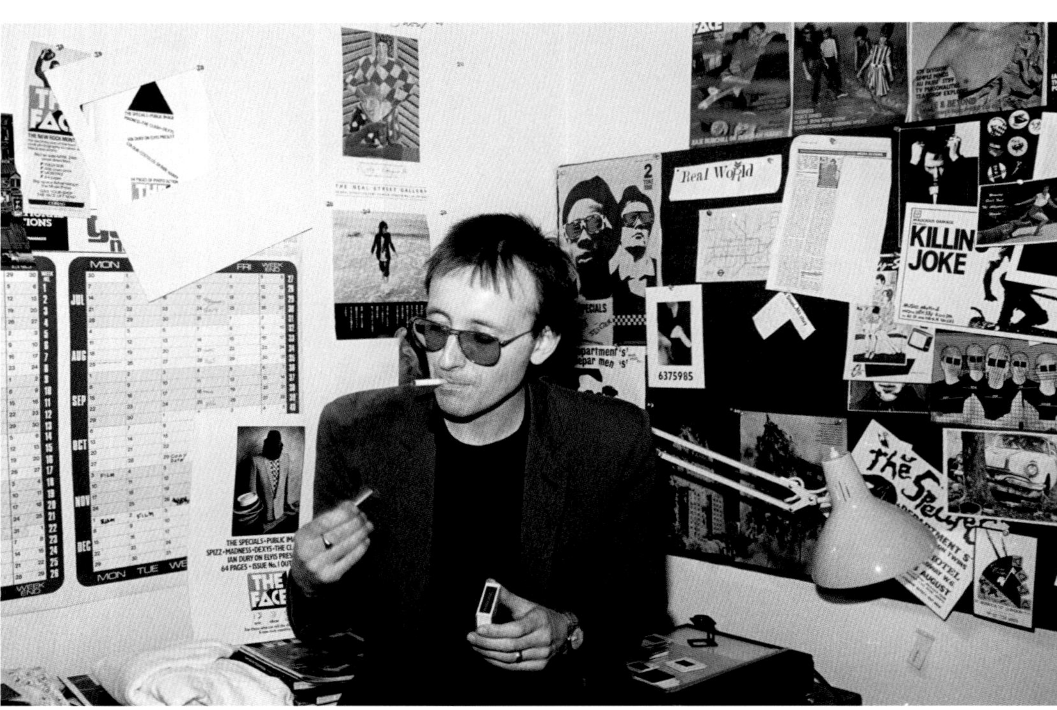

NICK LOGAN
By Sheila Rock
Autumn 1980

JERRY DAMMERS
By Chalkie Davies
May 1980

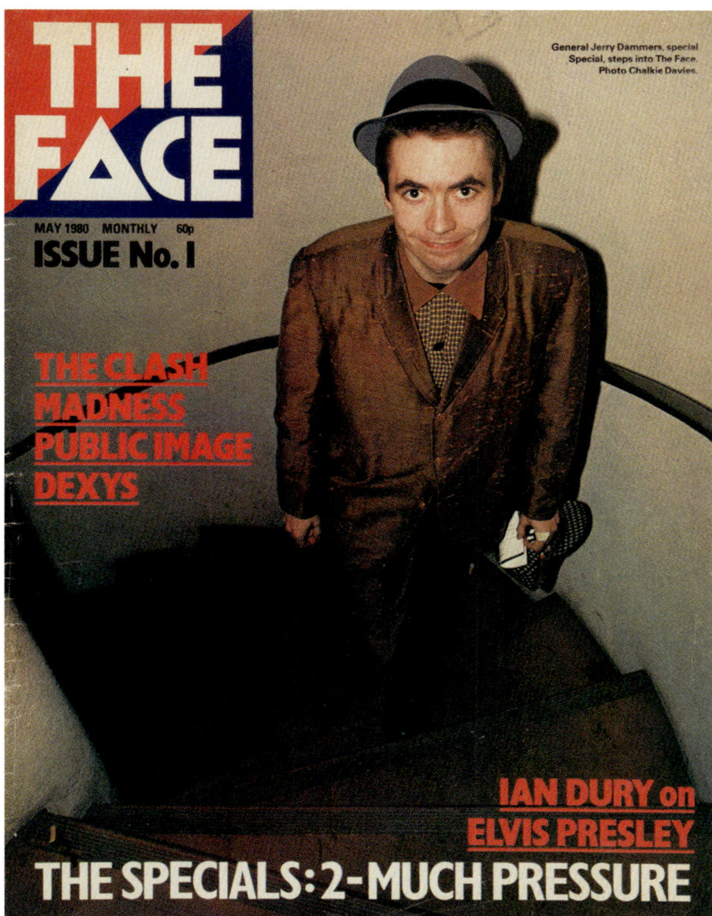

Sheila Rock painted her own backdrops, played with dramatic light and shadow to evoke mood, and experimented with distorting lenses and long exposures to give a sense of movement. Rock recalled, 'The Face in the beginning was like the Wild West. Nick had very little money. He relied on young, energetic creatives, and responded to people with enthusiasm and vision.'[8]

The cover of The Face quickly became the place to be seen and, with popstars clamouring to appear on the magazine's pages, Logan could afford to be selective. As Davies recalled, 'No-one could get Kim Wilde for an afternoon – but she did it for The Face. The photographers put out the idea that it was a magazine where you could be taken seriously – photographically but also journalistically.'[9] Increasingly, the portraits published in the magazine became the images by which music stars were defined.

While Logan prioritised innovative portraiture, the design of the magazine was equally important to his vision, and he sought out the best new talent here too. Neville Brody was a young graphic designer who had quickly become known for his avant-garde record sleeves. He had no experience of designing for magazines but – much like the photographers who were exploring new approaches in the studio – Brody used the magazine as an opportunity to disrupt conventions, noting, 'The Face was a living laboratory where I could experiment and have it published. Our golden rule was to question everything.'[10]

Brody introduced a new graphic style that integrated photography within experimental layouts and hand-drawn typefaces.

'I was using The Face as a platform to explore new ways of doing layout,' he later recalled, 'thinking about typography and how to use images in media – crop them differently, place them in different places, use juxtaposition to bring out new stories.'[11] Brody's cover crops were particularly radical, pushing images to their extremes. As Rock recognised, Brody's brilliance lay in the way he 'thought beyond portraiture'.[12] His approach not only defined the magazine's visual identity in the Eighties, it inspired the design aesthetic of the decade. Photographer Nick Knight acknowledged, 'That was really where [the magazine] shot to fame – it looked so good. If you look that great, that sharp, you attract a lot of people wanting to be in it.'[13]

Brody's September 1982 cover featured a closely cropped pair of ripped jeans, worn by Sade's manager, Lee Barrett, and photographed by Rock. The cover was a prelude to an article by Robert Elms which observed a 'hardening of attitudes in music and fashion' that reflected the difficult economic situation in Britain under Thatcher's Conservative government where unemployment was rife and heroin use was on the rise.[14] For Elms, the cover marked a new era for the magazine, 'This was the end of the first period of The Face when it had been a kind of "music mag plus". From here on in, music was just one part of a much broader spectrum.'[15]

THE WORLD'S BEST DRESSED MAGAZINE

From May 1980, when the first issue was published on a prayer, The Face *struggled for more than 18 months to find its feet … But what we had, it dawned on us as we inched towards commercial viability, was the rare chance to do something daring. By 1982,* The Face *was poised to break free of its roots in the music press and explore an altogether wider universe.* – Nick Logan [16]

The magazine initially billed itself as 'Rock's Final Frontier' but, by the end of the first year, it boldly proclaimed itself 'The World's Best Dressed Magazine'. 'There had always been fashion in The Face,' Logan acknowledged, 'implicit in the way we photographed and presented musicians.'[17] The name he had chosen for the magazine already indicated this: Sixties mod subculture coined the term 'face' to describe 'someone with the right clothes, the right haircut, and the right taste in soul music and ska'.[18] Logan had come from north London's mod scene and The Face manifested his interest not just in the musicians of the time, but also his appreciation for the clothes that they were wearing – 'the fashion end of music.'[19]

London's music scene was thriving, with musicians increasingly

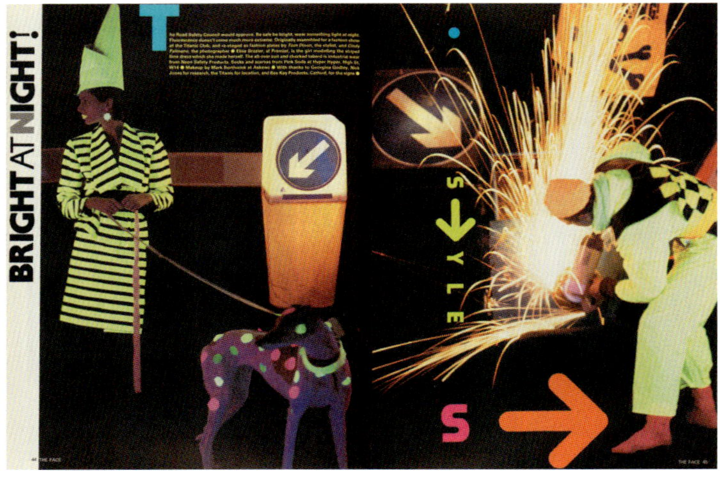

revered as style icons. Logan quickly aligned his magazine with the nascent new romantic scene, playing out in the capital's clubs, in which music and fashion were intertwined. Elms's November 1980 article, 'The Cult with No Name', described 'a colourful, exotic world which has set the styles to be copied in terms of both look and sound'.[20] Derek Ridgers photographed the key players of the scene, including Boy George, Marilyn and Steve Strange, and the flamboyant outfits they were fashioning.

At the same time, music photographers began to produce fashion stories, which they conceived and directed themselves, mostly featuring musicians. As Davies acknowledged, 'they were the only people that we knew, so we used them for shoots.'[21] Logan recalled, 'I'd had a bit of a dilemma over the photographs … of musicians posed in new fashions … What heading did they come under? I didn't want to use "fashion". That had connotations that didn't fit what we were doing, which was more from the street, so might prejudice readers who were only used to [fashion] appearing in places like *Vogue* or in women's magazines. "Style" seemed right.'[22]

From 1983, a new approach to fashion photography emerged, as a fresh fleet of photographers began to work for the magazine, including Robert Erdmann, Andrew Macpherson, Jamie Morgan and Mario Testino. In contrast to the music photographers who were honing their skills on the job, these new names had received more formal training in the fashion industry.

In addition, photographers increasingly began to collaborate with a new kind of contributor: the stylist. Morgan initiated this change, working with both Ray Petri and Helen Roberts in 1983; the following year, Caroline Baker, a noted fashion editor who had made her name at *Nova* magazine in the Sixties, began styling shoots with Testino and Erdmann; while fashion designers emerging from the London club scene, including Judy Blame and Stephen Linard, also turned their hand to styling. This changed the dynamic of the shoots, with photographers and stylists

BRIGHT AT NIGHT!
By Cindy Palmano
Styled by Tom Dixon
April 1984

collaborating to conceive increasingly ambitious and innovative fashion stories.

In 1985 an exhibition was held at The Photographers' Gallery in London celebrating five years of the magazine's trailblazing photography. Reflecting on this moment, writer David Brittain observed, 'the photography press became very interested in *The Face* because it seemed to represent something that had been forgotten: magazines as patrons of interesting, innovative photography.'[23]

BUFFALO: LOOKING GOOD'S A STATE OF MIND

As a team, talking up madcap ideas, talking up maverick pictures, taking risks and daring us to do the same, they were irresistible … Could we run this stuff? How could we not? – Nick Logan [24]

The stylist who had the most significant influence on the magazine was Ray Petri, or Stingray to his friends, whose collaborations with Jamie Morgan would take fashion at *The Face* to a new level. Petri brought a distinct approach to styling men's fashion, showing an irreverence to established codes of masculinity, and forging a new sensibility that was simultaneously camp, tough and, most importantly, cool.

Petri placed less emphasis on designer fashion and, instead, drew inspiration from an eclectic range of visual references to create looks that incorporated sportswear, classic tailoring, items from army surplus stores and vintage accessories. An early fashion story from May 1984 included the instruction: 'Read these pages as IDEAS rather than designer garments.'[25] For Petri, style was about attitude; it was not just about the clothes you wore, but how you chose to wear them.

Generous and charismatic, Petri did not work alone, but assembled a group of west London creatives – his tightknit 'Buffalo' family – who would all feature in or contribute to *The Face*. From diverse backgrounds, the group members were united by a shared love of music – in particular reggae, soul and R&B – and a common approach to style. Petri explained how the group adopted the name Buffalo because it characterised their attitude, 'It's a Caribbean expression to describe people who are rude boys or rebels. Not necessarily tough, but hard style taken from the street.'[26]

During photoshoots, Petri managed the styling and the ambience – playing music, loading cameras, shaping and pinning clothes between frames – while Morgan focused on the technical aspects. They worked in the studio, with sophisticated lighting and a clean backdrop, which gave prominence to the nuances of Petri's styling and subtle choreography, through which he carefully manipulated his models into position. The refinement of Morgan's photographs made Petri's radical styling all the more powerful.

Their first cover ran in January 1984: a key moment in the magazine's history, when the fashion, the photography and the discovery of a new face all coalesced to create an iconic image that defined a new zeitgeist. The cover featured the model, Nick Kamen, sporting a Puma hat with aviator sunglasses, zinced-out

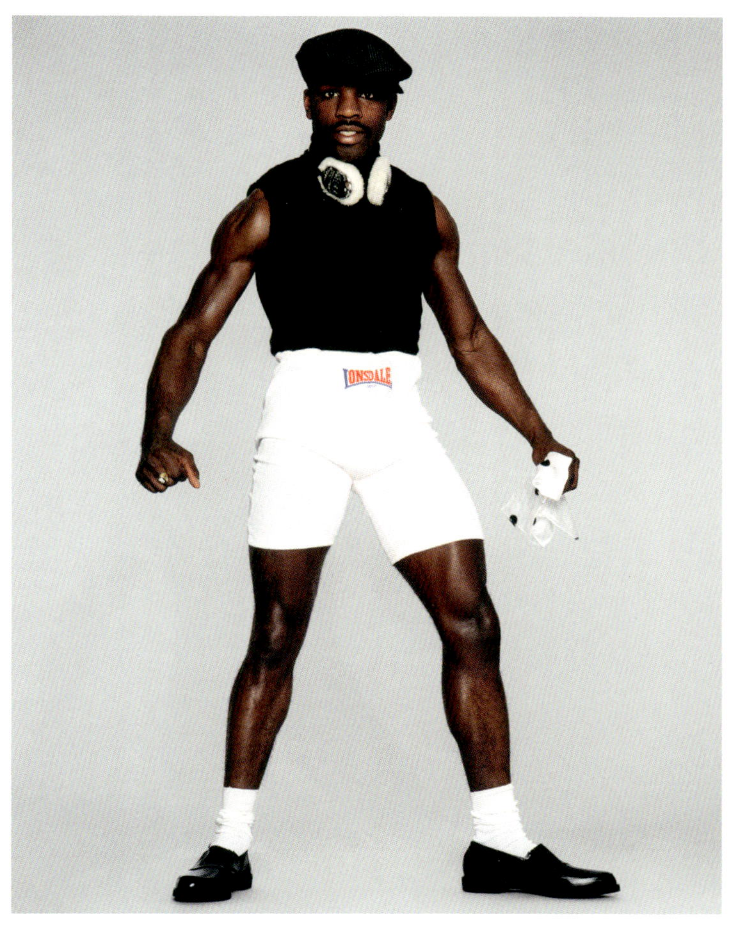

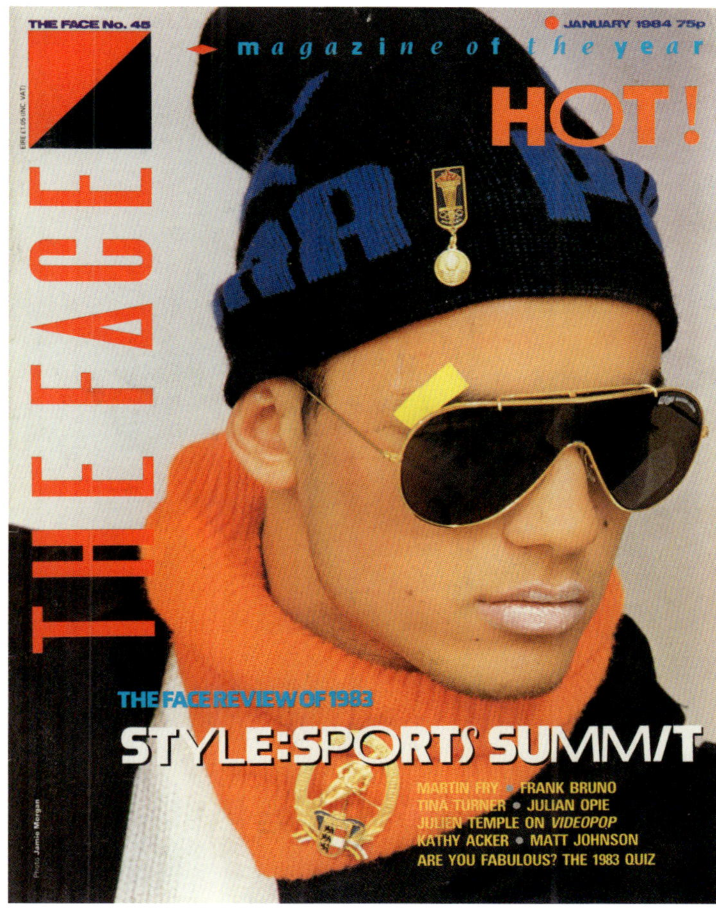

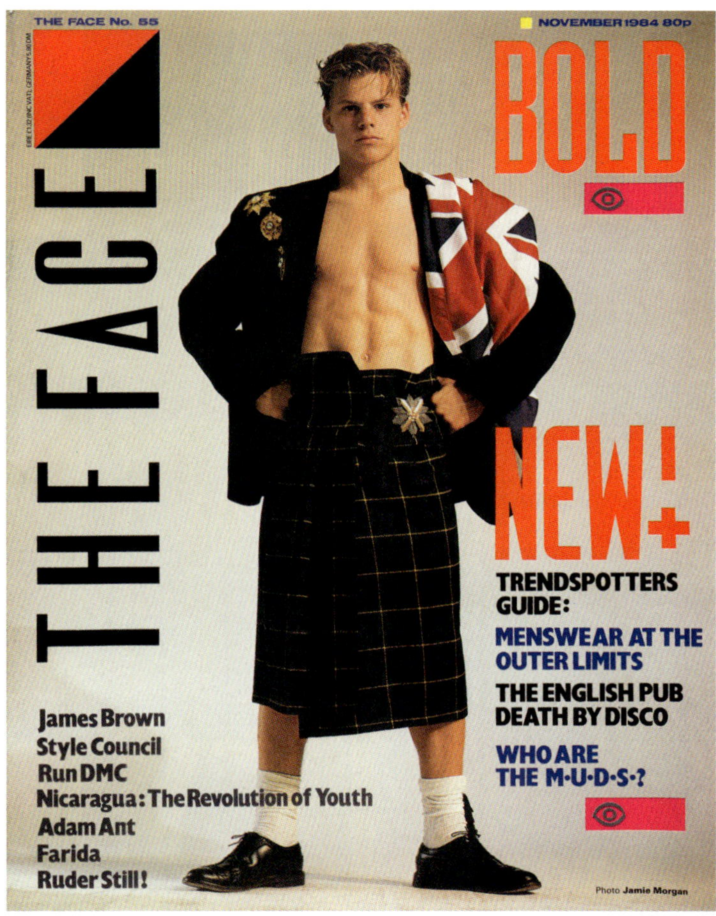

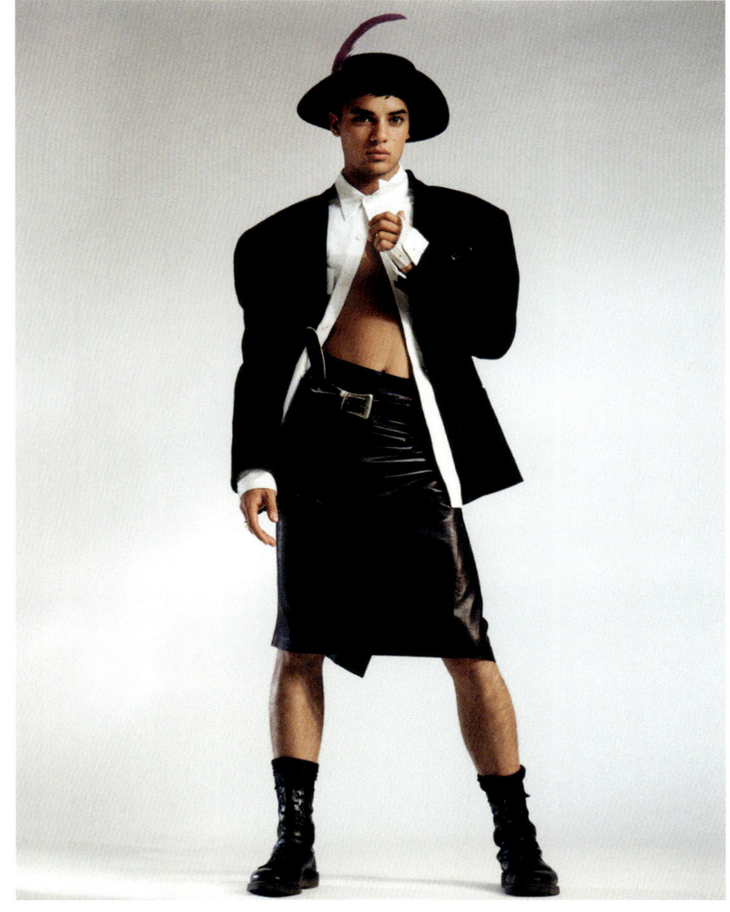

Clockwise from top left

FLOAT LIKE A BUTTERFLY
By Jamie Morgan
Styled by Ray Petri
June 1985

WINTER SPORTS
By Jamie Morgan
Styled by Ray Petri
January 1984

MEN'S WHERE?
By Jamie Morgan
Styled by Ray Petri
November 1984

MEN'S WHERE?
By Jamie Morgan
Styled by Ray Petri
November 1984

lips, a Benetton jumper and vintage brooches. The yellow plaster over Kamen's eyebrow was a styling note Petri often utilised, a reference to boxing.

This was one of the first 'style' images that Logan ran on the cover – a commercial risk but a bold statement about the direction of his magazine, made all the more radical by the fashion it featured: affordable, high-street clothes. 'I struggle to recognise the editor who presided over it,' Logan later admitted. 'I can't imagine now what readers thought when they saw it on the bookstalls, this fuck-off image from another planet!'[27]

Petri and Morgan's images were radical not just because of the fashion they presented, but also because of the models they featured. 'The important thing in good styling is casting,' Petri confided to *The Face* in 1985. 'Once you have the right face, it all falls into place.'[28] British-Burmese brothers Nick and Barry Kamen were discovered by Petri on a casting at Holborn Studios in London, struggling to find work at a time when few opportunities arose for diverse models. Within two years of appearing on the cover of *The Face*, Nick Kamen was starring in an iconic Levi's 501 advertising campaign, undressing in a laundrette.

Other models were street-cast: martial-arts champion Tony Felix was scouted at The Standard, a restaurant in Westbourne Grove; Simon de Montford was discovered in Mayfair

nightclub Legends; champion boxer Clinton MacKenzie was spotted at Thomas A Becket gym on the Old Kent Road. Petri created space for black models at a time when they were rarely visible in the fashion industry. Buffalo member and musician Neneh Cherry concluded, 'Ray was radical. It was the first time black male beauty was allowed to be admired.'[29]

Petri redefined men's fashion within the pages of Logan's magazine, and his unique approach and attitude made *The Face* the decade's most significant chronicler of style. While his influence lived on in the work of subsequent generations, Petri's career was cut tragically short due to his death from an AIDS-related illness in 1989. His obituary in *The Face* read:

At its most prosaic, a stylist is the person on a fashion shoot who selects the clothes for the models. Ray Petri was never prosaic, and 'styling' was always an inadequate term to describe what it was he excelled at. Ray used clothes to create a mood, to construct an 'attitude', and in so doing he defined the look of men's fashion in the Eighties.[30]

THE BATTLE FOR PLANET FASHION

Logan later conceded 'we unwittingly helped invent the term "Style Press"', and as a result the magazine began to attract 'photographers looking for creative licence unattainable elsewhere'.[31] Robin Derrick took over from Brody as Art Director at *The Face*, having joined from *i-D* magazine in November 1984. He sourced inspiration from London clubs, bringing a new fashion set to the magazine and commissioning increasingly subversive fashion and portrait photography from his contemporaries. 'Everything was very collaborative. Fuelled by naivety and poverty. We were all broke and on the dole', Derrick recalled.[32]

The second half of the decade proved to be a fertile time for photographic experimentation – both in-camera, playing with distortion and focus, and in the darkroom. Techniques such as cross-processing – where a photograph is developed in the wrong chemical solution to produce dramatic colour shifts and increase contrast – were popularised by master printer Brian Dowling at BDI Colour Lab, and utilised by photographers to imbue their images with altered colours and heightened ambience.

In September 1987 Phil Bicker assumed the role of Art Director and encouraged work by emerging photographic talent including Andy Bettles, Stéphane Sednaoui, Nigel Shafran and Juergen Teller. Bicker acknowledged, 'I knew I couldn't compete in terms of Neville's typographic legacy – I determined to build my approach around supporting and championing new

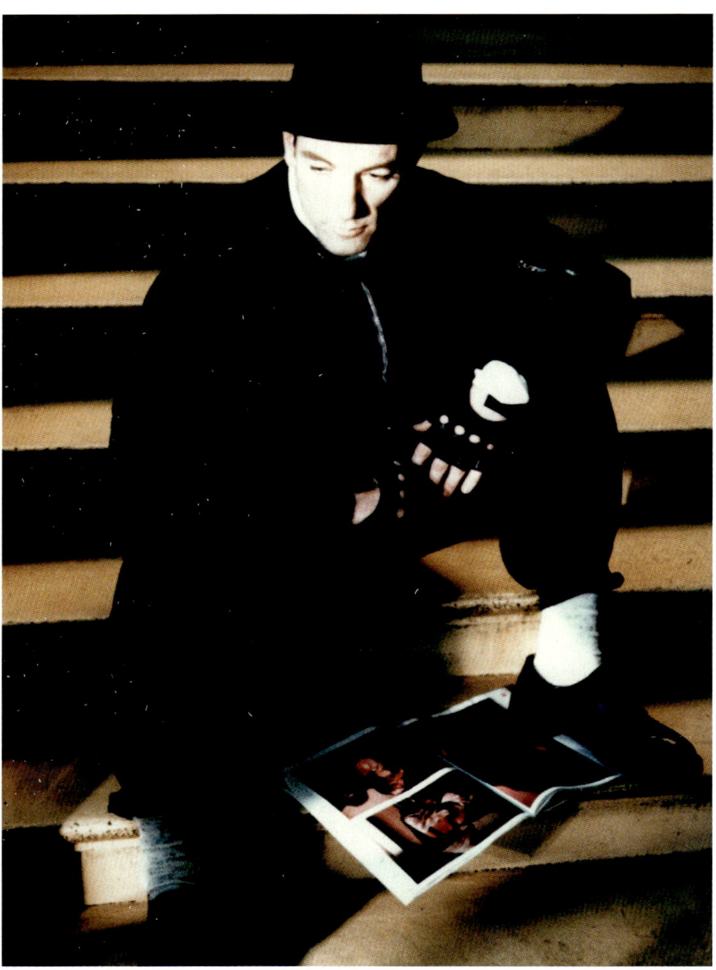

photography.'[33] The mood was beginning to shift, as was the soundtrack of the moment, led by cutting-edge British stars such as Jazzie B, Bomb the Bass, Neneh Cherry and S'Xpress. All had been championed by the magazine in the late Eighties, culminating in the November 1989 feature 'Drop the Bomb', which celebrated the increasing global influence of British dance music.

The decade closed with a 24-page fashion spectacle produced by French photographer and filmmaker Stéphane Sednaoui and Fashion Editor Babeth Djian, in which 'Fashion Heroes' Azzedine Alaïa, Jean Paul Gaultier, Thierry Mugler, Martine Sitbon and Vivienne Westwood fought to save the world of fashion from the dangers of conformity. It took Sednaoui more than two months to complete the story: individual portraits were photographed separately, meticulously cut out and arranged into collages on glass, then rephotographed with luminous haloes traced during long exposures. Significantly, the story marked Sednaoui's first use of digital technologies. He used Quantel Paintbox to scan and duplicate the hand-collaged figures – the first tentative steps into the world of digital post-production, which would be built upon by a new generation of photographers at the magazine in the Nineties.

ENGLAND'S DREAMING

The late Eighties and early Nineties saw a new lease of life for the magazine. The arrival of acid house music and the subsequent explosion of rave culture in warehouses and fields across the country, together with new music scenes emerging in Bristol and Manchester, were revolutionising youth culture. Recalling the 1967 Summer of Love in San Francisco, the music scene in the UK offered an opportunity to bring people together. One commentator described 'a euphoric high that lasted a year and a half and engulfed Britain's youth in a hedonistic haze of peace, love and unity'.[34] Sheryl Garratt, soon to take the helm as the magazine's Editor, recognised this could give *The Face* a new sense of direction. She recalled, 'Acid house had turned clubland day-glo, British dance music was exploding, fashion was finding exciting new directions, and it just felt as if *The Face* was needed.'[35]

A new generation of photographers whose work reflected this new mood – Corinne Day, Glen Luchford, Nigel Shafran, David Sims – began to coalesce around the magazine, championed by Bicker. Sims observed, 'People were already changing their attitude towards the way they were dressing and socialising, and there were a lot of social structures that were eradicated for a short period of time. Rave culture made it all possible – we were just creating a visual to accompany that.'[36] Bicker was seeking photographers who could present fashion in a new way, for a new audience. 'It was a very fertile time,' he later recalled. 'Everybody was quite young and they were all new to photography. They didn't have fully formed identities and I thought *The Face* was a good place for them to experiment.'[37]

Stylists Malcolm Beckford, Adam Howe, Karl Templer and Derick Procope brought a new focus on casual youth style, while Melanie Ward often made and customised clothes herself. 'A chill wind is blowing through the houses of fashion,'

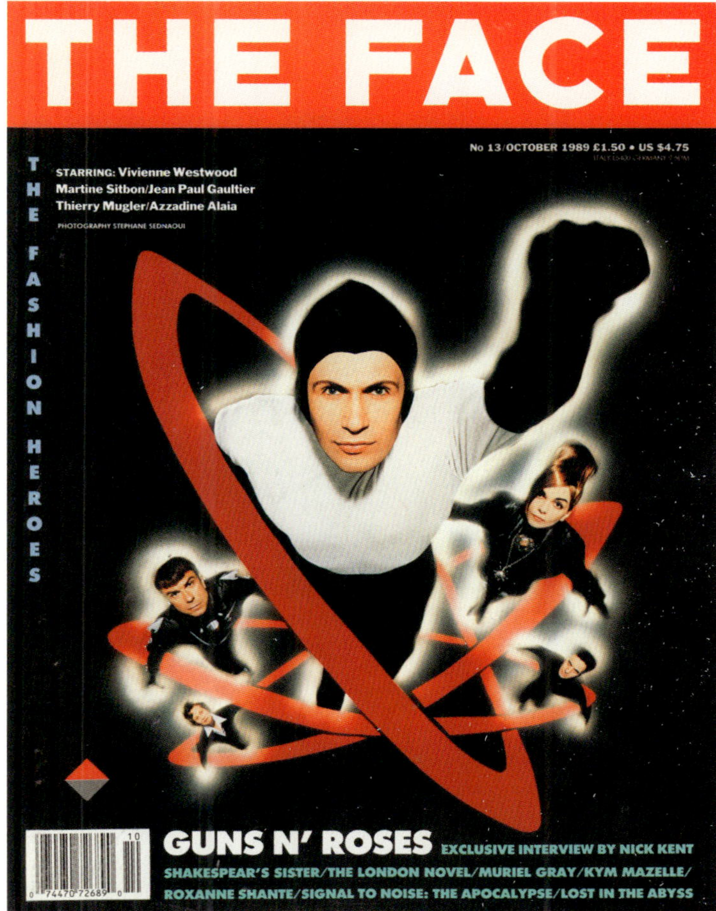

The Face declared in March 1990, 'The prevailing statement now is understatement.'[38]

These photographers and stylists shared an interest in authenticity, a desire to incorporate 'real life' into their images – the antithesis of commercial fashion photography, with its impossibly glamorous supermodels and elaborate shoots. As stylist Simon Foxton noted, 'The style of photography that had been prevalent up until then just felt very manufactured, very laboured, very hands on and untouchable and then, suddenly, there were pictures of people who looked like your next-door neighbours.'[39]

Shafran's photographs inaugurated this new approach in the magazine. His images, which situated his sitters within London's post-industrial landscapes, read more as documentary photographs than fashion images. A 1989 shoot, published to mark 20 years since the moon landing, blended sci-fi with suburbia. One image, styled by Ward, featured her six-year-old brother posed outside the Safeway supermarket in Finsbury Park. Shafran later said, 'I never really considered myself a fashion photographer … I wanted to put real people and issues into magazines.'[40]

Collectively, this new school of London photographers – often labelled 'grunge' or 'anti-fashion' – were radically disrupting fashion photography, but each had their own nuances of style and

RAY PETRI
By Jean Baptiste Mondino
Styled by Ray Petri
1986

THE FASHION HEROES
By Stéphane Sednaoui
Styled by Carlos Taylor
and Rommel Wilson
October 1989

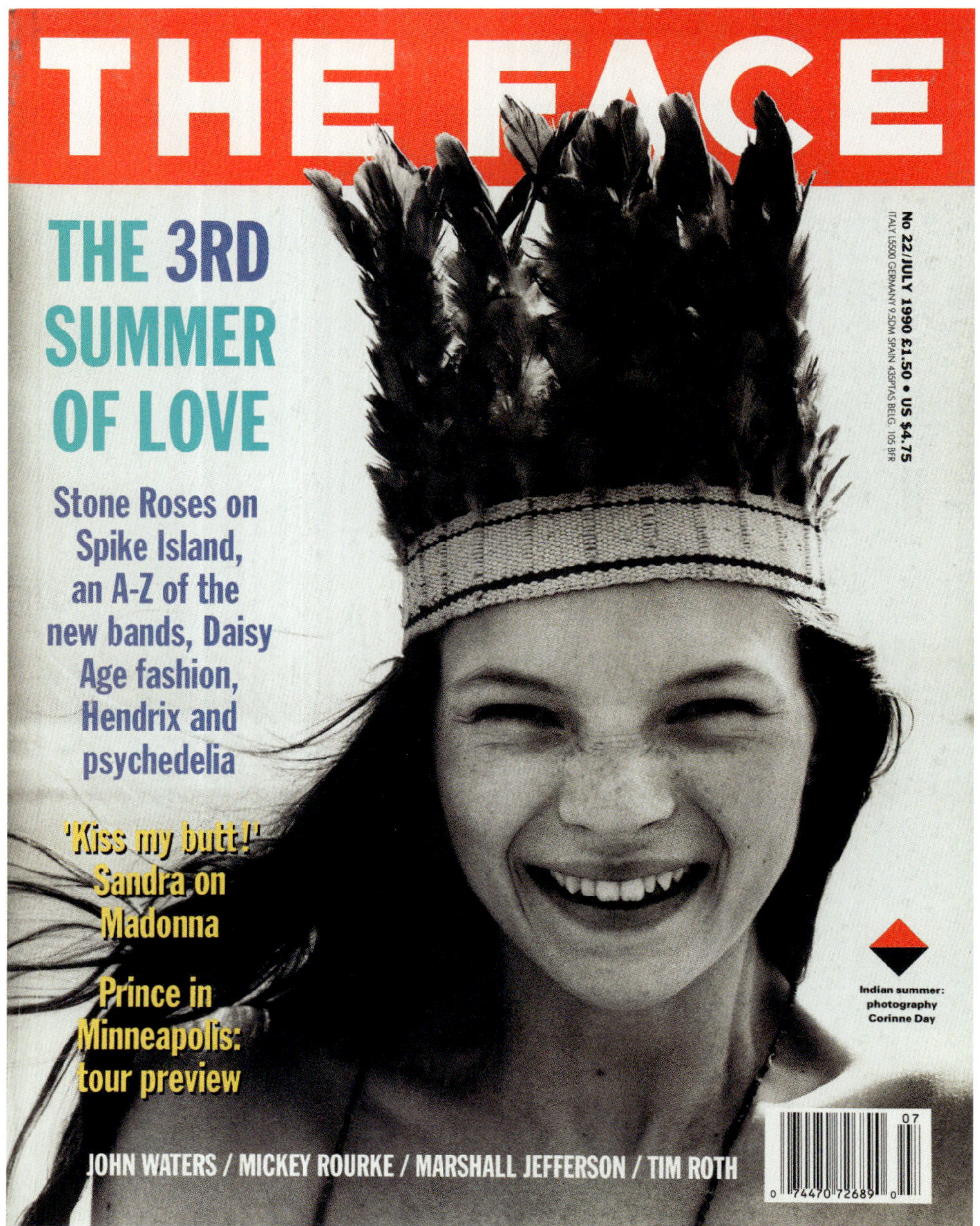

Fashion magazines had been selling sex and glamour for far too long. I wanted to instil some reality into a world of fantasy.

CORINNE DAY, PHOTOGRAPHER

THE DAISY AGE
By Corinne Day
Styled by Melanie Ward
July 1990

approach. Sims's early shoots for *The Face* were photographed in daylight, with no hair styling or make-up, and explored new ways of posing in an attempt to think 'beyond the usual parameters' of a fashion picture.[41] His point of reference was the portraiture of Richard Avedon, whose ability to convey 'character and a certain kind of spirit' he sought to emulate.[42] In contrast, Luchford experimented with different photographic formats, using an 8×10 inch plate camera or 35mm film, and increasingly took inspiration from American photojournalism to create environmental images imbued with cinematic narratives.

The models in their pictures also challenged mainstream fashion stereotypes. Sims featured unconventional male models; for the story 'Modern Love', Luchford photographed Filipino designer Zaldy Goco in androgynous drag; and a new generation of women, including Emma Balfour, Rosemary Ferguson, Kate Moss, Sarah Murray and Lorraine Pascale, looked very different to the supermodels dominating the covers of *Vogue*. As stylist Anna Cockburn recalled, 'It felt like the beginning of a recognition that ... the standard of beauty needed to be more flexible.'[43]

It was Day who brought Moss to the attention of *The Face*. She showed a photograph of a then unknown model from south London to Bicker, who immediately saw something in Moss. 'I had been looking for a model who reflected the demographic of our readership and projected the spirit of the magazine,' Bicker recounted. 'I knew at once I had found her. I realised she was the face of *The Face*.'[44] The cover of the July 1990 issue – featuring a joyful-looking 16-year-old Moss, grinning out at the viewer from a cold and windy beach on Britain's south coast – launched the careers of both Moss and Day.

Moss has since acknowledged the discomfort she felt at undressing and exposing herself before Day's lens, but she none-theless imbued the photographs with personality and emotional authenticity. Day shot in black and white – she was a young, self-taught photographer with no experience of working with colour film – and Ward's styling felt natural and believable for a teen-ager: plaited hair, daisy chains, Birkenstocks. The photographs appeared spontaneous, irreverent, full of optimism and energy for the new decade. For Bicker, the images perfectly 'embodied a new attitude and spirit for the age'.[45]

Three years later, Day's story 'England's Dreaming', set in the photographer's London flat, featured Rosemary Ferguson lying languidly on a sofa, watching daytime television, surrounded by dirty coffee mugs and used ashtrays. Day recalled, 'I was broke, still on the dole … I wasn't recording anything more than the way we were living.'[46] Ferguson concurred, 'We were all the same age, and all friends, and that's how it worked. It was like hanging out with extended family … it felt collaborative.'[47] Comparisons are frequently drawn between Day's work and that of American photographer Nan Goldin, in particular *The Ballad of Sexual Dependency* (1986), which candidly documented Goldin's friends. For American writer Glenn O'Brien, however, Day's work owes more of a debt to Seventies punk, 'She was sort of to fashion what The Clash were to rock – socially revolutionary, anti-snob, idealistic, funny, blunt.'[48]

'England's Dreaming' shares its title with Jon Savage's 1991 novel about the history of punk in London: a tale of ordinary young people, bored with suburban Britain, telling their truth to the establishment.[49] This group of young photographers appeared to pick up that mantle. Their images represented a powerful moment of youth rebellion in British photography – a statement about life in early Nineties Britain, marked by unemployment, poll tax riots and economic recession. The strapline to Day's fashion story read: 'This Is the Modern World'.[50]

This approach to fashion photography, forged in the pages of *The Face*, changed the zeitgeist. Initially many commentators were unable to comprehend the casting, styling or aesthetic, but the work of these photographers was quickly assimilated into the mainstream. It also coincided with 'one of the golden ages of journalism', according to Features Editor Amy Raphael.[51] Before the rise of the publicist and the PR machine, writers and photographers were allowed unfettered access to the biggest names of the day, resulting in some iconic covers. One of the most memorable was Sims's 1993 portrait of Kurt Cobain from American grunge band Nirvana, dressed in a floral tea dress and sporting kohl-rimmed eyes.

Having photographed fashion stories for *The Face* since 1987, Juergen Teller arrived at his now-signature style in the early Nineties, when he began to use a low-fi, verité aesthetic to transform celebrity portraiture. He offered an alternative gaze on the faces of the day by picturing celebrities with a frankness and honesty that would have been unimaginable only a few years before.

WILD TECHNICOLOR FUTURISM

In 1993, Conservative Prime Minister John Major was evoking a vision of Britain as the country of long shadows on cricket grounds, warm beer, green suburbs and 'old maids bicycling to Holy Communion through the morning mist'.[52] This seemed a long way from the Britain of *The Face*. Rave culture lived on in the 'free party' movement, organised by collectives such as Spiral Tribe, sparking parliamentary outrage and amendments to the 1994 Criminal Justice and Public Order Act, which famously banned parties of more than ten people from playing 'a succession of repetitive beats', and forced the free party movement into Europe. In its place came the rise of regional super-clubs and festivals, and the commercialisation of mainstream dance culture, documented by the photographs of Elaine Constantine and Ewen Spencer.

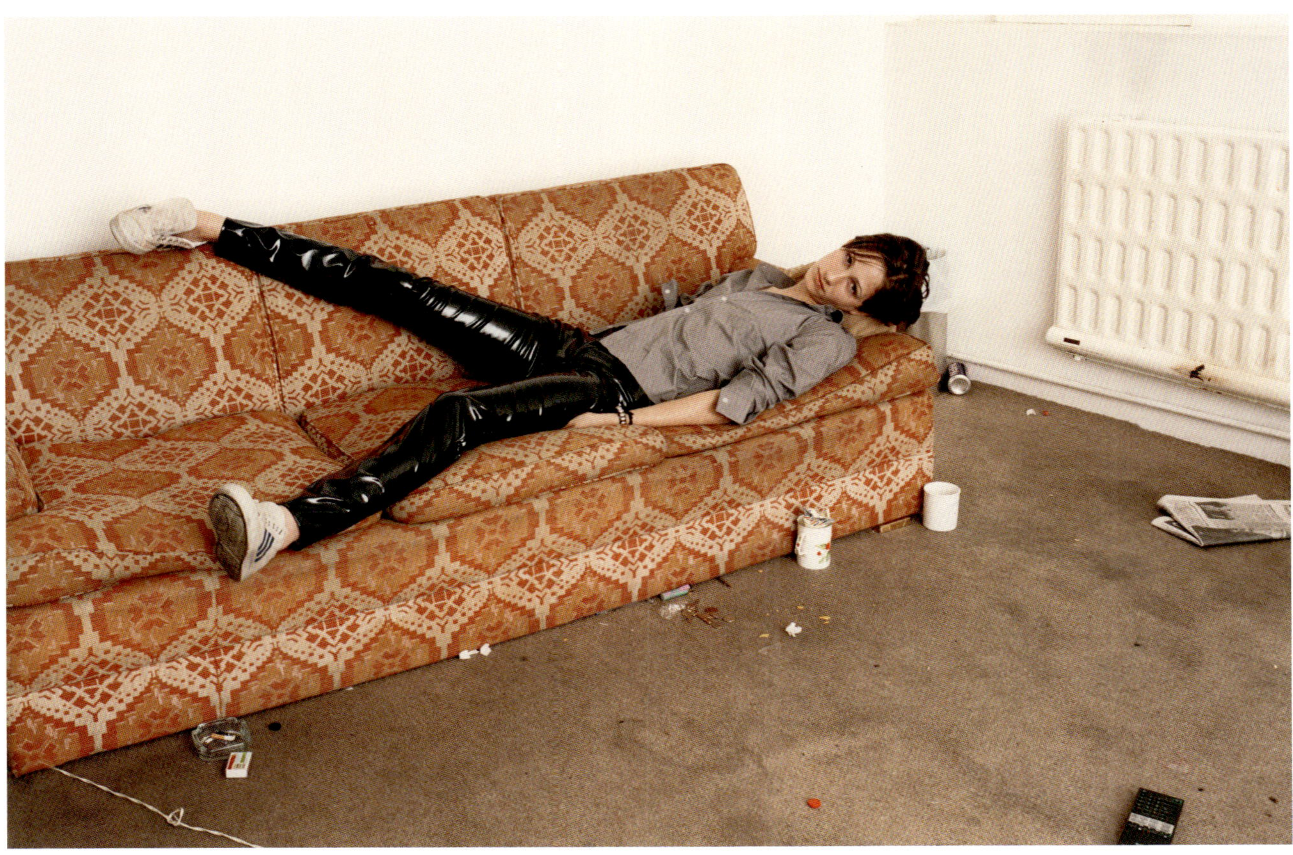

ENGLAND'S DREAMING
By Corinne Day
Styled by
Melanie Ward
August 1993

By the mid-Nineties, an explosion of different photographic approaches and styles had emerged, and a new vibrant mood had seeped into the pages of *The Face*, far removed from the black and white realism of Shafran and Day. As curator Charlotte Cotton concluded, it marked a 're-establishment of glamorous fashion photography, albeit with a contemporary twist'.[53]

Innovation was spearheaded by the magazine's new Art Director, Lee Swillingham. 'The culture was changing; music, art and cinema were evolving', he recalled, 'I was young but steeped in the magazine's history, and knew that it was the perfect time for *The Face* to visually change gears again. I was seeing incredible photographic talent in London and further afield, and I wanted to offer these image-makers a platform.'[54]

Swillingham recognised that the advances in digital post-production presented by image-manipulation and computer graphics programs such as Quantel Paintbox and Photoshop were offering photographers a new age of creative potential. Art Editor Stuart Spalding noted, 'We were at the forefront of using Quantel Paintbox, which was for high-end advertising campaigns, but we encouraged photographers to work with it for our editorial. We all take digital manipulation for granted now, but then it was a bit of a call moving away from the traditional ways of presenting clothes.'[55]

Together, they actively collaborated with photographers to conceive and develop ideas for shoots that could harness these tools to spur innovation and keep *The Face* at the vanguard of fashion publishing. Swillingham recognised, 'We weren't using technology for the sake of it; we were using it to create a new visual language.'[56]

For some, the advent of new post-production technologies generated anxiety around the truthfulness of the photographic image, stemming from an enduring – albeit naïve – belief that photography could offer an accurate depiction of the world. Digital technologies liberated photography from this function, and shifted the photographer's role from image-taker to image-maker: rather than capturing a single decisive moment, the photograph became the starting point from which to manipulate an image, visualise a concept and build a narrative.

For photography duo Inez van Lamsweerde and Vinoodh Matadin, it was time for a changing of the guard: 'It was just what people wanted to see: colourful, hyperrealistic work.'[57] Introduced to Quantel Paintbox in 1991, they had been early adopters and quickly recognised that it could be a creative tool for their work. 'Suddenly, there were no limits.'[58] For their April 1994 story, 'For Your Pleasure', models were photographed in the studio by Lamsweerde, wearing fashion styled by Matadin, then digitally montaged onto vividly coloured stock slides from image libraries.

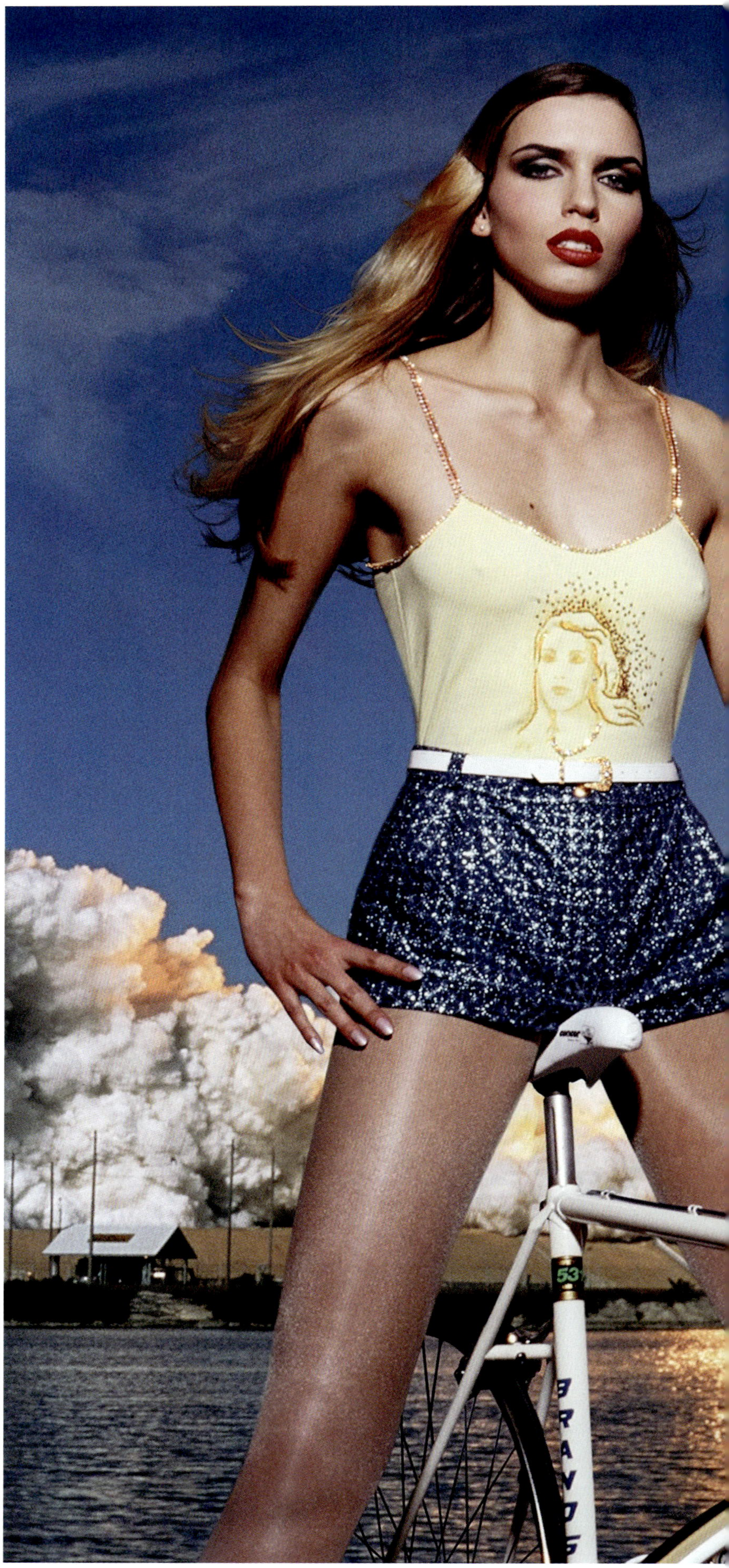

FOR YOUR PLEASURE
Photographed and styled by
Inez & Vinoodh
April 1994

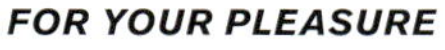

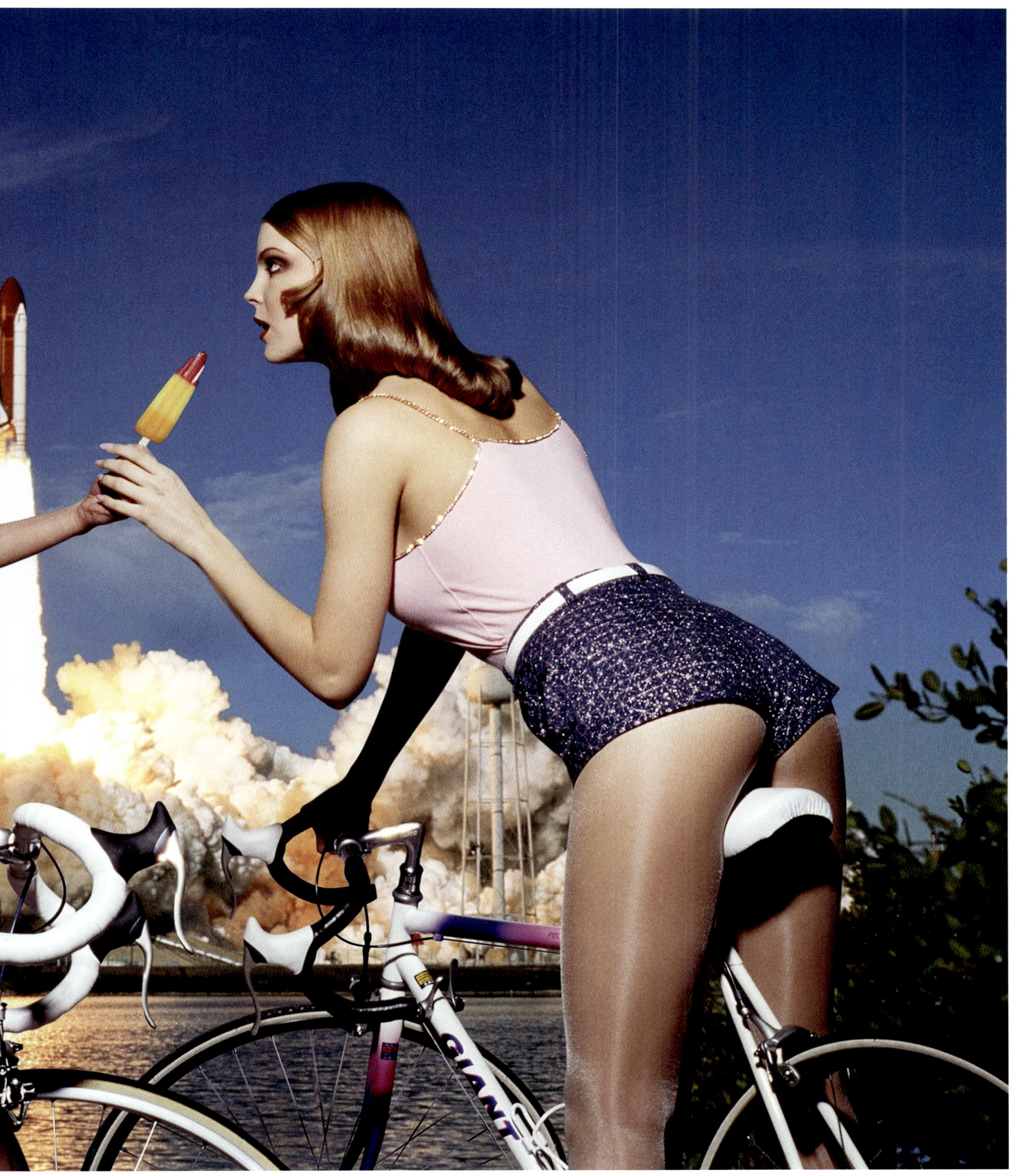

GIANT

We weren't using technology for the sake of it;
we were using it to create a new visual language.

LEE SWILLINGHAM, ART DIRECTOR

Swillingham later observed, 'It was what would happen if Ziggy Stardust and J.G. Ballard got together to take fashion pictures. It was so ahead of its time.'[59] Their images seemed to invoke French philosopher Jean Baudrillard's commentary on Postmodern image culture: that reality was being replaced by representation, and artificial images were becoming more definitive of the real than reality itself – 'a real without origin or reality: a hyperreal.'[60]

Norbert Schoerner was one of the first to experiment with these new possibilities, harnessing their potential for generating emotional impact and narrative. An early story from 1994, 'Bad Boy Memory', was photographed at a British Gas-owned waste-land in Greenwich, south London – also the location for Stanley Kubrick's war film, *Full Metal Jacket* (1987). In post-production, Schoerner altered textures and colours to render the urban landscape surreal and create a Japanese manga-inspired vision of a post-apocalyptic future. Ekow Eshun, then Assistant Editor at *The Face*, later described how Schoerner's photographs 'seem to have been culled from the subconscious; dream fragments redolent with ambiguity and unease'.[61]

Photographer Andrea Giacobbe pursued a 'purely subjective' vision of reality, in collaboration with the stylist Maida Gregori

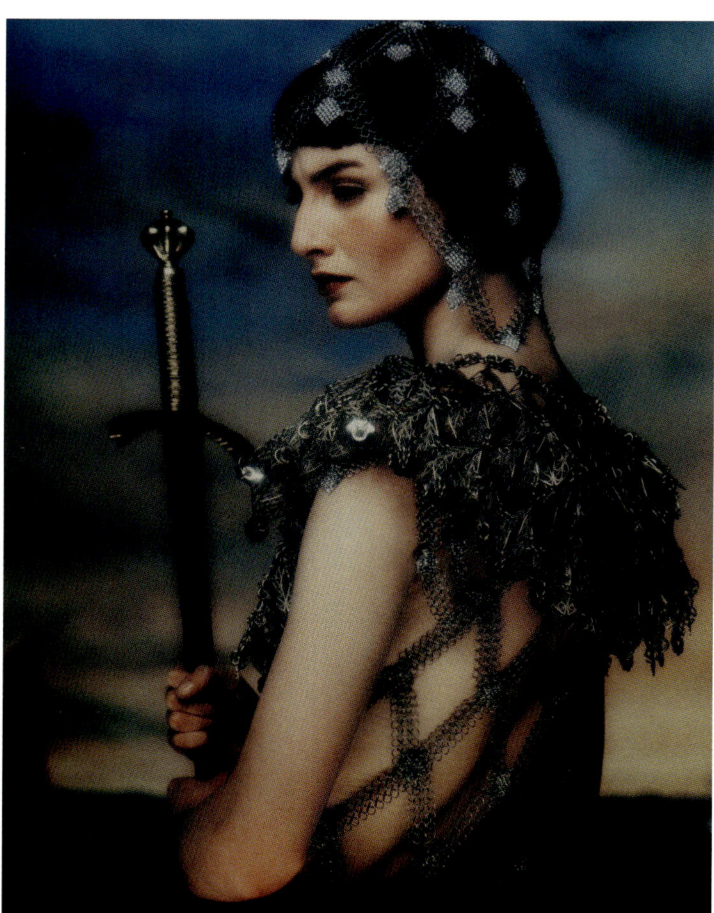

Boina.[62] Together, they produced fashion stories in which familiar settings – nightclubs, apartments, motorways – were made strange through unnatural colours and incongruous juxtapositions. Openly exhibiting their artifice, these surreal images seemed to tap into the global media frenzy around genetically cloned sheep and presaged the emerging millennial paranoia as the world approached Y2K.

The embrace of digital coincided with the rise in popularity of Britpop, whose key players were all championed by *The Face* in 'hyperreal' photographs that pushed the boundaries of portraiture in new and innovative ways. Every element of Inez and Vinoodh's November 1994 portrait of Suede frontman Brett Anderson, for instance, was digitally tweaked and adjusted to create an impossible level of perfection, the gleam of the singer's skin heightening a sense of separation from real life.

Unusual for the time, this approach ensured the magazine's photography stood out. As Garratt elaborated, 'If a rock band was going to feature in *The Face*, then they had to do something different. They weren't just going to be lined up for five minutes against a wall for the photograph, but [they'd] have to commit to a day in the studio.'[63] Despite increasingly fierce competition on the newsstands, *The Face* still had cachet. The *Independent* noted: 'There is no better place to be than on the magazine's cover.'[64]

The Face reached its highest readership during the mid-Nineties, fuelled by a zeitgeist it had helped to create. These were the years of Blur vs Oasis in the battle for Britpop, the meteoric global domination of the Spice Girls, a group of Young British Artists promoting unmade beds and sharks in tanks, Moss spilling out of the Met Bar in Mayfair, and a New Labour government proclaiming, 'things can only get better'.

Fashion Editor Ashley Heath brought in a new fleet of stylists, including Greg Fay, Justin Laurie and Seta Niland. At the same time, an increased number of fashion stories in each issue necessitated more photographic content and variety. Swillingham made space within the magazine for this plurality of approaches, commissioning work from new photographers, each with their own recognisable aesthetic. David LaChapelle's surreal photo-graphic tableaux pictured constructed image worlds, mediated by consumer culture, while at the other extreme, photographers Sean Ellis and Steven Klein, together with stylists Isabella Blow and Nancy Rohde, used their images as an outlet for the darker depths of their imaginations.

Another exponent of the 'hyperreal' aesthetic, Elaine Constantine eschewed digital technologies and photographed her images using flash to create intense and vibrant colours. She had been photographing celebrities and documenting clubbers across the nation for the magazine's 'Hype' section since 1993, but her first fashion stories appeared in 1996. Some of her most memorable shoots for *The Face* evoke nostalgic memories

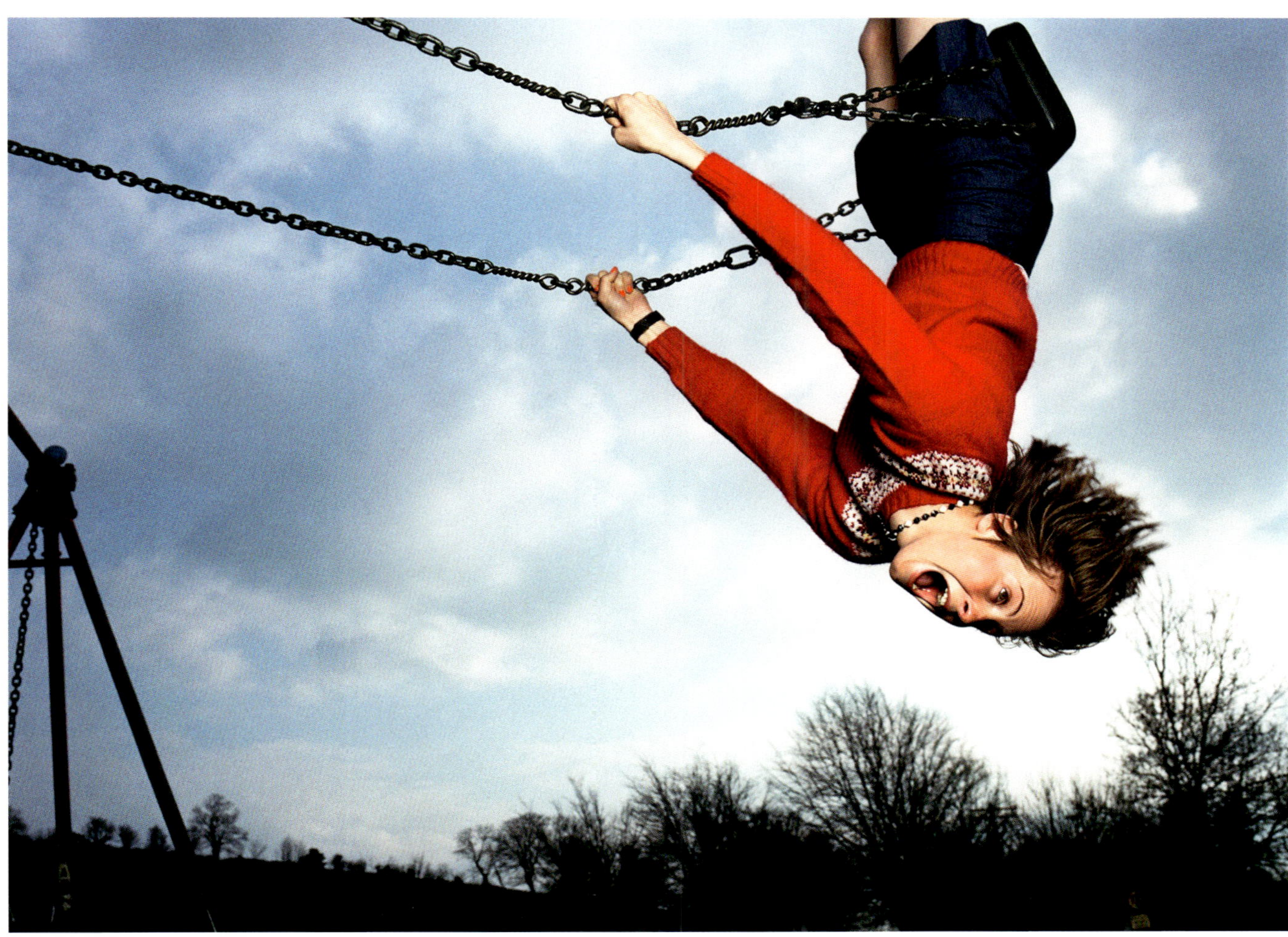

of carefree teenage rebellion, inspired by British documentary photographers such as Chris Killip and Martin Parr and the photojournalism of *Picture Post*. As Constantine noted, 'The Face had a reputation for pushing the genre of fashion photography and taking risks, which allowed me to use the fashion platform to find my own voice as an artist.'[65]

WHERE NEXT FOR YOUTH CULTURE?

In 1999, Logan made the decision to sell *The Face* to Emap, a large multimedia publishing company, which inevitably resulted in a turn towards more commercial content and covers. Promoted to Editorial Director, Heath brought in influential stylist Katie Grand as the magazine's Fashion Director, who amplified the fashion content with exciting new photographers including Vincent Peters and Sølve Sundsbø.

As the magazine had become more successful, it attracted contributions from more established names, and many of the later covers were shot by photographers who had launched their careers at *The Face* over the preceding decades. This signalled a move away from nurturing new photographic talent in favour of well-known names whose styles were now recognisable rather than rebellious. Two decades after Logan launched *The Face*, style journalism had proliferated and the market was increasingly overcrowded. In many respects, *The Face* was a victim of its own trailblazing success. The title ceased publication in 2004.

Fifteen years later, *The Face* was relaunched in print and online, returning to a radically altered publishing landscape. Navigating this new terrain, *The Face* has continued Logan's original vision for a disruptive, creative and inclusive magazine, championing fresh talent in photography, fashion, music and graphic design.

Reflecting on the legacy of the style magazine, artist Wolfgang Tillmans wrote, 'There have repeatedly been periods in which constellations of individuals, places and times, and economic circumstances have allowed for pictures and stories of extraordinary clarity and poignancy to emerge.'[66] Remarkably, *The Face* has been the platform for more than one such constellation, with the magazine reinventing and reshaping the cultural landscape on multiple occasions throughout its history.

Looking back at the photographs that filled the pages of the magazine across its first 25 years – most of which have only ever existed in print – *The Face* has excelled precisely when contributors are given the creative freedom to react against the prevailing mood, to create a shift in culture. *The Face* stands out for providing image-makers with a platform to freely reimagine and revolutionise the visual language of fashion and portrait photography and, in doing so, it has empowered photographers to define the spirit of their times. ∎

Sabina Jaskot-Gill is Senior Curator, Photographs, at the National Portrait Gallery, London.

THE DARK KNIGHT RETURNS
By Sean Ellis
Styled by Isabella Blow
August 1998

3.45
By Elaine Constantine
Styled by Cathy Kasterine
June 1999

IF YOU KNOW

NICK LOGAN AND LEE SWILLINGHAM

Having edited *NME* and then launched *Smash Hits*, in 1980 Nick Logan set about creating a new title that better fitted his vision of what a magazine could be – one that reflected more than just music or fashion, encompassing a wider creative culture and spirit of innovation. Here, he looks back on the legacy of *The Face* with Lee Swillingham, the magazine's Art Director from 1992 to 1999.

LEE SWILLINGHAM: When you first launched *The Face*, it very much seemed to be marketed as a music magazine…

NICK LOGAN: It was more focused on music because that was my background and also nobody conceived a general interest magazine working in the market. But it was always my intention to broaden it out, so we started to cover film, politics, cultural stuff, anything. And for everyone, not just for men or just for women. If you're creating a magazine, it has to have a personality and it has to have integrity. It mustn't patronise the readers.

LS: There was always a link with style wasn't there?

NL: Totally. Rather than more commonly used stage shots, I'd go for Pennie Smith shots of The Clash in an alleyway. Or David Bowie on the train, or Paul Weller in an overcoat walking through a crowd of mods on scooters…

LS: …Which is an incredible photograph. He has already moved on to the Style Council era of his career, but the fans waiting for him are still dressed like Jam fans. We also shouldn't forget the women you featured. You had that amazing Sheila Rock cover of Siouxsie Sioux where everything was just red and black.

NL: *The Face* was an idea that was rolling around in my head. And where I wanted it to go to could change in a day, in an hour.

SIOUXSIE SIOUX
By Sheila Rock
February 1982

THE HARDER THEY COME
By Jamie Morgan
Styled by Ray Petri
March 1985

BODY ROCK
By Tony Viramontes
Styled by Ray Petri
September 1985

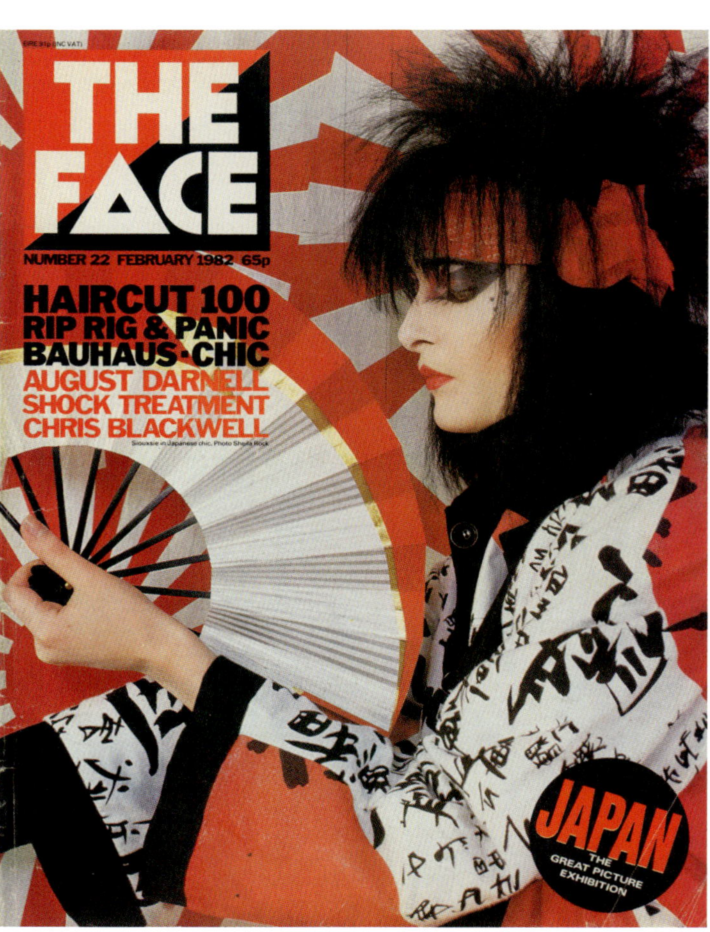

YOU KNOW

I wanted it to feel like reportage, like *Life* magazine or *Paris Match*.

LS: If you look at the John Lydon cover from December 1980, that is basically a men's fashion picture that could have been in *L'Uomo Vogue*.

NL: It's probably not a great cover. It's very dark. But it is a great image.

LS: It is very well art directed by Sheila Rock. You can see Lydon's already moved on from his punk days, he's more stylish. It's a powerful image. I wasn't buying the magazine then, I was too young. But you clearly had an eye for style and fashion – but doing it in a stealthy way, because you were selling it as a music magazine. You were probably the only magazine in the country that was publishing these kind of well-art directed, well-photographed images.

NL: I met Sheila Rock while I was editing *Smash Hits*. She showed me all these great colour images she was shooting for Japanese magazines and I thought, 'Wow, no-one in this country's doing that'. So access to that work – like Chalkie Davies's and Jill Furmanovsky's – was a big part of it. I had the photographers but I didn't have strong writers to start with. I couldn't just go and steal writers from the *NME*; that would have been wrong for them and for me.

LS: As a reader, I picked up on the writing, because although I trained as a designer, I was also a fan of journalism…

NL: It was always a journalistic project. Right at the beginning I was trying to get non-writers to write, it was more of a fanzine approach. I'd come from the *NME* and *Smash Hits* where you could throw things around and mess with tradition, but essentially I wanted it to be good journalism and great photography: a combination.

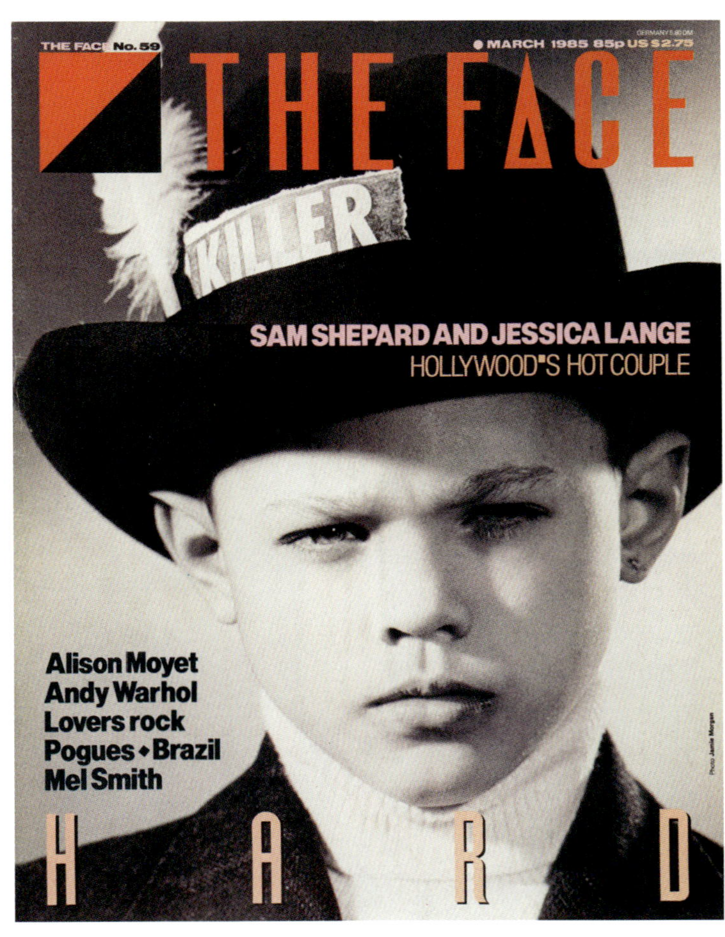

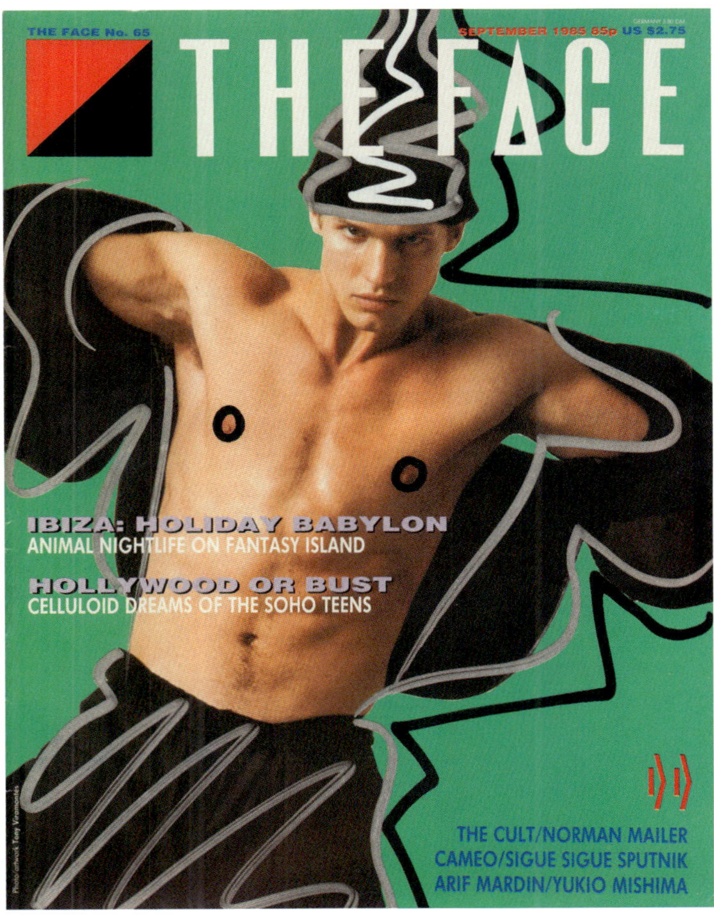

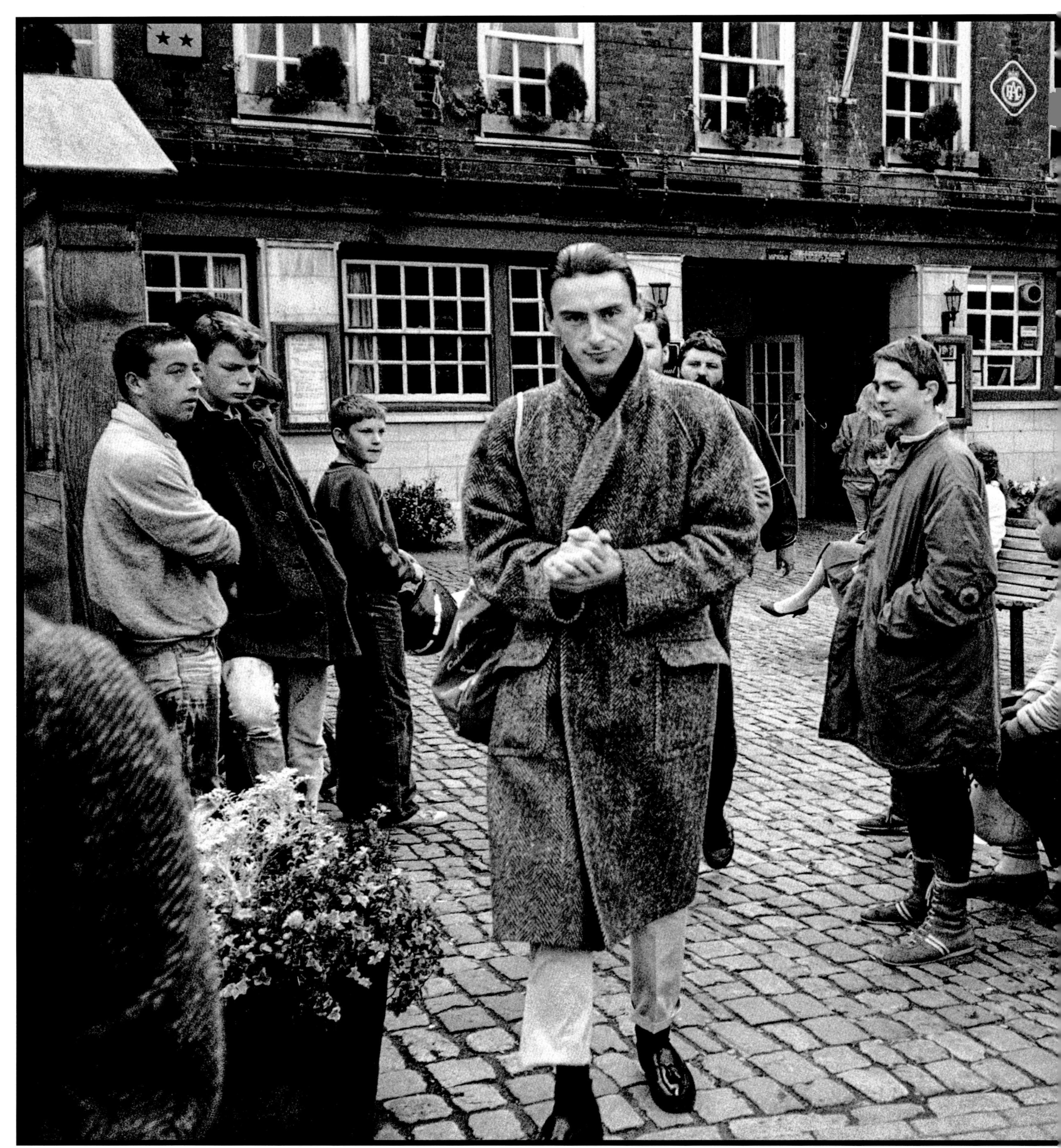

PAUL WELLER
By Steve Pyke
November 1984

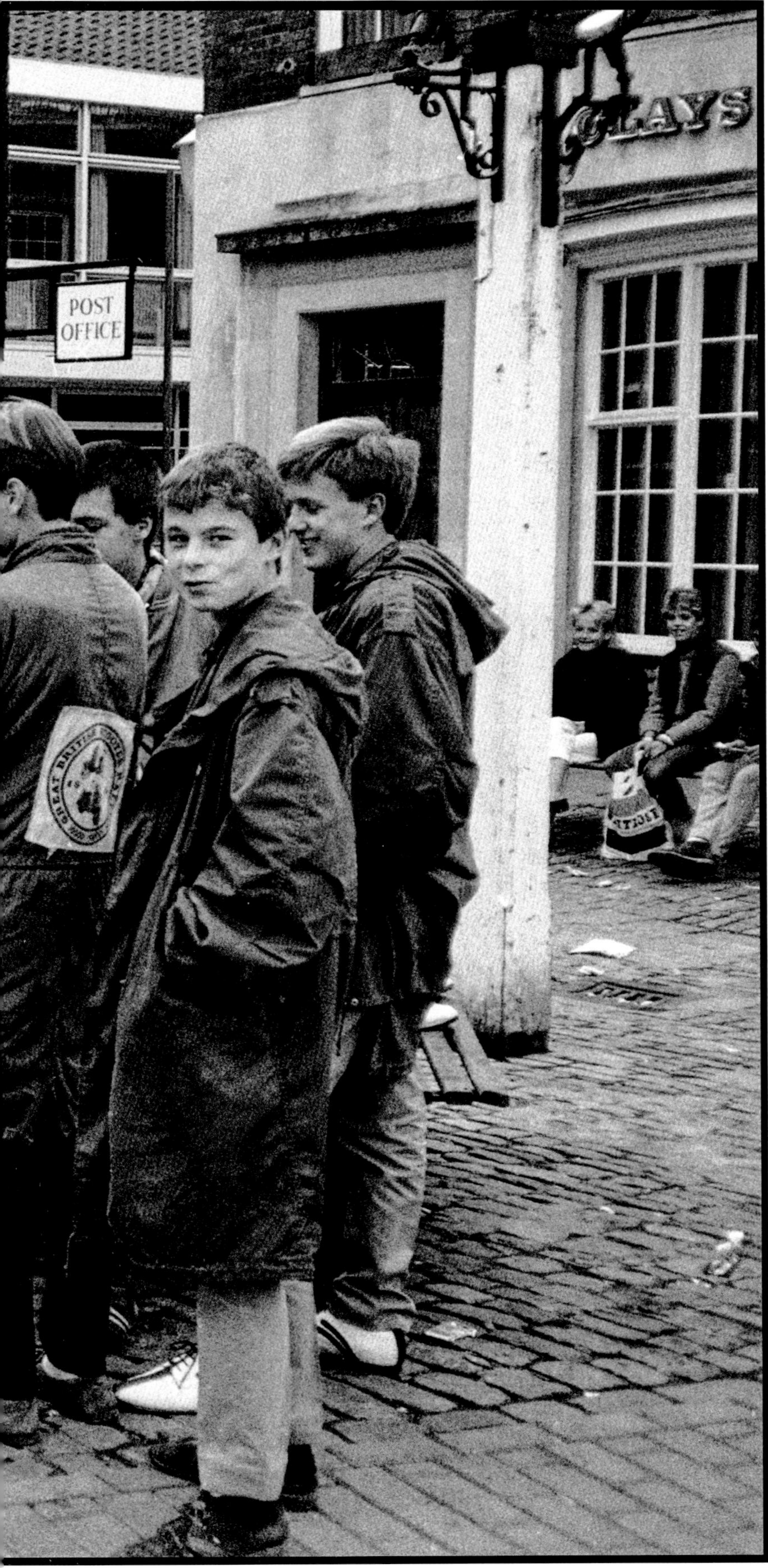

LS: And what about fashion?

NL: I had some pictures at the back of the first issue called 'You're Not Going Out Like That…' – I wanted to cover street style, but very quickly *i-D* came along and claimed that turf, so I backed off.

LS: You also had a feature on Johnson's, this great shop that everyone in the know went to that sold West Coast-inspired Americana clothing, in issue 1…

NL: That was crucial, that story. It was in my head for three or four years. It gives you music, it gives you fashion, it gives you culture.

LS: It was so brilliant how you introduced that branding of 'style' rather than 'fashion', which for me always felt a bit snobby back then.

NL: Well, that's exactly why I thought, 'How do I handle this? I can't call it fashion. What is it?'

LS: Whereas now, the influence of magazines like *The Face* has completely upended the whole fashion industry. For me, the 'Hard Times' cover [September 1982] was incredibly inspirational because it made me understand what art direction was.

NL: That was Neville. I did all the covers and many of the layouts on *NME* but I didn't know what art direction was until he came along.

LS: I think it's the crop plus the copy that really makes it sing. And you can't get more 'Face' than these coverlines: Kevin Rowland, Phillip K. Dick, La Resistance Graphique, Imagination, The Soul Band and Nam June Paik. I mean: no other magazine in the world! It's the combination of the words and the image that make it so powerful.

NL: It is. Neville was just a joy to work with, we worked really well together. I made suggestions about crops and pictures to use. I think, to be honest, I was just looking at other people's stuff and thinking, 'Can I add to that?' I never wanted to be similar to anyone else. But I was never interested in just talking to a small group. You can argue *The Face* did, but it was a *big* small group.

LS: And something like the first Nick Kamen cover by Ray Petri and Jamie Morgan [January 1984]; that really felt like the birth of fashion for *The Face*.

NL: By that point, Ray and Jamie didn't ever have to ask us what we wanted them to do. They would just come in with an idea. Ray might scribble three or four words down as a reference while we talked. And then they would bring in the photos and we'd pull them together as a story. Sheila was the same, taking ABC or Heaven 17 or The Human League, dressing them in linen suits or workwear. I wasn't sure what to do with that. But then I thought, 'If I put those together, they become a fashion feature'. I used to switch around the sections and the titles. I was always obsessed with the fact that it had to have a name: 'Thrills' or 'Expo'…

There's one issue, with the cover image 'Electric Ladyland', shot by Jean Baptiste Mondino [October 1987], where there's hardly any music in it at all. I actually thought 'maybe I've gone too far here' and pulled back a little after that. But that's my favourite magazine cover of all time.

LS: I'm glad you love that, because I remember seeing that on the newsstands when I was doing my A-Levels, and it was one of the most stunning things I've ever seen. If you look at Max Vadukul's

Essentially I wanted *The Face* to be good journalism and great photography: a combination

NICK LOGAN, FOUNDER OF THE FACE

'Good to Gaultier' fashion story [November 1986], that was the pinnacle of sophisticated image-making for me as a young person, wanting to go to art college and interested in fashion and photography. Also there's humour there – I always like to have a bit of humour in my own work too.

NL: Yeah. It definitely has a European feel, doesn't it?

LS: The 'Killer' cover, with the photograph of Felix Howard, by Ray Petri and Jamie Morgan [March 1985], has become iconic…

NL: I loved the story but I was very hesitant to put him on the cover, his age worried me. I thought, 'How are newsagents going to react?' I would have gone broke if they had refused to handle it. But I was persuaded by Paul Rambali [Assistant Editor] and Lesley White [Features Editor].

LS: By making that decision, you basically made the coolest magazine cover of all time.

NL: That was one where, when the issue came back from the printers, I thought 'Wow! *That's* why people buy magazines – just to have that cover'.

LS: Gut instinct has been key throughout your career. I was very young when you hired me to be Art Director, I was an assistant on the magazine. I was really surprised when you called me in and offered me the role, I was only 23 and fresh out of St Martins. There's this internet slang – 'IYKYK' – 'If You Know, You Know'. For me, that is what *The Face* always was. If you know, you know – and if you don't know, you're never going to know.

NL: You either get it or you don't.

LS: That also sums up why you were really good at hiring people. You met people, and thought, 'You get it, you can work on my magazine because you understand it.' I remember when you made me Art Director, the size of that responsibility suddenly dawned on me. I realised – because the magazines had such an amazing legacy by that point – that I had to make sure that whatever was shot didn't look like anything that had been done before. I remember thinking 'We can't do 'Killer' again: this has got to be *new, new, new*'. There was a pressure of having that responsibility for the visual output of what I think is the best magazine of all time … but after a while I got into my stride and I was commissioning things like the 'Leisure Lounge' story by Andrea Giacobbe [October 1994] or the Excalibur-style shoot by Sean Ellis with Isabella Blow ['The Dark Knight Returns', August 1998]. And Ashley [Heath, Fashion Editor] was getting really great results from the stylists.

NL: Yeah, that was good.

LS: In retrospect, I think those shoots represent how I moved into commissioning this more cinematic, very colourful work, after the whole grunge thing, with Corinne Day's photos – which I loved. People like Norbert Schoerner or Inez van Lamsweerde obviously are now very established photographers, but they were launched by *The Face*.

NL: Yeah, I loved it. And Elaine Constantine's work always stood out.

LS: Yes, Elaine's energetic, super colourful photography. Her 'Sarf Coastin'' story with Polly Banks [December 1997] has become widely celebrated. I was interviewed by a photography magazine and they asked me to describe this new style of imagery I was commissioning and, having been interested in Postmodern theory, I dubbed it 'hyperreal'. I think that was an apt description. I was realising I could no longer just be a fan, I had to actually do something as good or better than before, that was right for the era. Trying to mix fashion, style, imagery, music … doing things like the pink Prodigy cover by Peter Robathan [July 1996]. You see pink everywhere now, but back then you would never see a cover like that, and certainly not with a man on.

NL: It's really good. The humour is great. There is definitely a glamour to it as well, but on an accessible level. It's not *Vogue*, when *Vogue* was, in previous eras, all about unattainable glamour.

LS: That's exactly what I was trying to do – Modern Glamour. Looking at Phil Bicker's 'Summer of Love' cover with Kate Moss [July 1990] – that was another game changer.

NL: The minute I saw this cover, I thought '*Fantastic*!' And then Sheryl [Garratt, Editor] said we could tie it in with what was already in the issue and make it work… That's pretty much the last issue I was directly responsible for. I wasn't the biggest fan of what was going on, with grunge. It didn't do much for me. I suppose because it is anti-glamour, and I like glamour. I always wanted to give the reader an issue that felt out of their world, and I worried that this was going the other way.

LS: By the time I arrived, I wanted to bring some glamour back. I was very inspired by Bowie and Roxy Music. I didn't grow up with those artists because I was too young, but I bought their records.

NL: There was an element of 'Stranded' or 'Country Life' to some of those images. I was very happy to see that. I've always liked glamour, that's what attracted me to Japanese and Italian magazines.

LS: The other thing I was conscious of at *The Face* was how influential the design was, how you'd see ideas getting picked up in the wider culture. The two I remember from my time was when we used the stencil typeface, which got copied everywhere from the poster and graphics for *Trainspotting* to a car advert. And then the hyperreal photography, which Levi's memorably copied for a TV ad. But there's a power with that also, because you're coming up with something new and influential.

NL: I honestly never looked at the opposition. I wasn't even bothered what they'd done. I didn't care about exclusives. I think you can get hung up on that. But we tended to get them anyway! Like with the Jean-Paul Goude stuff, when he masterminded the celebrations for the French Republic's 200th anniversary: they

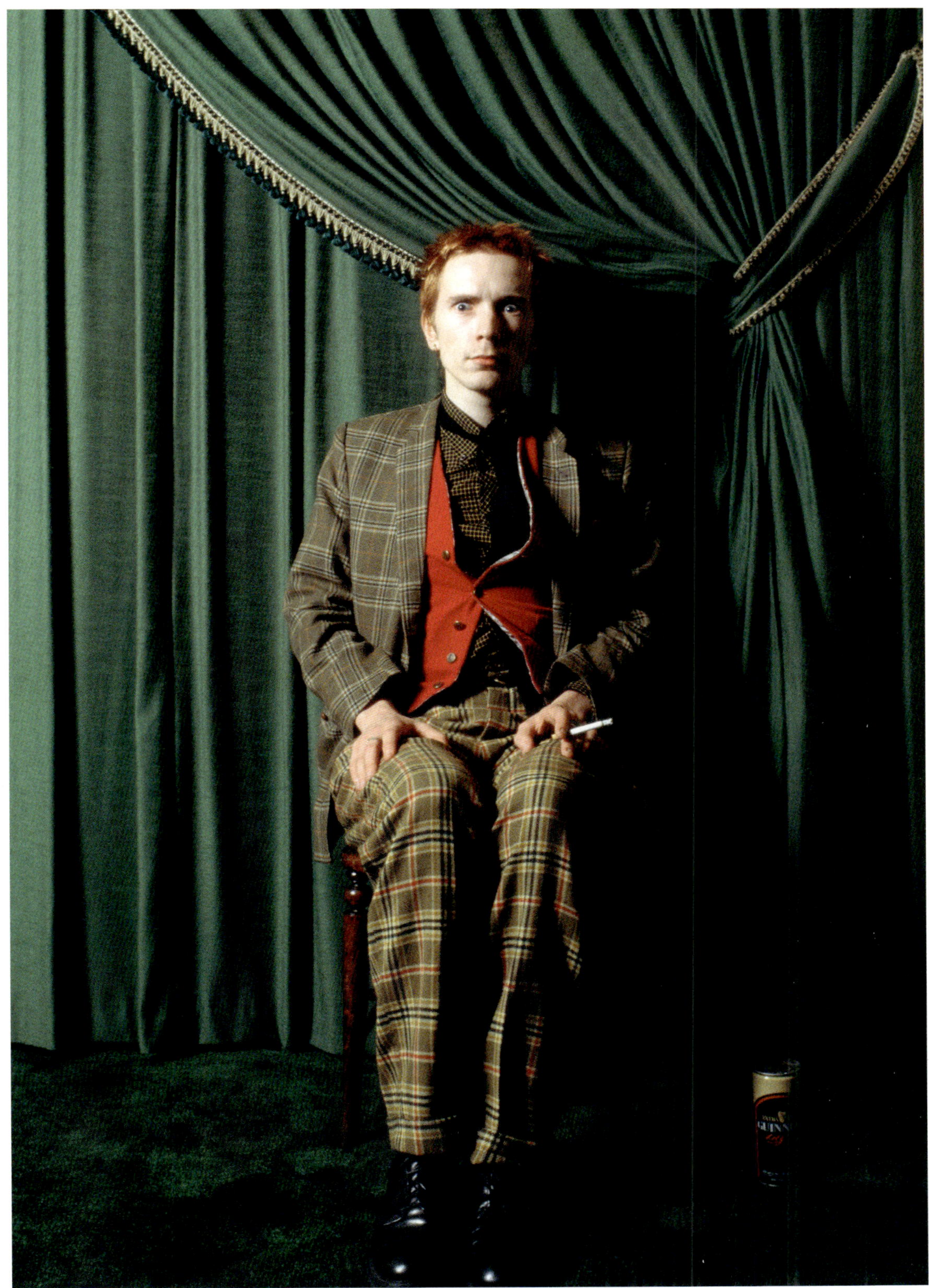

JOHN LYDON
By Sheila Rock
December 1980

John Lydon could be difficult, but he had great style and was very photogenic. The image I took of him in a tartan suit for the November 1980 cover looks like it's been styled by *L'Uomo Vogue*, but it's just what he was wearing that day.
Sheila Rock

gave us all the sketches and I was thinking, 'How come I've got these? Is no-one else interested?'

LS: I think that's why *The Face* was so important, because you knew about it and then you shared that with other people.

NL: I'd like to think that *The Face* invited people to feel they could be different, be creative and do things that otherwise they couldn't. It opened a window and it encouraged diversity and tolerance, and very much a European sensibility. Obviously I'm proud of *The Face* and I'm most happy when I see somebody say, 'Yeah, it changed my opinion on everything: politics, music, art.'

LS: It was also instinctively LGBTQ+ friendly, there was generally a diverse selection of people being photographed.

NL: What would've been the first issue you saw?

LS: I really remember the Tony Viramontes cover with the green background [September 1985] – and thinking how sophisticated it was to grasp all that was going on – this super cool image on the cover of a mainstream magazine, with club culture, art and fashion all wrapped up. That was quite an edgy cover. You know, you created a whole new category of media that took over the world: the style magazine…

NL: Yeah, 'style' again…

LS: But you created that, and that still lives on today. ∎

FEARLESS MODERNITY

PETE PAPHIDES

Because history has a way of removing risk from triumph, it's easy to imagine that *The Face*'s success was a done deal from the outset. To be reminded that was anything but the case is to read the typewritten pitch letter circulated by Nick Logan at its inception in autumn 1979. 'The Face', he wrote, 'is a new rock magazine for the Eighties.'[1] In a sector dominated by venerable inkies such as *Melody Maker*, *Sounds* and Logan's alma mater *NME*, *The Face* was not conceived as a rival to those titles. 'It might help to think of *The Face*', continued Logan, 'as a kind of "unofficial" monthly colour supplement to these weekly tabloids.' Perhaps it was closer to the mark to see this fresh contender as a sharper older sibling to Logan's previous creation, *Smash Hits*. Certainly, that was the impression given by the inaugural issue. Whereas much of the rock press piously hymned the supremacy of substance over style, cover star Jerry Dammers spearheaded a label and a movement – 2 Tone – whose very essence was the interweaving of style and substance.

If Logan had a superpower, it was his lack of bolshiness. He revelled in the talent of his music writers and remained curious to see what they could deliver if sufficiently emboldened. He knew this would bring out the best in them because of his own experience in committee rooms where the prospect of speaking up had filled him with terror. Early examples of this approach include a 1980 piece headlined 'What The Rude Boy Doesn't Know', in which ingenue scribe Vaughn Toulouse chronicled his journey from dole-money subsistence in Plymouth to full-time disciple of The Clash. Within months of publication, Toulouse would find himself on *Top of the Pops* with his group, Department S, singing 'Is Vic There?' (1981), thus setting set the tone for a trend that recurred throughout the decade. By inviting political science graduate Robert Elms to write about the nascent scene around London's Blitz club, Logan ensured his magazine would be the first to play host to characters such as Boy George, Sade, Spandau Ballet and Steve Strange – artists who would all play a pivotal part in heralding a second 'British invasion' in America.

For the first time, serious music fans looking for something substantial to read had the option of buying a mainstream music magazine where rock was not the default. Previously, devotees of black music genres in this country would have had to look to 'specialist' titles to find out what their favourite artists were up to. Yet, within the first few months of its existence, *The Face* had run in-depth profiles of Laurel Aitken, Burning Spear, Desmond Dekker and Linton Kwesi Johnson. By far the most extensive coverage of Bob Marley's funeral was also to be found in *The Face*, with photographs by Adrian Boot running alongside the last-ever interview with Marley by journalist Roz Reines.

When it came to music, *The Face* benefited from a more curatorial approach. Unlike the music weeklies, the editors were under no obligation to cover artists they disliked simply because they were big names and their new record had just been released. This created a triangle of complicity between writer, musician and reader that repelled cynicism or any suggestion that pop's golden age was over, doomed never to return.

Steve Taylor's 1982 interview with Kraftwerk saw the group's founding member Ralf Hütter describe the vanguard of synth groups championed in the pages of *The Face* as a 'resistance to cultural imperialism'. The Neo-Constructivist design for that feature – Art Director Neville Brody's first for the magazine – served to announce that, from hereon in, the experience of reading *The Face* would reflect the full synaesthetic reach of the music covered within it. Other later examples that spring to mind include Mark Hooper's 1998 interview with Air, with photos by Jean Baptiste Mondino that mirrored the somniferous retro-futurism of their just-released album *Moon Safari*, and Kevin Braddock's 2000 feature on the UK garage phenomenon, with accompanying shots by Elaine Constantine.

STEVEN MORRIS
By Kevin Cummins
July 1983

SADE
By Jamie Morgan
April 1984

ELECTRO
Designed by Neville Brody
May 1984

LIAM GALLAGHER
By Norman Watson
Styled by Jason Kelvin
August 1994

DAFT PUNK
By Toby Mcfarlan Pond
February 2001

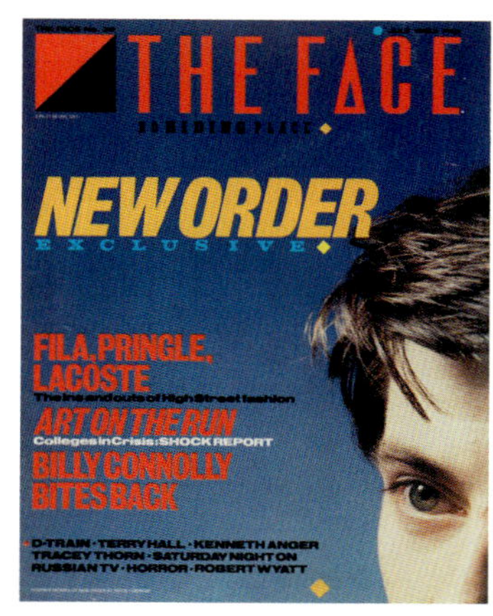

PORTRAITS OF MUSICIANS

Bold visual choices frequently reflected the fearless modernity of the music being championed. A case in point was the stark yellow and blue cover of the May 1984 issue announcing a report from New York club the Fun House, in which music writer David Toop hymned the wild, forward-facing creativity of electro in all its myriad subgenres, from the 'direct-to-disc wall poems' of Run-DMC to Jonzun Crew's 'Pack Jam', 'a video-game record' from which 'if adults wanted to run scared that was their business'.[2]

Two years later, soon-to-be Editor Sheryl Garratt hit the clubs and recording studios of Chicago and got the scoop on the city's emerging house scene – in the process becoming the first UK writer to bag an interview with one of the movement's prime innovators, Marshall Jefferson. The resulting feature is, in its way, as much a masterpiece as the records it exists to champion – music journalism that compels the reader to climb inside the world it describes and re-create the experience by seeking out every track mentioned. By the time the piece ran in 1986, one of its stars, Farley 'Jackmaster' Funk, was at number ten in the UK charts with 'Love Can't Turn Around'. The second summer of love was still 18 months away, but this was undoubtedly a catalyst for the flowering of rave – a movement documented by Garratt in a series of celebrated essays for the magazine.

To watch *Top of the Pops* or to rifle through the racks of your local record shop in the mid-to-late Eighties was to realise the extent to which the visual language of *The Face* had permeated pop. It could be the reissued Sam Cooke and Marvin Gaye songs that scaled the top ten as a result of Levi's adverts whose styling – along with that of contemporaneous teen idols Curiosity Killed the Cat – seemed to spring fully formed from the pages of *The Face*; or Neneh Cherry's 'Buffalo Stance' (1988), whose title referenced Ray Petri's Buffalo collective of west London creatives. Whilst this all served to affirm what *The Face* had already achieved, it was important for the magazine's coverage to maintain its connection to the streets. Speaking about the extraordinary wave of support that followed the defamation lawsuit brought against the magazine by Jason Donovan in 1991, Garratt said, 'the readers felt like they owned *The Face*' and future music coverage needed to honour that bond.[3]

The May 1994 cover depicted Damon Albarn, lead singer of Blur, in a suit and school tie against a Union Jack backdrop. The headline reads 'Blur: Brit Up Your Ears', one of the first uses of the word 'Brit' in connection with a genre that – catalysed by the art-school panache of Blur, Elastica, Pulp and Suede – would, in time, come to be known as Britpop. The cover line reads 'London Calling: British Art Special', in itself a bellwether of what was to come: a conversation between British art, fashion and music that gained global traction under the 'Cool Britannia' banner. Oasis would swiftly follow with their first glossy magazine cover just three months later. Were it not for the chain of events kicked off by these bands, it's almost certain that the March 1997 cover featuring the bikini-clad Spice Girls would never have happened.

To casual observers, it might have felt like *The Face* was unrecognisable from the post-punk street bible of its infancy. In fact, the enthusiastic, unpatronising, cultural curiosity that informed its inception still formed the core of its editorial ethos. But the way we were consuming music was changing. The Nineties would be the final decade in which pop would still be defined and demarcated along tribal lines. Back in 1980, you might have felt surprised to see Dammers declare, 'I listen to anything basically … it doesn't matter how good or bad it is, if you listen to it enough, you learn to like it.'[4] Two decades on, everyone was eclectic. Music no longer had a monopoly on cultural identity. ■

Pete Paphides is a music journalist, author and broadcaster.

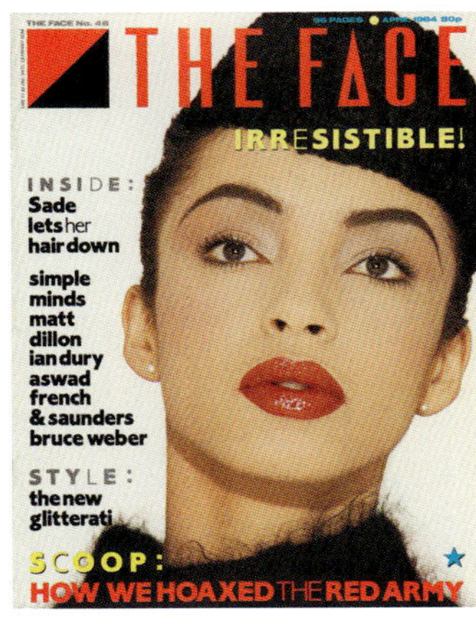

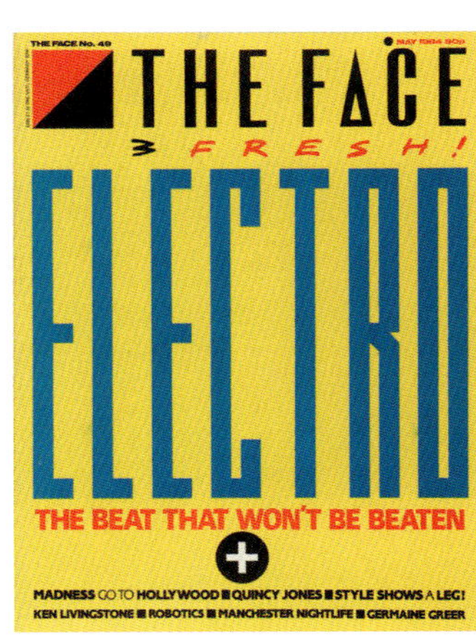

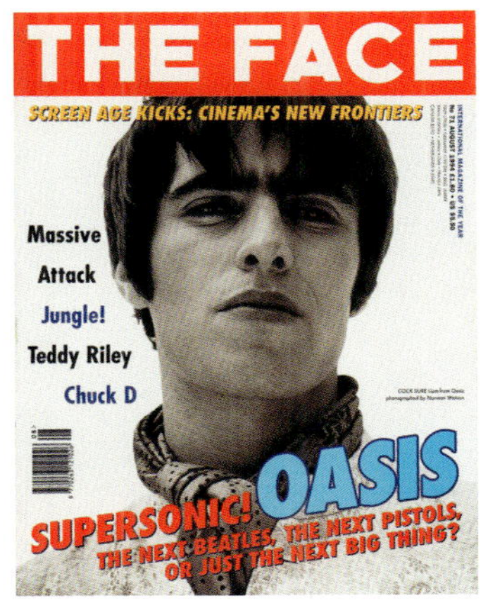

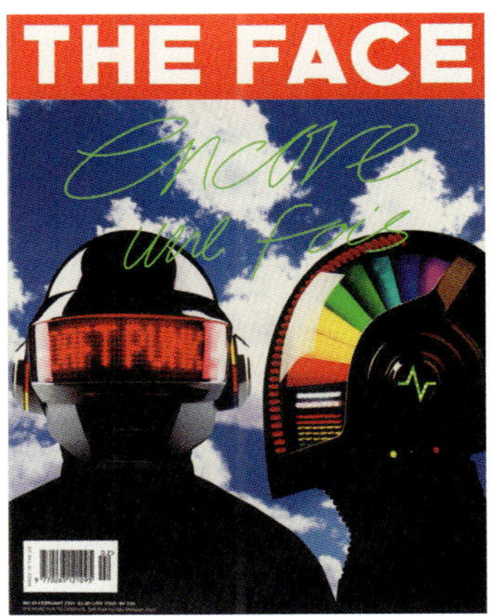

1980

1989

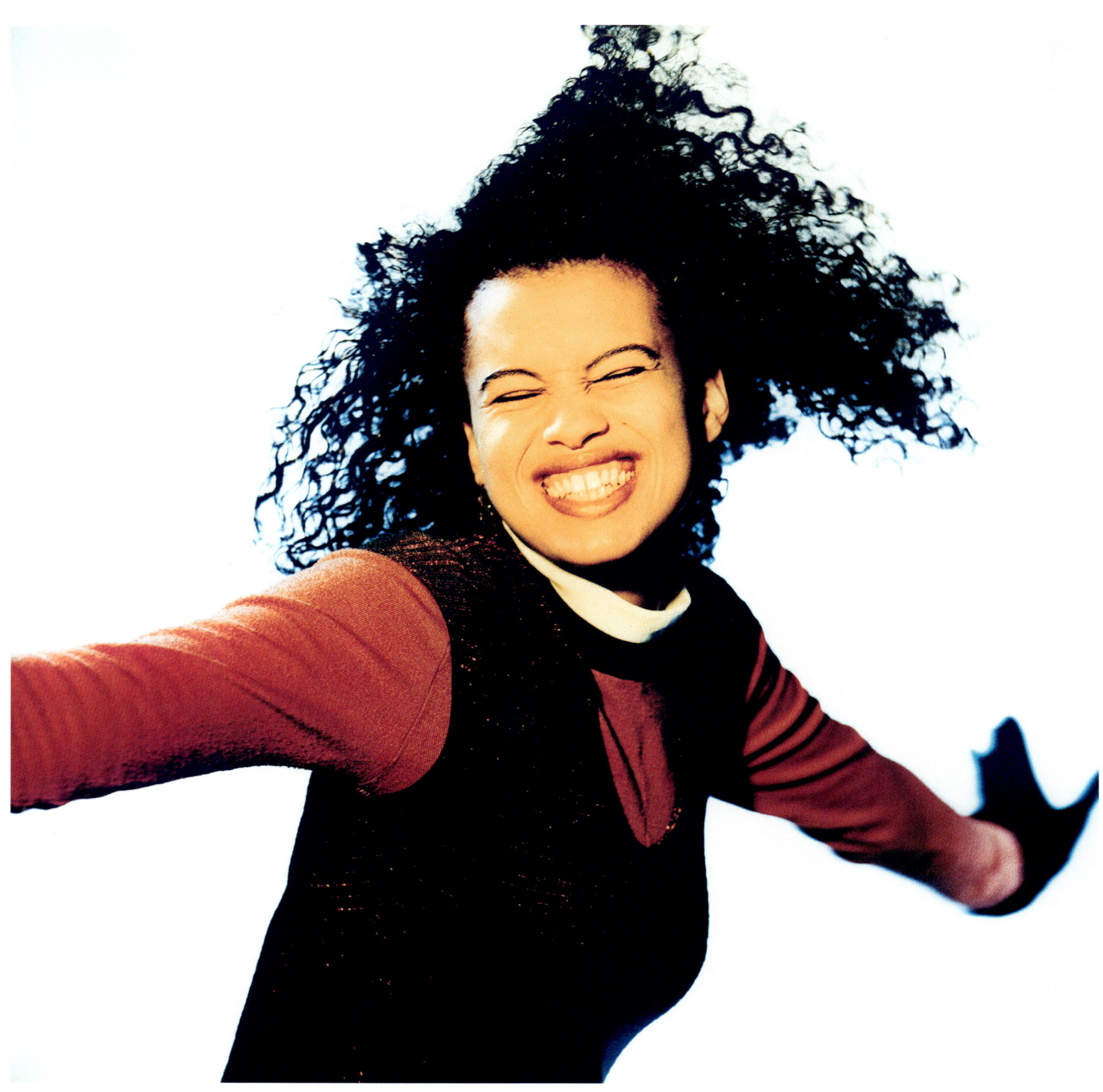

NENEH CHERRY
By Eddie Monsoon
Styled by Judy Blame
November 1988

ELECTRIC LADYLAND
By Jean Baptiste Mondino
Styled by Babeth Djian and Beatrice Carle
October 1987

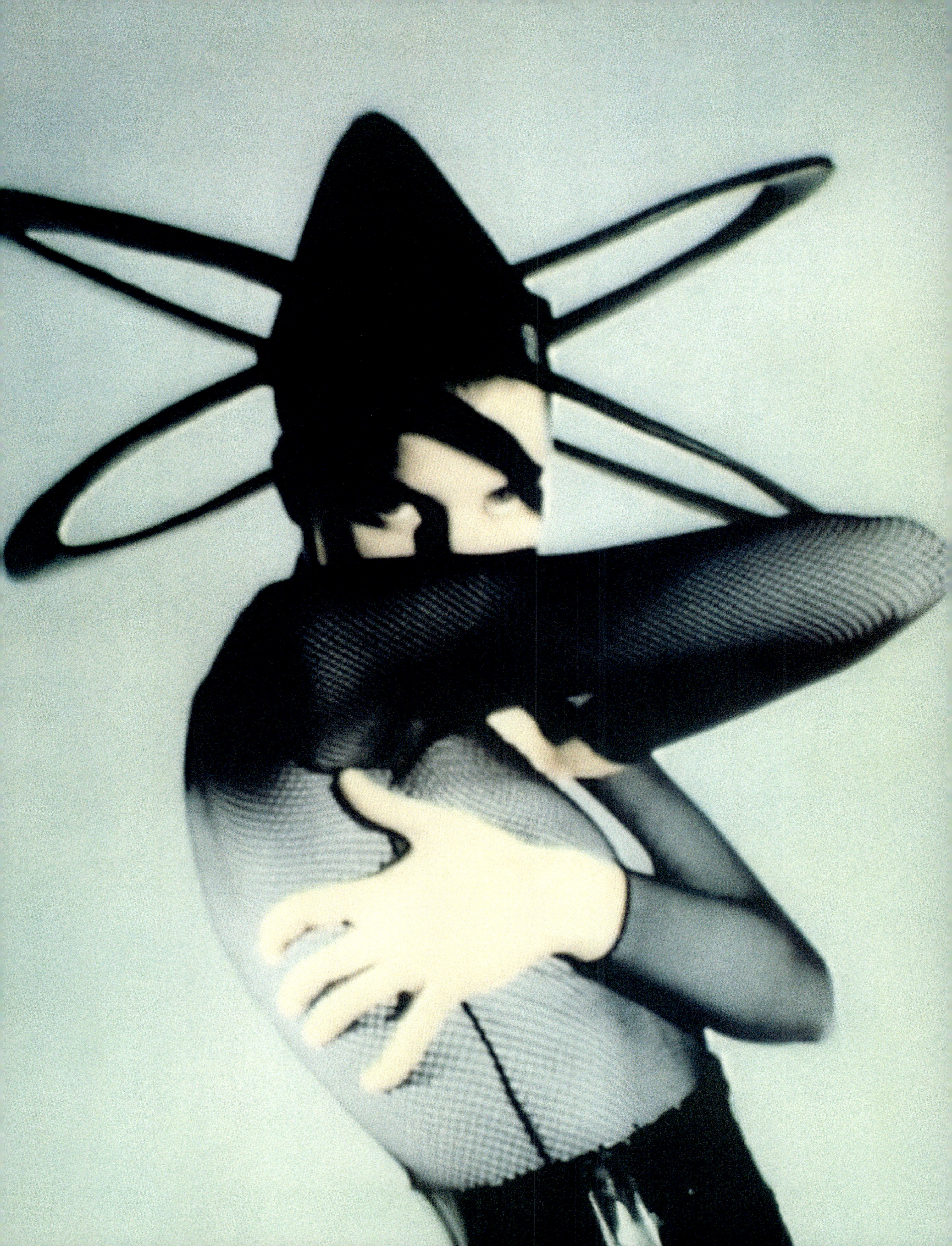

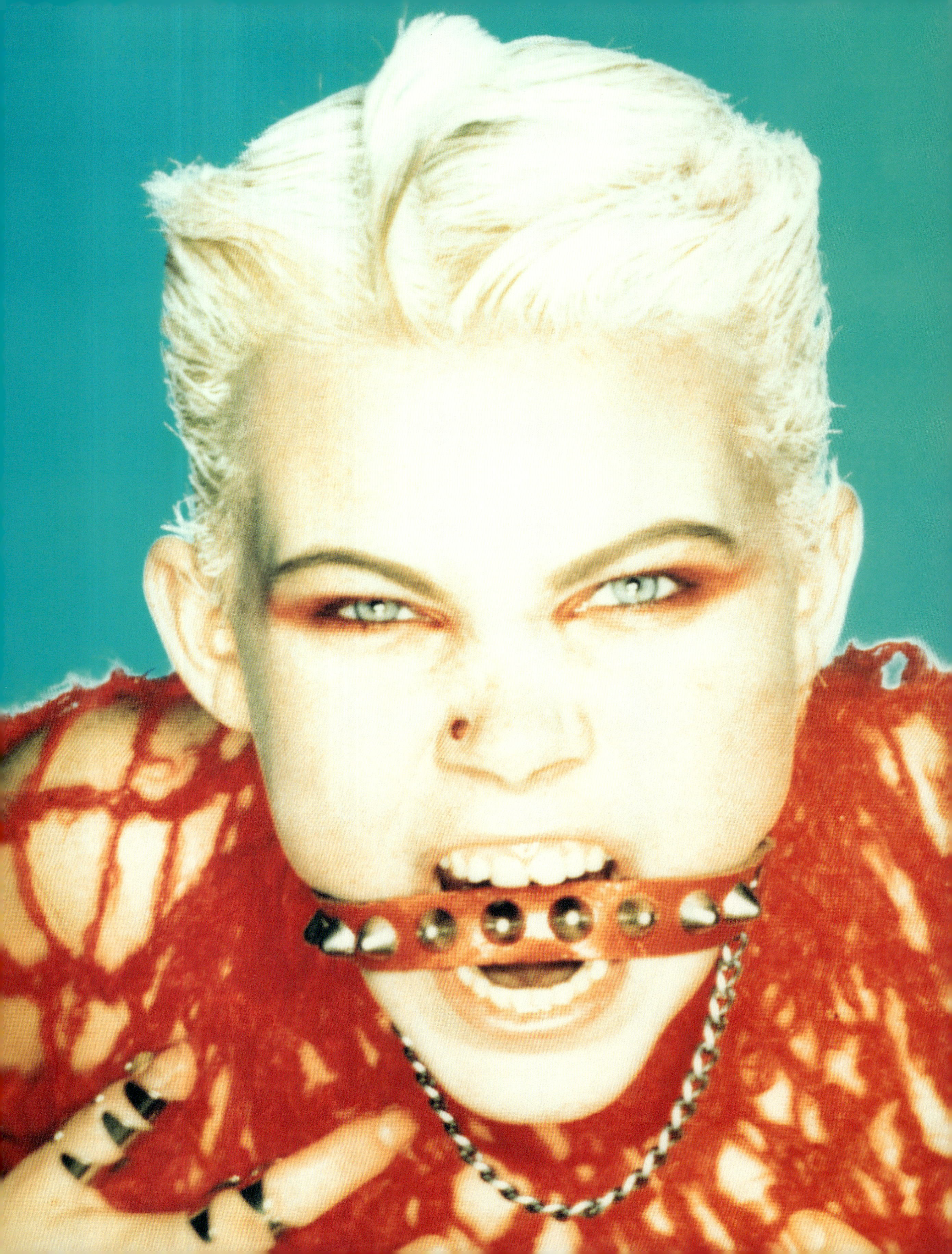

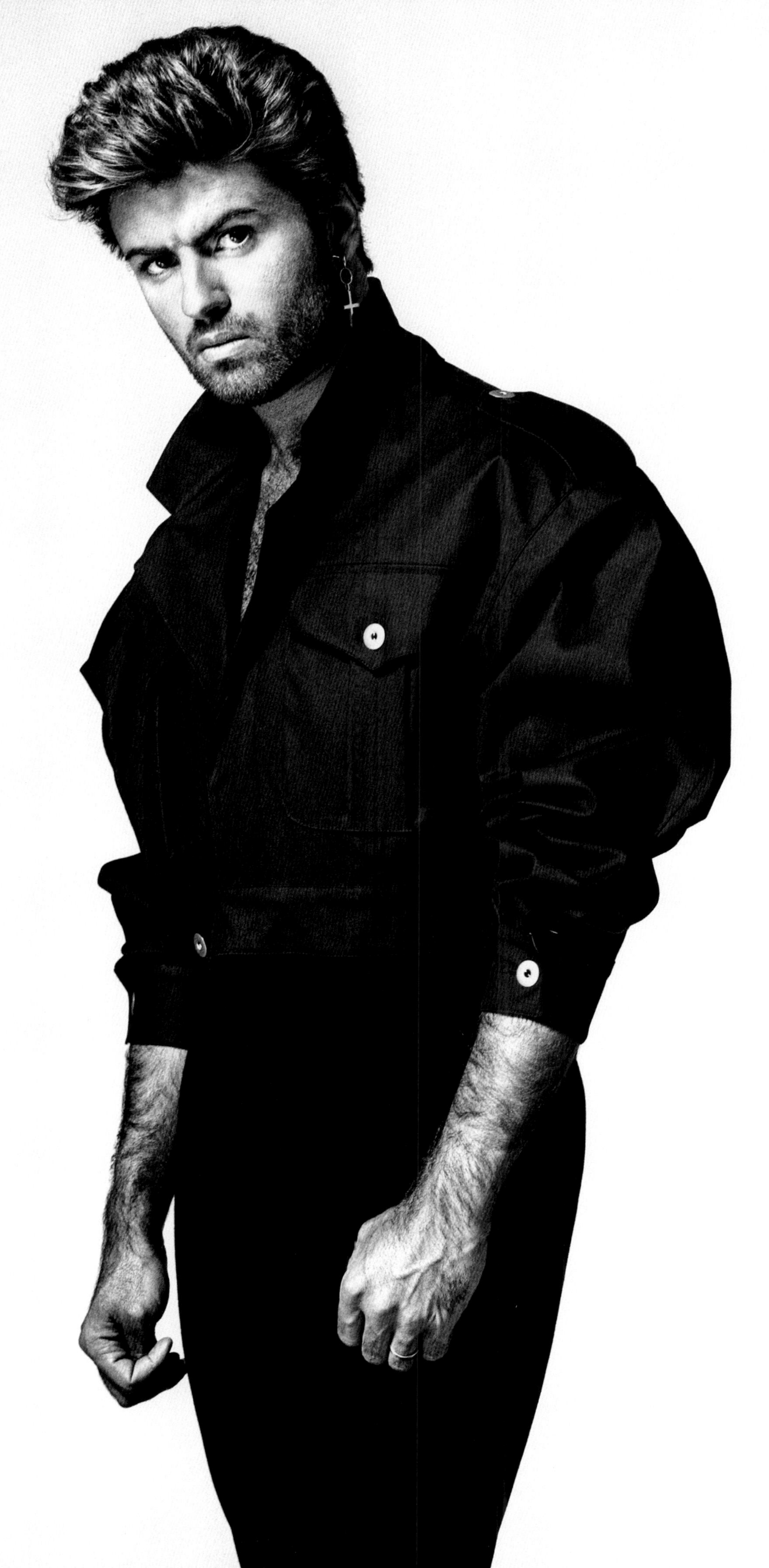

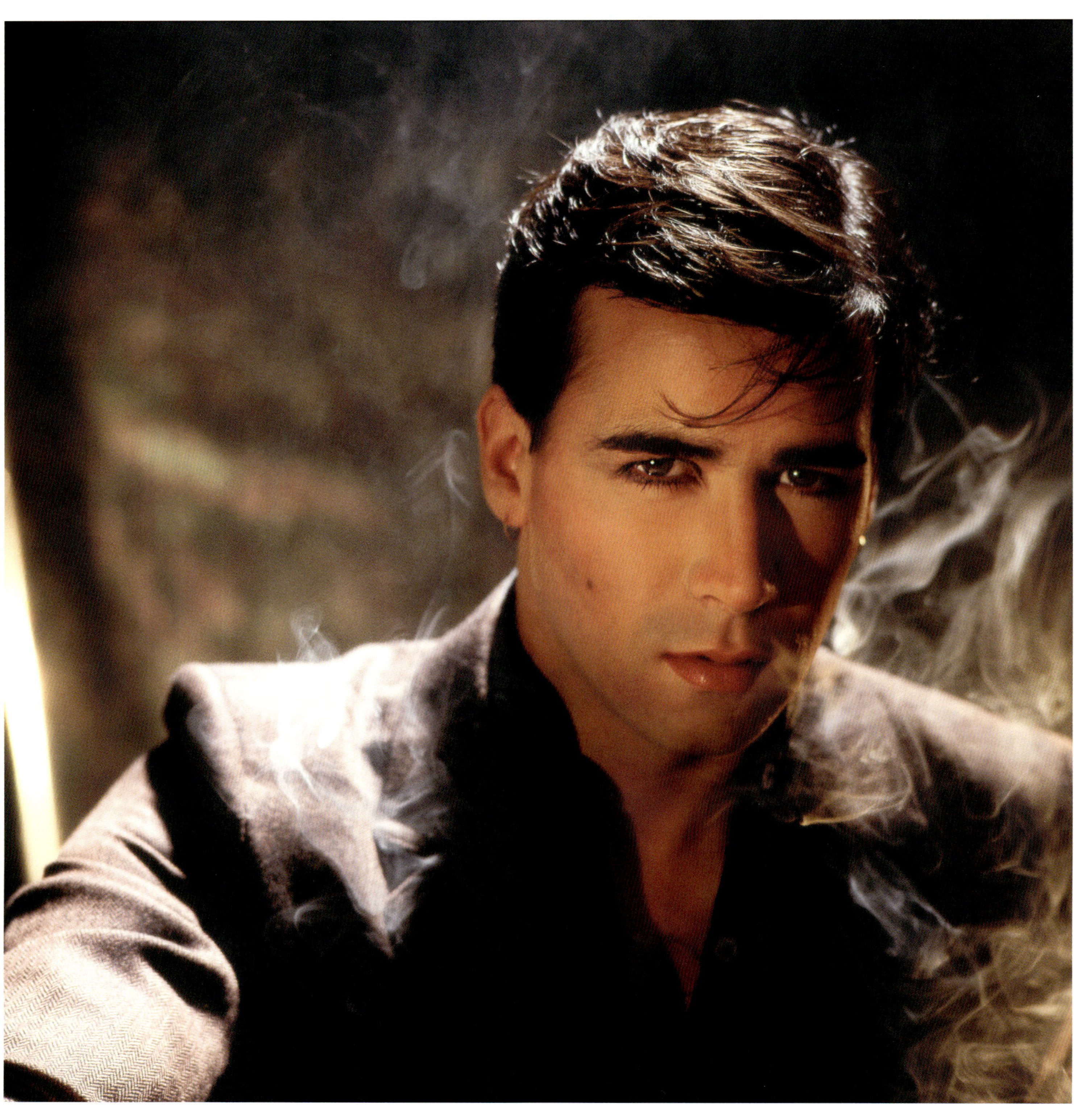

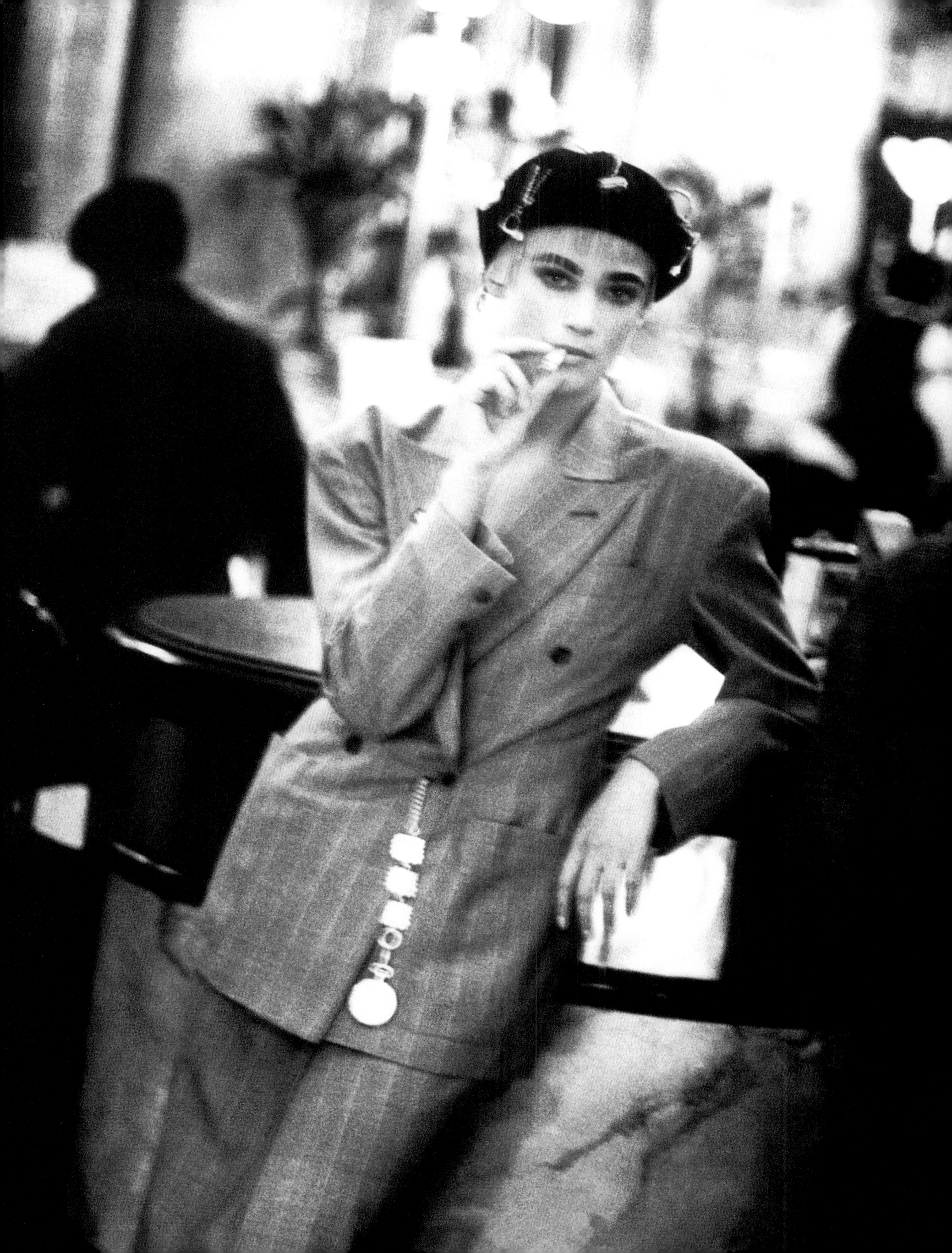

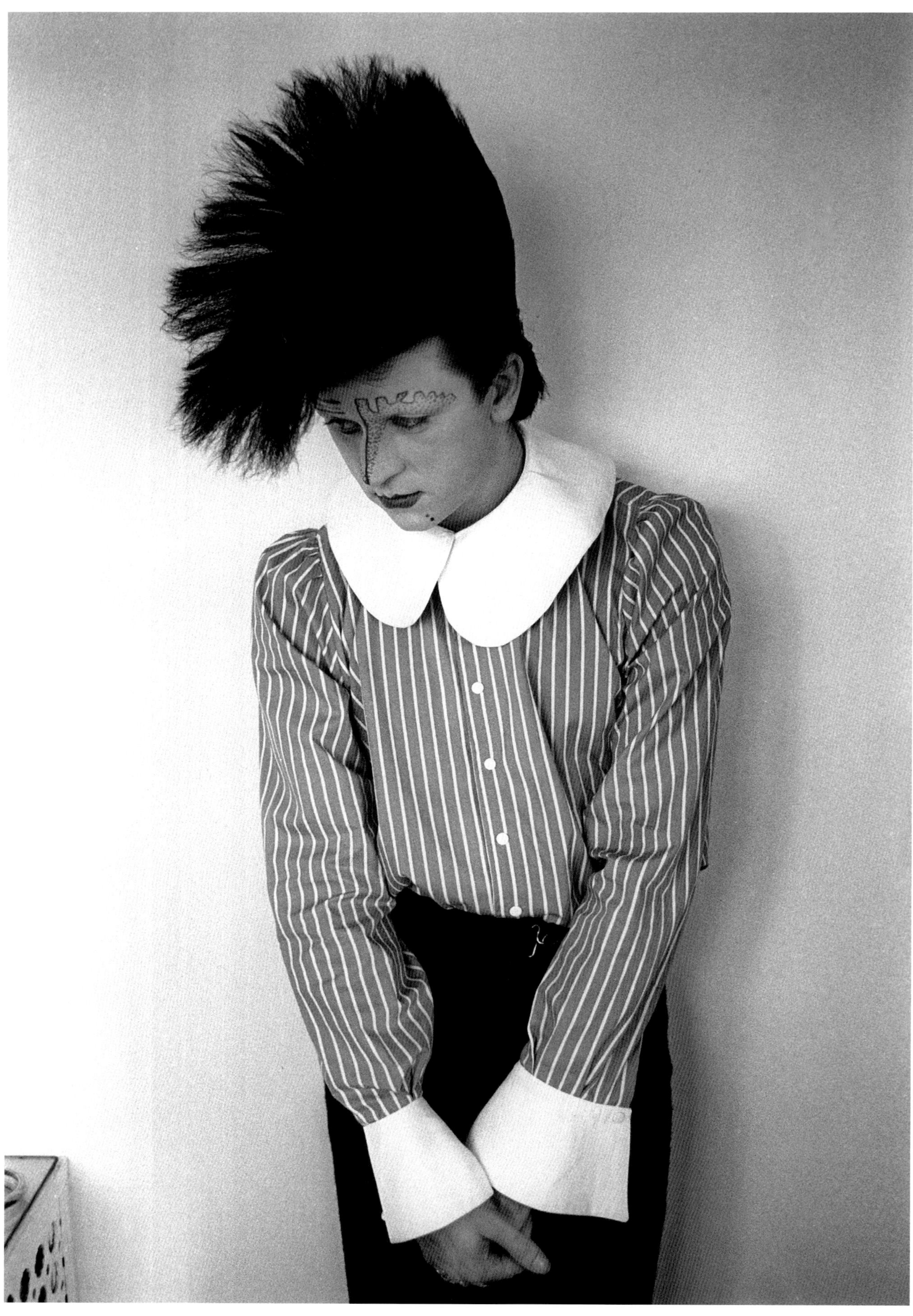

STEVE STRANGE
By Janette Beckman
October 1980

THE CLASH
By Pennie Smith
October 1980

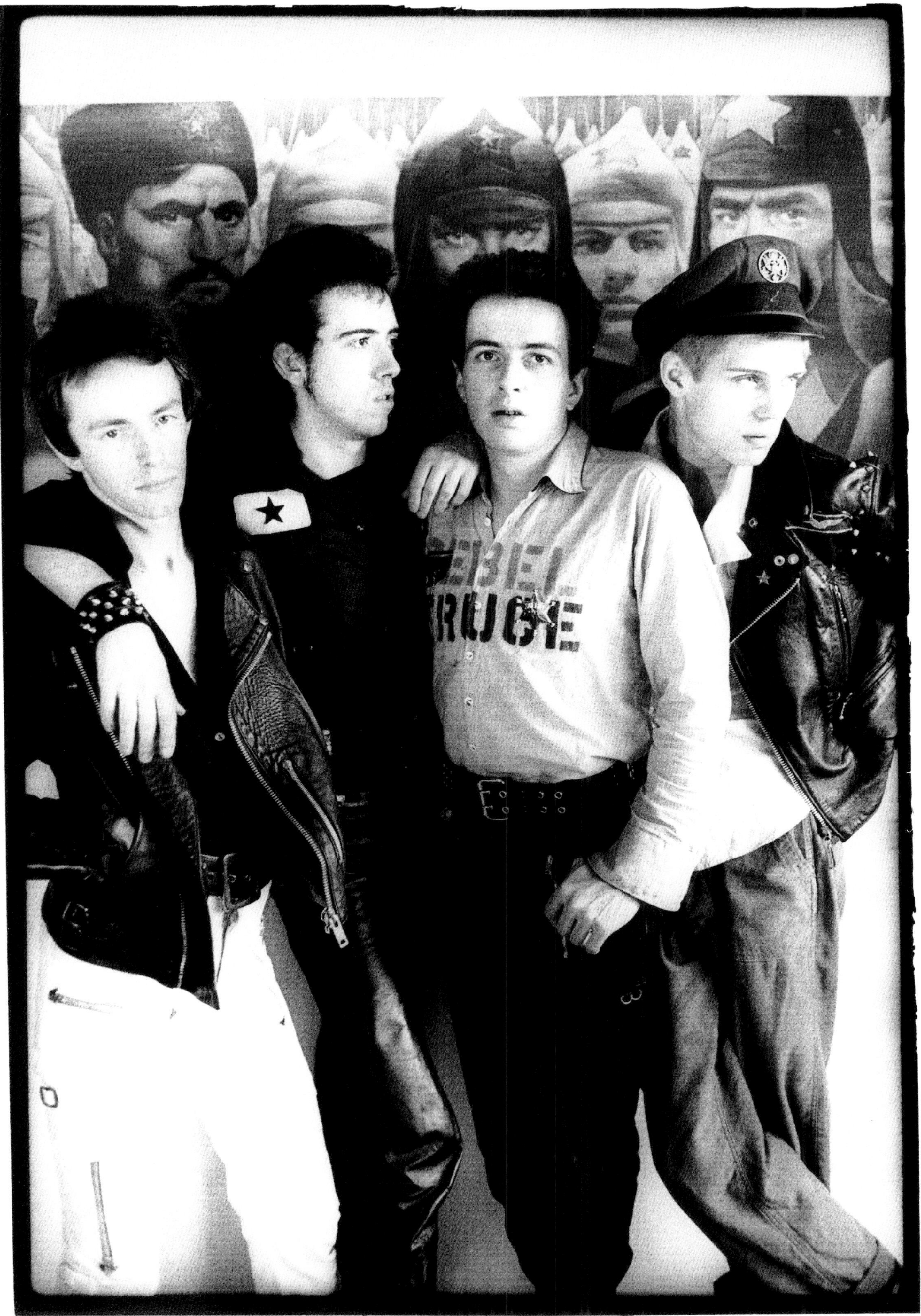

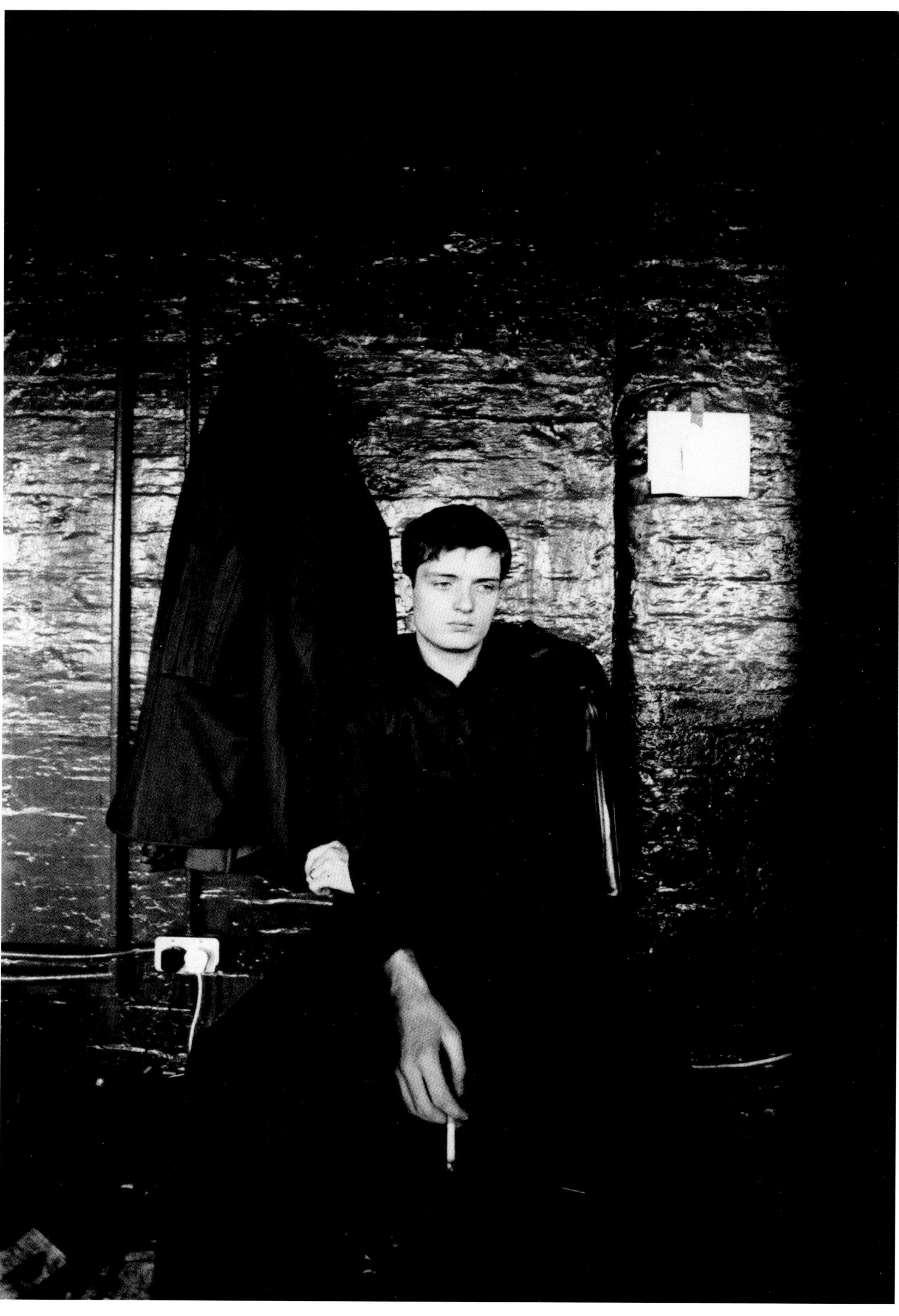

IAN CURTIS
By Kevin Cummins
November 1980

MADNESS
By Jill Furmanovsky
May 1980

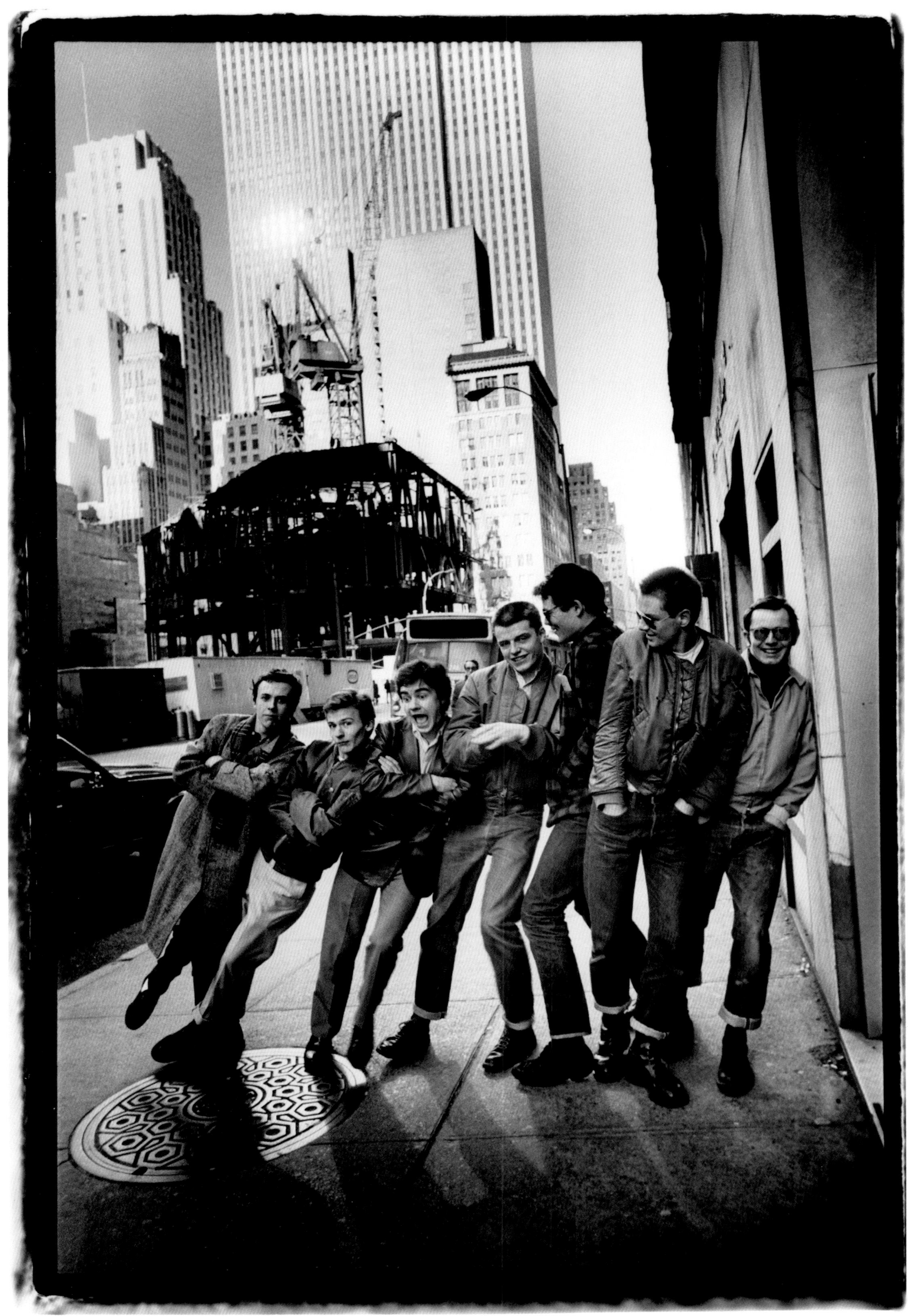

There was a direct lineage from the underground press, through the music press, to *The Face*. It was the natural conclusion. What set *The Face* apart was the calibre of the photographers who wanted to work there. Nobody worked for *The Face* for the money, you did it because you believed in the magazine and for the creative freedom that came with that belief.

CHALKIE DAVIES, PHOTOGRAPHER

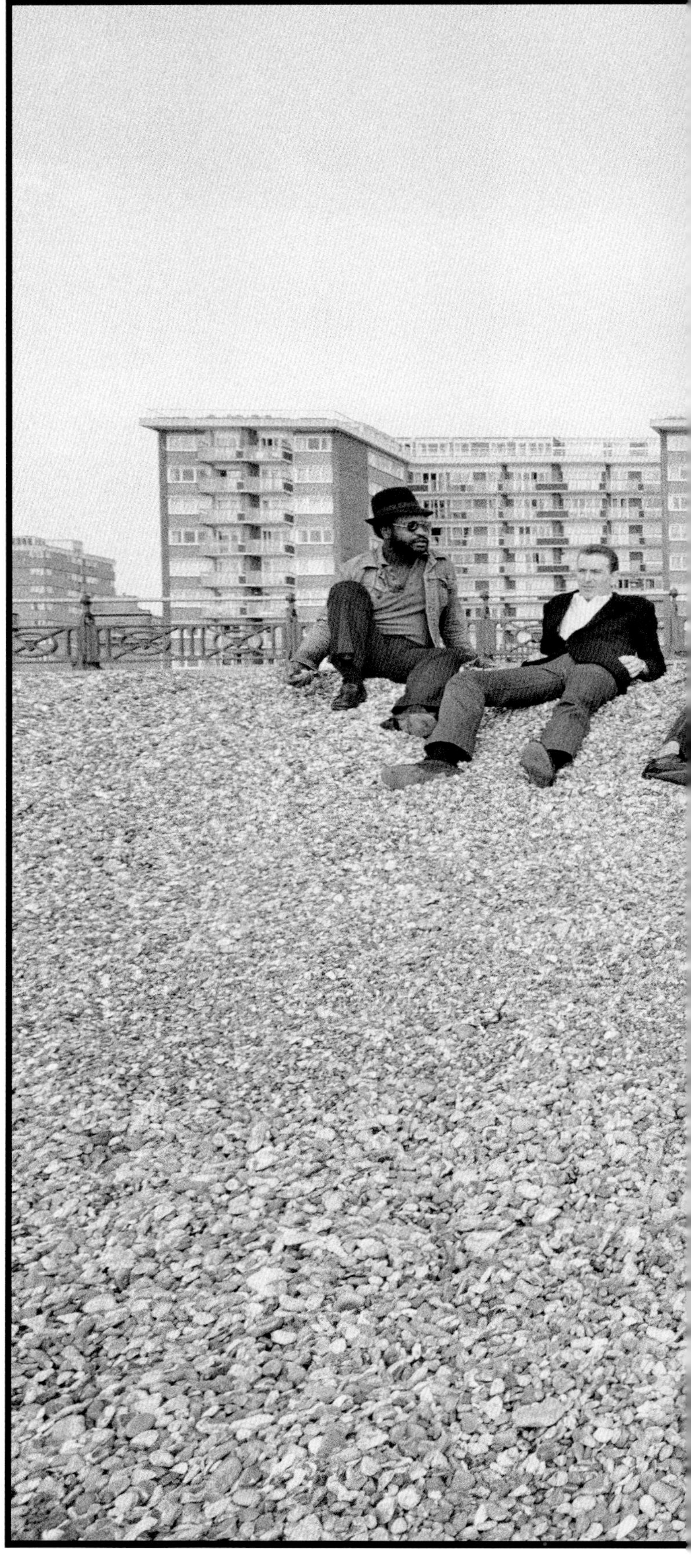

**MADNESS, THE SELECTER
AND THE SPECIALS**
By Chalkie Davies
May 1980

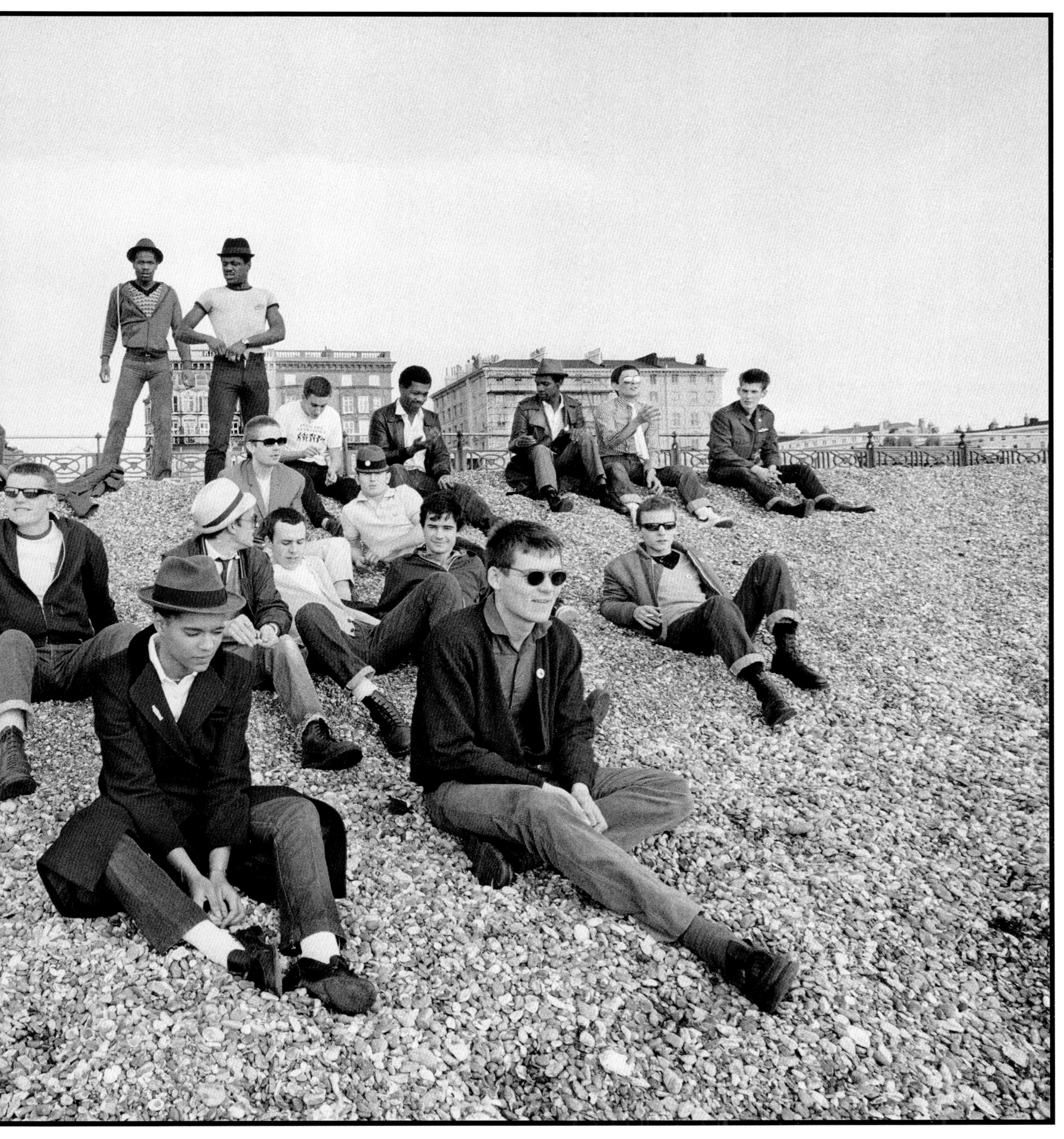

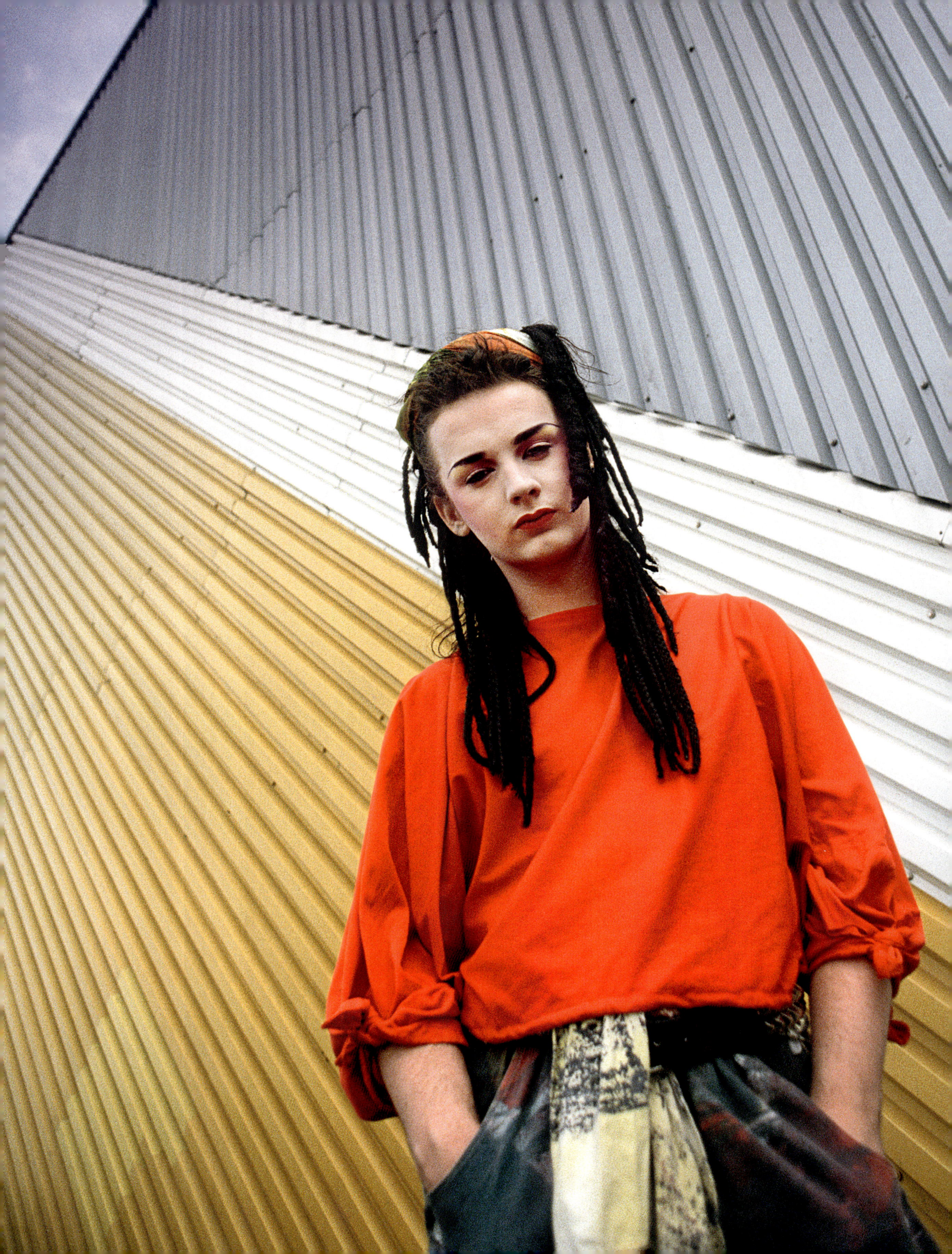

With almost all my early commissions for *The Face*,
I'd drive all over London to find interesting backgrounds
– including this warehouse on the North Circular Road.
I didn't have any photographic training, but wanted
to shoot images that were graphically strong and that
would look good on the page.
Derek Ridgers

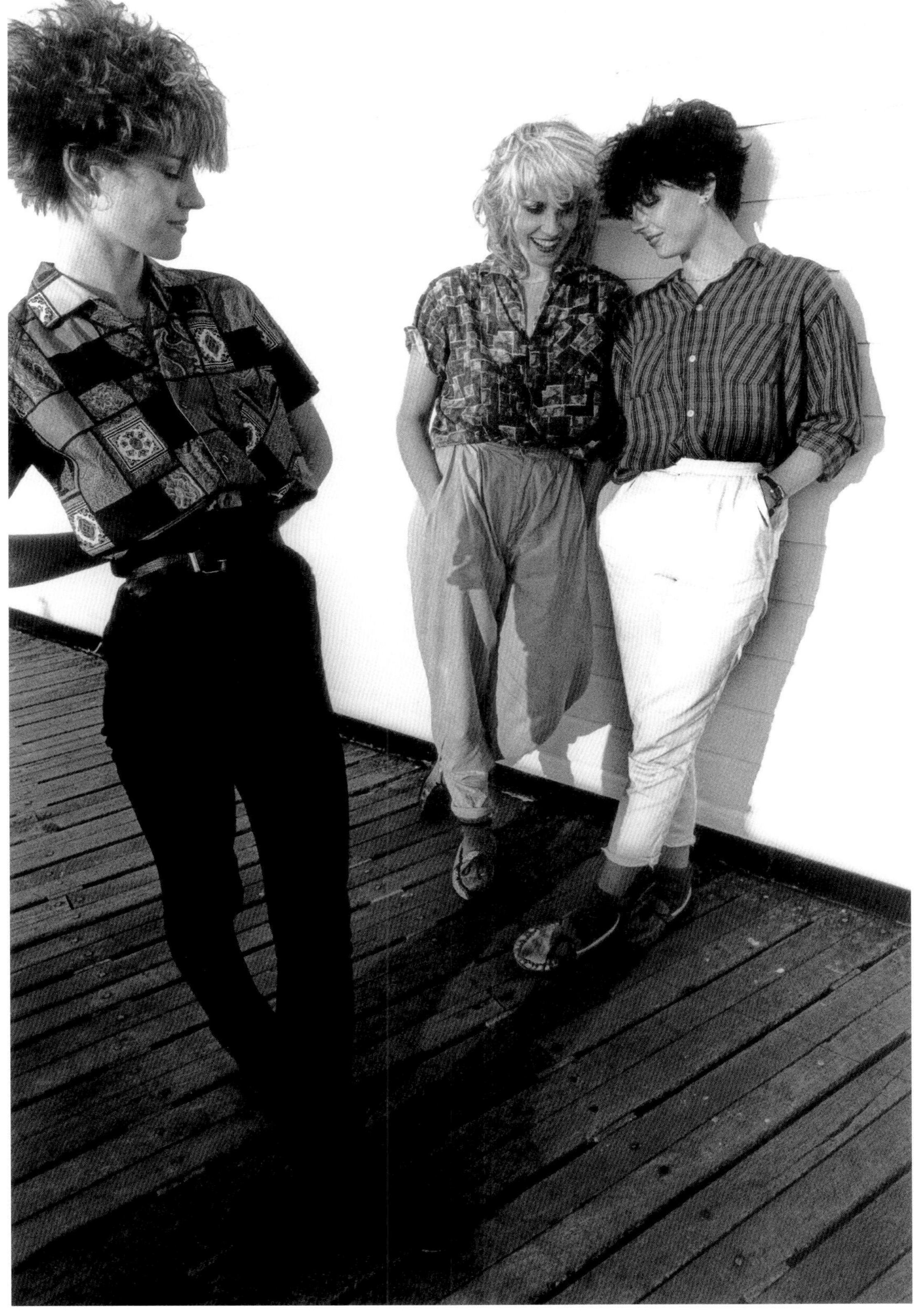

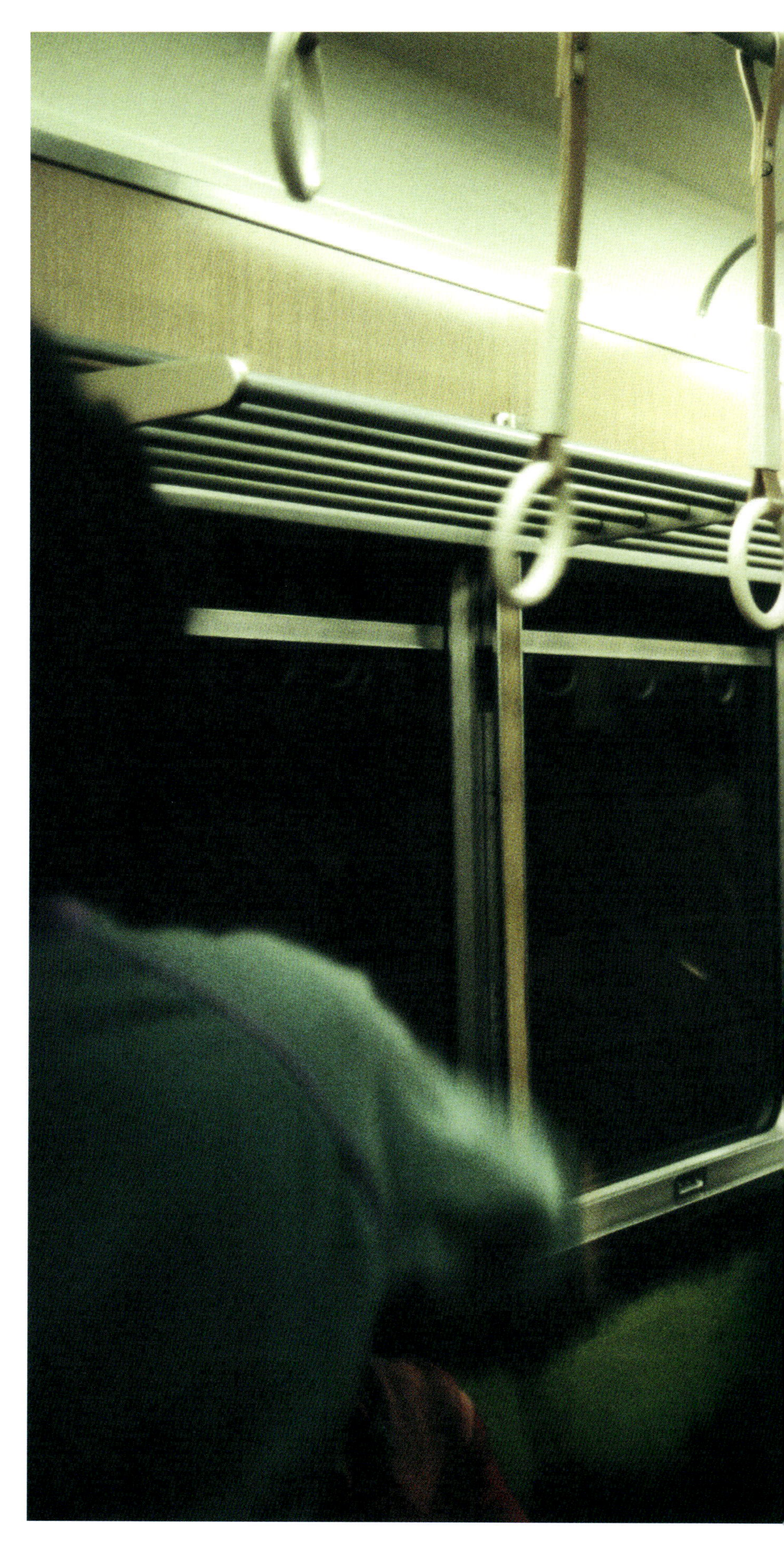

DAVID BOWIE
By Masayoshi Sukita
July 1980

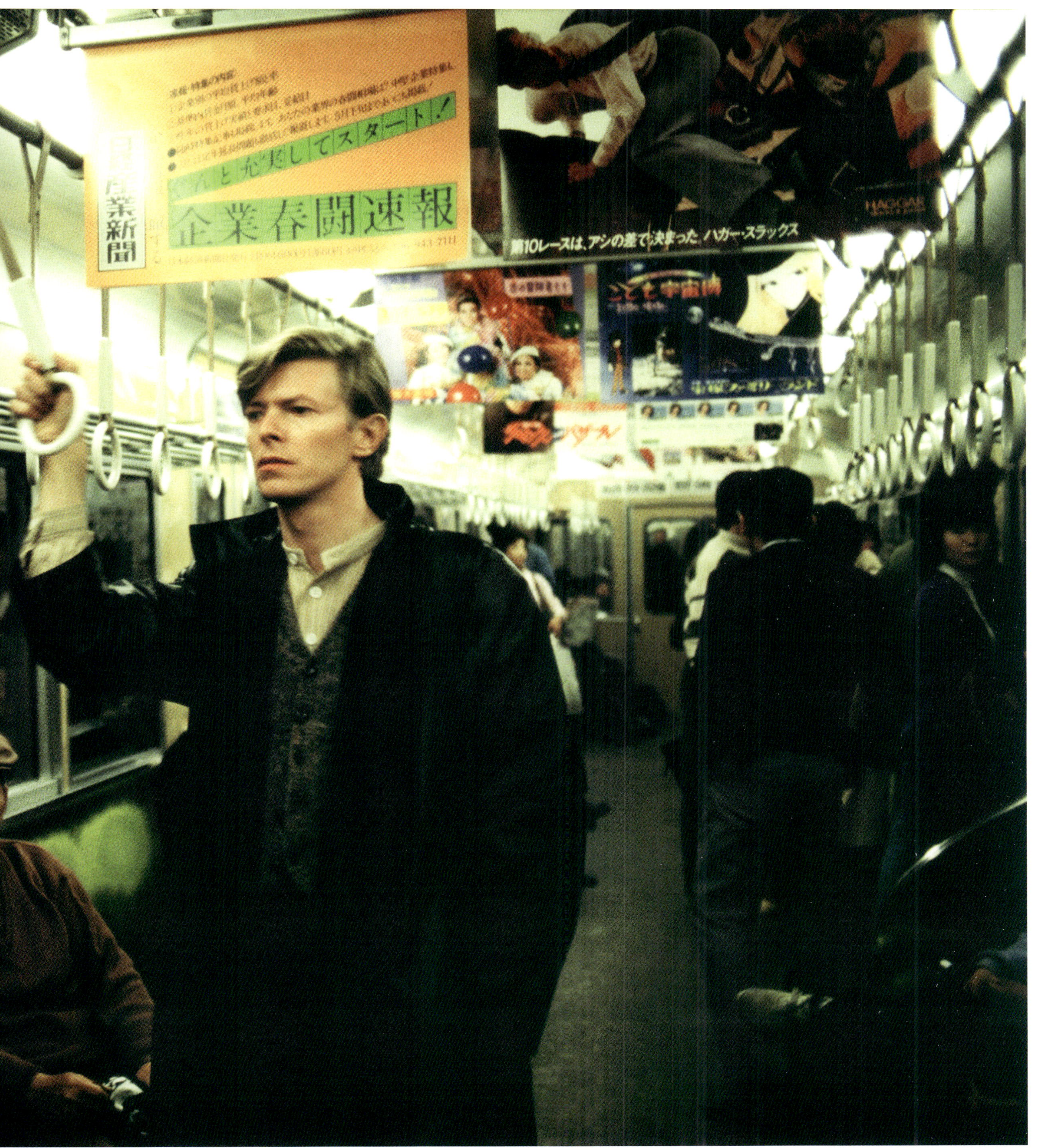
企業春闘速報
日本工業新聞
第10レースは、アシの差で決まった ハガー・スラックス
こども宇宙博

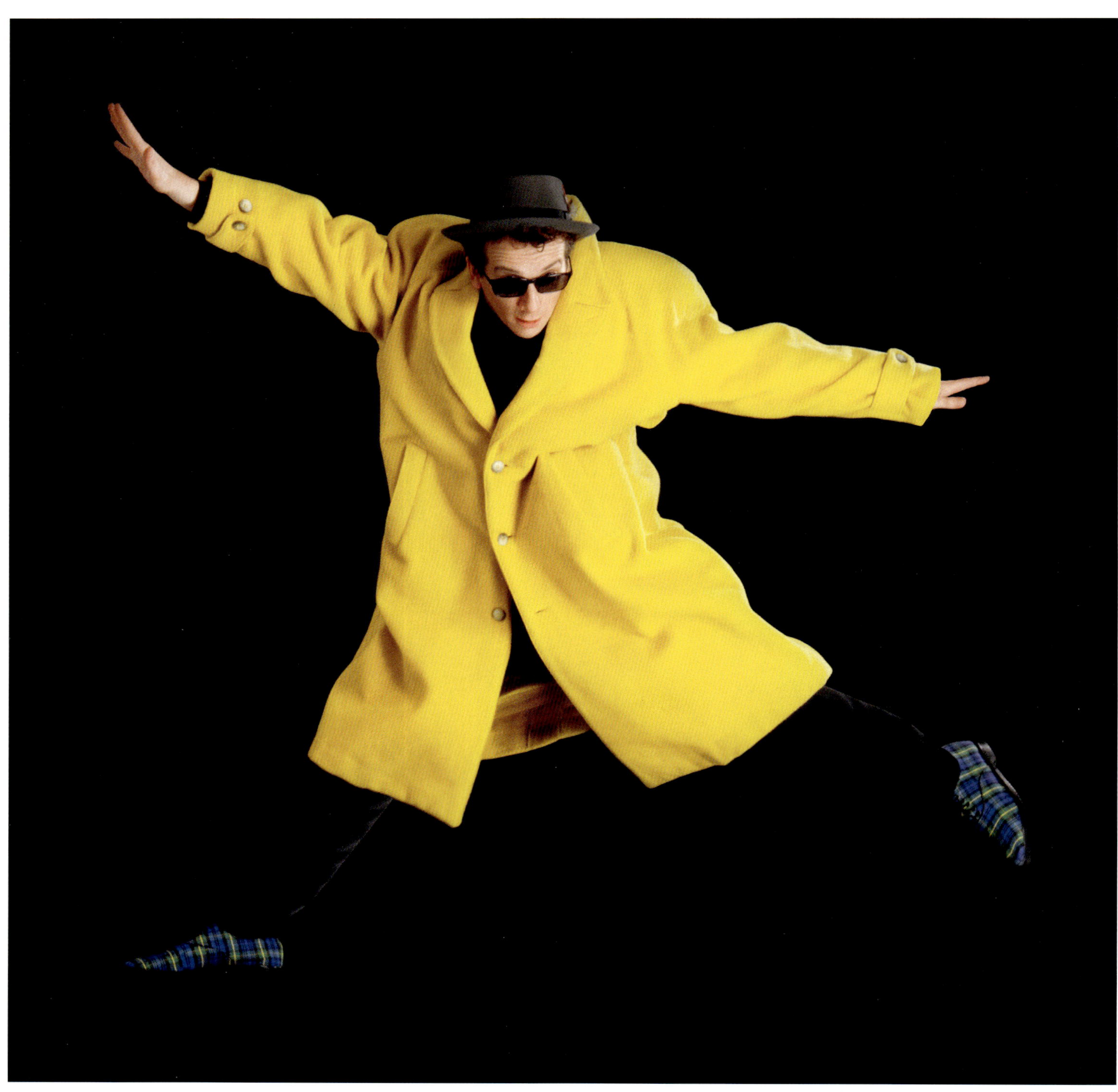

ELVIS COSTELLO
By Davies and Starr
March 1986

Studio portraiture is the purest
form of all. You control the light,
the atmosphere, and you carefully
manoeuvre people into revealing
themselves through the lens.
Carol Starr and I made these
photographs together, often using
two cable-release cords connected
to the same Hasselblad camera.
Chalkie Davies

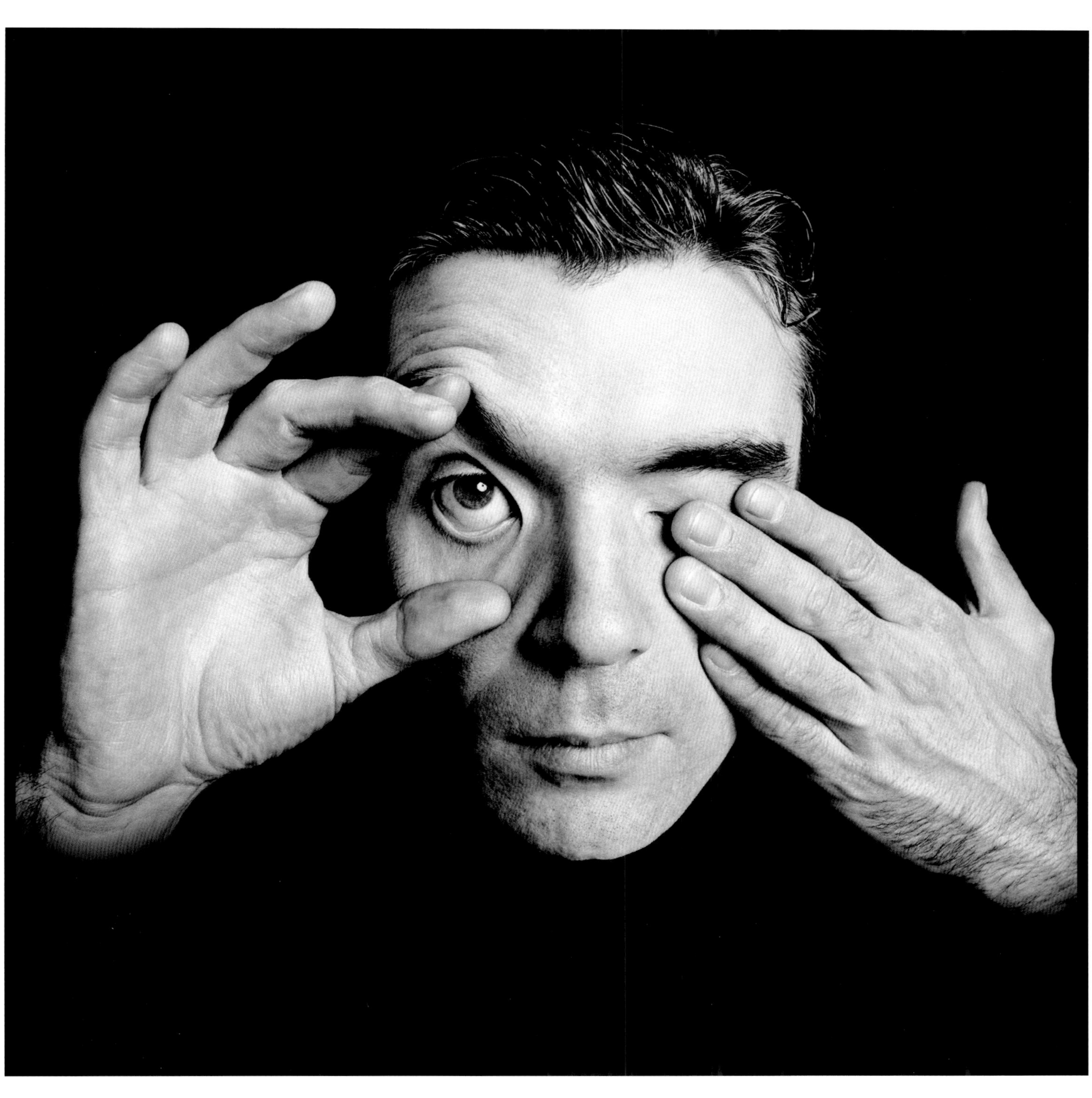

DAVID BYRNE
By Davies and Starr
June 1983

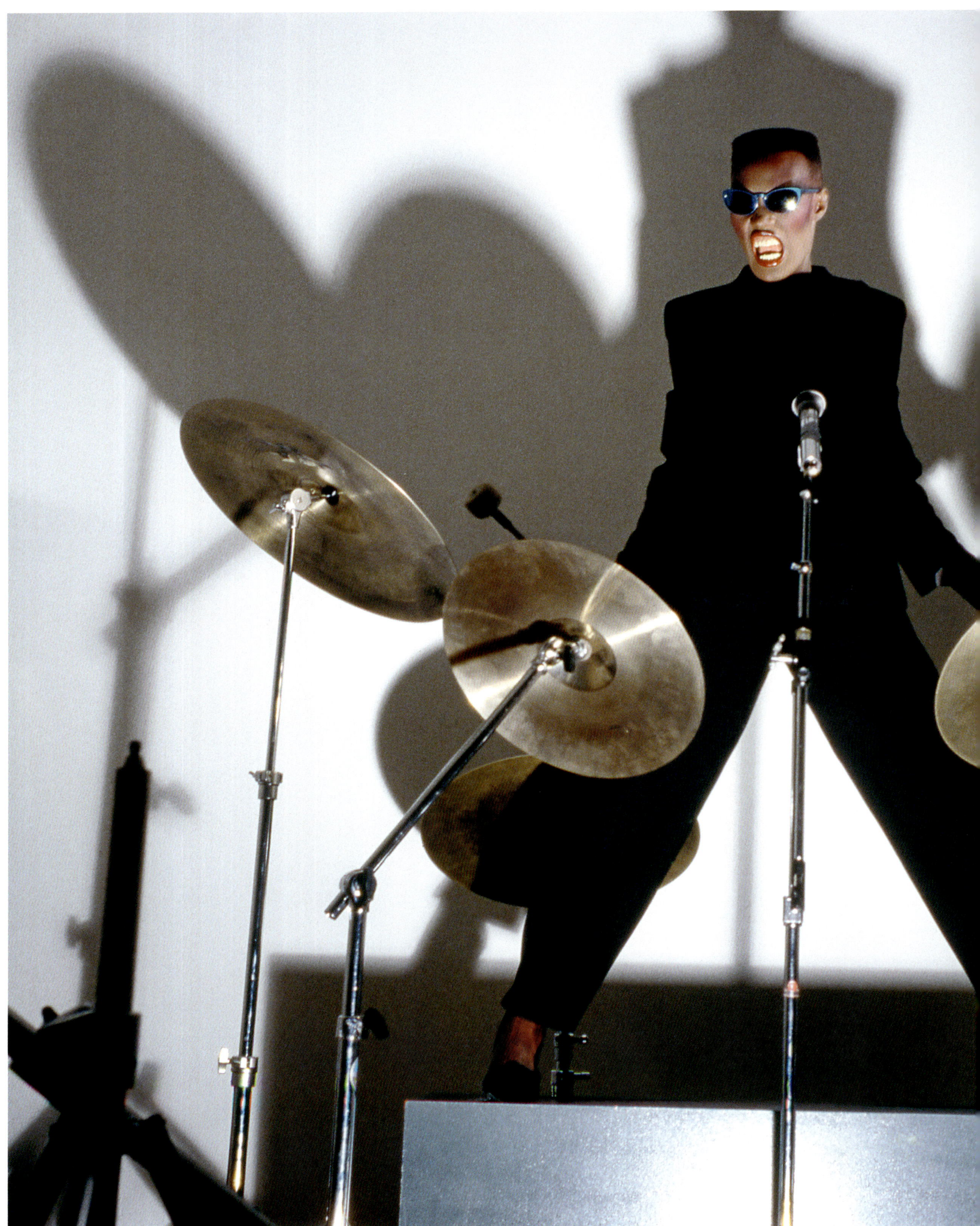

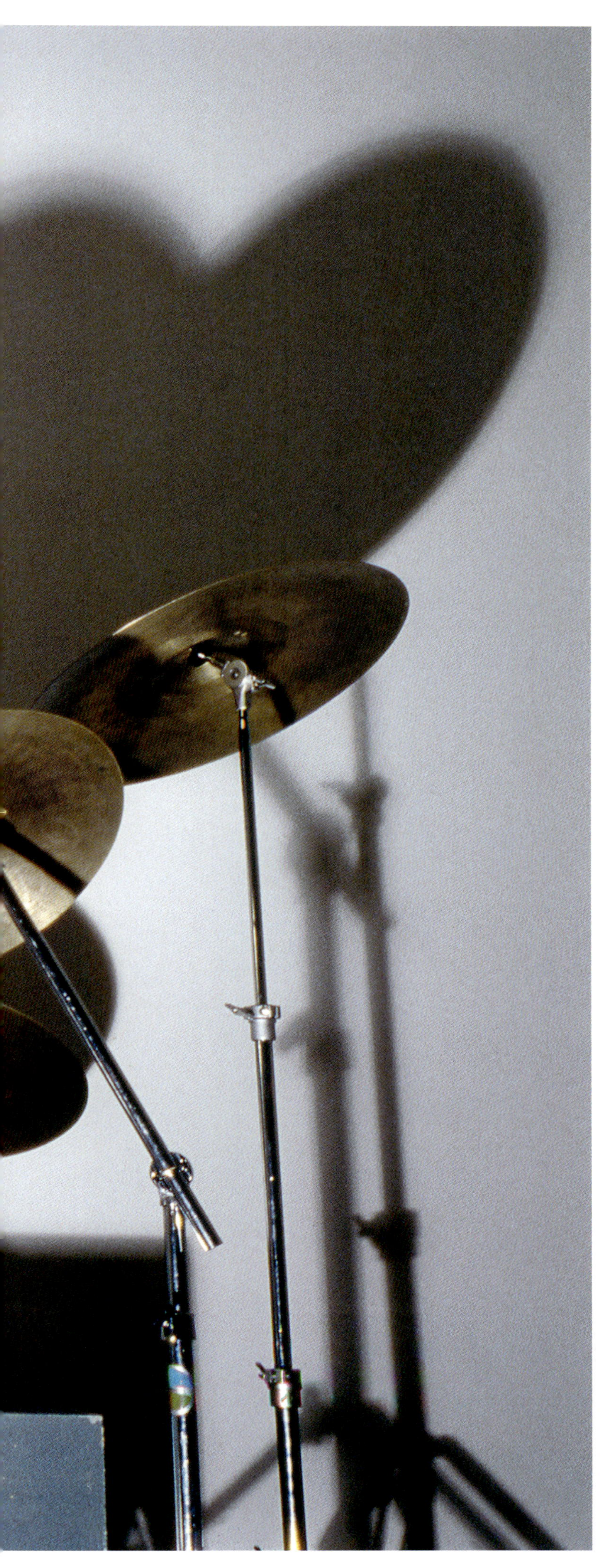

GRACE JONES
By Jean-Paul Goude
May 1981

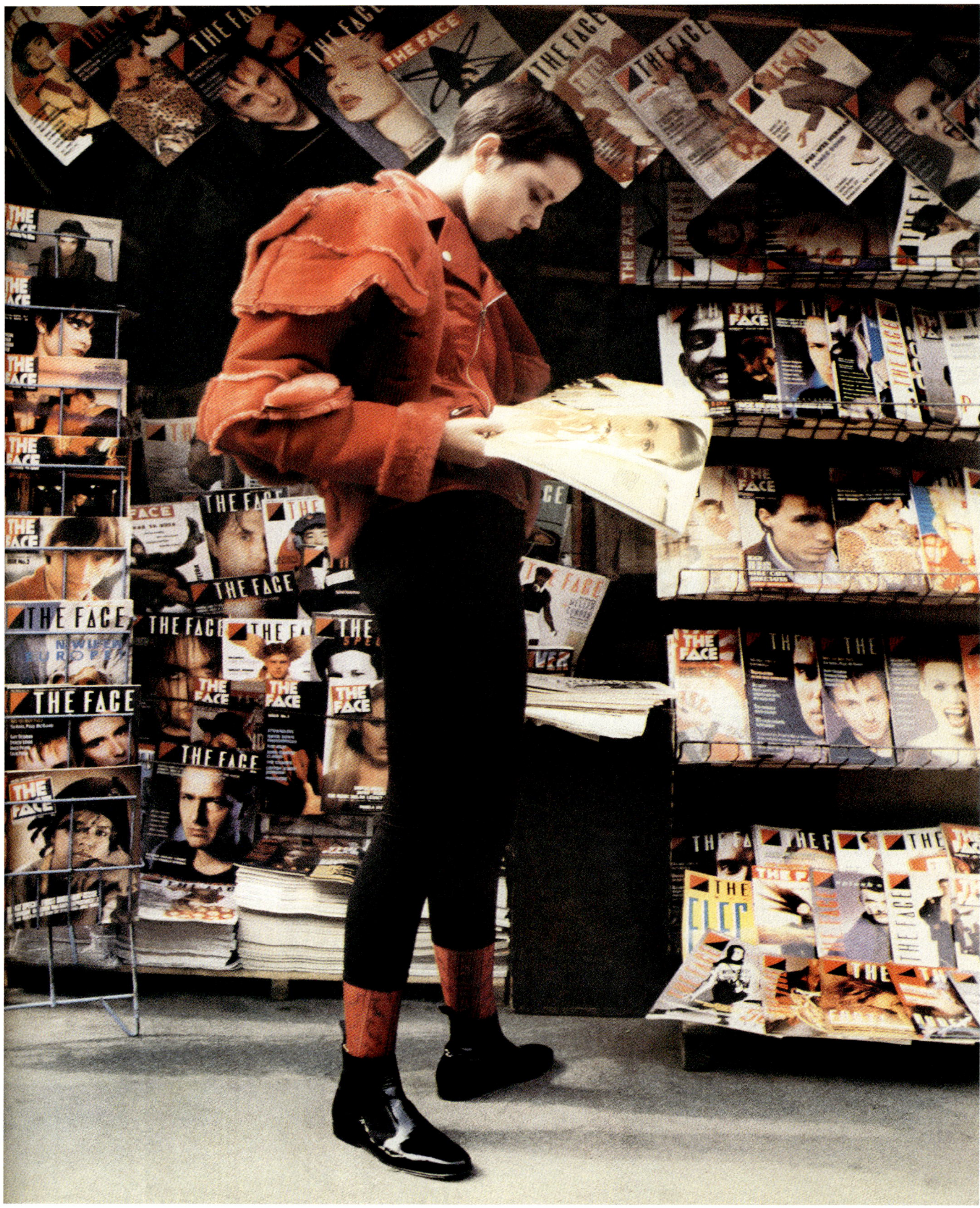

ALEX WORKS
By Anthony Gordon
Styled by Kathryn Flett
September 1988

We wanted to do a fashion shoot for the 100th issue
that showcased clothes but also said something
about the times in which we lived, from the
perspective of a woman. It was a tongue-in-cheek
look at the idea that a woman's work is never done.
We raced around town, doing everything
on a shoestring in a couple of days.
Kathryn Flett

SADE
By Jamie Morgan
April 1984

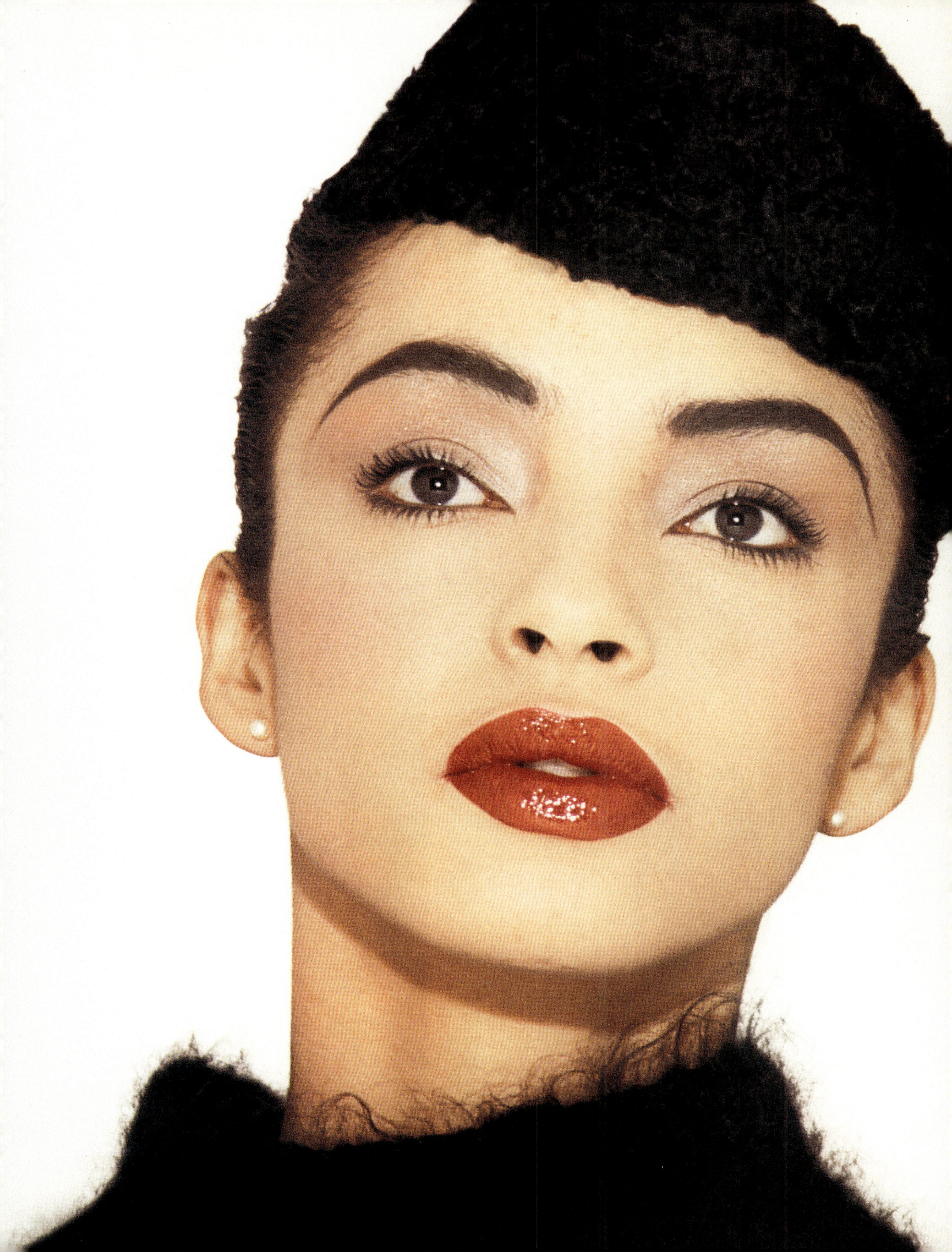

A NEW VOCABULARY

NEVILLE BRODY, JILL FURMANOVSKY AND SHEILA ROCK

Celebrated photographers Jill Furmanovsky and Sheila Rock contributed to *The Face* from the early Eighties. We reunited them with graphic designer Neville Brody, who was the magazine's Art Director from 1981 to 1986, to reflect on their experiences.

NEVILLE BRODY: I was working at Rocking Russian, a record-sleeve design agency in Soho, when Nick [Logan] approached me about designing a Kraftwerk spread for *The Face*, about a year after he'd launched the magazine. I quickly put something together for him and he jumped right in and appointed me as Art Director soon after.

SHEILA ROCK: Nick gave so many of us opportunities. The atmosphere at *The Face* was about allowing people to express themselves individually and, from a personal perspective, it really helped me evolve because, at the start, I didn't always know what I was doing – I was learning on the fly – but I could use *The Face* as a platform to try out different techniques. It fuelled my creative spirit. Nick was very much a hero to me.

JILL FURMANOVSKY: Likewise. I knew Nick from working for *NME*, before he launched *The Face*. He was the best editor of the tabloid music press. He was a picture man.

NB: Nick was a shrewd businessman. Not only did he discover young talents, he also knew they would help his product. So, he peopled his magazines with young writers and photographers, and the Buffalo movement. Nick had a sense of where things were going.

SR: I remember going to Nick's dark little office down some rickety stairs. It was pretty grim but, as a young person, everything in Soho seemed exciting. I remember pitching him ideas all the time. None of us got a lot of money from *The Face* – I got paid £50 for a job once, which was a big deal at the time – but it was about having the opportunity to express yourself in a magazine with an energy that resonated with so many young people. I remember being called up by record labels to do photoshoots and they'd ask me to send my portfolio. I'd say: 'I'm sorry, I don't have a portfolio.' And they'd say: 'Oh, that's cool. It doesn't matter: you work for *The Face*.' Doing photography for *The Face* and being in the music business was my education.

NB: Soho back then was an amazing community of clubbers, actors, fashion designers, architects, musicians and filmmakers. *The Face* was a magazine for that community by that community, but its influence went way beyond. Advertising agencies would copy what *The Face* was doing in terms of typography, portraiture or photography and turn it into a style. Then it became known as 'the style magazine' and I hated that because we were trying to do something that wasn't about style; it was about changing culture and society. There were a lot of serious articles in *The Face*: cultural observations by writers like John Savage and Paul Morley; stories about oppressed people in other countries. Yet, despite the magazine's political undertone, some people just hijacked its stylistic attributes and iconic images.

SR: I would use the word 'inspired' rather than 'hijacked'. You inspired other designers! I never heard the word 'style' in London during the 1970s then, suddenly, it became a new vocabulary. *The Face* was a publication for young people who were dressing up and trying to express themselves through what they saw in the clubs and on the street.

NB: Despite resenting the fact it was called the style bible, the term stylist was essentially invented by Ray Petri, the creator of Buffalo. Before then, you'd have people putting the fashion together, but they weren't stylists in the way Ray was, using models that were mates or people he'd seen on the street.

JF: When it started, *The Face* was subtitled 'Rock's Final Frontier' and its content was mainly about rock. But it became

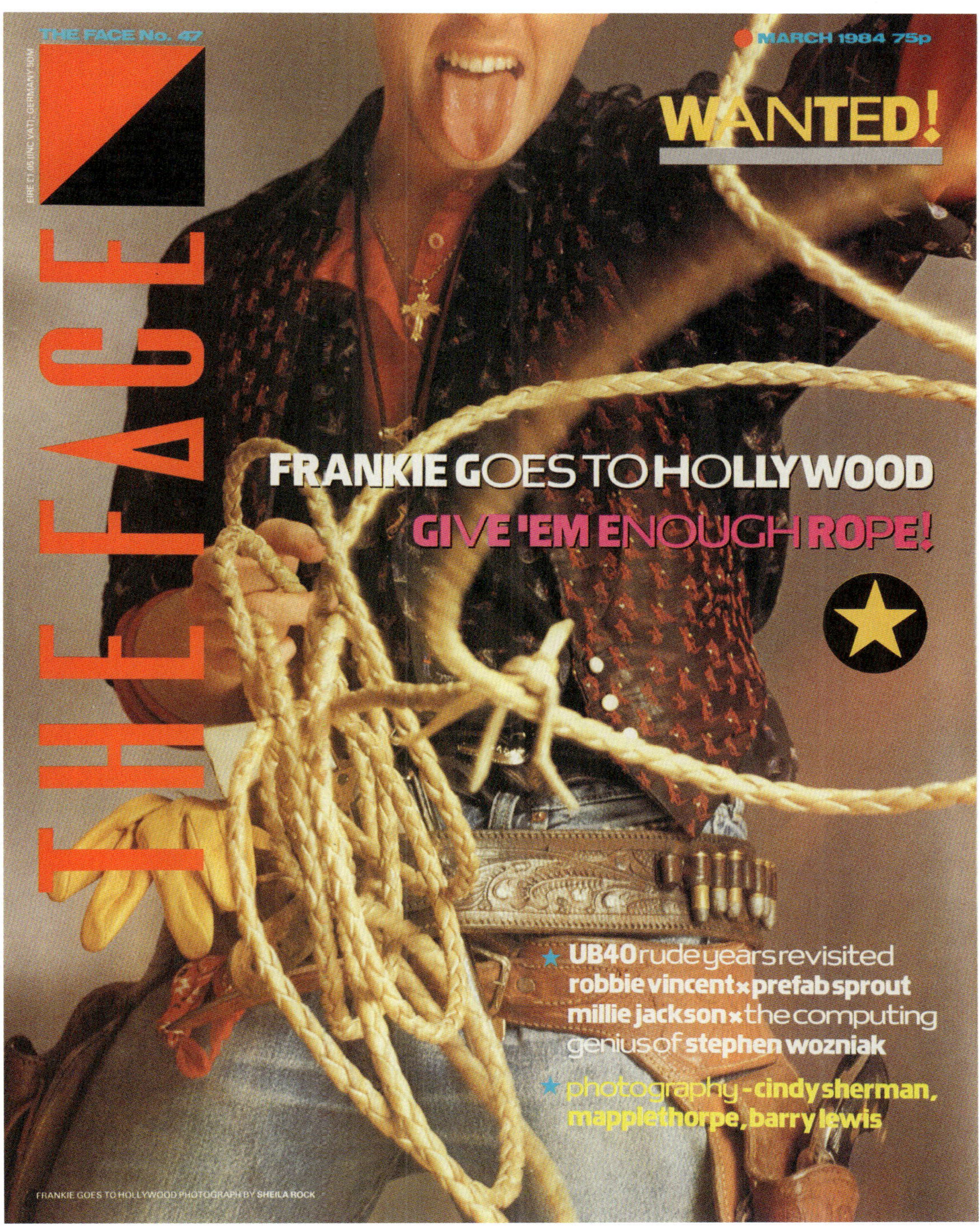

HOLLY JOHNSON
By Sheila Rock
Design by Neville Brody
March 1984

such an iconic magazine that fashion photographers wanted to work for it. Sheila's photography has always been elegant, and her portraits of rock musicians were like fashion shoots. I came from photojournalism – from shooting bands on tour – so, when *The Face* started to get fashion-y, I felt a bit lost. I had people asking me what they should wear and I had absolutely no idea. At first, I didn't get on too well with stylists coming along with racks of clothing or faffing with hair and make-up. For me, *The Face* was at its best during those first five years, when it was still commissioning quite a lot of rock work, and there was this fantastic mixture of photographers, from Anton Corbijn's gritty portraits to Mike Laye's original and memorable covers.

SR: I was always interested in the extraordinary marriage between youth fashion, music and poverty. The way punks and new romantics dressed was so creative because they couldn't afford to buy their clothes in fancy shops. It really inspired me. I got to meet people like Judy Blame, who would pitch ideas to me that I would then pitch to *The Face*, and the response was always: 'Why not?' I never had anything rejected.

NB: One of the reasons the magazine was so creative was because no-one art directed the photographers.

SR: I agree; it was organic. Someone would have an idea, then suddenly you'd be in the middle of it, with everyone working on the fly and Neville orchestrating.

JF: We hadn't had anything like Neville's beautiful layouts in the music press before. Previously we were known as 'snappers': we'd come along for a few minutes at the end of a journalist's interview. But in *The Face* our work was credited. Combined with what Neville was doing with the spreads, it elevated our status in line with fashion photographers. Previously, the journalist was king: they had all the time and you had ten minutes at the end. *The Face* inverted that: the photographer got an hour and the journalist got ten minutes at the end. That's an exaggeration, of course, but the image became king, and it was all thanks to the

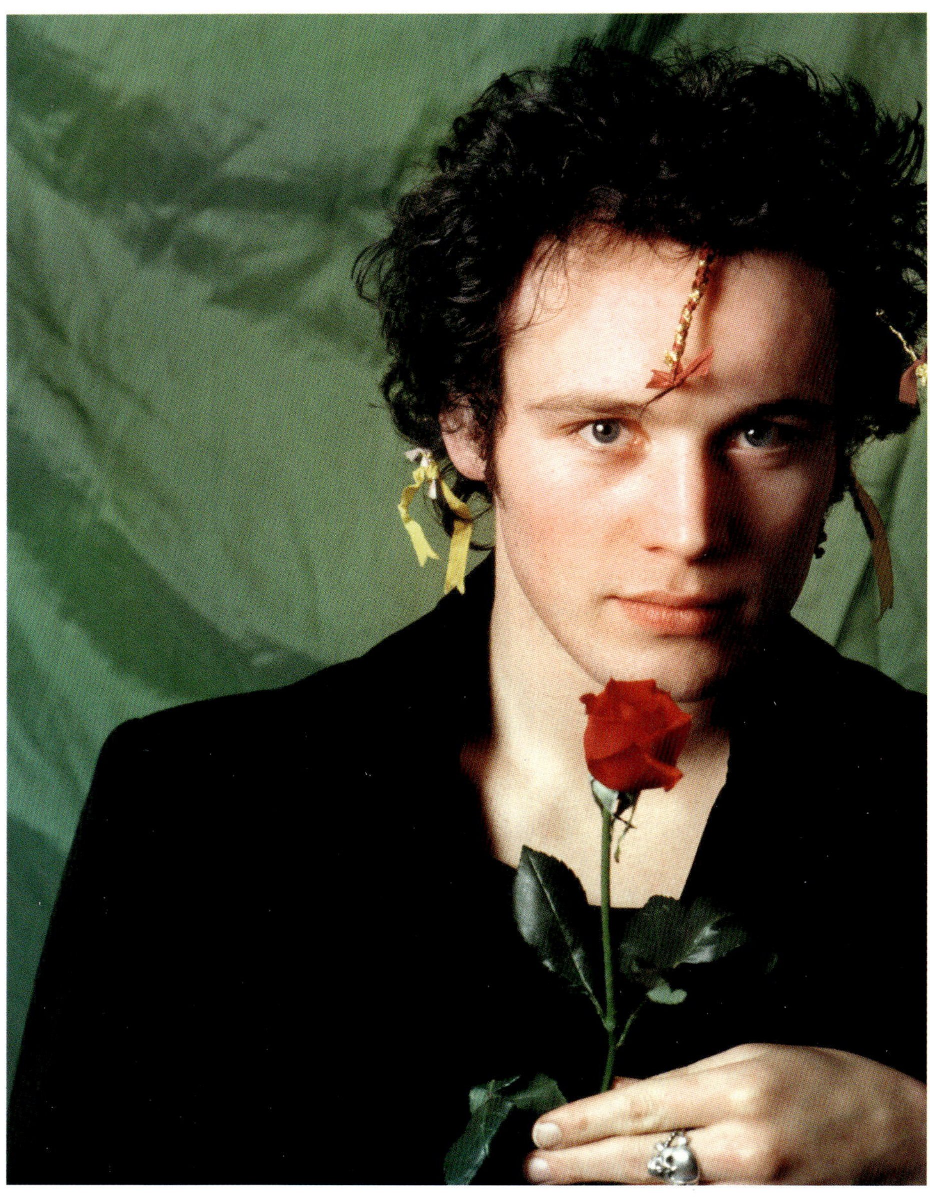

ADAM ANT
By Jill Furmanovsky
Styled by Liz Gilmore
April 1981

way Neville and Nick were packaging it. It was a really important moment for us as music photographers.

SR: I agree.

NB: The whole magazine was art directed, designed and sent to production in a week. It was the maddest. We'd do at least two or three all-nighters in that week. Bike messengers would be waiting to rush a layout over to the printer while we were still trying to design it. At the same time, we'd also be thinking ahead to the next issue, so texts would be coming in and we'd be deciding who to commission for the photography. But, as I said, we art directed by choosing the right people for the right jobs. So, in selecting a photographer, we were saying: 'We're gonna give you the story. Let's see what you do with it.' It was a unique approach and only happened for a small window of time because photography is quite heavily art directed again today and, I suspect, apart from reportage, it had been quite heavily art directed in the past. For *The Face*, interviews were never pre-structured and imagery was never pre-imagined. Ideas came from everyone. So, I might be involved in headline-writing and a writer might suggest a photographer. It was beautiful in that sense: there were no boundaries as to what you could contribute.

SR: At the time, I didn't feel I was doing anything radical, but *The*

Face gave me the privilege to work with some iconic people. All my photo shoots are spontaneous. I usually have a vague idea of how I want to approach something, but I respond to the moment – to the person or to the clothes they're wearing. Most of the people that I photographed had an extraordinary sense of their own style.

NB: Nowadays, you have to sign a contract and get permission to crop a photograph. But, in those days, we'd crop images and use them with the words and headline to create a narrative. Everything came alive on the page as an integrated whole and that was really important to us. Generally, the photographers loved what we did with their images because we were bringing a different eye to them. And, unusually, we worked with the same stable of brilliant photographers for years.

JF: Most of those photographers had come from the music press, but there were others like Sheila and Nick Knight who brought their own natural stylishness. If you combine that kind of photographer with Neville's graphics and a picture man like Nick, you've got this magic moment in design and journalism, which I think was pivotal to the whole culture.

NB: More than anything else, we were just really excited by what we were doing. Excited to be discovering talented new fashion designers, writers and photographers. *The Face* had its finger on so many pulses that it was like a creative magnet: people would just walk into the office with a photo session or an article already done. It was brilliant.

SR: A major shift *The Face* brought to my own practice was collaborating with stylists. I used to do my own styling, but through the magazine I met some extraordinary creatives, like Judy Blame. I thought everything he did was phenomenal. I would base an entire photoshoot around some found objects he'd gotten together. Everything we did was slightly provocative. I think all of us gravitated toward things that were not run-of-the-mill.

NB: The stylist was an entirely new role and a complete change in approach because, unlike someone simply doing fashion and make-up, they would often choose the photographer they felt was appropriate to the story.

JF: Nick commissioned a fashion shoot from me, despite my ignorance about clothes. I photographed a model wearing an exquisite linen suit made by John Flett, a contemporary of John Galliano's from Saint Martins [school of art]. It was styled by Paul Frecker with make-up by William Falkner. I learned a great deal from that dynamic duo. I just thought: 'I know nothing about this stuff. Go for it! I'll light it nicely.' I had started out with a second-hand Hasselblad that I couldn't even connect the flash to properly. But, when I began working with *The Face*, I had taken a leap of faith and rented my own studio. I remember thinking: 'I can do this!' My time at *The Face* went on to influence my entire career.

SR: Like you, Jill, the more work I started to get, the more I had to up the ante, so I bought a second-hand Hasselblad and really focused on improving my technique, because I never went to photography school.

JF: Me neither. I'd get given jobs then not know how to use the equipment! I mean, we were winging it, weren't we?!

NB: Even though *The Face* was of its era, when you show it to people now, they think it's contemporary. It has this timeless quality, which I think we felt, even if we didn't entirely recognise it. For me, this period was magical: dynamic and serendipitous.

SR: It was an inspiring environment, because if you had an idea, you could run with it. The result was a defining moment in British cultural history.

JF: *The Face* was certainly pivotal to my career, and I think it was truly ground-breaking in terms of journalism and magazine publication.

NB: Coming out of the 1970s, there was this explosion of punk and underground youth culture. The whole of the UK was buzzing, with bands coming out of Leeds, Manchester, Sheffield. *The Face* was the culmination of an incredibly powerful set of energies – a rare moment of connection. ∎

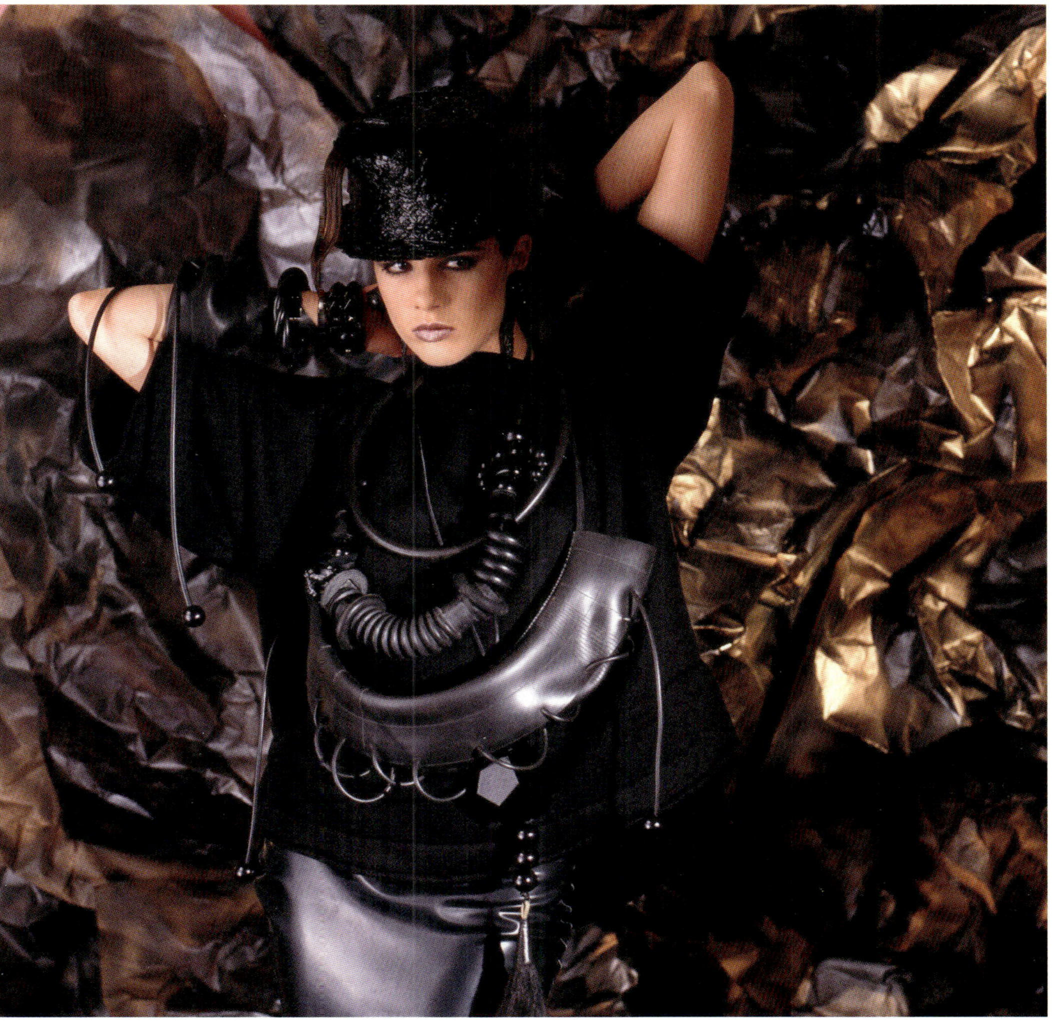

CASH FROM TRASH
By Sheila Rock
Styled by Judy Blame
January 1984

RUN-DMC AND FRIENDS
By Janette Beckman
November 1984

I was commissioned to photograph a new group. It was before cell phones and emails, so I called the telephone number I was given – it was Jam Master Jay's mom's house. Jam Master Jay arranged to meet me at a subway stop and we walked over to meet the group and some friends on a tree-lined street in Queens. Run-DMC and their friends Fludd, Butter Love, Cool Tee and Runny Ray were perfectly styled, wearing Adidas, Kangol hats and Cazal glasses. They were just hanging out in the dappled sunlight on a spring day on the street where they lived. *Janette Beckman*

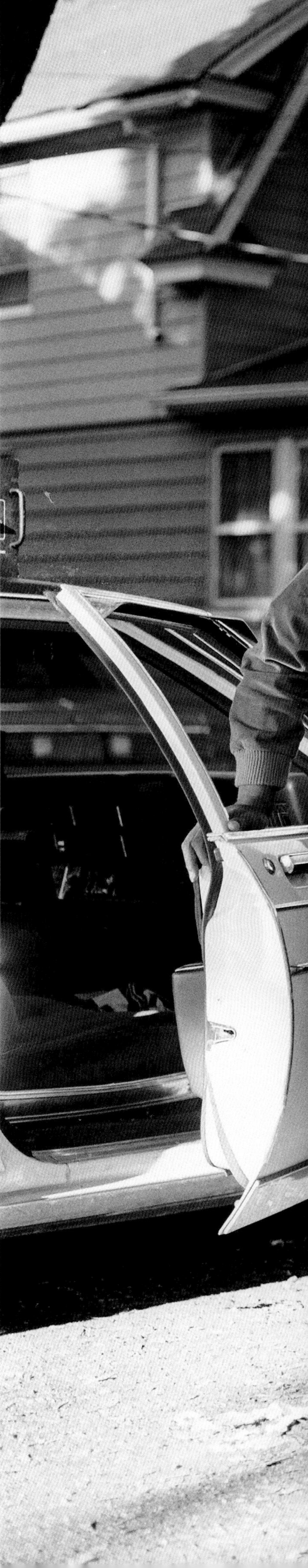

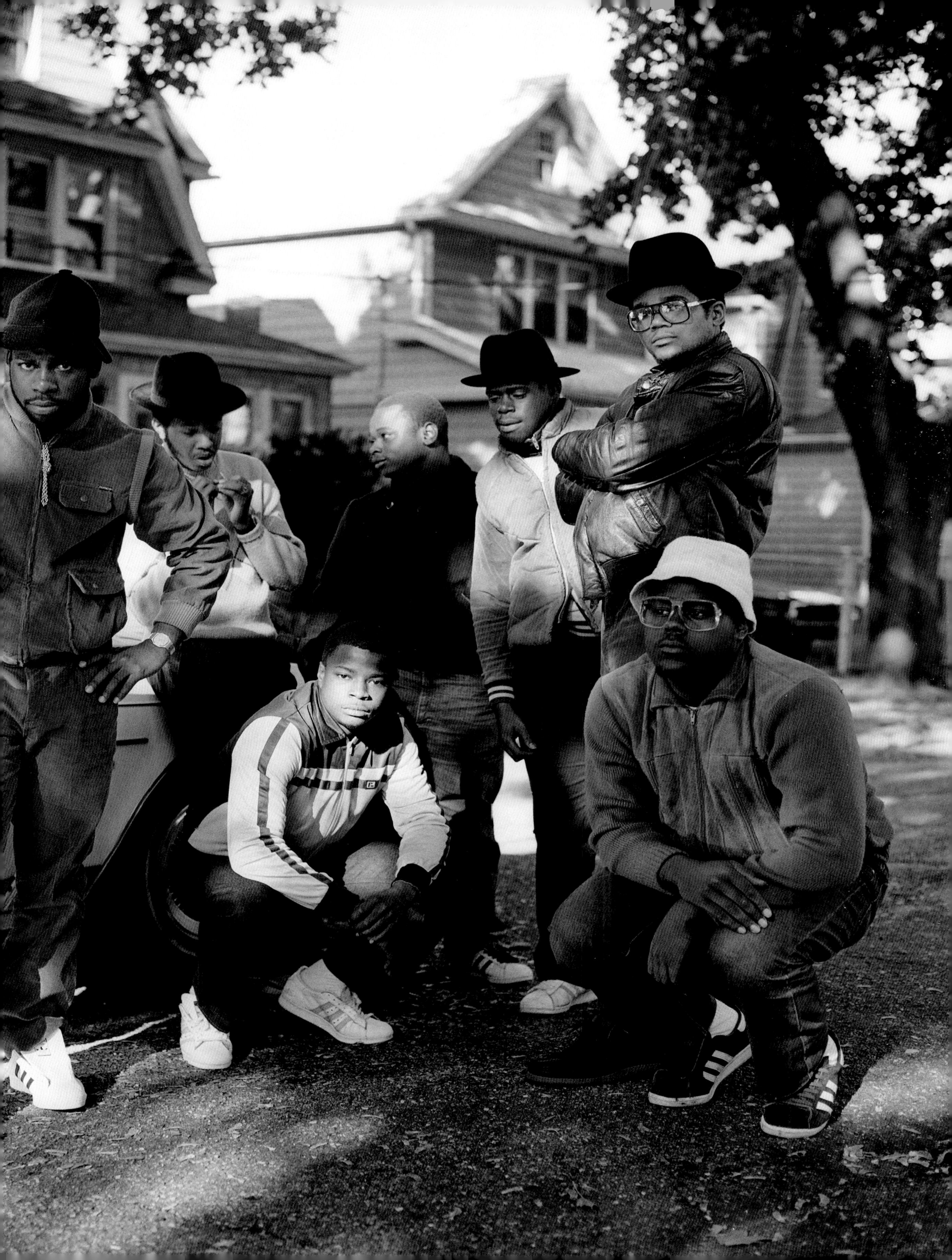

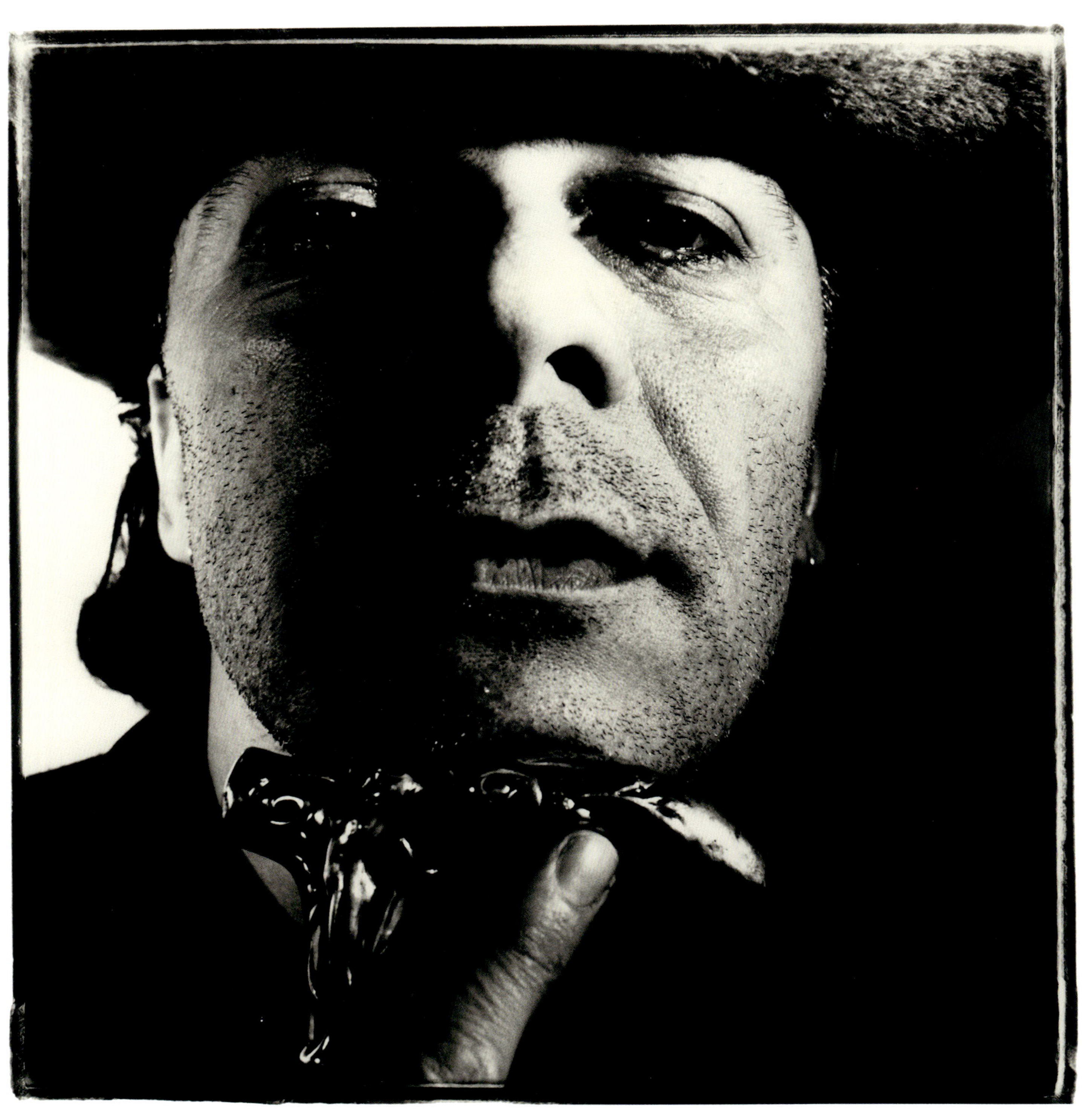

IAN DURY
By Steve Pyke
April 1984

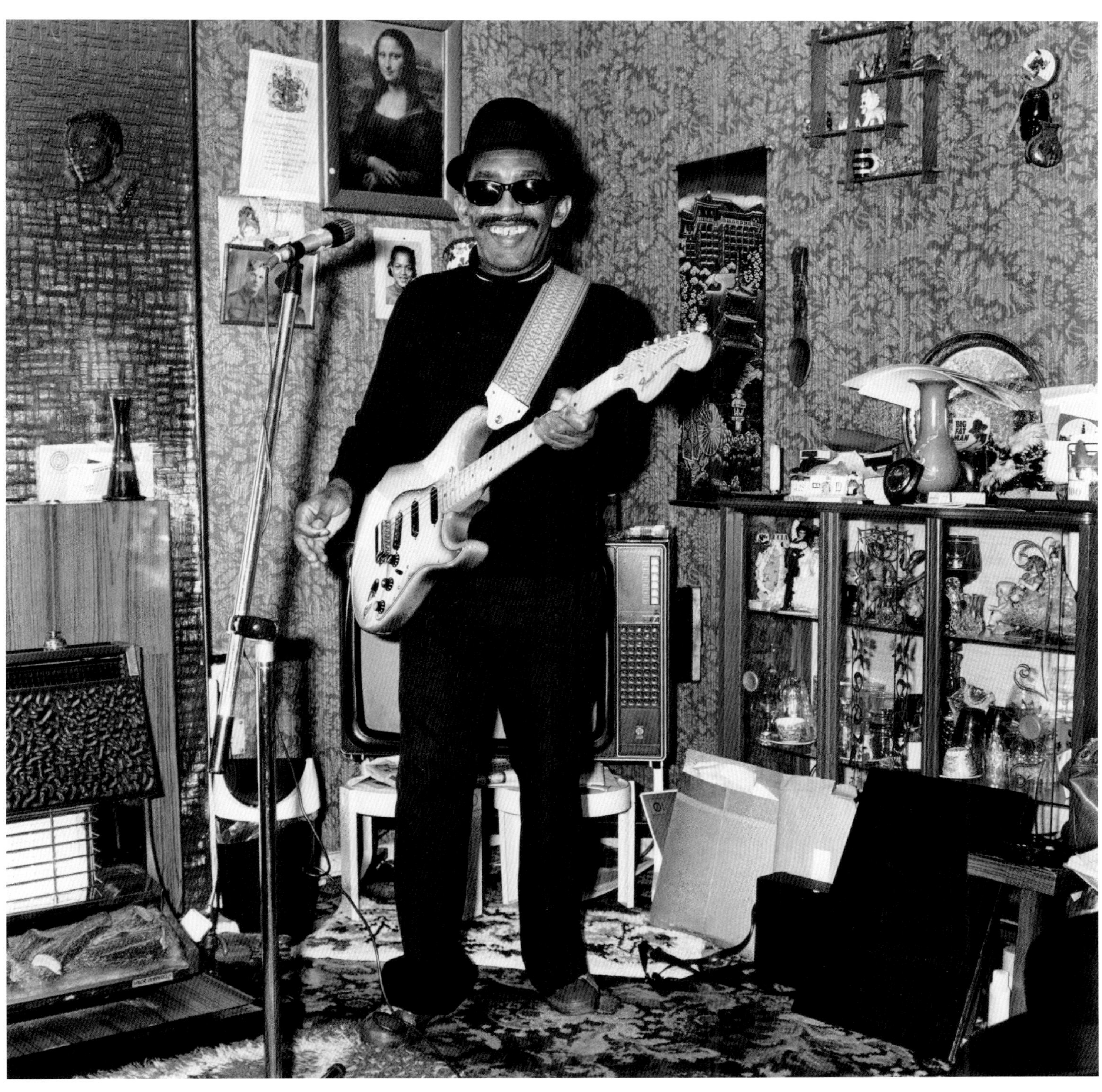

LAUREL AITKEN
By Janette Beckman
September 1980

The Face sent me to Leicester to take
a portrait of the 'Godfather of Ska',
Laurel Aitken, at home. We got on
immediately. I loved his small flat,
with the Mona Lisa and his family
pictures on the wall, teacups in a
cabinet. He was Cuban-Jamaican,
and so much of his history as an
immigrant is in that photo.
Janette Beckman

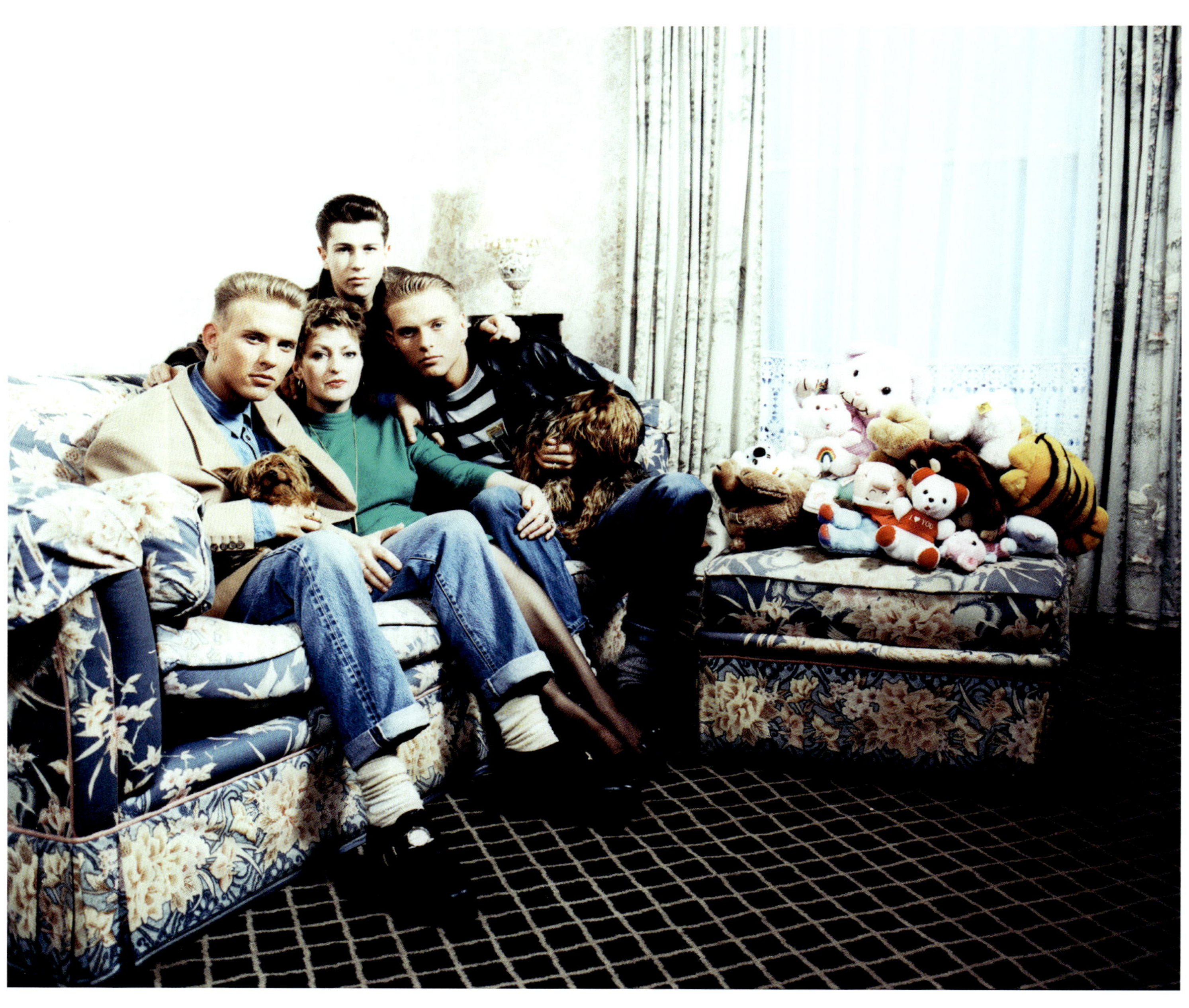

BROS AND CAROL GOSS

By Christian Thompson

April 1988

IGGY POP

By Robert Erdmann

December 1986

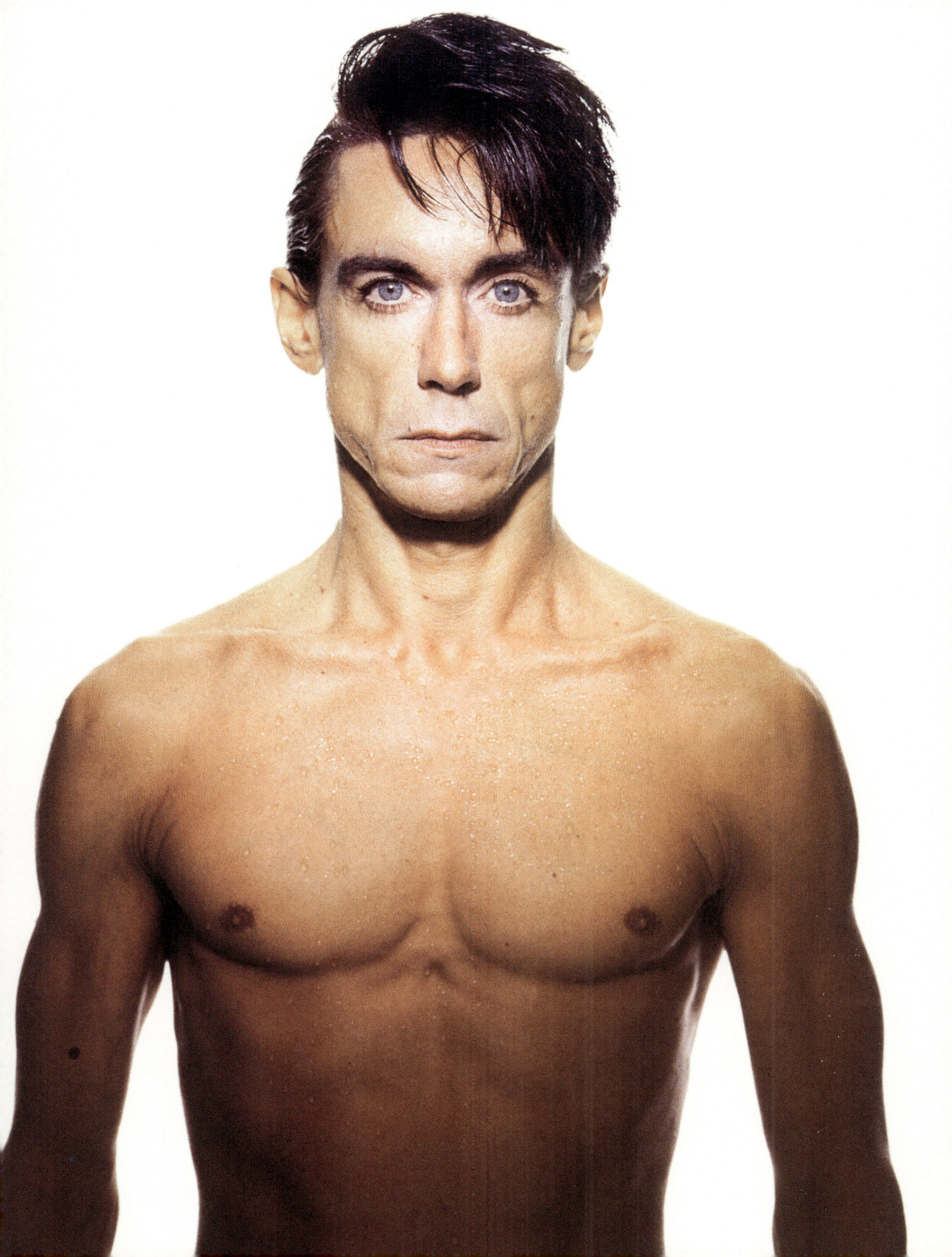

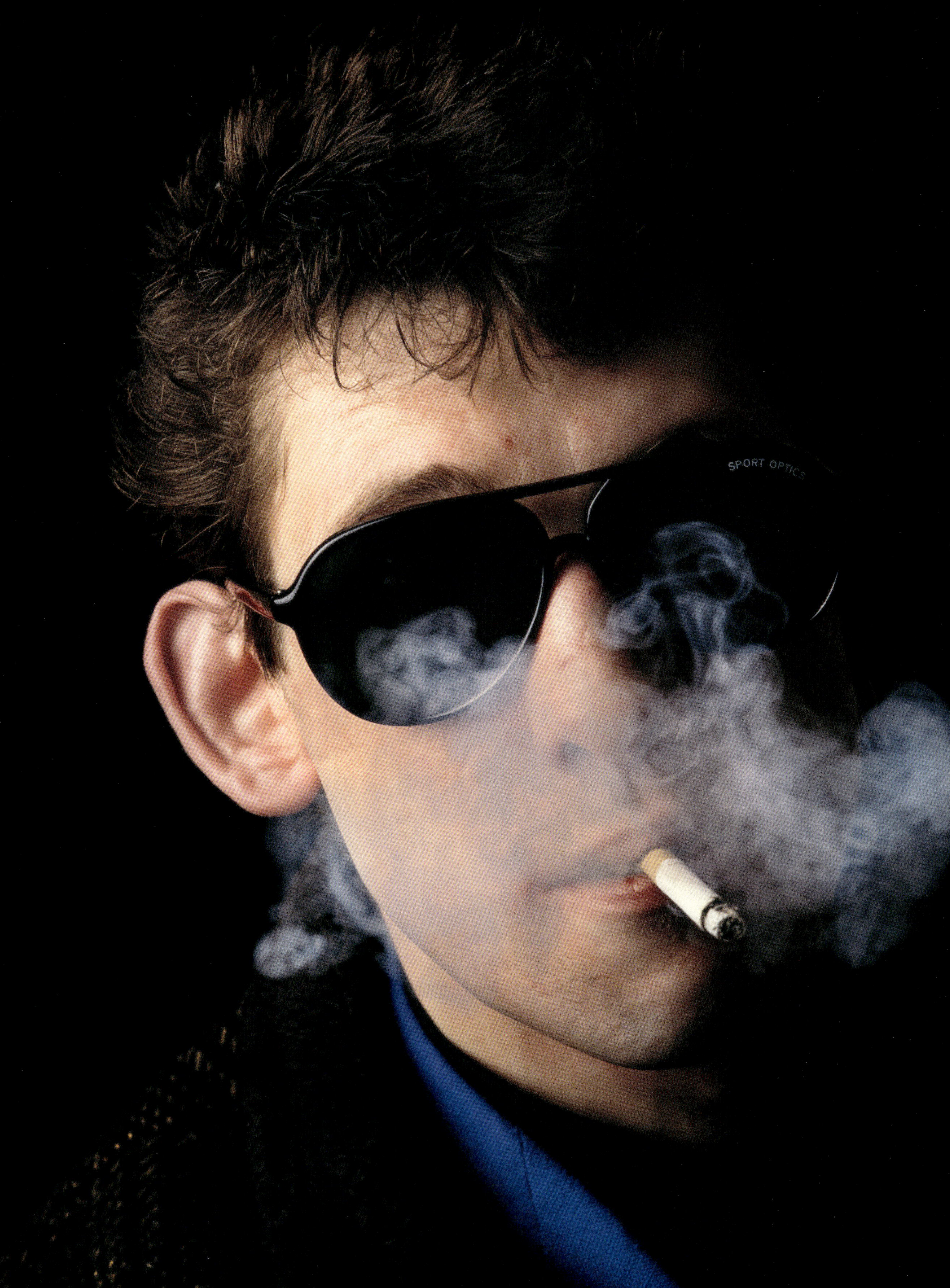
SPORT OPTICS

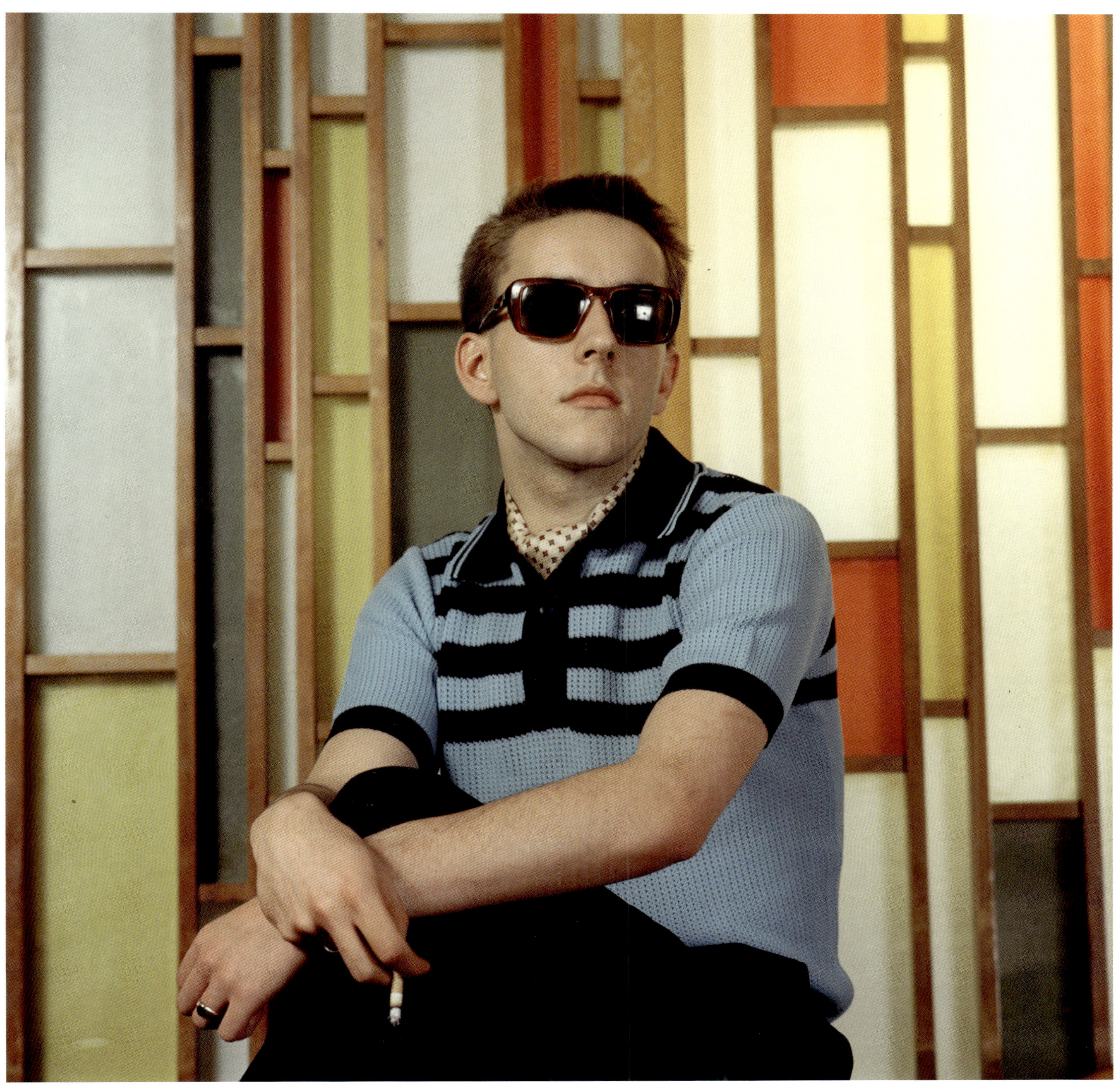

SHANE MACGOWAN
By Kevin Davies
April 1988

The shoot was at the Birmingham
NEC and Shane MacGowan had
literally just walked off stage. I held
the camera two feet from his face.
He sat down, lit a cigarette and
asked if his feet were in the shot,
because he wasn't wearing socks.
Kevin Davies

TERRY HALL
By Davies and Starr
July 1980

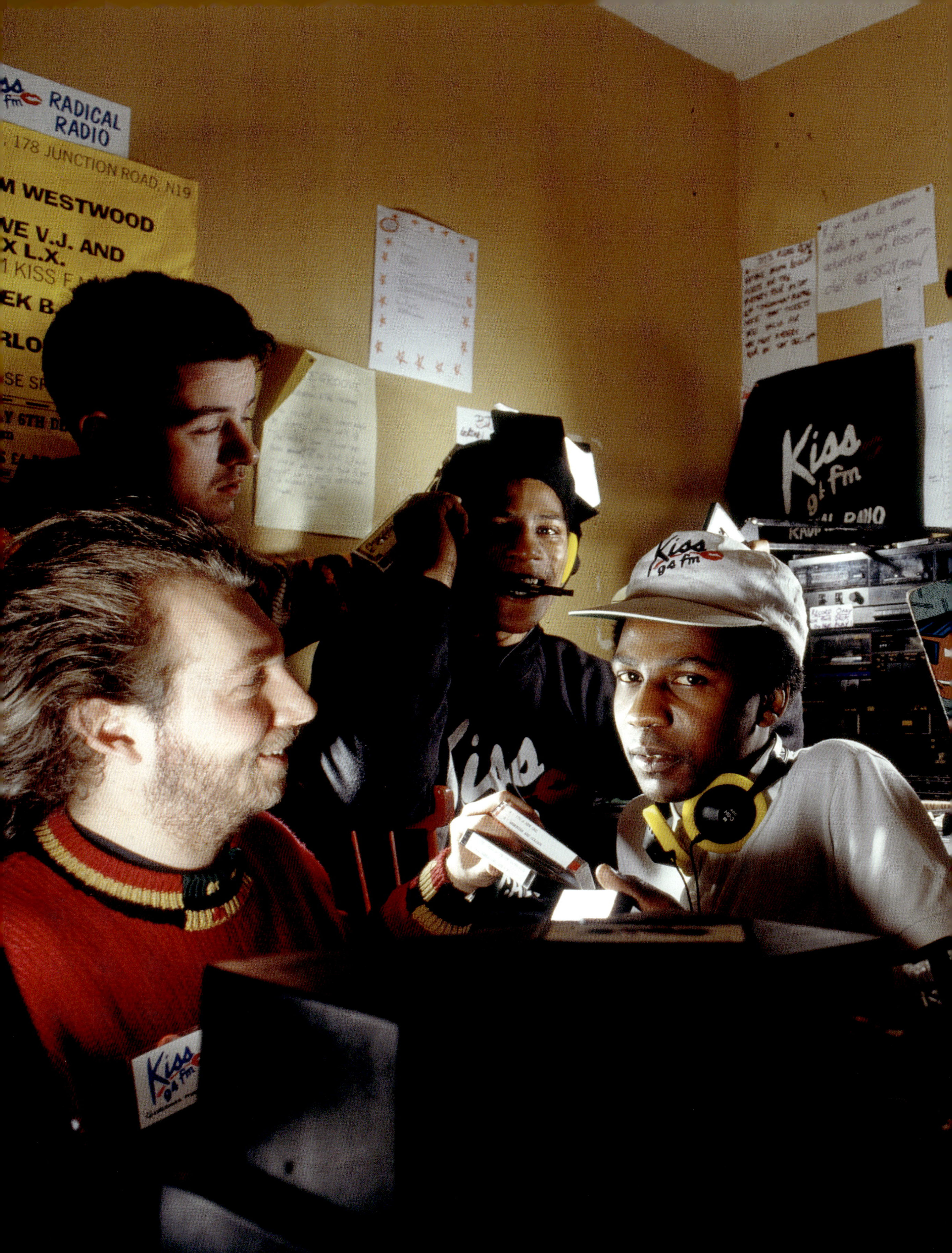
Kiss
fm
RADICAL
RADIO
, 178 JUNCTION ROAD, N19
M WESTWOOD
VE V.J. AND
X L.X.
M KISS F
EK B
RLO
Kiss
94 fm
RADIO
Kiss
94 fm
Kiss
94 fm

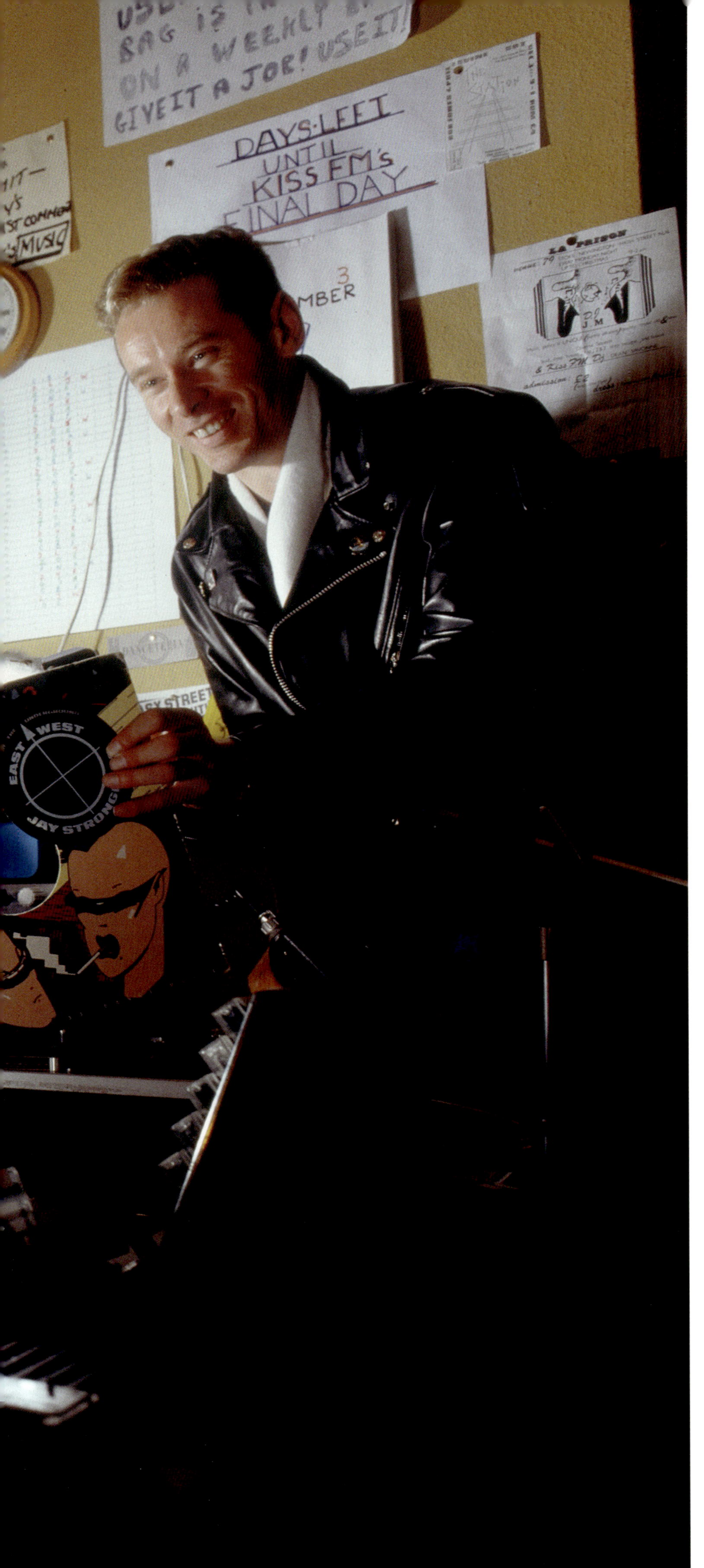

KISS FM DJS

Left to right: Gordon Mac,
Judge Jules, Paul Anderson,
Norman Jay, Jay Strongman
By David Gamble
January 1989

The location was a council flat
in South London; Kiss FM
was still a pirate radio station
then. There was no room for
light stands and no daylight
in the room, so I just got them
to hold the flash heads and
light themselves. I didn't really
know until I processed the film
whether I had made it work.
David Gamble

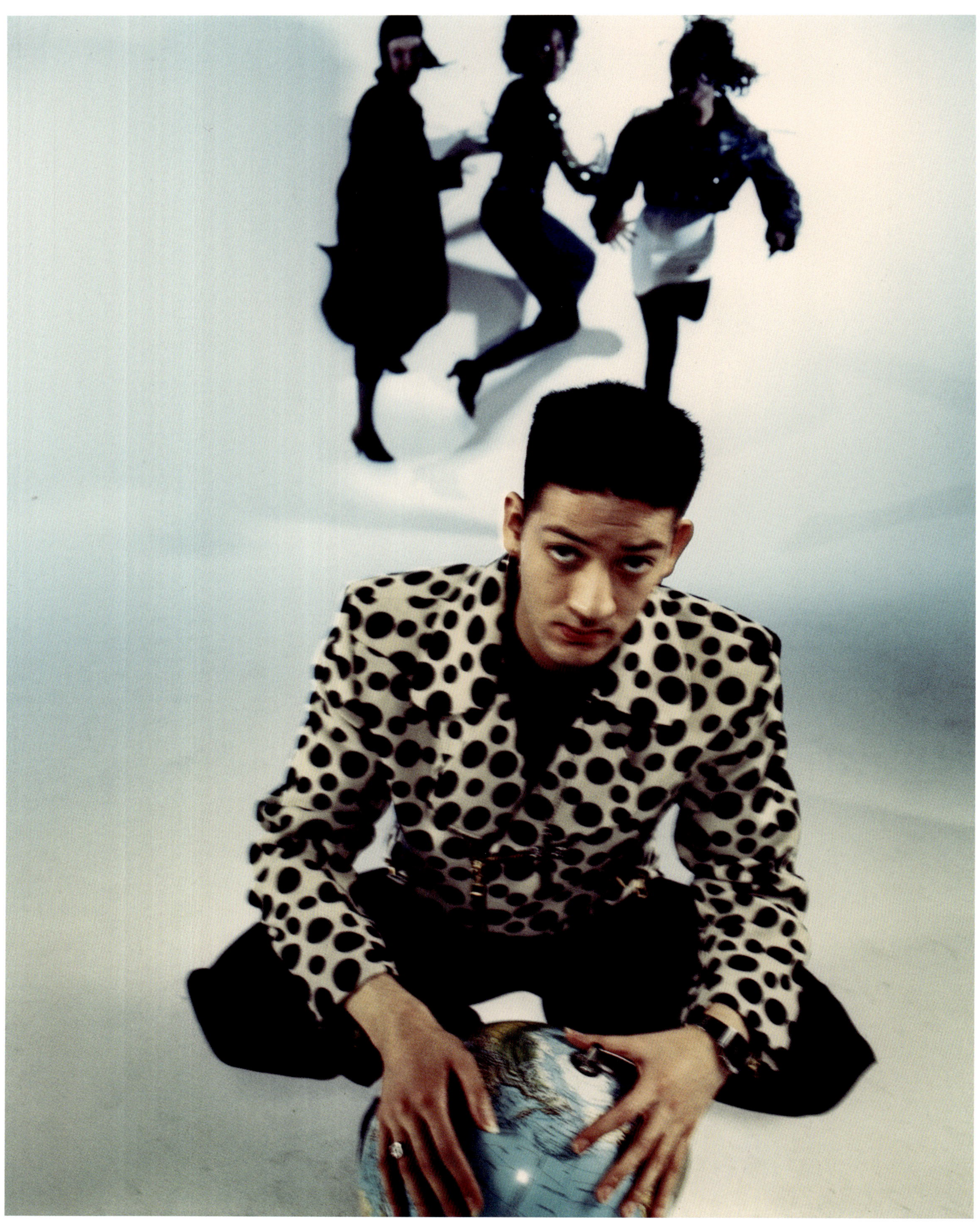

S'XPRESS

By Christian Thompson
January 1989

JAZZIE B

By Enrique Badulescu
Styled by Adam Howe
April 1989

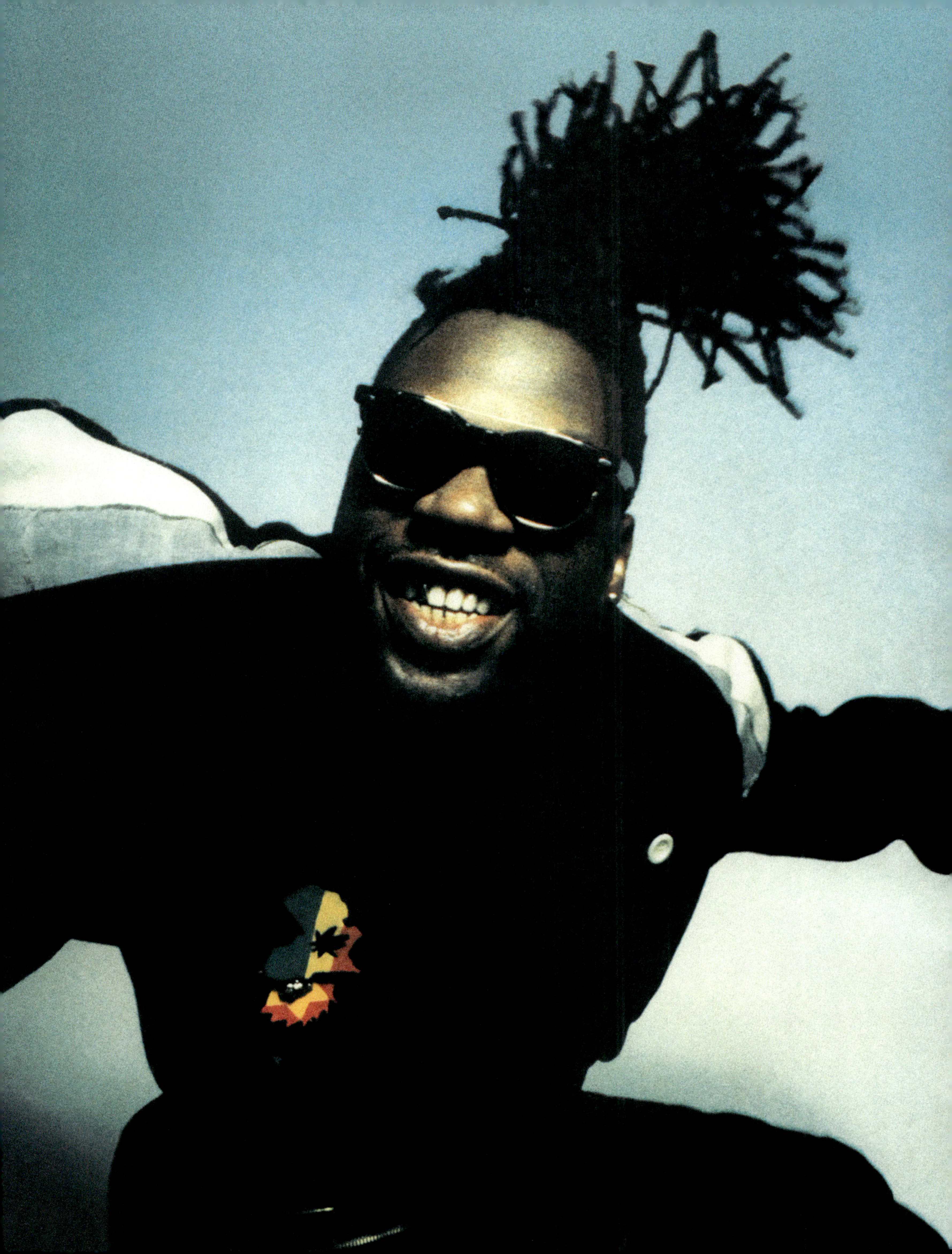

There was a political stance of championing inclusiveness, establishing that culture through fashion. There was a definite sense of purpose, an intent to create a brave new world through fashion imagery.

ROBERT ERDMANN, PHOTOGRAPHER

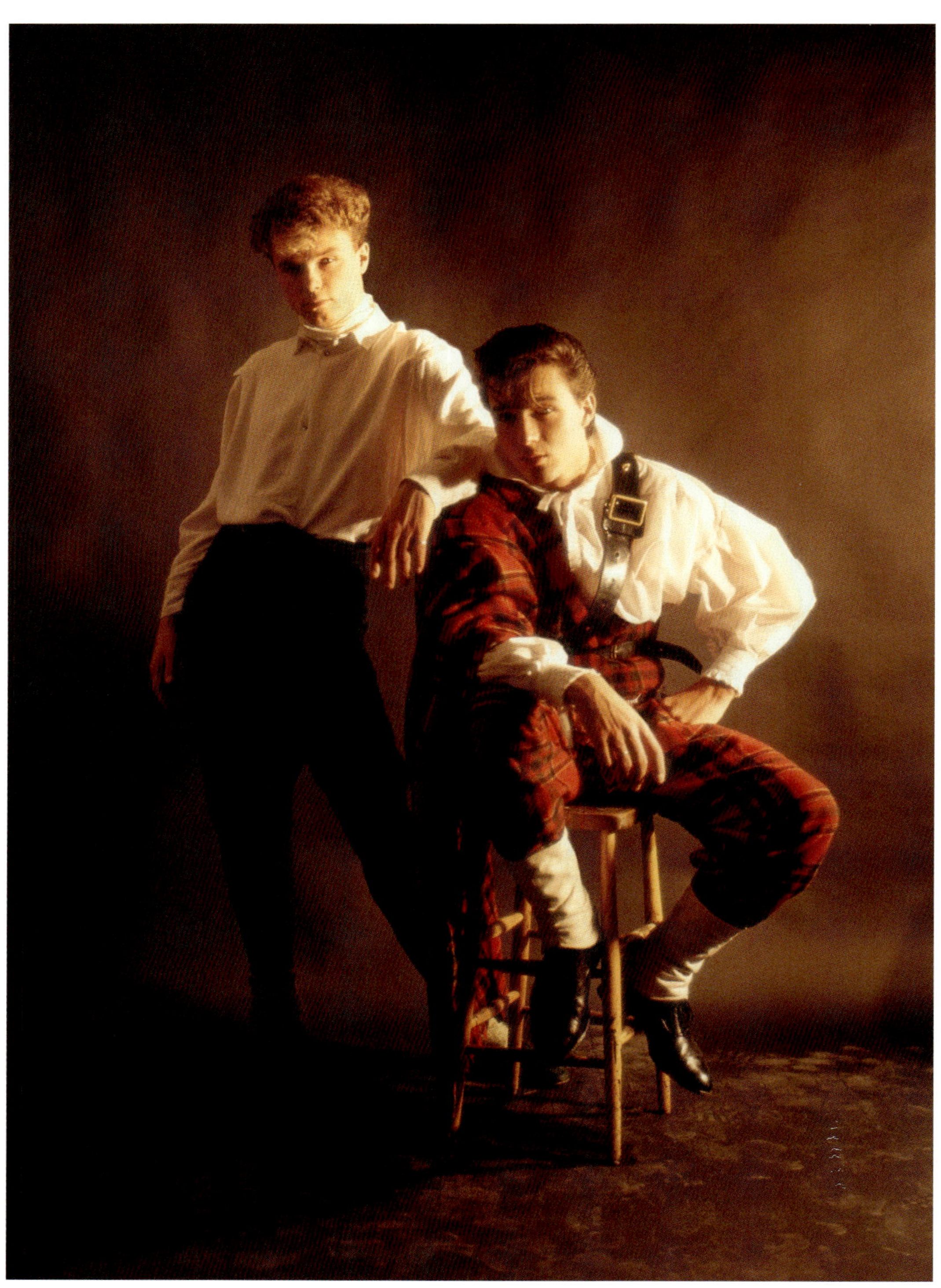

GARY AND MARTIN KEMP
By Graham Smith
February 1981

THE COCKY GENERATION
By Robert Erdmann
Styled by Caroline Baker
September 1984

At the time I was irritated by the way women and their breasts were such a universal focus in film and photography. So I thought, 'What if men had to show their bumps?' Clothing had gone all soft with the influence of sportswear so I pulled together sweatshirts, pull-on pants and knitted tights from ballet shops that would be a bit clingy. We wanted to shape up people's ideas and perceptions.
Caroline Baker

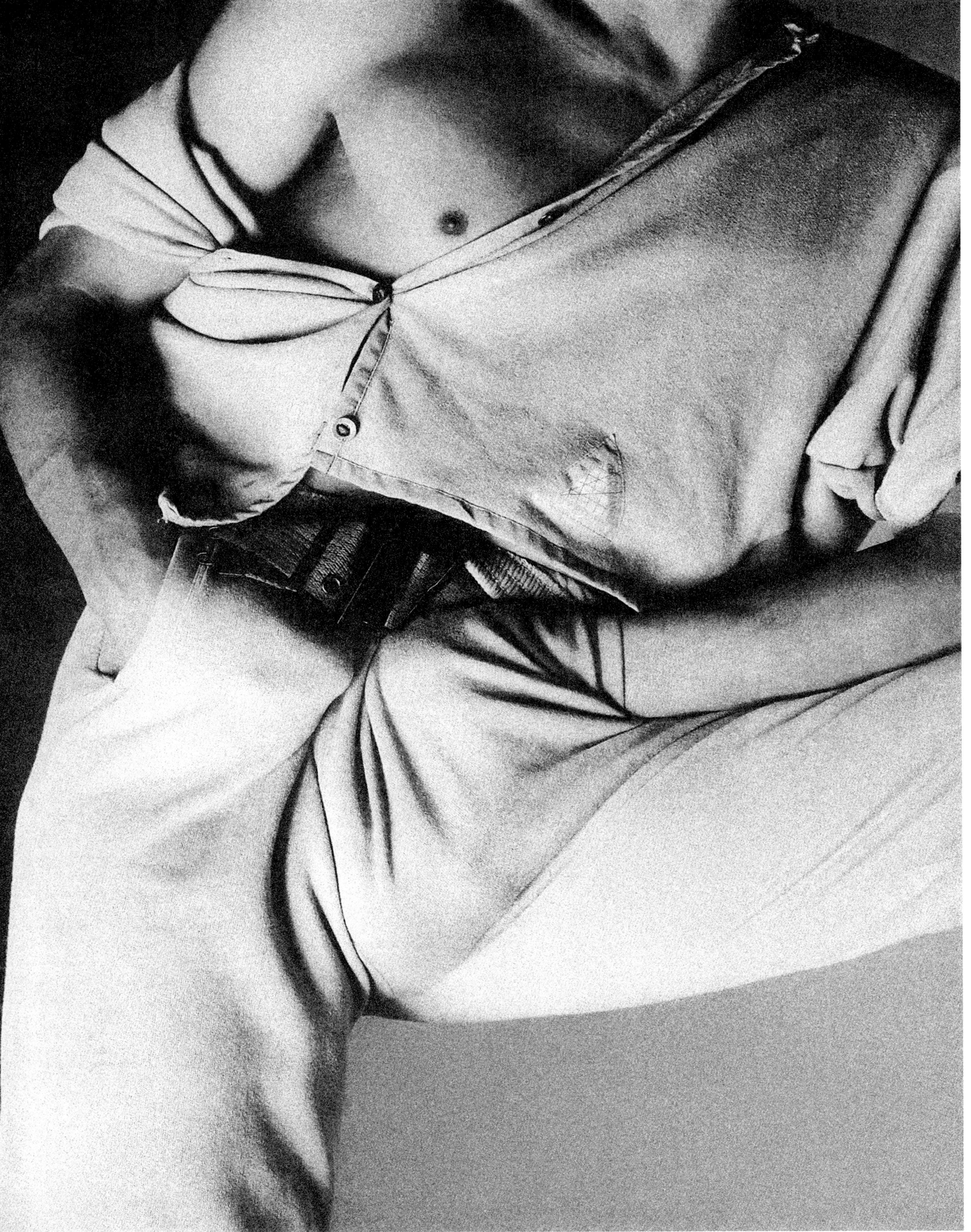

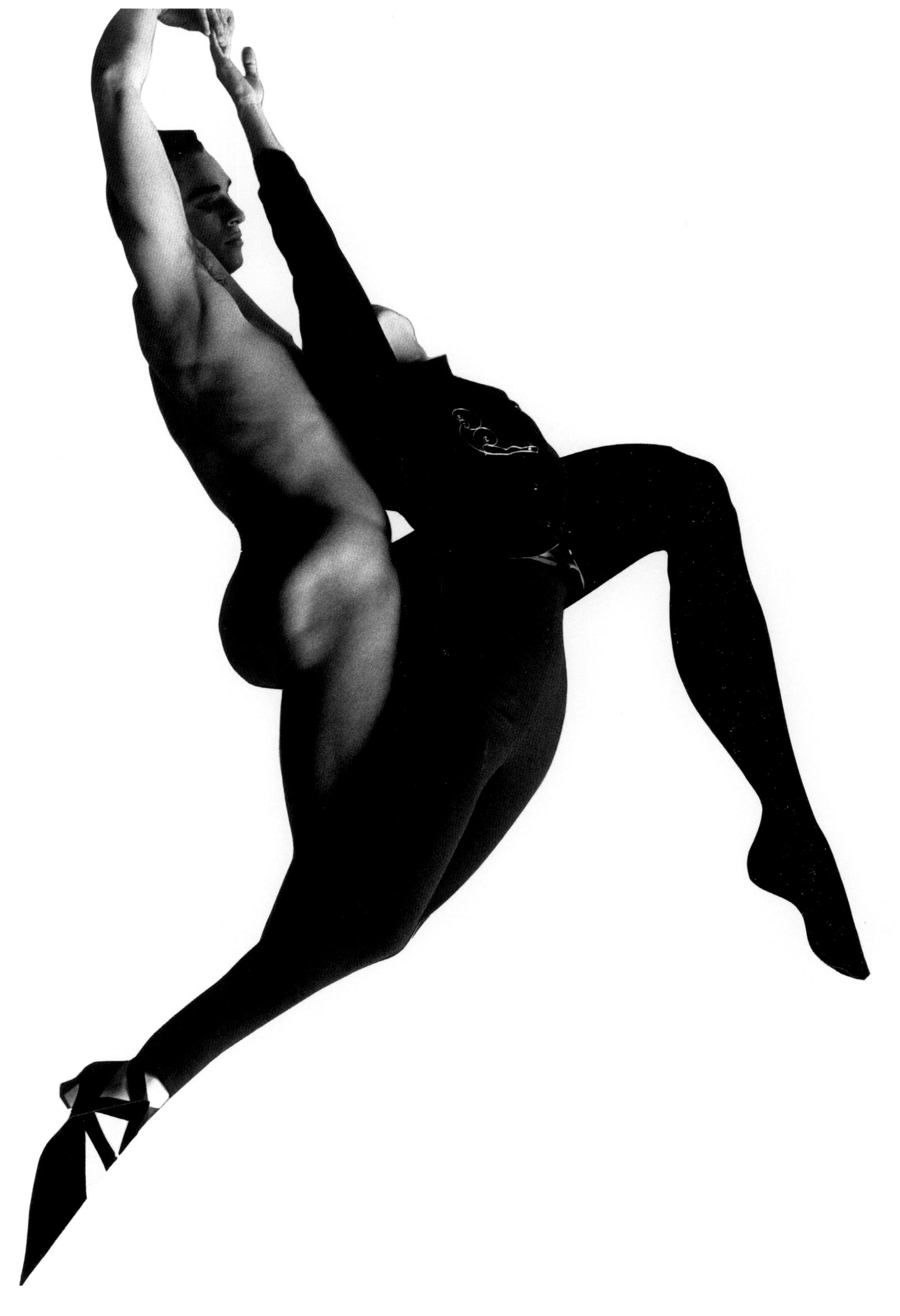

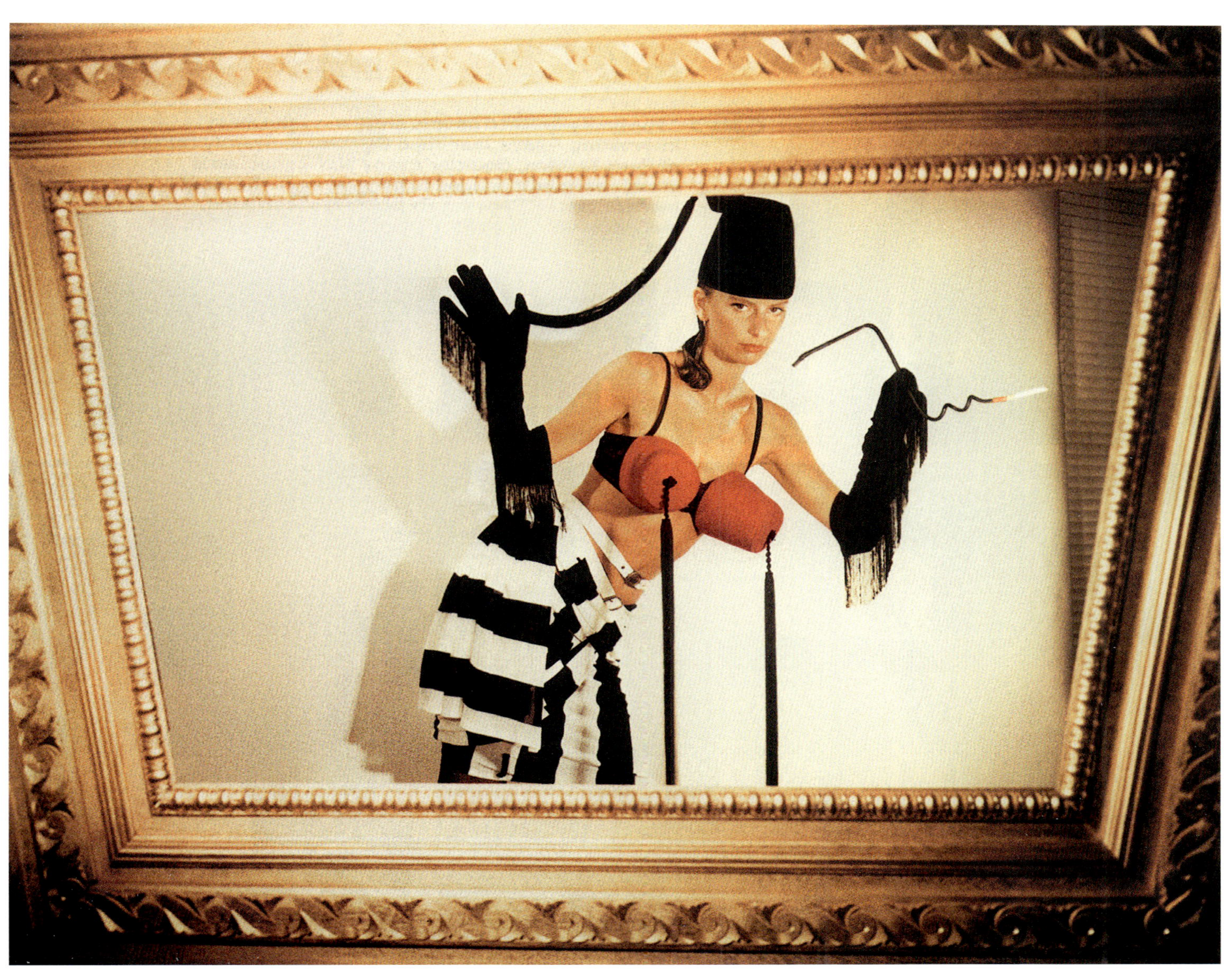

RIFAT OZBEK
By Tony Viramontes
Styled by Sarajane Hoare
June 1986

**THE SIX INVENTIONS
OF JEAN PAUL GAULTIER**
By Jean Paul Gaultier
February 1984

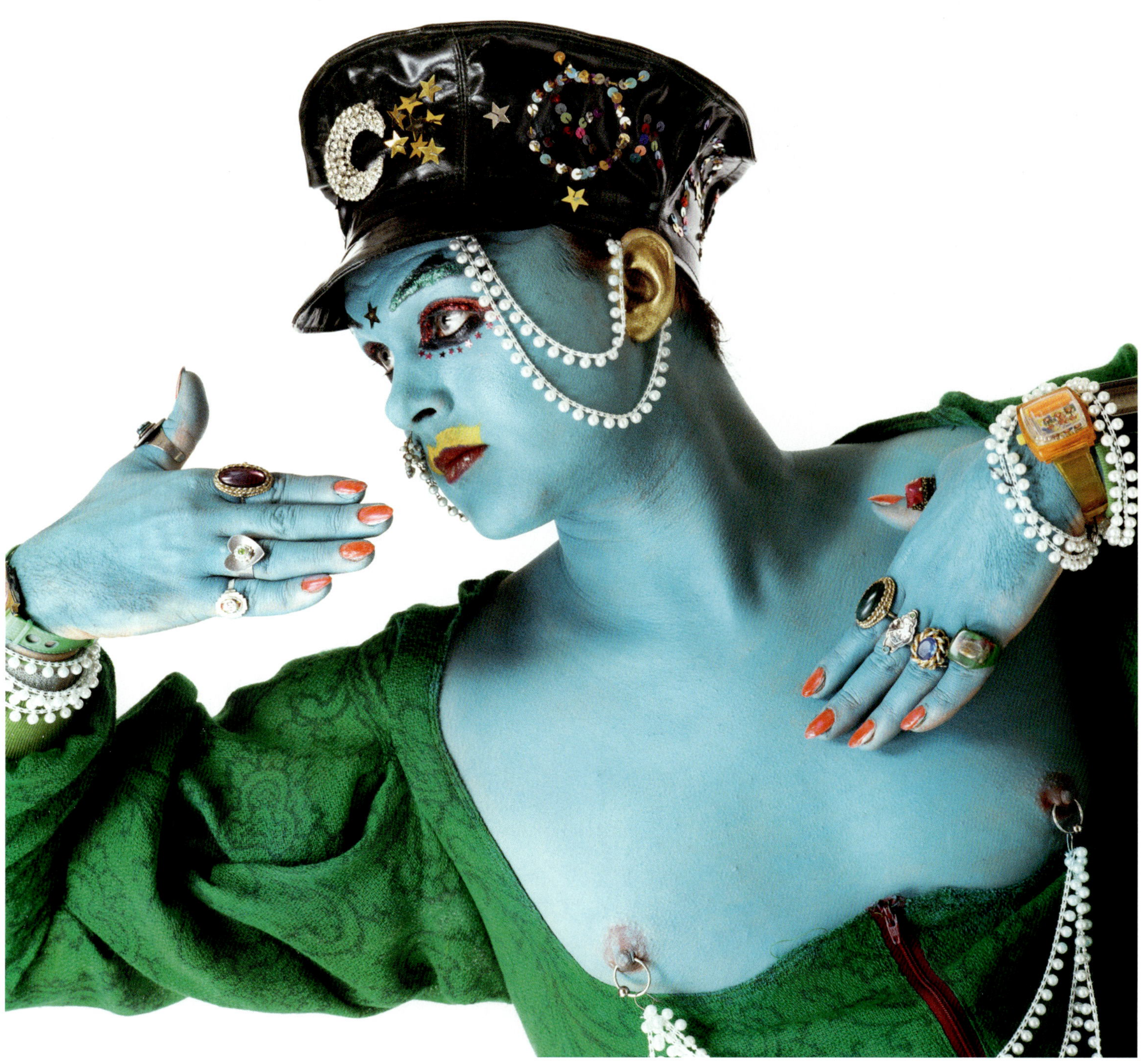

We were big clubbers, and would all meet at the
Criterion, Soho Brasserie and Leigh Bowery's Taboo.
I was sourcing inspiration from the clubs and brought
that more wacky fashion crowd into the magazine.
The magazine was all about being zeitgeisty.
Robin Derrick, Art Director

74

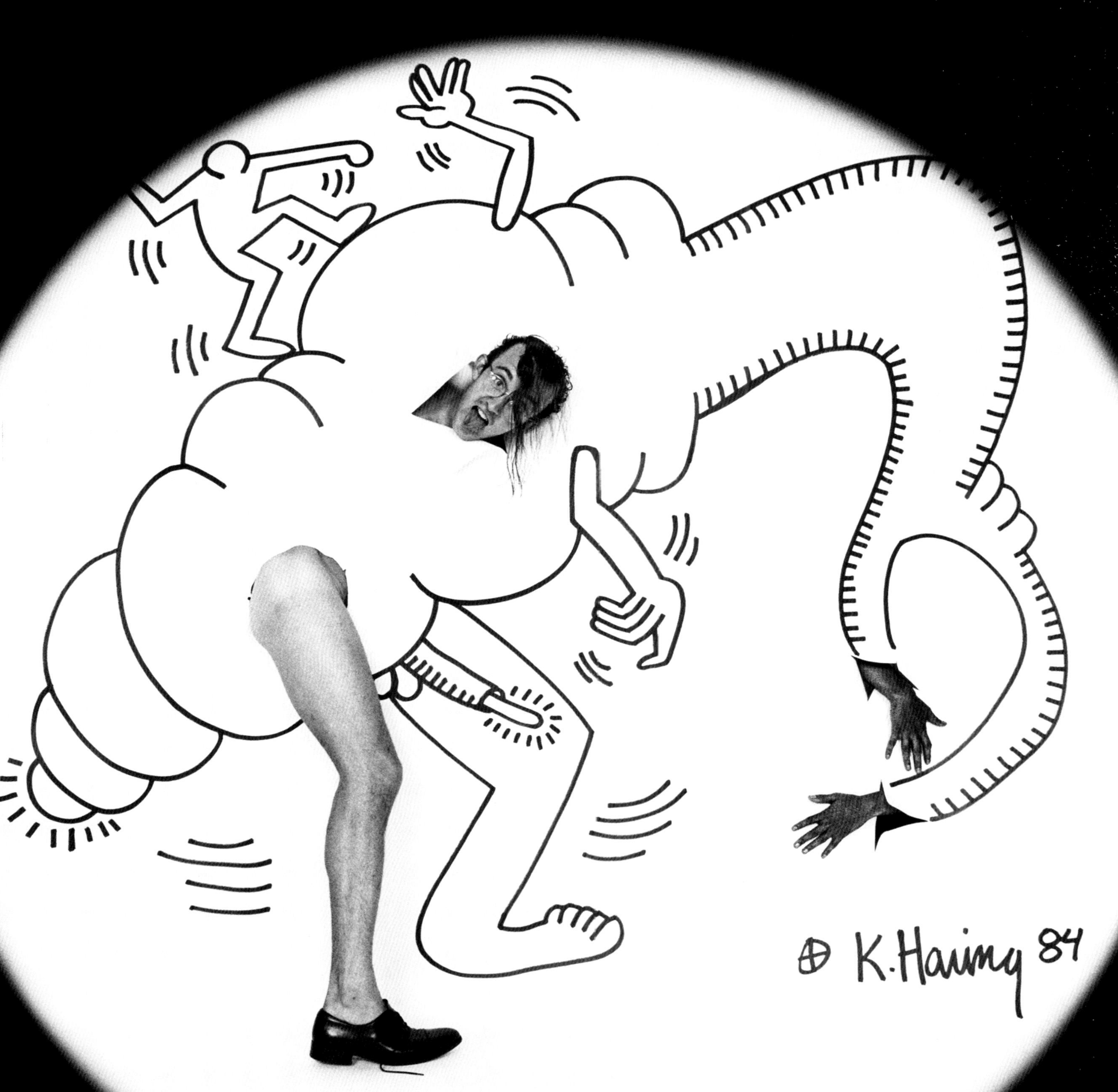

⊕ K. Haring 84

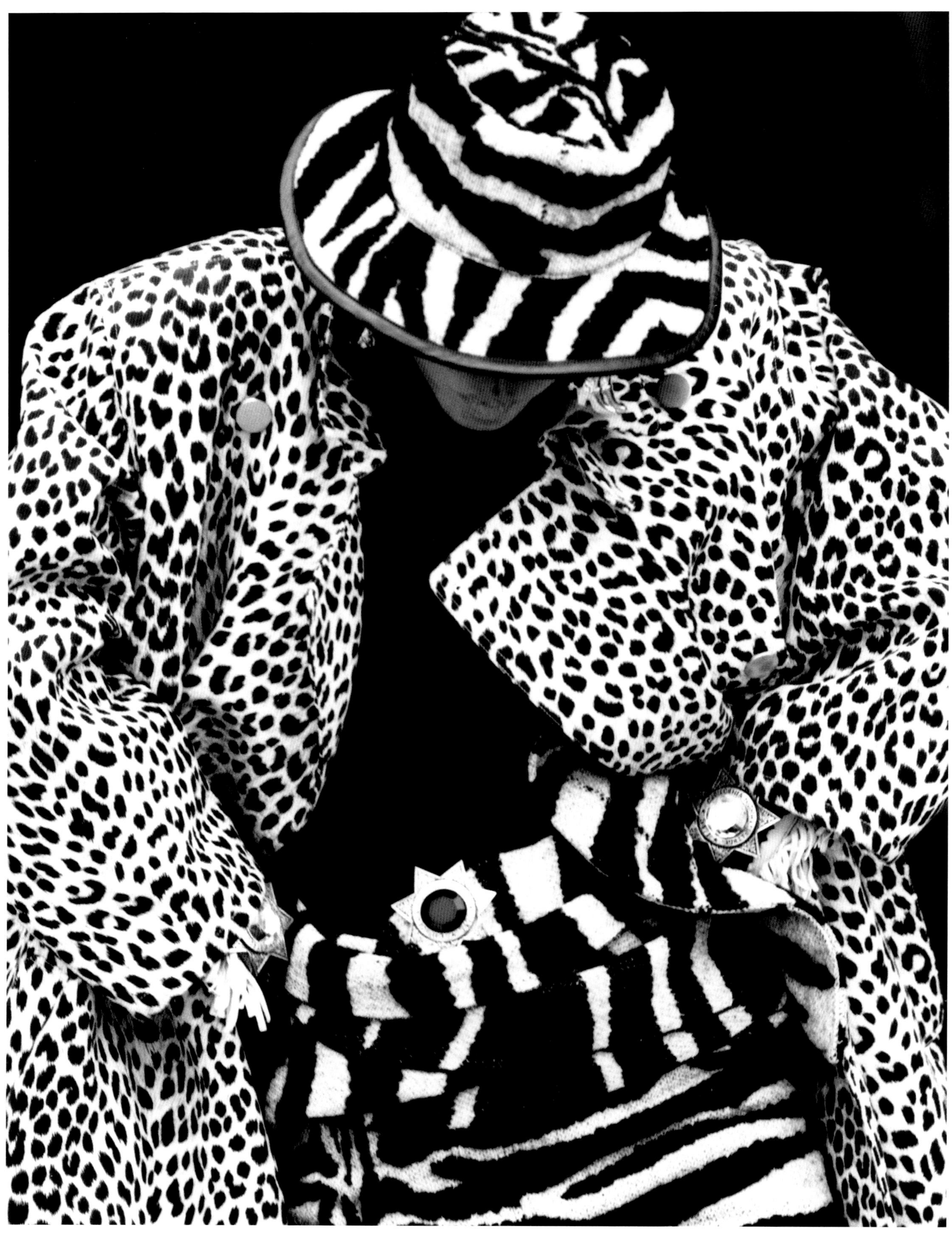

JAPANESE DESIGN:
THE THIRD WAVE
By Sheila Rock
March 1985

PARIS: THE LEGACY
By Andrew Macpherson
Styled by Babeth Djian
July 1986

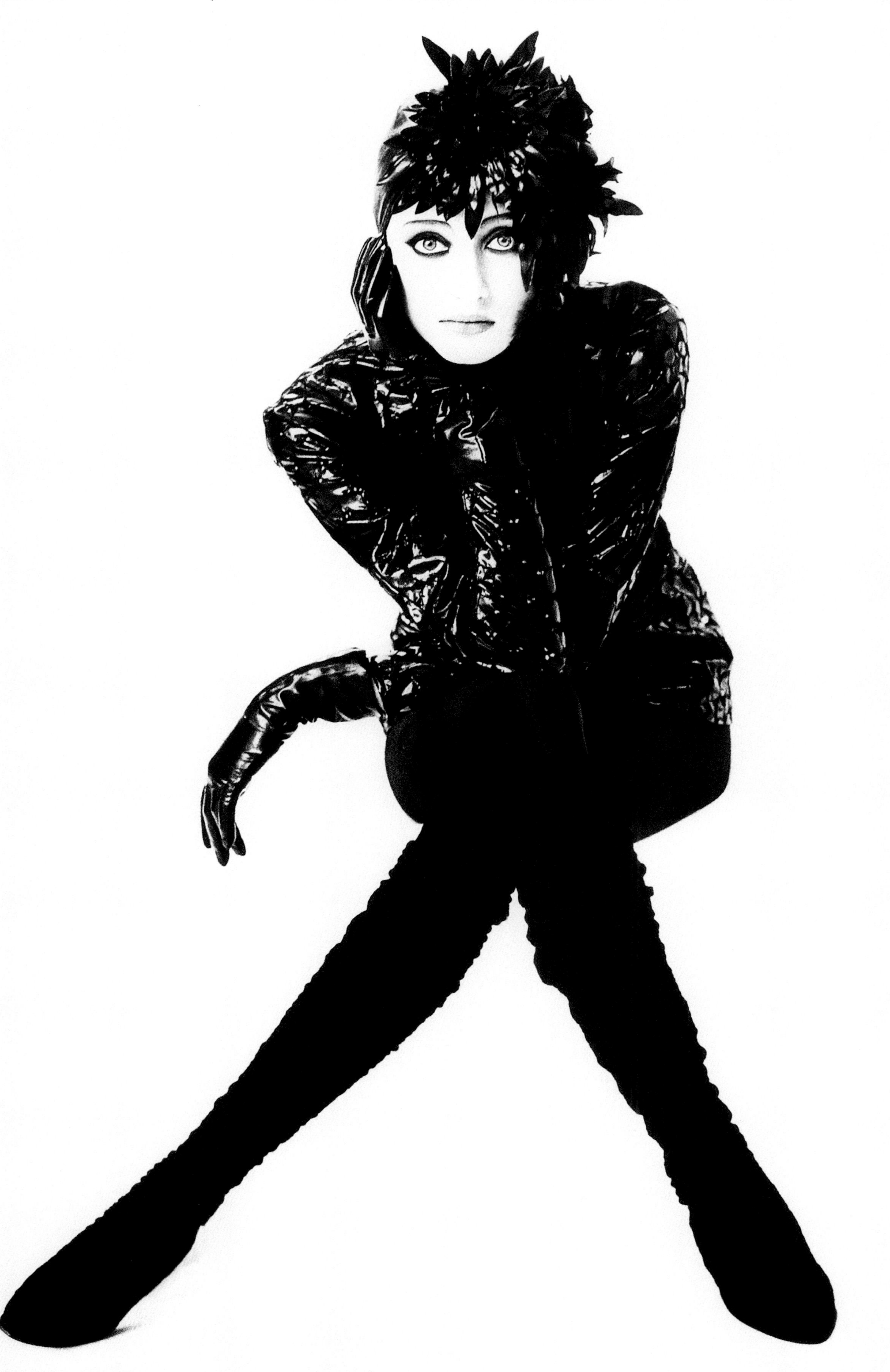

SPIRIT OF BUFFALO

JAMIE MORGAN

Jamie Morgan is a photographer who worked closely with the legendary stylist Ray Petri until Petri's death from an AIDS-related illness in 1989, at the age of 40. Petri and Morgan are credited with forming Buffalo, a collective, style and attitude brought to the public by magazines including *The Face* and into the mainstream by Neneh Cherry in her hit song 'Buffalo Stance'. Morgan reflects on his time collaborating with Petri, working for *The Face* at the beginning of the Buffalo movement.

No magazine is more than the people who work there, and this is totally true for *The Face*. The founder Nick Logan and Art Director Neville Brody created an atmosphere of openness and creativity. *The Face* gave us a platform that no-one else would.

When I first shot for *The Face*, I was 19 and still a photographic assistant, looking for a home for my work. I was inspired by a

WINTER SPORTS
By Jamie Morgan
Styled by Ray Petri
January 1984

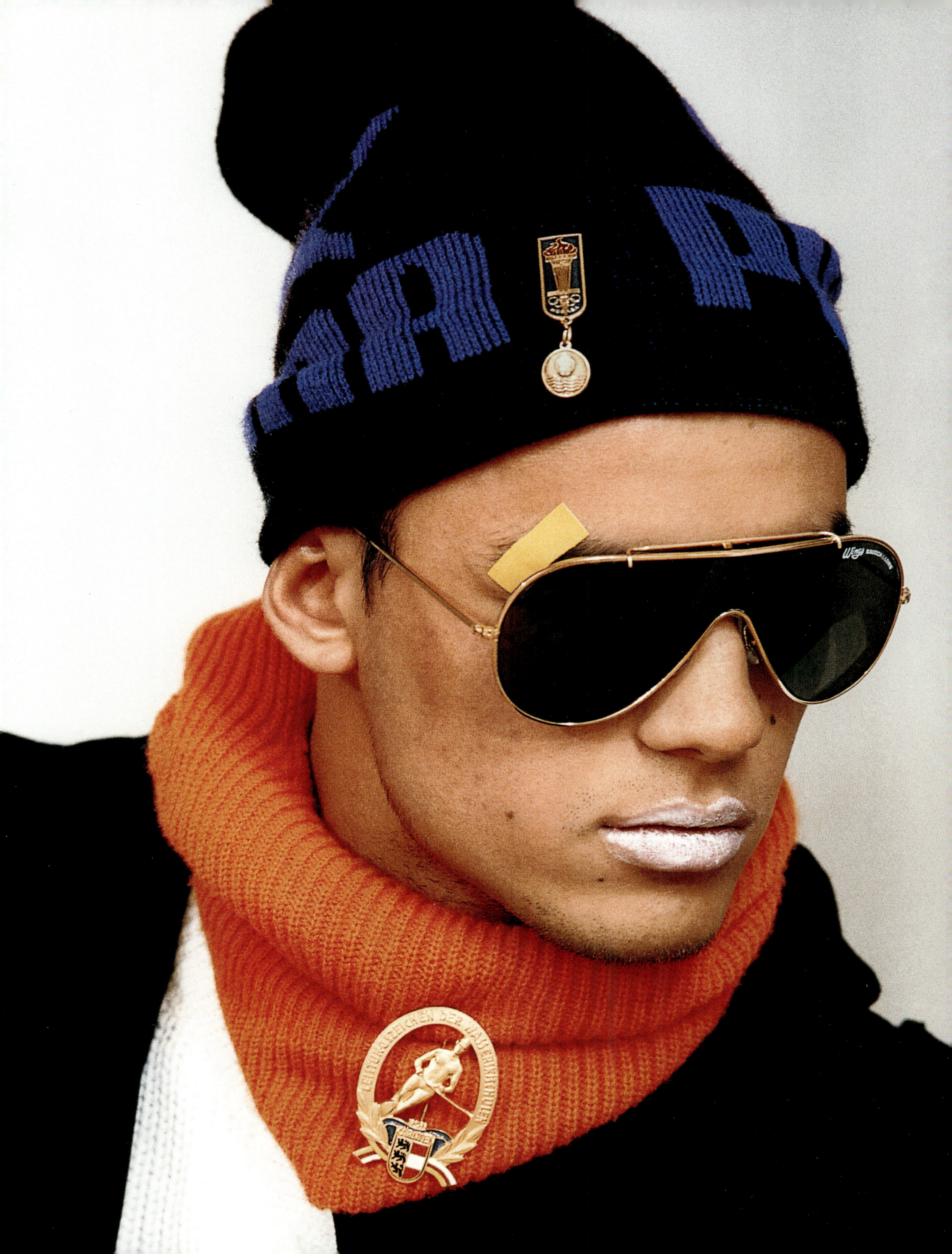

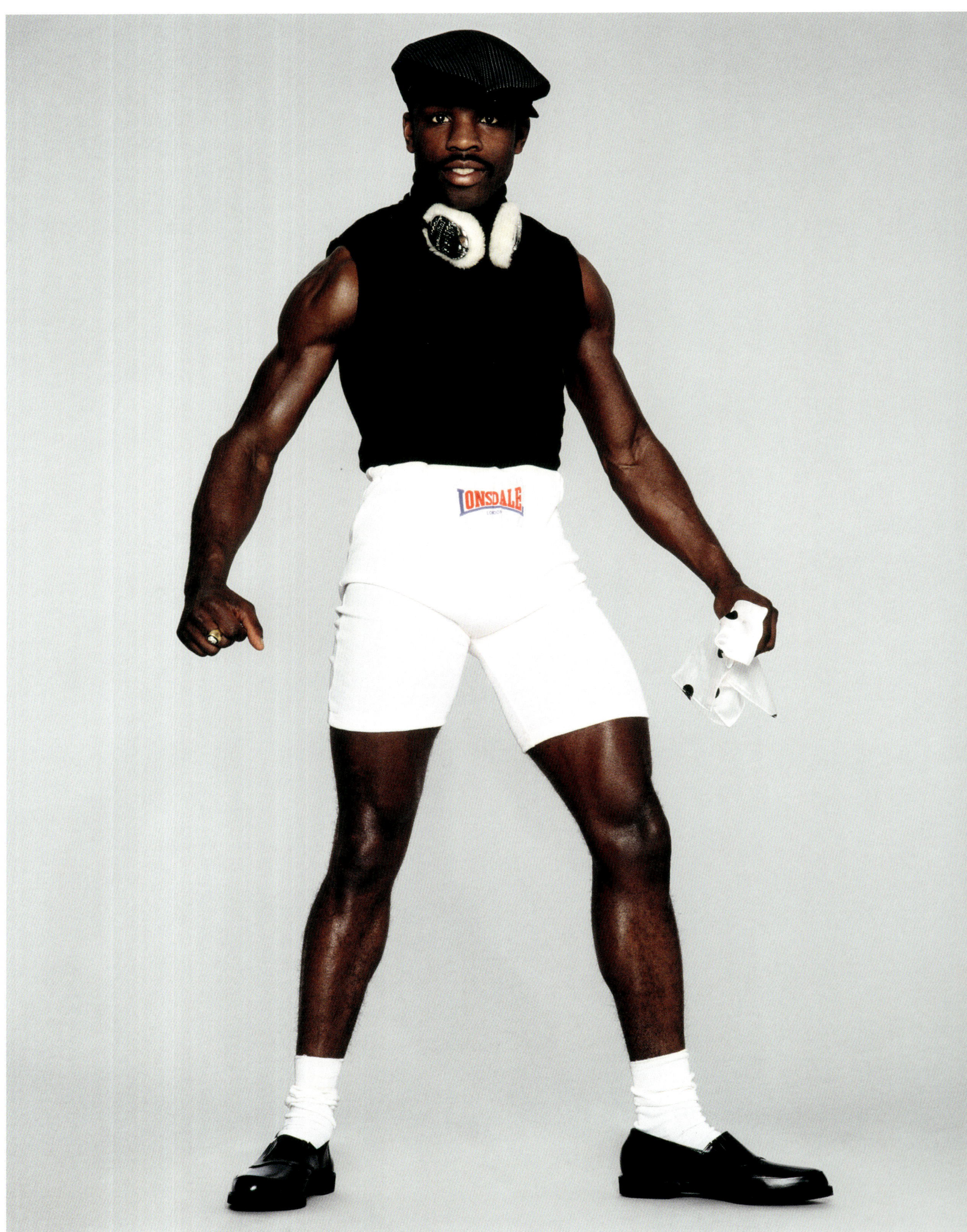

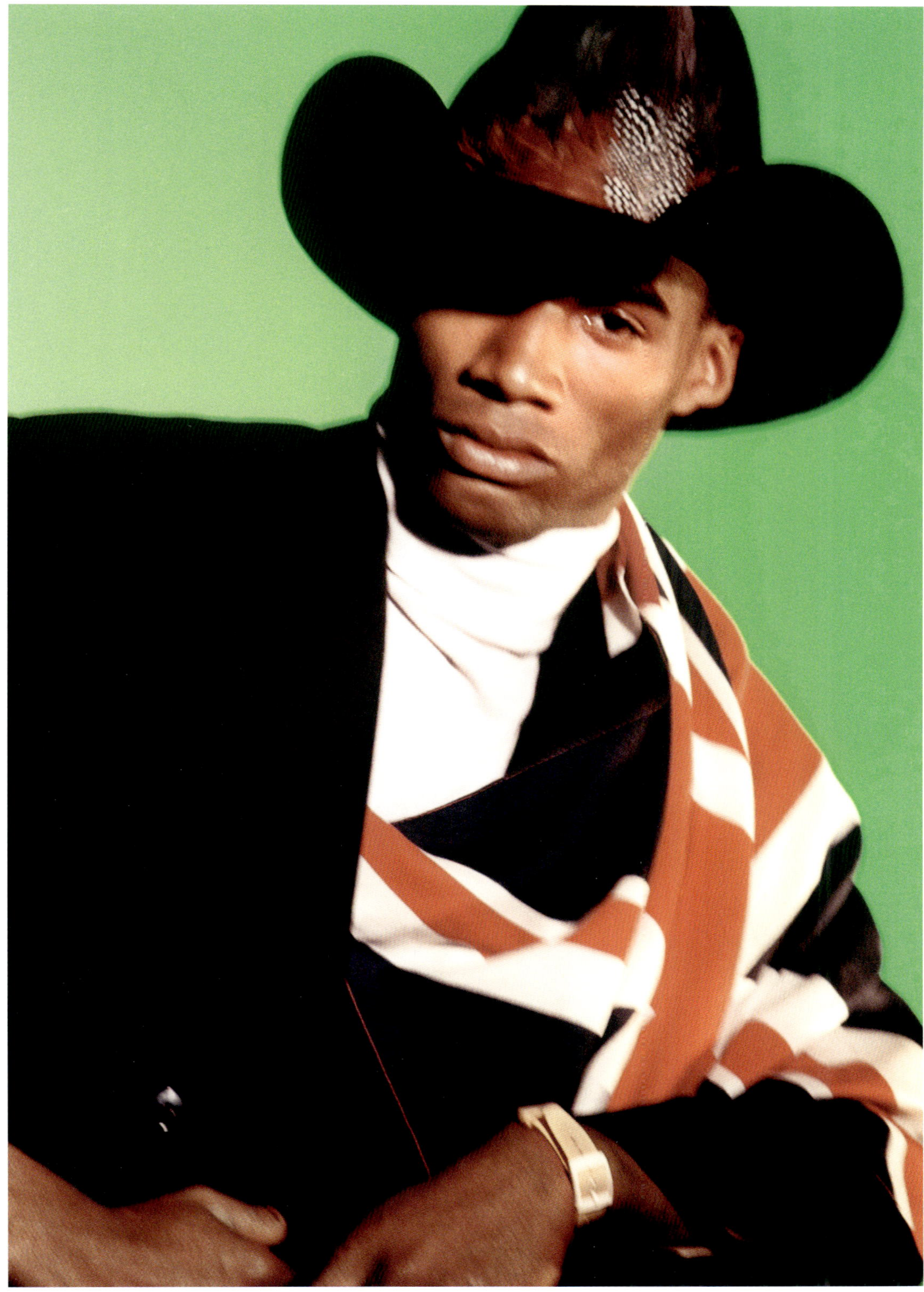

rebellious DIY punk attitude and knew the establishment magazines had nothing to offer me, in fact they didn't represent any of the people I was hanging out with or was seeing on the streets and clubs of London.

I began working with *The Face* by photographing music people; Sade was one of my first covers. I did a small shoot for them about girls in swimming hats and Nick asked me if I could do the same with men. The only person I knew who I thought could do this with me was Ray Petri. Ray was introduced to me by a friend and asked if he could assist me on any shoots. Ray had the best style I had ever seen, not wild like the club kids, but classy and cool. We went to Nick and Neville with the idea of shooting full fashion stories. We told them that we wanted to shoot fashion not as it was then seen, but to mix it with everything that inspired us. We were referencing all types of culture from all over the world, inspired by music, sports, high fashion, news: everything that interested us.

They agreed to hold eight pages and a cover for us! We had total freedom to create anything we wanted and the pages and cover were secured. It was that security and encouragement from *The Face* that allowed us to fly.

We decided to photograph mostly men. The reasoning was that men's fashion was so boring in the West and when we looked out across the world or went travelling it was the men who were the Dandies, the show-offs, the style kings. We thought: 'why can't

Buffalo saw beauty in mixing culture, race, age and gender. Boys were softer and women stronger.

MITZI LORENZ, STYLIST AND FASHION EDITOR

we be peacocks, be sexy and cool? Why is it only the girls that get to dress up and groom themselves?' We wanted men to look fabulous too. When we shot women we flipped the script, thinking 'why do girls need to be girly? Let them embrace their power and show off their strength'. We were intent on shattering any preconceived idea of gender.

Ray Petri's love for beautiful, tough men drove us forward in our casting choices. We could find almost no diversity or interesting characters in model agencies, so we started casting on the streets. Ray had an eye for beauty and found our models everywhere, from the guys in the local shop to men from boxing clubs, anywhere was our casting net. We just approached guys in the street. I think in retrospect me being straight and Ray being gay was the perfect match to shoot men in the way that we did. Ray was a very gentle, subtle and classy man, I was younger and more of a maverick.

It was this yin and yang that worked so well between us. We were hardly ever apart. We lived together and worked together. We'd get up in the morning, put on a killer Ragga tune, then take the same cassette, head to the studio, put it on, set up, and wait for guys we had cast that week to turn up, and shoot. I was the worker, creating the photographs, and Ray was the maestro creating the vibe, the elegance, the style. It was very organic, more a way of life than work. It was our deep friendship and a mutual love of art and music that fuelled our collaboration. We travelled the world together, bringing back styling items. Hats from Jamaica, patent leather shoes from the army shops in NYC, cycling shorts from the Tour de France in Paris. The world was our education and styling ground, and London was our studio, where we put it all together.

Ray would style a look from head to toe in absolute perfection and I would light it, create the image, deciding if it was full length, colour or black and white. Just before we shot, Ray would spray perfume on the model; Ray wanted everything to be perfect, including how the model smelled. I think one of the reasons that our work was so well received so quickly was that it appealed to both straight men and gay men, and to women. It seemed to resonate with everybody.

We just kept going. The story 'Men's Where?' was inspired by the kilts from Ray's upbringing in Scotland, and the sarongs from his time in Africa. I would push and say 'if he can wear a kilt, why can't we put him in a punk leather skirt and Doc Martens?' We would create a look in a shoot and as soon as *The Face* came out, we would see people wearing the look in the clubs and on the streets.

We started to pull together a large crew, always working with same models, Nick and Barry Kamen and Simon De Montford, and Ray was also working with other photographers like Mark LeBon and Jean Baptiste Mondino. We were gathering an extended family of creatives, including Judy Blame, Naomi Campbell, Neneh Cherry and Mitzi Lorenz.

We decided to begin calling our work by a collective name, and Buffalo was born. Why the name Buffalo and what that was, and what it became, well … that's another chapter in the story.

When I look back at my work with Ray Petri and *The Face*, we only actually did five main shoots: 'Winter Sports', 'Men's Where?', 'The Harder they Come', 'Float Like a Butterfly', and 'Pure Prairie'. We knew we were creating something magic – if only because we were creating from our hearts inspired by the music, culture, art and the streets that we loved so much – and that this mix of ideas had never been seen before, which was one of our main inspirations for doing it, but we had no idea of the cultural impact or influence that the work would garner over the years. ∎

STYLE SHOWS A LEG!
By Jamie Morgan
Styled by Ray Petri
May 1984

THE HARDER THEY COME
By Jamie Morgan
Styled by Ray Petri
March 1985

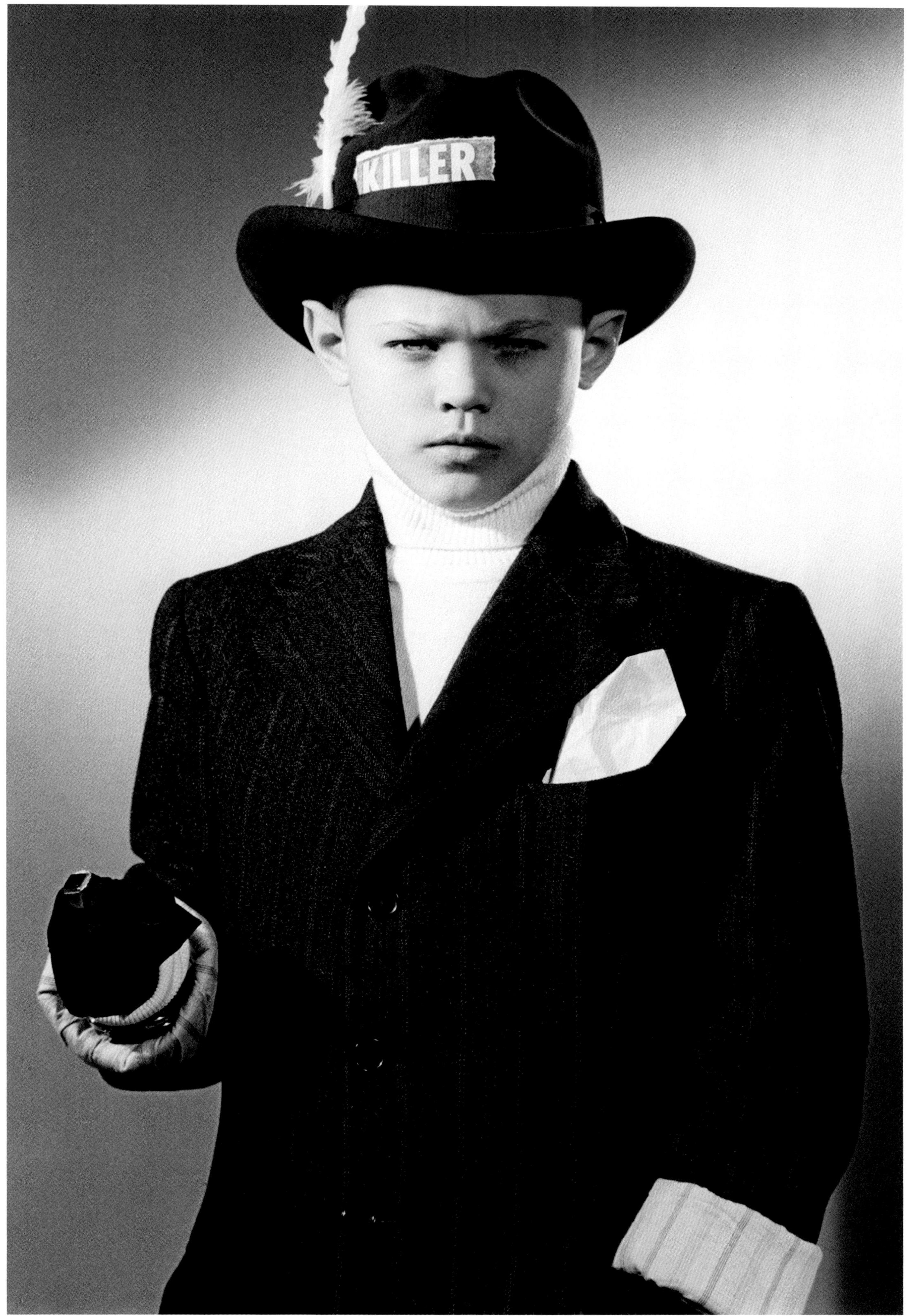

KILLER

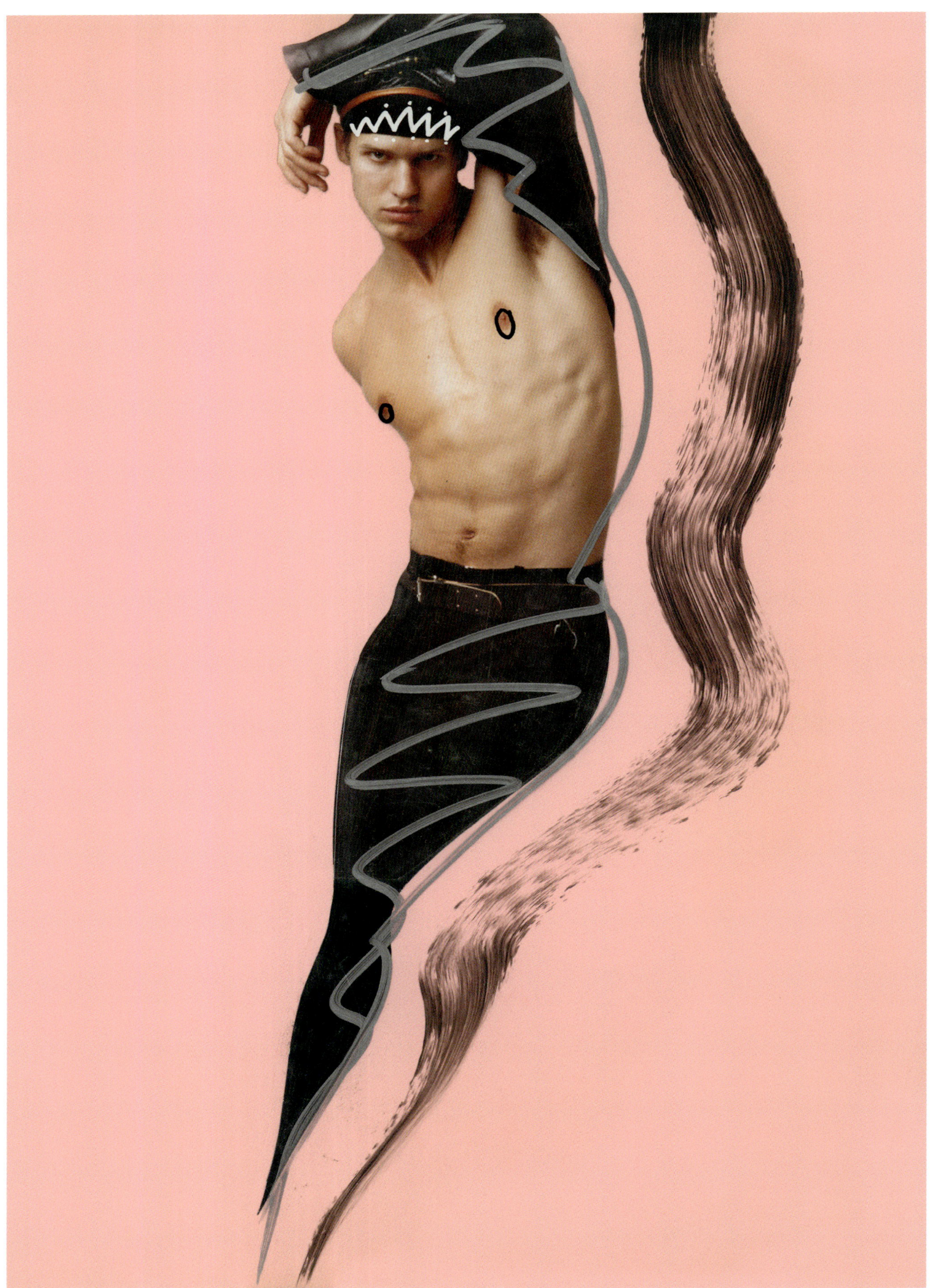

BODY ROCK
By Tony Viramontes
Styled by Ray Petri
September 1985

**NEW HATS FROM LONDON
AND PARIS**
By Jean Baptiste Mondino
Styled by Ray Petri
February 1988

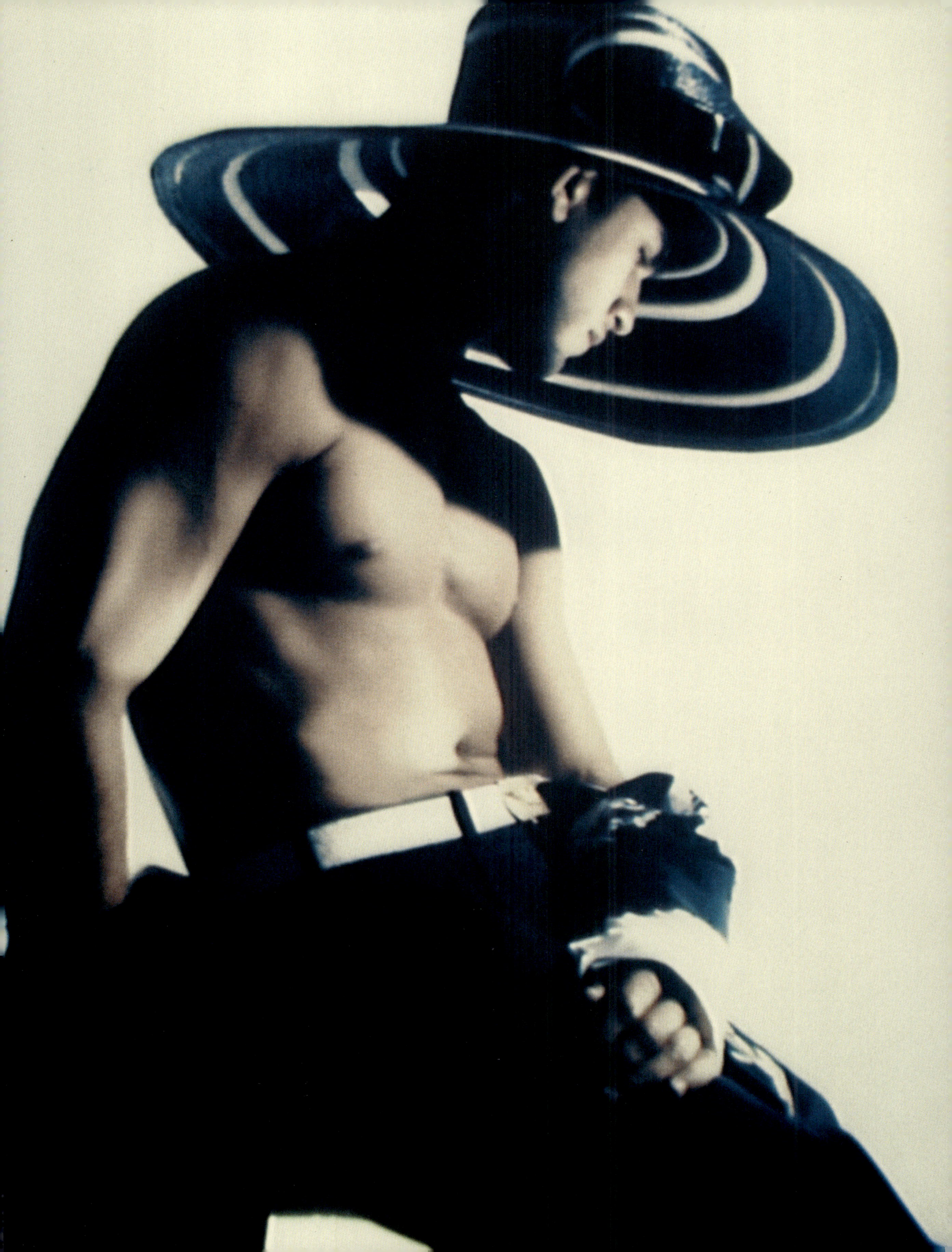

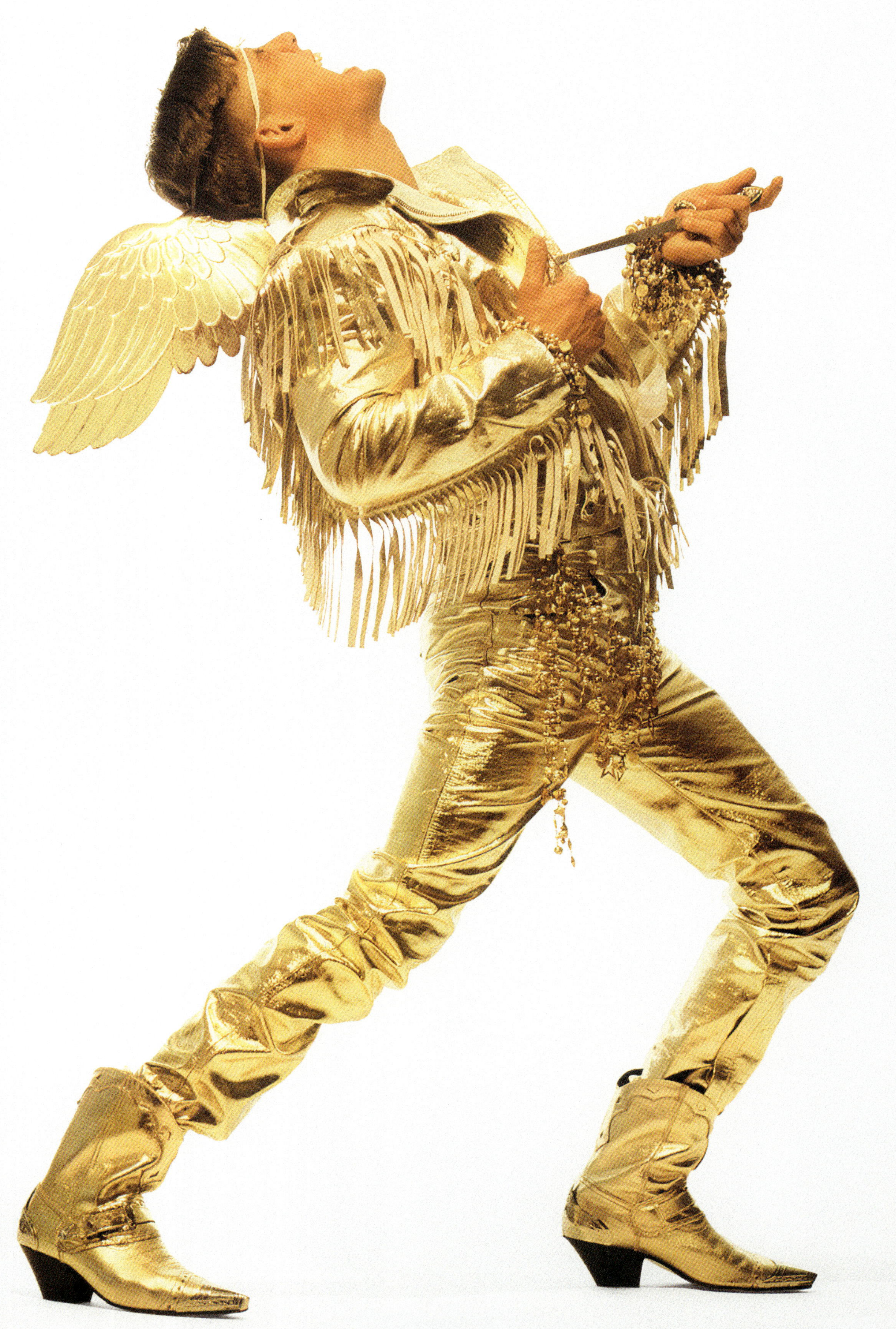

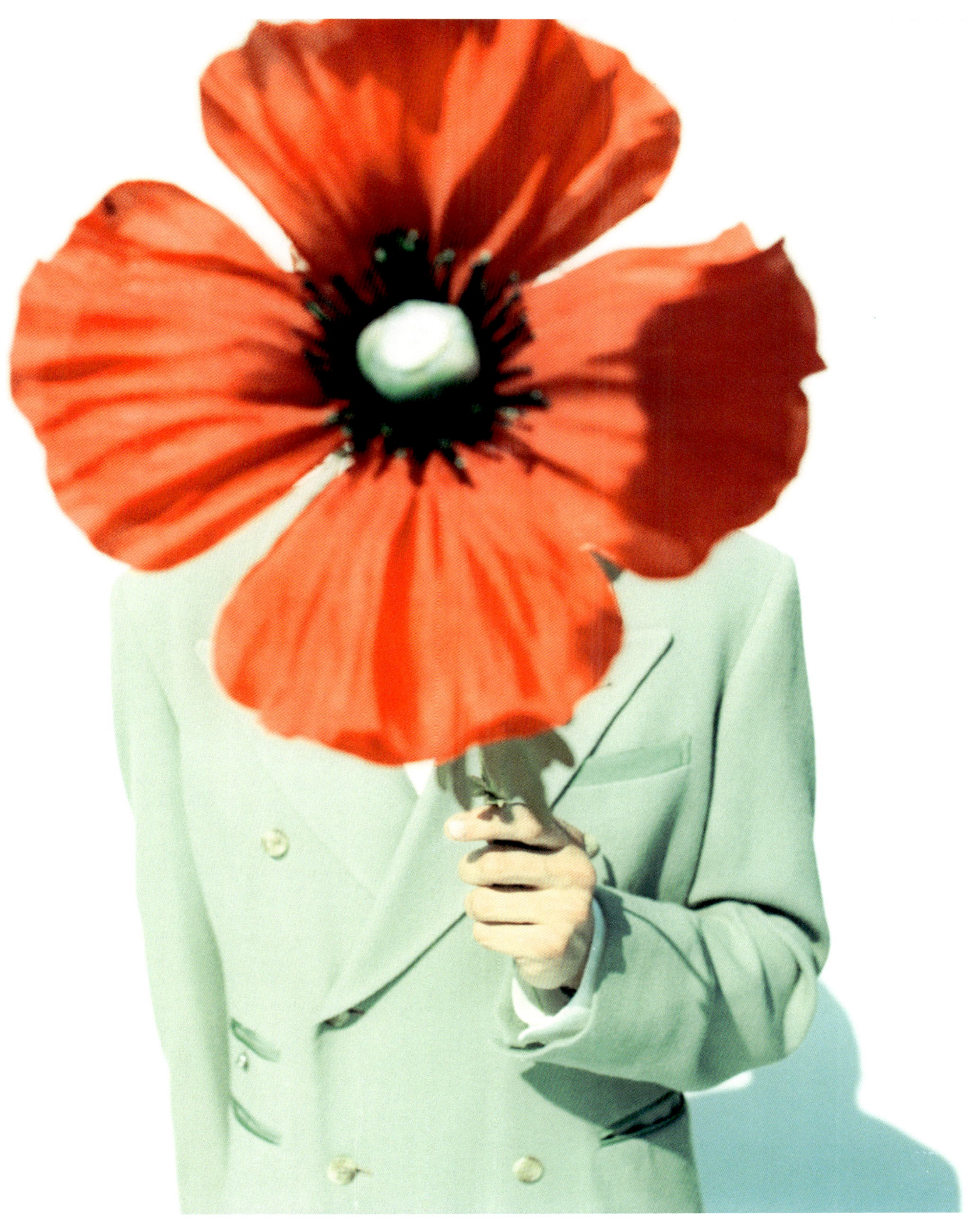

LONDON CALLING

By EJ McCabe
Styled by Stephen Linard
September 1986

There was a new buzz in the fashion world, with so much talent coming out of Central Saint Martins. I was asked to shoot with Stephen Linard, using clothes from his new collection. The designs were so unique, so visually exciting, I had a duty not to get in the way of what the designer was expressing.
EJ McCabe

SPELLBOUND

By Andy Bettles
Styled by Wayne Shires
August 1987

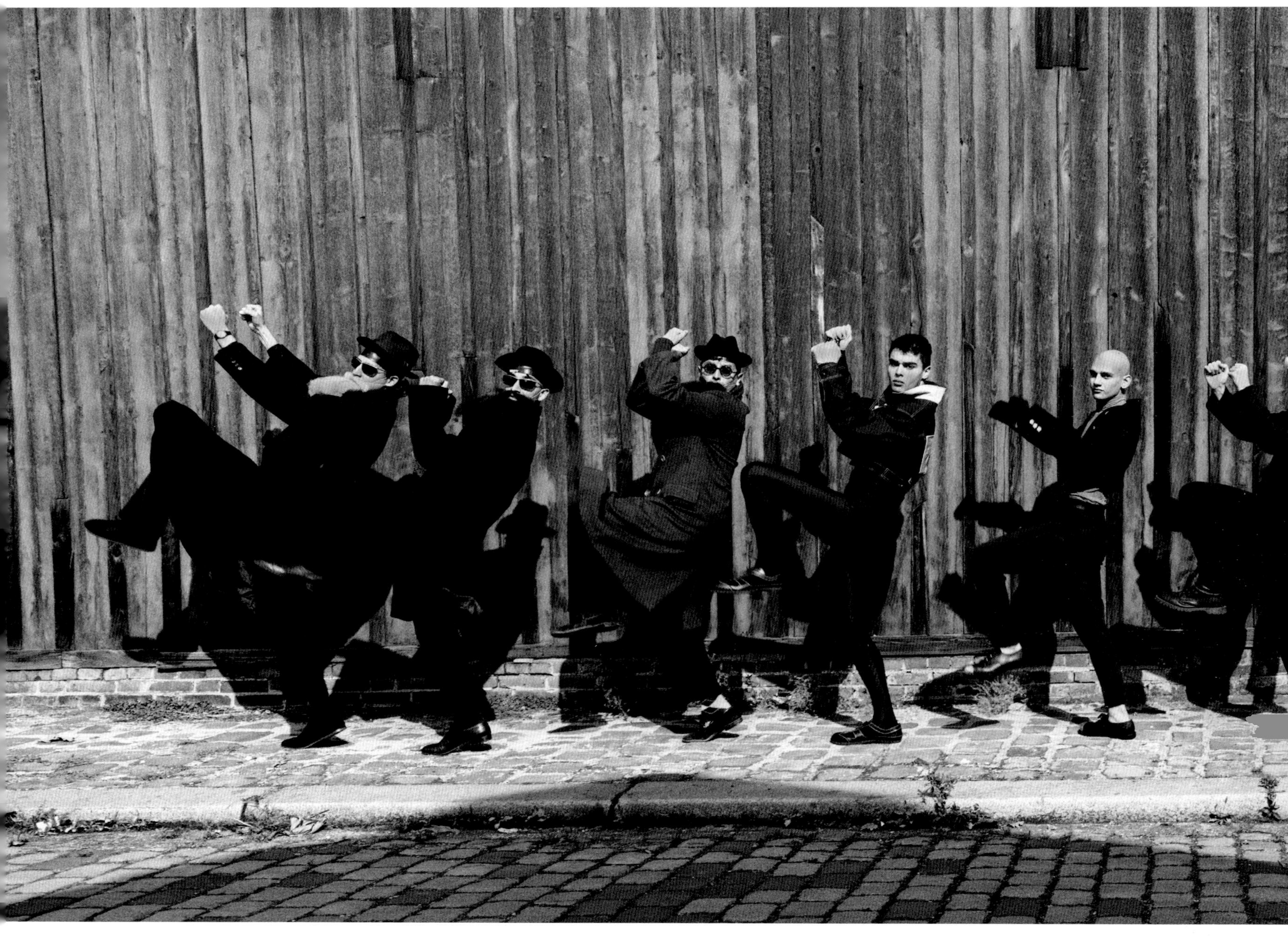

I invited Jean Paul Gaultier and his
Atelier team to my favourite spot
in Paris, an old train station that
used to store wine. It had tram lines
but was pretty empty at that time.
I loved photographing there, and
miraculously, the whole crew from
Jean Paul Gaultier showed up. I had
this quirky idea to have them pose
in a unique move: both arms at 90°,
one leg up, arching the body back,
facing the camera, and looking
like they were moving forward but
suspended. After a few tries with my
panoramic Fuji 6×17cm camera – an
unusual format back then – it all
worked perfectly. It was a blast.
Max Vadukul

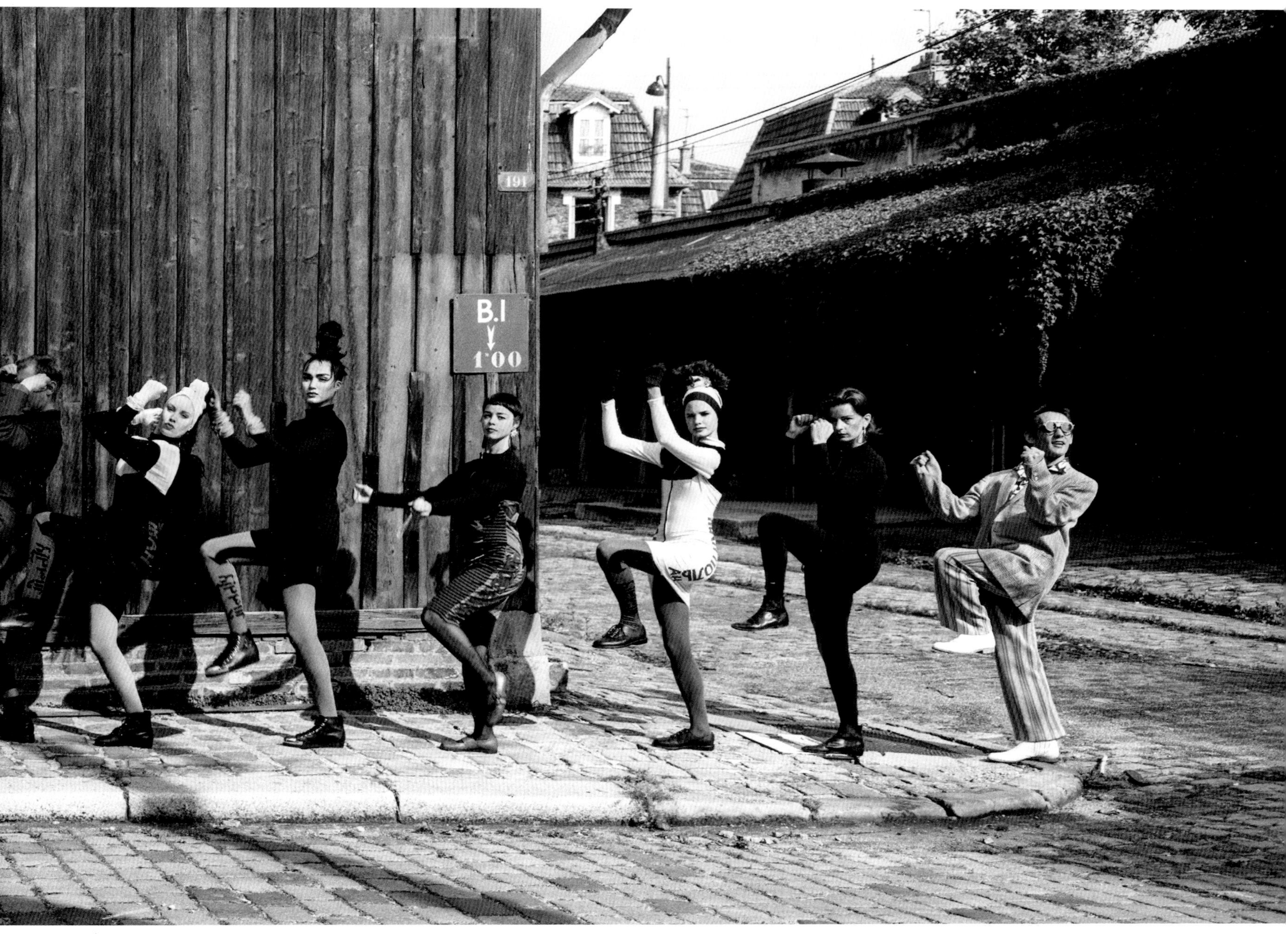
191
B.I
↓
1ºº00

VOICI PARIS
By Stéphane Sednaoui
Styled by Babeth Djian
June 1988

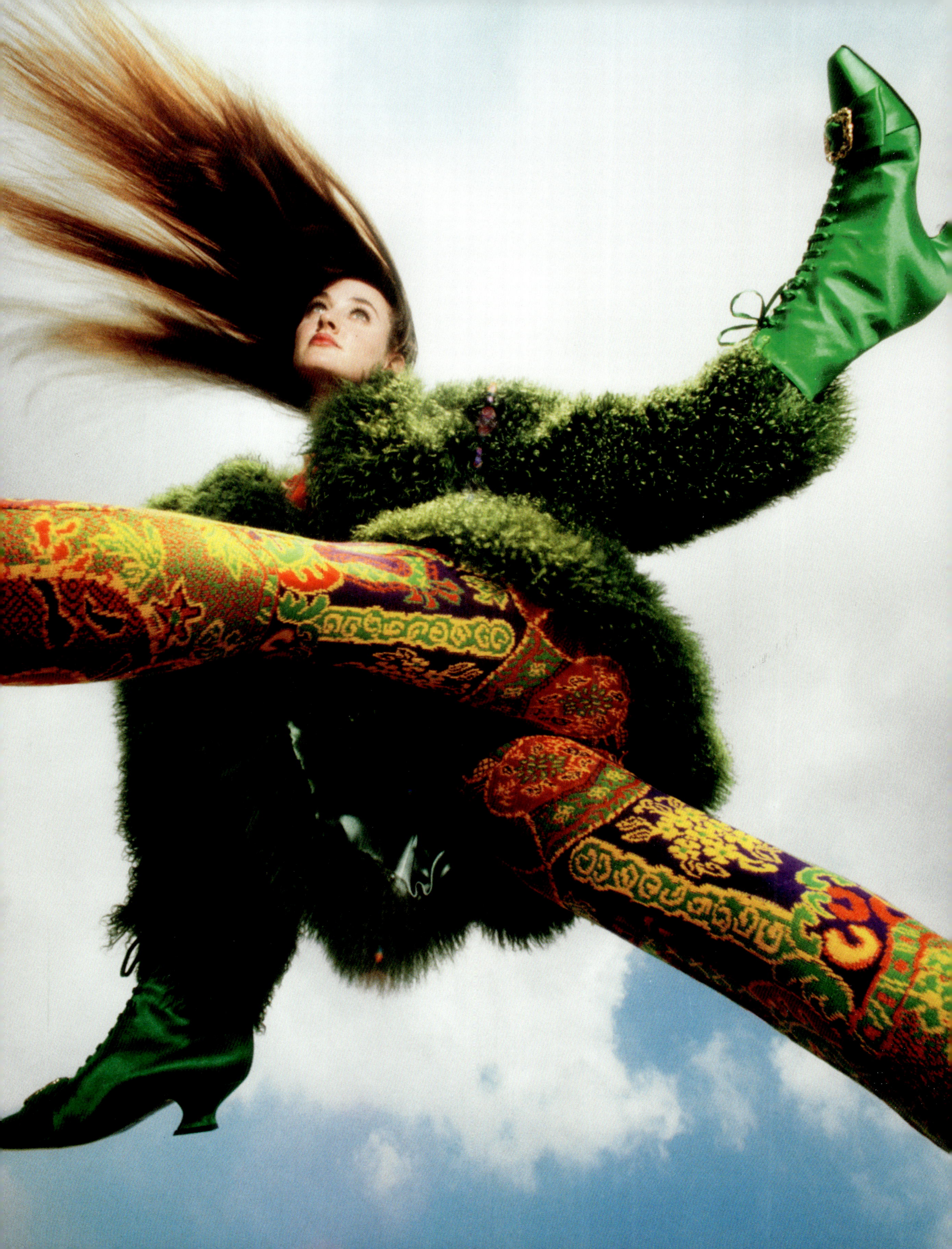

SCHOOLGIRLS AND MATADORS
By EJ McCabe
Styled by Mitzi Lorenz
April 1986

BRITISH SUMMERTIME
By Andrew Macpherson
Styled by Tanya Gill
December 1988

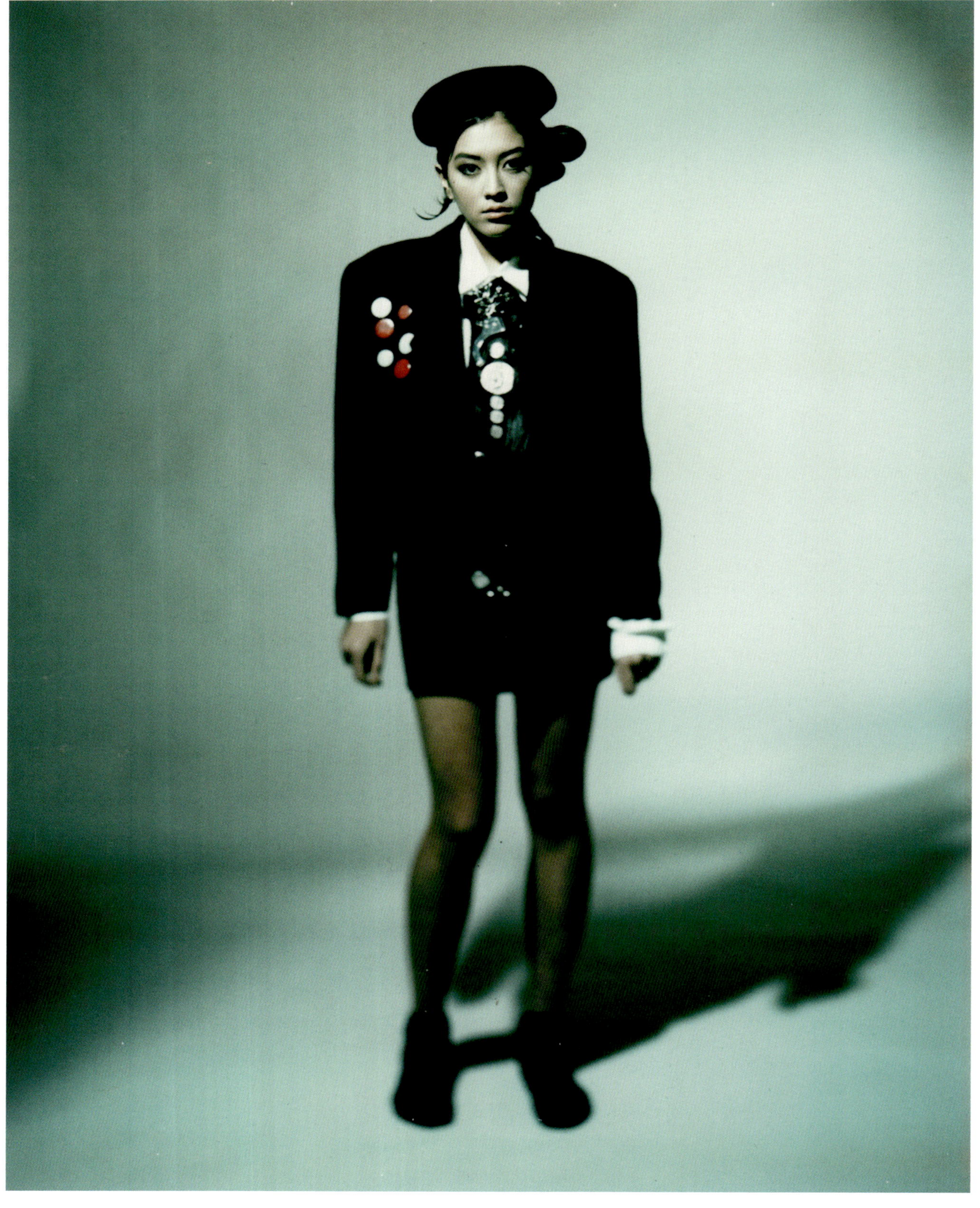

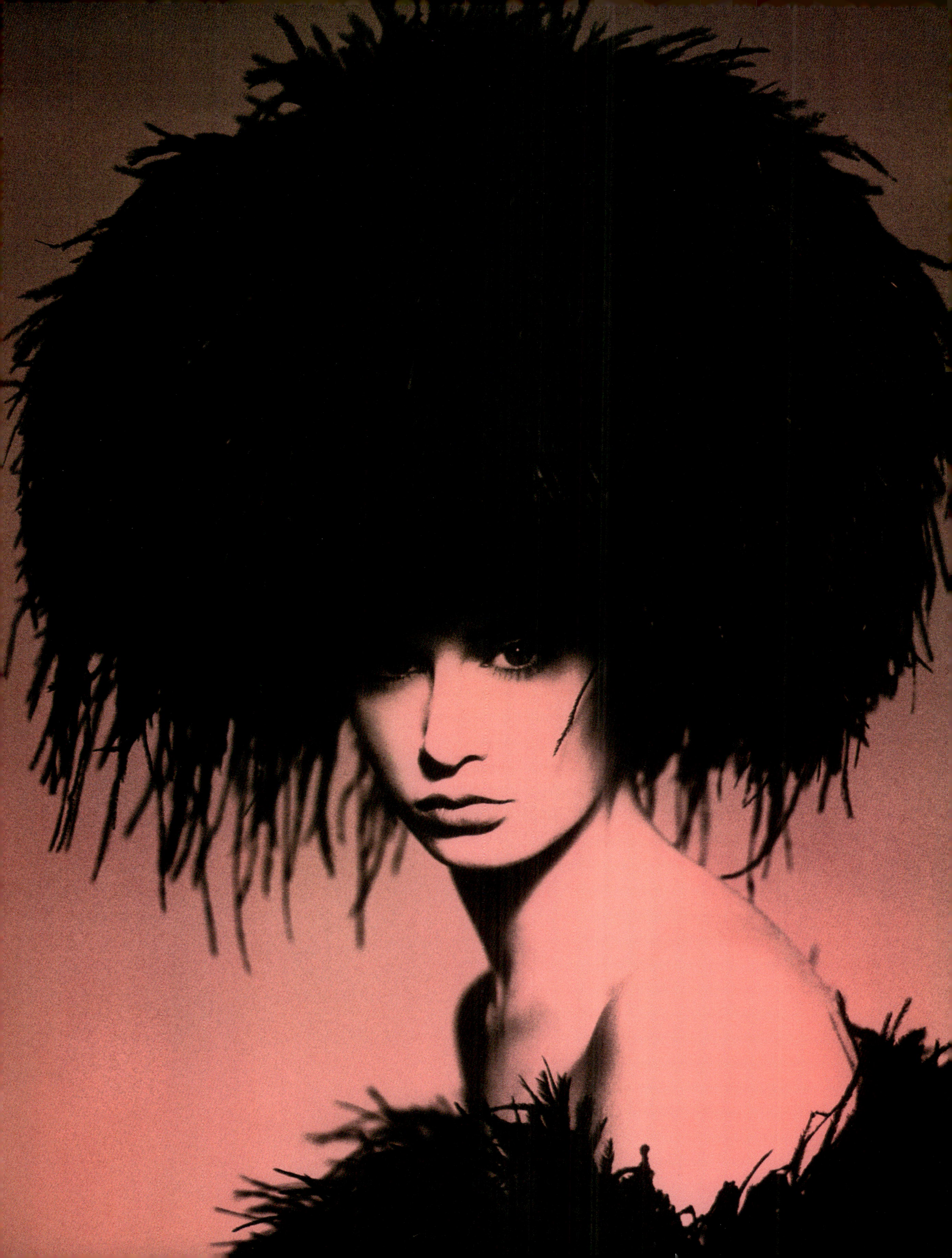

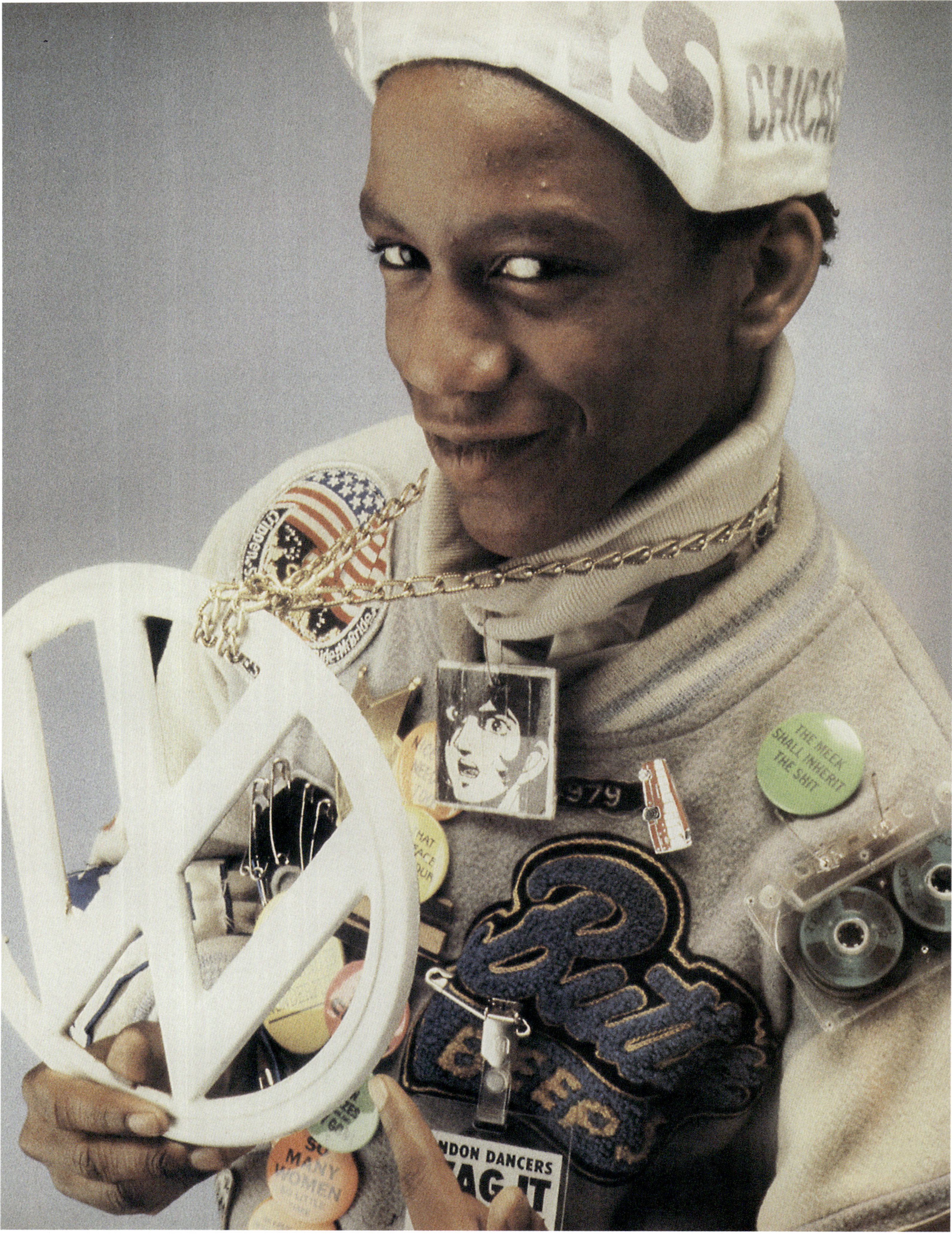
CHICA
THE MEEK
SHALL INHERIT
THE SHIT
1979
SO
MANY
WOMEN
NDON DANCERS
AG IT

Rap changed the musical landscape and ushered
in new ways of looking, being, dancing and lyricising.
These young rap fans were influenced by Public Enemy,
the American hip-hop group who addressed American
racism through their music.
Sheila Rock

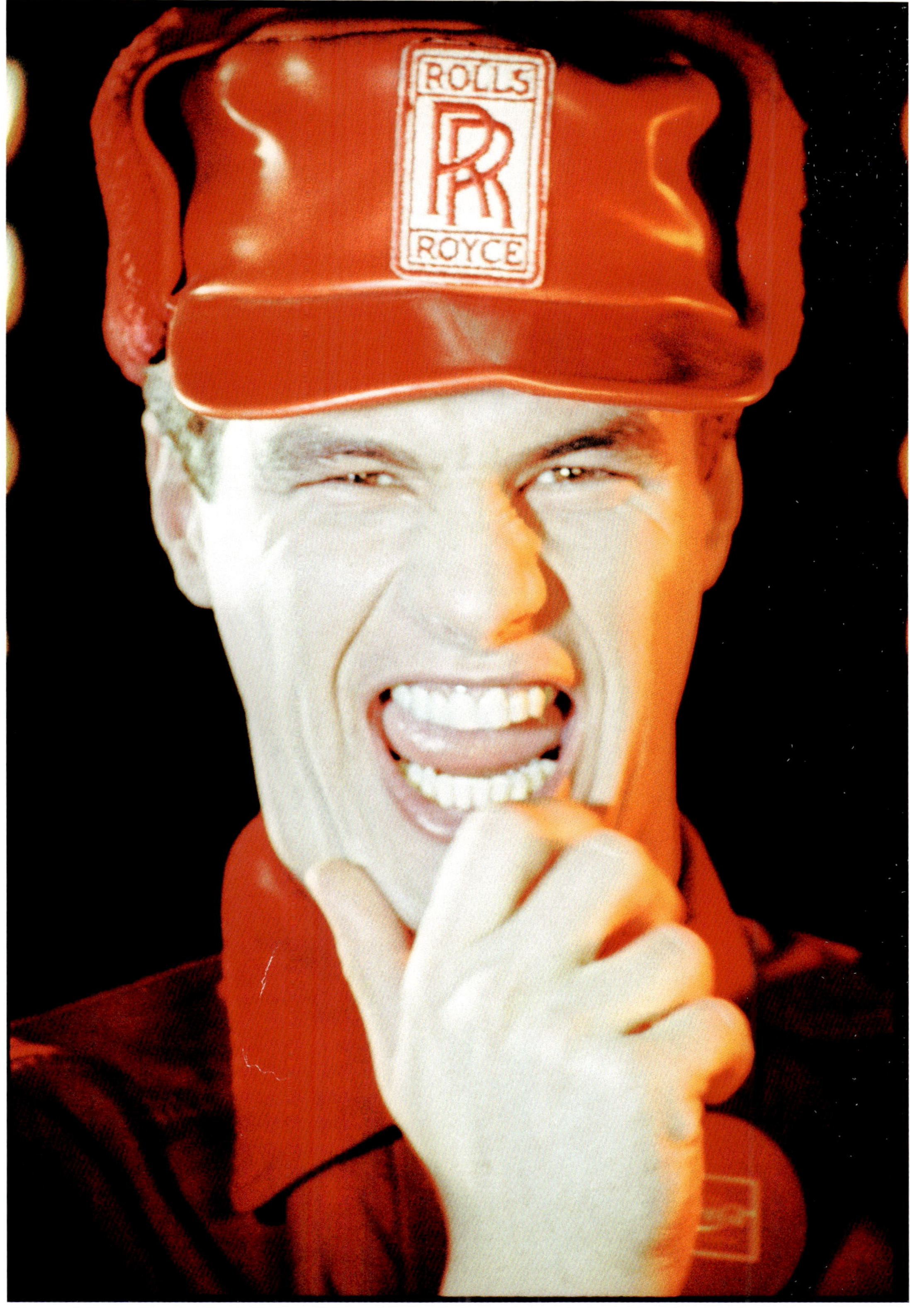

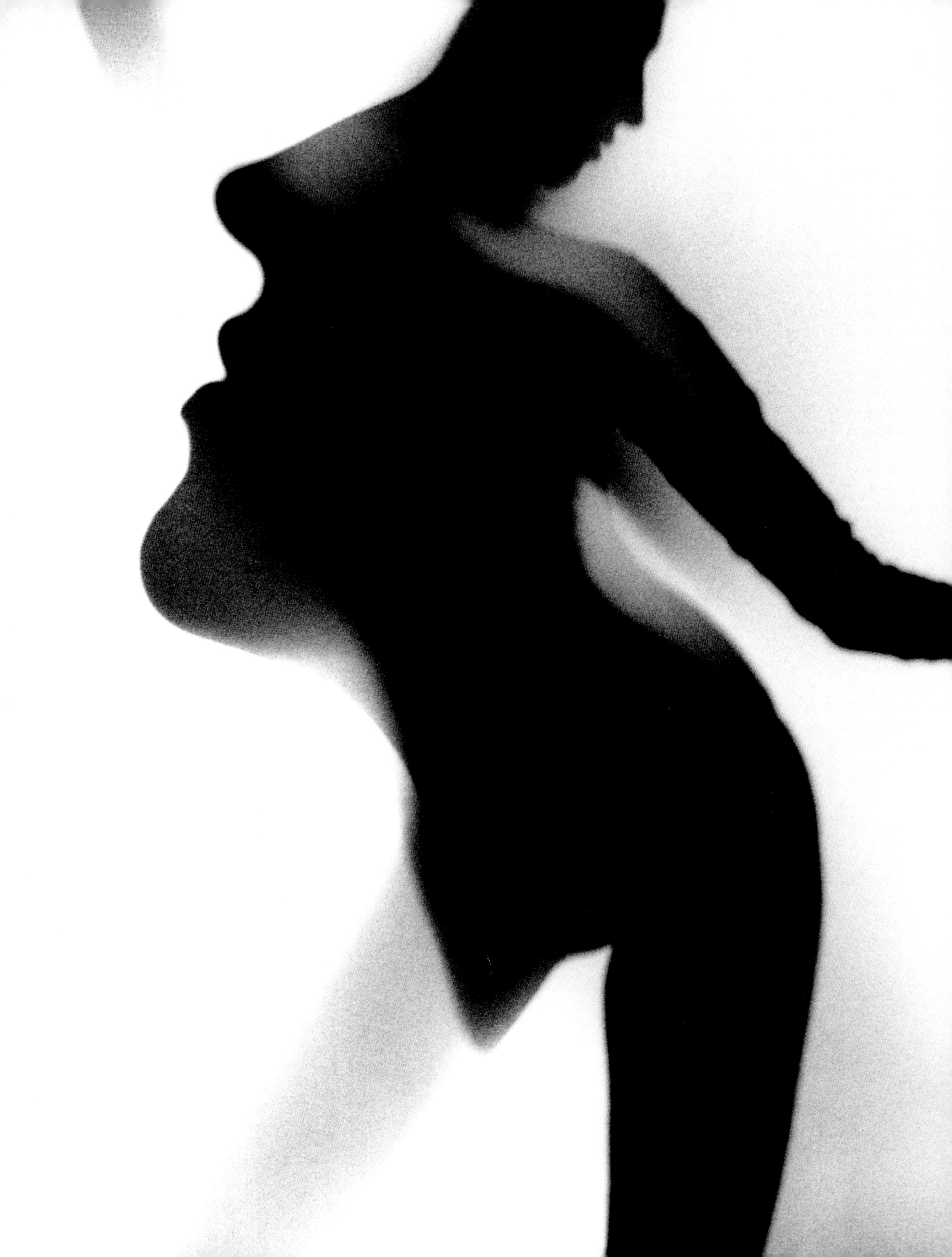

DATELINES
By Andy Bettles
Styled by Alicen Hunter
October 1988

Andy Bettles took a classical
approach that had its origins
in the graphic fashion imagery
of Erwin Blumenfeld and the
darkroom experiments of Man
Ray, and updated it to the
(then) present day.
Phil Bicker, Art Director

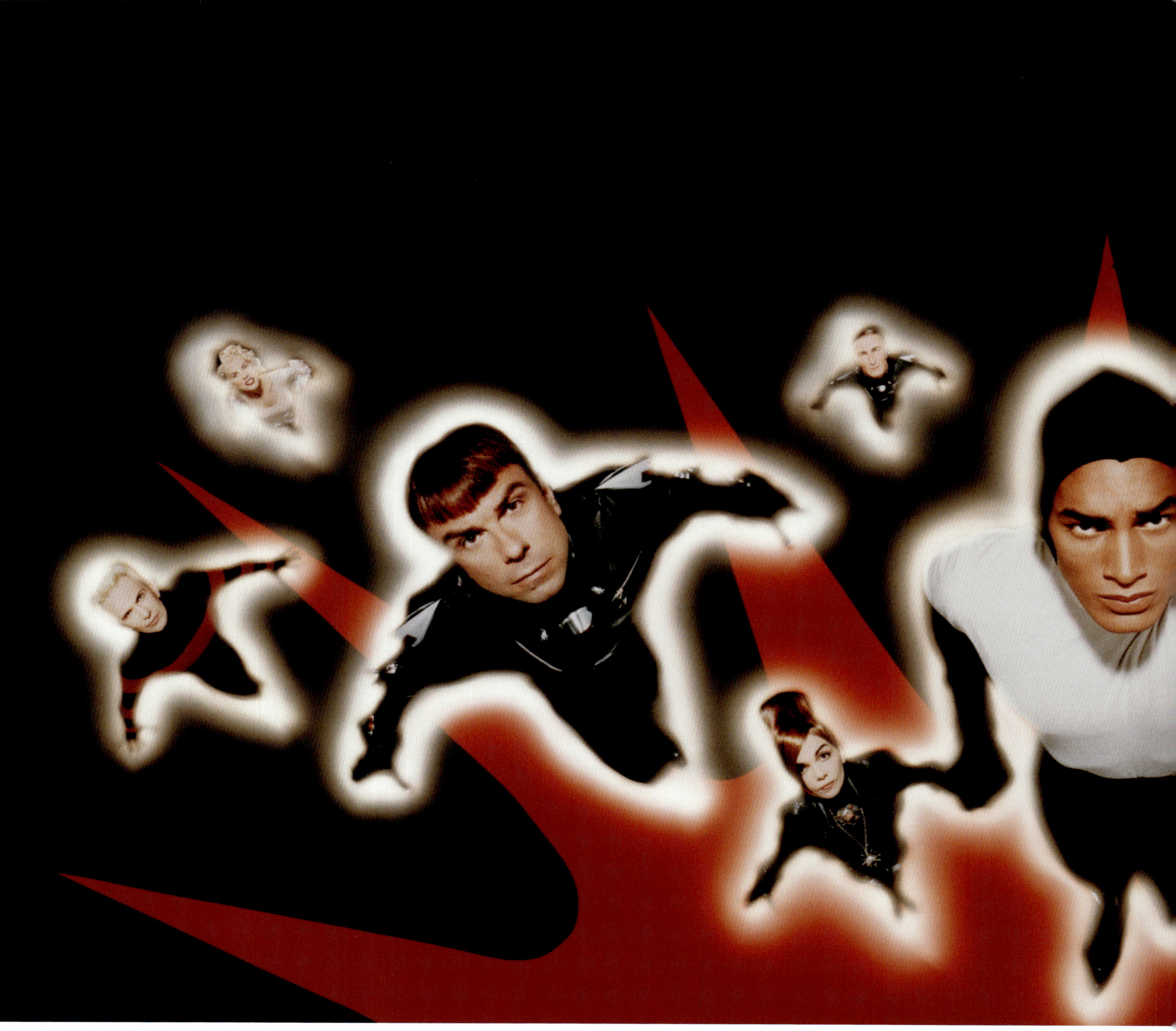

This stylised fashion-forward comic book story was art directed by Babeth Djian and cast the most prominent fashion designers of the day as 'fashion heroes' battling to save our planet. The perfect storm for Stéphane and Babeth's conceptual and creative talents.
Phil Bicker, Art Director

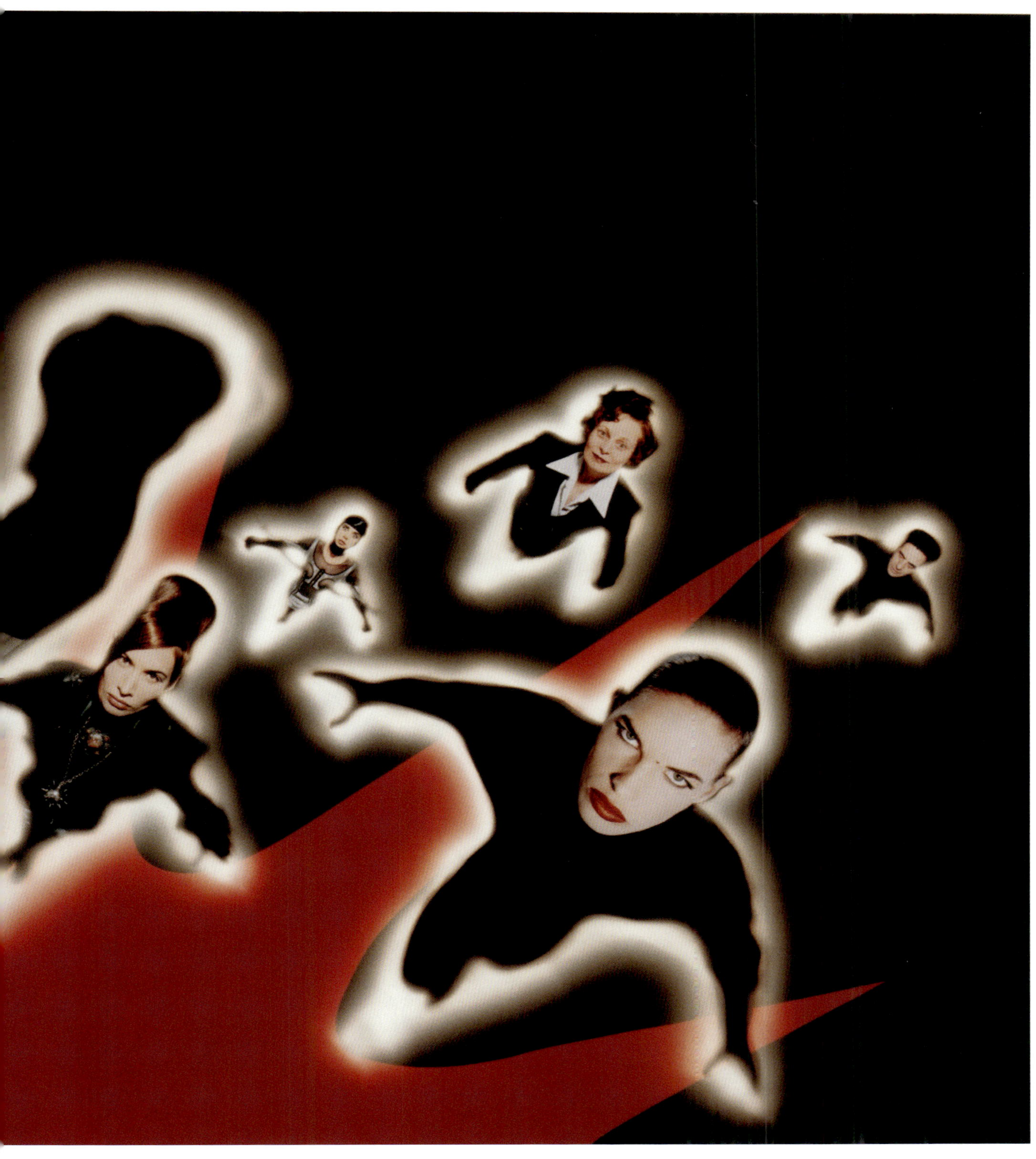

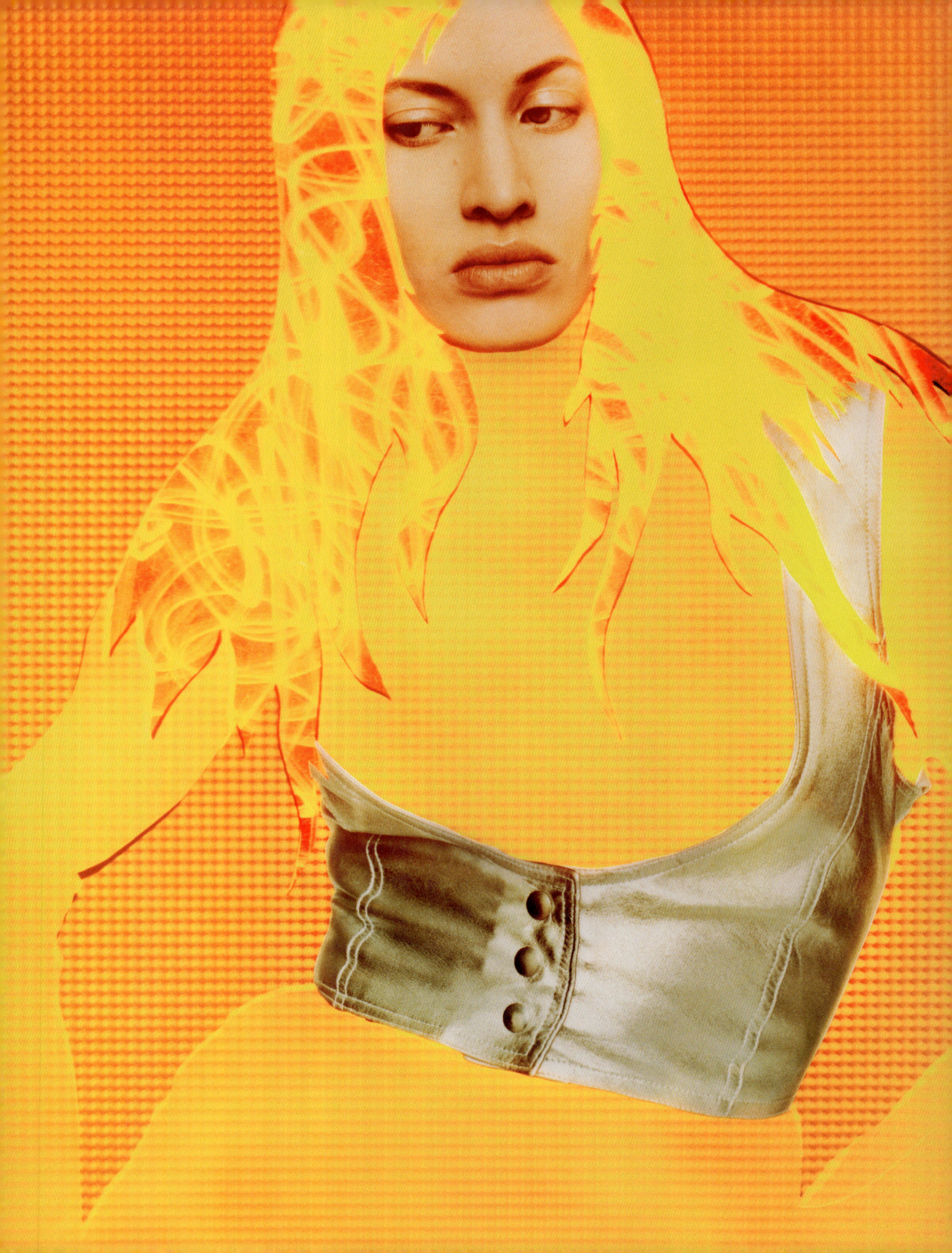

BROTHERS IN YARNS
By Richard Croft
Styled by Malcolm Beckford
February 1989

I met the Joseph twins, Nick
[pictured here] and Richard,
at the Wag Club and thought
they had a unique look.
They had never modelled
before, but were eager to give
it a try. The shoot marked
the beginning of the twins'
successful modelling career.
Malcolm Beckford

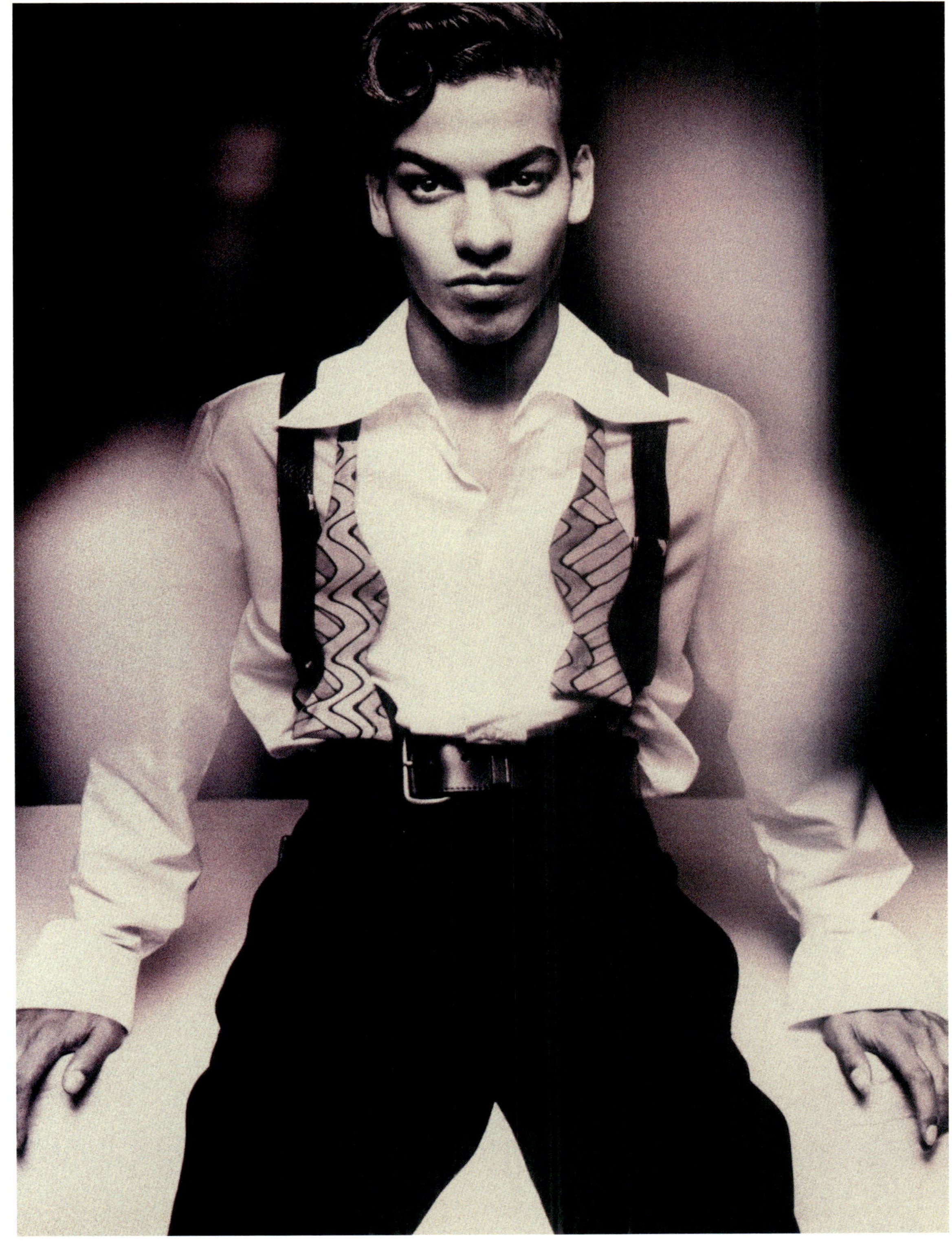

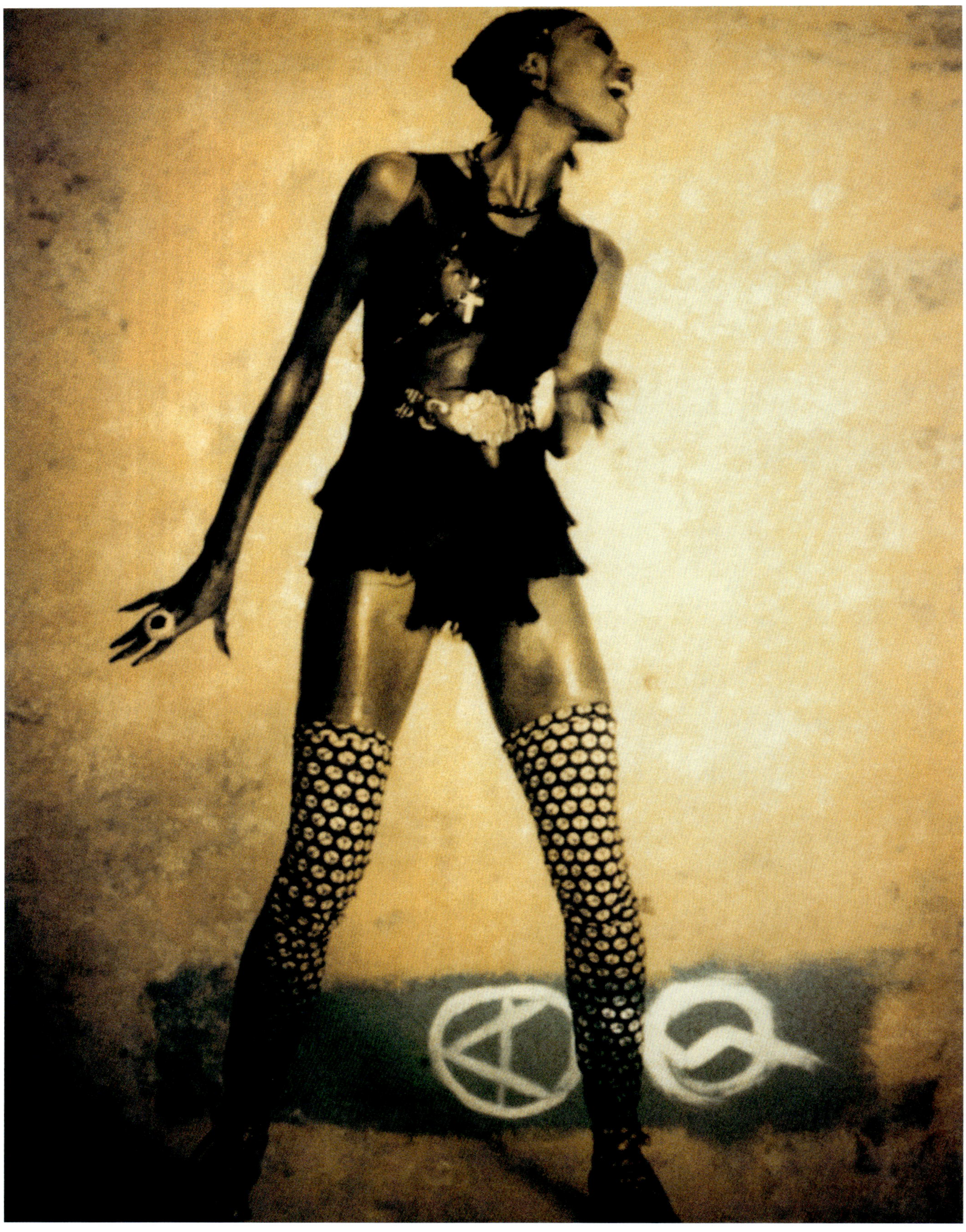

FUCK ART, LET'S VOGUE
By Enrique Badulescu
Styled by Judy Blame
and Adam Howe
May 1989

I remember Enrique being so energetic,
he always used a hand-held camera, music
LOUD, and he would never ask a model
to dance if he wasn't dancing himself.
Adam Howe

STORMY LEATHER
By Julian Broad
Styled by Christian Logan
August 1989

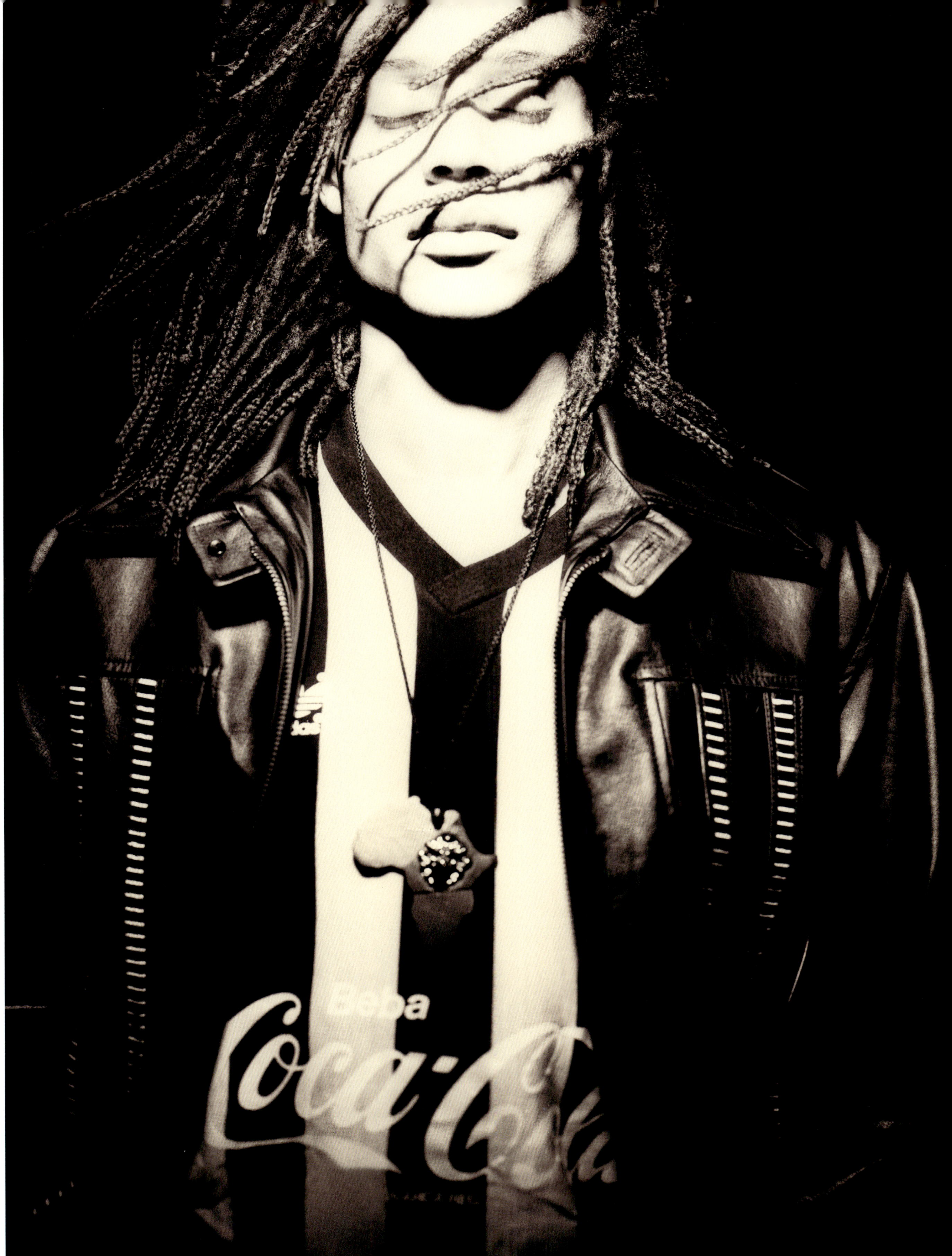

Beba
Coca-Cola

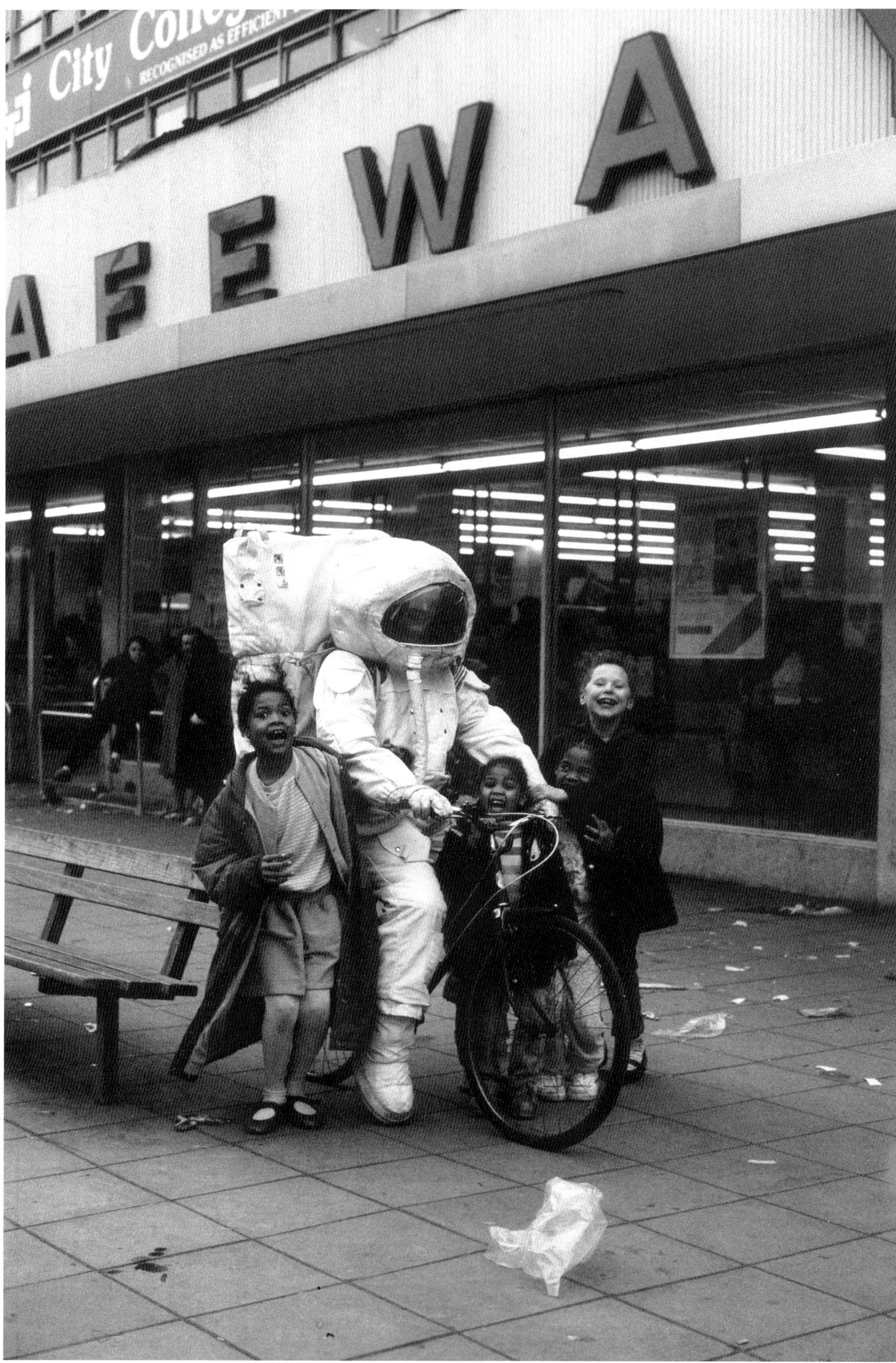

City Colleg
RECOGNISED AS EFFICIENT
AFEWA

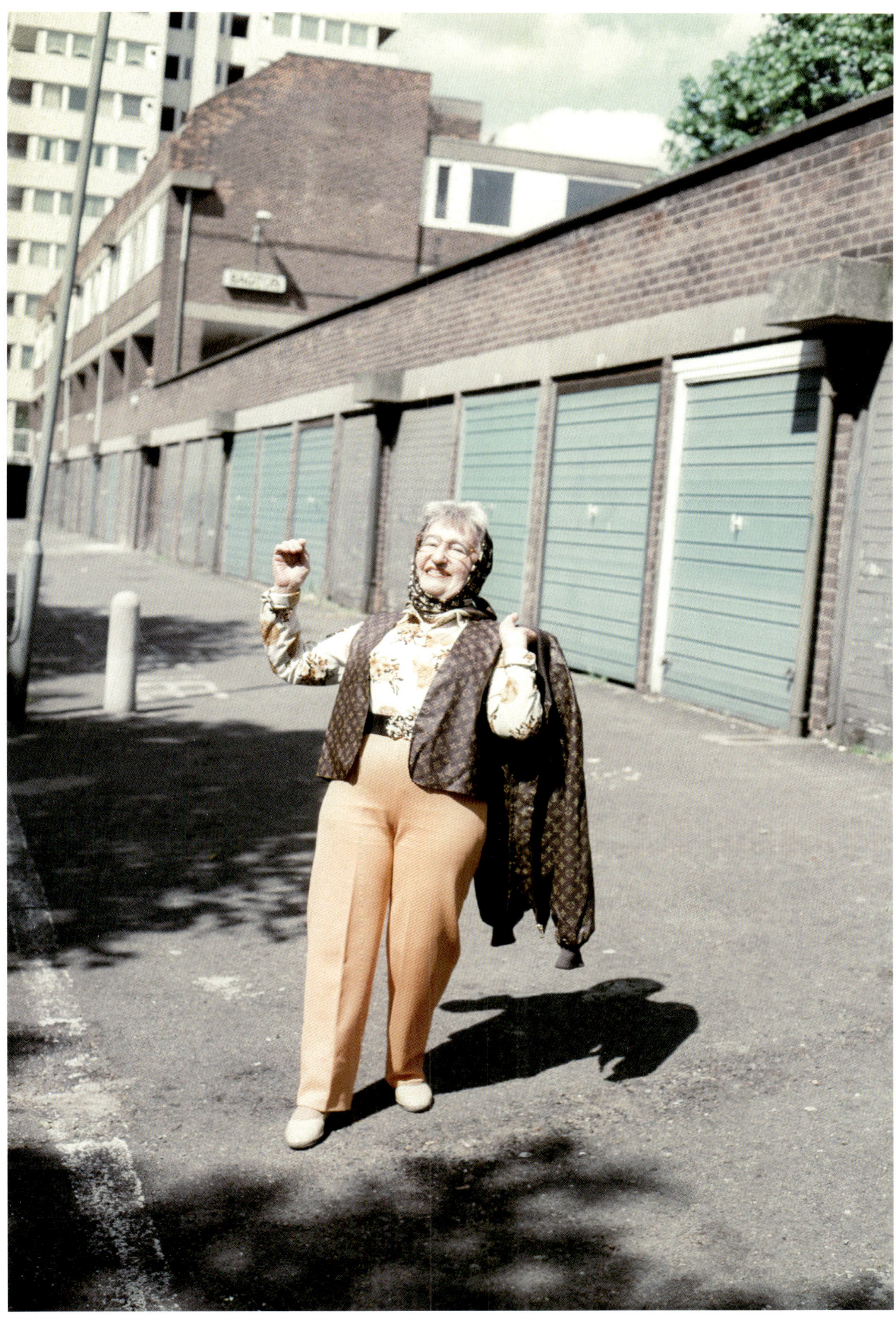

LOST IN SPACE
By Nigel Shafran
Styled by Melanie Ward
July 1989

FAKING IT
By Nigel Shafran
July/August 1988

Nigel's approach to his subject matter
is intimate and unpretentious, and full
of youthful energy.
Phil Bicker, Art Director

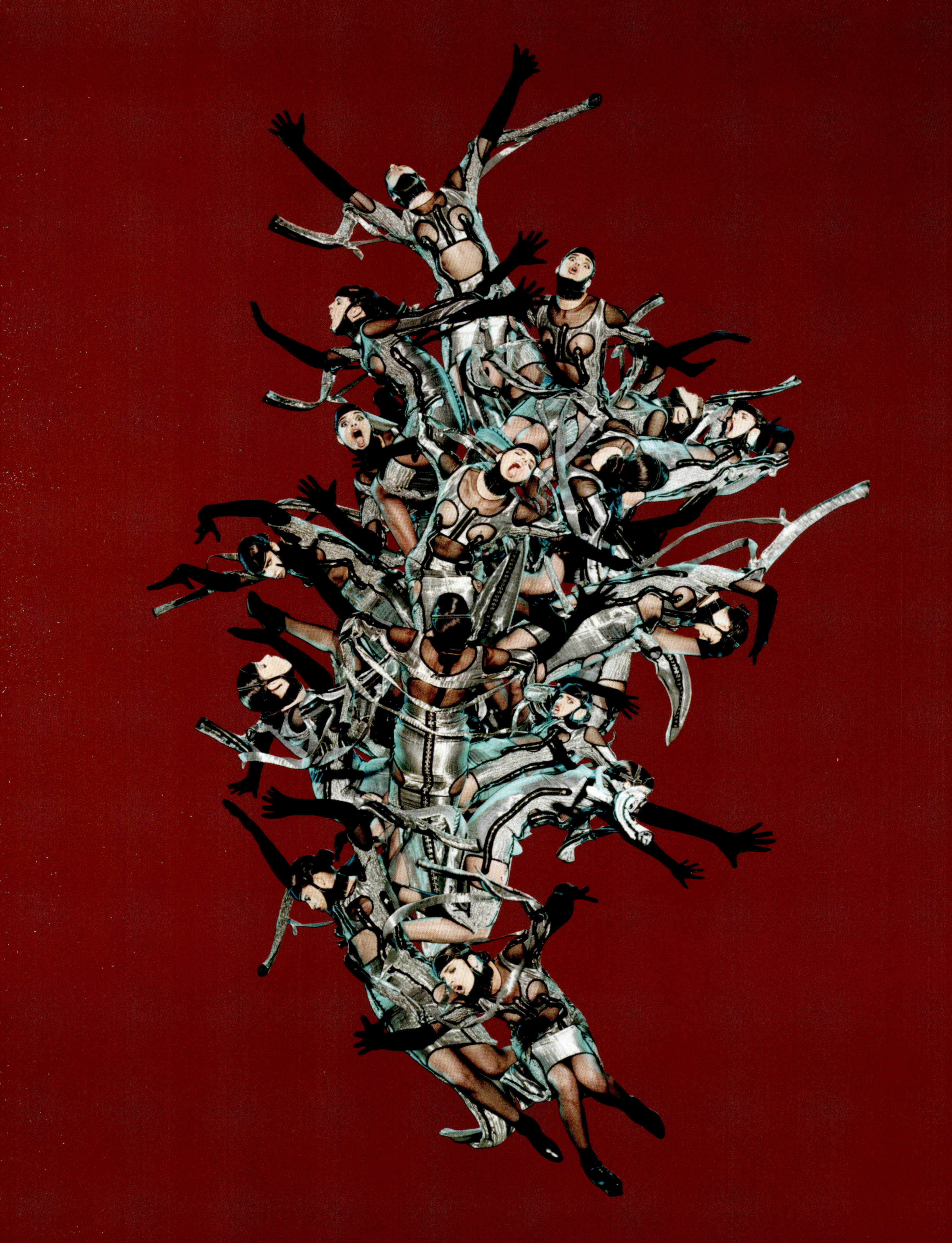

ENHANCED

NORBERT SCHOERNER AND STÉPHANE SEDNAOUI

Norbert Schoerner is a photographer and filmmaker whose work featured in *The Face* from 1990 onwards. Stéphane Sednaoui is a fine artist, filmmaker and photographer who began contributing to the magazine in the late Eighties. The pair met to discuss the role of *The Face* in their practice, and the impact of evolving digital and photographic technologies on the images they made for the magazine.

NORBERT SCHOERNER: How did you first hear about *The Face*? Was it famous in Paris in the Eighties?

STÉPHANE SEDNAOUI: I discovered *The Face* through Jean Paul Gaultier, who had his eye on London street culture. The first time I went to his studio, Boy George from Culture Club showed up. Another time, it was the New York artist Keith Haring. I thought: 'This place is insane. This is fantastic!' In Paris, I worked with Gaultier, helping in the studio and modelling for him, but pretty soon I had one foot in New York and one foot in London, because for a photographer starting out there wasn't much going on in Paris.

NS: Before I started working for *The Face* myself, I remember seeing your 1989 'Fashion Heroes' feature. It really stood out to me for the different techniques you used – classic collage, superhero cartoons and a sense of colour I hadn't really seen before. It felt completely new.

SS: Andy Warhol was definitely an influence for me. Also, William Klein. In 1989 the Museum of Modern Art in New York held an Andy Warhol retrospective and I got the exhibition catalogue when it toured to the Centre Pompidou. I was flipping through its pages, while also looking at French editions of Marvel comics, and the colours and aesthetic had a big impact on me, and on that series.

NS: I grew up in Munich and bought *The Face* in the mid-Eighties. For me, it represented a completely different world, a place where it was possible to create new things and upset the status quo. When you started working for *The Face*, were you aware of just how far-reaching the magazine's impact was?

SS: My first story for *The Face* was 'Voici Paris', with models Susie Bick and Eugenie Vincent, in 1988; I was 25 years old. I was aware of its impact, but more on an emotional level. I was never thinking strategically. Of course, I knew it was good to have a story in *The Face*, but I was driven more by the fact that I loved the magazine and wanted to be in it.

NS: I felt the same – actually, I moved to London because I wanted to work for *The Face*. Why do you think it became so successful? What made it so unique?

SS: I think it was because it stayed true to street culture and was full of energy. Nowadays, magazines think they have to put models or famous people on the cover but the message of *The Face*, at

REALITY

least until the mid-Nineties, was that anybody from any background could be fantastic: we all have creativity and we can all express it. It was the same with fashion. Five years earlier, before meeting Gaultier, I hated fashion because to me it felt so elitist. That was not the creative environment that I aspired to. Gaultier and Vivienne Westwood changed that impression. When I discovered *The Face*, it was bad boys, bad girls, rock and roll, punk and street culture. It was fashion but unpretentious. The message was right. You didn't have to put somebody famous on the cover: it could just be a great character. Look at the cover you did with [artist] Hanayo as a geisha.

NS: That was very special. We wanted to do a story about the generation after the economic bubble burst in Japan. Hanayo just happened to be chewing gum in the studio, so the fact that she blew a bubble just as I took that picture was a complete coincidence but it really did work perfectly for the story.

SS: Yes, everything was perfect, and they picked it for the cover. Another big difference with *The Face* was that they would decide which was the best image for the cover while they were putting together the issue, as images came in. Nowadays, editorial teams all have a plan and certain pages have been sold to big-brand advertisers, so they already know three months in advance what's going to be on the cover.

NS: I was very lucky because about two weeks after my arrival the stylist Adam Howe introduced me to Phil Bicker, who was *The Face*'s Art Director, and he gave me a commission two weeks later. I didn't have any fashion pictures: like you, I wasn't that interested in fashion. I just showed him my portfolio, which had 50 landscape images in it, and he said: 'Oh, I love your work. Do you want to shoot this band next week?'

SS: It's like when Alexey Brodovitch [Art Director of *Harper's Bazaar*] invited William Klein and Robert Frank to do fashion shoots for the magazine because he thought they were interesting artists. Phil is our Alexey Brodovitch, I love Phil!

NS: It's fascinating to look back now and remember that, especially in London, there was a whole community of photographers who would go to the same labs to develop their images. BDI Colour Lab on Old Street had a particularly big influence and helped to create a visual style. By the early Nineties, of course, photography technology was evolving, and people were starting to use Quantel Paintbox or other forms of digital manipulation.

SS: I discovered Paintbox at a lab called Dahinden when I did a campaign for the Parisian department store Printemps in 1988. While the images from the 'The Fashion Heroes' were done by hand, I wanted to make a few double-page spreads, so I multiplied the images using Paintbox.

NS: You were a true pioneer! Paintbox was very difficult to access because it was so expensive and not many companies had it. I remember using Paintbox for a story in *The Face* and having to call in favours because there was no budget for it. I used a printing company in London called Ad Plates, who had it. The core team weren't creatives – they were print technicians – there were only a couple of retouchers, and I built up a relationship with them. By the late Nineties, Photoshop was evolving and fashion and style magazines began to use digital post-production more widely.

SS: I moved to New York in 1991 and, as I shifted all my creative energy into music videos, I only worked sporadically for *The Face* until the last story I did for them in 1998. Juergen Teller had been working with *The Face* for some time but in the early Nineties he started to bring a more natural, 'snapshot' feel, both to his portraits and fashion photography. For me, your work fell somewhere in between, because you kept that pop approach, continuing to experiment with light and colour, but your aesthetic was more natural. Your work was conceptual but you were making concept out of reality.

NS: That is an interesting description because I think it hits the nail on the head for that particular period of my work. I would also call it enhanced reality.

In the early Nineties, especially after Lee Swillingham became Art Director of *The Face*, you suddenly had so many different styles coexisting. You had the grungy thing, fashion became much more self-aware and a much more stylised type of music photography emerged. Younger generations now are so used to seeing a flood of visual information that it's quite hard to explain how much it meant at the time to see these different references and styles. How do you look at the legacy of *The Face* in the context of digital media and social media today and this whole overload of information? Was *The Face* more powerful back then because there weren't as many competing channels?

SS: Nowadays, there is an infinity of choice, not only in terms of magazines, but in how you communicate on social media platforms. Anyone can produce their own show or magazine online, which is fantastic. However, the counter-productive aspect is that everything is becoming more compartmentalised, so we end up only seeing content produced by those people whose tastes already align with our own. We are becoming increasingly polarised as a society because we all constantly get our beliefs affirmed. If there are a hundred thousand people online that think like me, then I don't need to explore what's going on in the rest

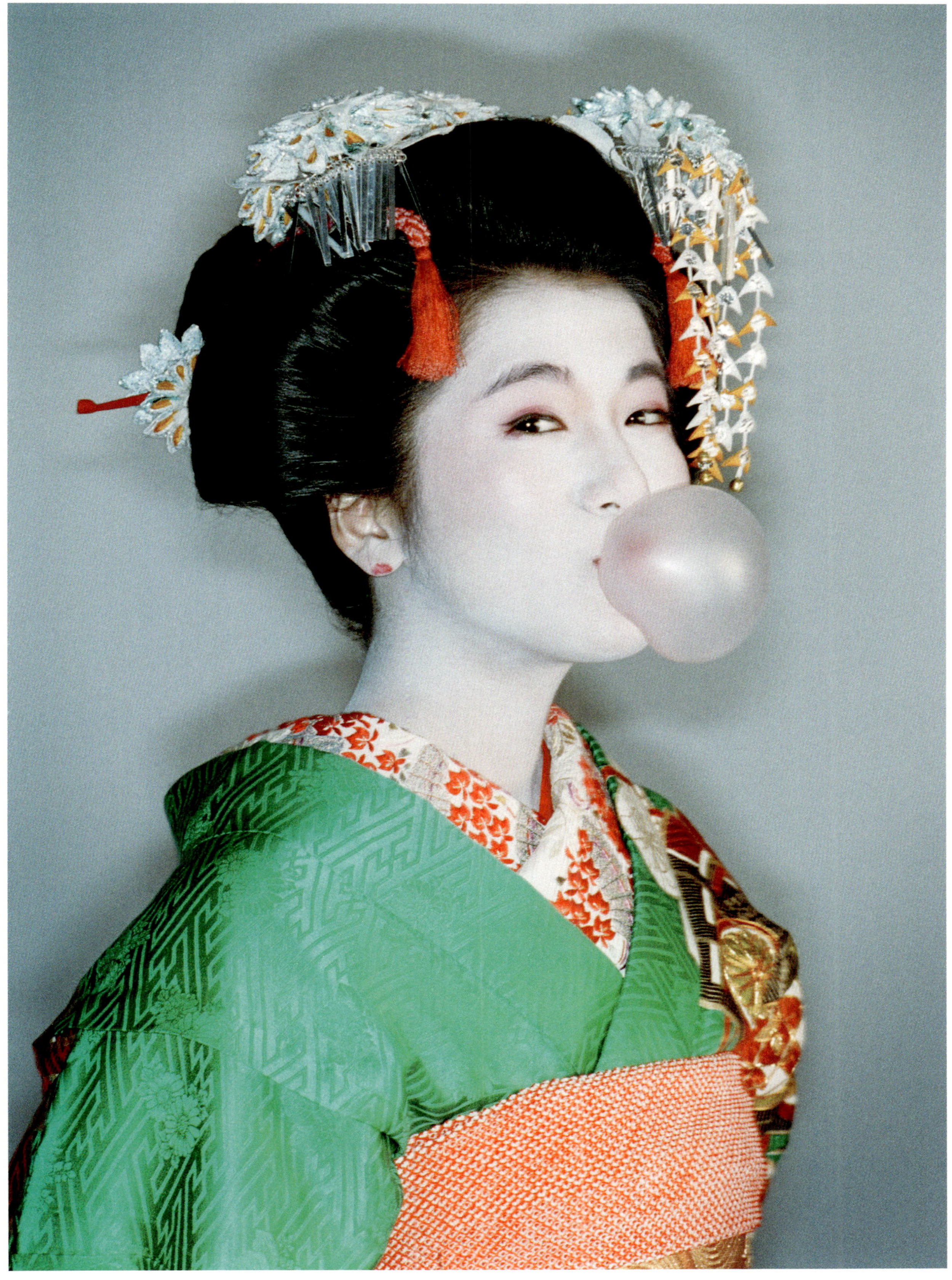

of the world. In the Eighties and Nineties, we only had a handful of pop-culture magazines and we had only one counterpart on television, MTV. So, we were forced to see things we didn't like. You'd turn on MTV and there would be an hour-long programme about some kind of music that wasn't your favourite, but you'd leave it on and you'd be exposed to things other people liked. Nowadays, you can pick exactly what you want to watch, so your worldview just gets narrower and narrower.

NS: I think that's such a valid point because increased choice is definitely leading to a fragmentation of society and culture. In *The Face*, you would have a fashion story next to a story about some rave clubs next to a story about civil war in Africa. It was multi-dimensional; it was engaged in social issues and politics as well as culture. Nowadays, it's a lot harder to get that breadth, because we are driven by the algorithm towards our own specific interest groups. It's a seismic, even cataclysmic, shift. ∎

1990

1999

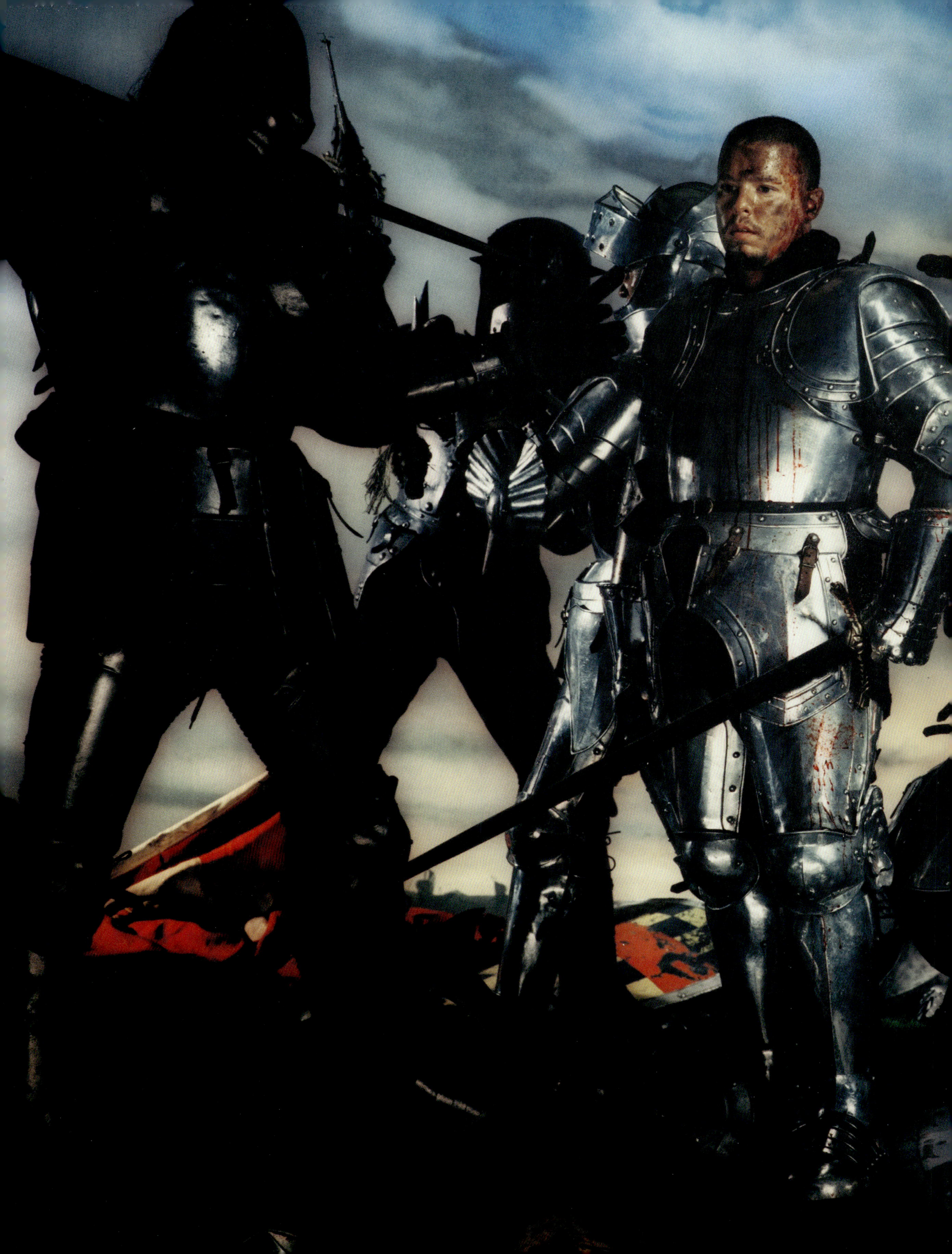

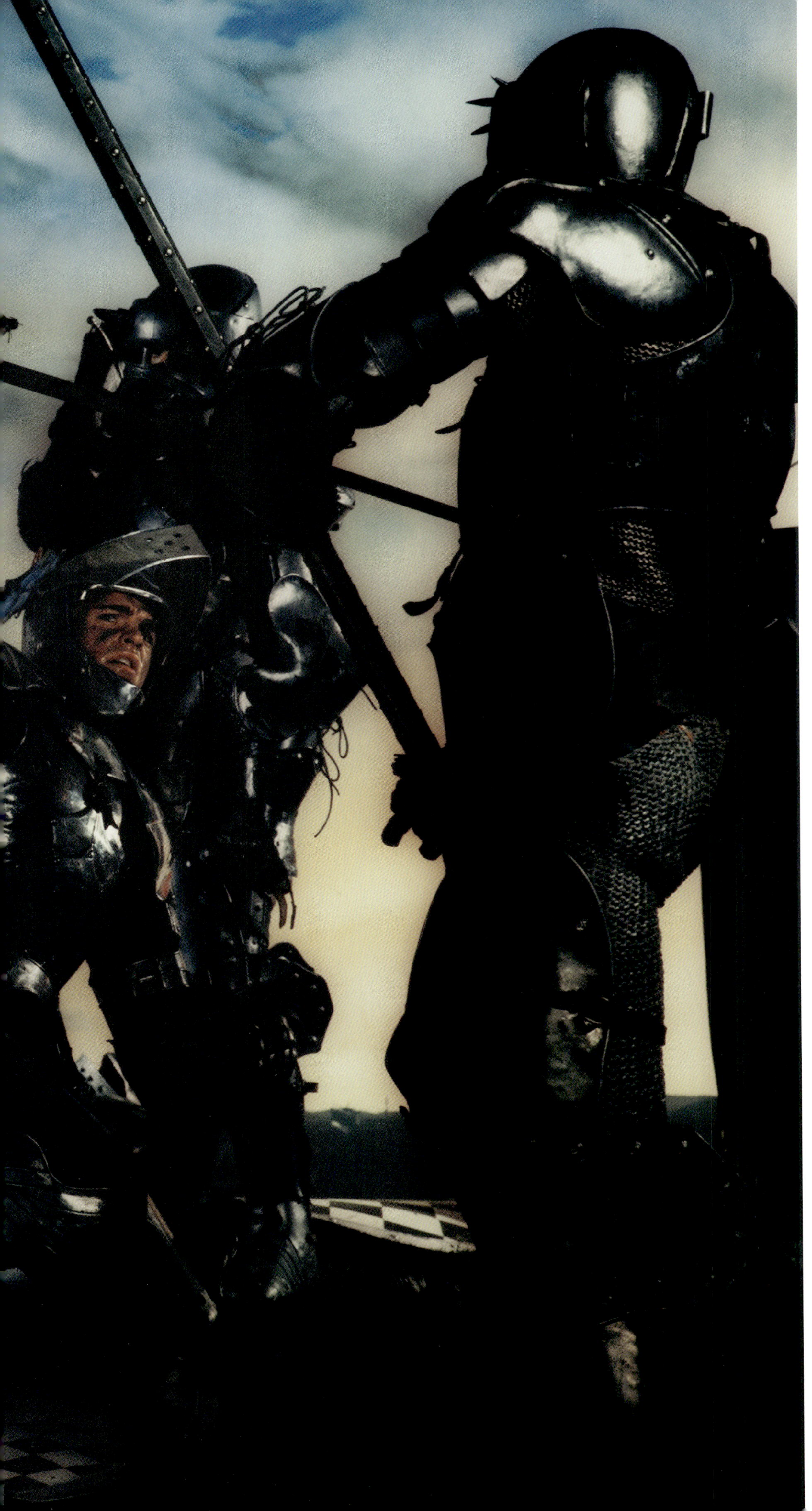

THE DARK KNIGHT RETURNS
By Sean Ellis
Styled by Isabella Blow
August 1998

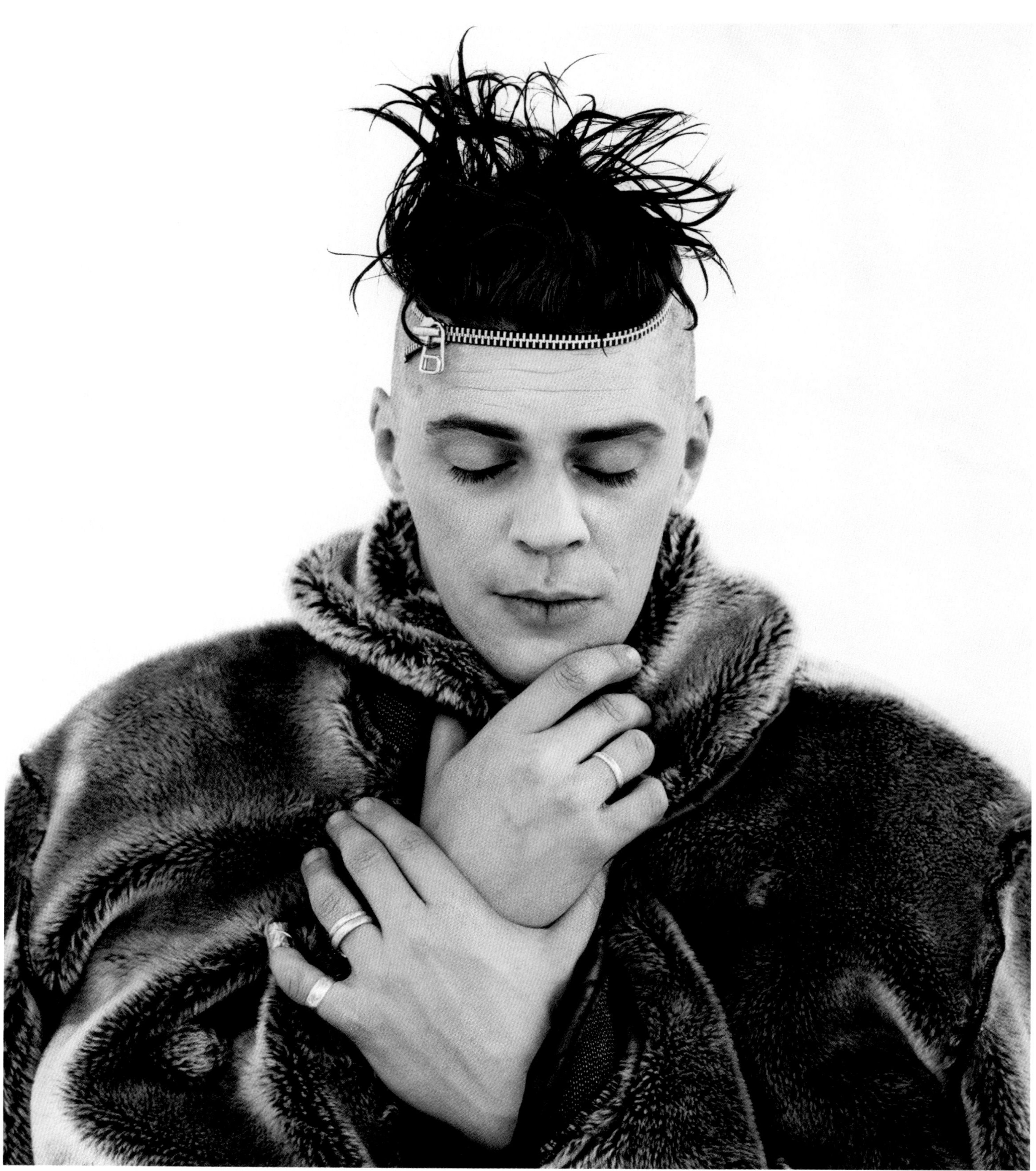

HEAD HUNTERS

By Jean Baptiste Mondino
Styled by Judy Blame
August 1993

LONDON GIRLS

By Corinne Day
Styled by Melanie Ward
June 1992

Casting and simplicity were integral to the fashion in
The Face from the mid-Eighties through the early Nineties.
There is an inherent authenticity in the imagery, which
is as much portraiture as it is fashion photography.
Phil Bicker, Art Director

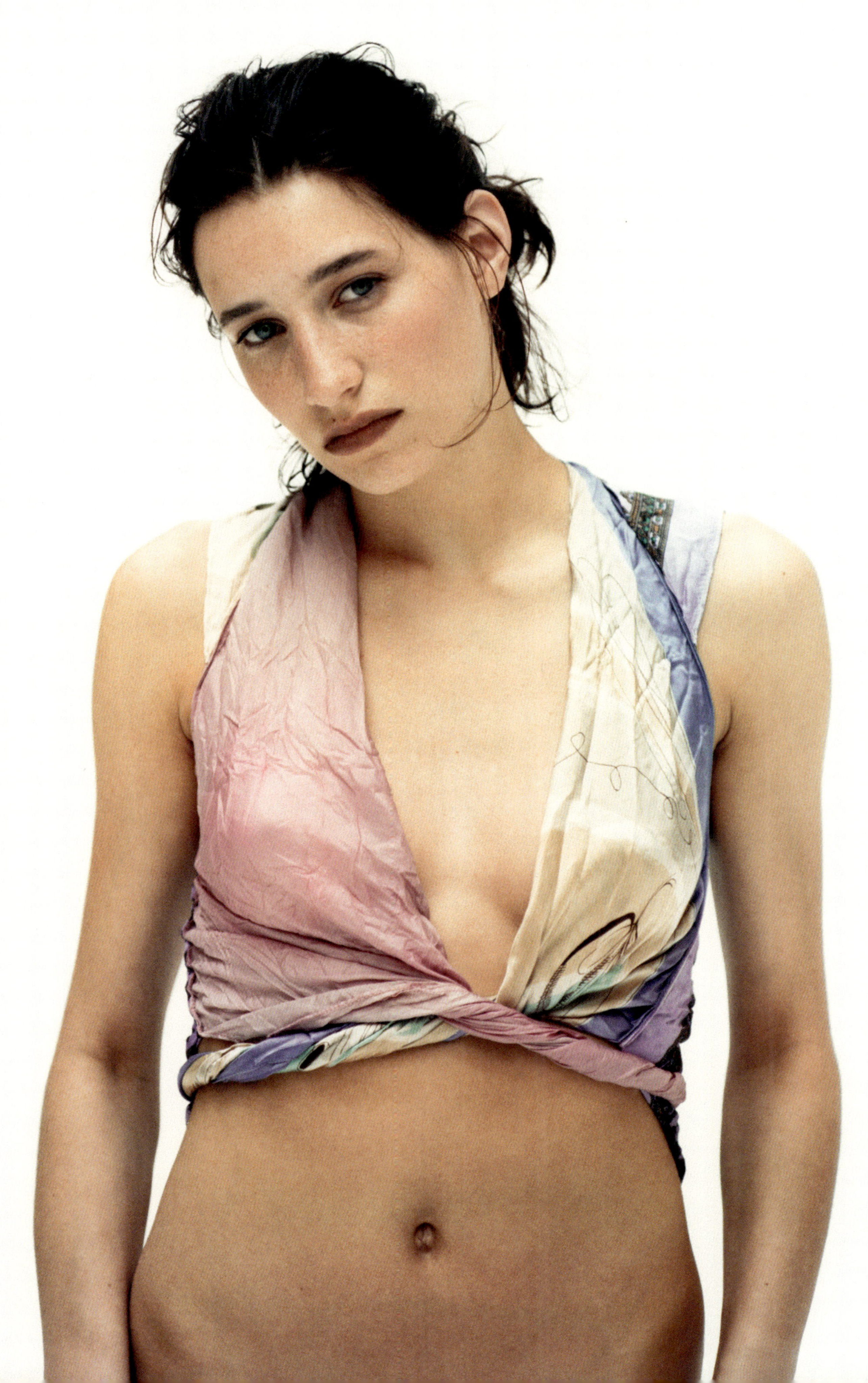

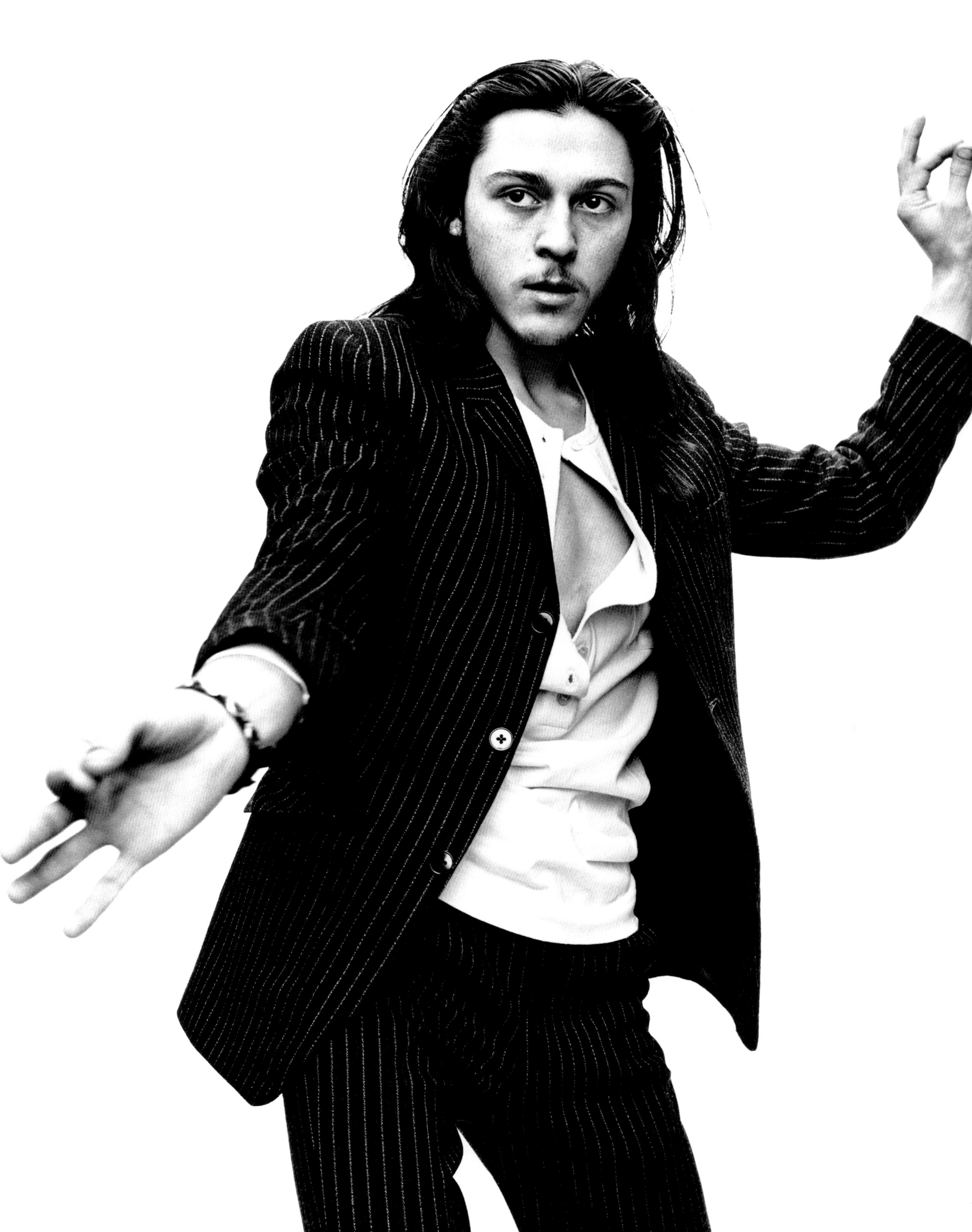

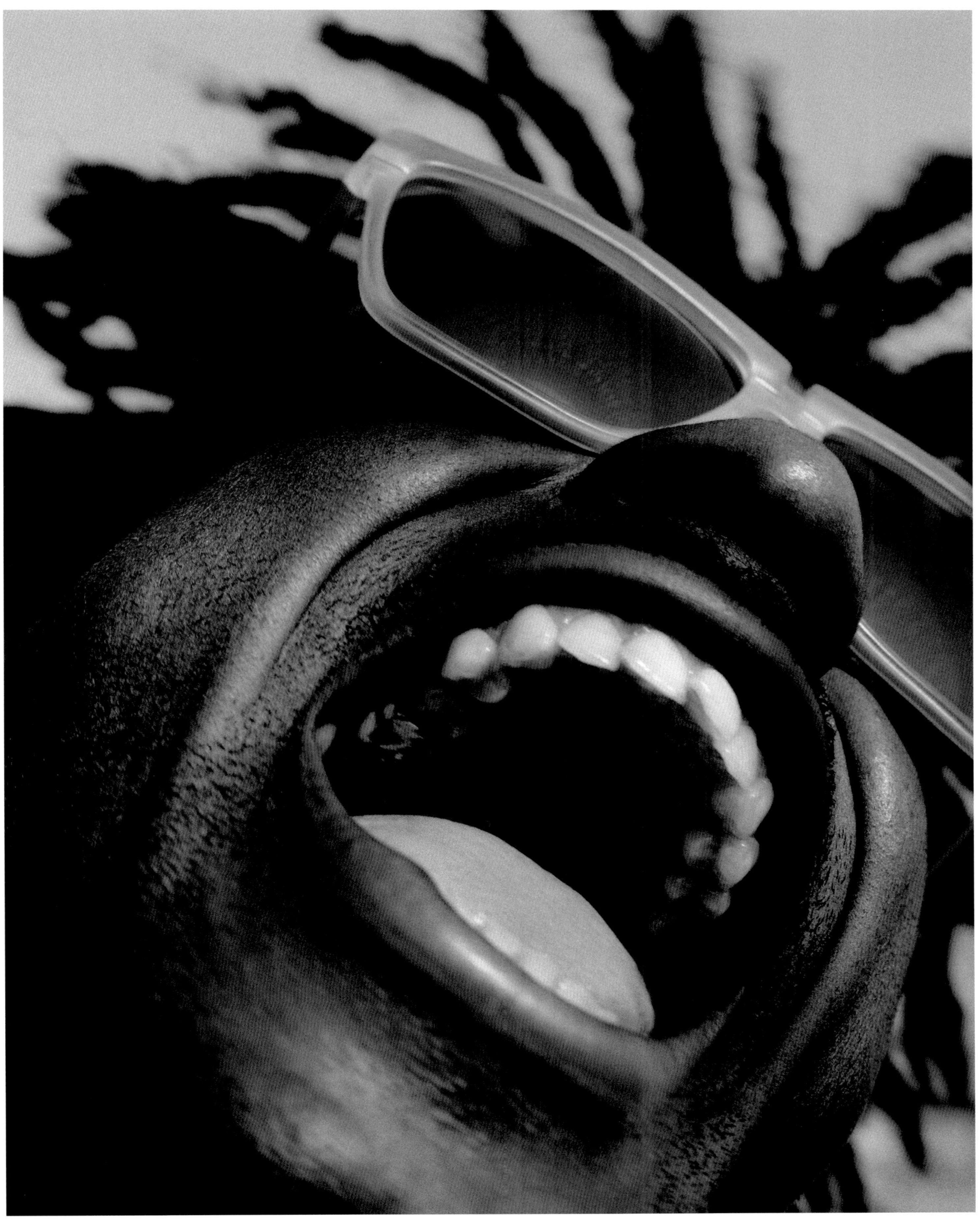

BACK TO LIFE
By David Sims
Styled by Melanie Ward
November 1990

NORMSKI
By Jake Chessum
December 1992

There was not only room to experiment – you felt like you owed it in return.
Working for *The Face*, you were granted the opportunity and freedom
to produce the kind of images that you wanted to see in the magazine.

DONALD MILNE, PHOTOGRAPHER

BEASTIE BOYS
By Donald Milne
July 1998

ONE LOVE
By Mario Testino
Styled by Mitzi Lorenz
December 1990

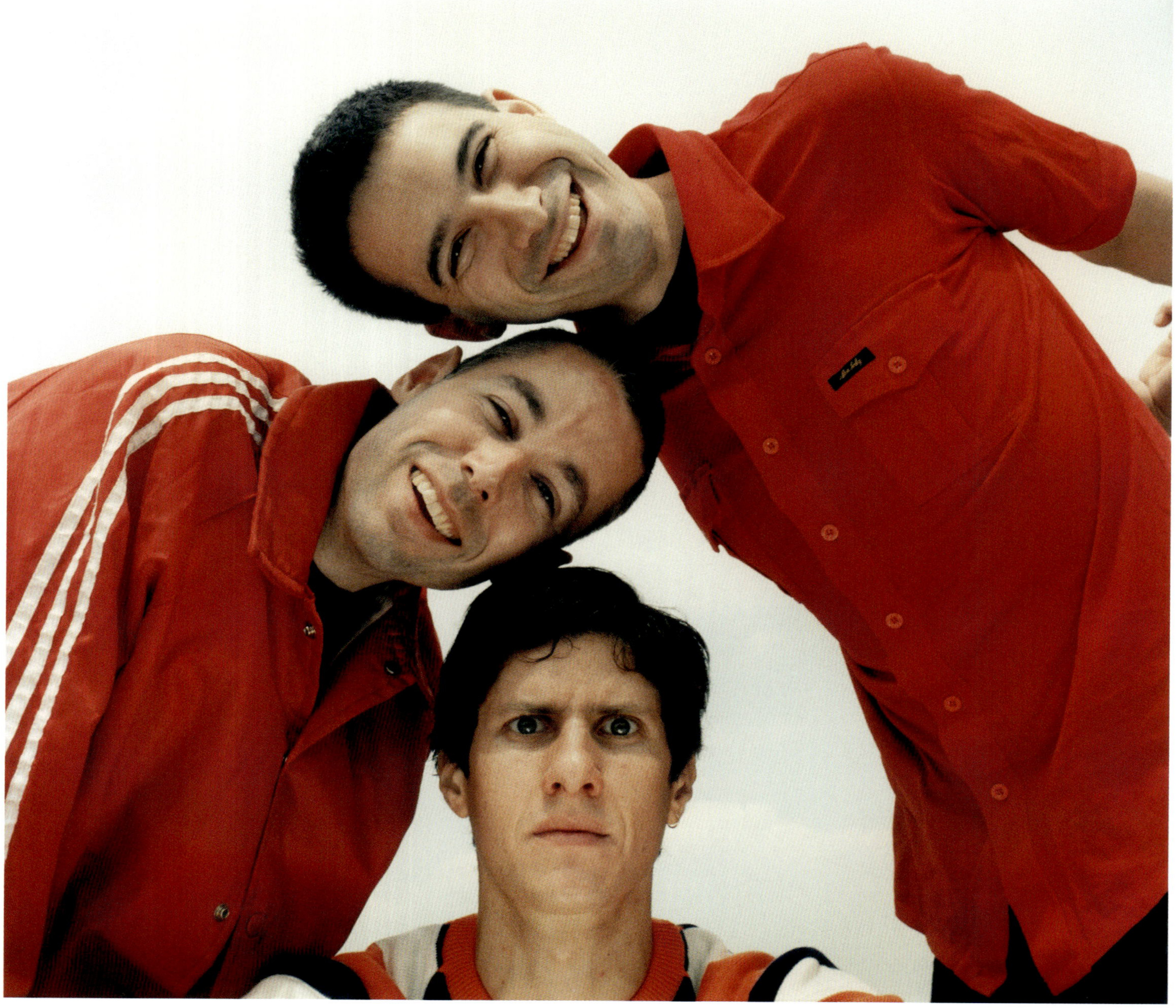

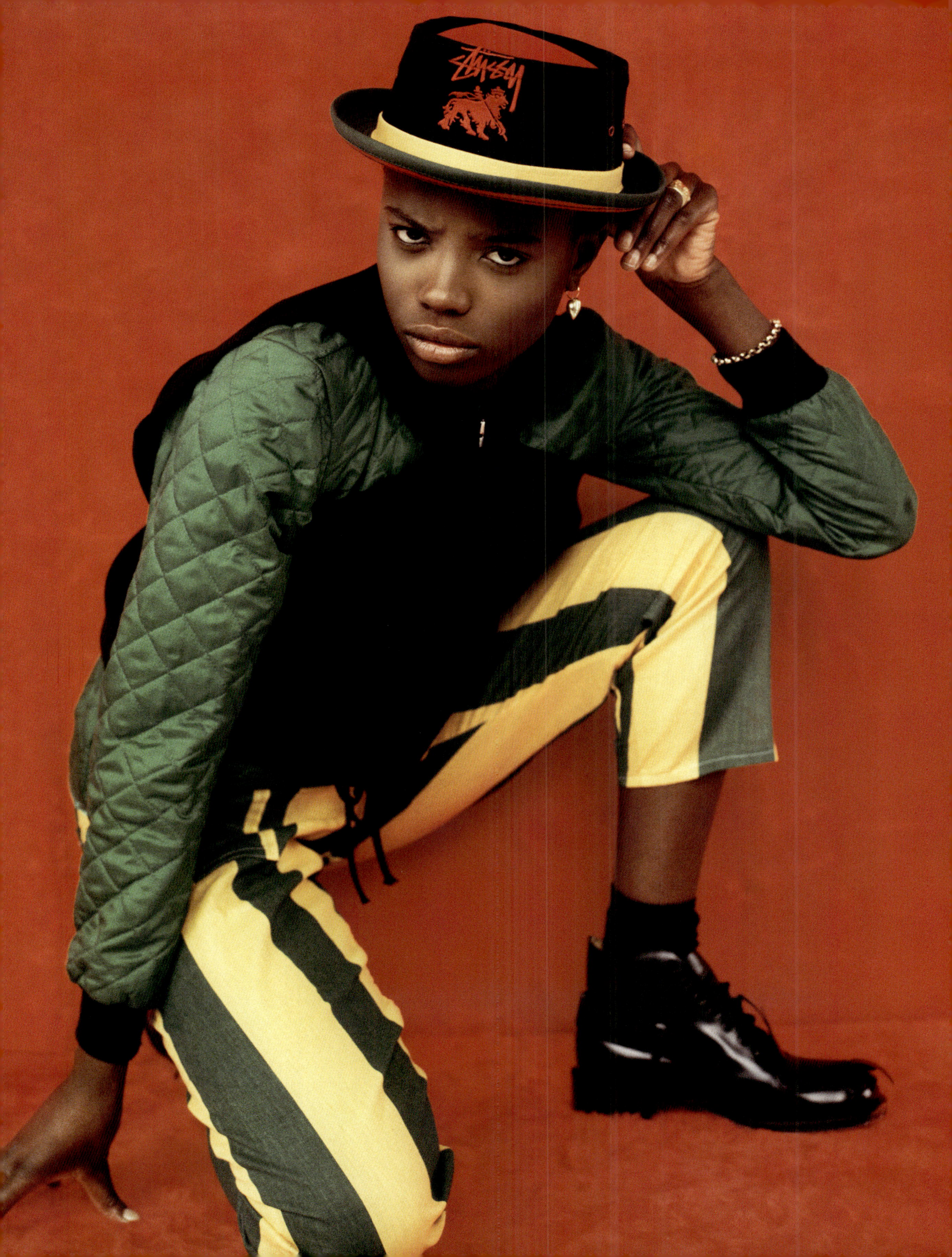
Stüssy

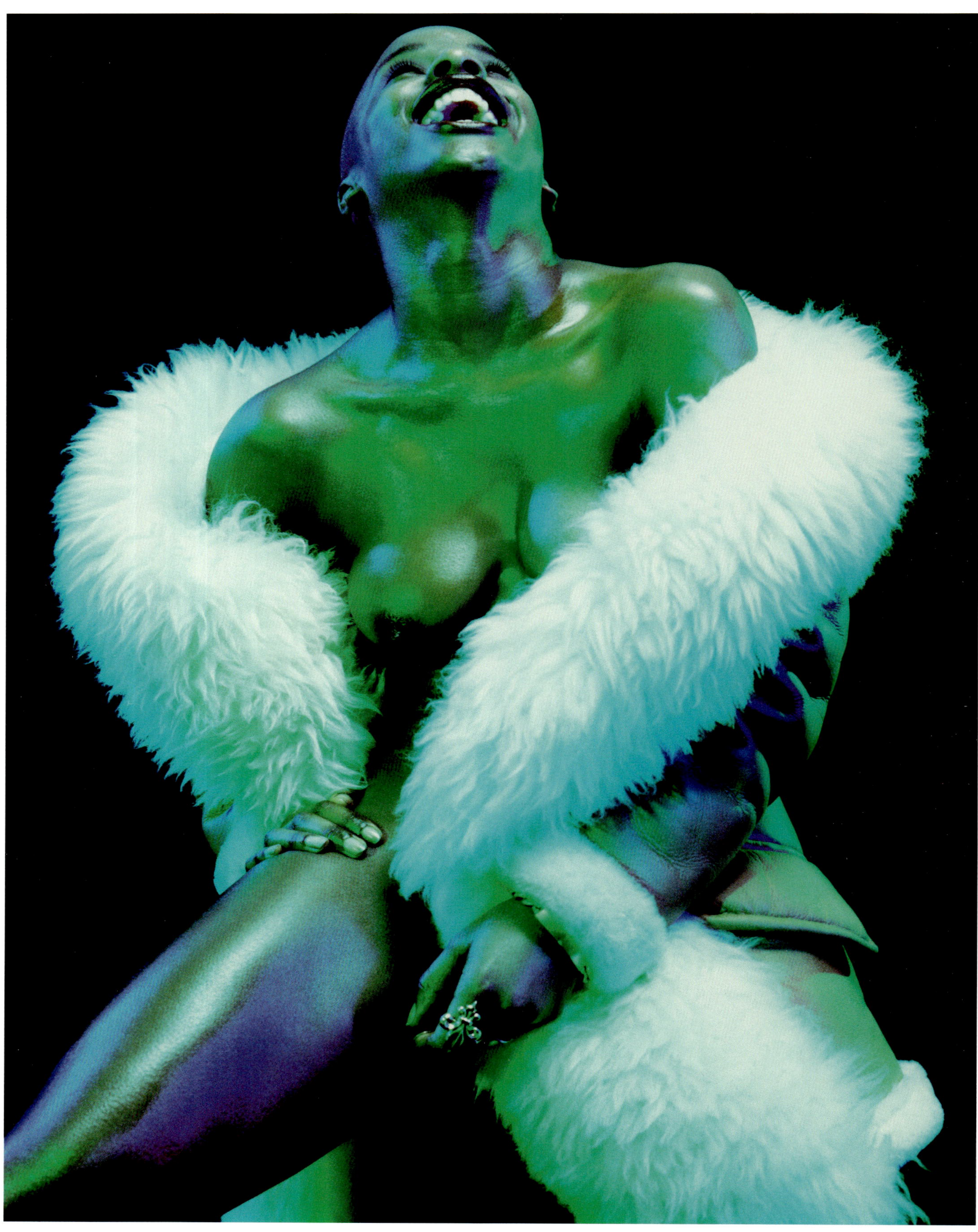

Black girls weren't really getting much attention in the Eighties. I wanted that to change and give them a platform wherever I could, celebrating black and mixed-race beauty and glamorising it in a stylish way. I was crazy about clothes: before styling, it was all about dressing up to go out. Then we did the same thing conceptually in the studio, but also leaving room for spontaneity, capturing the energy and spirit of the day.
Mitzi Lorenz

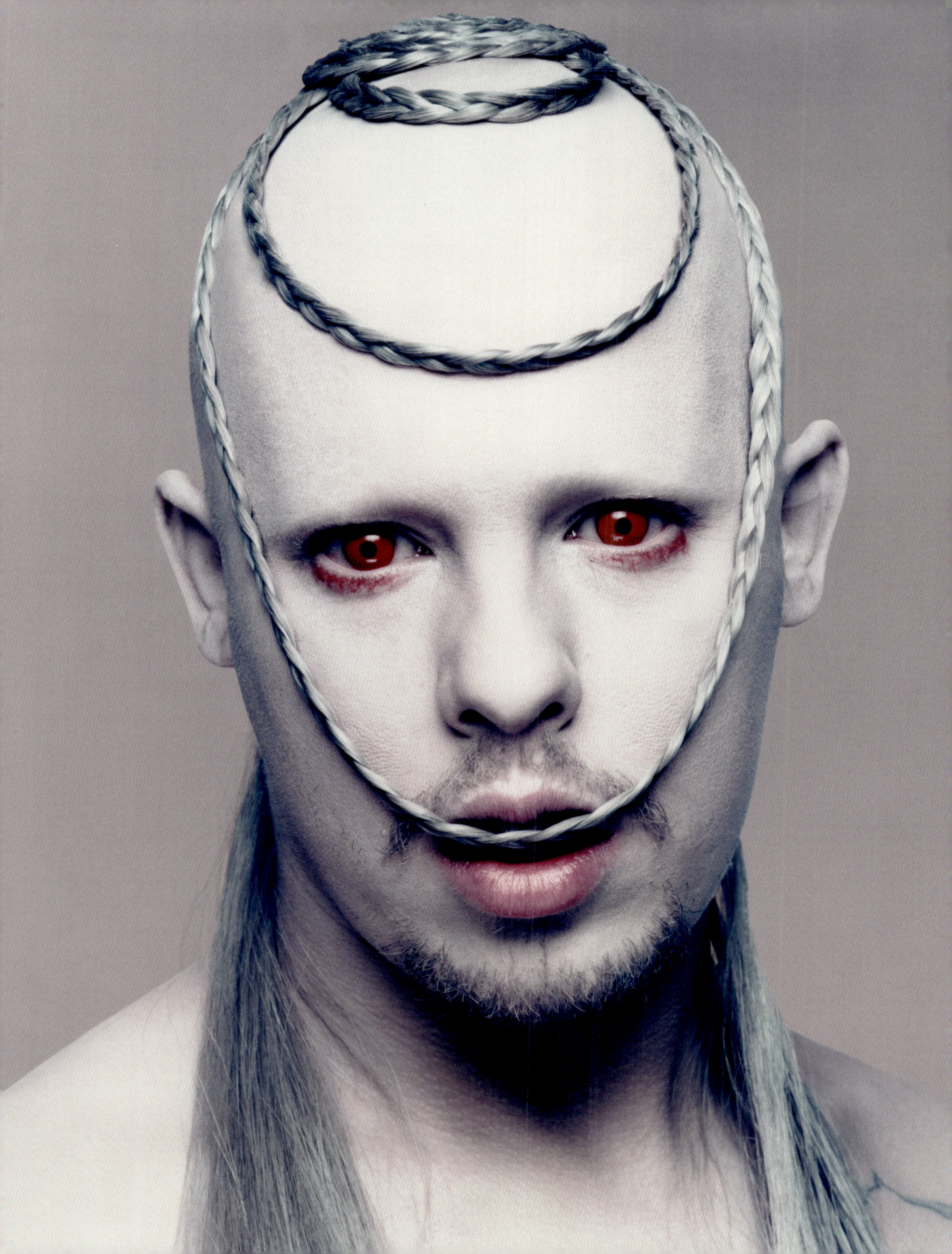

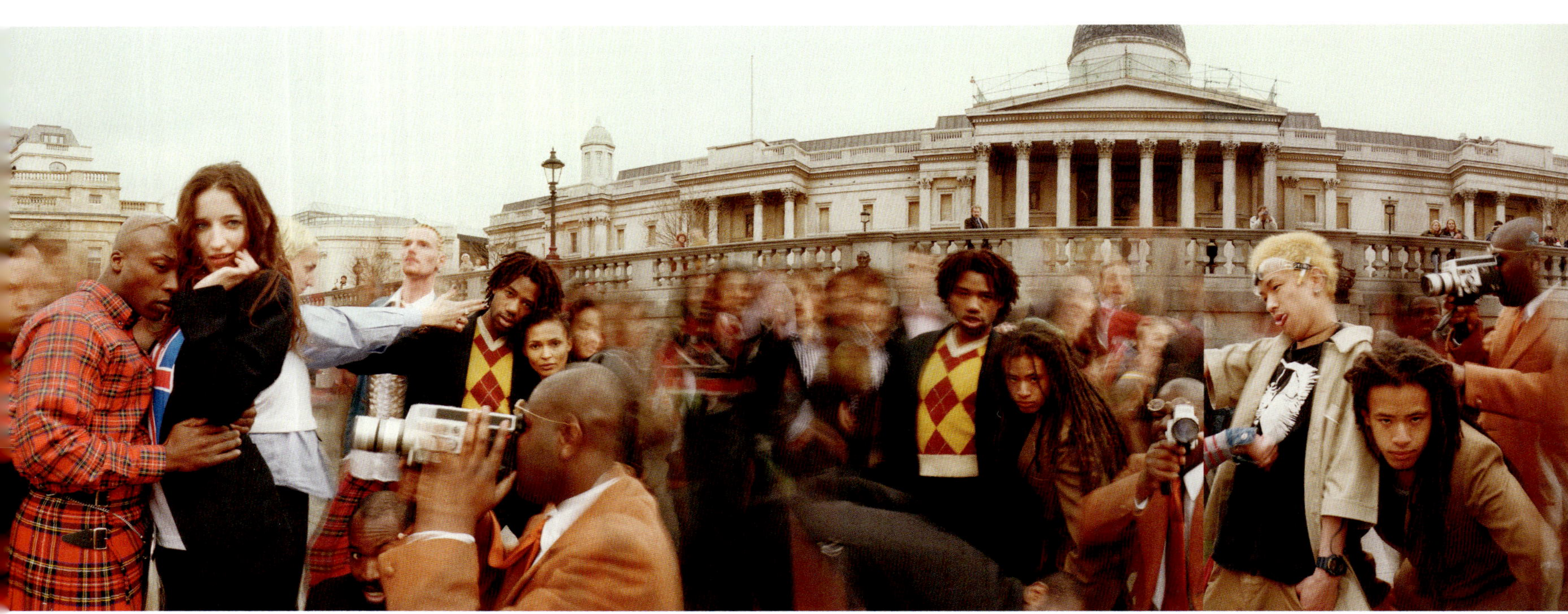

TRAFALGAR SQUARE
By Stéphane Sednaoui
Styled by Simon Foxton
May 1995

For *Trafalgar Square*
I was experimenting with
distortions. We positioned
a panoramic camera in the
centre of the square, and the
idea was to create one long
photo that would cover many
pages of the magazine.
Stéphane Sednaoui

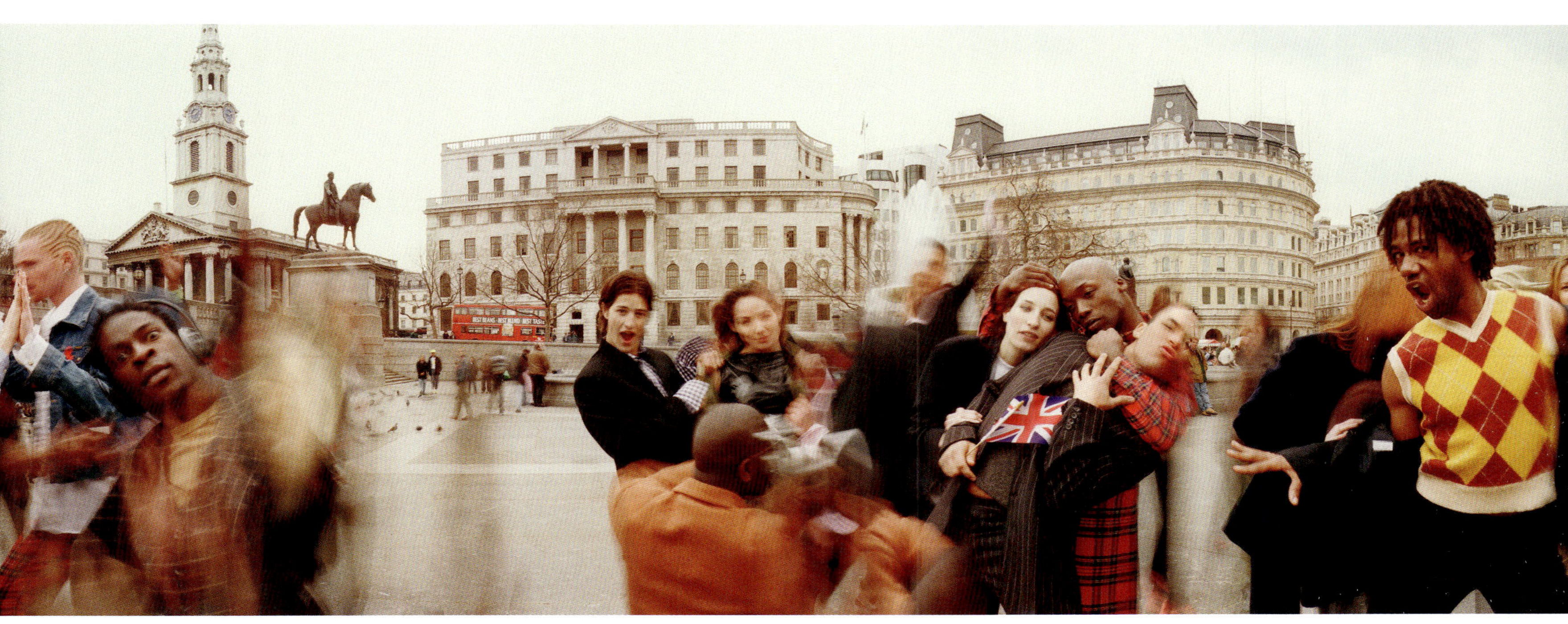

Following pages
FACE OFF
By David Sims
January 1998

KURT COBAIN
By David Sims
Styled by Anna Cockburn
September 1993

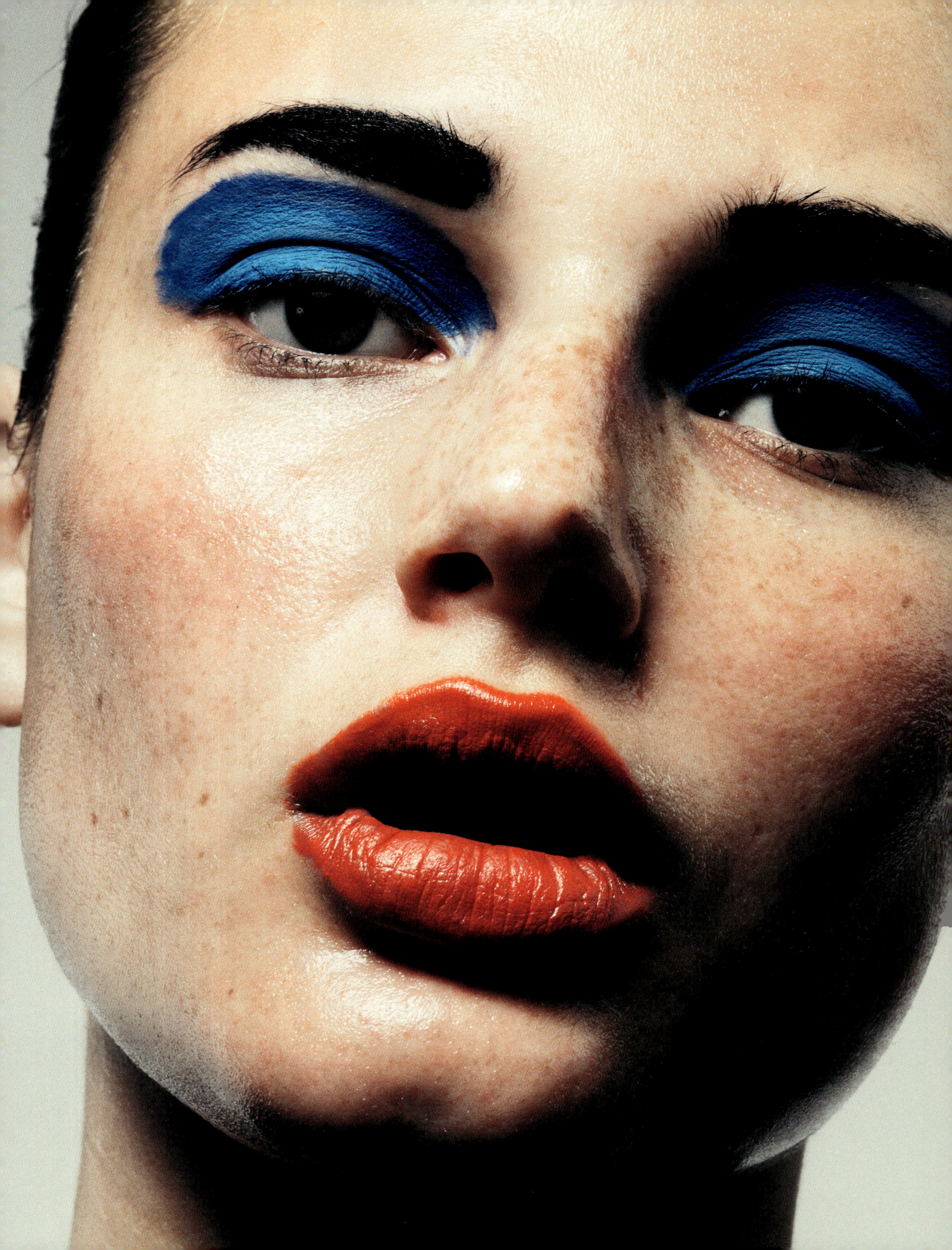

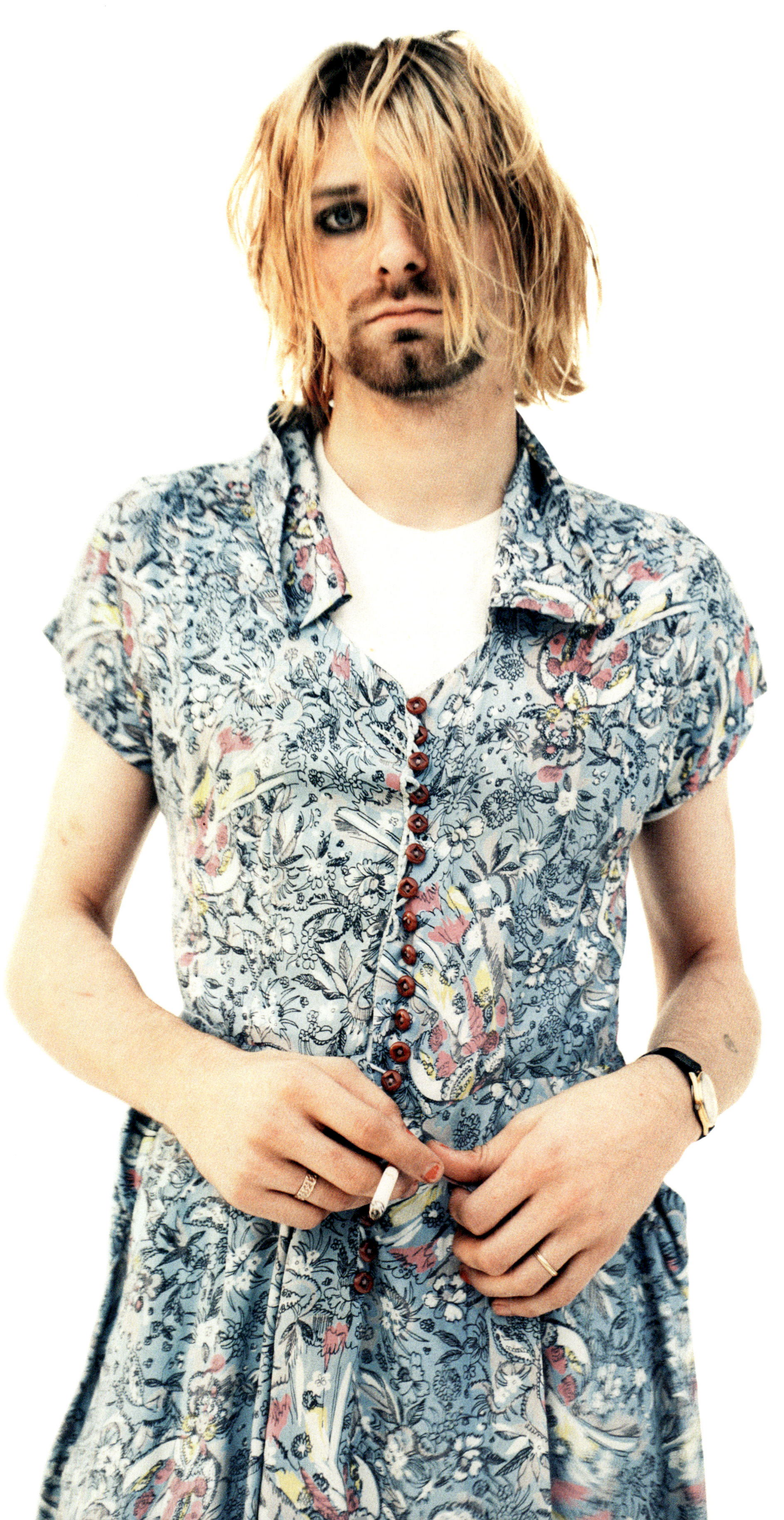

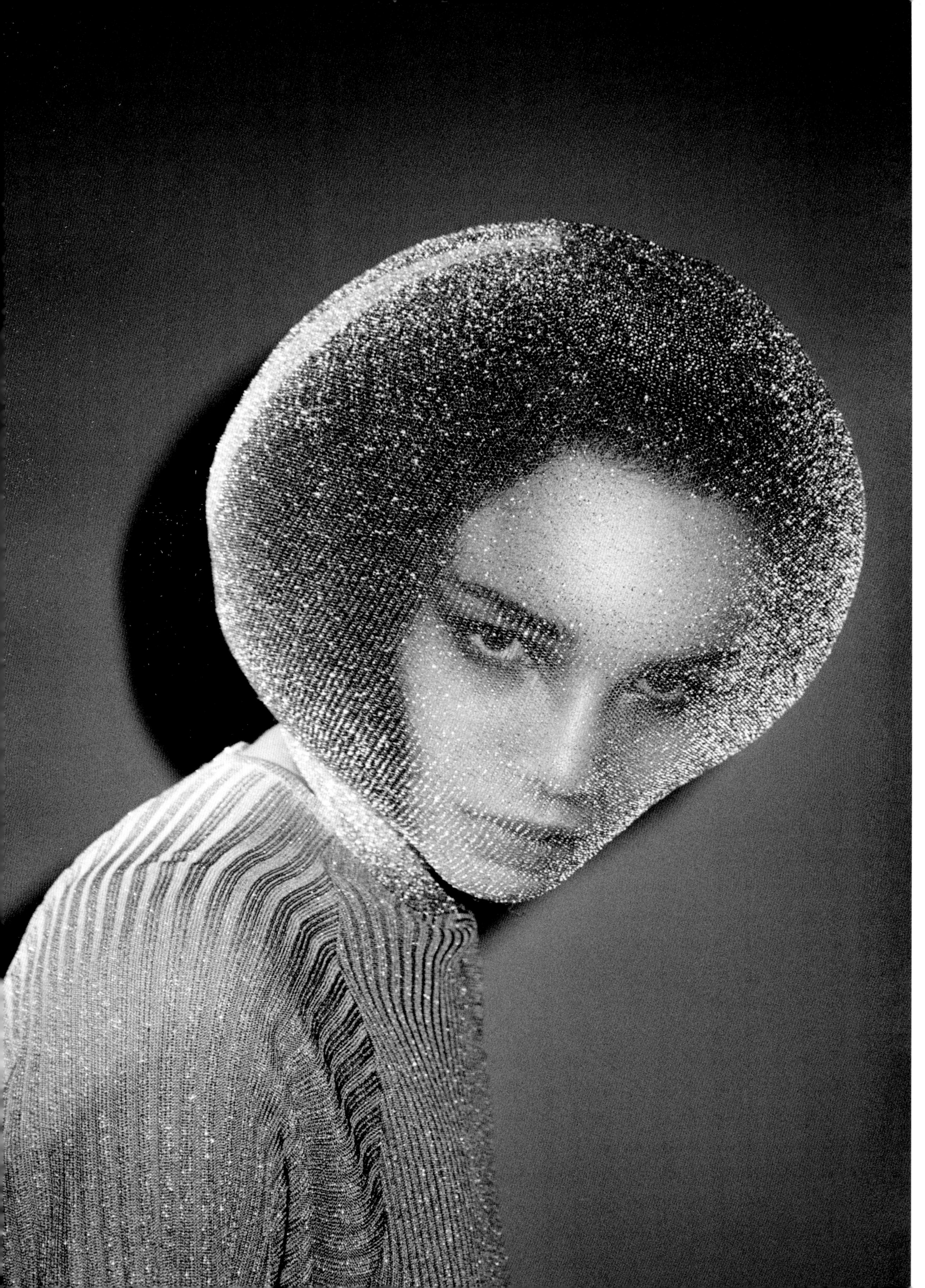

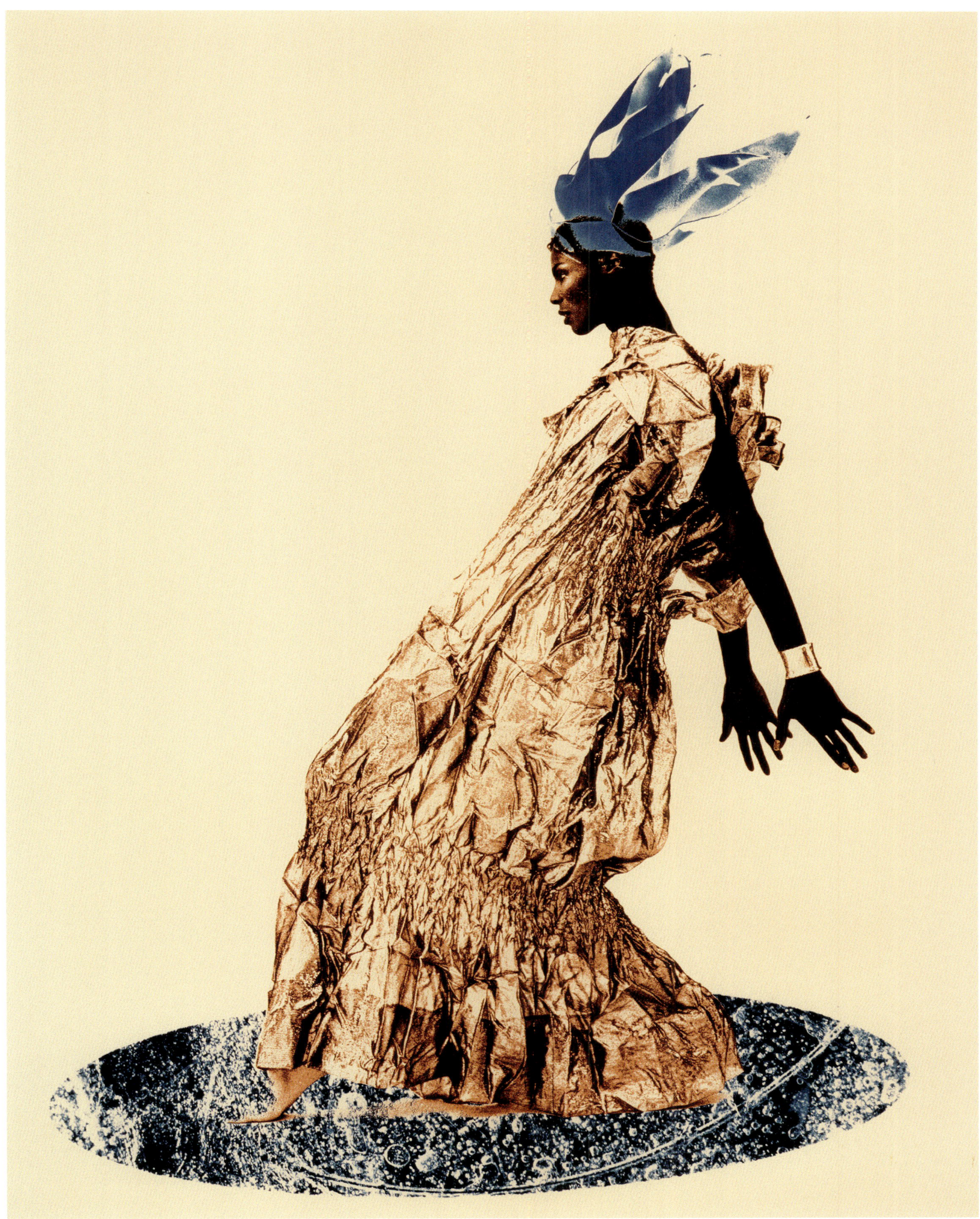

GIRL IN STOCKING
By Juergen Teller
Styled by Judy Blame
December 1990

COLD COMFORTS
By Marcus Tomlinson
Styled by Karl Templer
and Derick Procope
December 1991

I was working at a time when the transition from conventional analogue film photography to the digital format was only just beginning. For *Cold Comforts* I was still using collage stencils in the darkroom, as the digital world was massively expensive and generally out of reach for editorials.
Marcus Tomlinson

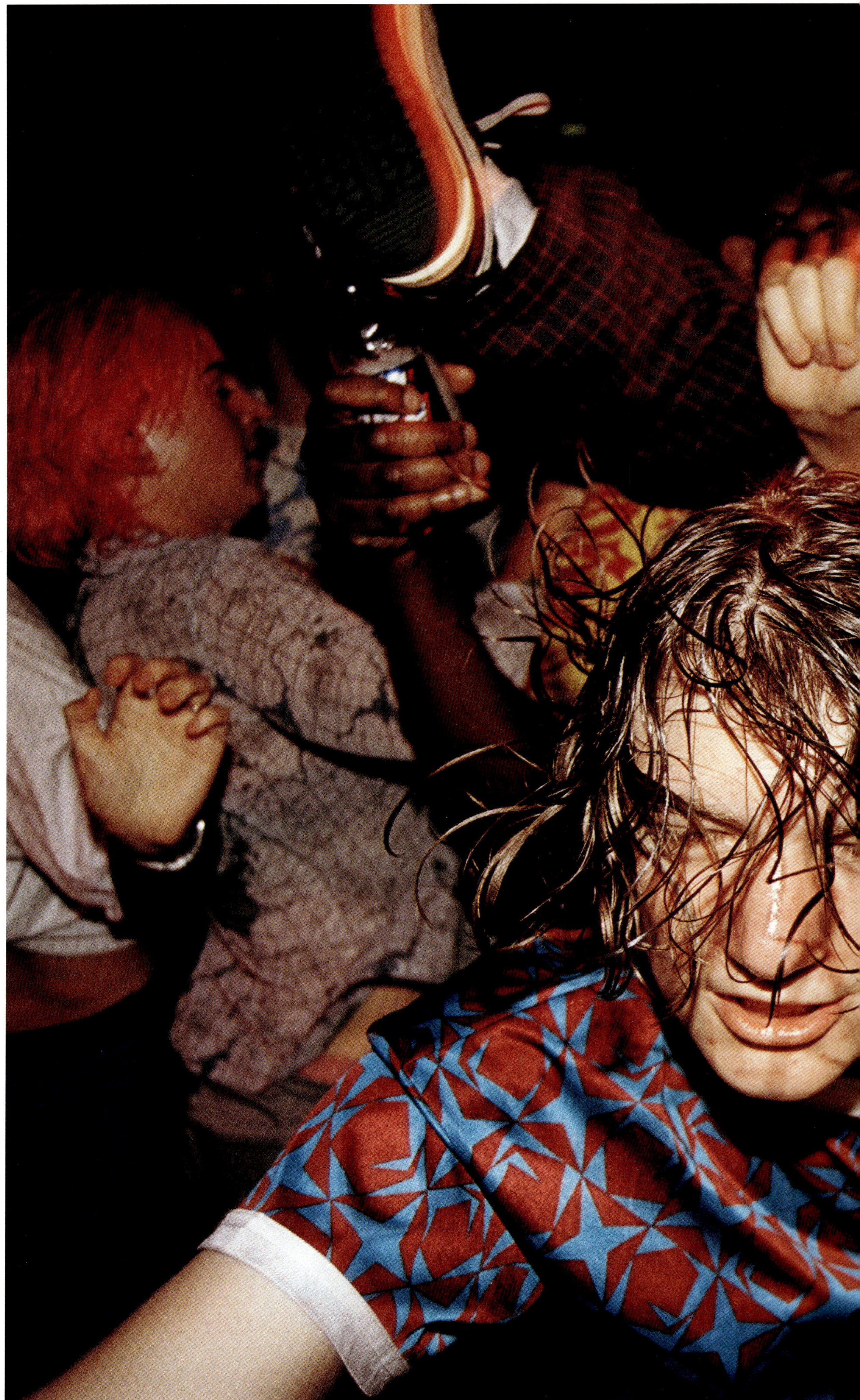

MOSH
By Elaine Constantine
Styled by Greg Fay
and Justin Laurie
October 1997

I loved that for *The Face*
I could make a fashion shoot
using a completely democratic
casting process. I fly-posted
clubs where I knew kids did
a lot of stage diving. I made
it an open invite without a
casting appointment, everyone
was welcome, and we piled
clothes on trestle tables. There
was a huge turnout and it was
the exact amount of chaos
I needed to create the spirit
I wanted. By the end of the
shoot everything was covered
in beer and sweat and half the
clothes were pilfered.
Elaine Constantine

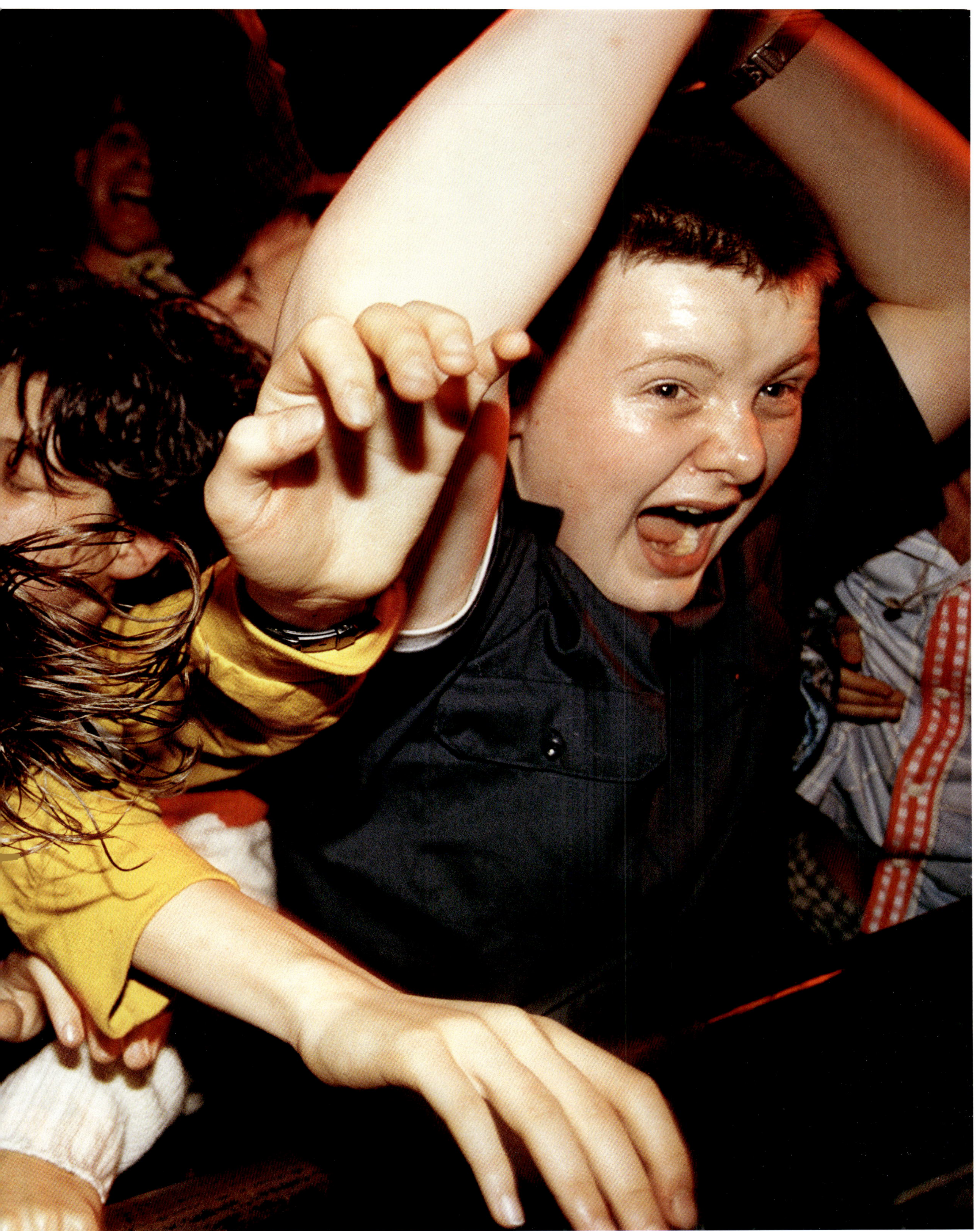

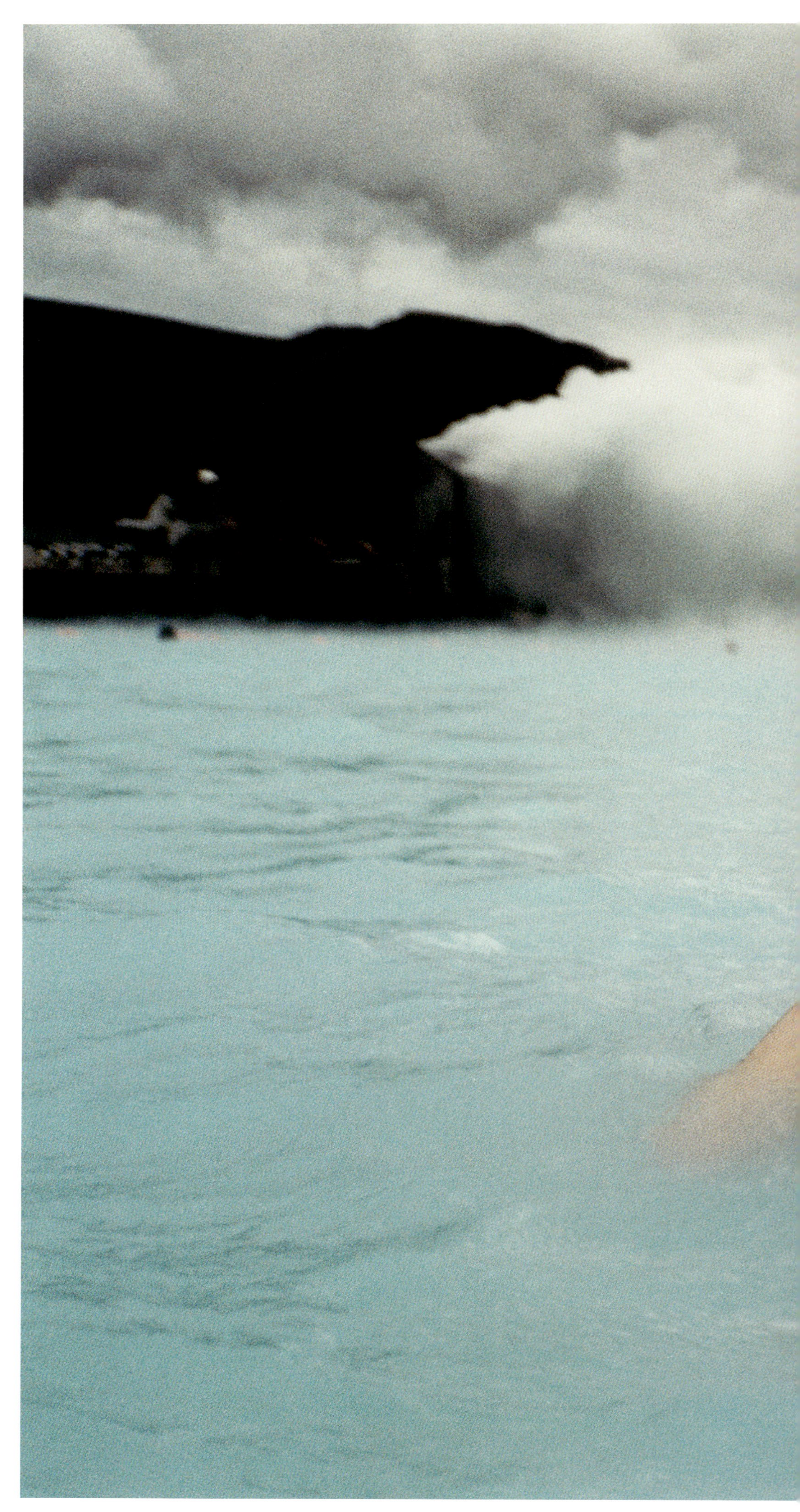

BJÖRK AND HER SON
By Juergen Teller
November 1993

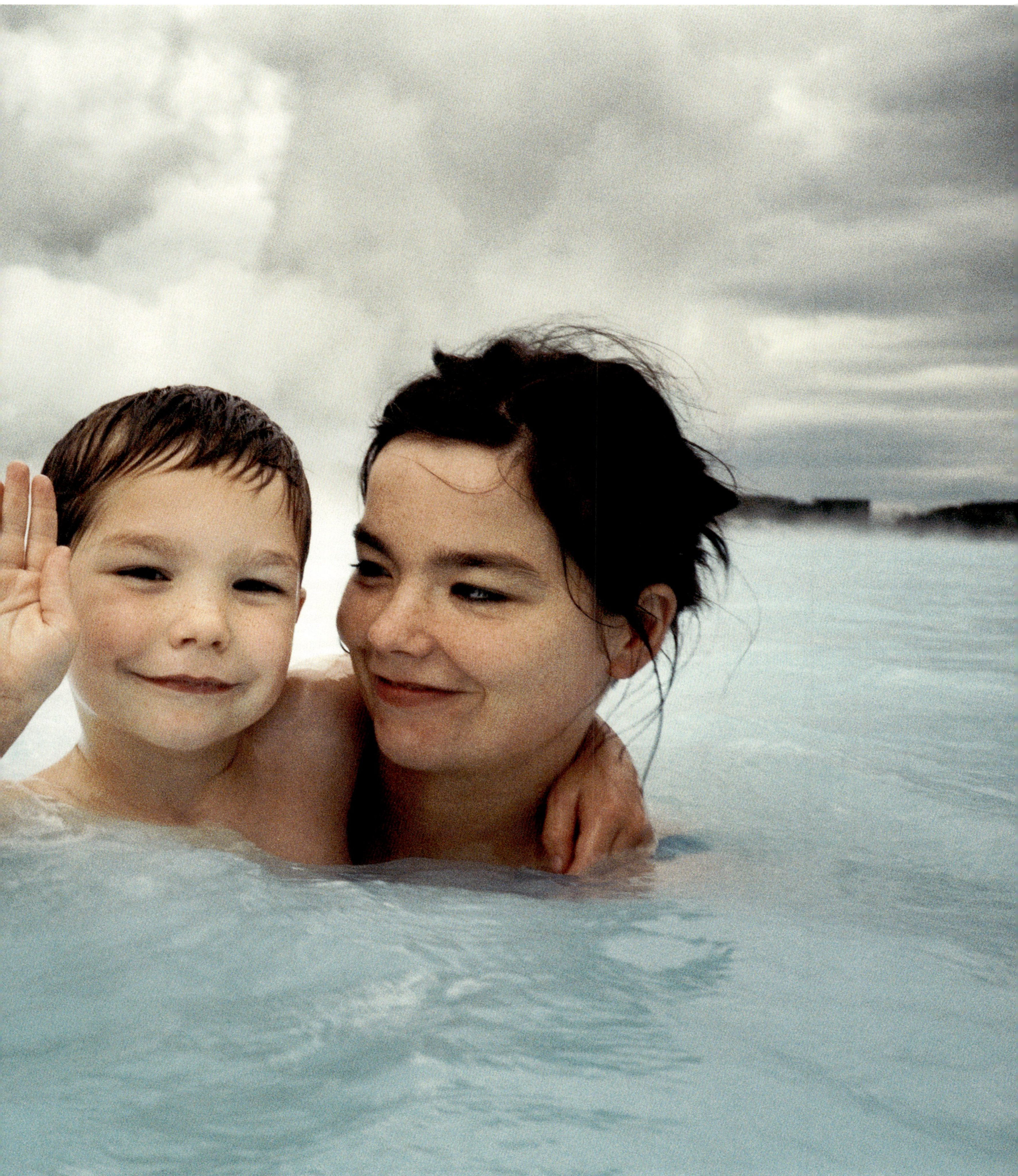

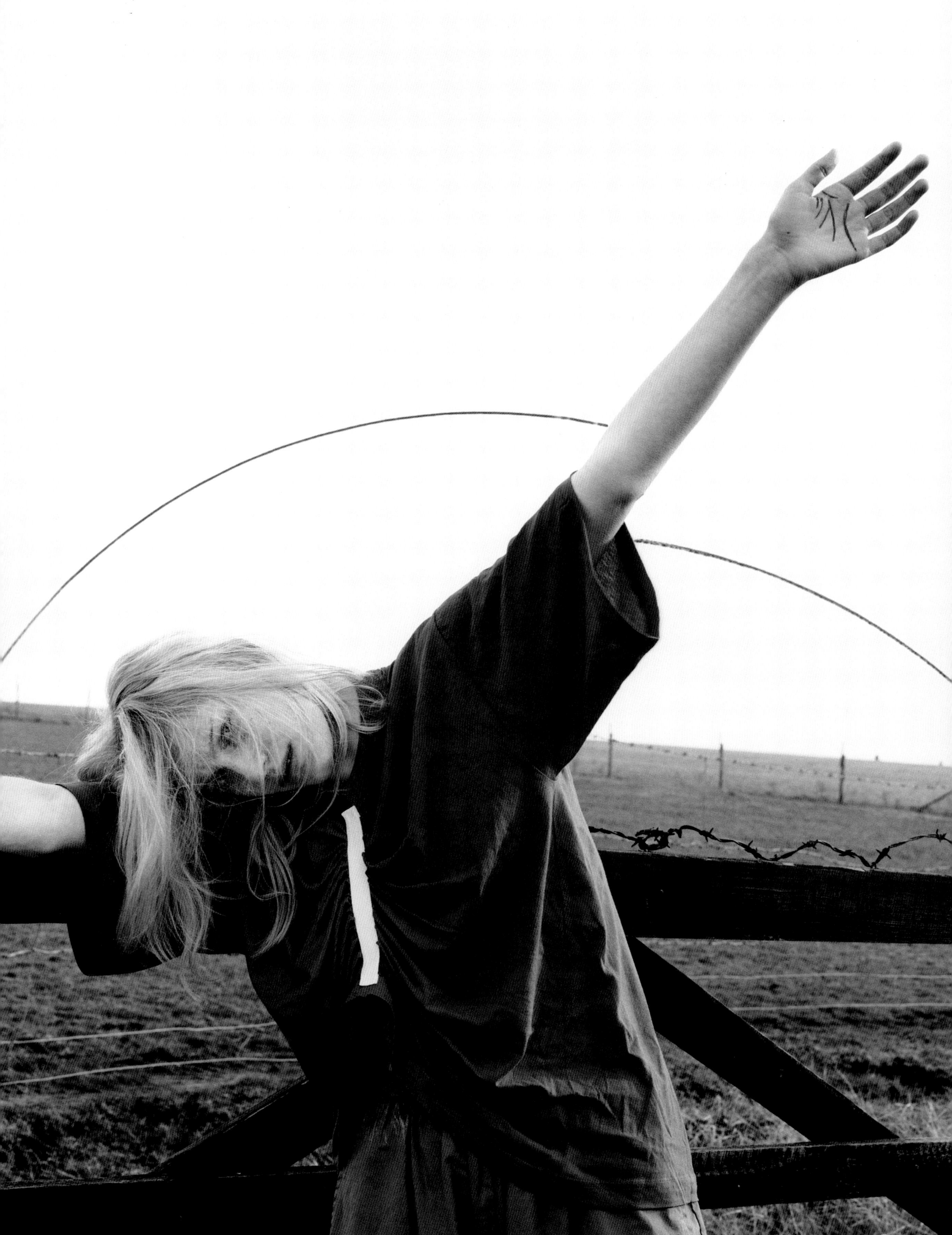

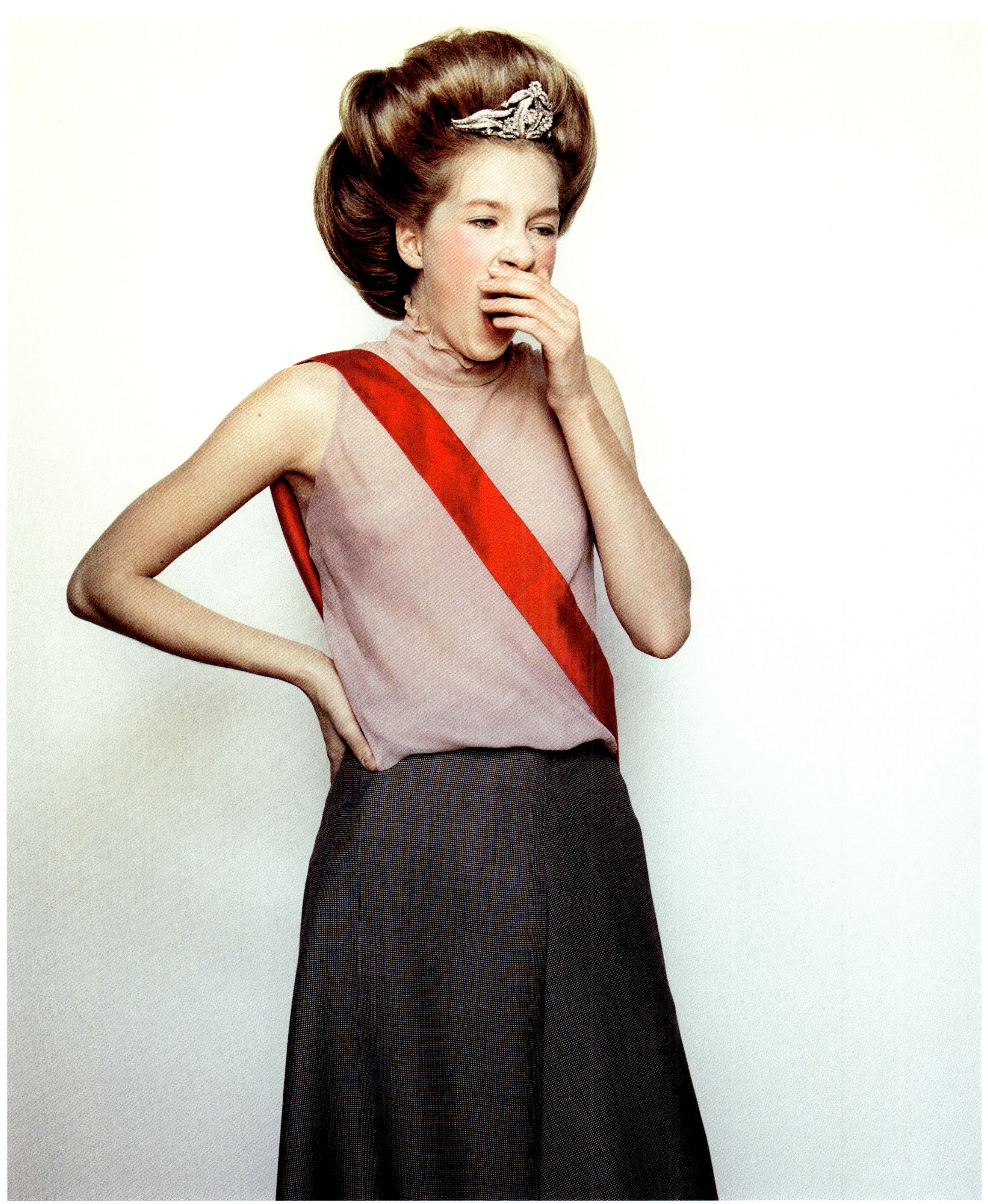

EAST OF EDEN

By David Sims
Styled by Anna Cockburn
May 1997

H.R.H. R.E.S.P.E.C.T.

By Mario Testino
Styled by Carine Roitfeld
July 1997

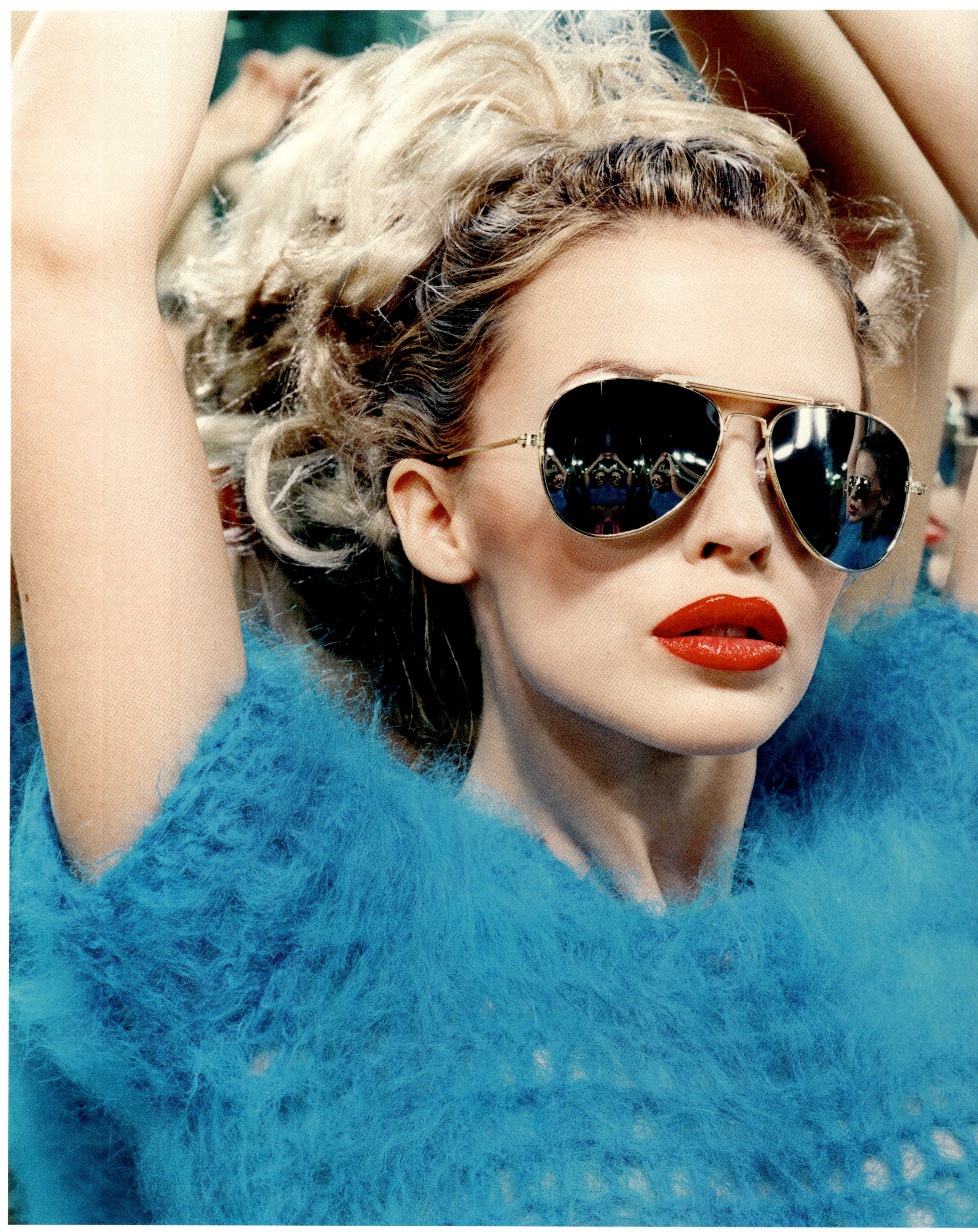

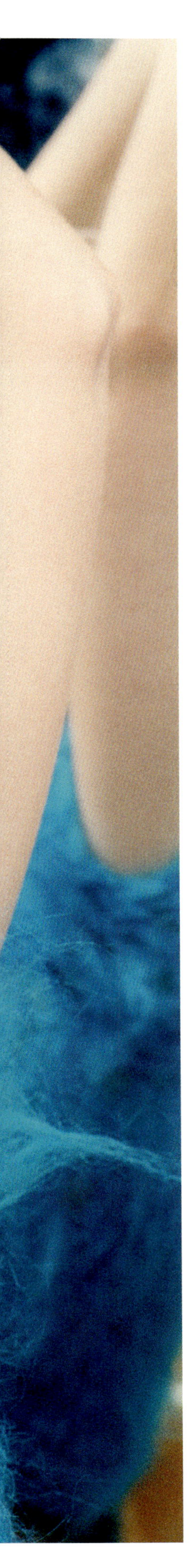

KYLIE MINOGUE
By Norbert Schoerner
Styled by Adam Howe
June 1994

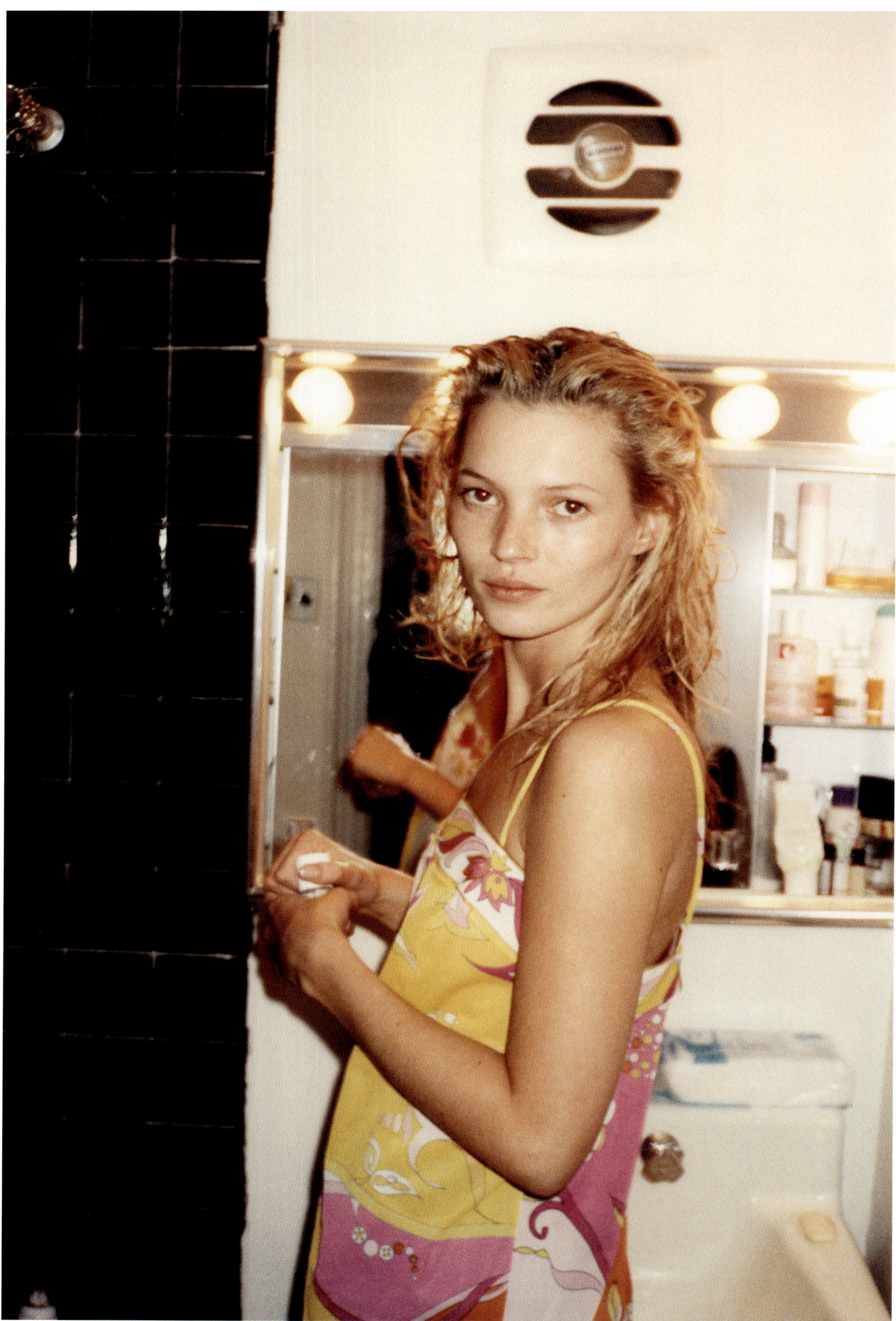

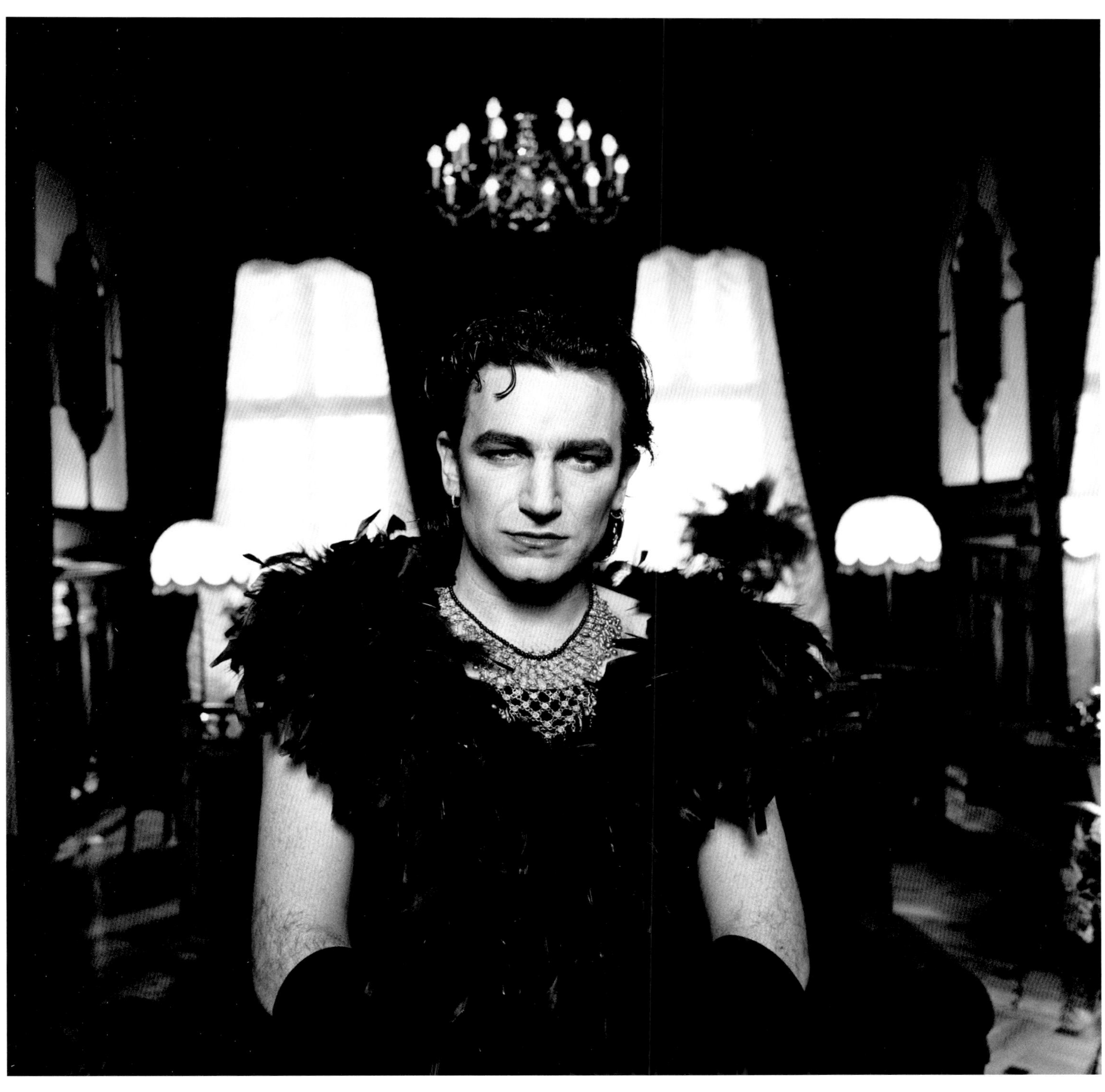

THIS GIRL'S LIFE
By Juergen Teller
May 1996

BONO
By Anton Corbijn
April 1992

RUFF JUSDIS
By Nigel Shafran
September 1990

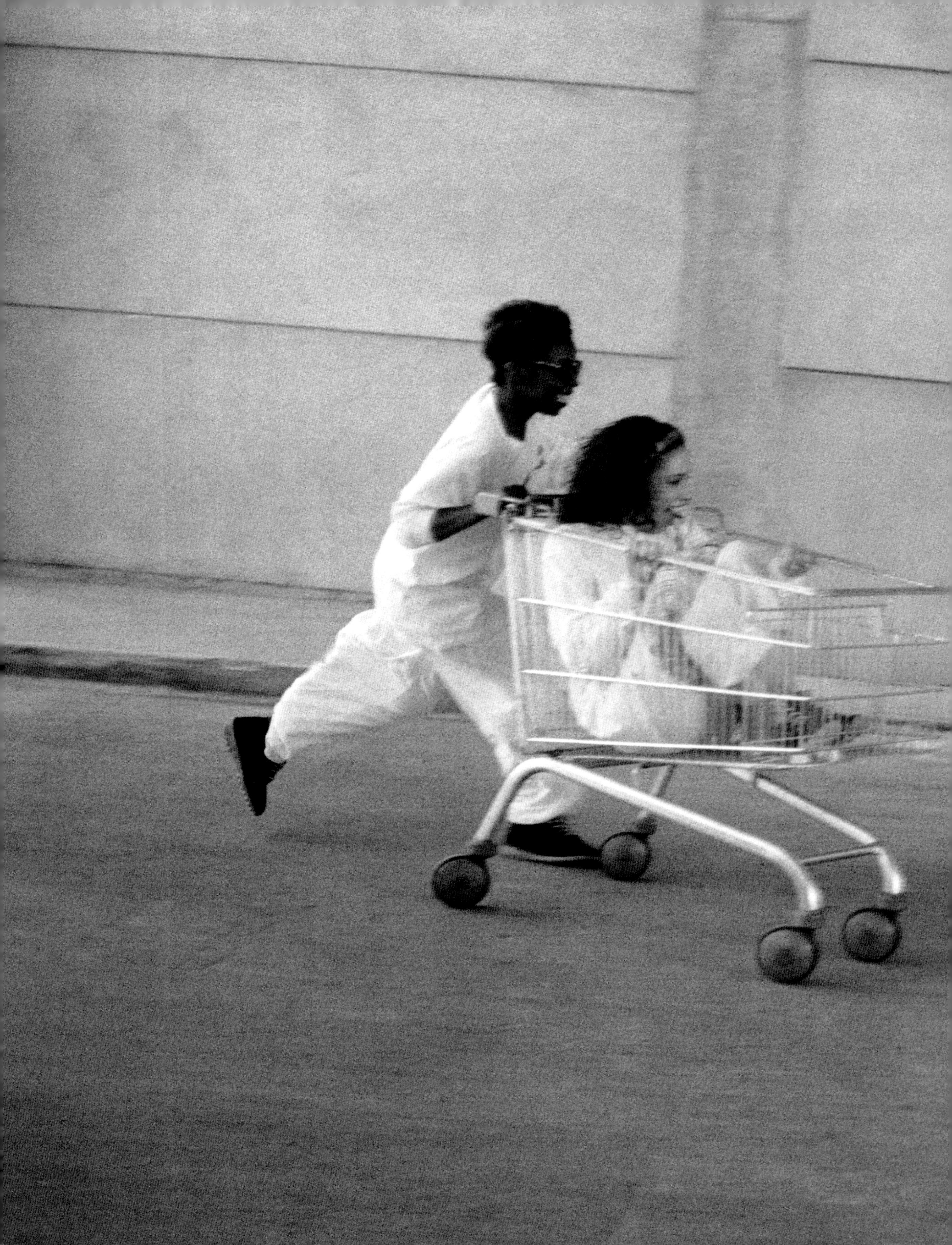

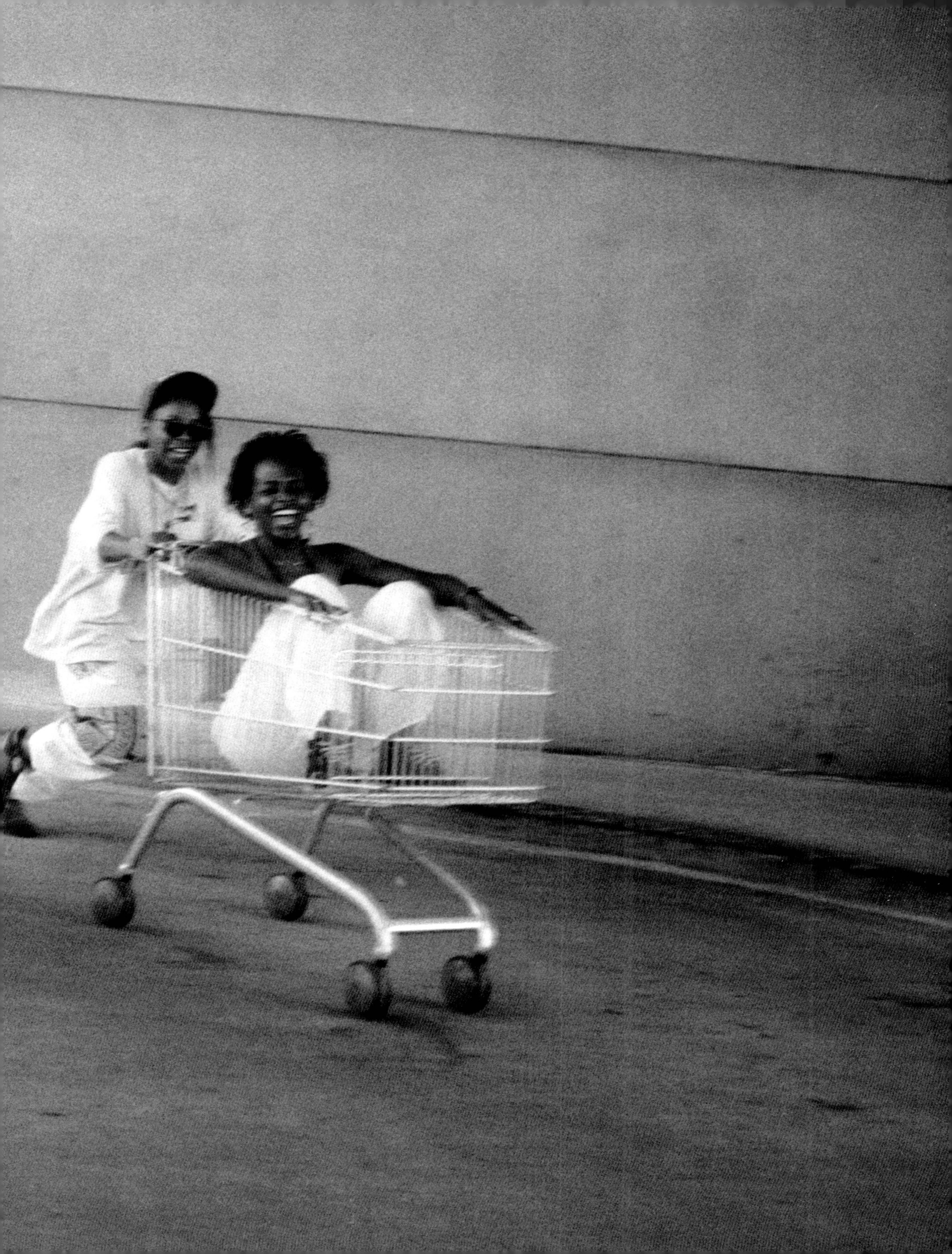

The Face is a distilled forbearer of niche social media culture, in the way it democratised information, disseminated trends, predicted the cultural zeitgeist and provided inspiration to its readers. It was a catalyst that challenged and changed broader culture.

PHIL BICKER, ART DIRECTOR

MADONNA
By Jean Baptiste Mondino
June 1990

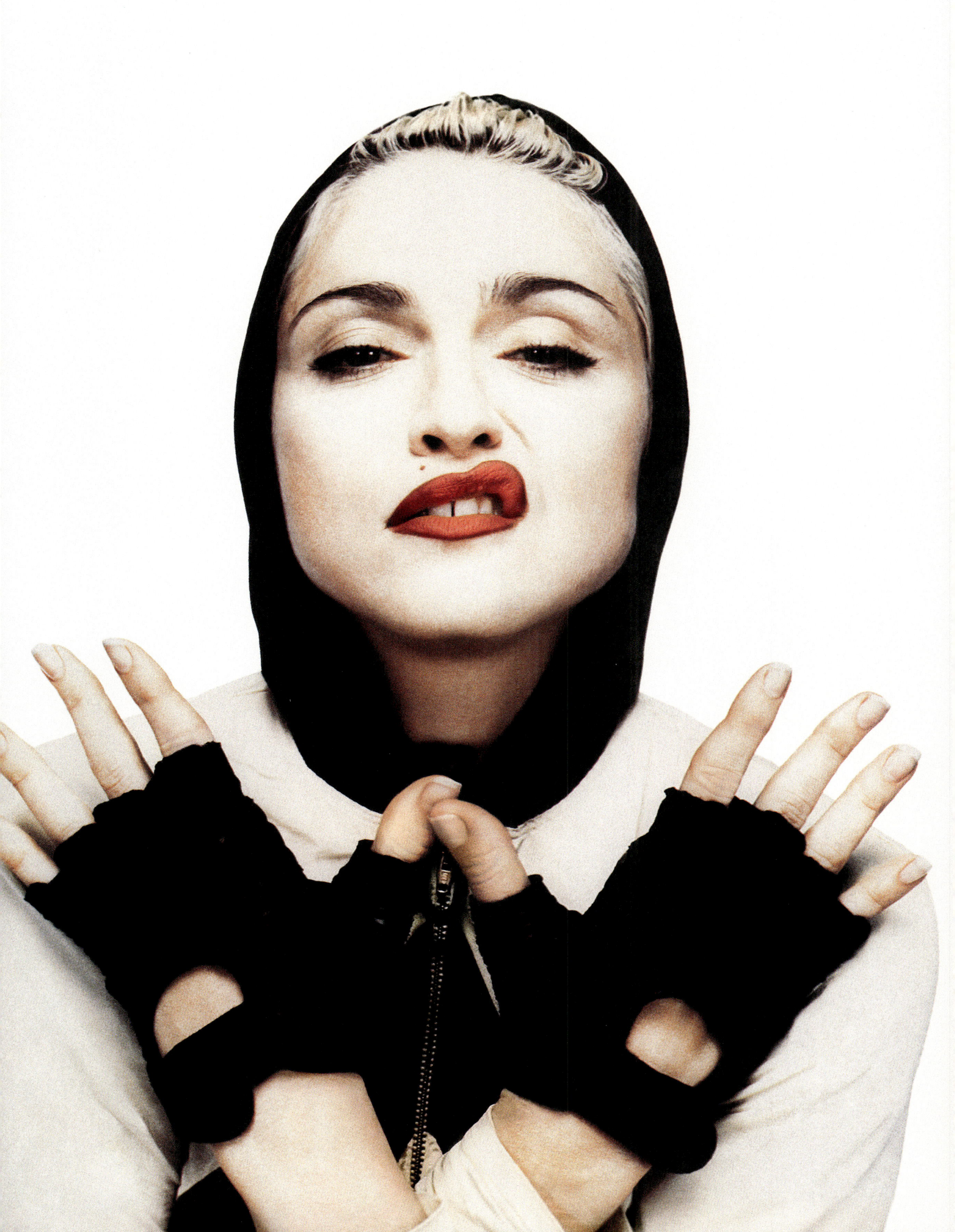

Always instinctive, from the gut; it was not a conscious revolt. Our motivation was purely creative, there were no commercial concerns: we were having fun expressing ourselves. We were unconsciously ushering in change from outside of the existing industry parameters. In contrast to the glossy, manicured images of the system featured in most other publications, our vision was effortless, tangible and authentic. We were friends documenting our friends.
Melanie Ward

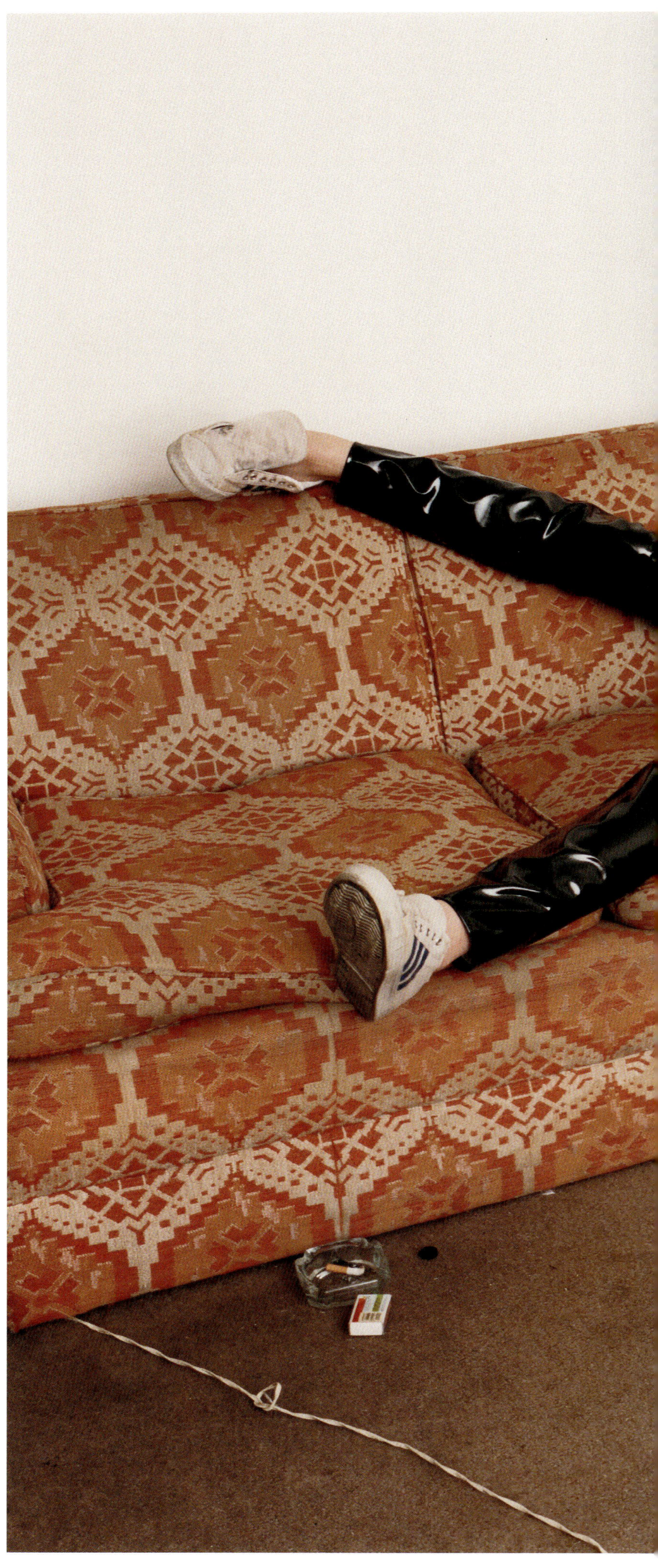

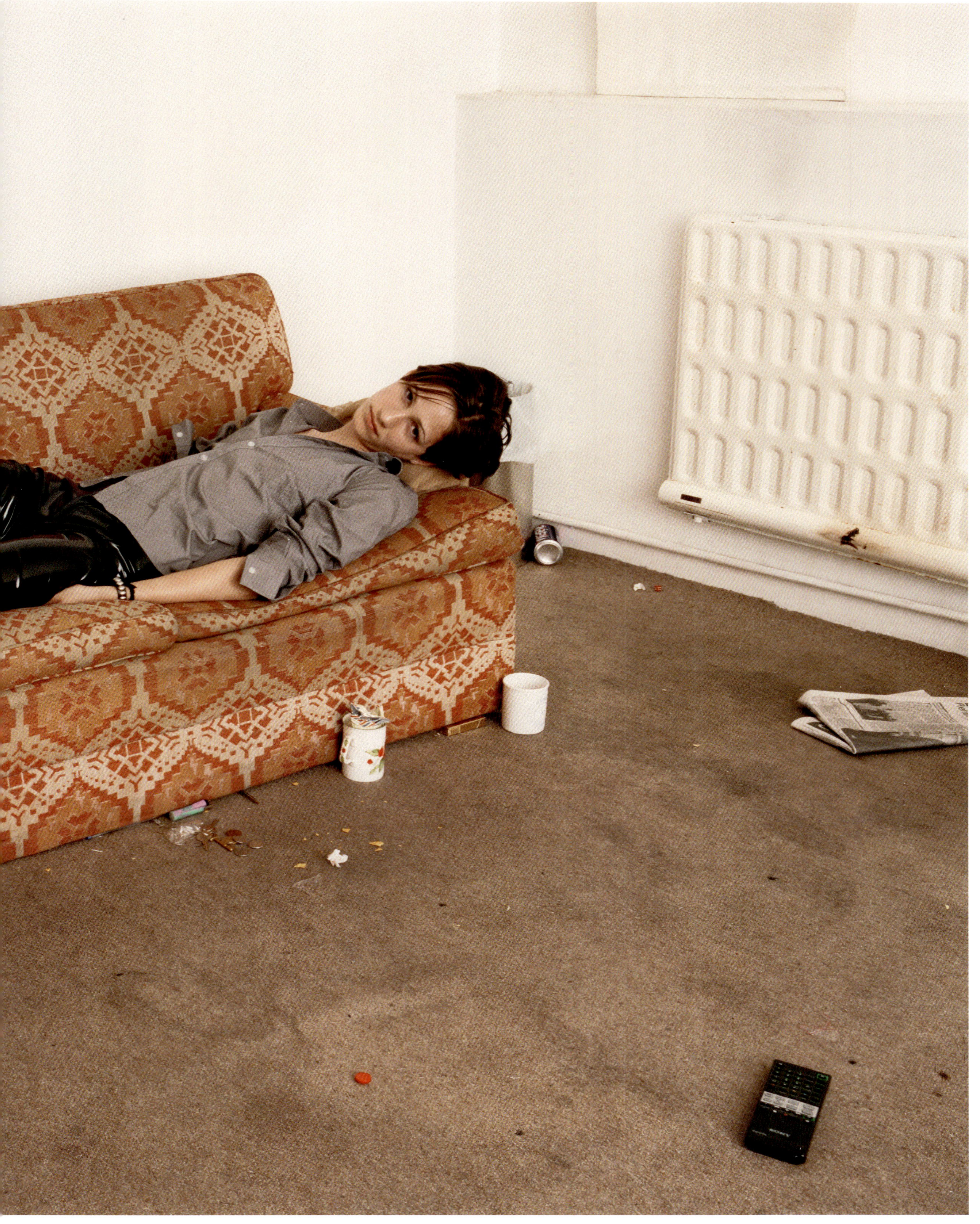

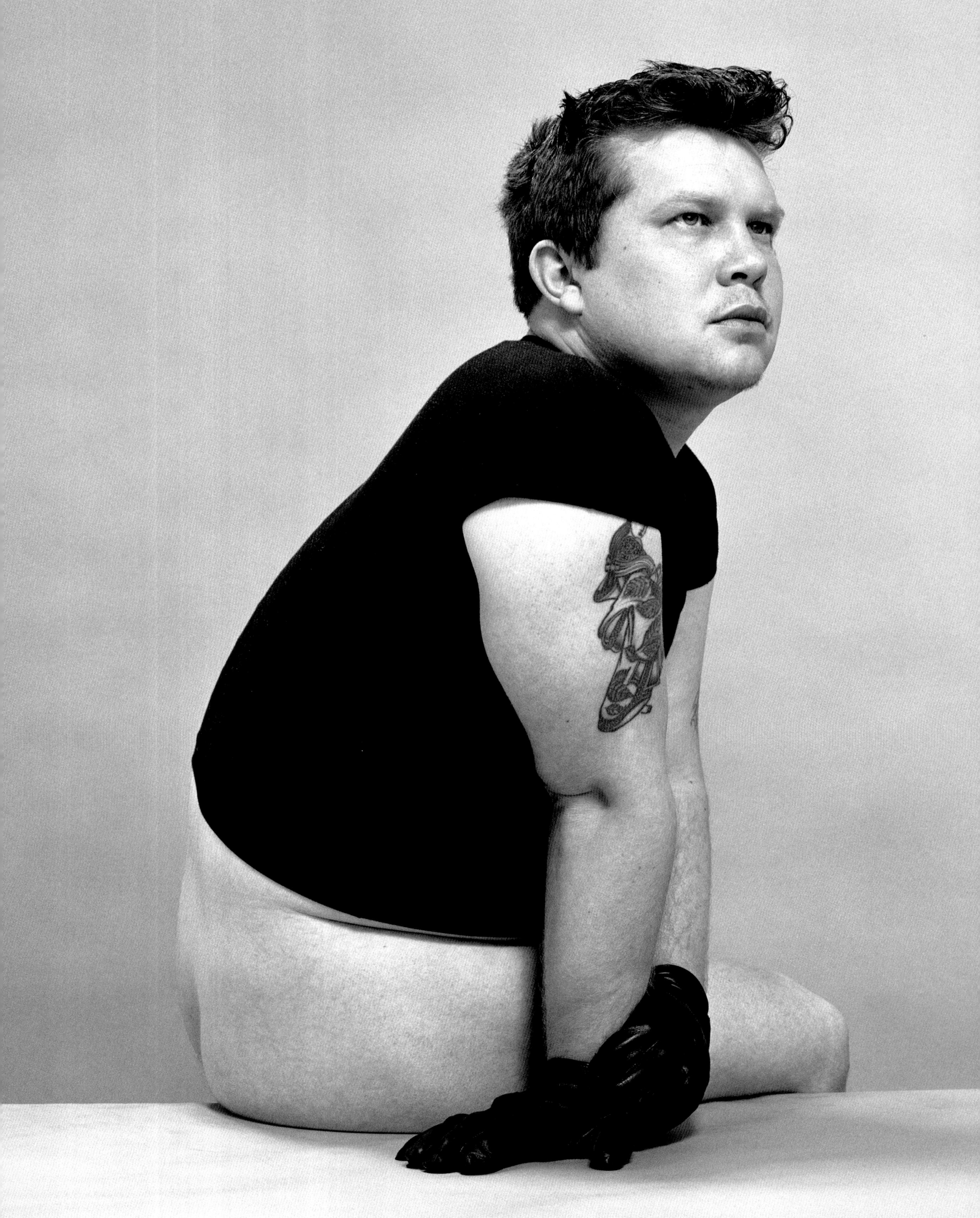

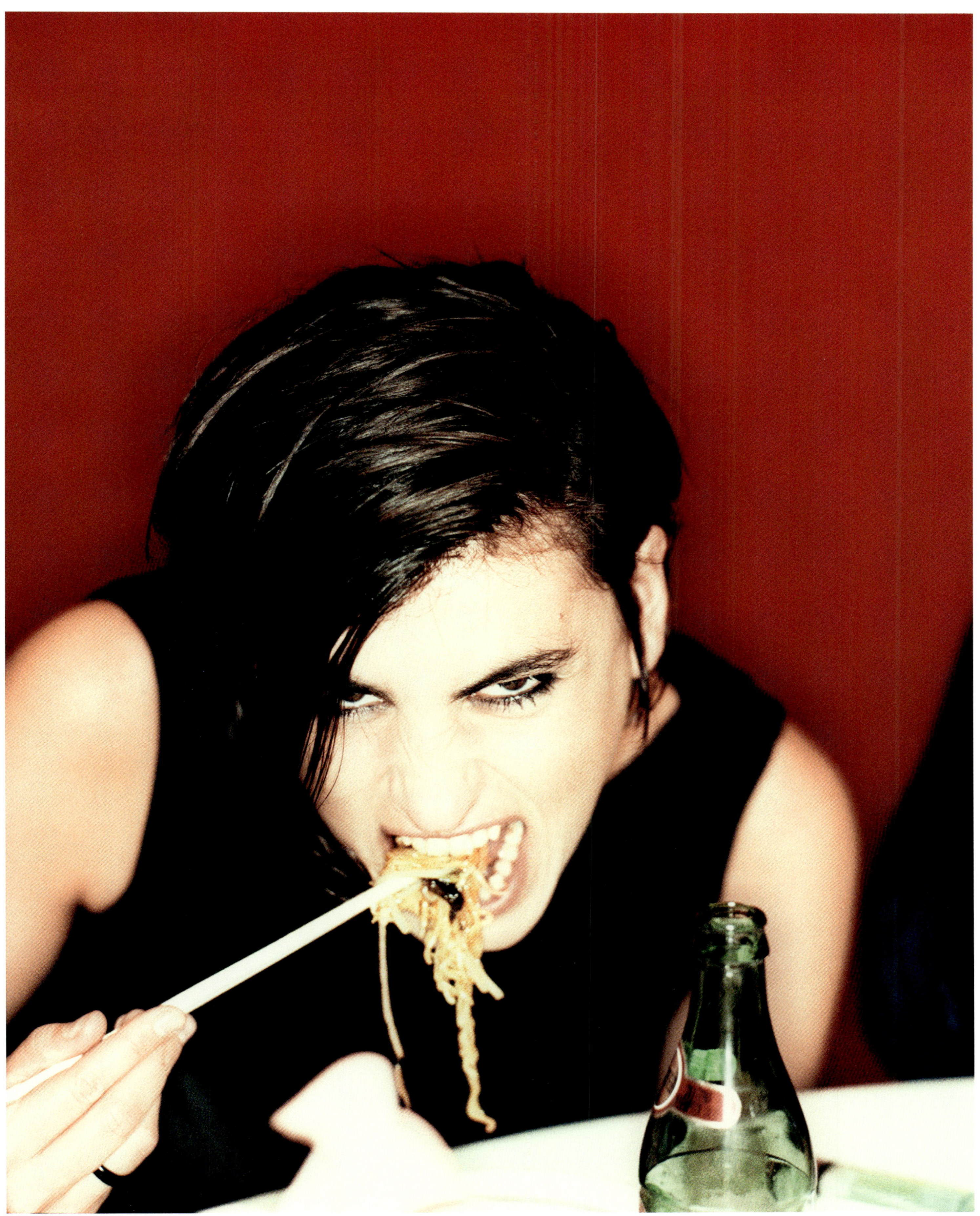

THE WARM JETS
By David Sims
Styled by Nancy Rohde
May 1995

JUSTINE FRISCHMANN
By Ellen von Unwerth
Styled by Andrew Richardson
June 1996

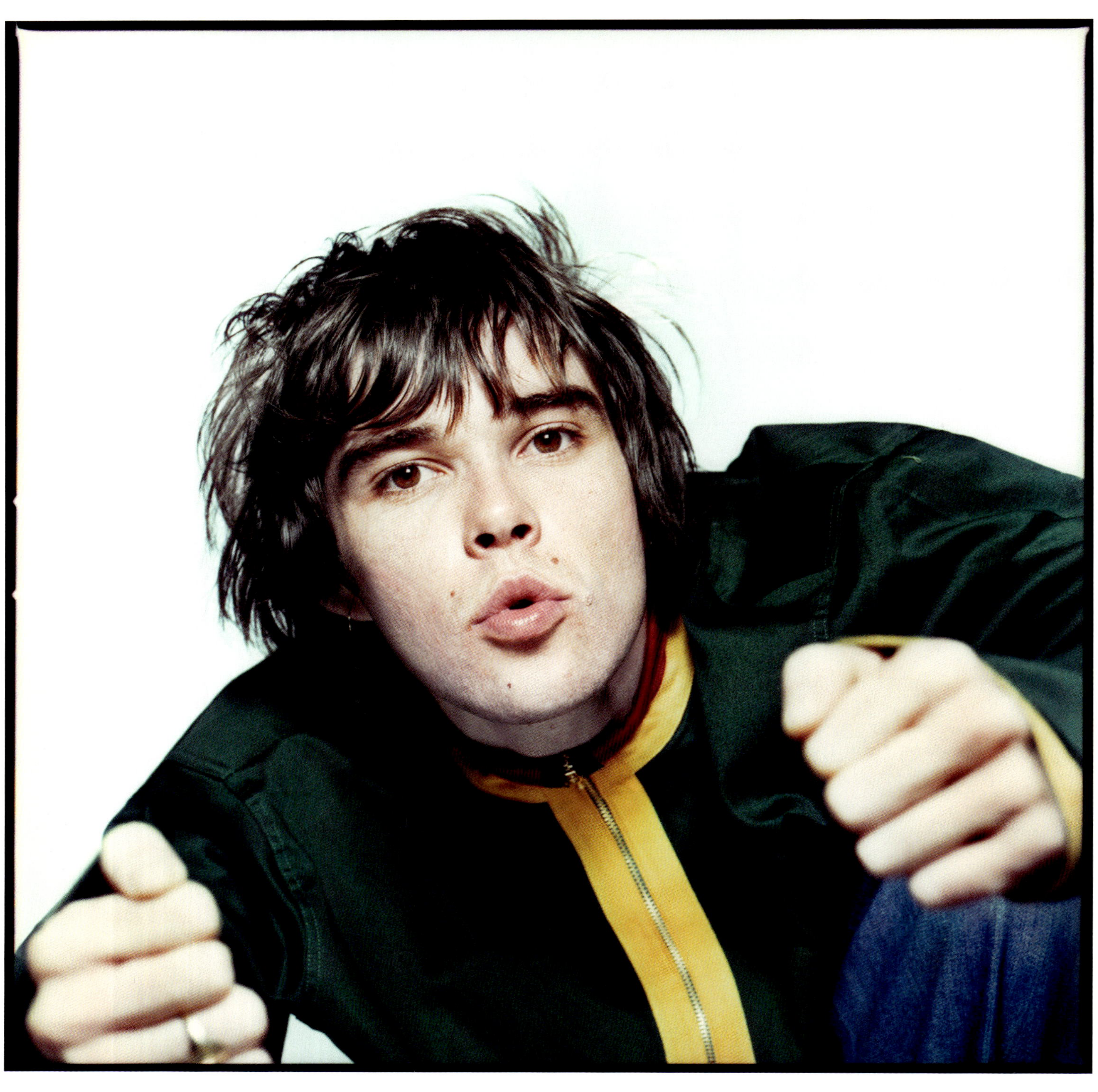

IAN BROWN
By Kevin Davies
January 1990

RAIN
By Norbert Schoerner
Styled by Greg Fay and Justin Laurie
December 1993

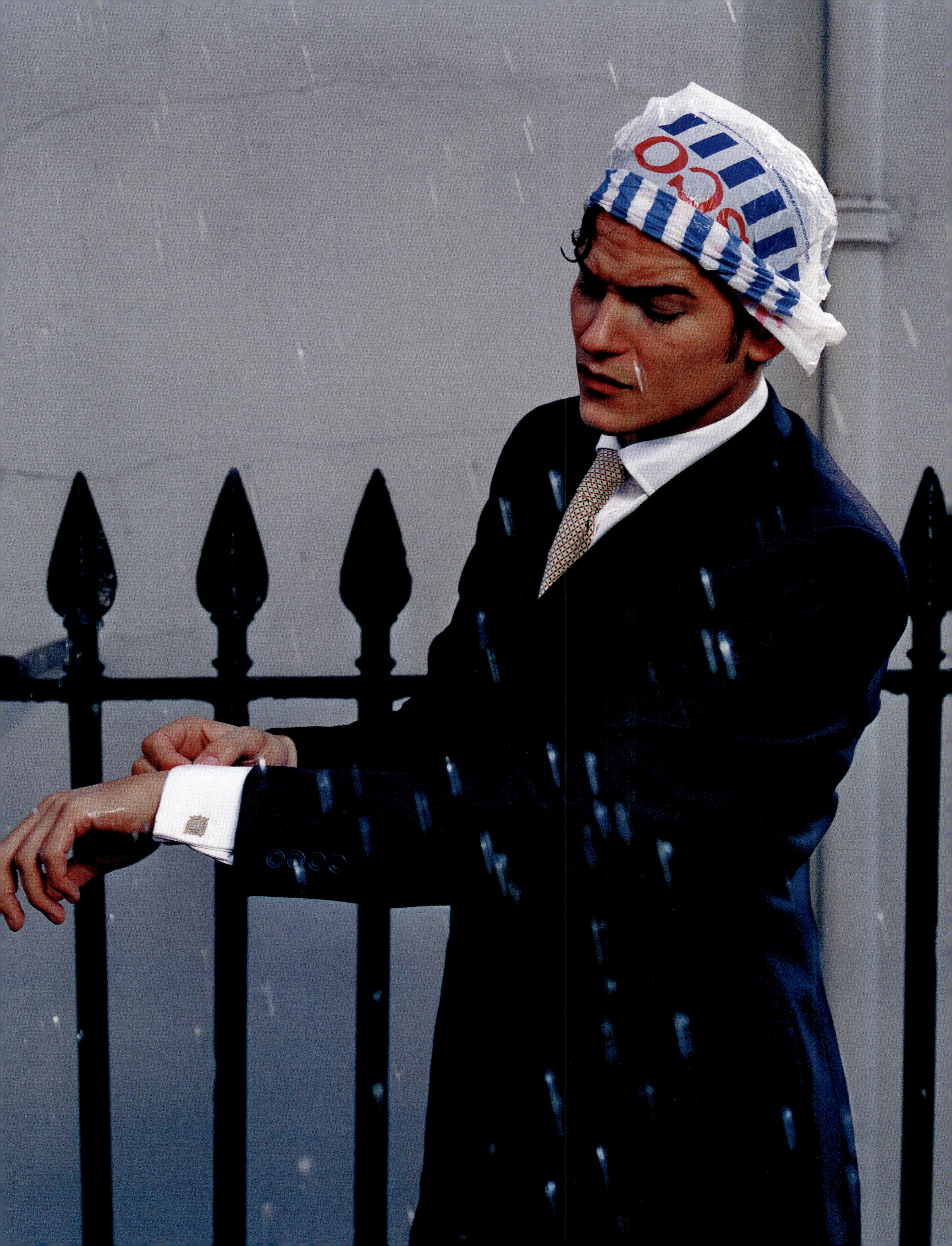

GLOBAL WARMING TV
Photographed and styled by
Inez & Vinoodh
September 1994

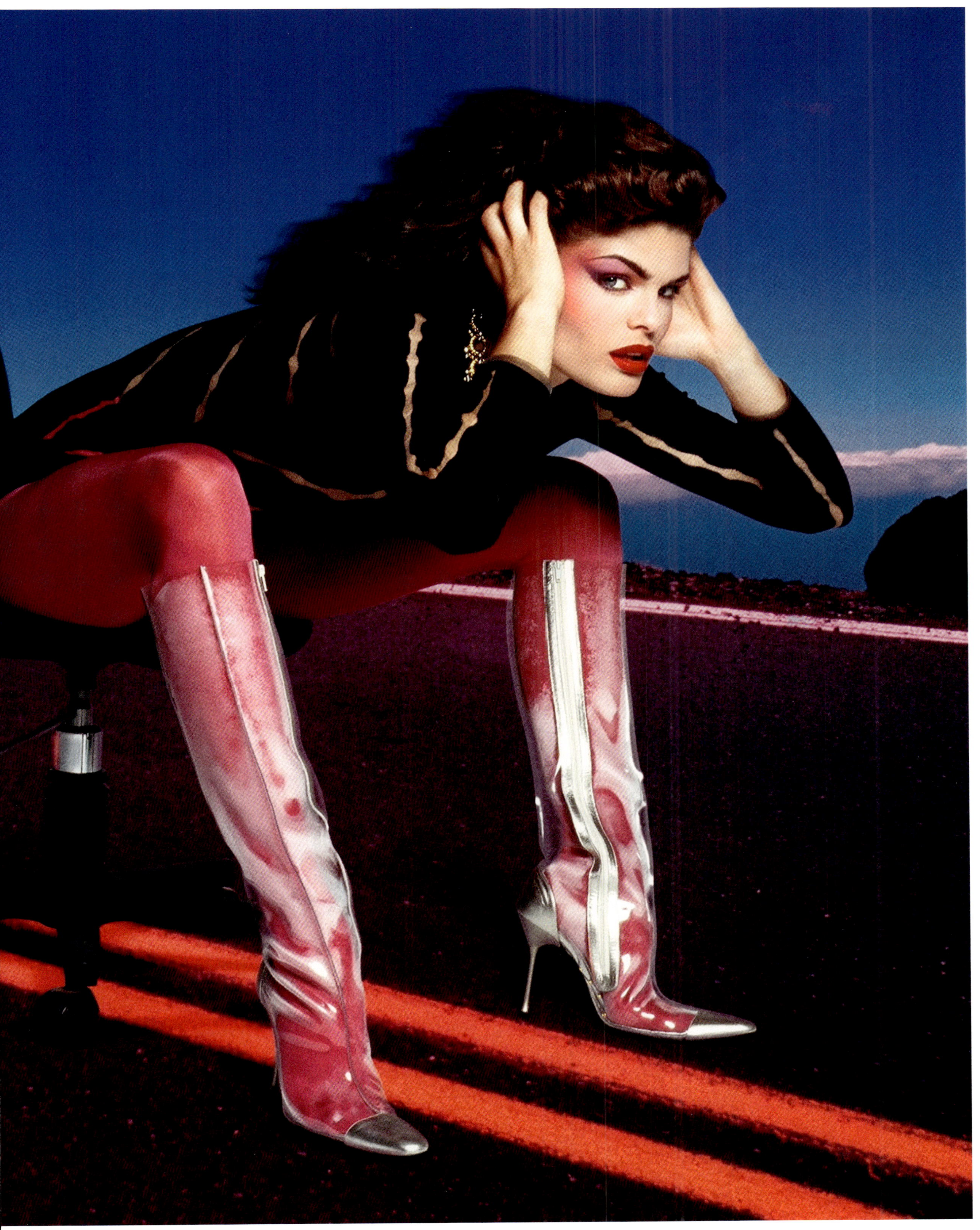

THIS IS IT! GROWING UP WITH THE FACE

ELAINE CONSTANTINE, GLEN LUCHFORD AND NANCY ROHDE

Glen Luchford and Elaine Constantine are photographers whose work featured in *The Face* from 1990 and 1993 respectively. Nancy Rohde is a stylist whose first commission came from *The Face* in 1993, and went on to become the magazine's contributing Fashion Editor. The group met to discuss how they got involved with the magazine, its distinctive creative approach and British youth culture in the Eighties and early Nineties.

KATE MOSS
By Glen Luchford
Styled by Venetia Scott
March 1993

NANCY ROHDE: All of us grew up during a period when British youth culture was at its most diverse. There were so many scenes, all with their own fashions. When we'd go clubbing at Subterfuge

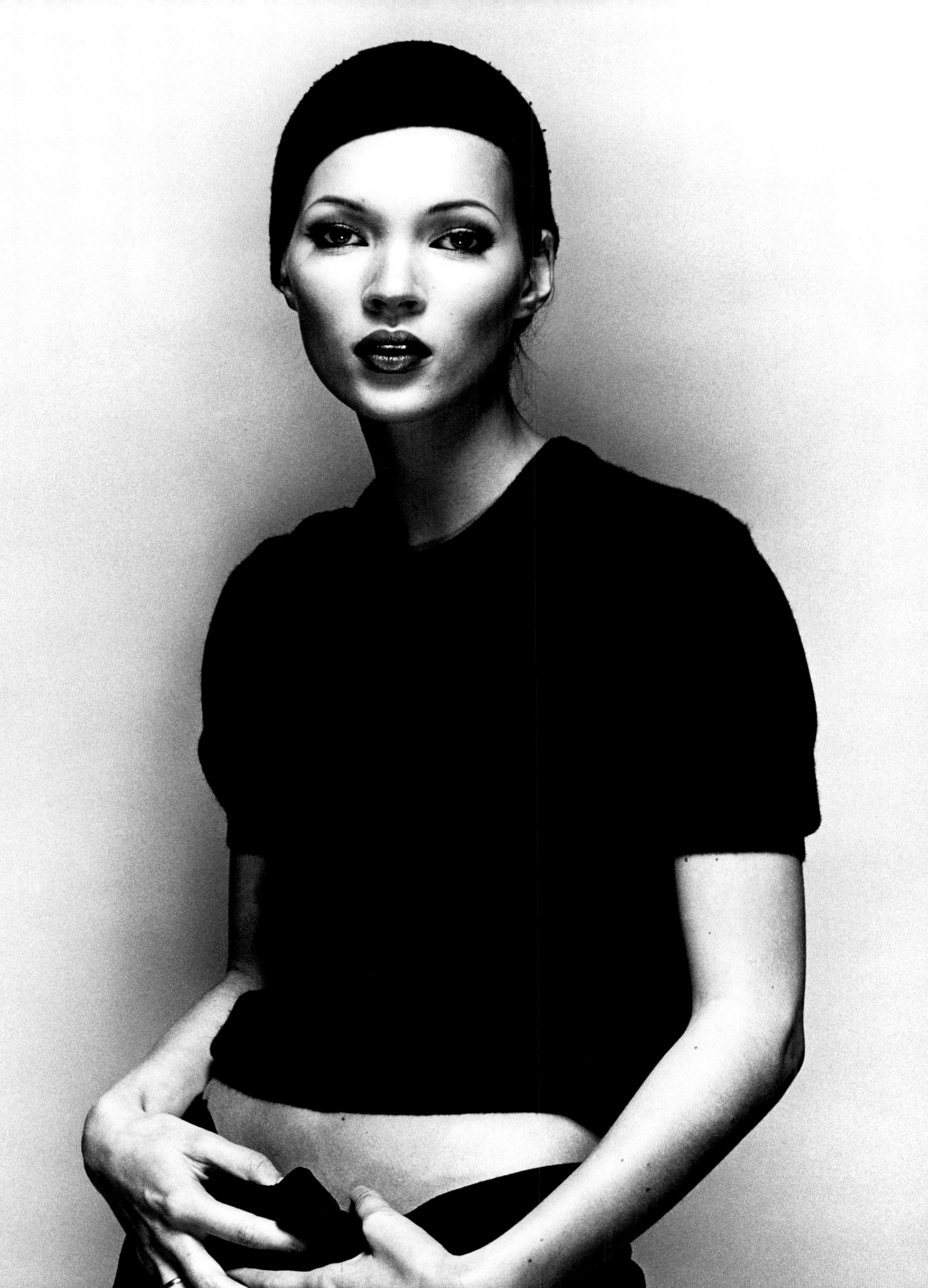

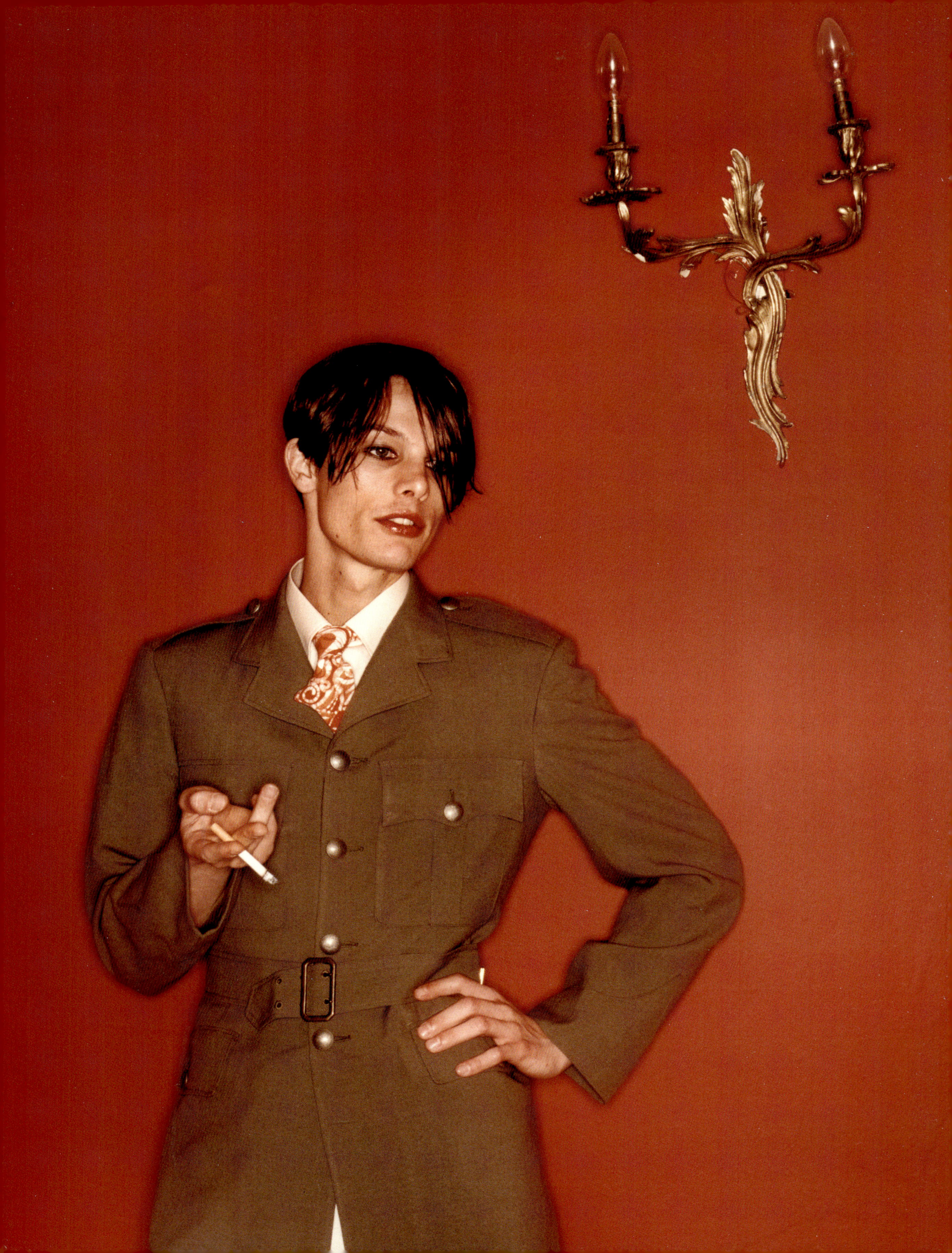

in Brighton, there'd be rockabillies, punks and psychobillies. Everybody was part of some kind of tribe, and I think that not only fuelled people's outlook but influenced how they took photographs. We were inspired by what we were experiencing around us, not by high fashion.

ELAINE CONSTANTINE: I never felt *The Face* and *i-D* were fashion magazines, even though they had lots of stories with stylist collaborations. They felt like a representation of that time.

NR: Mainstream fashion wasn't really available to us because it was very class-based. Public school girls went to work for *Vogue*, and that wasn't us. We had a different story to tell, which *i-D* and *The Face* allowed us to do. Classism had kept the door to fashion closed, but we knocked it down.

GLEN LUCHFORD: I got into *The Face* through skateboarding. I started taking pictures of skateboarders, and I showed them to some fashion students in Brighton, who wanted me to take pictures of their clothes. I was determined to get into *The Face*, so I kept going in with my little portfolio trying to see [Art Director] Phil Bicker. I became so annoying that, eventually, they relented. Phil looked through the pictures and said, 'Well, you haven't got much here, but I can see they're good, so we'll give you a job.' It was real beginner's luck.

EC: I was into Northern Soul and I had started out spray painting scooters and photographing them. Then later I worked as a technician at a college in Salford, photographing fashion students' collections. I was into the documentary side of things, so I really loved the photographers Chris Killip and Martin Parr. A lecturer who worked at the college said, 'My husband used to teach [photographer] Nick Knight. Do you want to interview to be one of his assistants?' So, that's how I ended up in London working in that world.

NR: I studied social documentary photography at Nottingham, but I was also influenced by magazines. I just didn't feel like I had a single photographic vision. So, I moved from behind the camera into styling for the camera, but I still found the photographic knowledge I had built up useful, because it gave me lots of visual references. Now, all stylists know about the history of photography but, when I started, a lot of them didn't.

EC: I remember seeing Nancy's work in *The Face* when I was still living in Manchester and thinking, 'This is it! This is what I want to get into!' It was the 'Army Dreamers' shoot you did in 1994 with [photographer] Donald Milne. It wasn't a fashion story – about people wearing orange or belts or whatever – which, to me, always seemed really naff. It felt like real photography. So, when I saw your work and a couple of other shoots from around that time, with stylists like Melanie Ward, I was really inspired and I remember thinking, 'I really want to create fashion editorial like that for *The Face*.'

GL: I wanted to work with Ray Petri. So, I ended up assisting Norman Watson, who was photographing for *The Face* and *Arena* at the time, just because he worked with Ray. Norman came from a very cultured background, so being his assistant was amazing, because growing up I hadn't had access to museums or books or anything like that. He was the first person who showed me the work of photographers like Larry Clark and Nan Goldin. And he introduced me to Ray.

At that time, a lot of us were on the Youth Training Scheme that Margaret Thatcher came up with to get people off the dole. If you could raise £1,000, the government would match it, give you a salary of £27 a week and pay most of your rent. Pretty much everyone I knew who was working for *The Face* in the beginning was on that scheme. It was amazing because the fact that they paid your rent meant you could take pictures all the time: you could borrow film from other people and the labs I went to often worked for free based on the premise that you'd become a client afterwards. So, you could sort of skim by.

NR: Everybody was on the dole. It was like internship money. Being on the dole enabled you to work for free and to build a career.

EC: You didn't have a choice. There weren't any jobs to go to, so it was a case of, 'How do I try and carve out a life for myself?' I'm never going to say that Thatcher was a good prime minister, but that scheme saved me from being factory fodder.

NR: It helped not only photographers and stylists, but bands, artists, so many people that just don't have that opportunity anymore. I used to do music videos or TV ads to earn money. All stylists did.

GL: In the Eighties and early Nineties, the London fashion world

ARMY DREAMERS
By Donald Milne
Styled by Nancy Rohde
November 1994

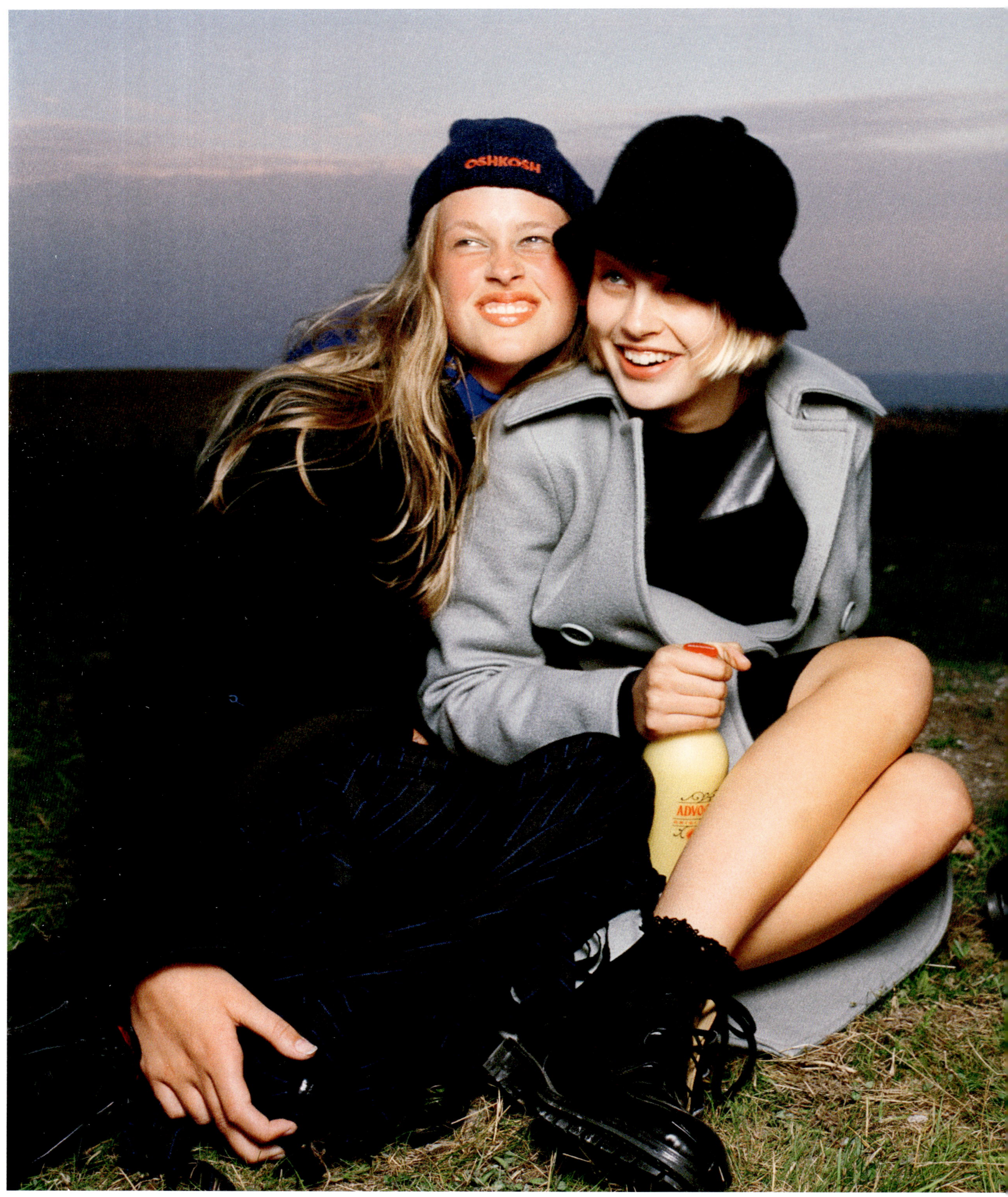

OSHKOSH
ADVO

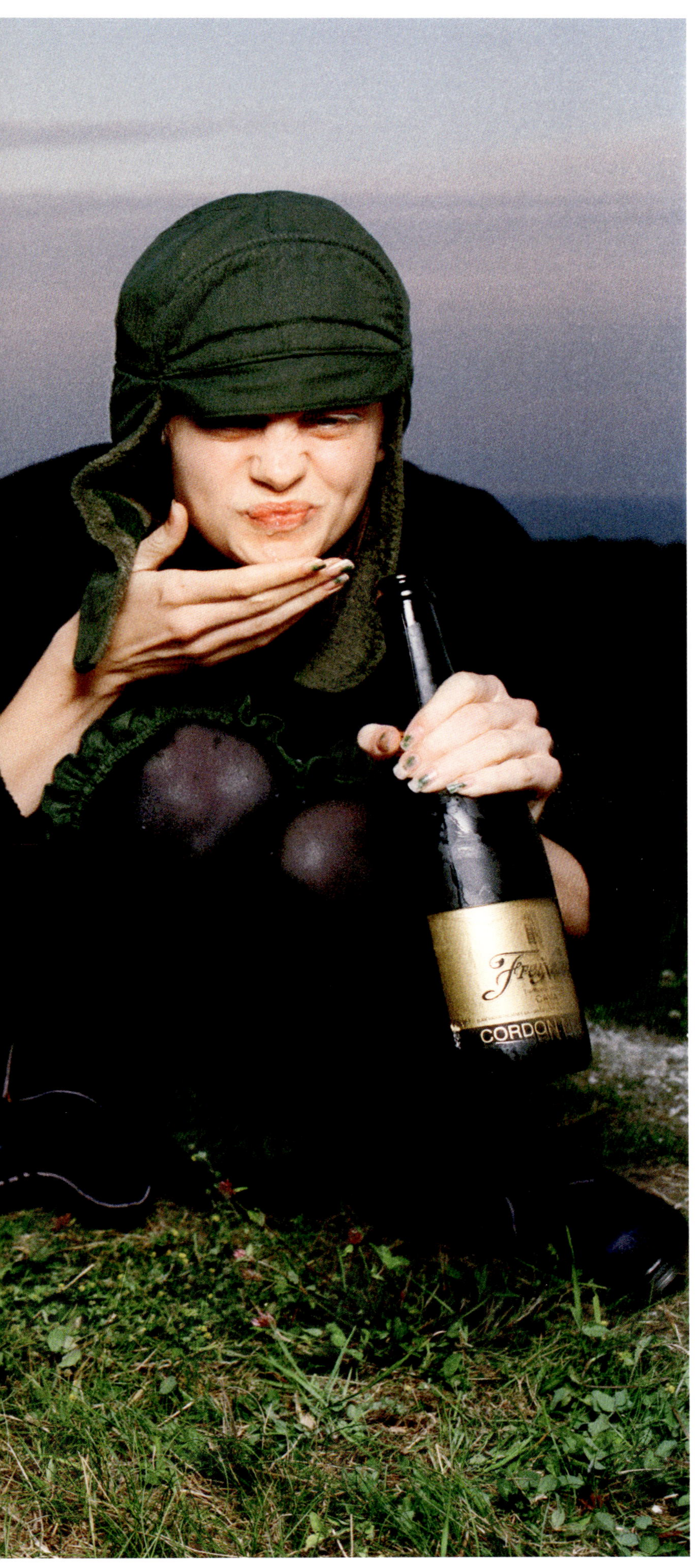

was a like a cottage industry. Things were on a completely different scale. There were a lot of small designers who would all put on shows. Everything was handmade and everyone would pitch in to help. There were no super brands. And *The Face* wasn't interested in designer fashion: they never questioned what clothes were going into a shoot.

NR: Fashion wasn't very accessible. It was quite difficult to get hold of those clothes if you didn't have the means of big magazines like *Vogue*.

GL: Yes, and it only became important when you started working for those bigger magazines.

EC: In hindsight, the special thing about working for *The Face* was that there wasn't this impetus to use big labels and I could use a democratic casting process. It was only later, after I began working for bigger magazines, that I was told what models I had to use.

GL: There were fashion editors at *Vogue*, but I think Caroline Baker was the first person to call herself a fashion stylist, and Ray was the second. They were part of a whole new culture: they wrote the rule book.

NR: People knew each other, so they would come up with a story, propose the idea to *The Face*, then go and do it. I only fully realised the cultural impact of the magazine when certain photographers and advertisers were accused by the press of promoting unhealthy-looking models. It was a bit of an eye-rolling moment: the establishment suddenly coming down on what we were doing without understanding the context – which was a reaction against the unattainable ideal of the supermodel, trying to create gritty representations that were closer to real life.

GL: In America, you had these powerhouse photographers like Richard Avedon, Patrick Demarchelier, Arthur Elgort, Steven Meisel and Irving Penn. Whereas we were a bunch of scrappy kids from council estates, mostly. The industry didn't understand us. I remember taking pictures of Kate [Moss] to show fashion designers in London and they didn't get it. Then she blew up and they knew they had to embrace it, but it was a subculture that they couldn't quite put their finger on.

NR: When the world decided *The Face* was cool, everyone from *Vogue* stylists to advertisers wanted a bit of it. Actually, the advertisers were pretty cool because they didn't pressure us a lot: they were just happy to be in the magazine. *The Face*'s art directors put a lot of faith in people, too: you could prove yourself by working for the magazine. I don't think that would happen again. It was a golden moment in magazine history. ∎

**GIRLS ON SOUTH DOWNS
(SARF COASTIN')**
By Elaine Constantine
Styled by Polly Banks
December 1997

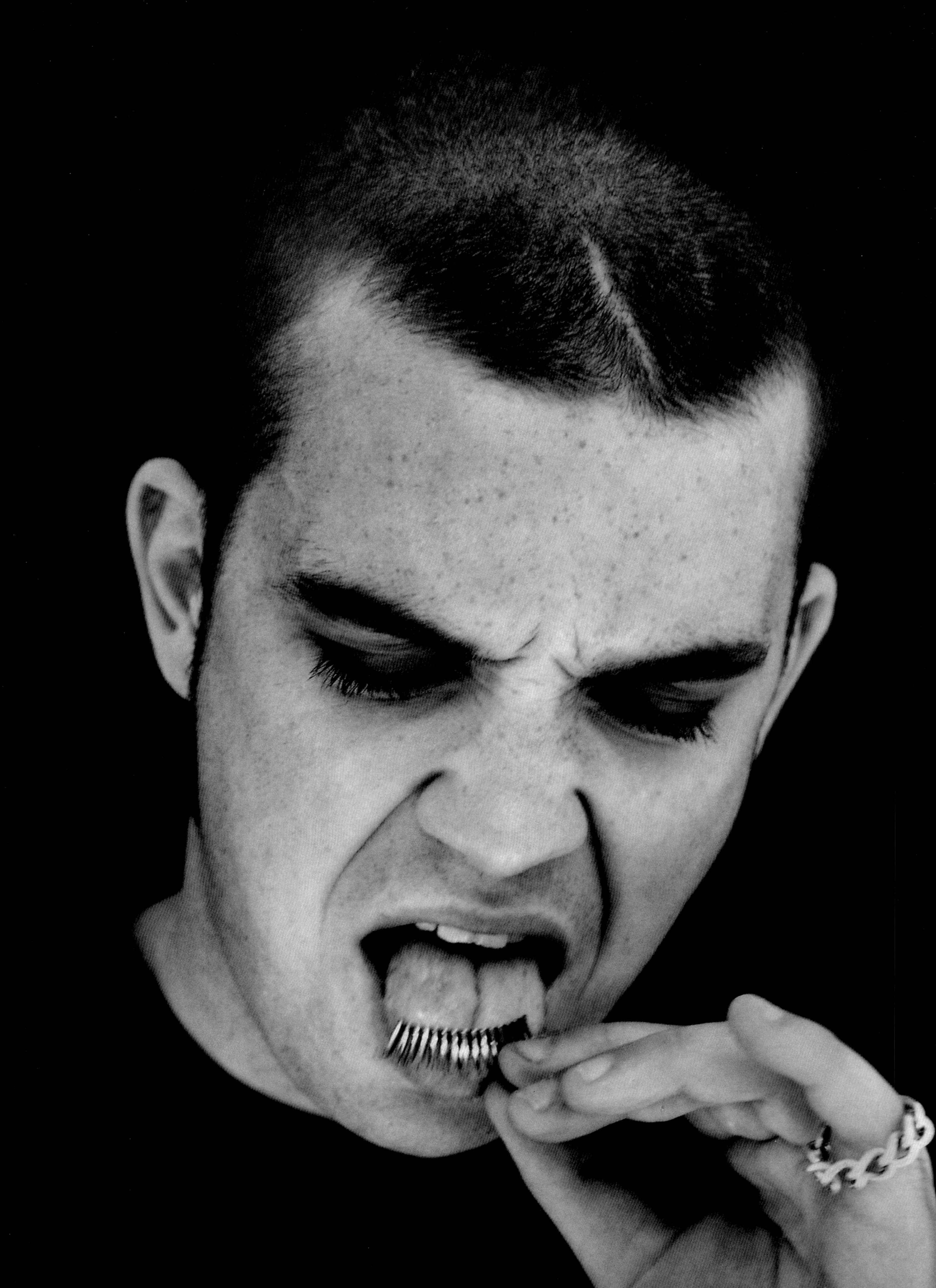

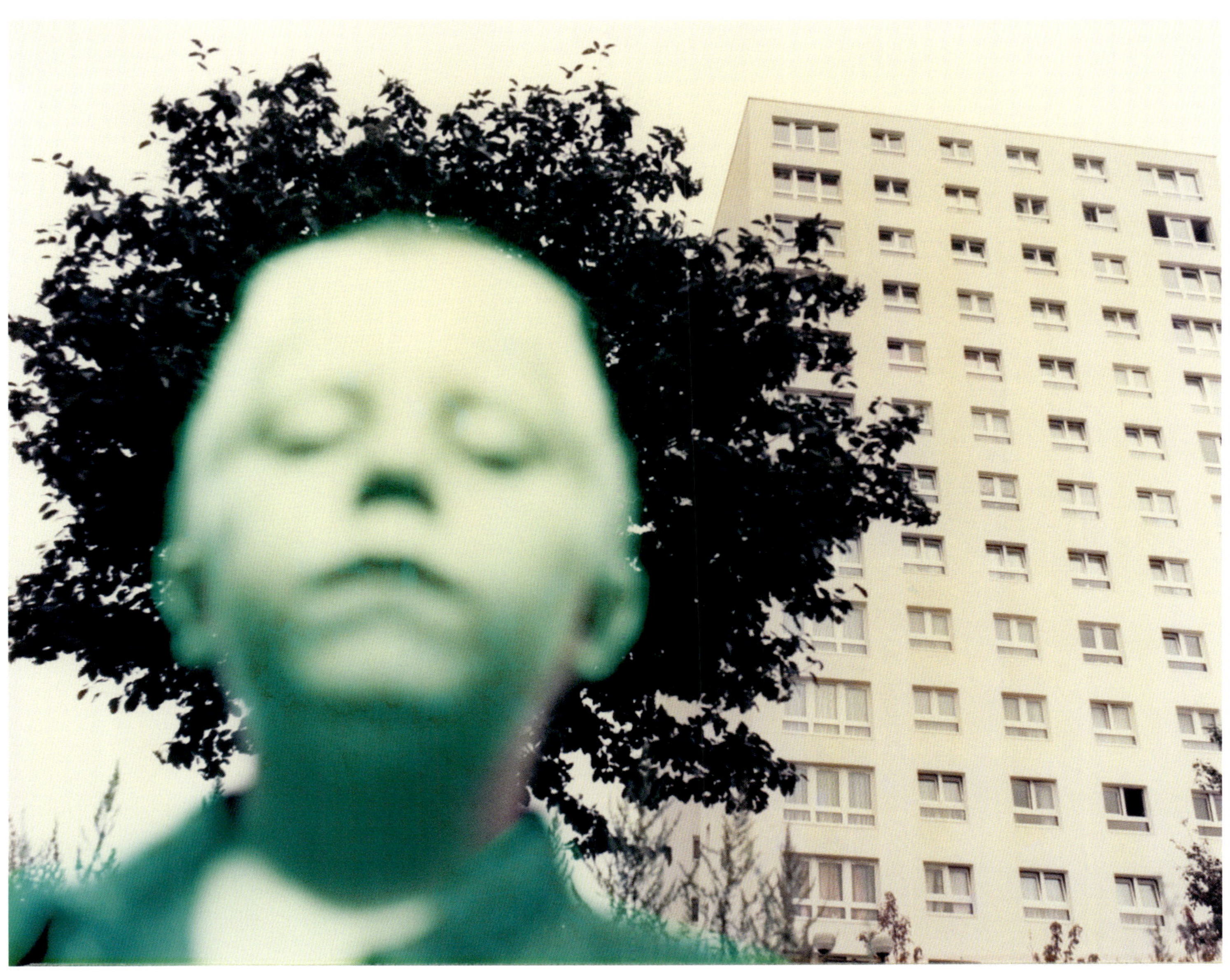

ROBBIE WILLIAMS

By Norman Watson
Styled by Judy Blame
and Giannie Couji
October 1995

KEV'S GHOST

By Lee Jenkins
Styled by Greg Fay
and Justin Laurie
October 1995

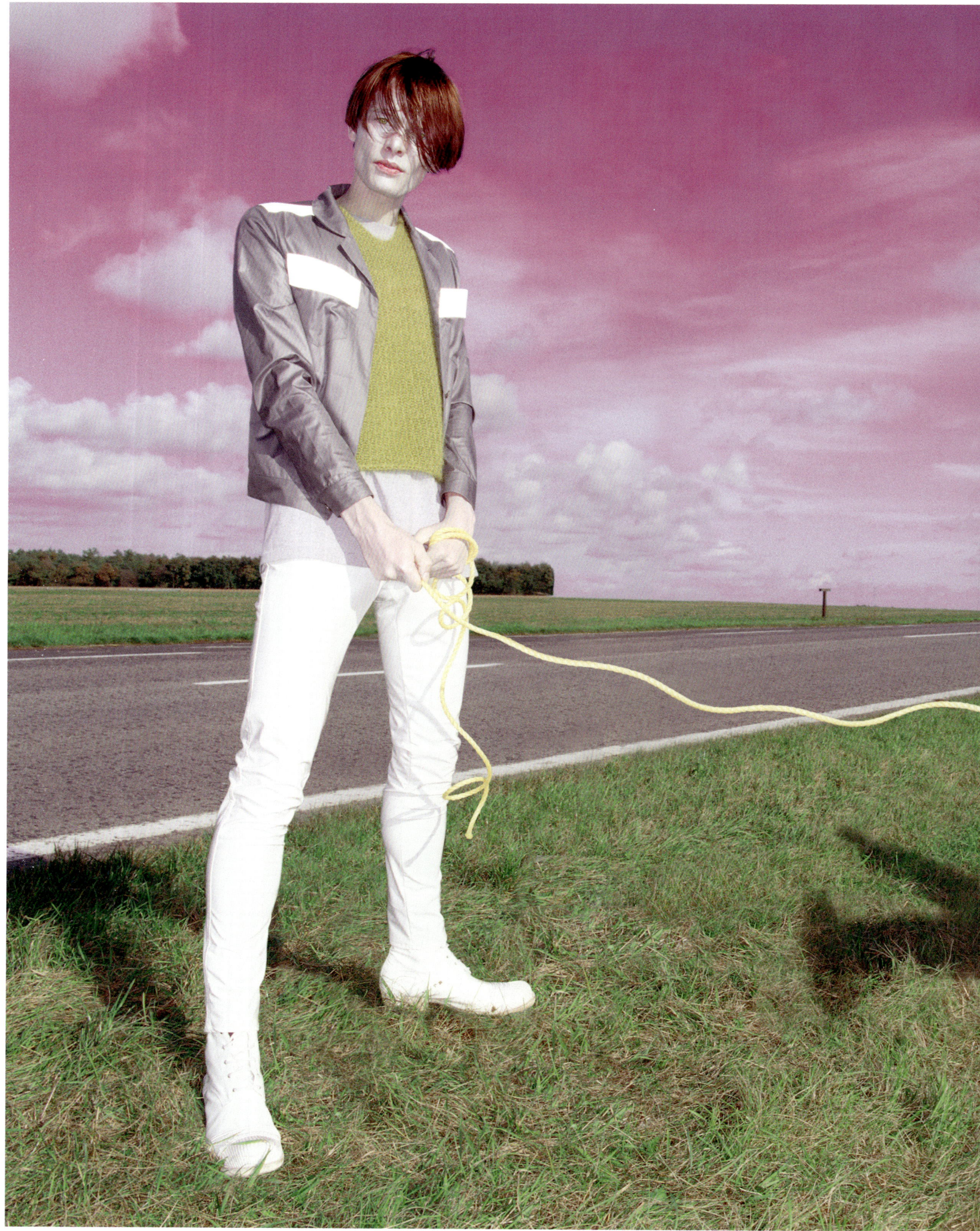

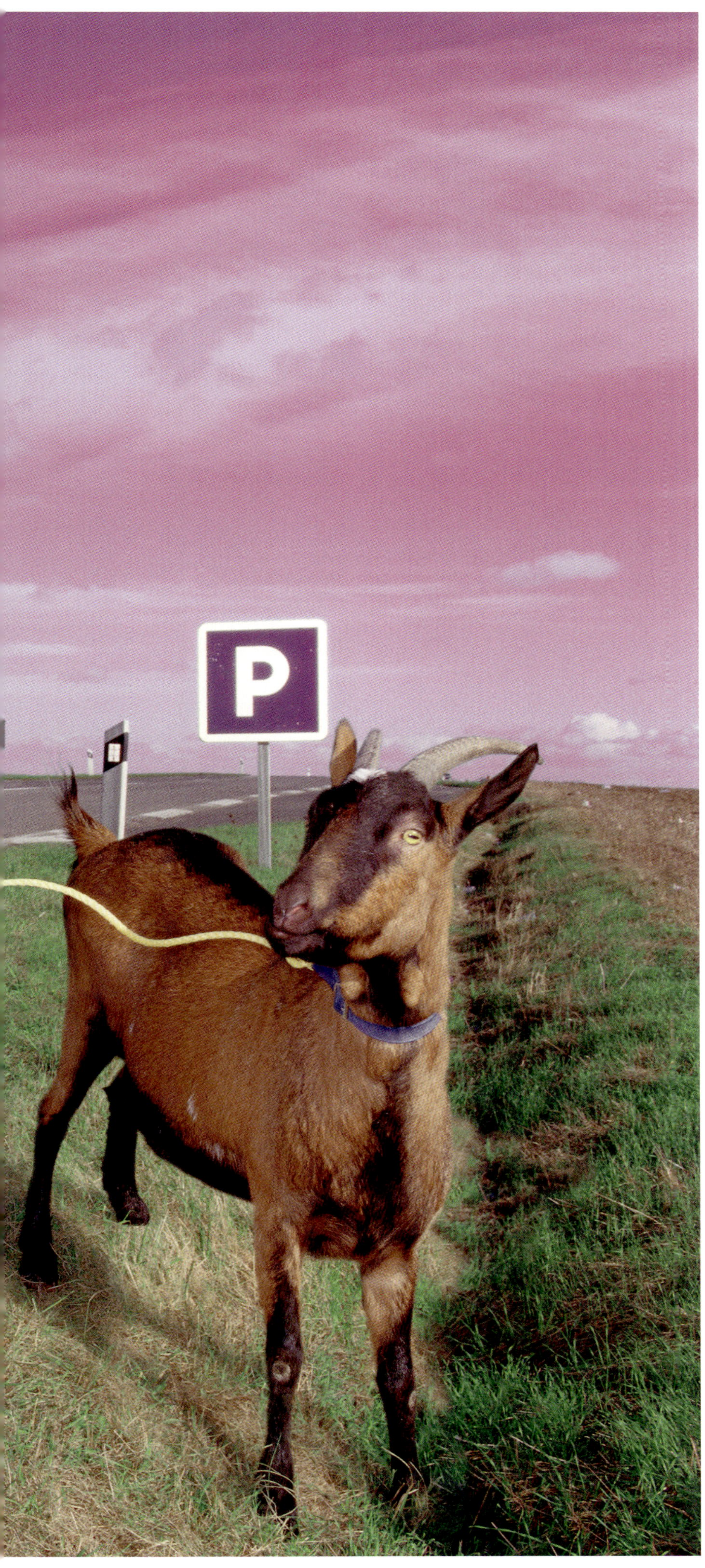

What struck me was the magazine's eclectic aesthetic mixture, remaining on the edge of contemporary styles, without cornering itself into any one youth culture niche.

ANDREA GIACOBBE, PHOTOGRAPHER

ARK LIFE
By Andrea Giacobbe
Styled by Maida Gregori Boina
March 1995

Following pages
THE DAISY AGE
By Corinne Day
Styled by Melanie Ward
July 1990

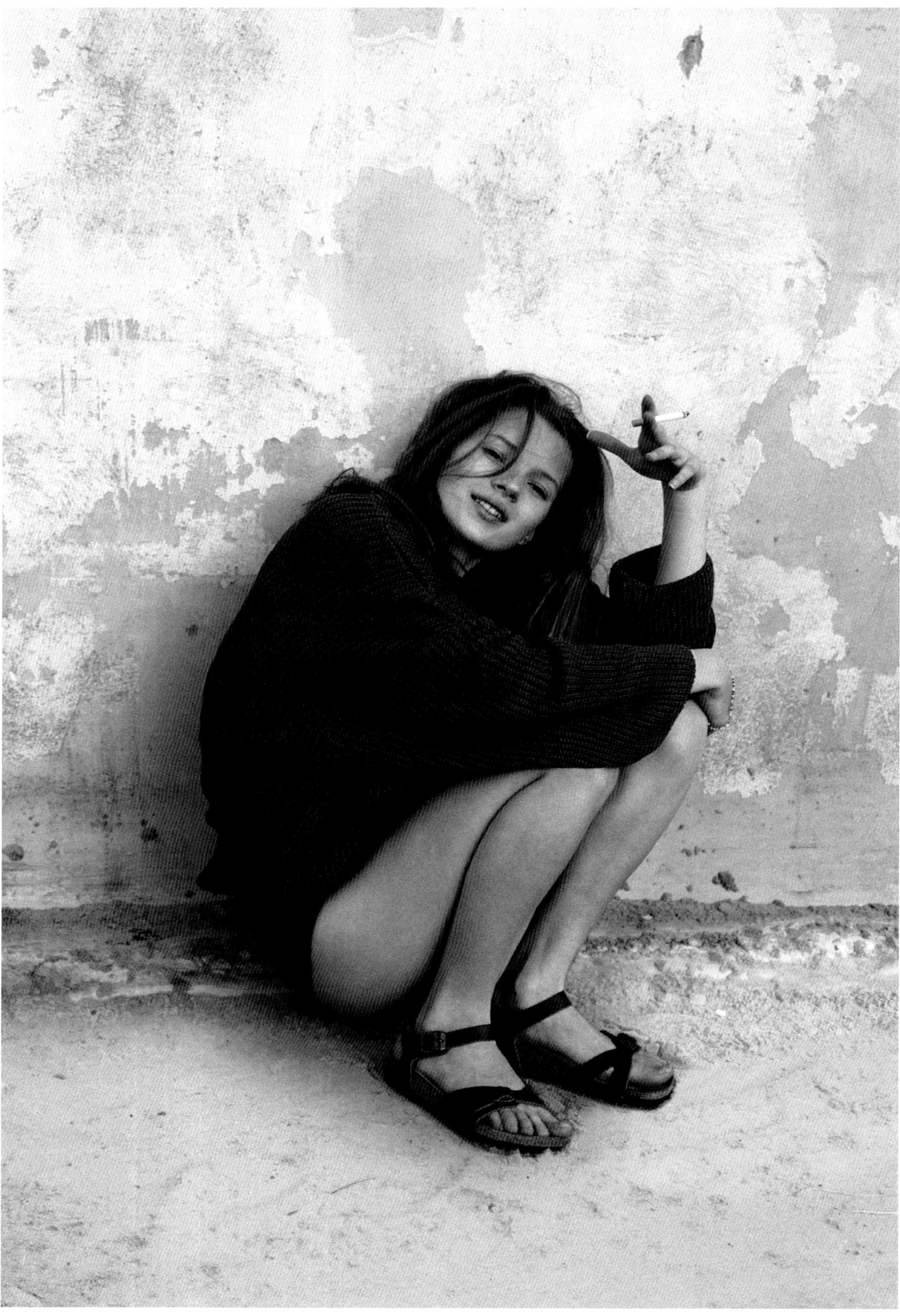

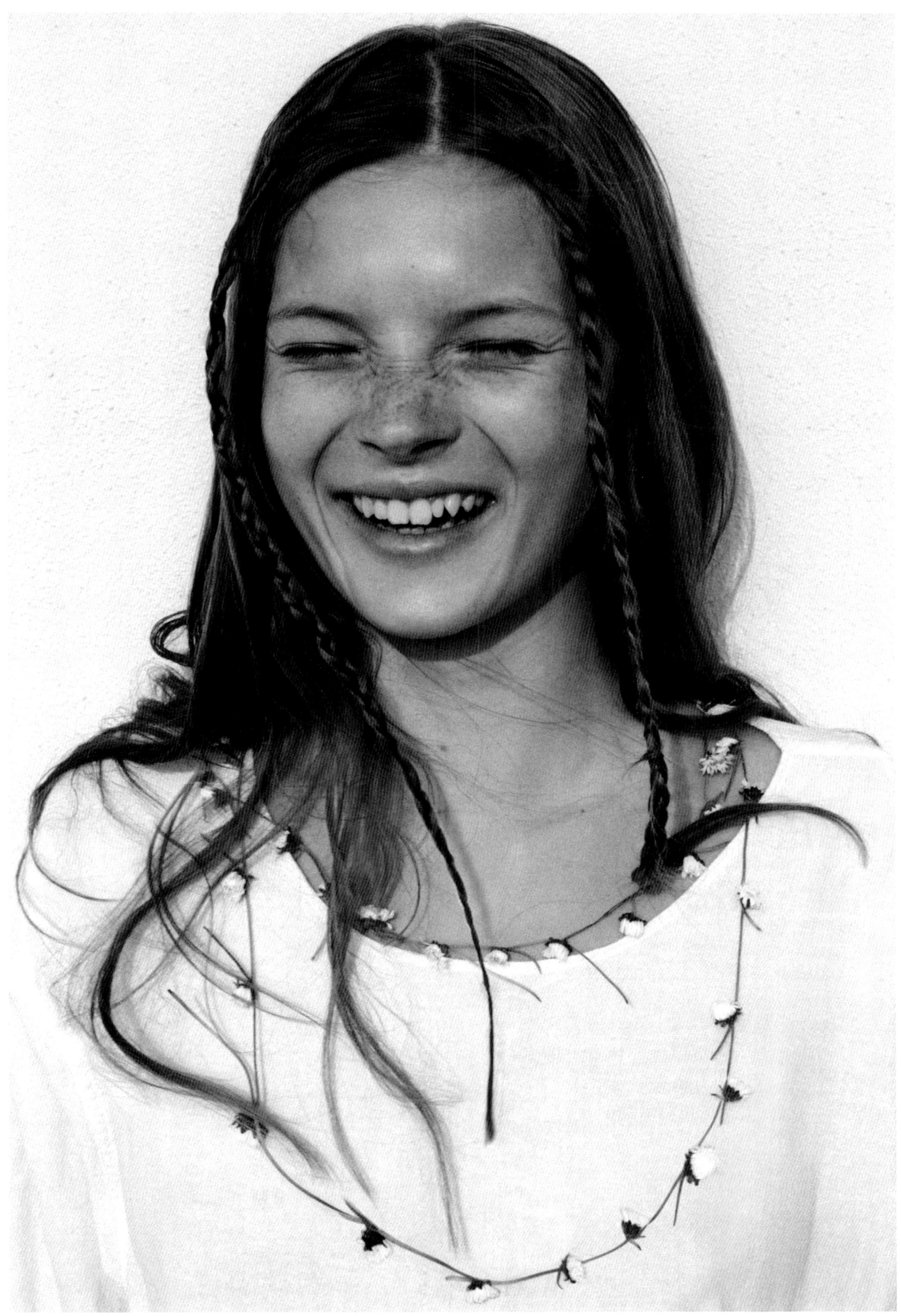

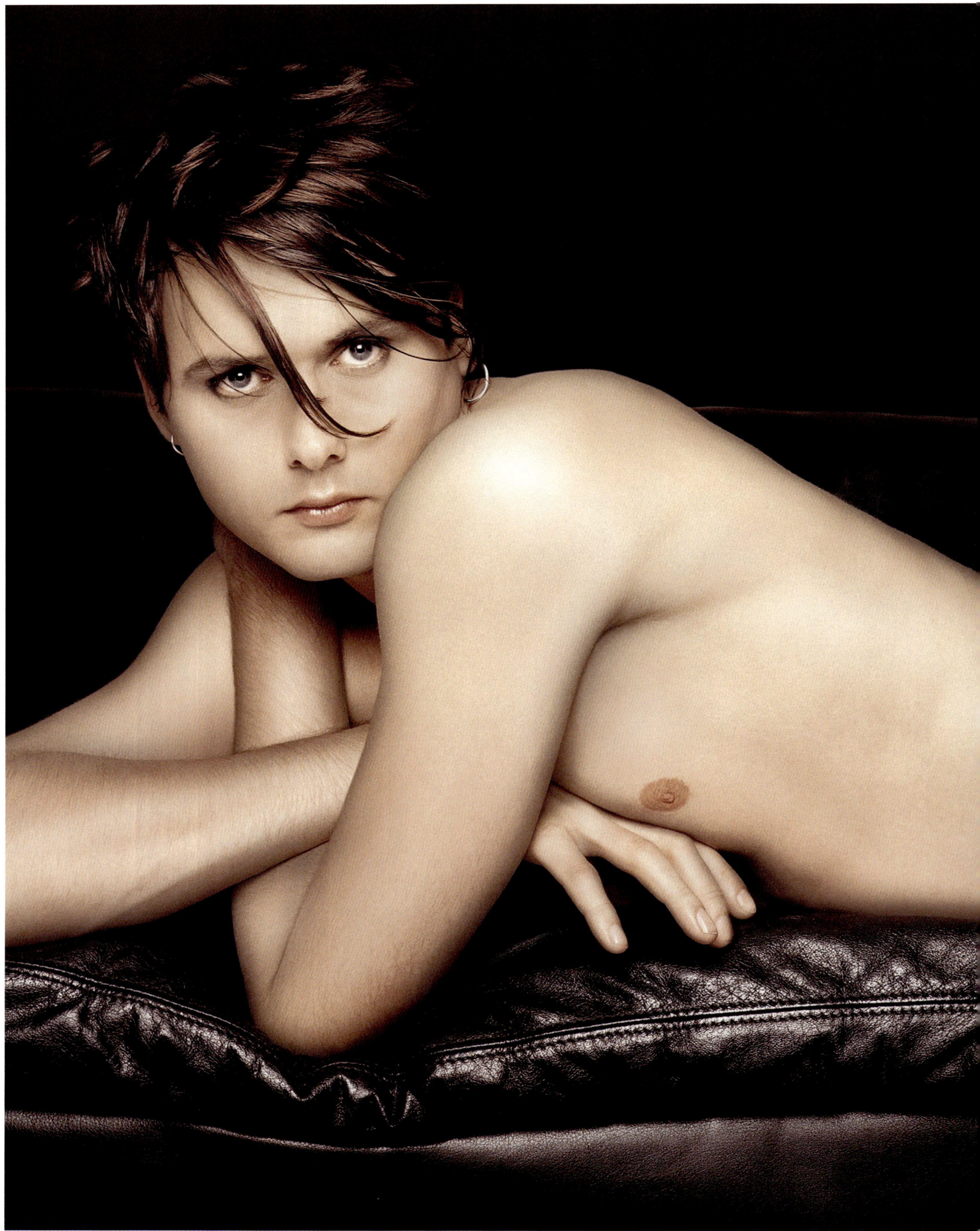

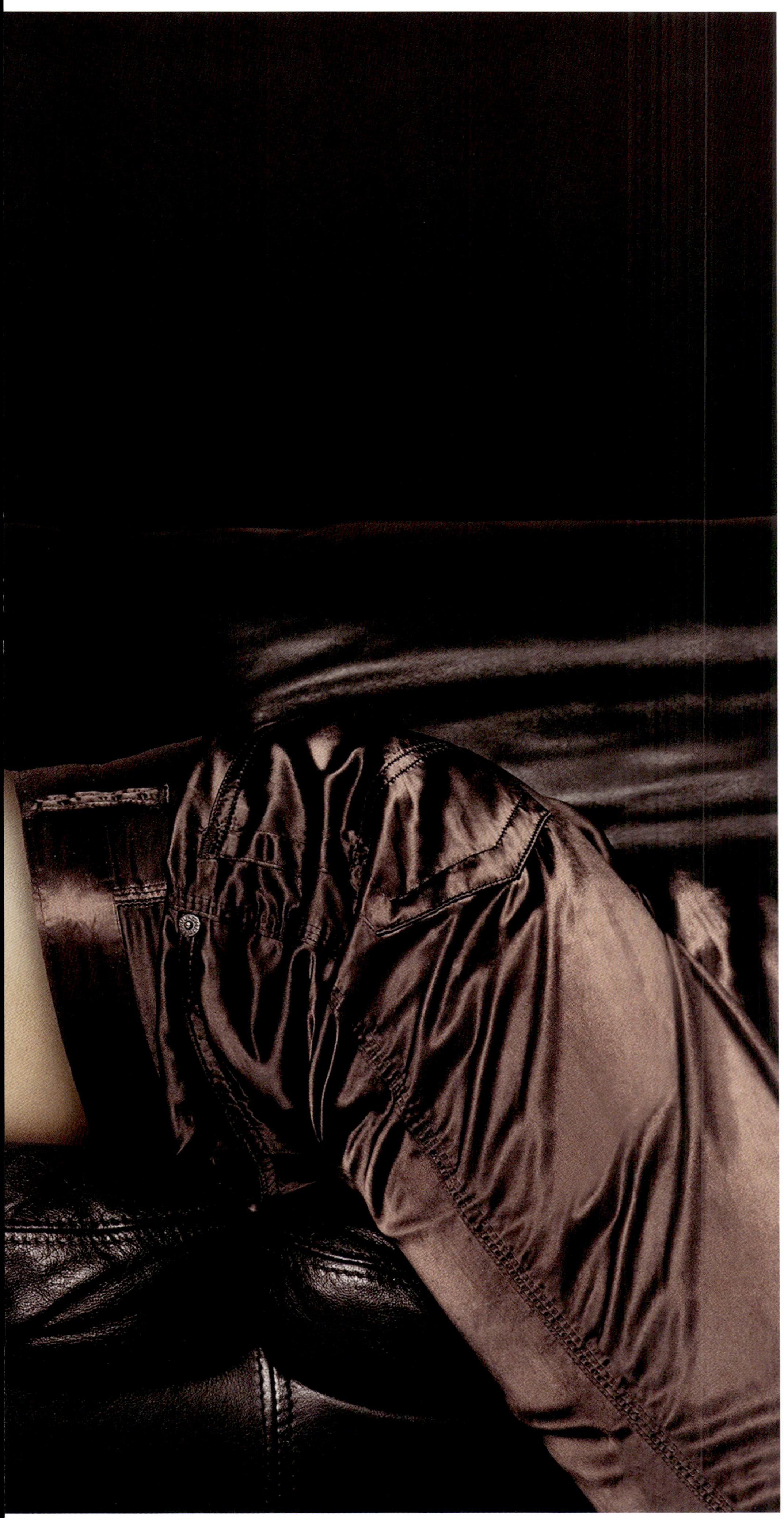

There was a certain glam affectation in Suede's music, a celebration of all things louche and decadent. I asked Inez and Vinoodh to make a Bowie-esque portrait of Brett Anderson: the more fake and plastic-looking, the better.

LEE SWILLINGHAM, ART DIRECTOR

BRETT ANDERSON
Photographed and
styled by Inez & Vinoodh
and Nancy Rohde
November 1994

Following pages
THE EGG
By John Akehurst
Styled by
Charlotte Stockdale
August 1997

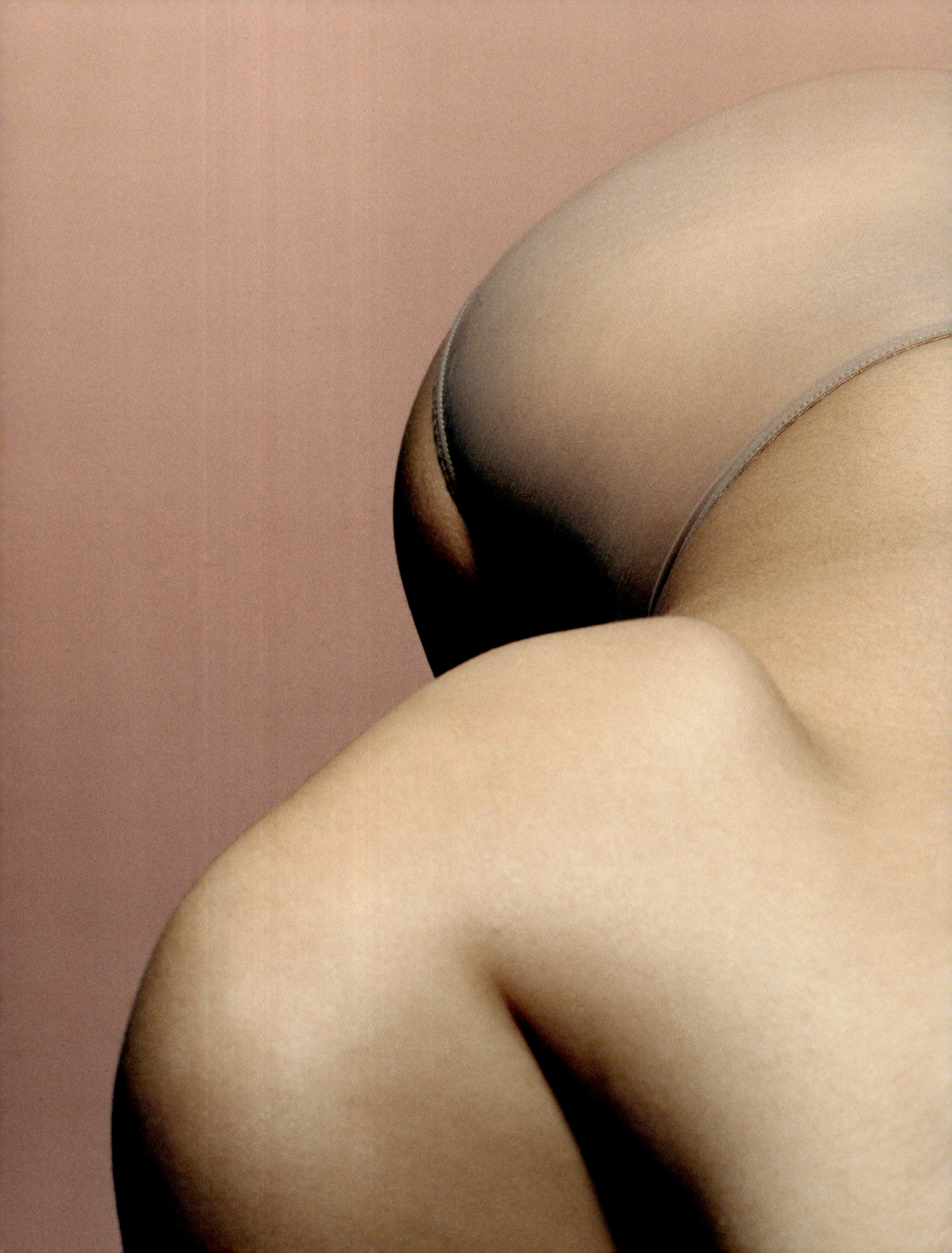

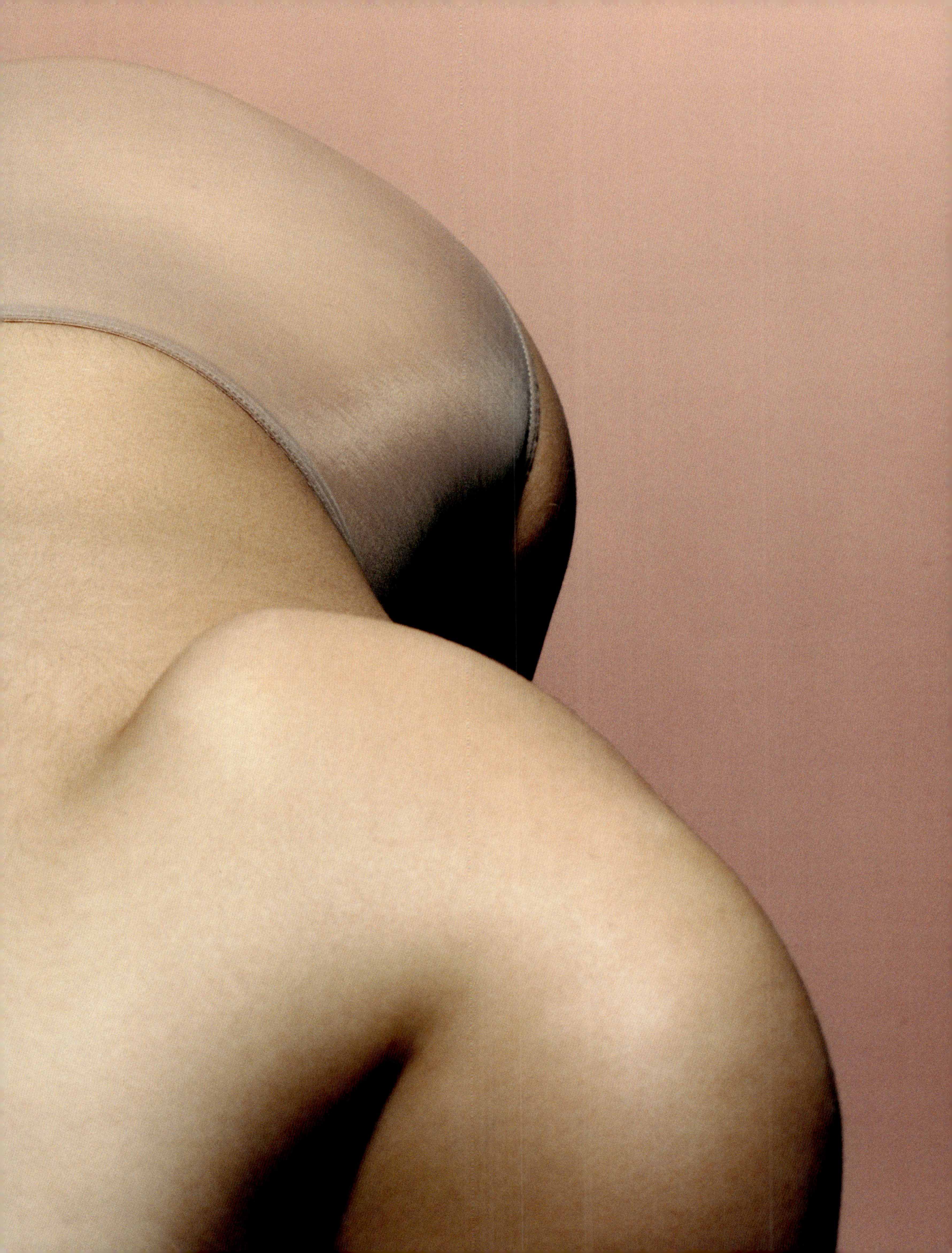

Magazines were much more distinct from one another then. *Vogue* magazine was very much about fashion, designers and high society. *The Face* stood for a culture that was at large in clubs and the music scene, bolstered by the attitude of journalism which was defiantly in opposition to the mainstream.

DAVID SIMS, PHOTOGRAPHER

These early images were instinctual and this translated to me making clothes, customising thrift and vintage – basically an extension of my wardrobe. My aesthetic was fundamentally more about personal style than fashion dictates, an allure, a high-low effortless way of dressing. I remember making the red quilted shorts from a sleeping bag. These editorials were influencing and inspiring designers, setting and leading trends.
Melanie Ward

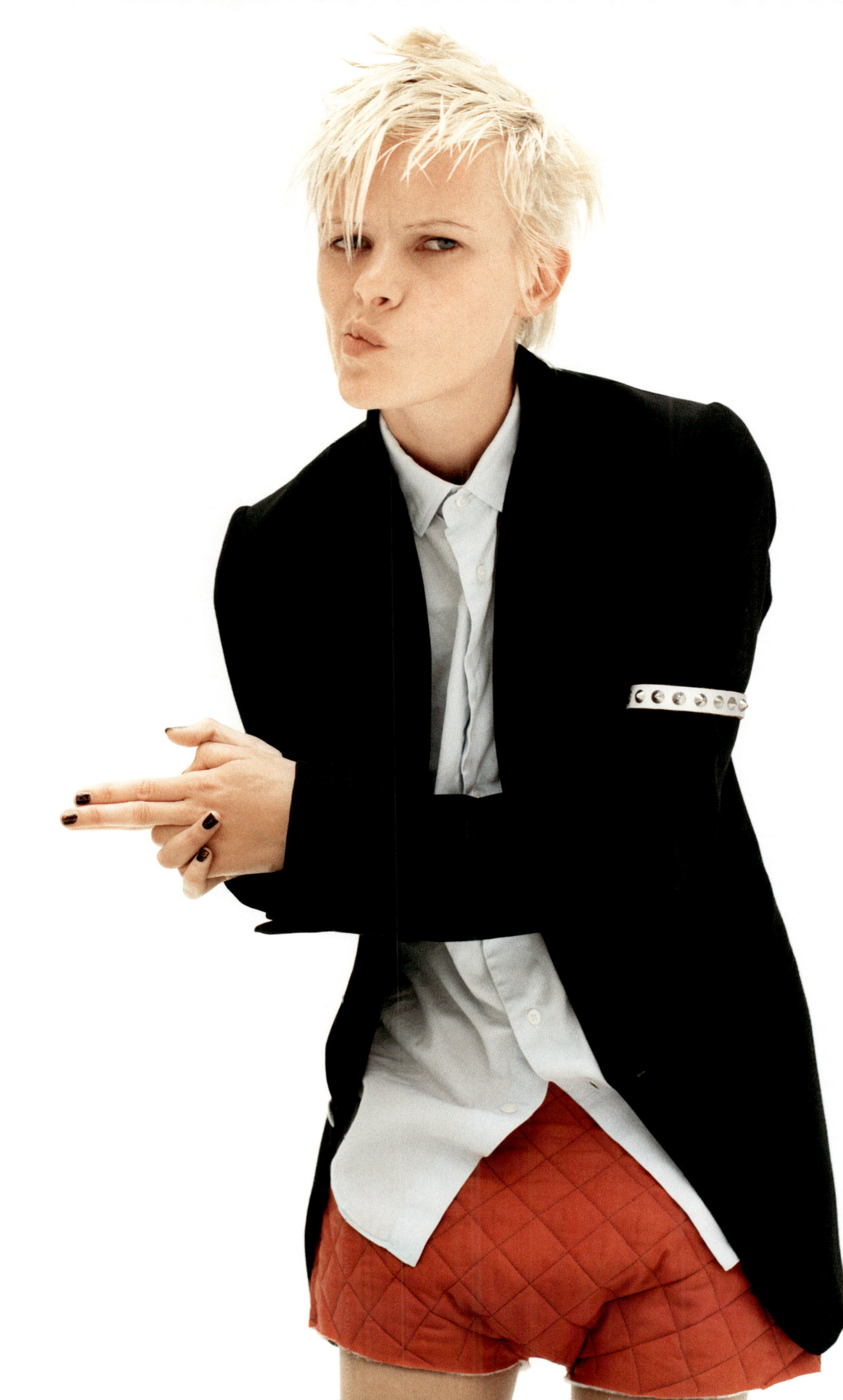

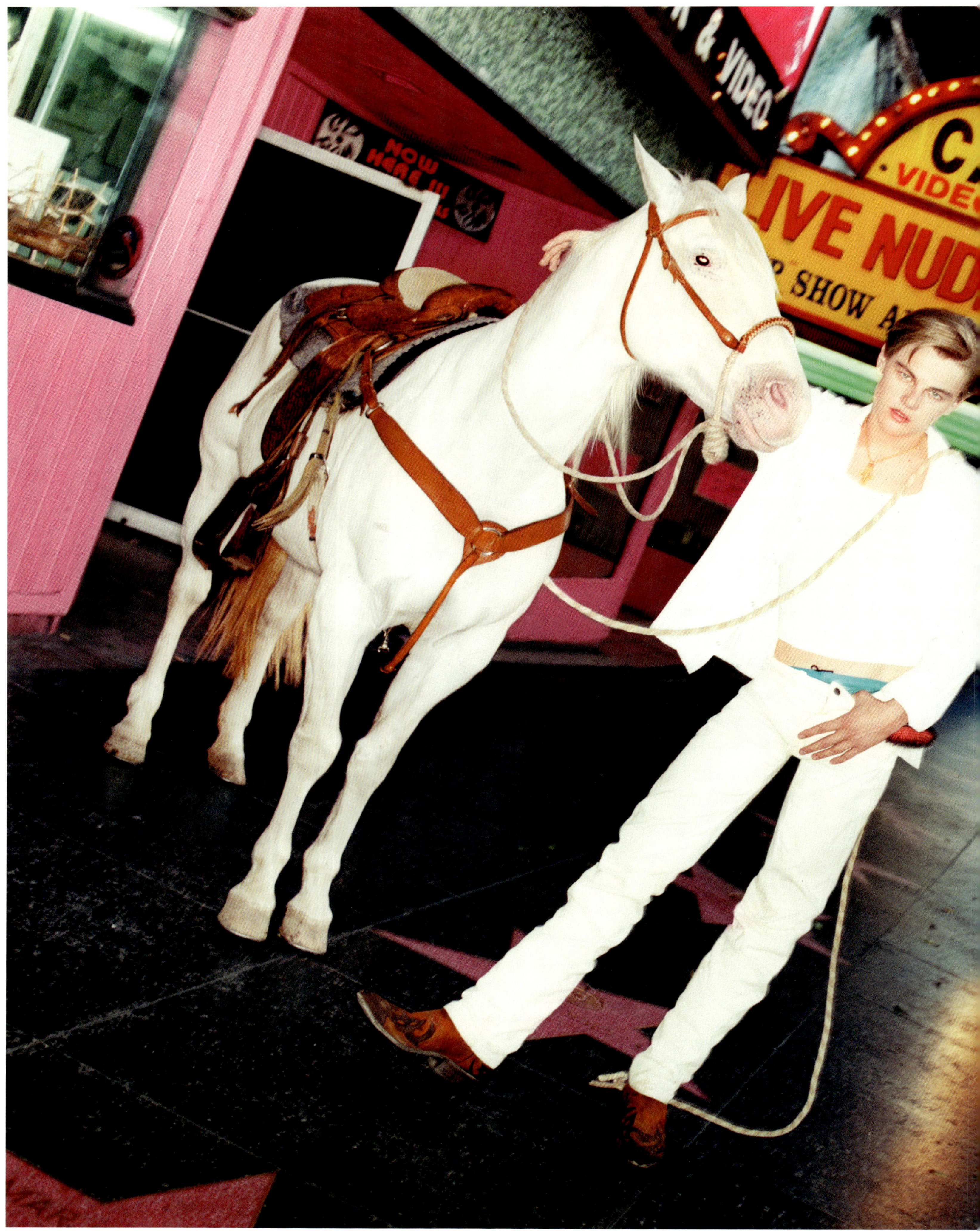

& VIDEO
NOW
HERE !!!
C
VIDEO
LIVE NUD
SHOW

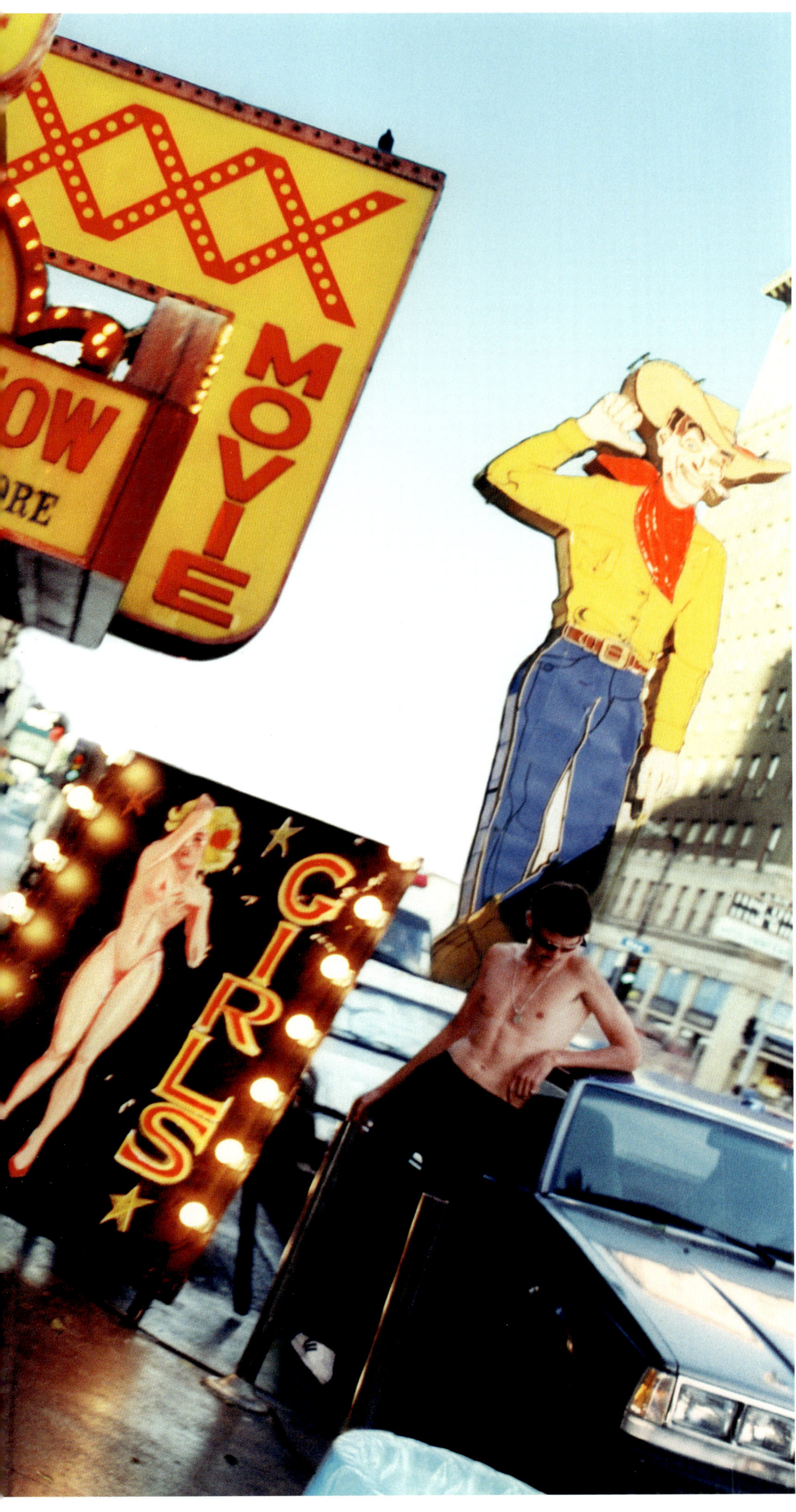

David LaChapelle is the master of his own universe, and people that work with him are really just visiting for a short period of time.

LEE SWILLINGHAM, ART DIRECTOR

LEONARDO DICAPRIO
By David LaChapelle
Styled by Arianne Phillips
December 1995

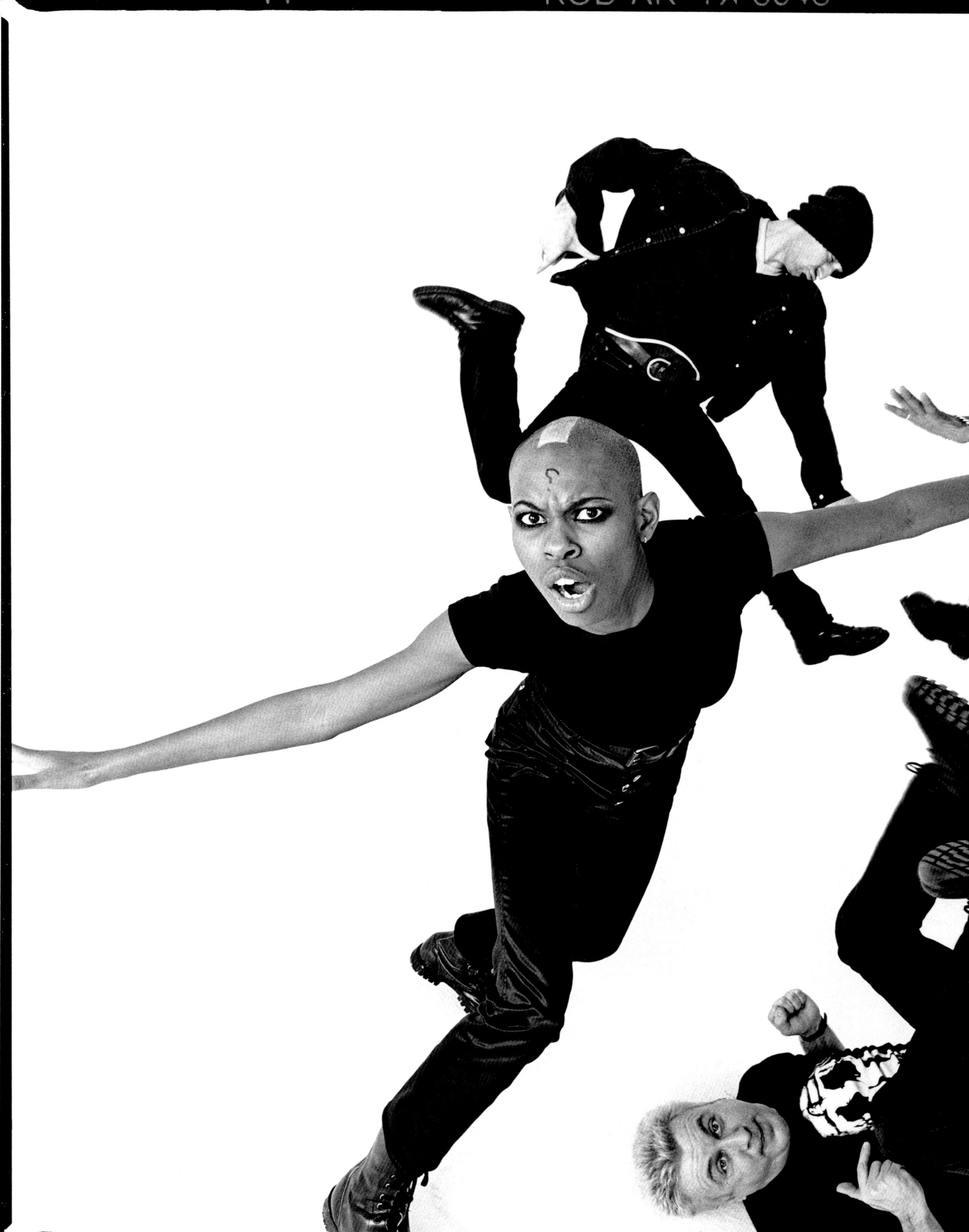

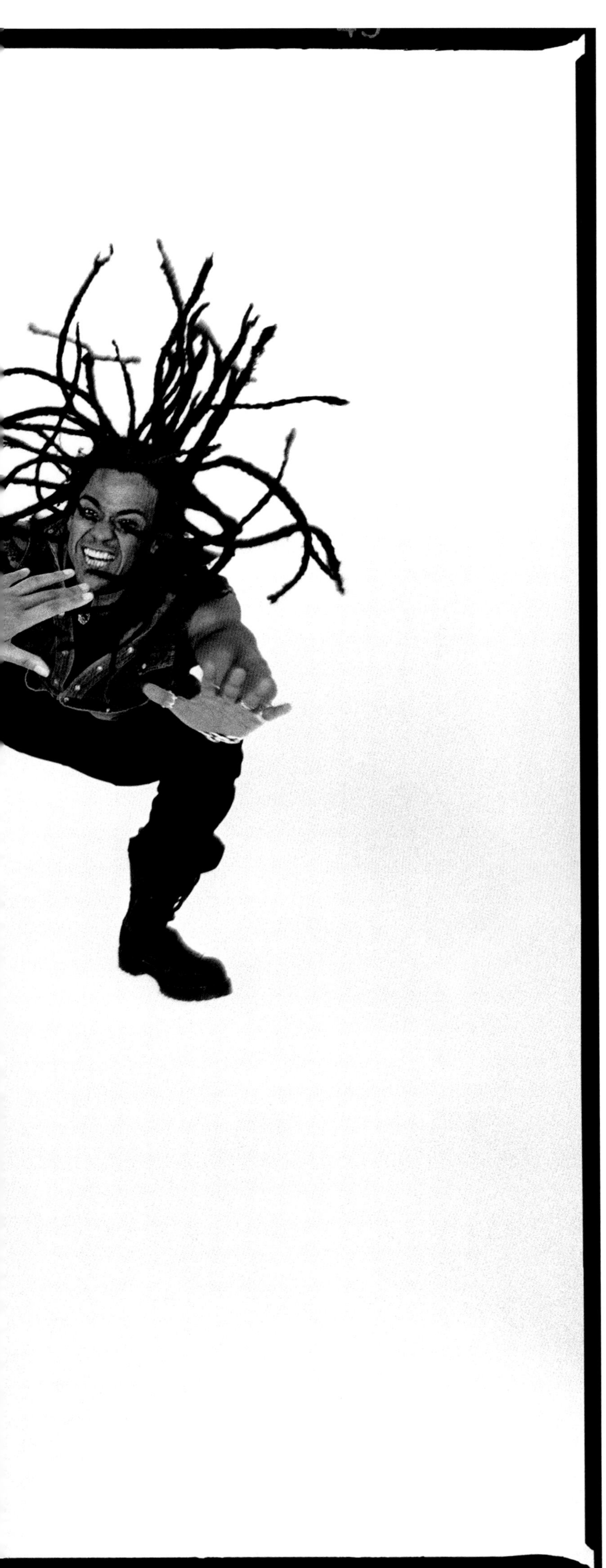

SKUNK ANANSIE
By Jake Chessum
March 1995

We photographed Naomi at the end of a *Vogue* shoot in New Orleans. The stylist had nothing left except a t-shirt and a pair of sneakers. That was enough for us. It was really about the intimacy between Naomi and me. I think my reportage, snapshot style, with its grain and blur, was something new at the time.
Ellen von Unwerth

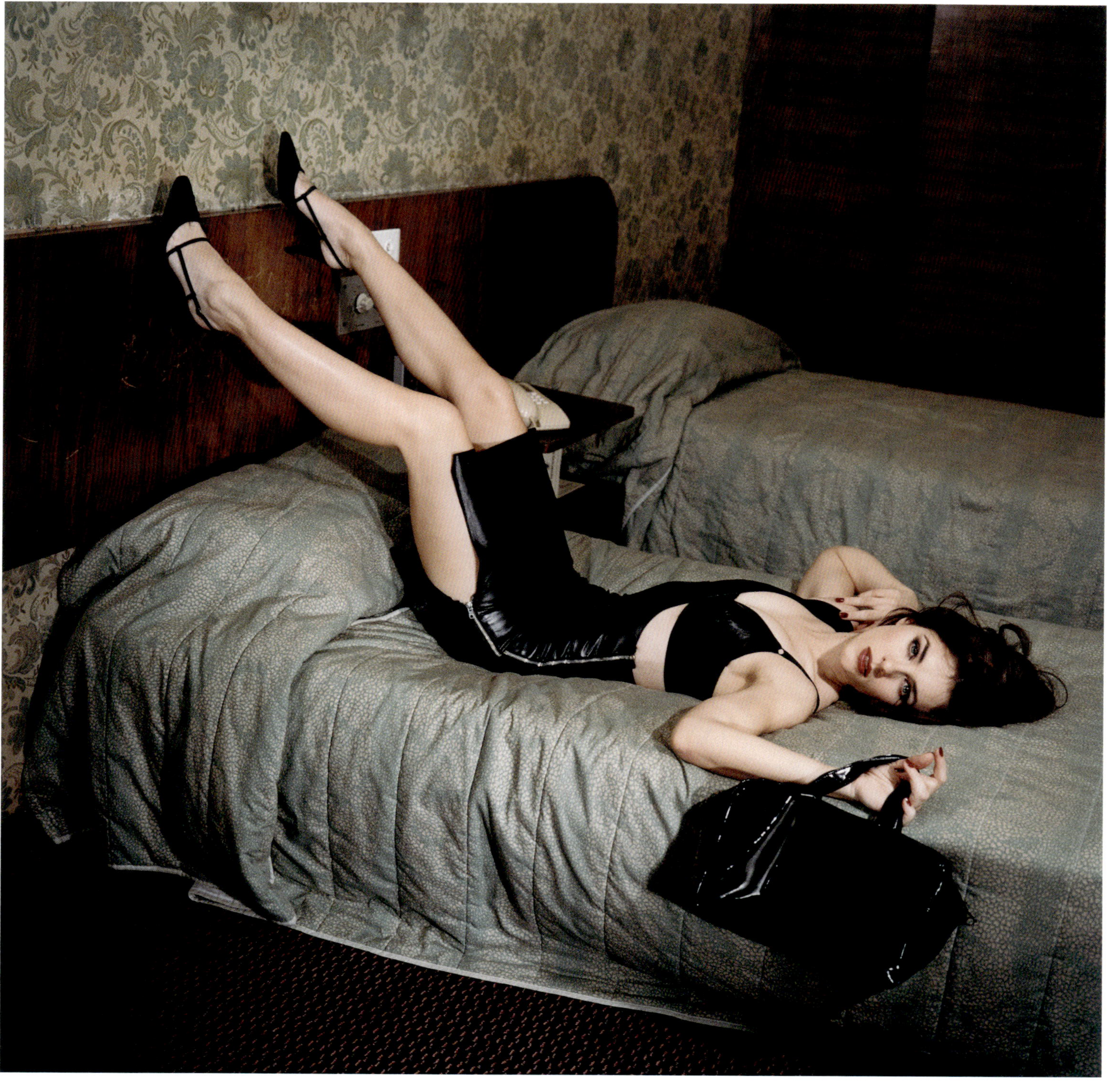

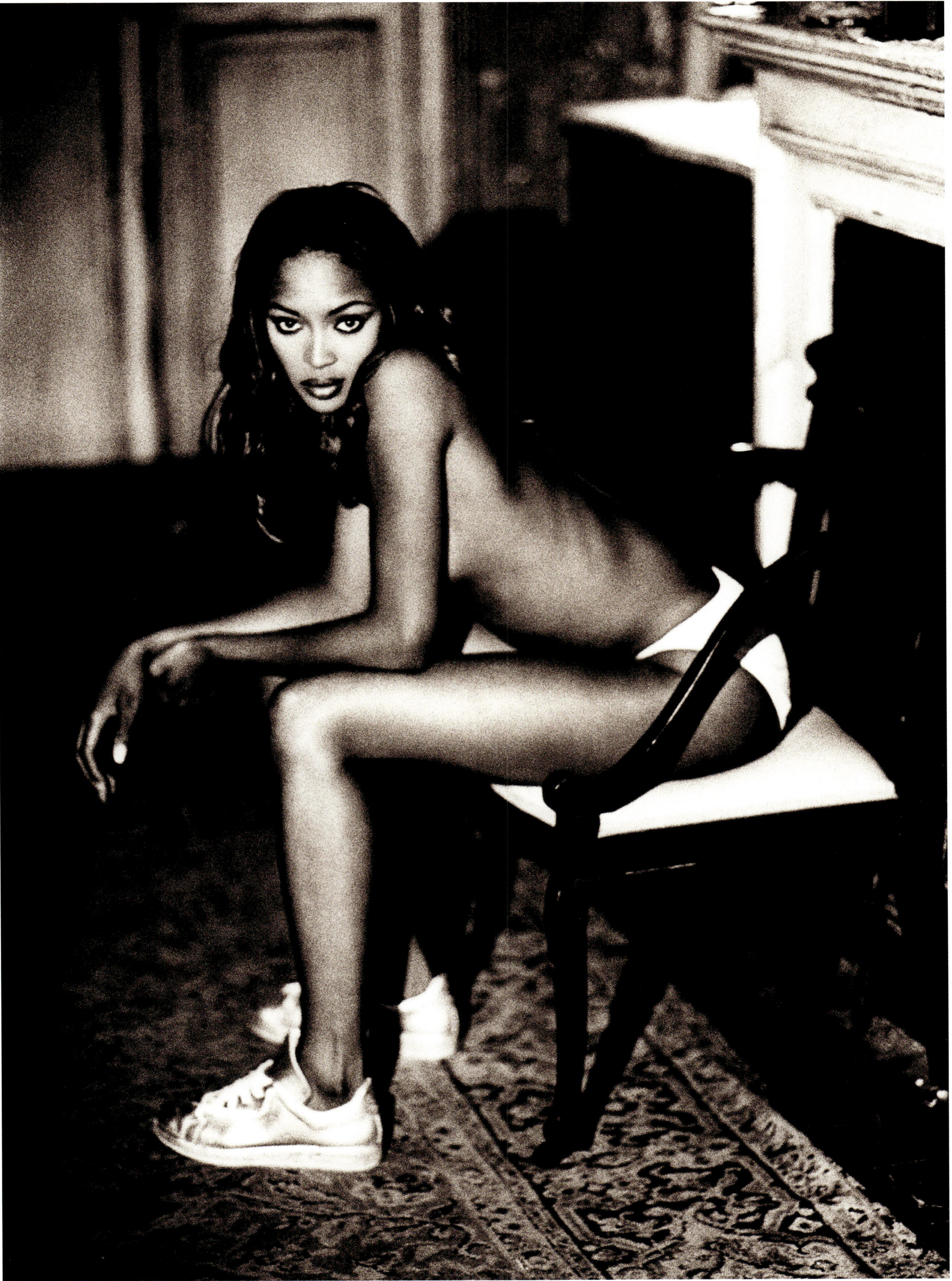

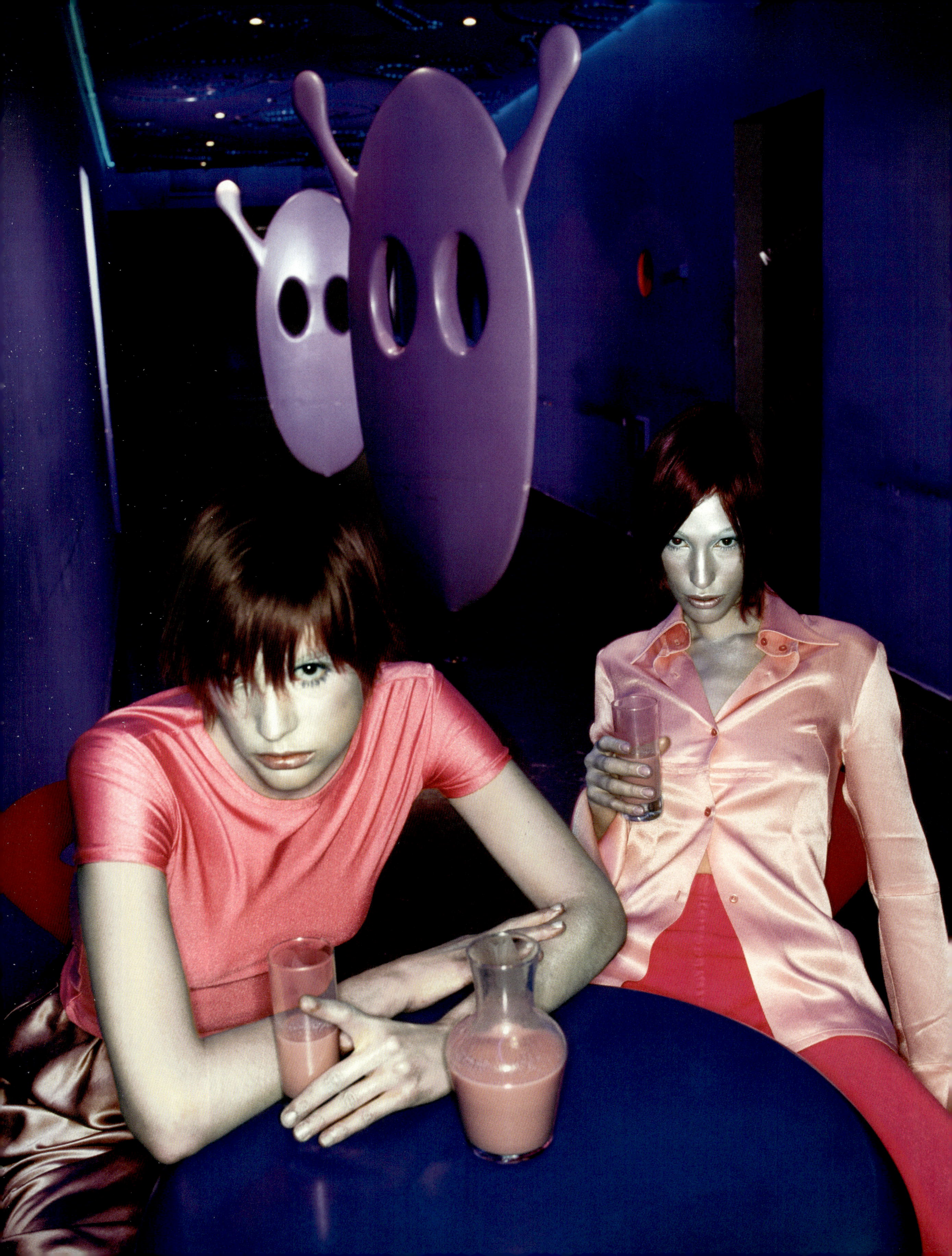

LEISURE LOUNGE
By Andrea Giacobbe
Styled by Maida Gregori Boina
October 1994

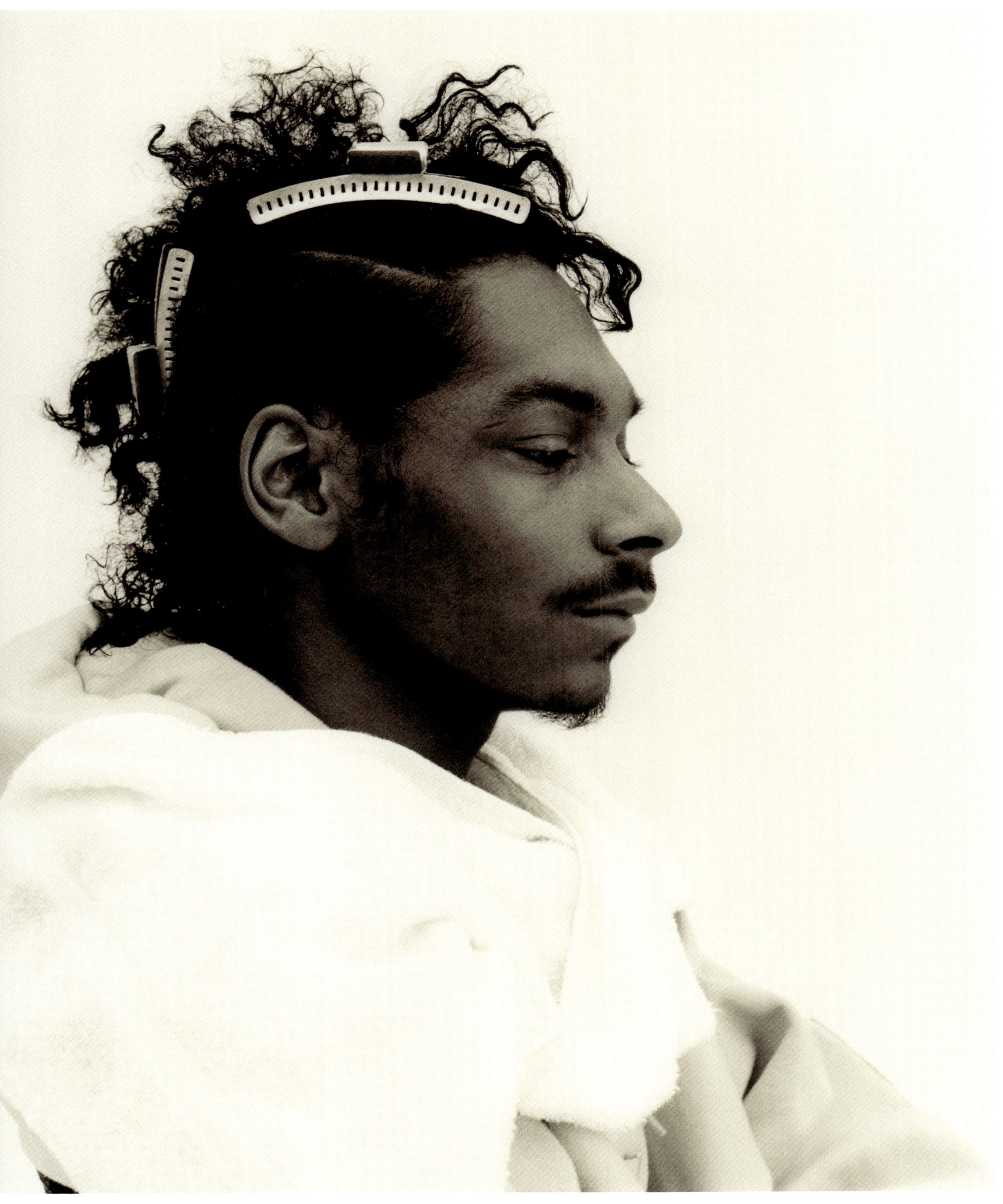

MASSIVE ATTACK
By Donald Milne
December 1995

ALL DAY I DREAM ABOUT...
By Antoinette Aurell
Styled by Cathy Dixon
October 1993

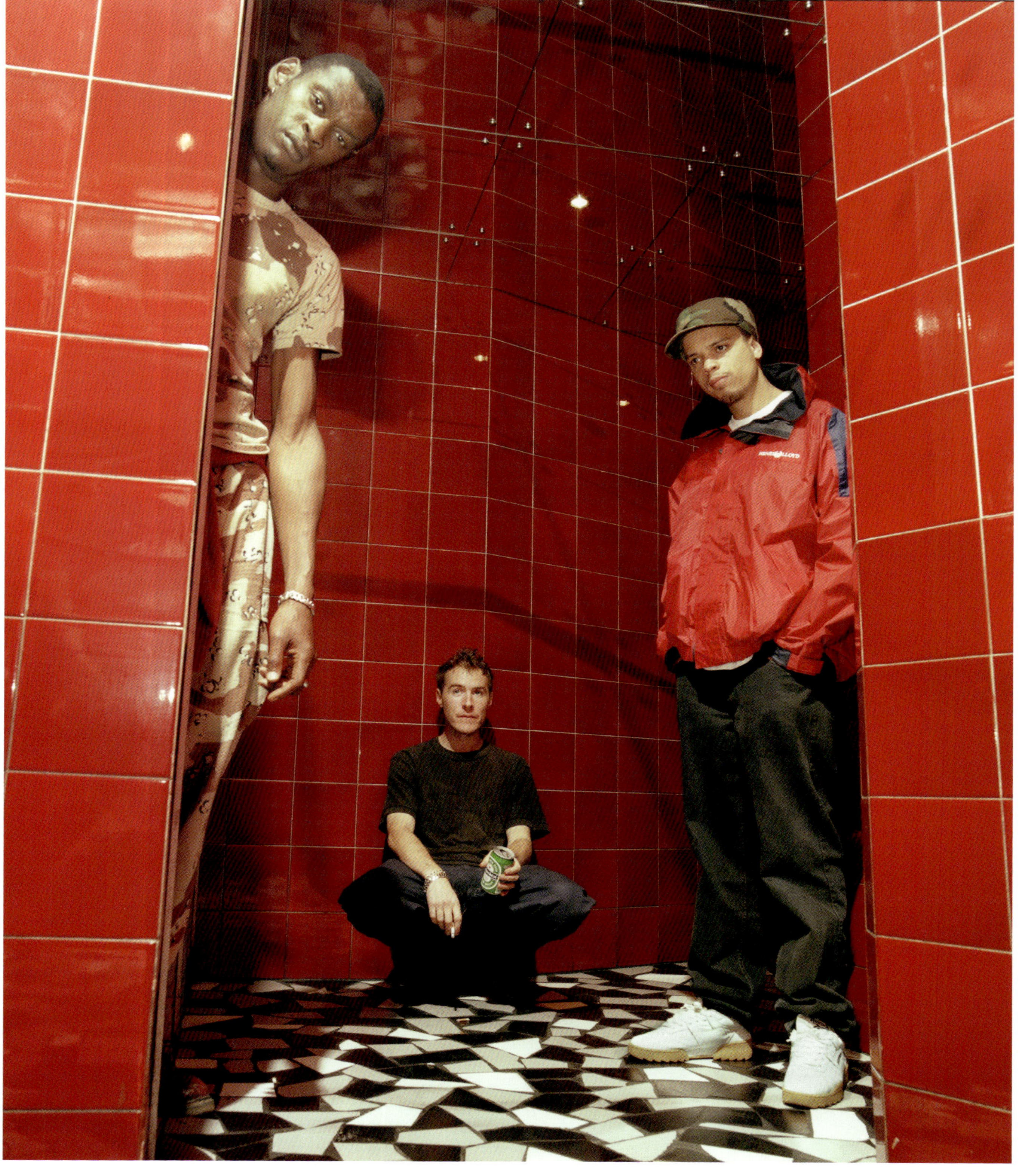

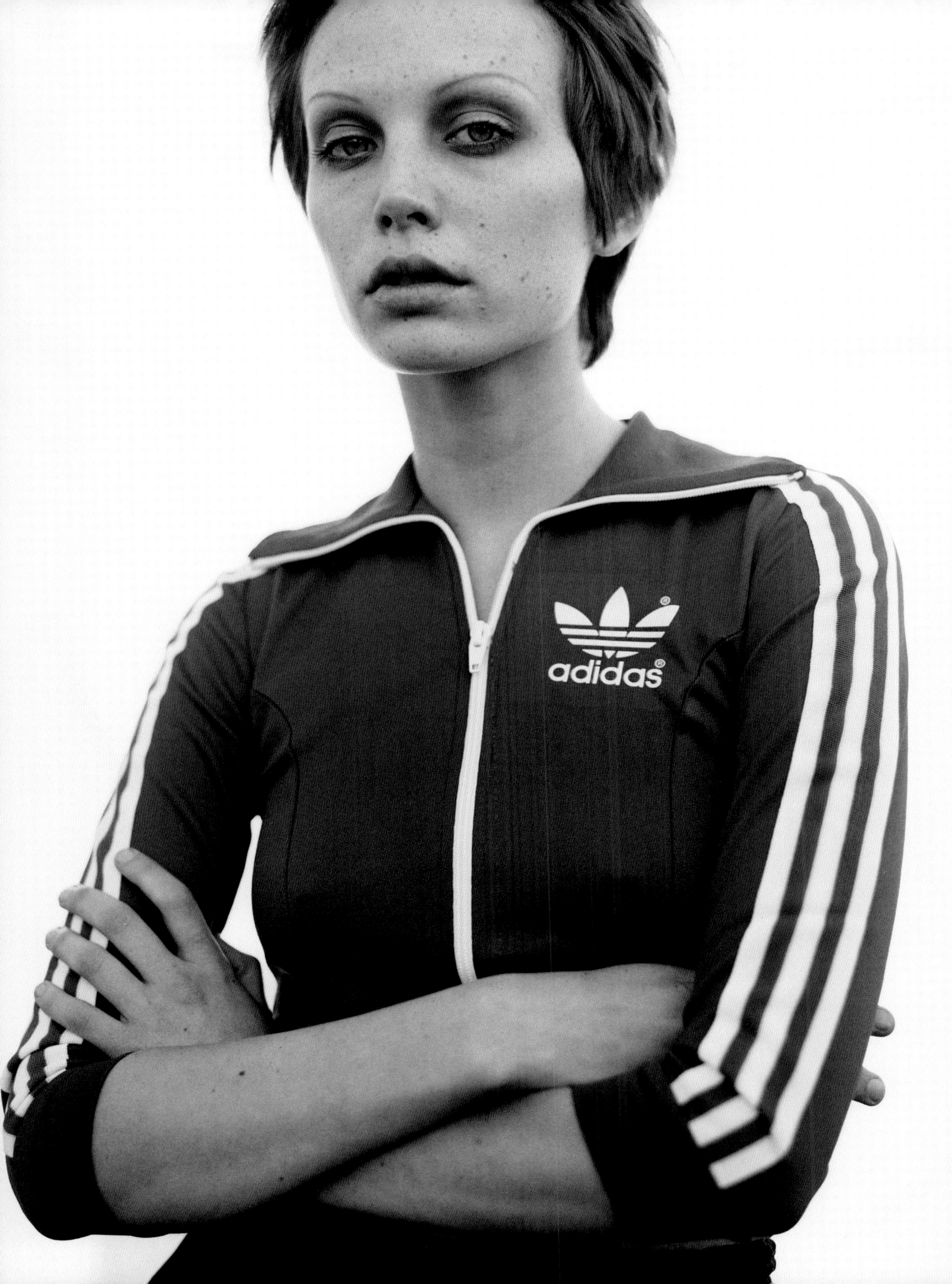

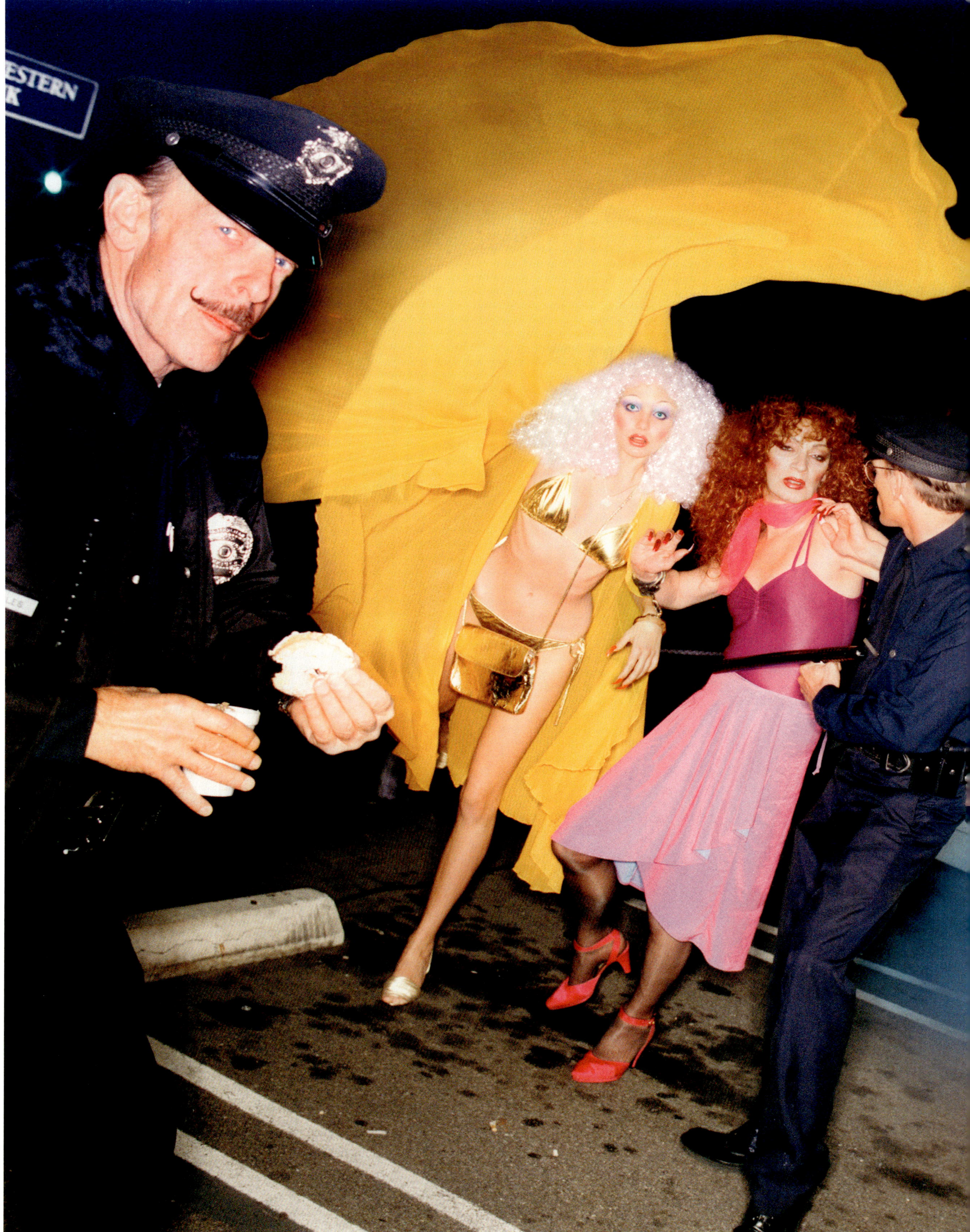
ESTERN
NK

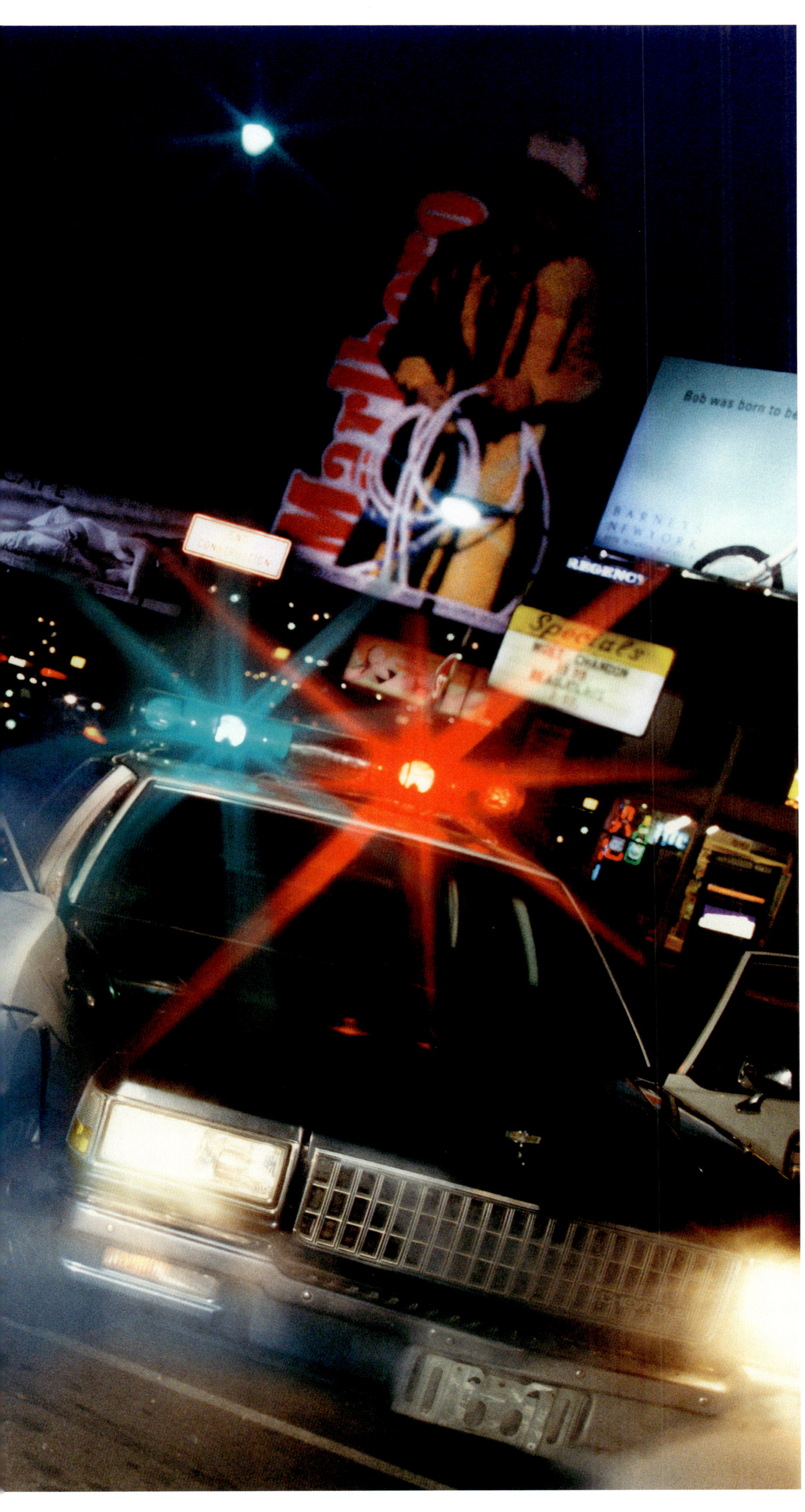

GLACE GIRLS
WITH HOLLY WOODLAWN
By David LaChapelle
Styled by Arianne Phillips
July 1994

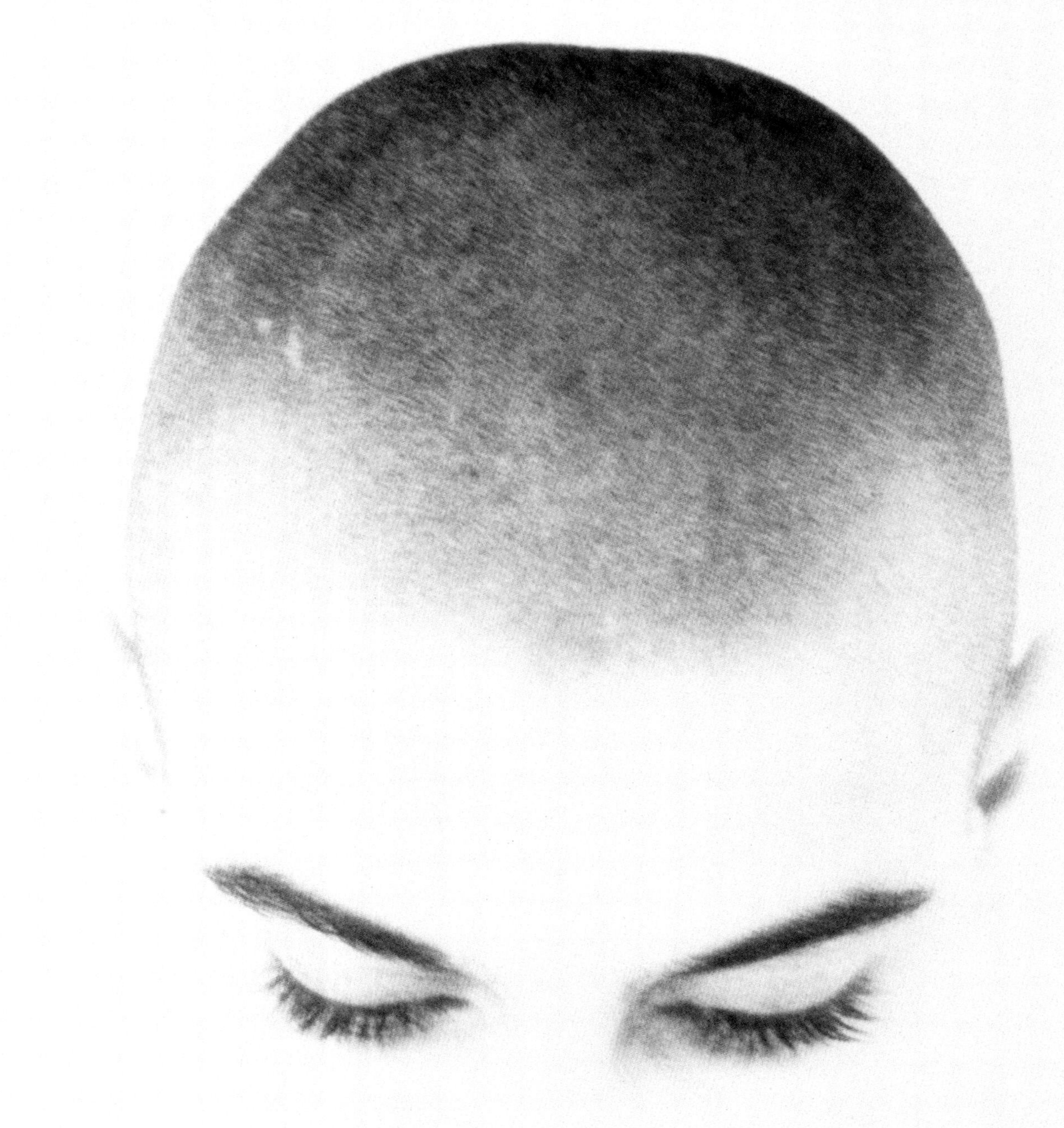

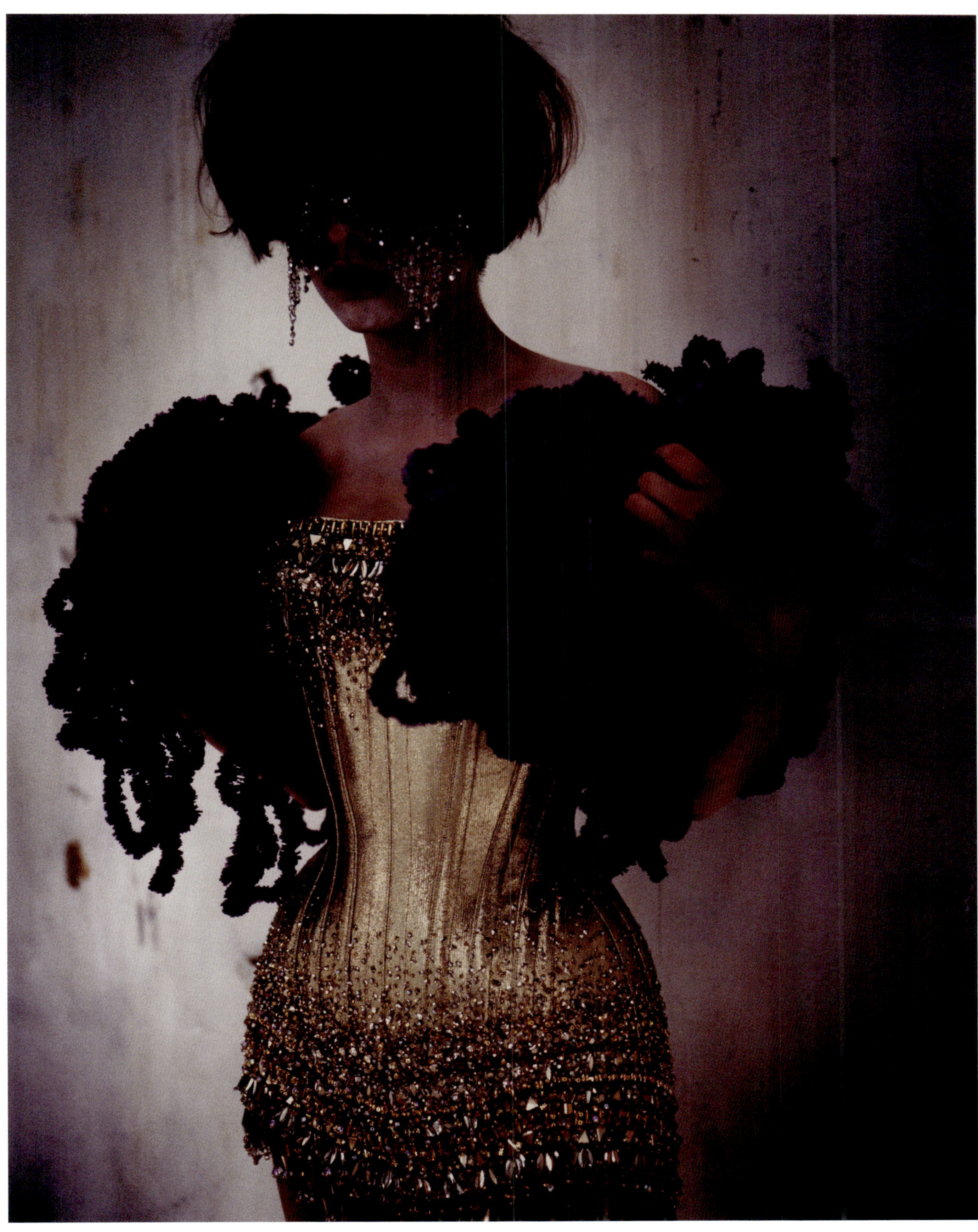

TASTE OF ARSENIC

By Sean Ellis
Styled by Isabella Blow
October 199€

Photographer Sean Ellis and stylist Isabella Blow conjured up cinematic opium-soaked images of dark romance. Their gothic fantasias resonated with the culture, a contemporaneous soundtrack provided by bands such as Nine Inch Nails and Marilyn Manson. Isabella was a close friend of Alexander McQueen, and his designs featured heavily in the duo's fashion stories.
Lee Swillingham, Art Director

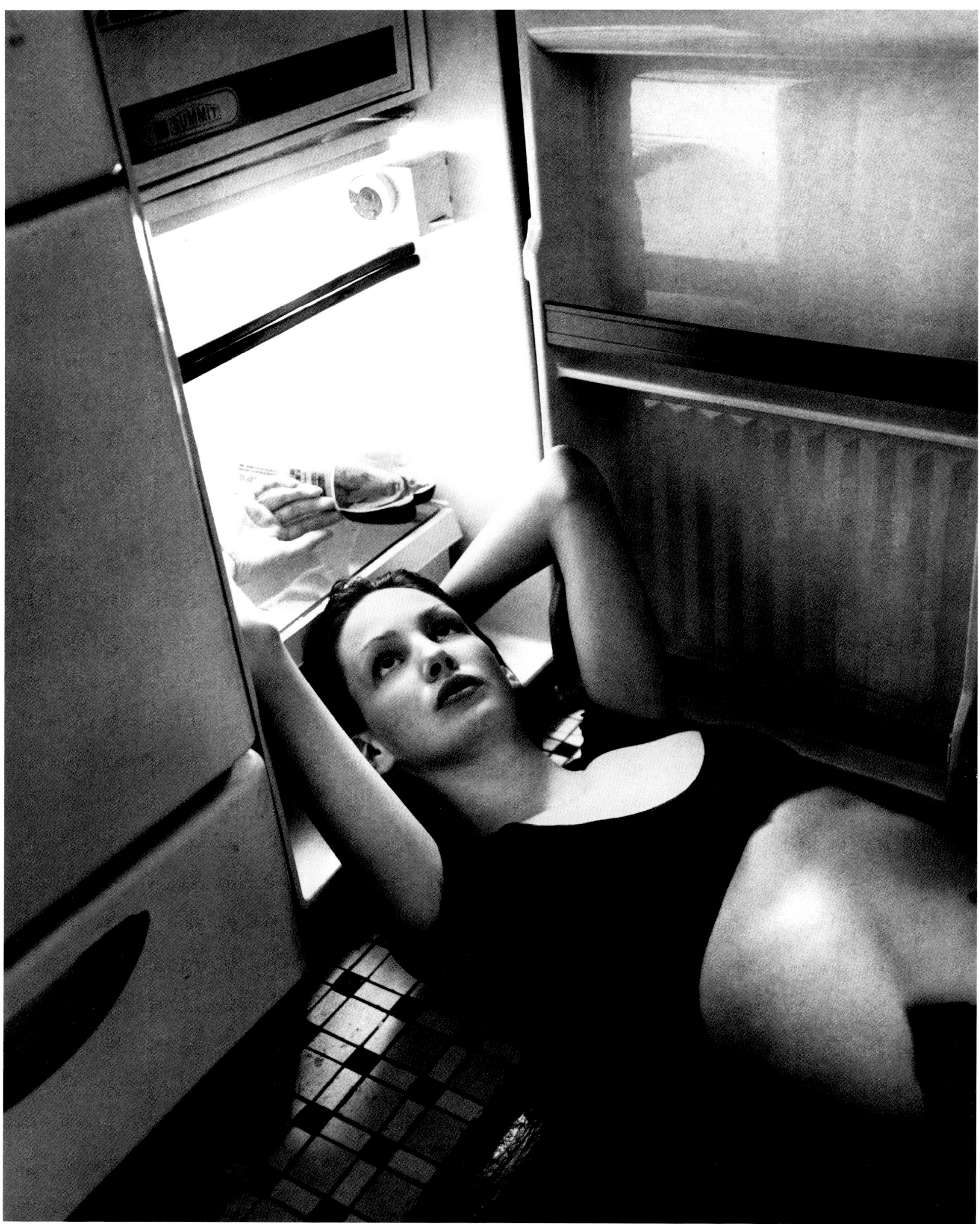

AMERICA EATS ITS YOUNG
By Glen Luchford
Styled by Dodi Greganti
July 1993

MEANWHILE...
By David LaChapelle
Styled by Arianne Phillips
February 1994

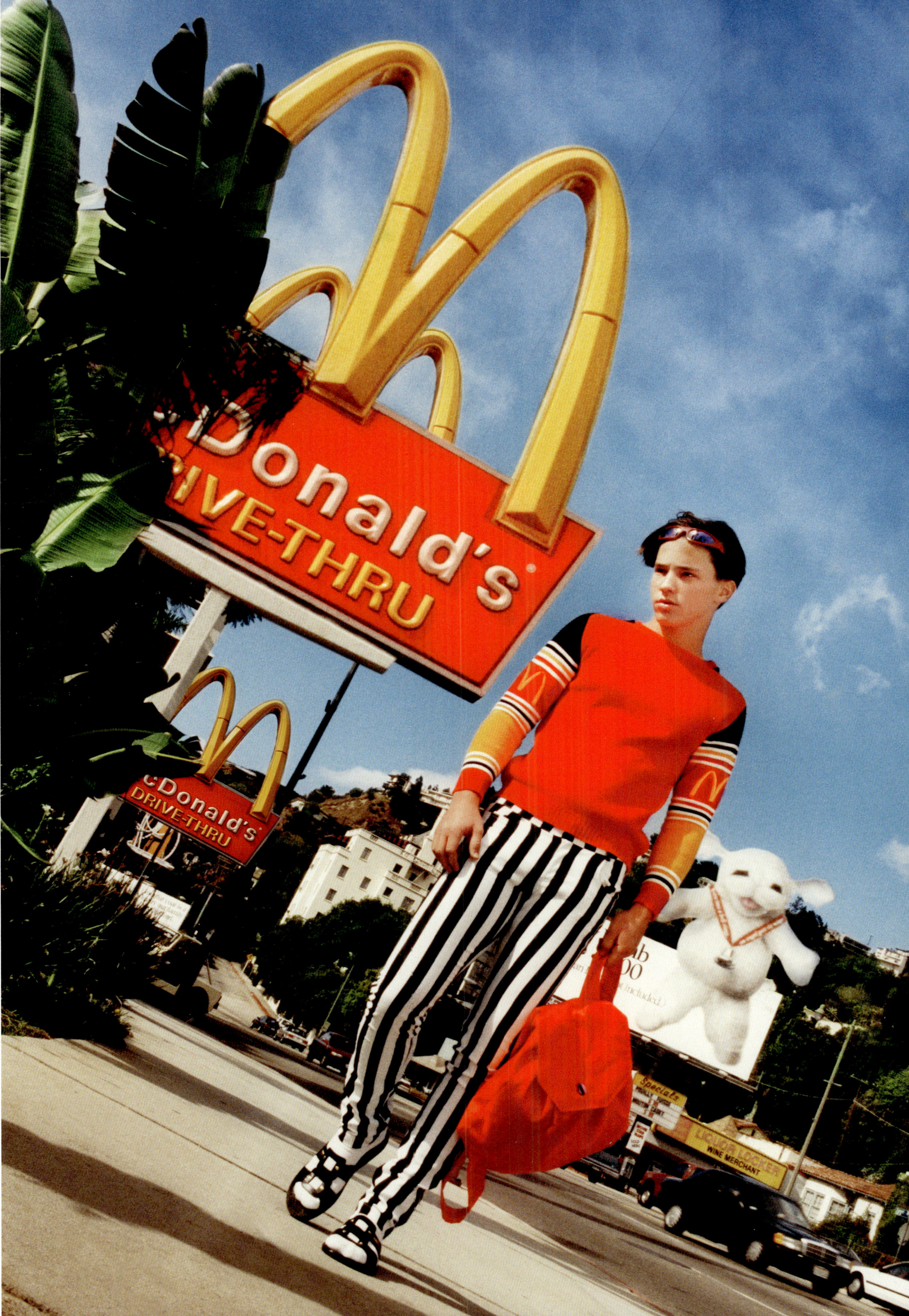

cDonald's
RIVE-THRU
cDonald's
DRIVE-THRU
LIQUOR LOCKER
WINE MERCHANT
Specials

MODERN LOVE
By Glen Luchford
Styled by Judy Blame
February 1992

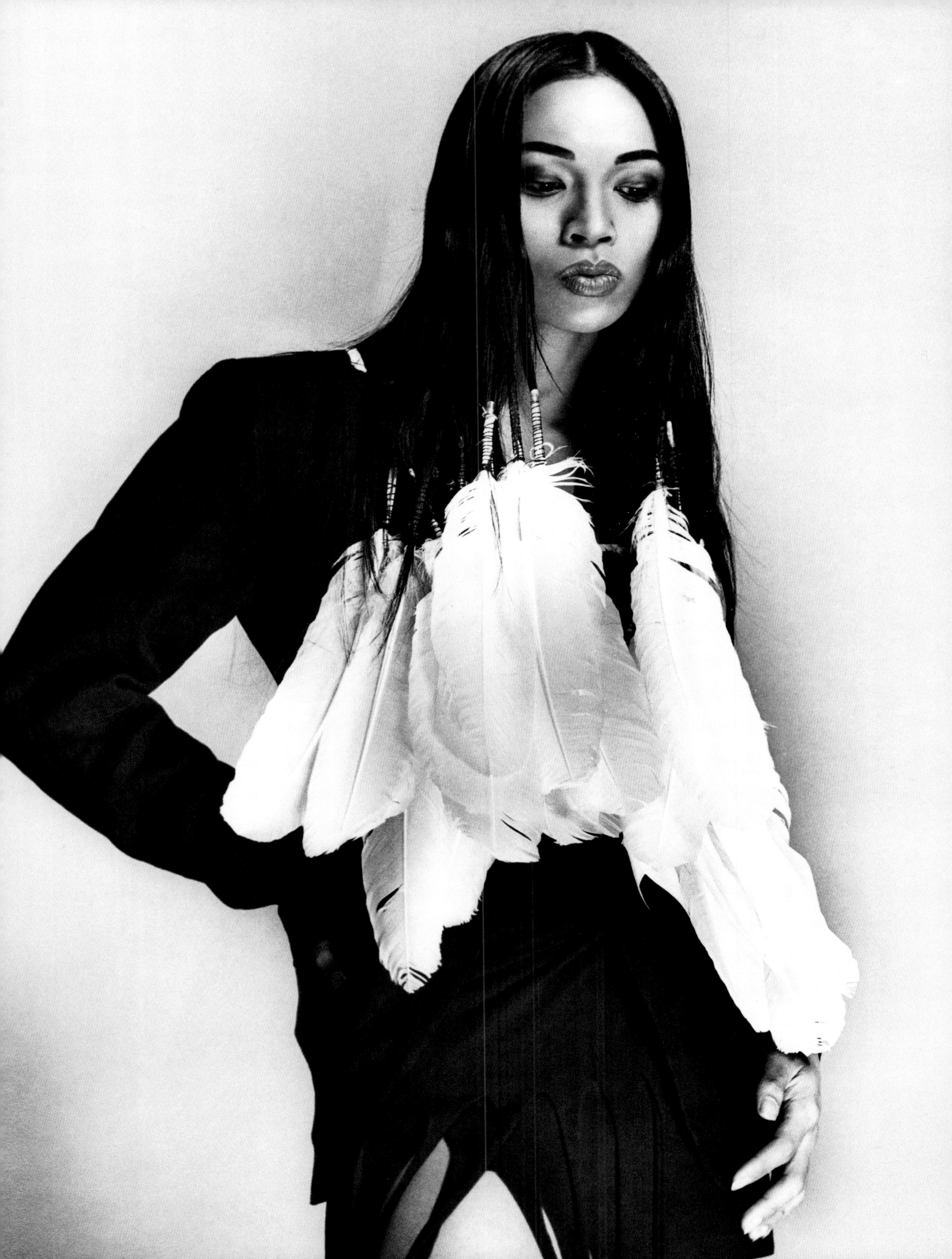

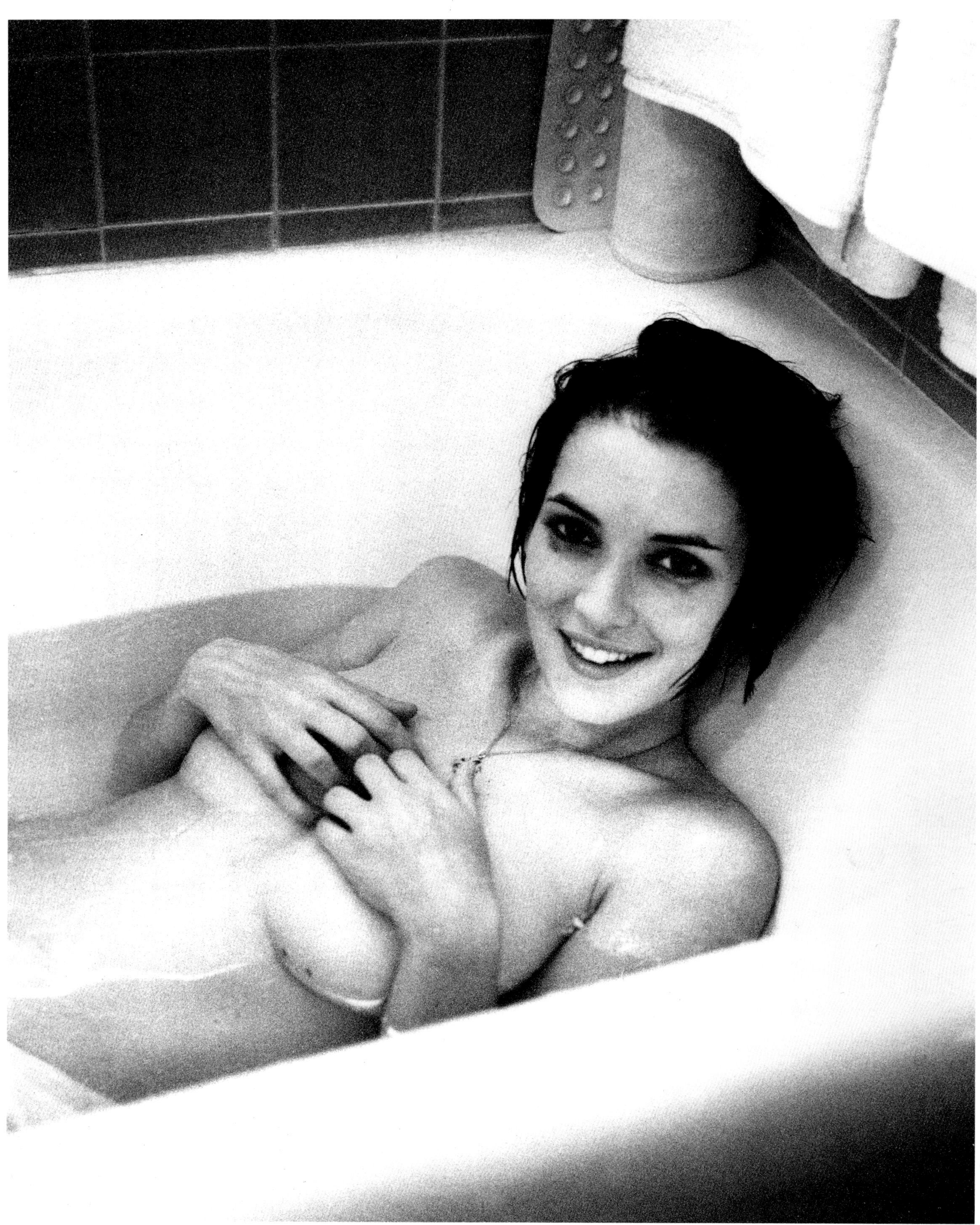

WINONA RYDER
By Ellen von Unwerth
Styled by Camilla Nickerson
July 1994

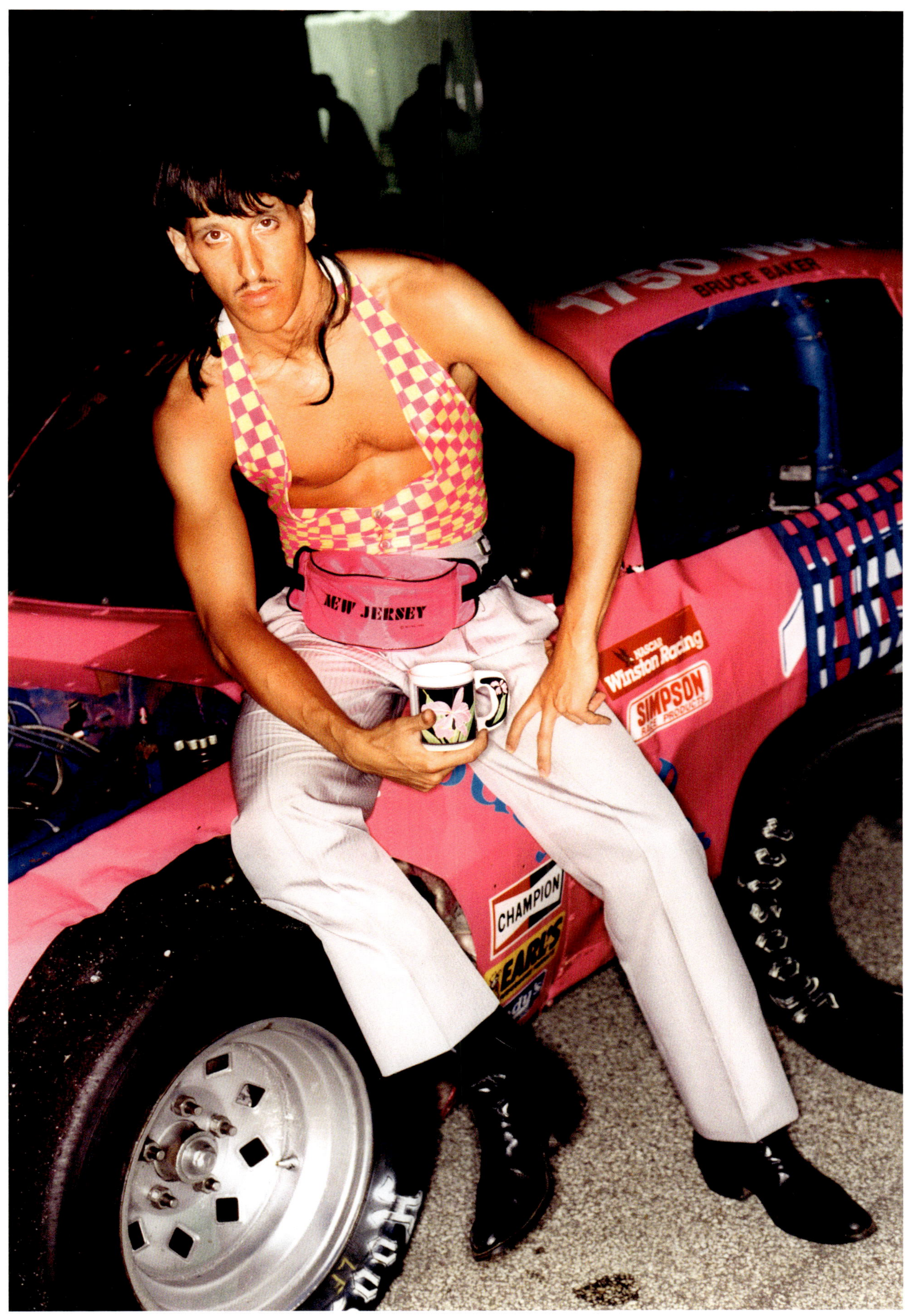

CRUISERS
By David LaChapelle
Styled by Justin Kelvin
and Martin Keehn
September 1994

Following pages
NEW SKOOL
By Norman Watson
Styled by Karl Templer
and Derick Procope
November 1991

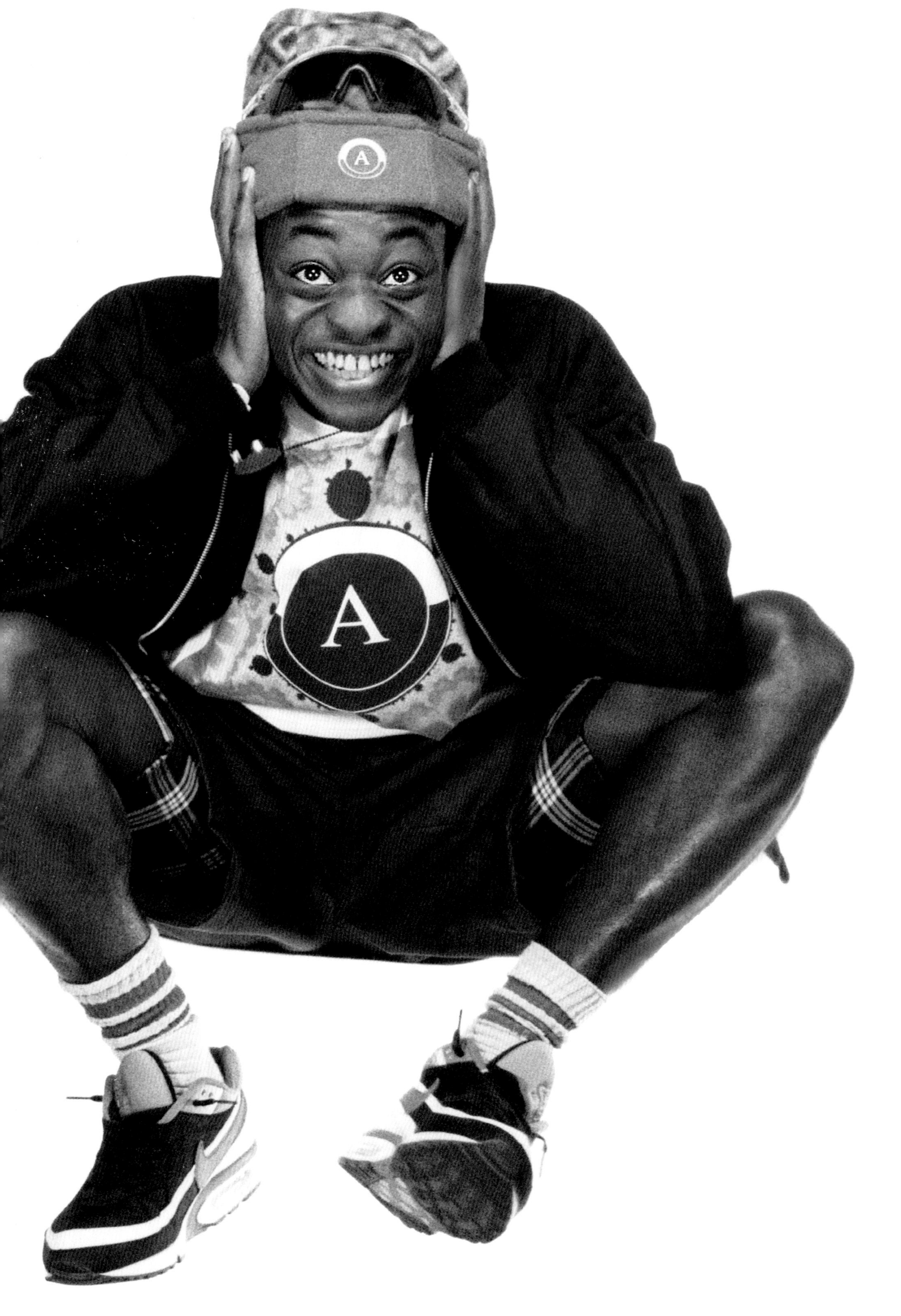

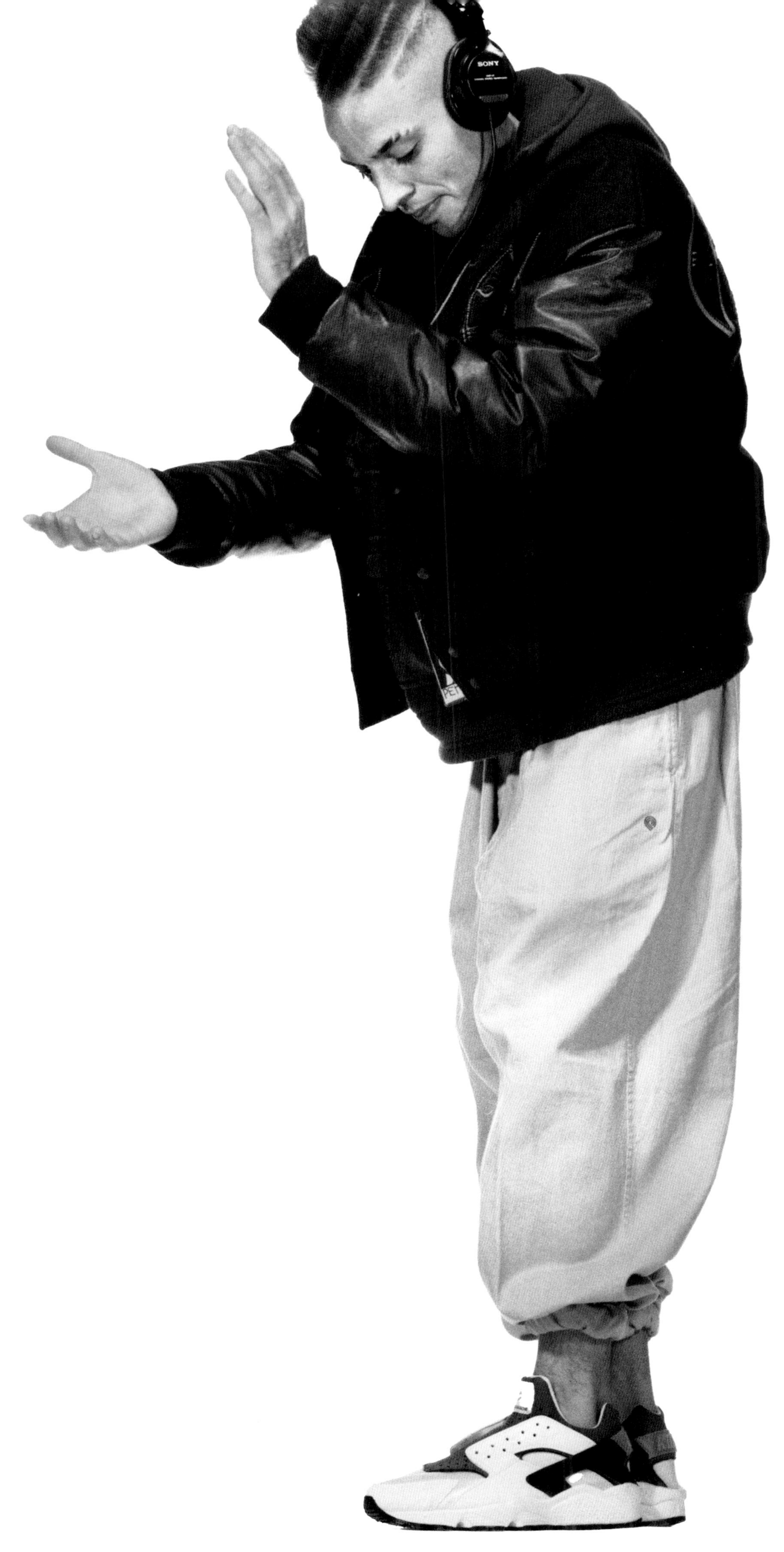

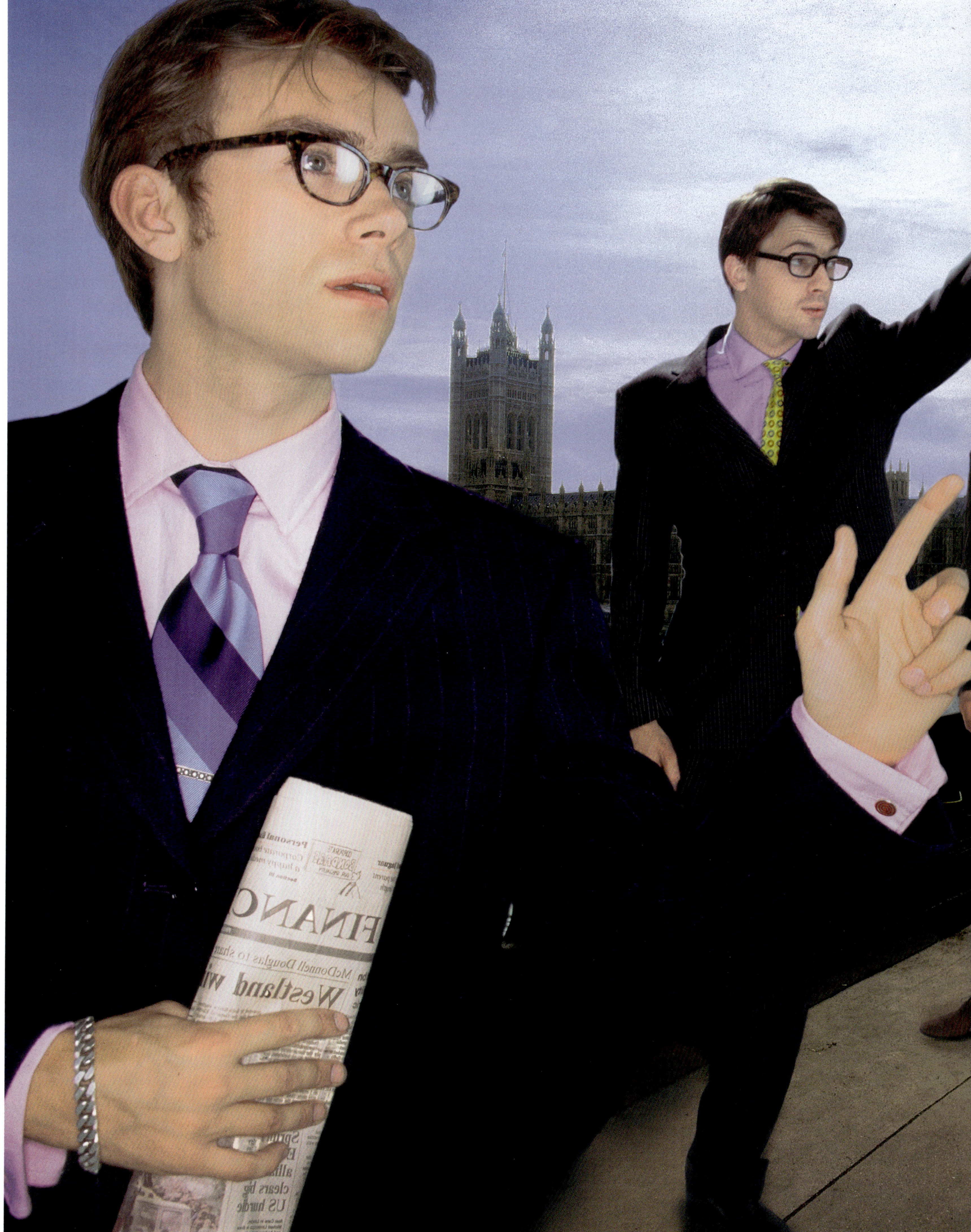

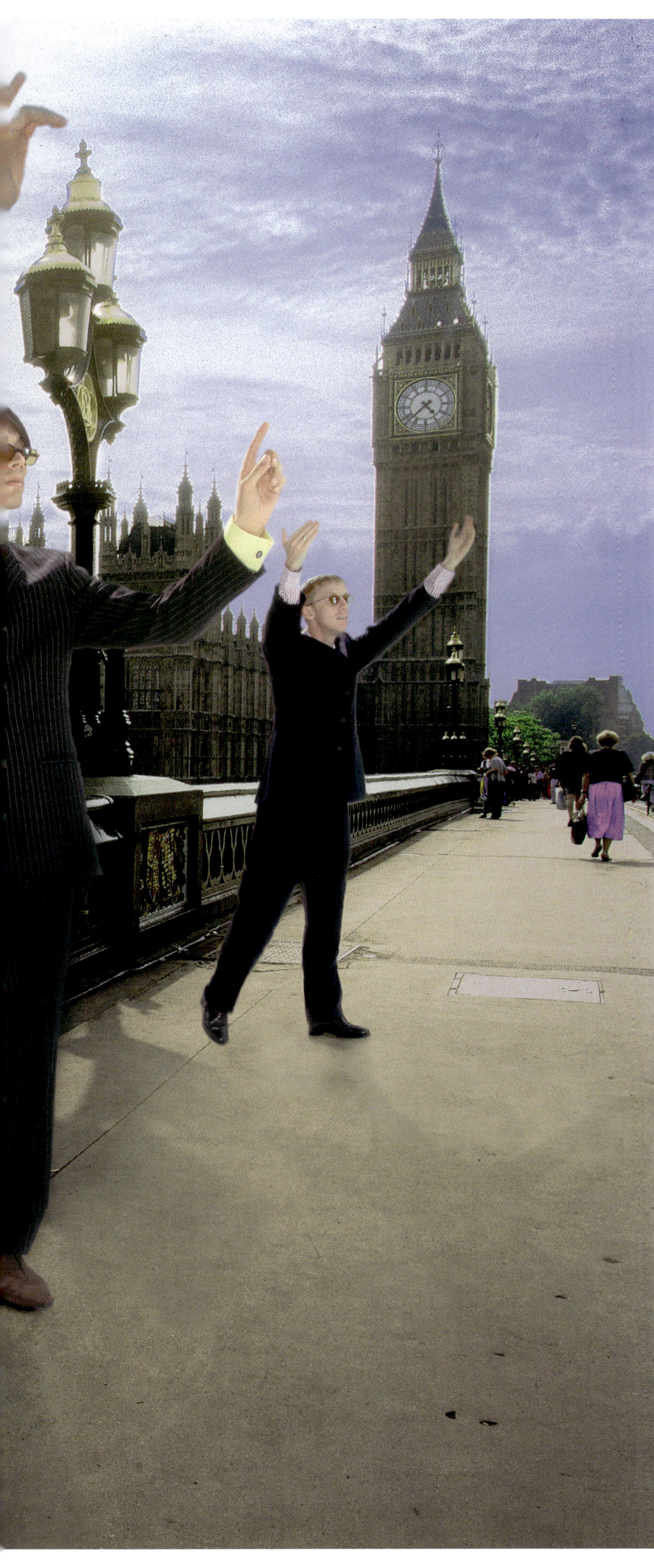

We were making editorial that was about the imagery first, not about the credits and stockists' lists. *The Face* wasn't a directory; it was visual entertainment.

BLUR
By Andrea Giacobbe
Styled by Greg Fay
and Justin Laurie
September 1995

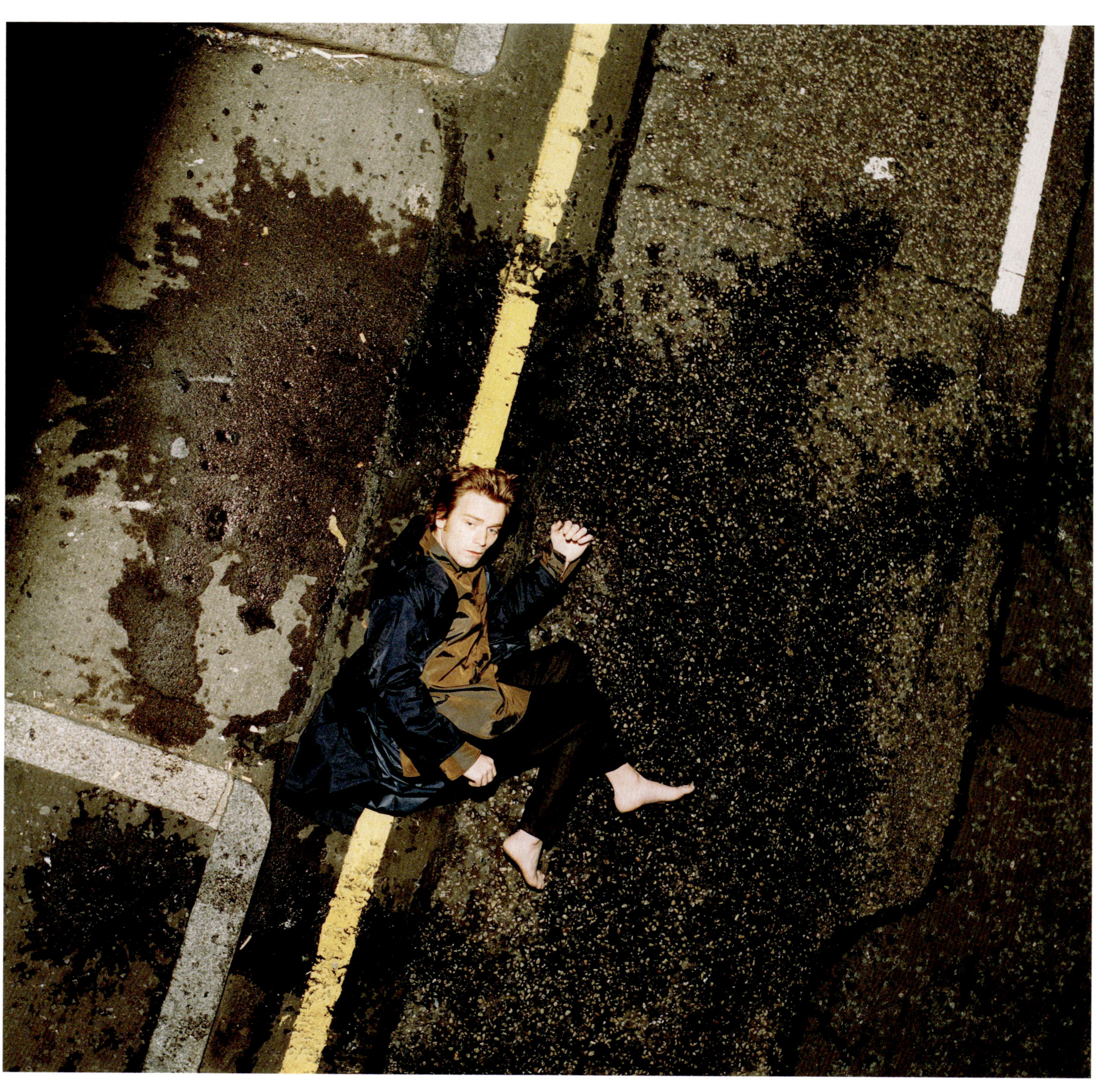

EWAN MCGREGOR
By Norbert Schoerner
Styled by Adam Howe
November 1996

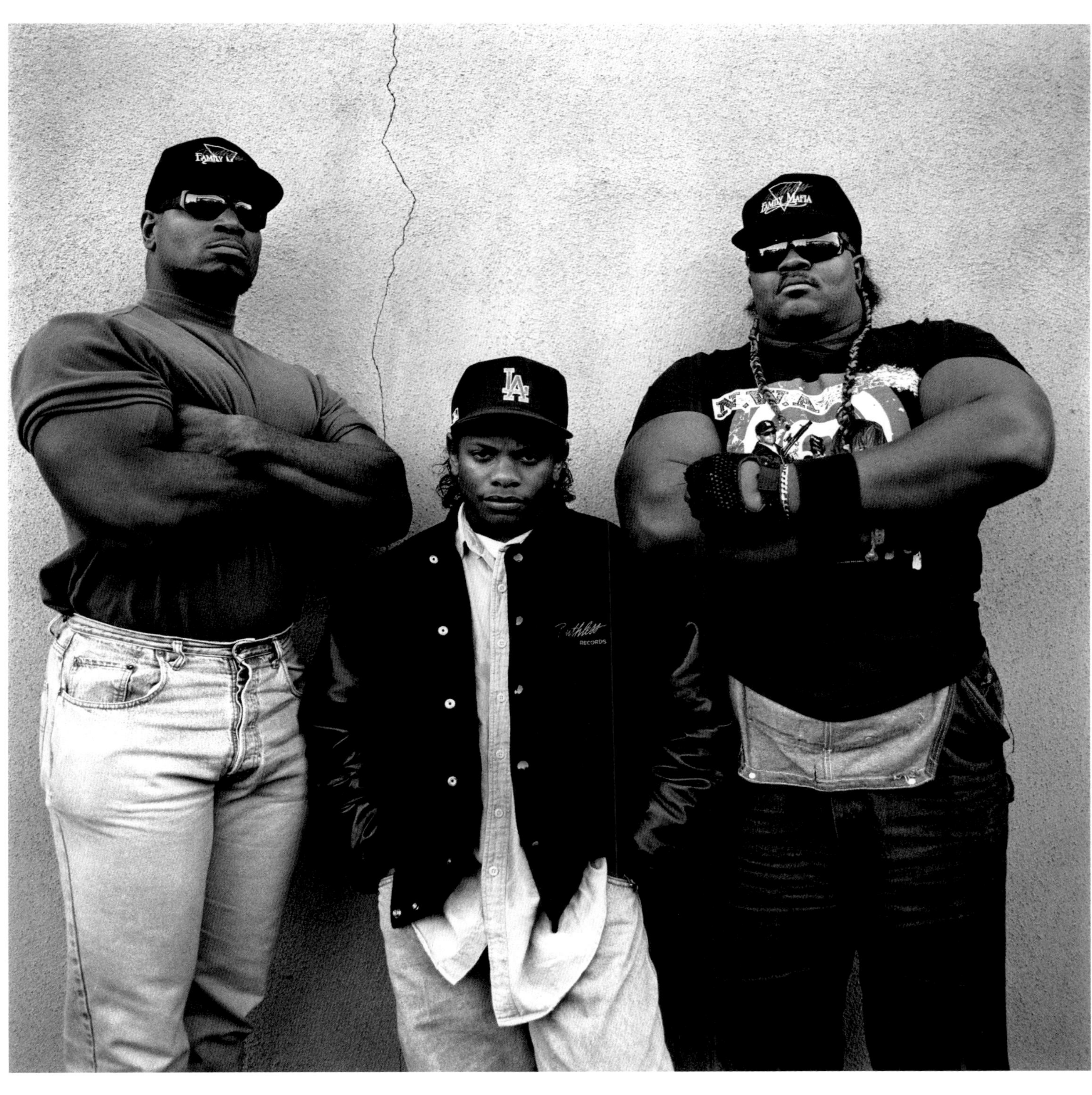

EAZY-E
By Anton Corbijn
January 1992

THE CHEMICAL BROTHERS
By Andrea Giacobbe
Styled by Greg Fay and Justin Laurie
April 1997

TOM JONES
By David LaChapelle
December 1994

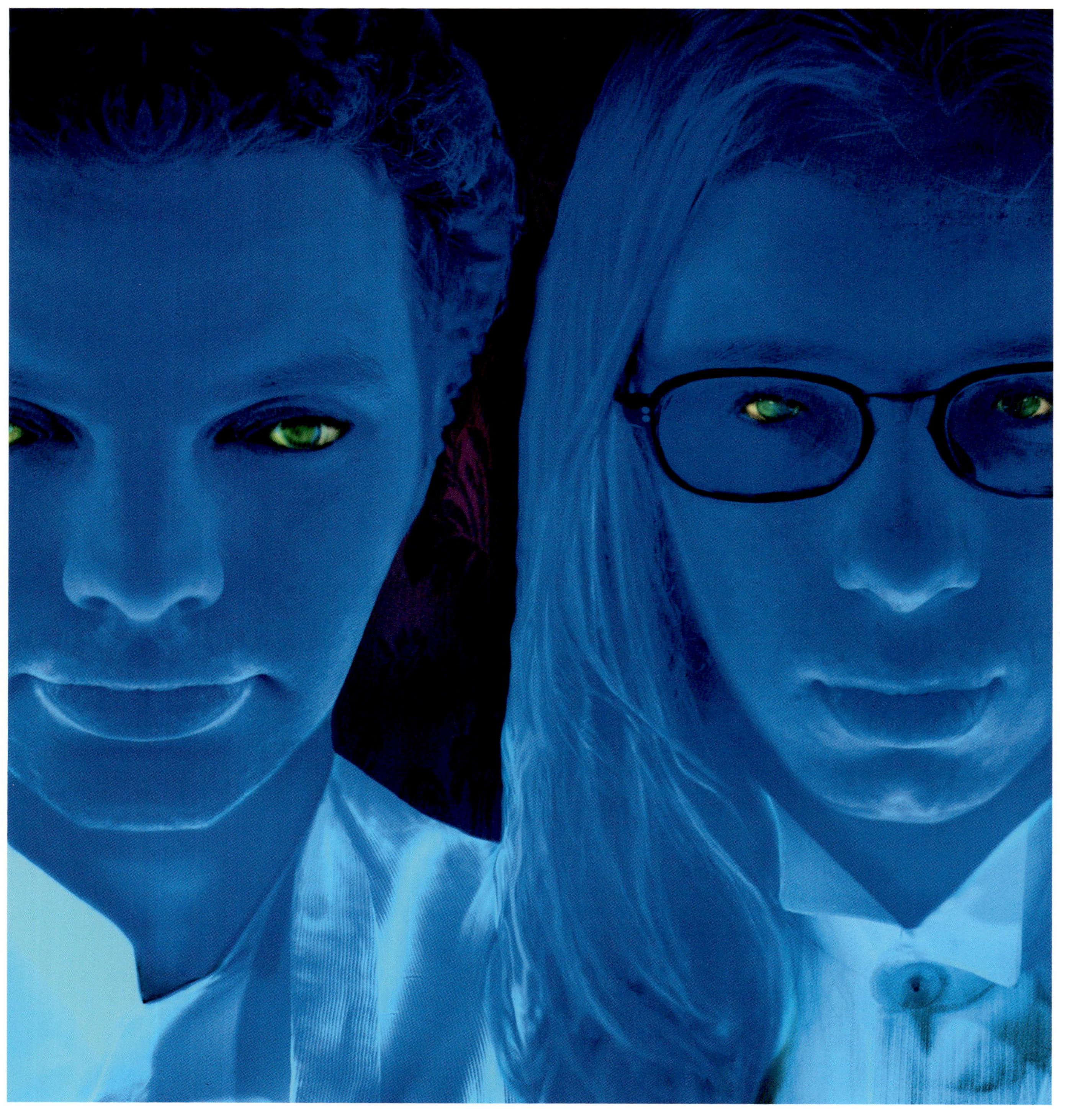

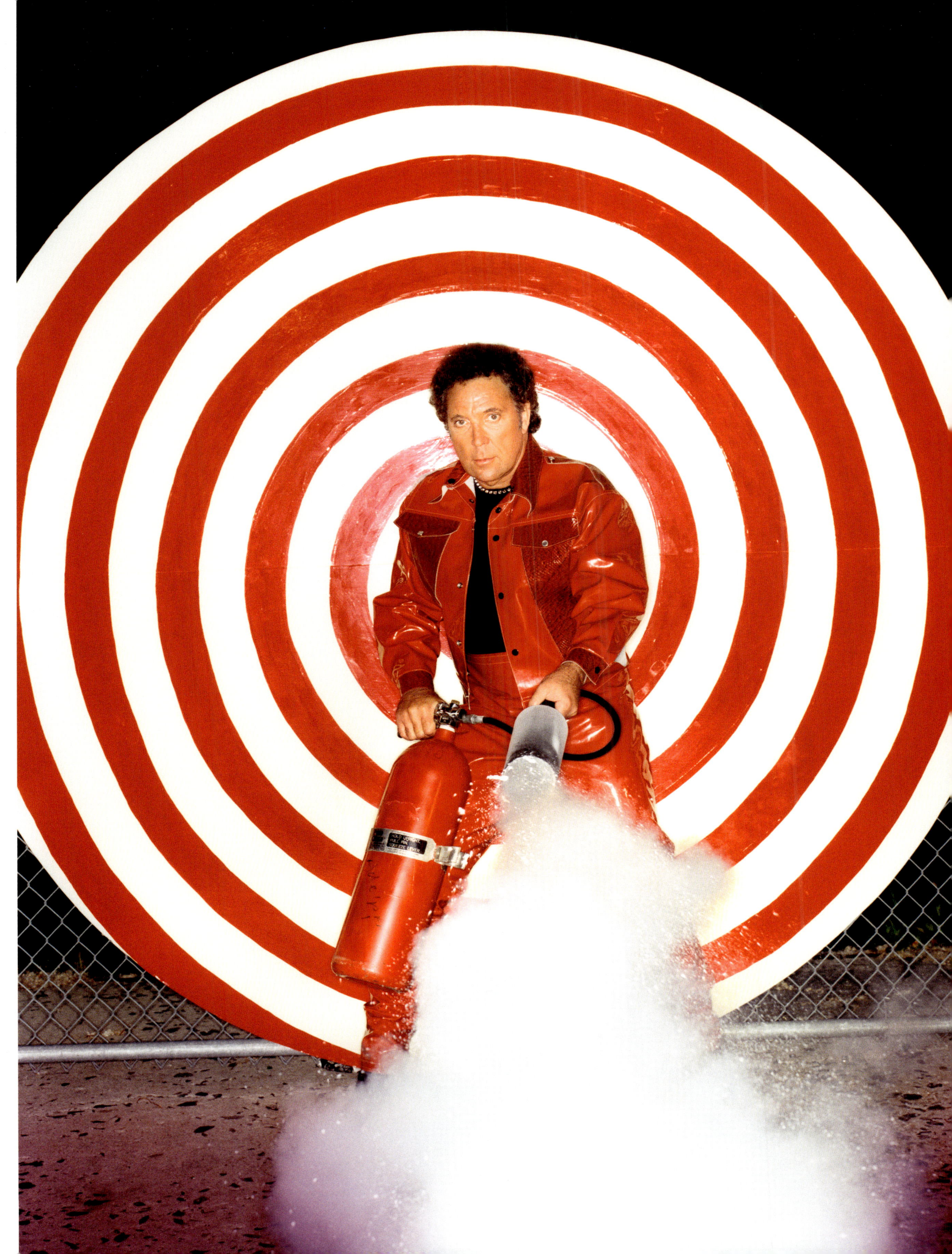

The Face was naturally open to observations from, say, a more casual point of view in terms of fashion coverage. Takes on what people were actually wearing felt totally normal. Street casting took over. The models all had character. The influence of music, raving, parties, football. All things being connected. *Sarf Coastin'* was all about a sense of exuberant realism, it's suburban but in technicolor. No sophisticated narrative, just girls making each other laugh.
Polly Banks

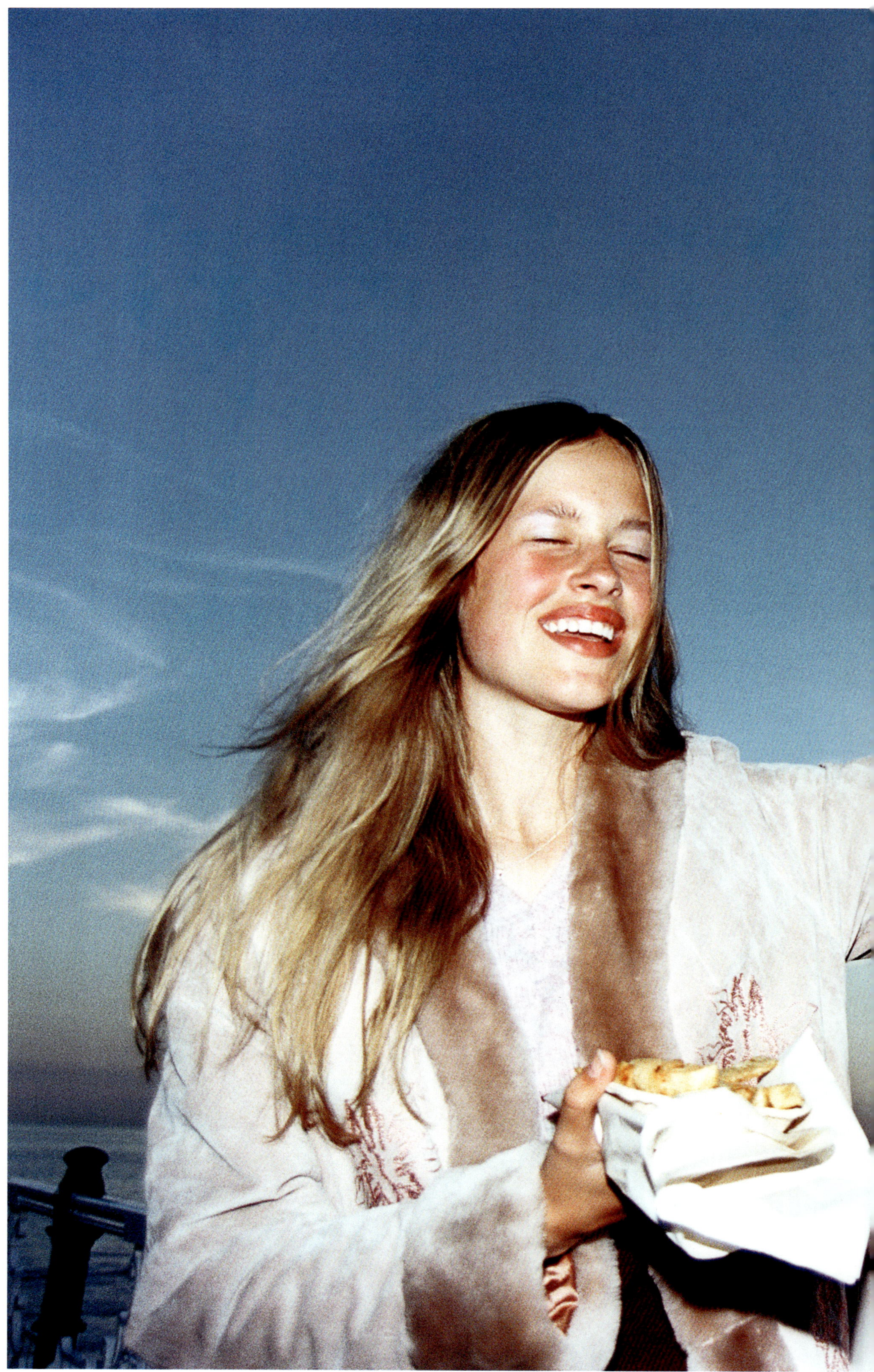

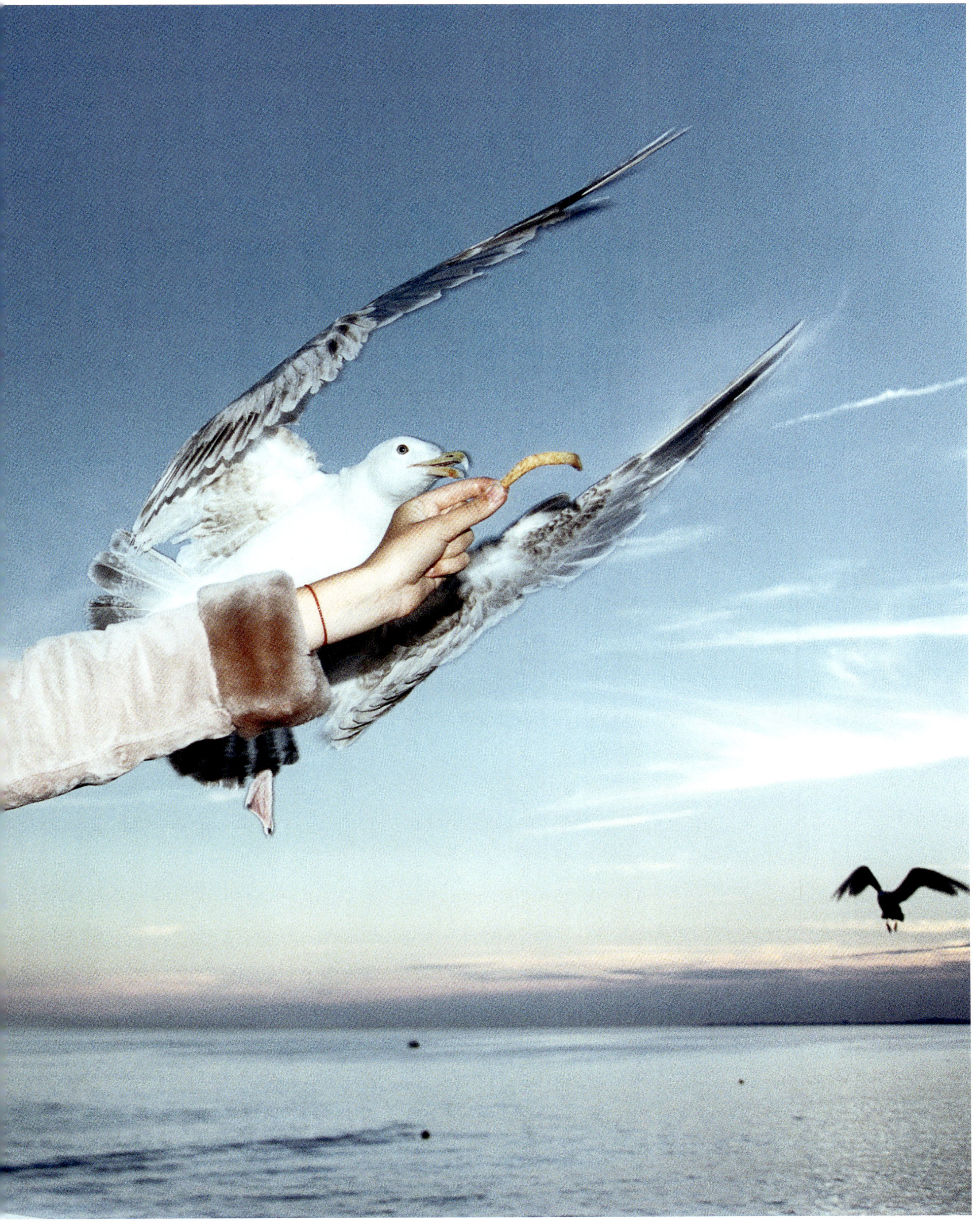

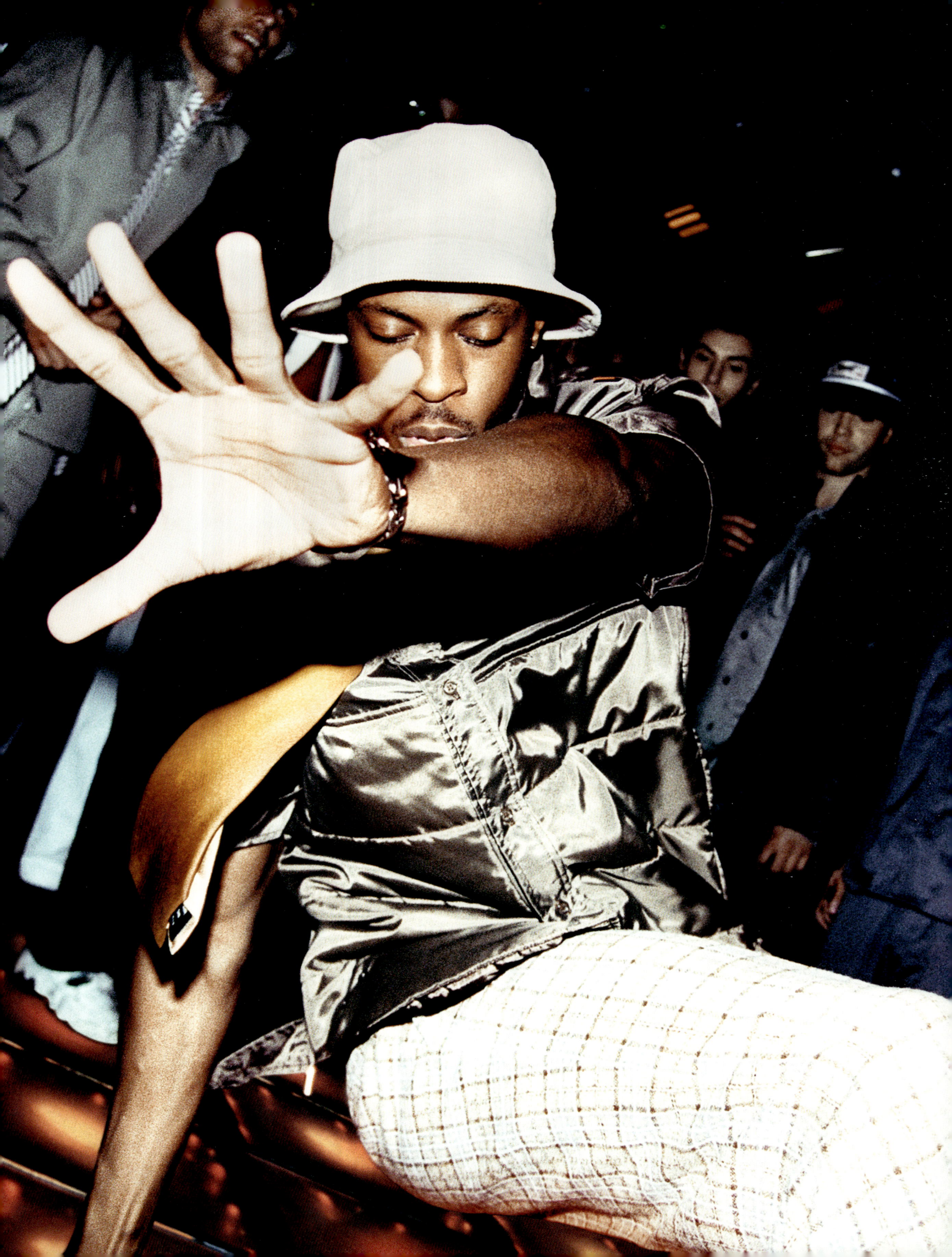

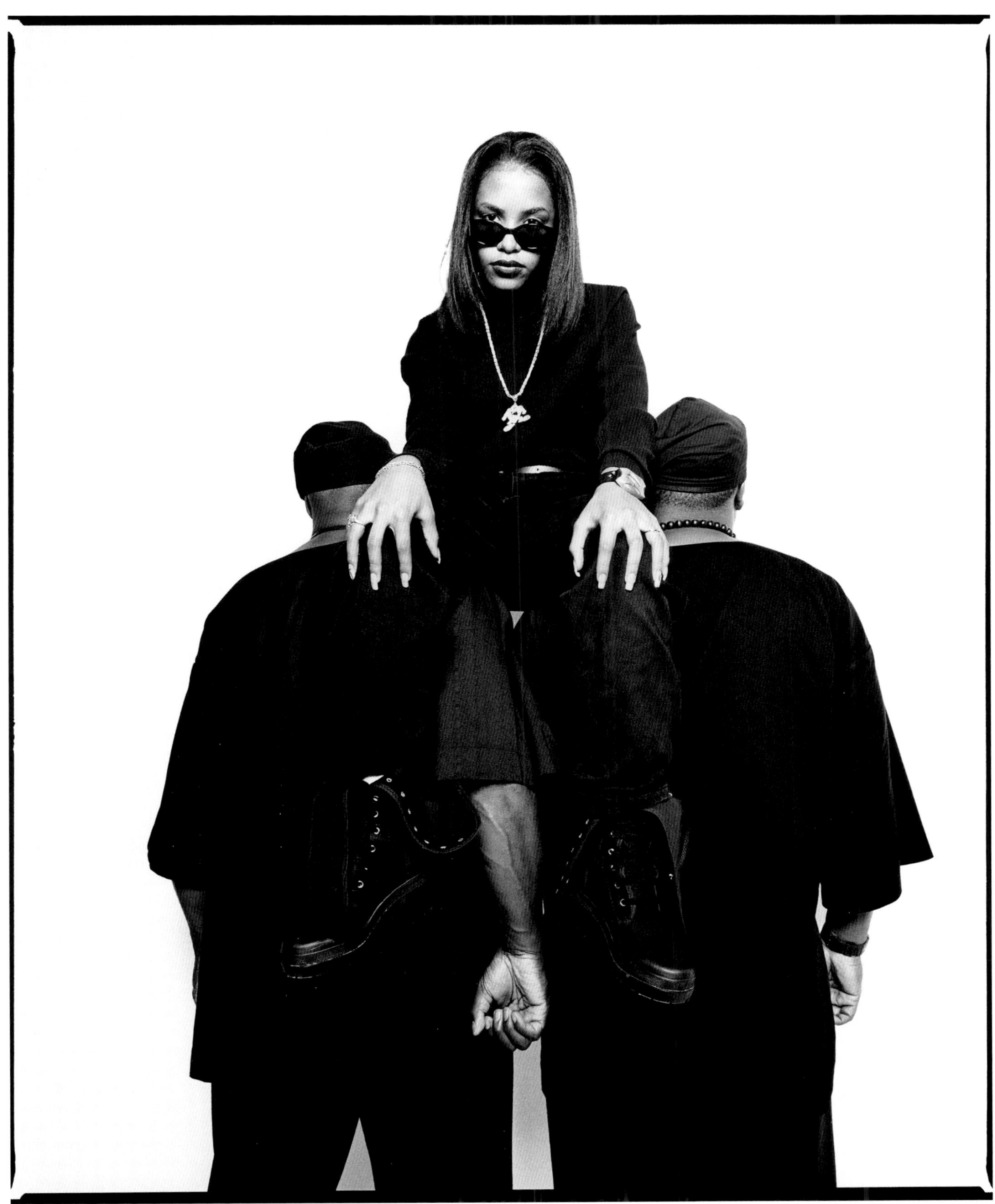

Up until this point, most of my shoots with celebrities had been pretty low key. There may have been a publicist, as well as hair and make-up, but often it was just me, an assistant and the subject. This shoot was my first experience with an entourage – friends, managers, hair and make-up, stylists – and two bodyguards. I asked the guys if they would be willing to pose, and they didn't need much persuading.
Jake Chessum

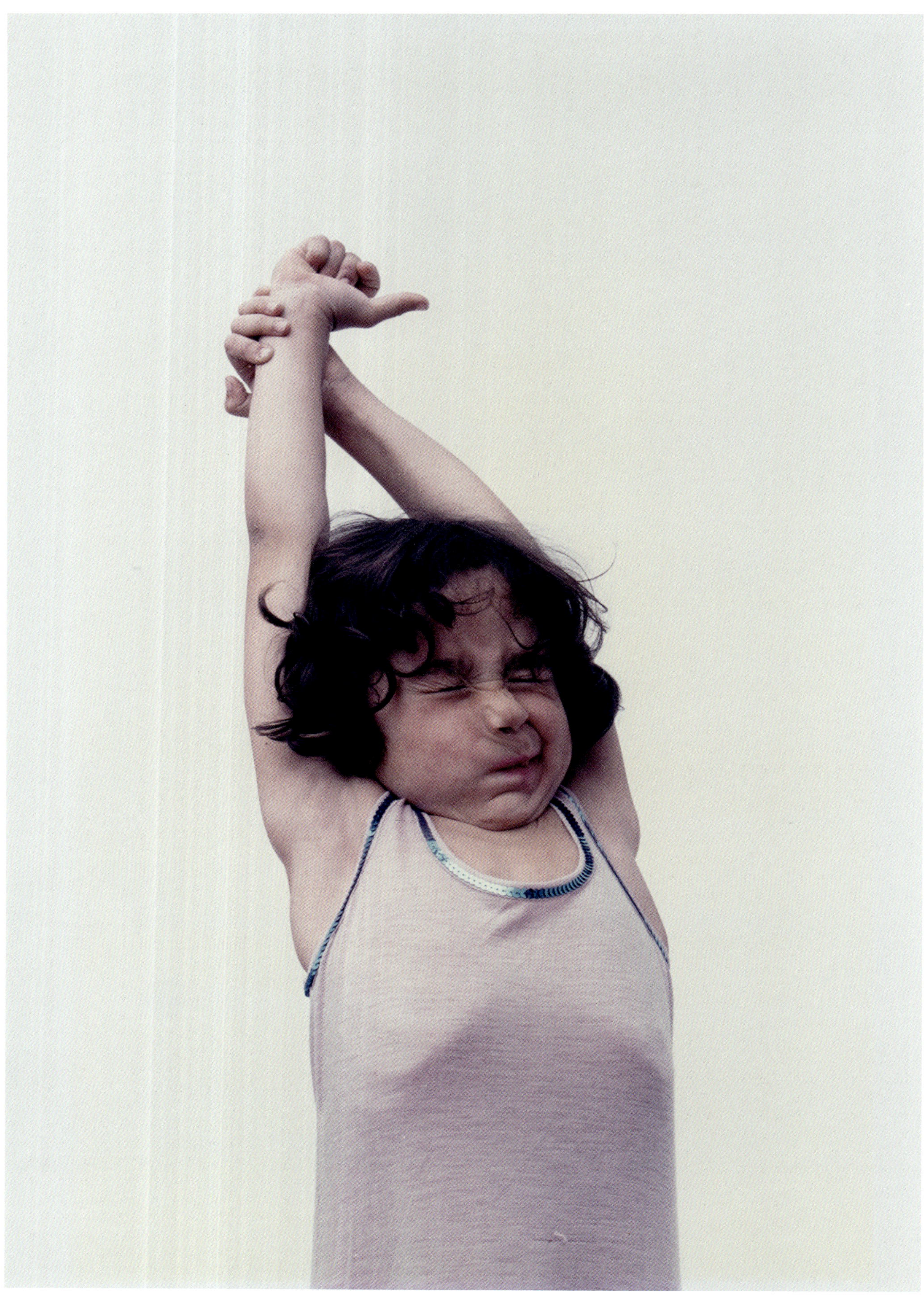

KINDER
By Bettina Komenda
Styled by Sabina Schreder
August 1997

THE PILGRIMS
By Martina Hoogland Ivanow
Styled by Alister Mackie
March 1998

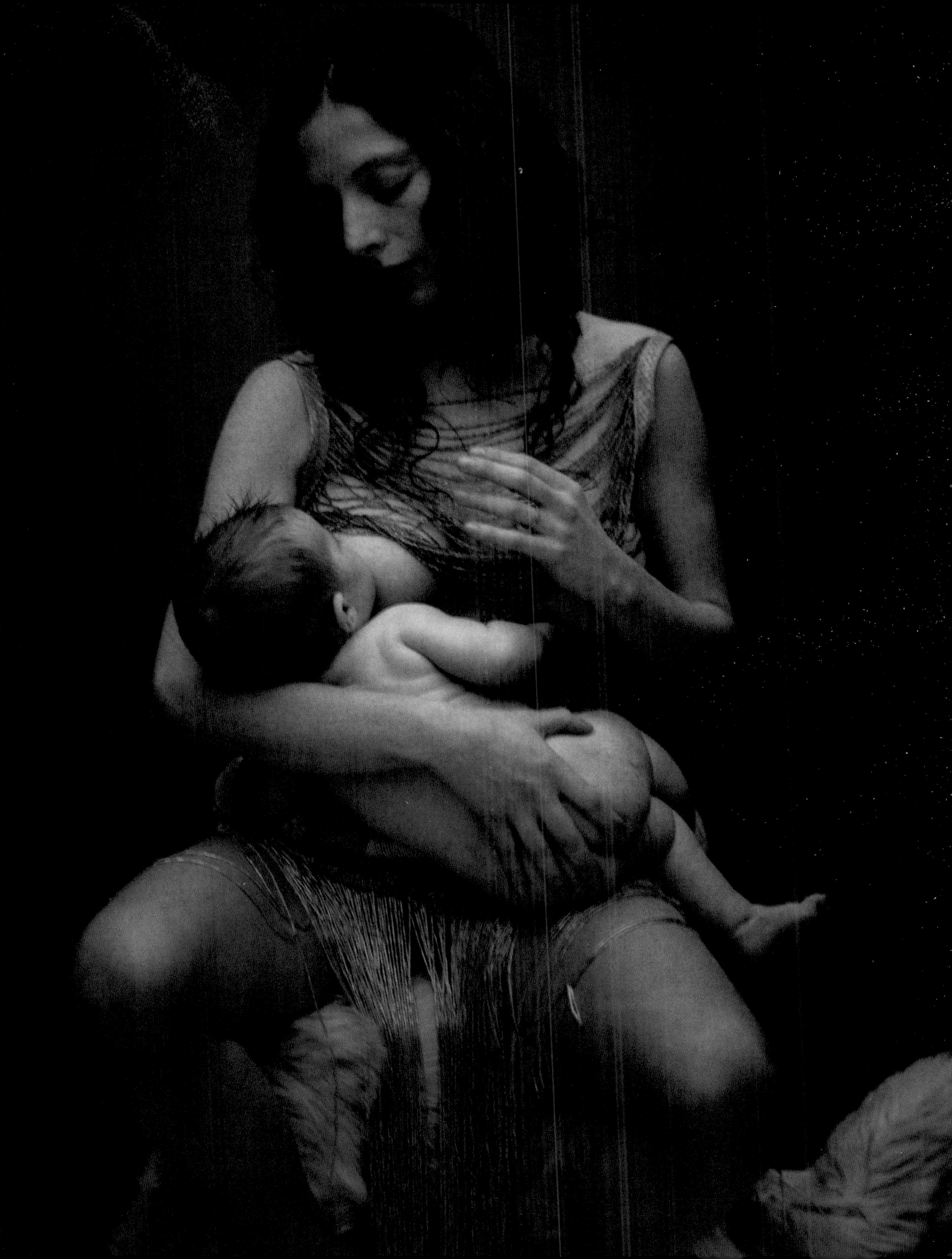

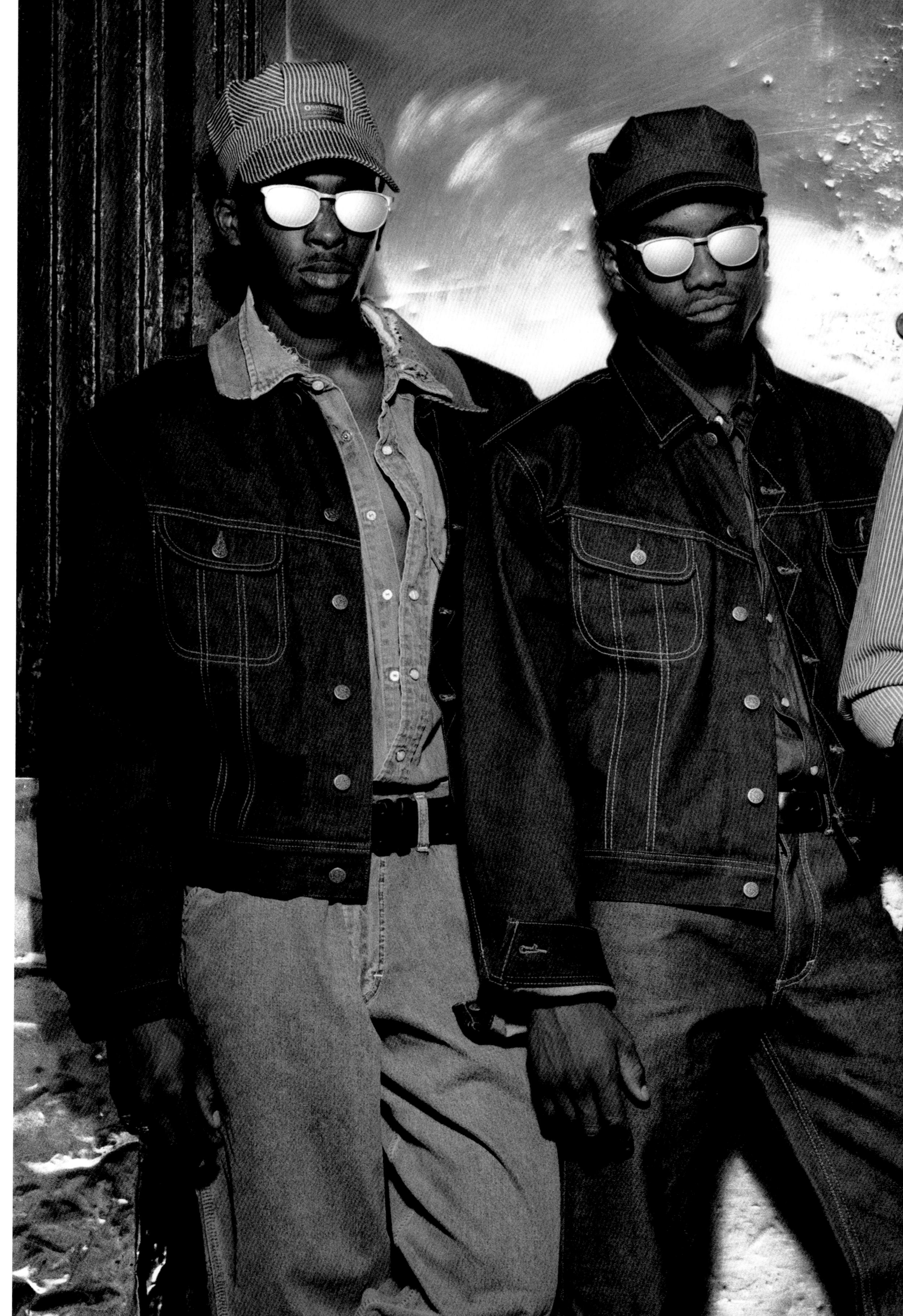

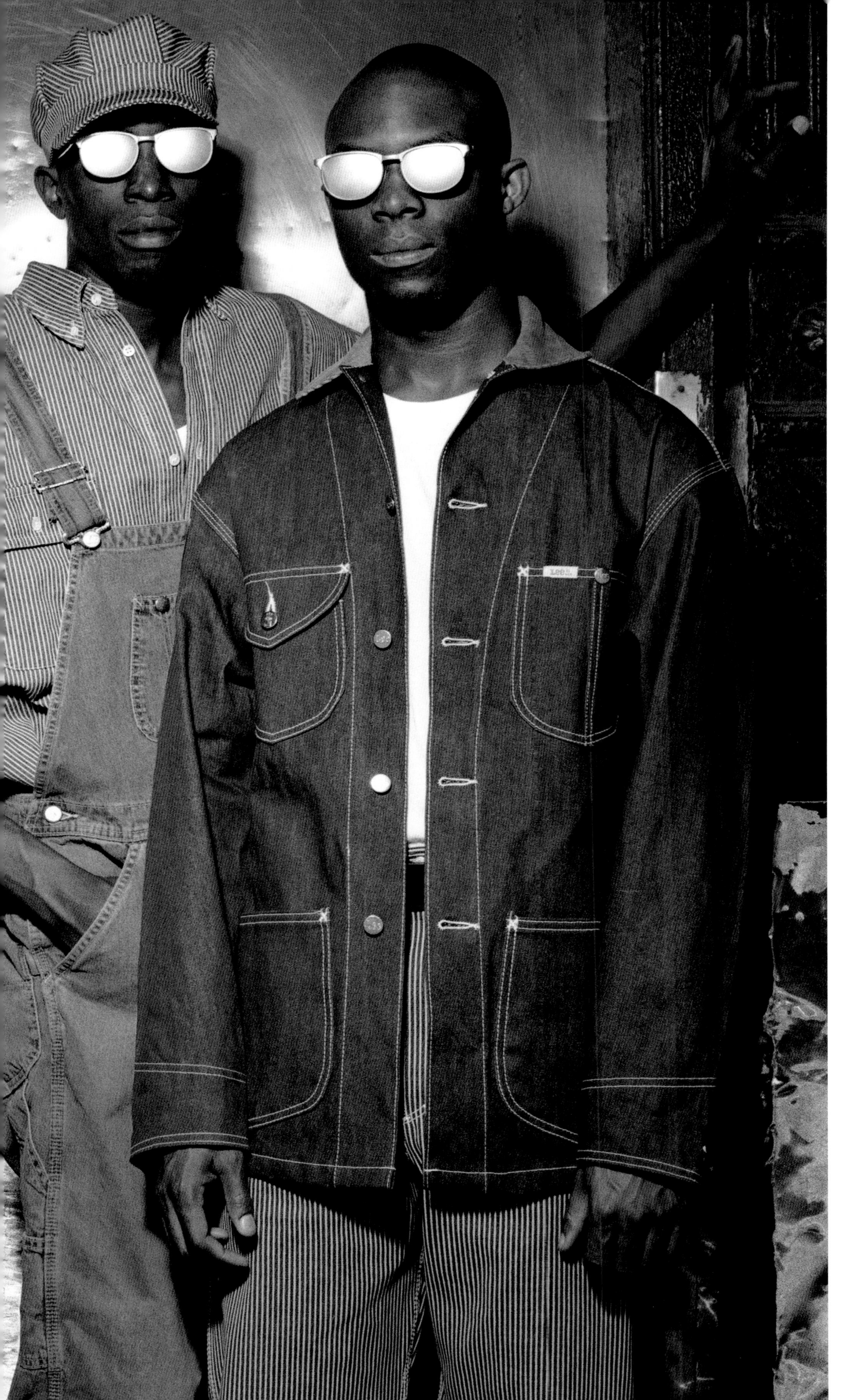

UNTITLED
By Albert Watson
Styled by Karl Templer
and Derick Procope
September 1992

I always bought
The Face from
the minute I was
aware of it. Then
when I was asked
to work for them,
I jumped at it.
Albert Watson

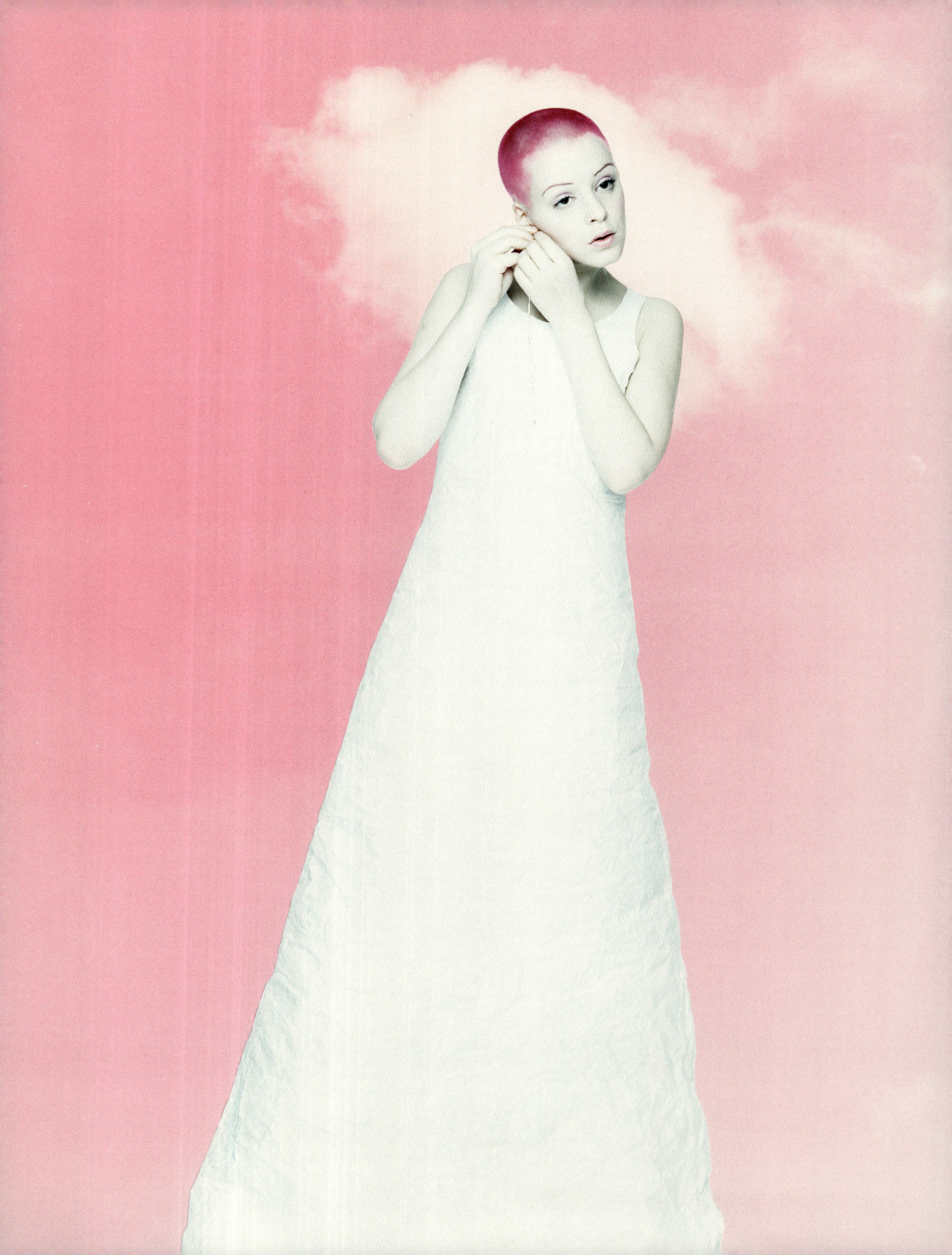

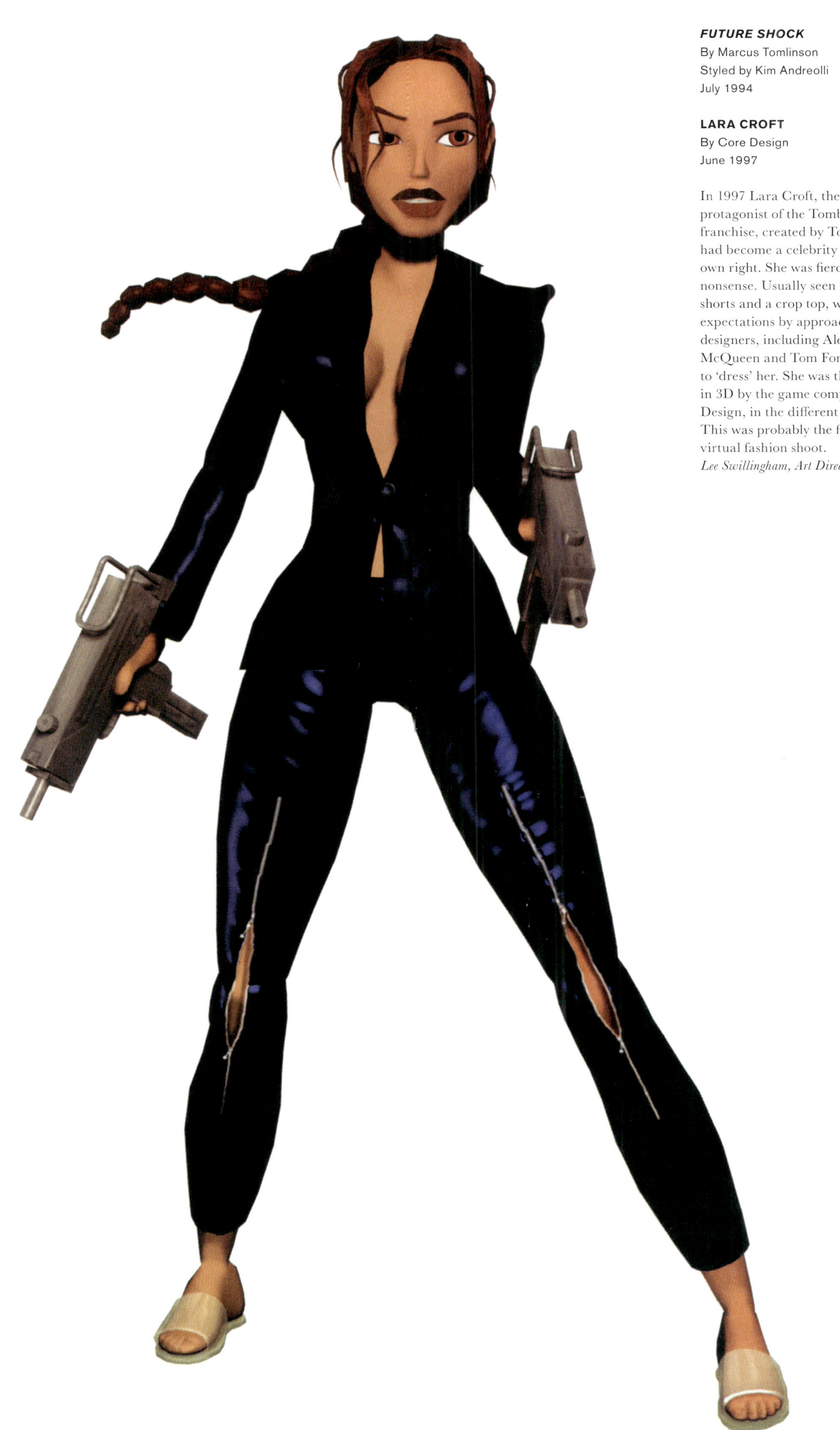

FUTURE SHOCK
By Marcus Tomlinson
Styled by Kim Andreolli
July 1994

LARA CROFT
By Core Design
June 1997

In 1997 Lara Croft, the fictional
protagonist of the Tomb Raider
franchise, created by Toby Gard,
had become a celebrity in her
own right. She was fierce and no-
nonsense. Usually seen in khaki
shorts and a crop top, we flipped
expectations by approaching
designers, including Alexander
McQueen and Tom Ford at Gucci
to 'dress' her. She was then rendered
in 3D by the game company Core
Design, in the different outfits.
This was probably the first ever
virtual fashion shoot.
Lee Swillingham, Art Director

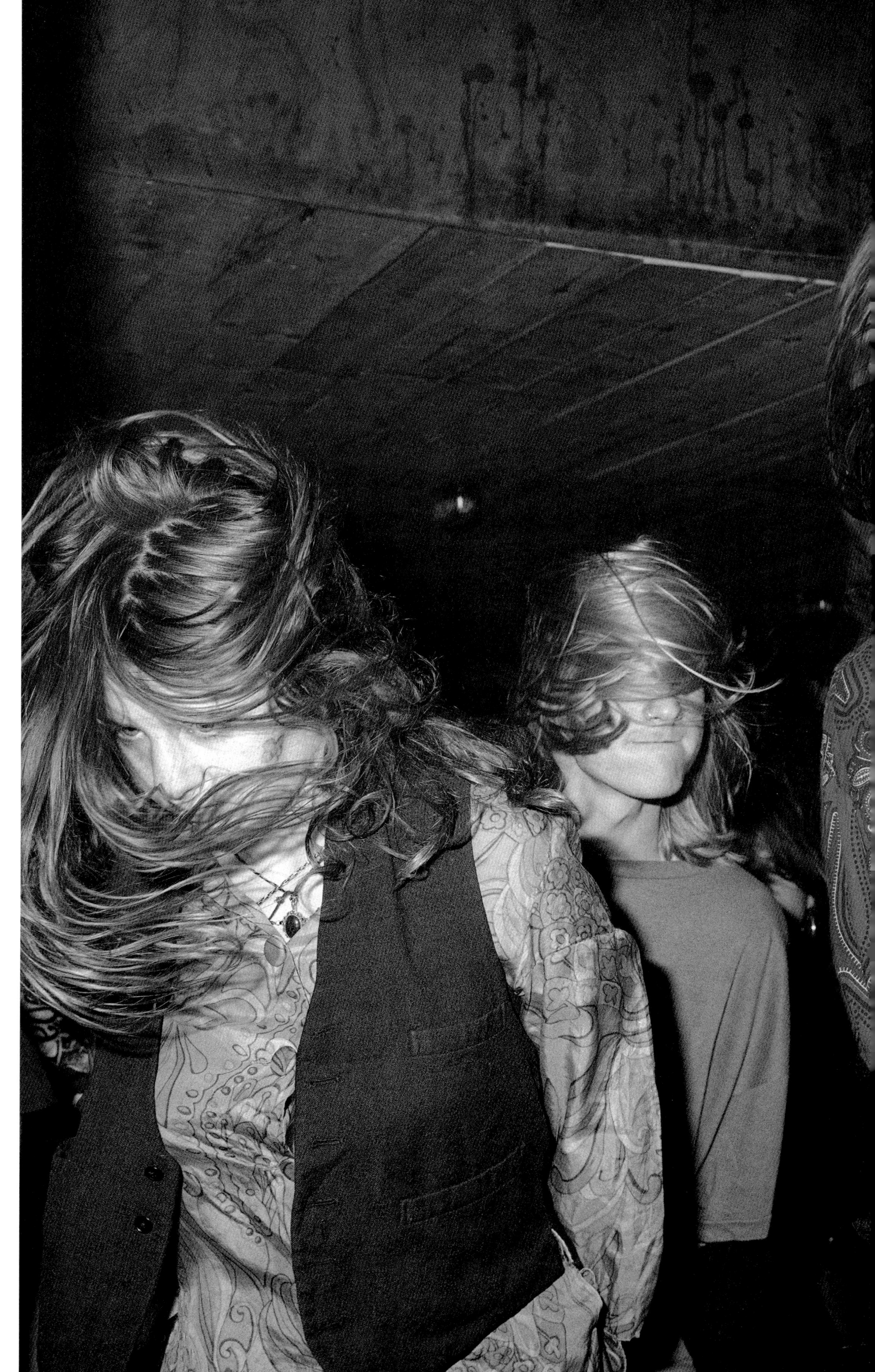

**MOONFLOWERS
AUDIENCE,
ONBOARD
THE THEKLA,
BRISTOL**
By Nigel Shafran
December 1991

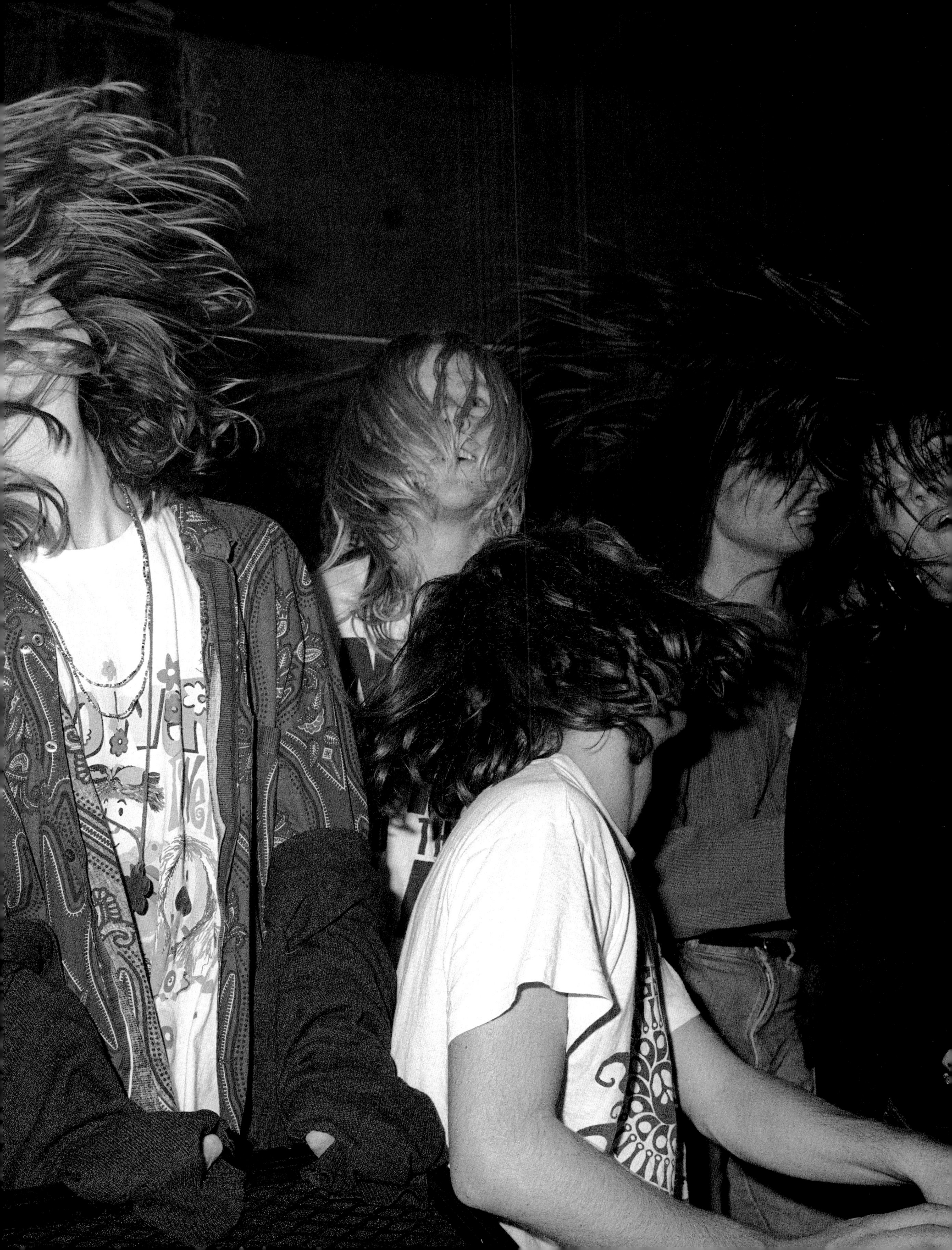

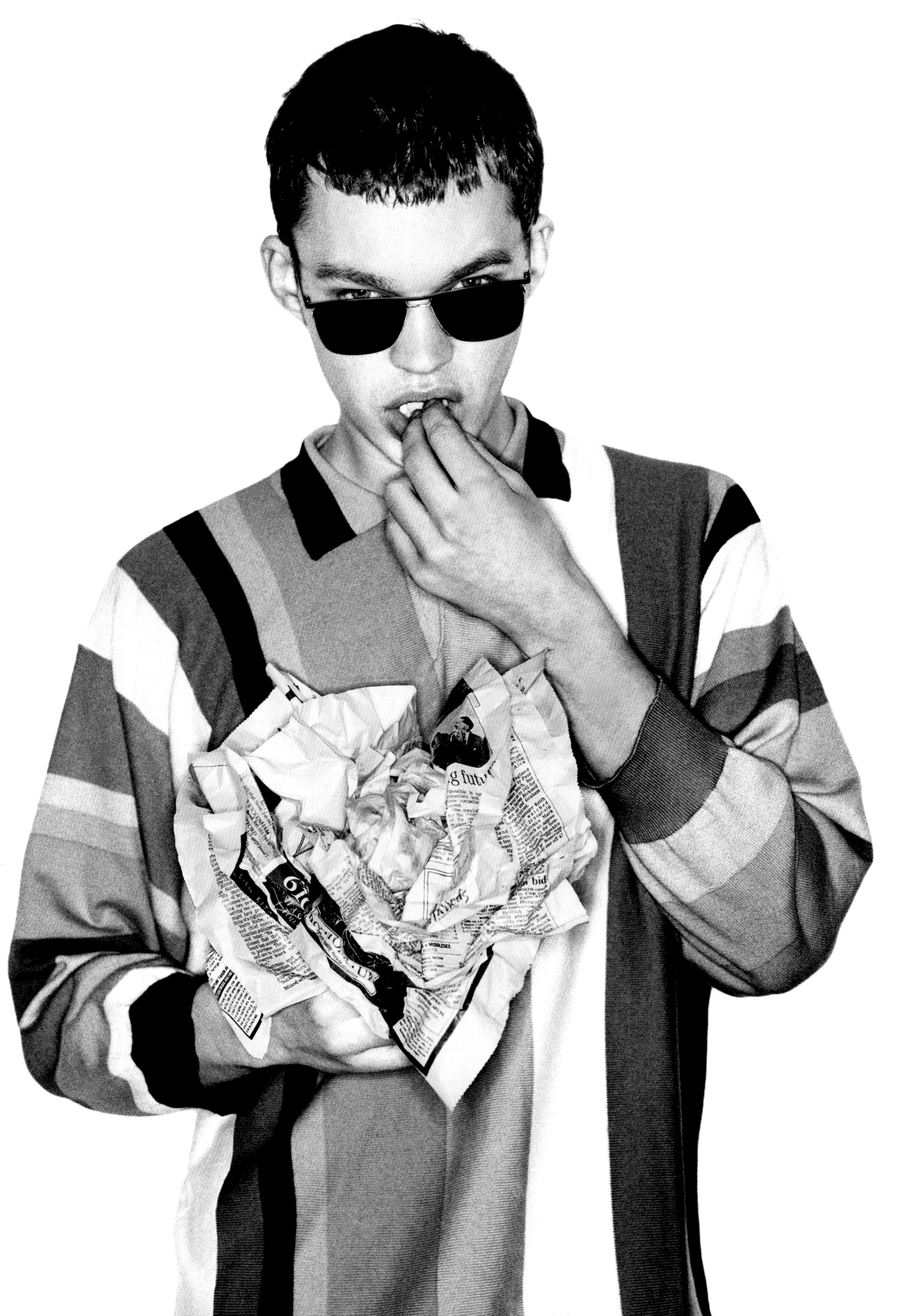

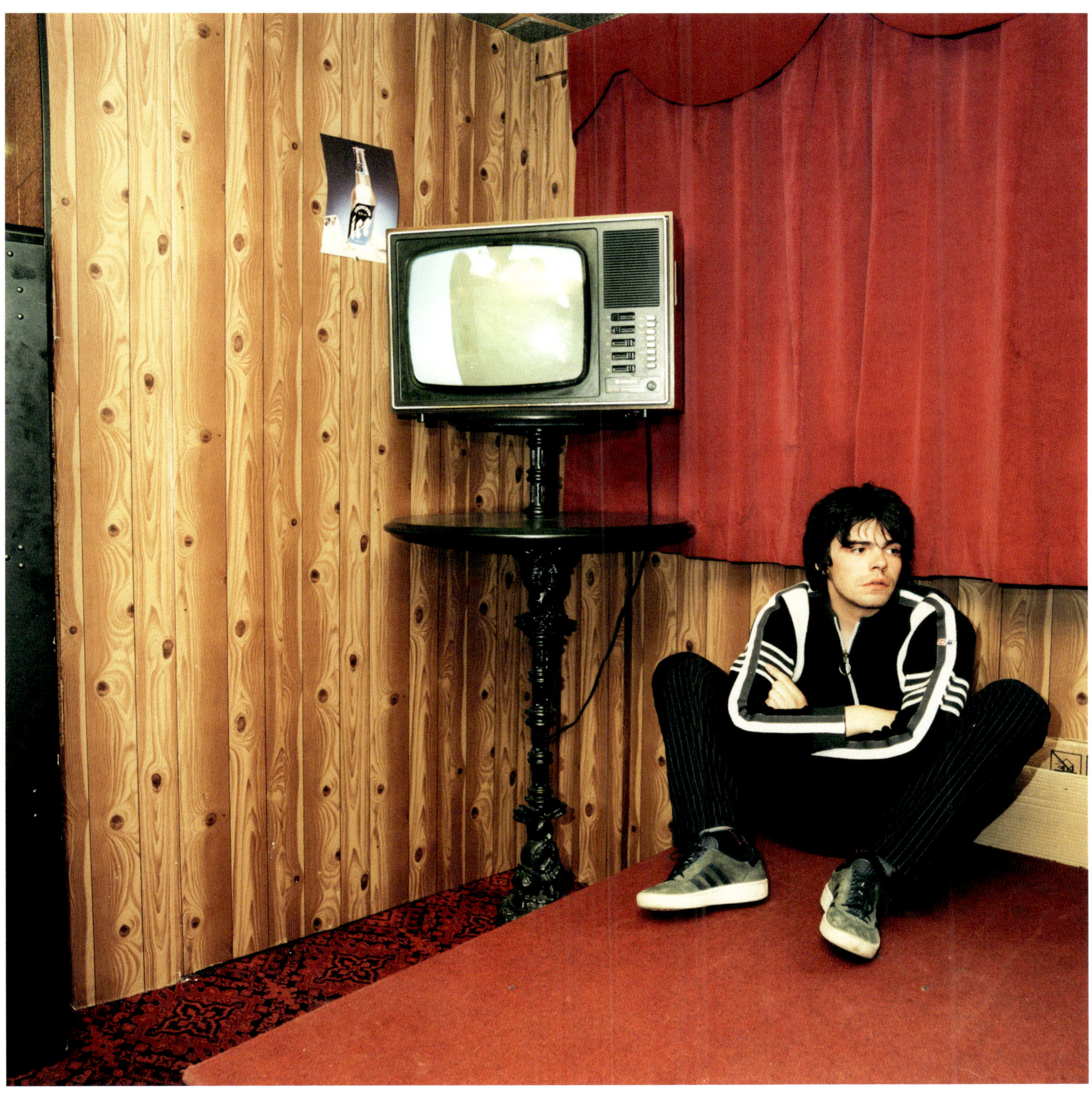

THE HIT

By Albert Watson
Styled by Karl Templer
and Derick Procope
June 1993

TIM BURGESS

By Donald Milne
Styled by Jason Kelvin
September 1996

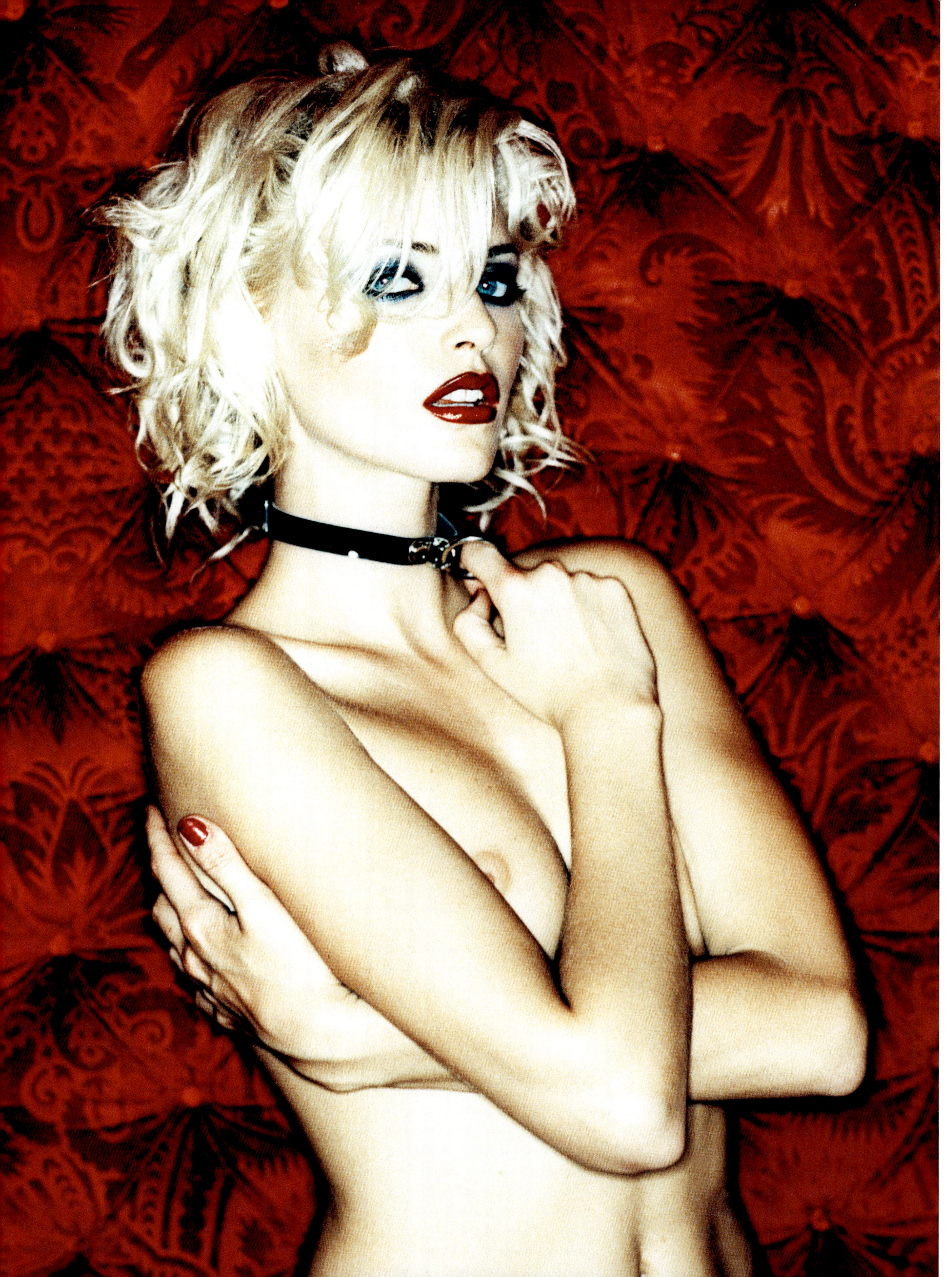

NADJA AUERMANN
By Ellen von Unwerth
Styled by Cathy Kasterine
September 1994

When you worked for *The Face*, you knew
you could push boundaries. You could be more
provocative, which is what I like.
Ellen von Unwerth

GAZ COOMBES
By John Scarisbrick
Styled by Greg Fay
and Justin Laurie
March 1996

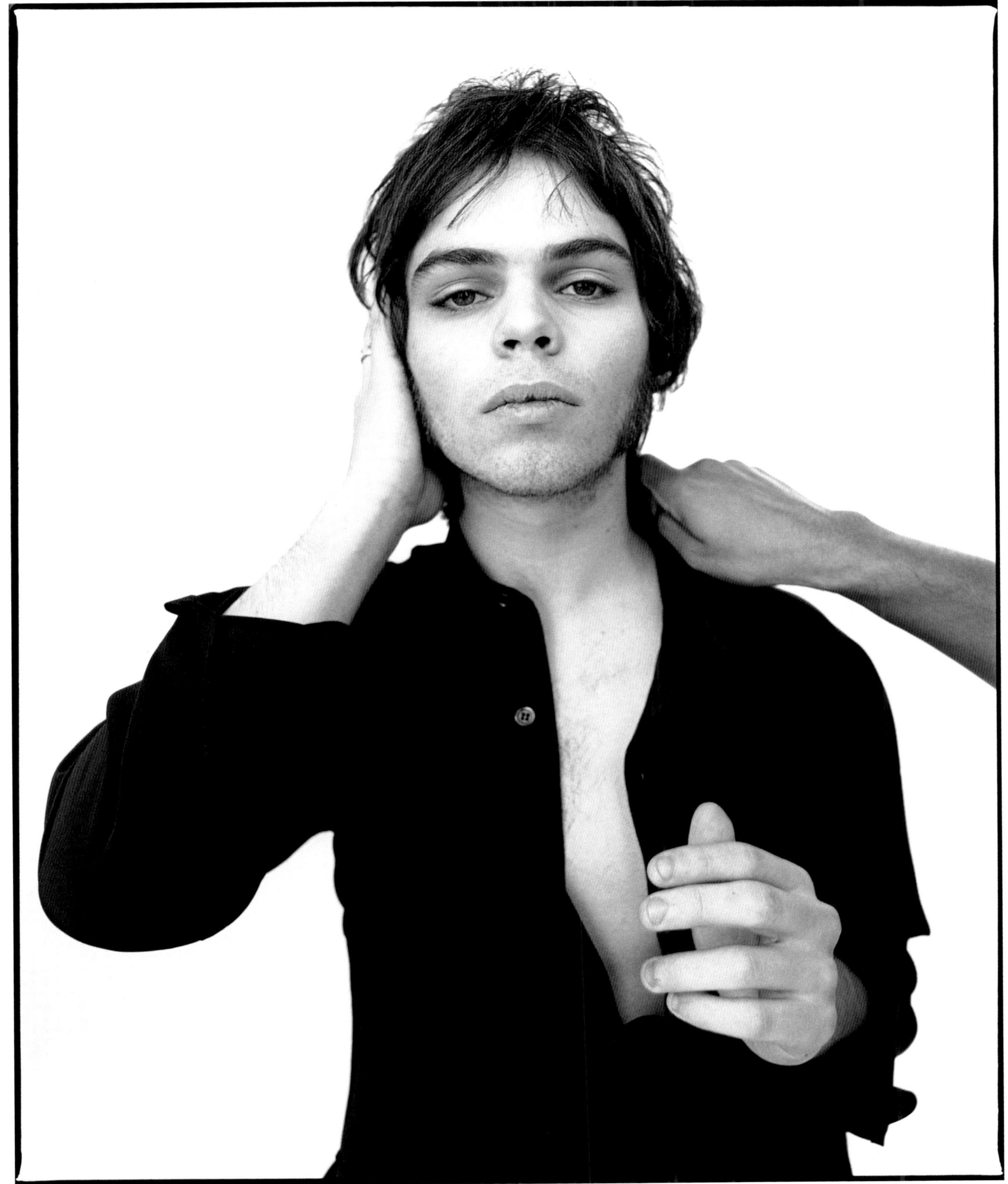

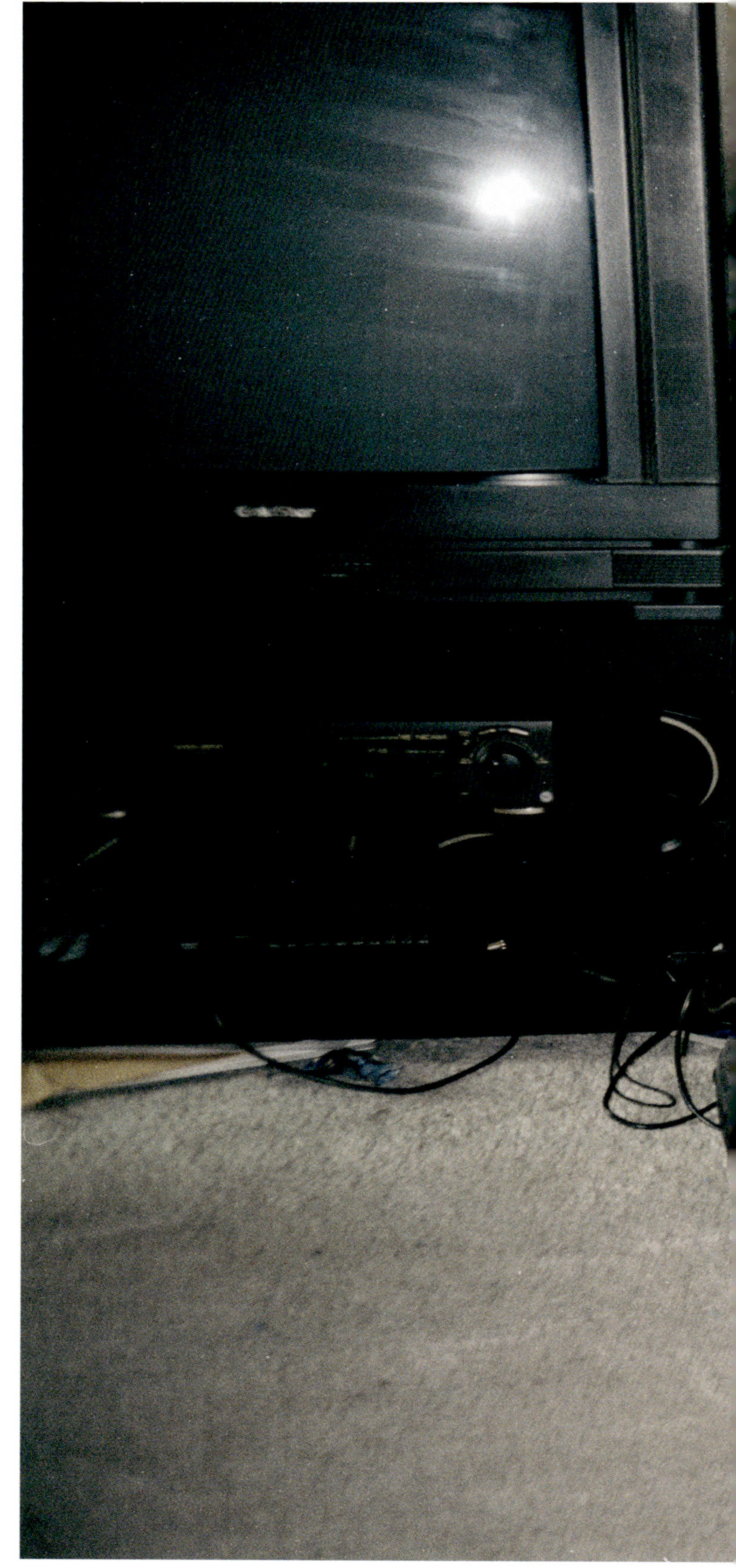

GOLDIE
By Juergen Teller
July 1995

Following pages
GIRLS ON BIKES
(SARF COASTIN')
By Elaine Constantine
Styled by Polly Banks
December 1997

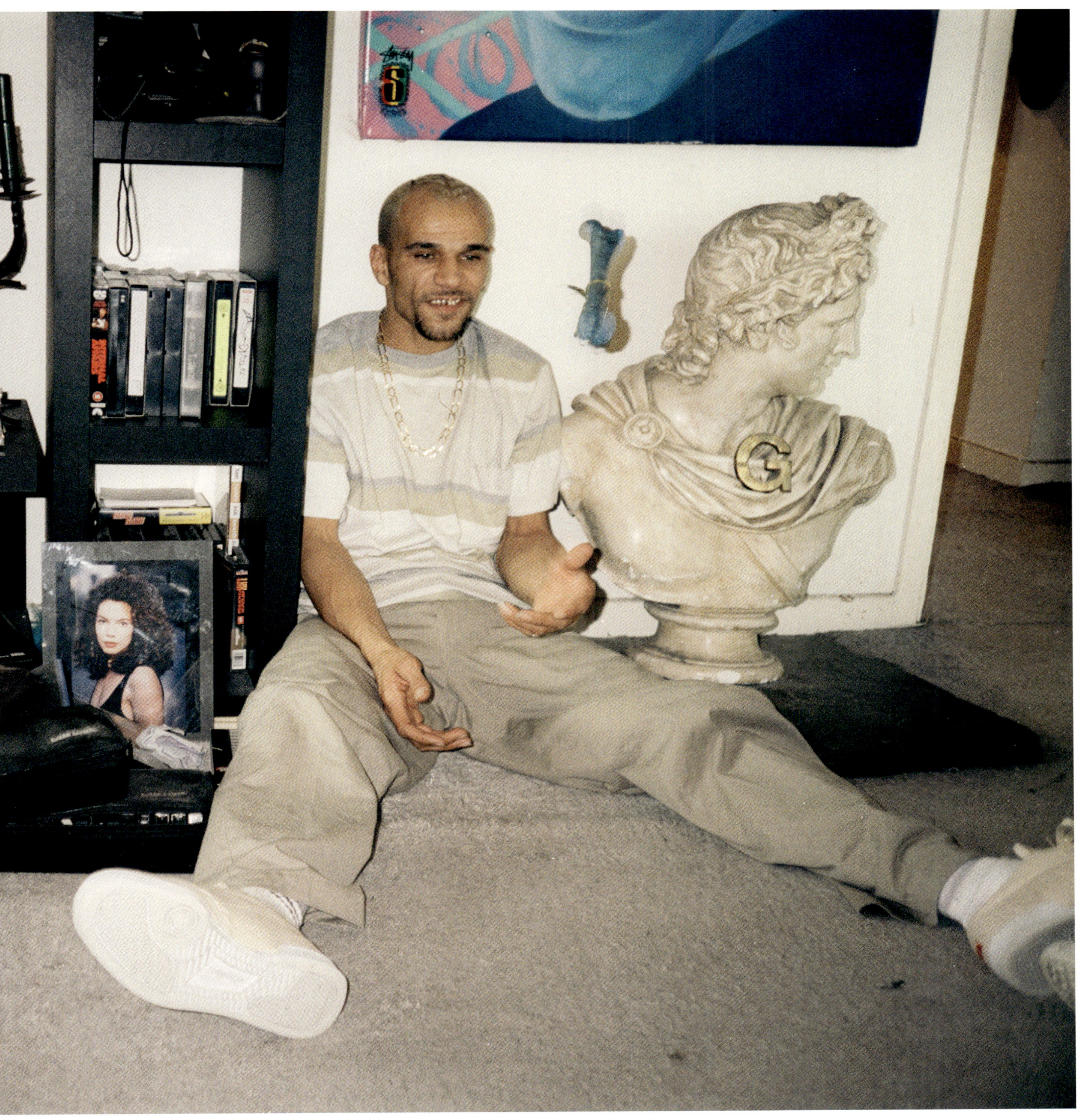

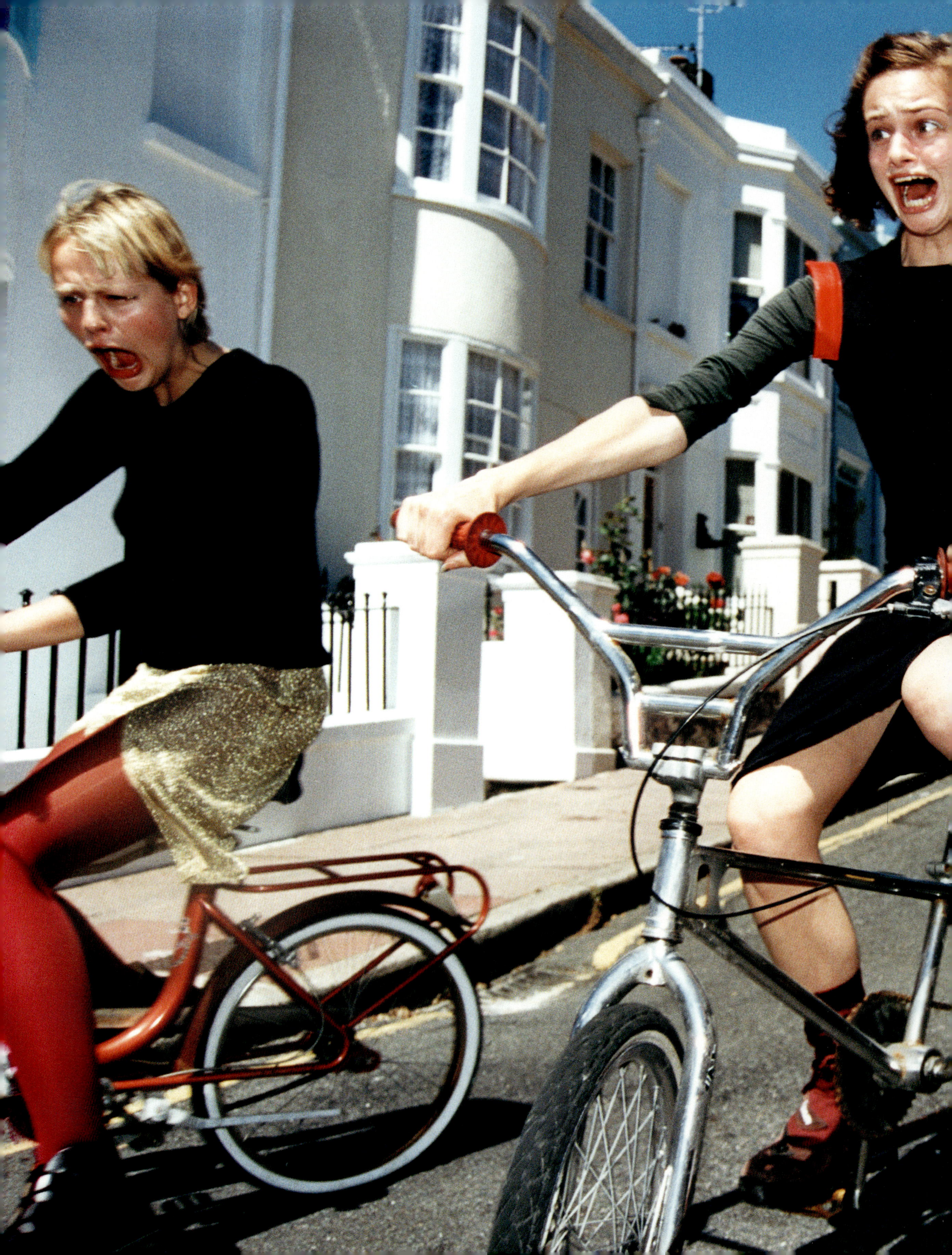

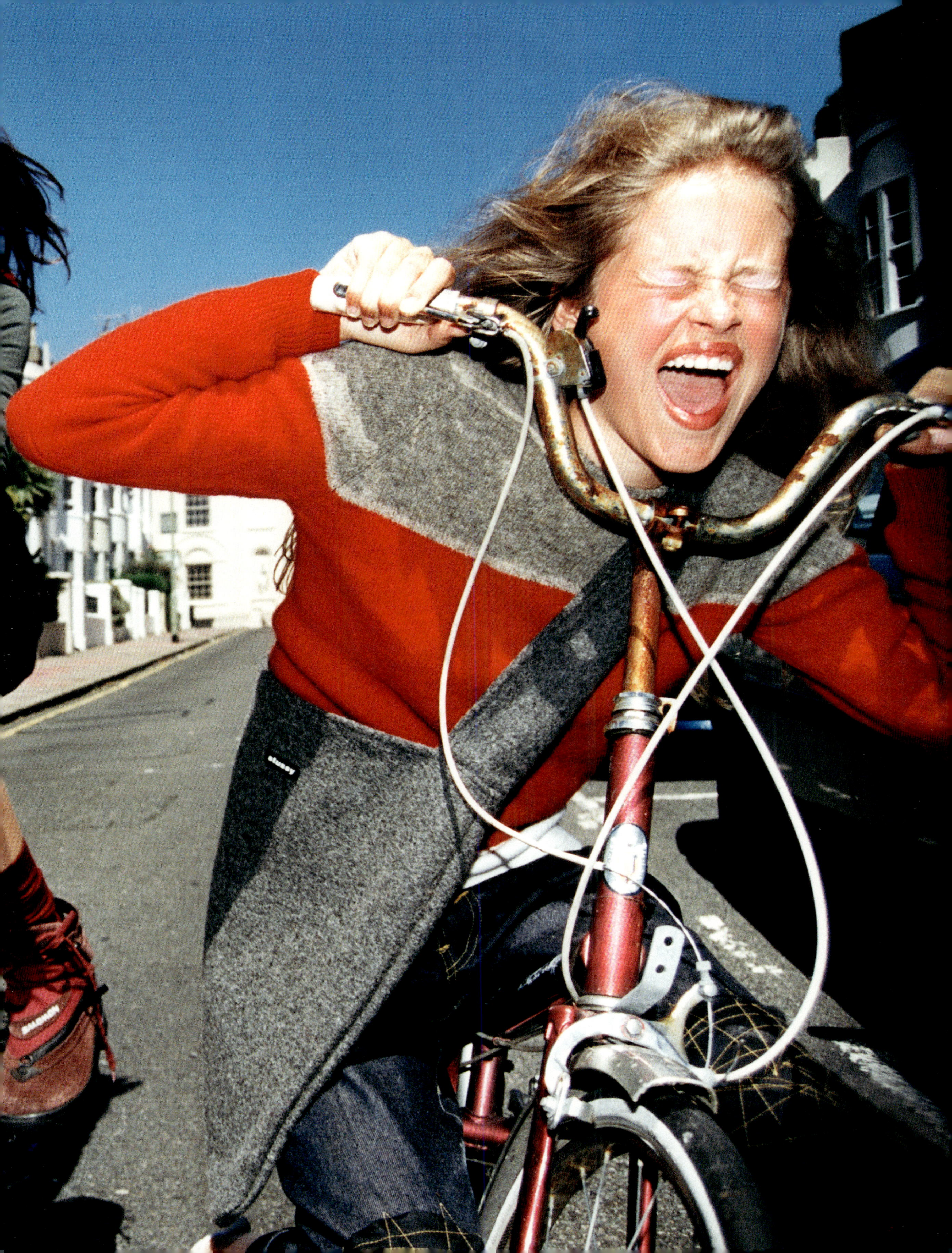

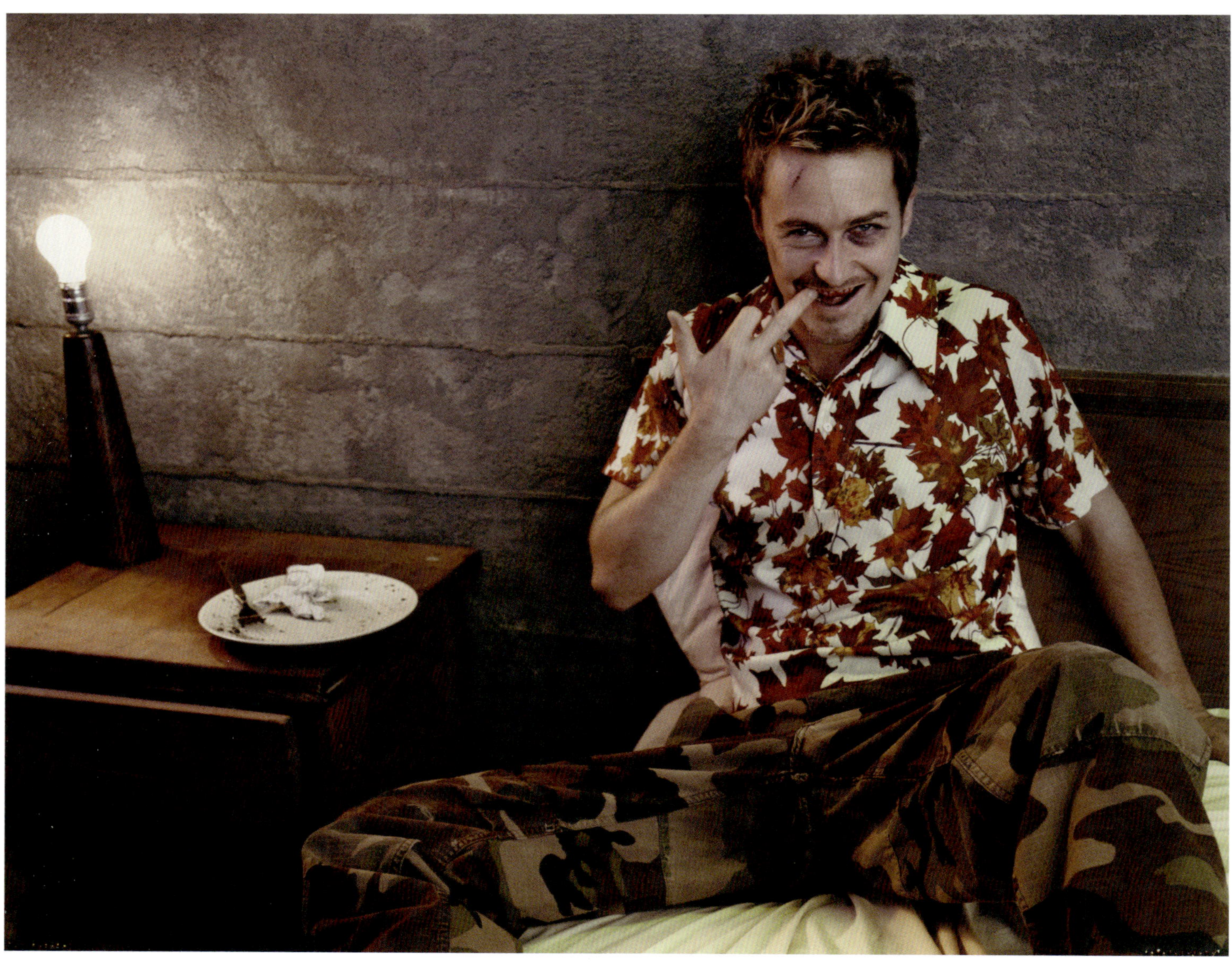

EDWARD NORTON
By Steven Klein
Styled by Michael Kaplan
December 1999

I'M IN LOVE WITH MY CAR
By Liz Collins
Styled by Katie Grand
March 1998

The relatable, aspirational dream of fixing the car up, driving it out on the weekend; it reflected a sense of pride that was instinctual to me as a working-class kid. Taking fashion pictures of people doing normal things like cleaning a car went hand-in-hand with the deglamorisation of fashion photography that was happening. I was simply reflecting life around me: the tone, the music, the politics.
Liz Collins

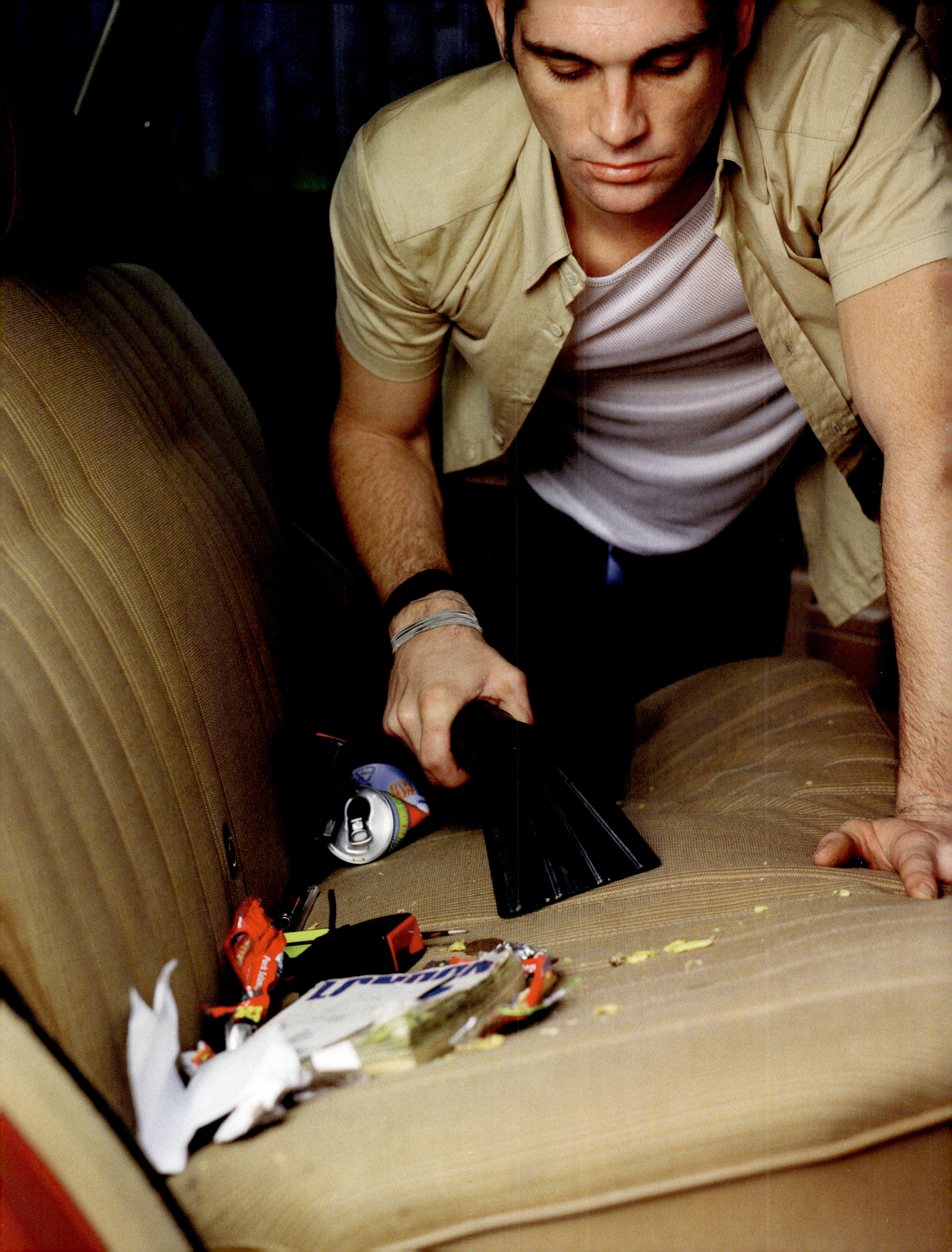

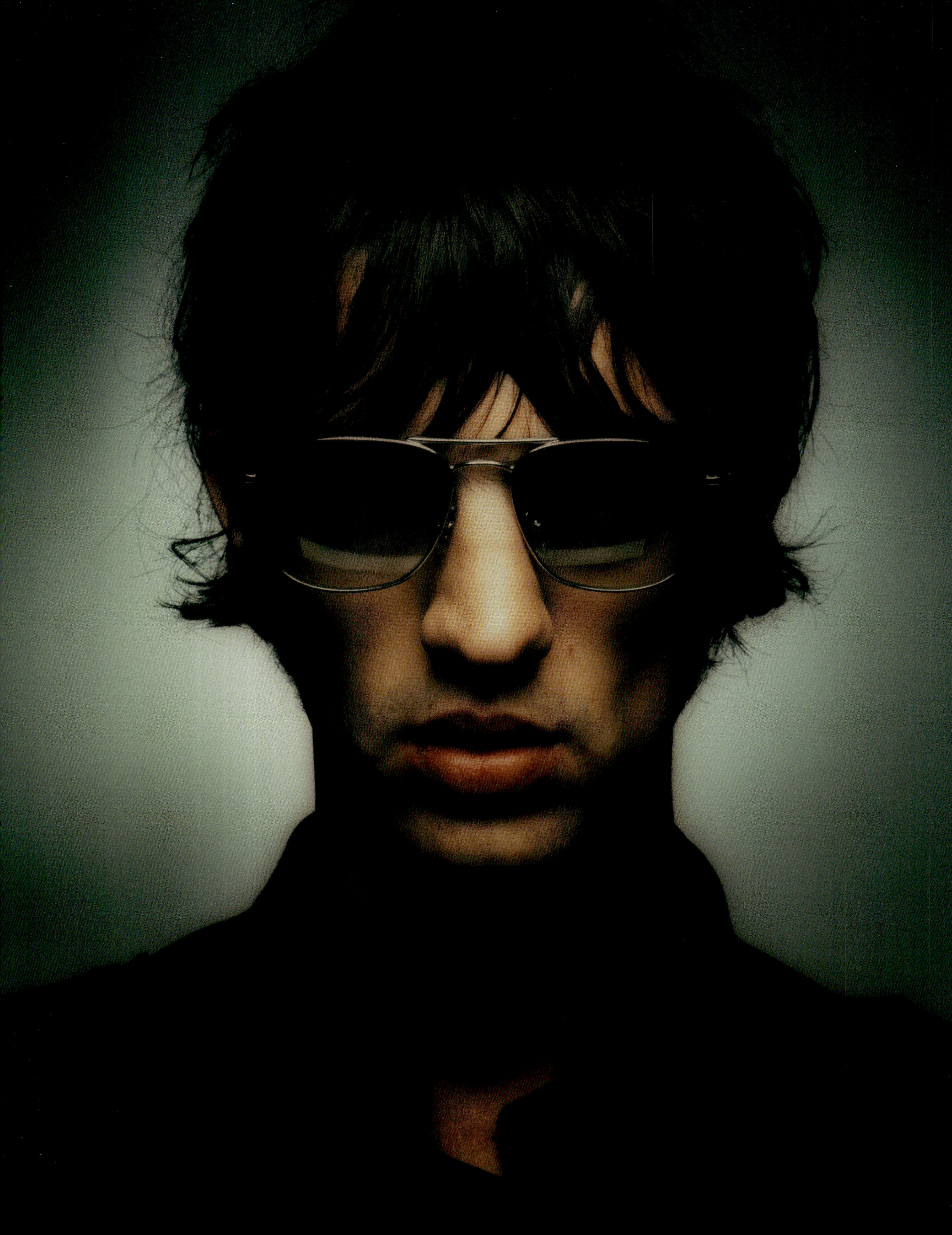

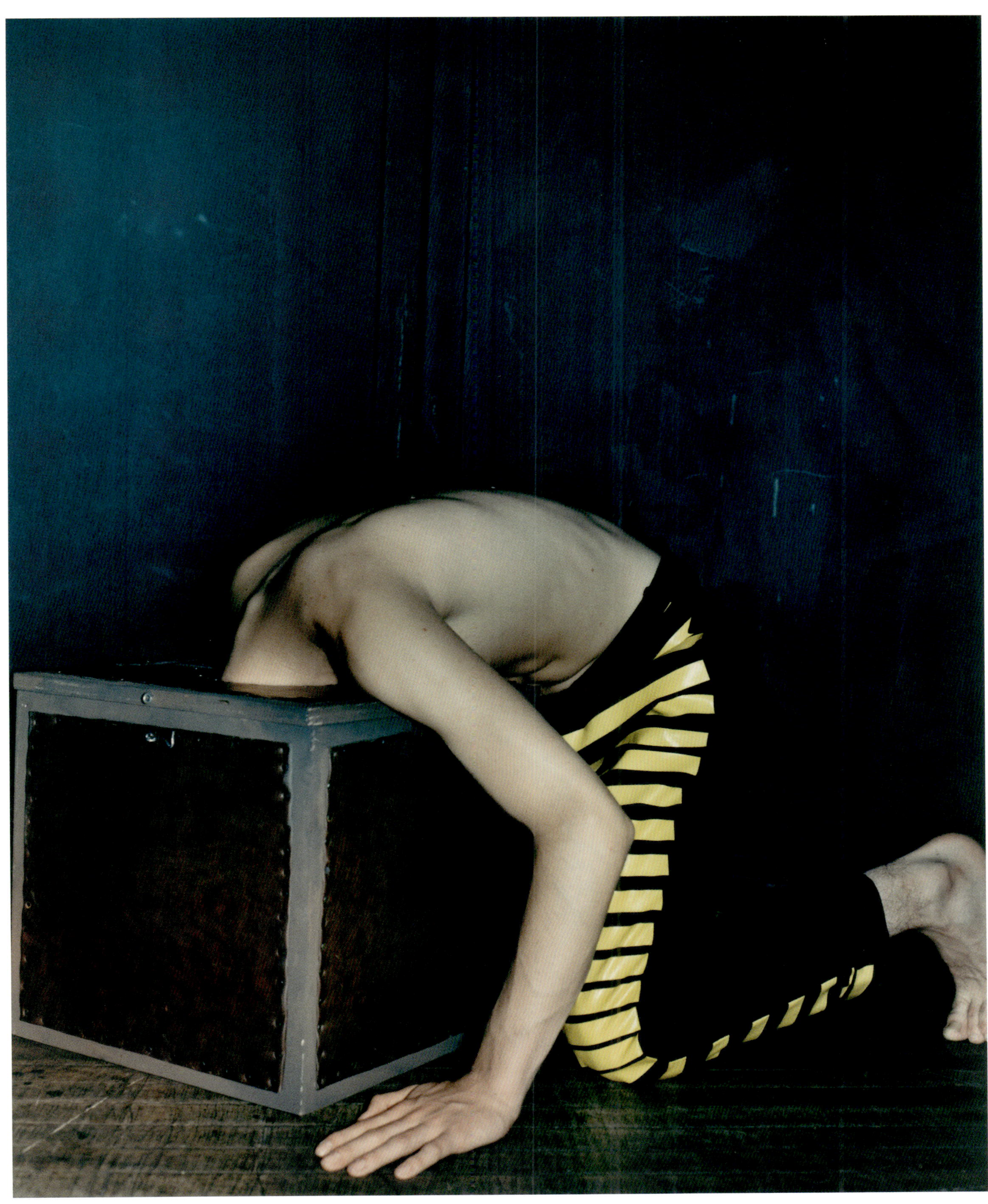

RICHARD ASHCROFT
By Sean Ellis
September 1997

PERFORMANCE
By Steven Klein
Styled by Nancy Rohde
December 1995

Following pages
BORDER LINE
By Norbert Schoerner
Styled by Katie Grand
September 1998

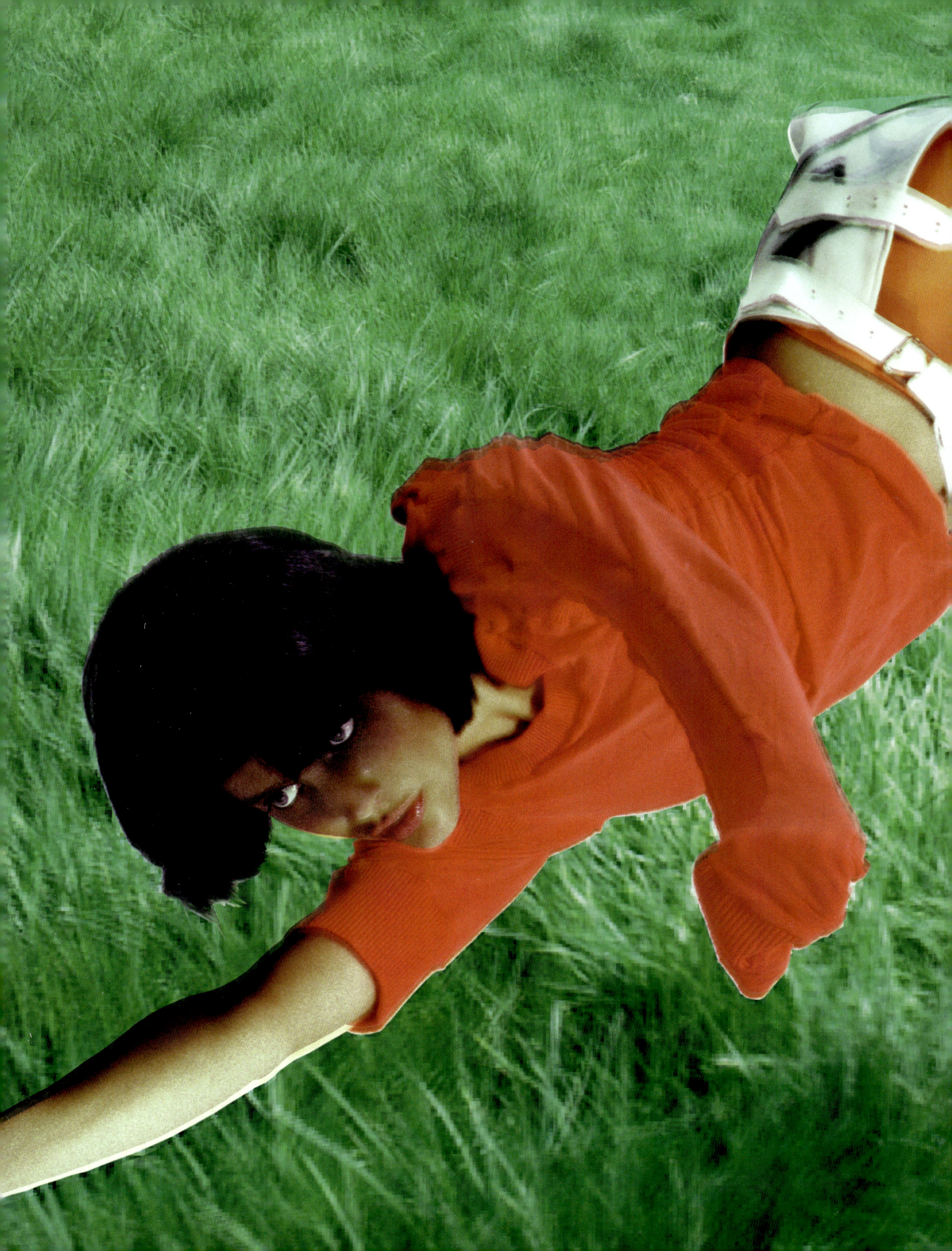

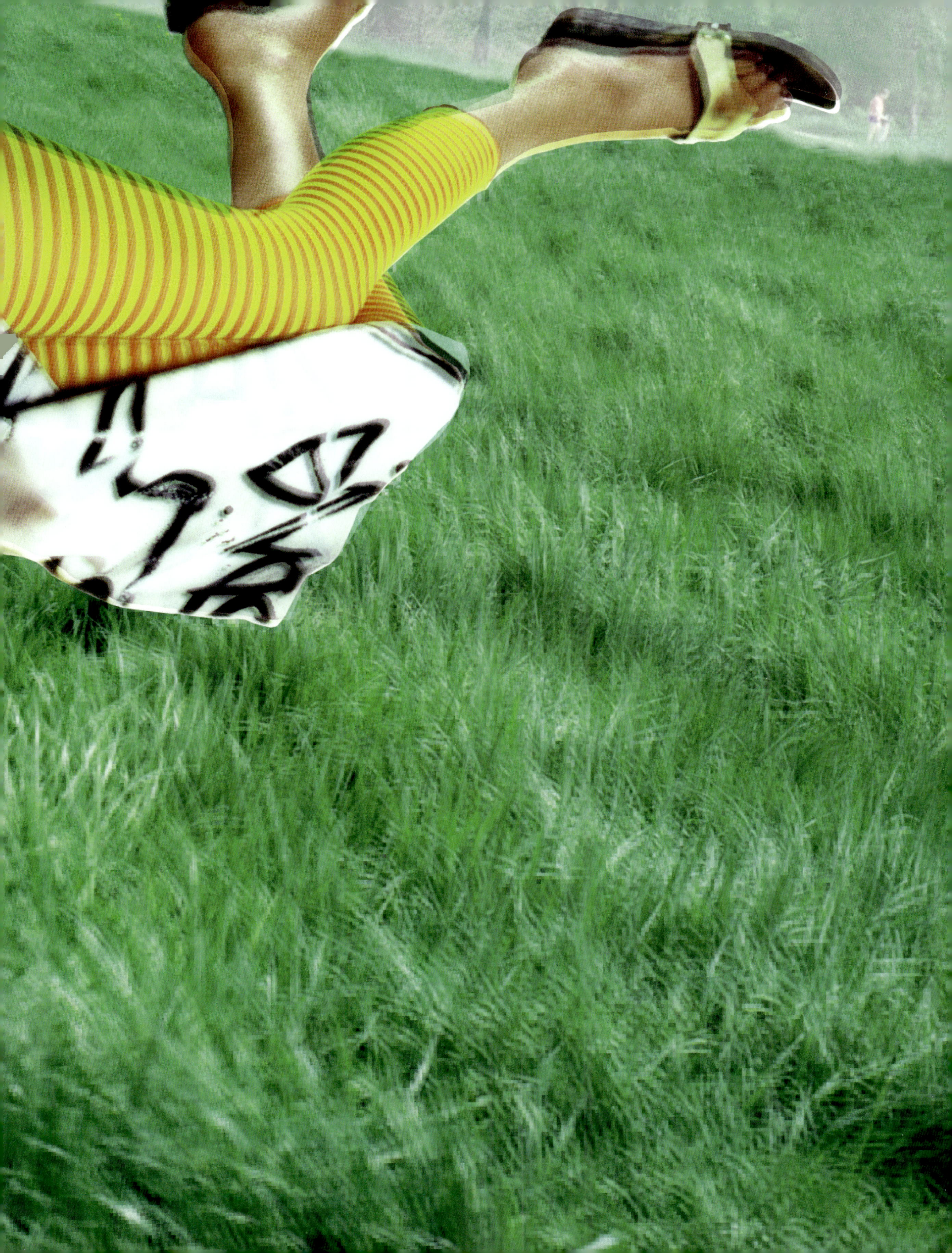

EMBRACE
By Toyin Ibidapo
Styled by Geriada Kefford
July 1999

RUDER THAN THE REST
By Richard Croft
March 1991

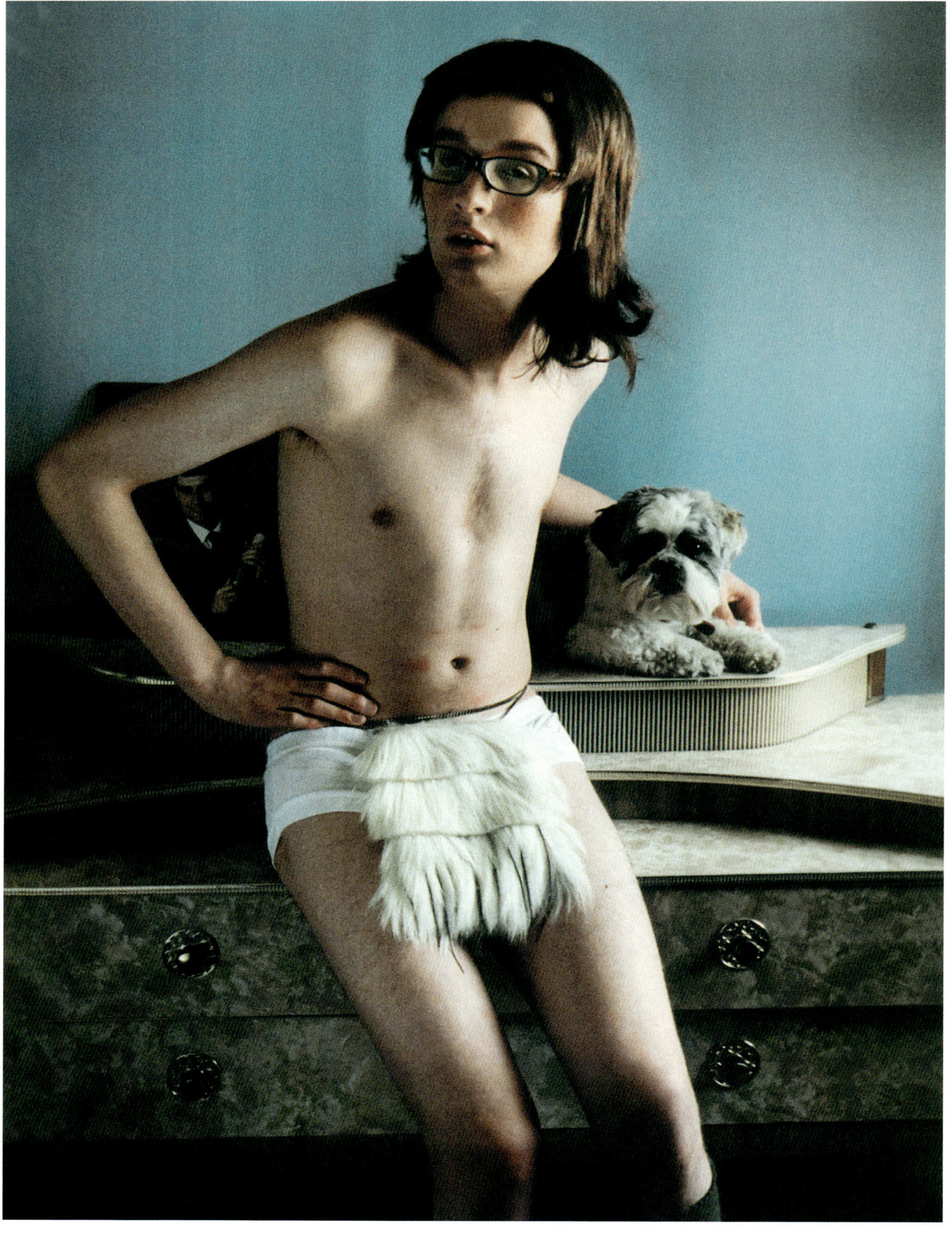

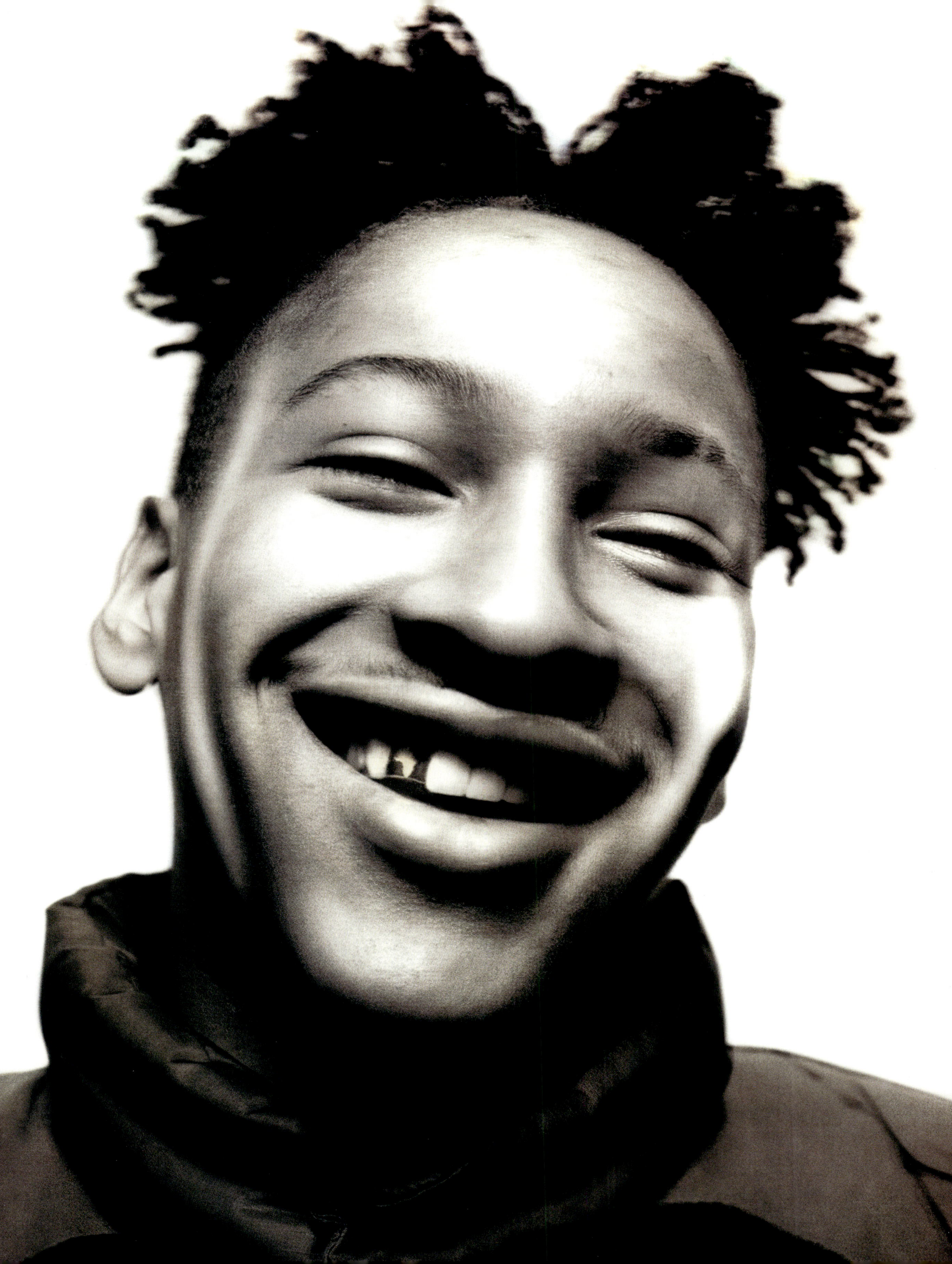

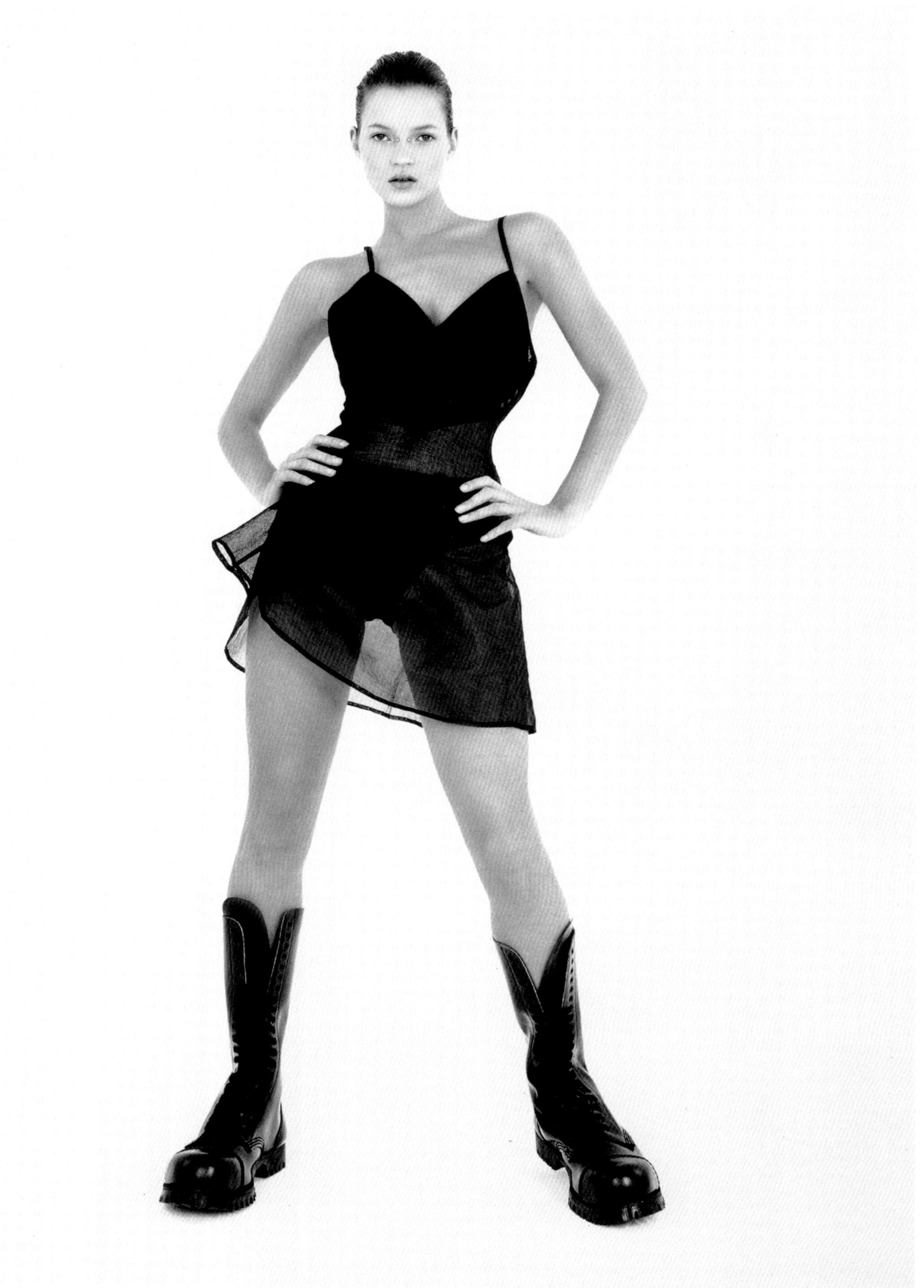

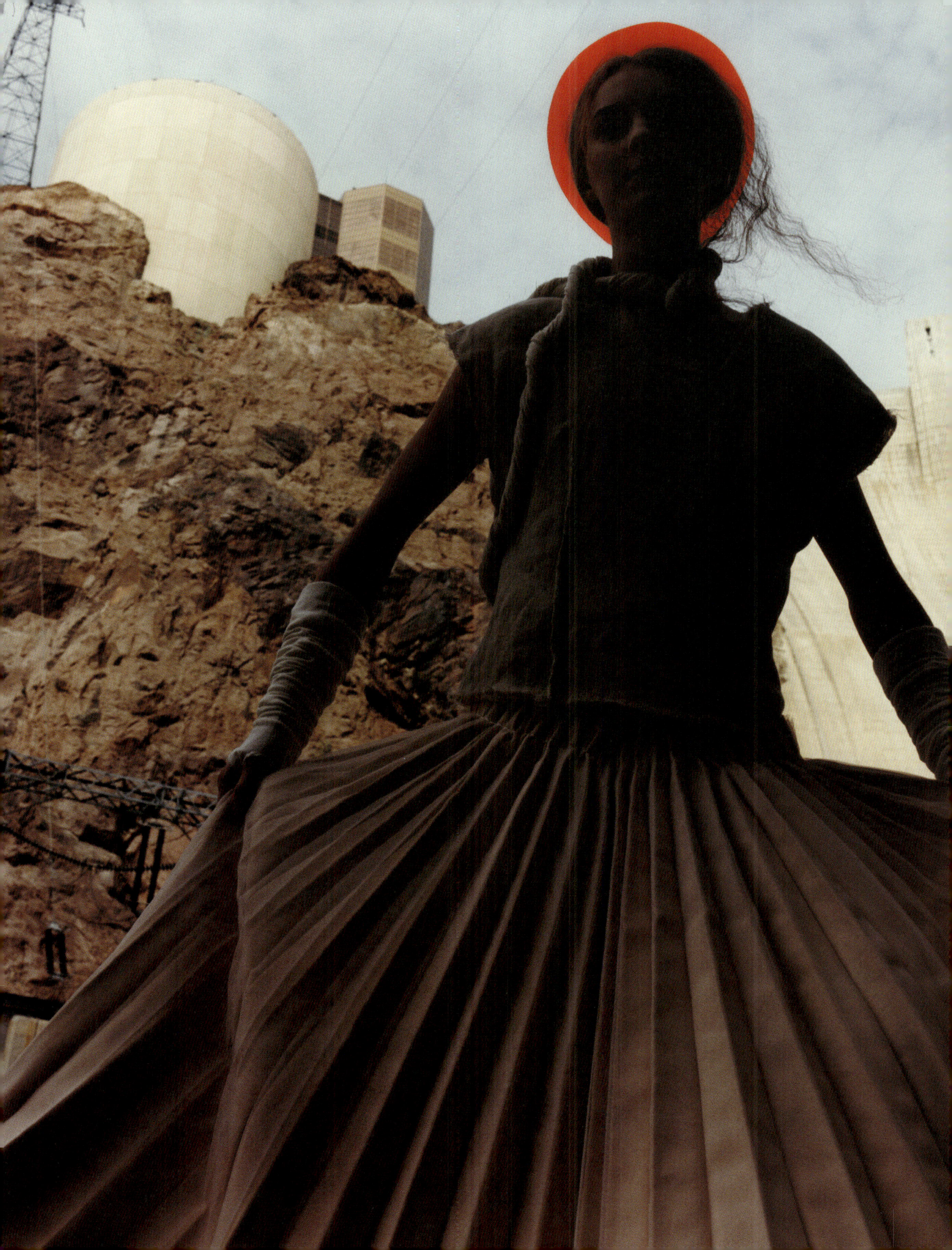

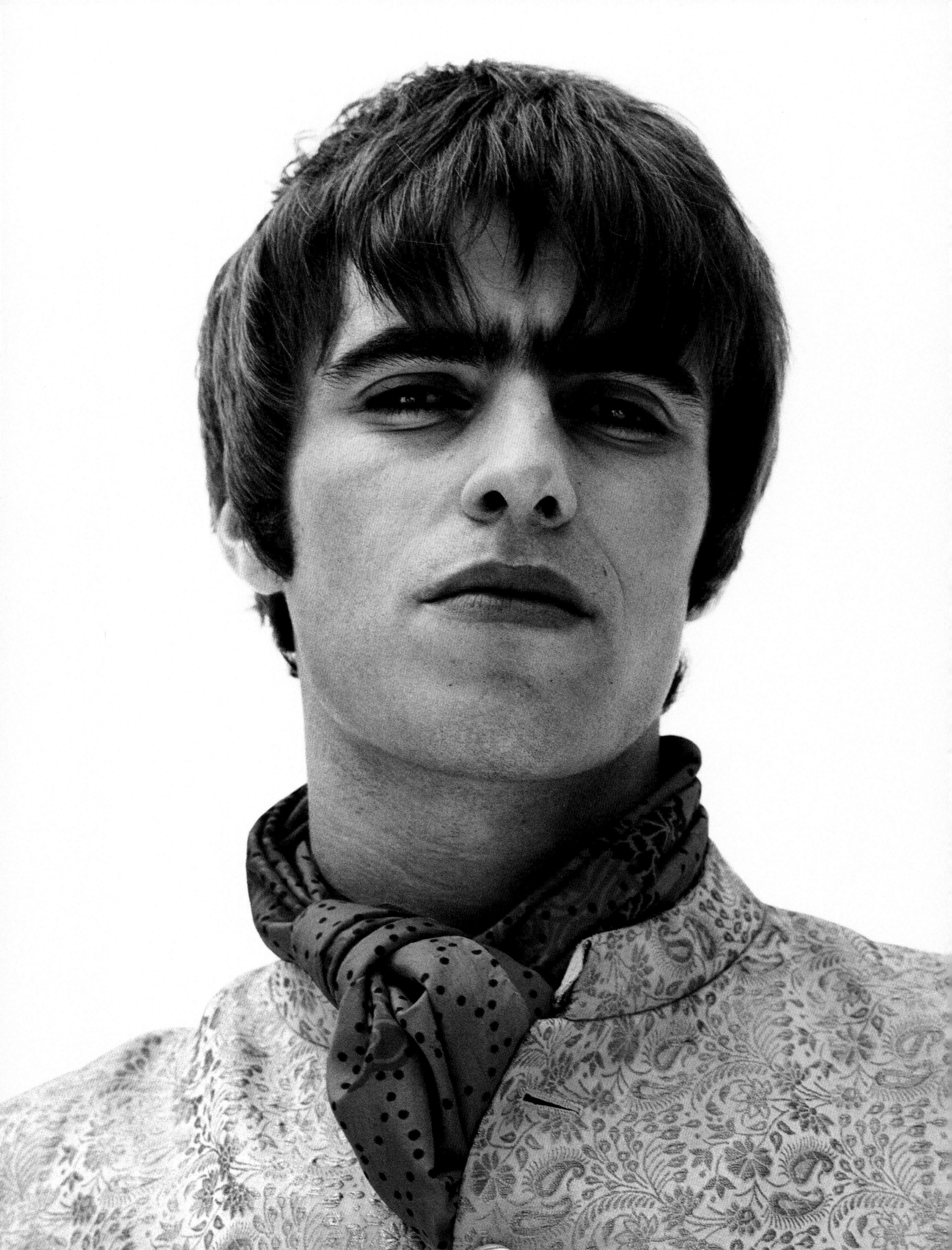

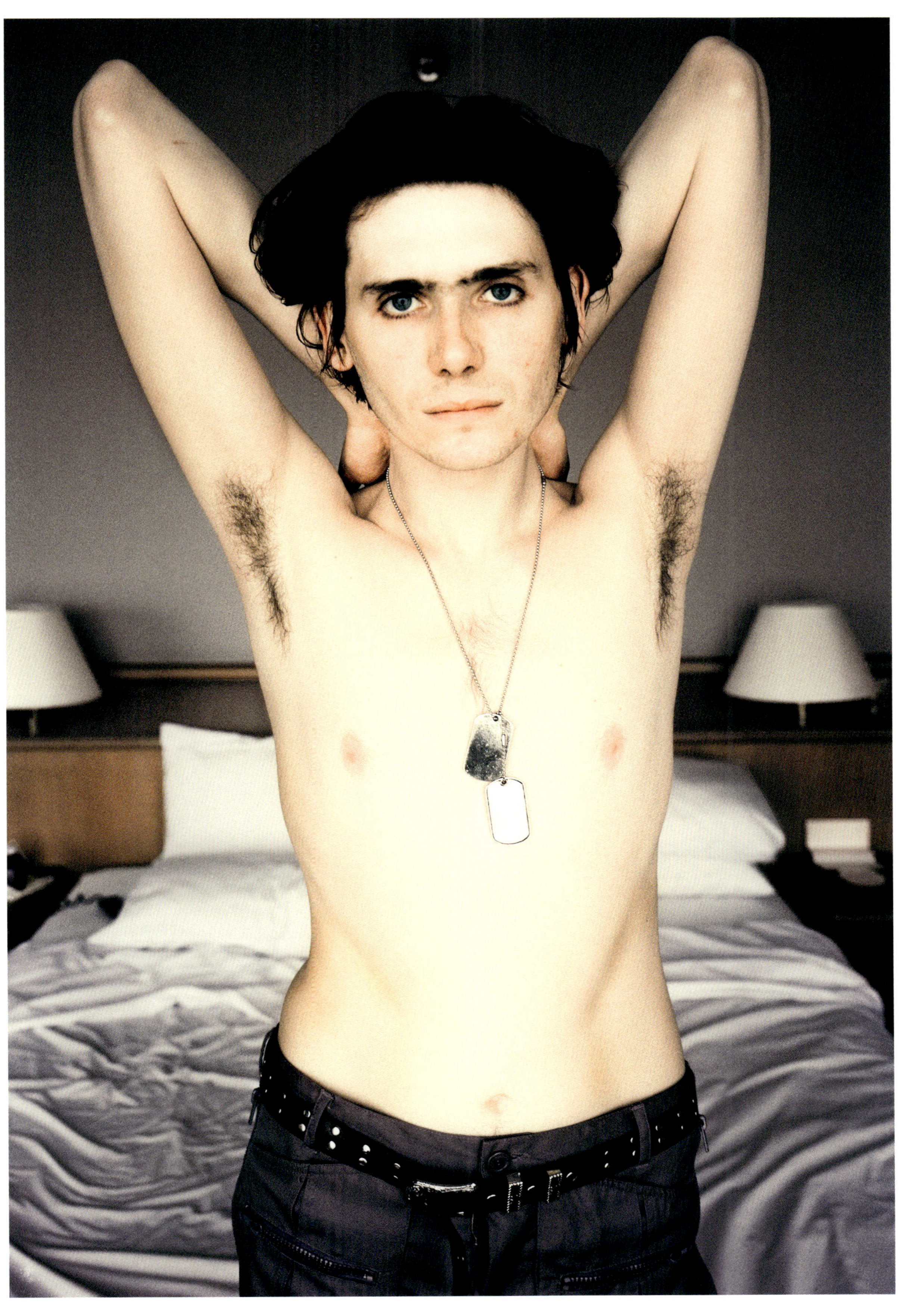

LIAM GALLAGHER
By Norman Watson
Styled by Jason Kelvin
August 1994

NICKY WIRE
By Donald Christie
June 1994

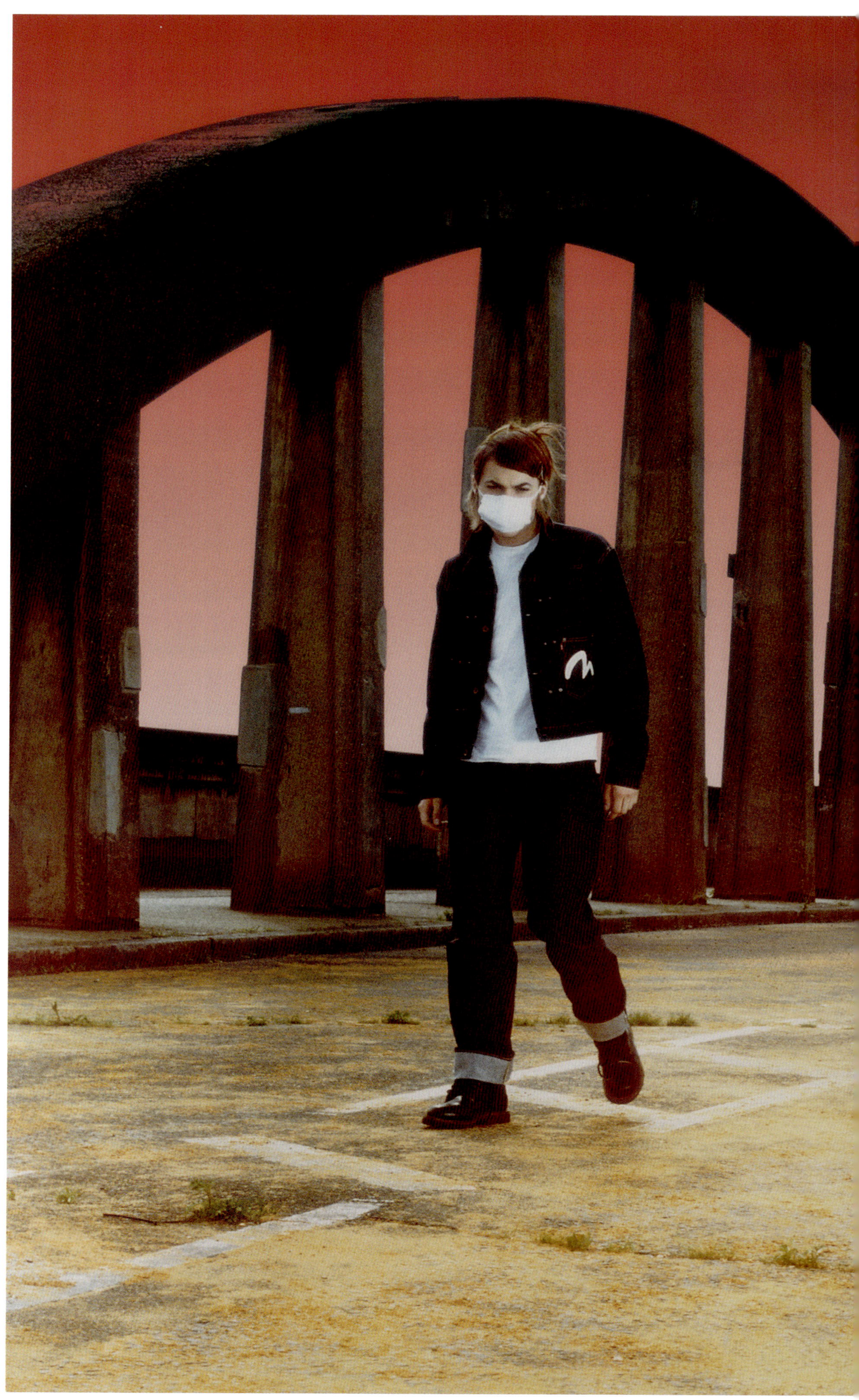

BAD BOY MEMORY
By Norbert Schoerner
Styled by Adam Howe
September 1994

I had relocated to Osaka with
my family. Norbert came
to visit and fell in love with
Japan. This story was a western
homage to manga and Japanese
cinema. We shot it in London's
Docklands, where Stanley
Kubrick filmed *Full Metal Jacket*.
Adam Howe

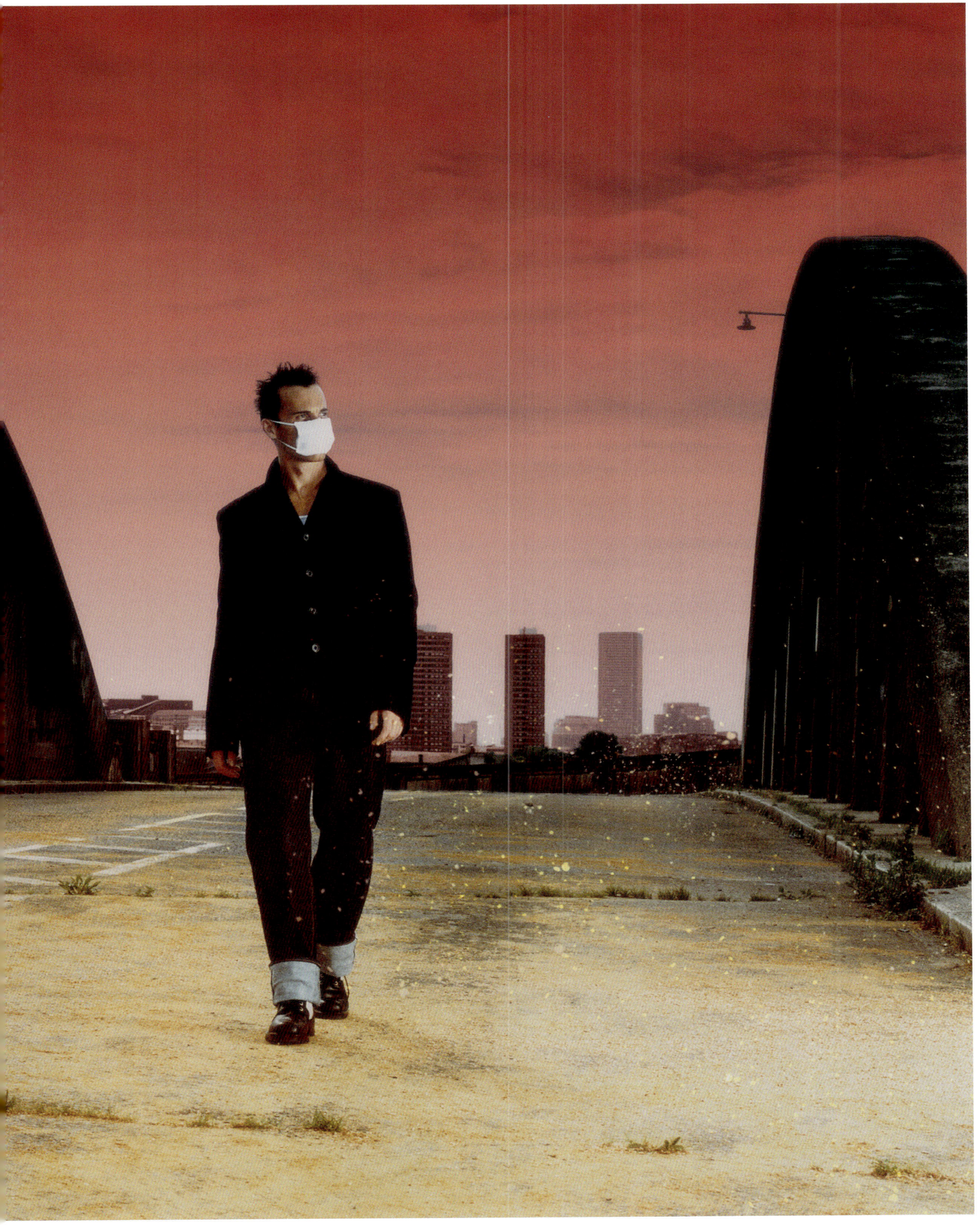

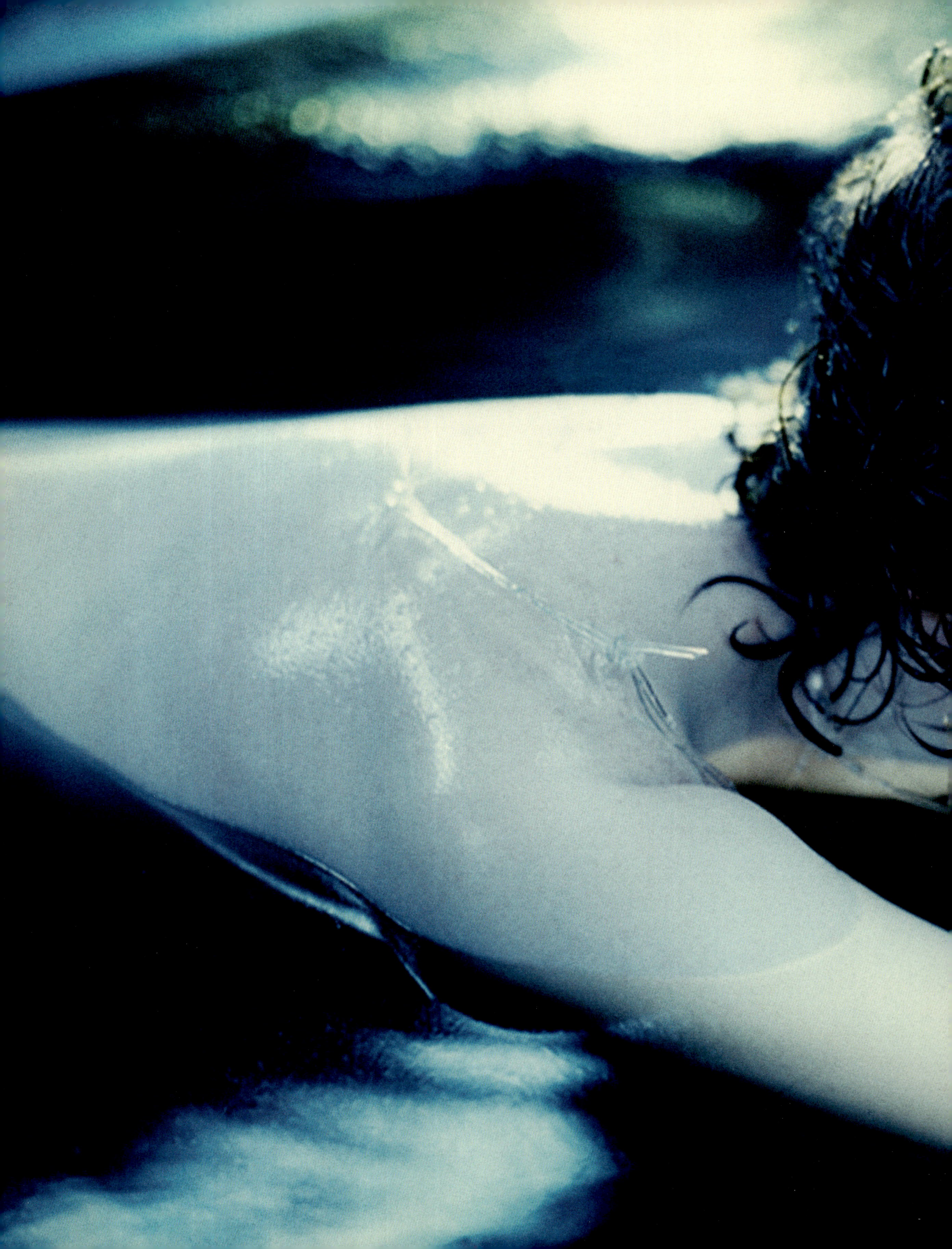

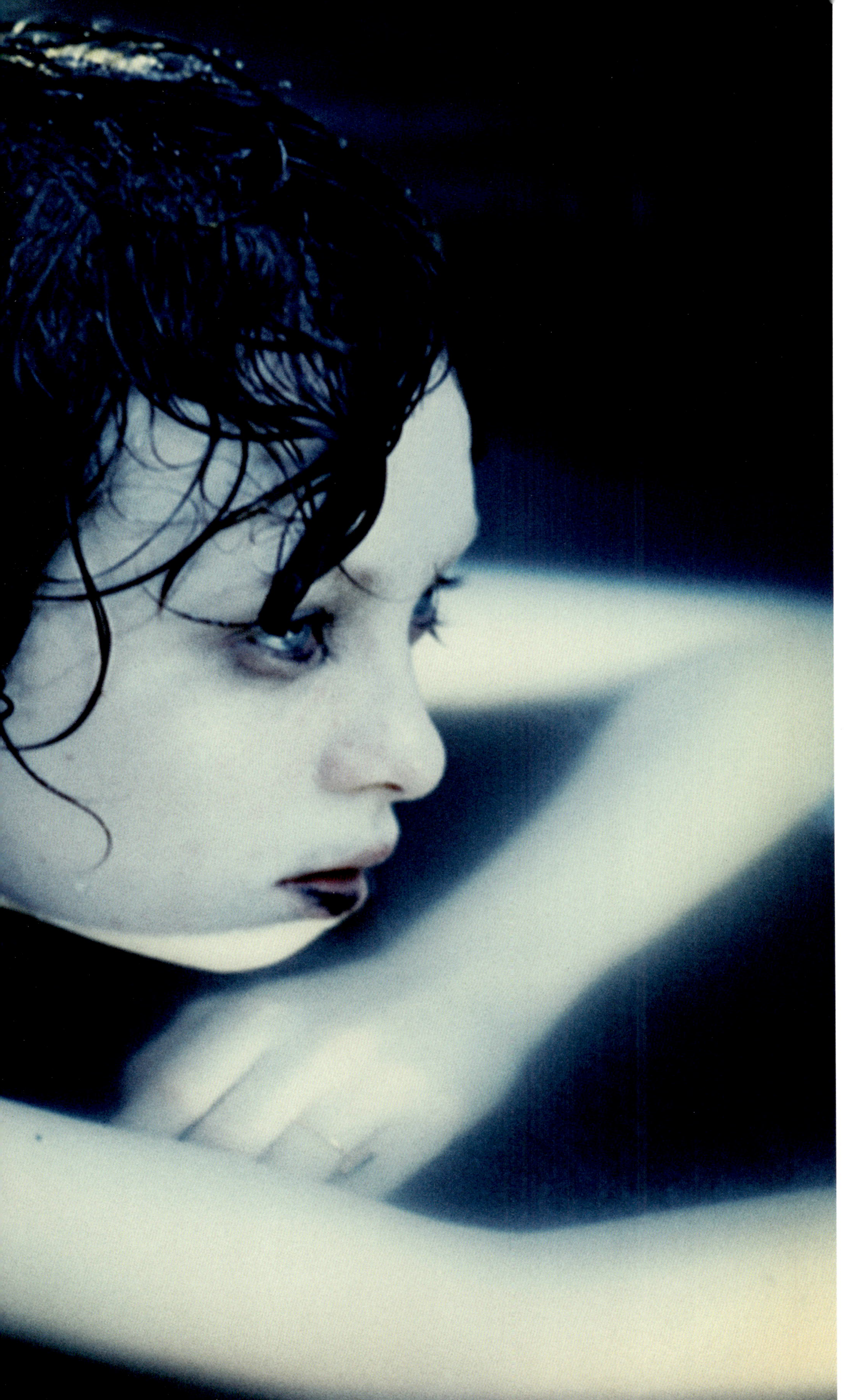

THE LAKE
By Luis Sanchis
Styled by
Gabriel Feliciano
April 1997

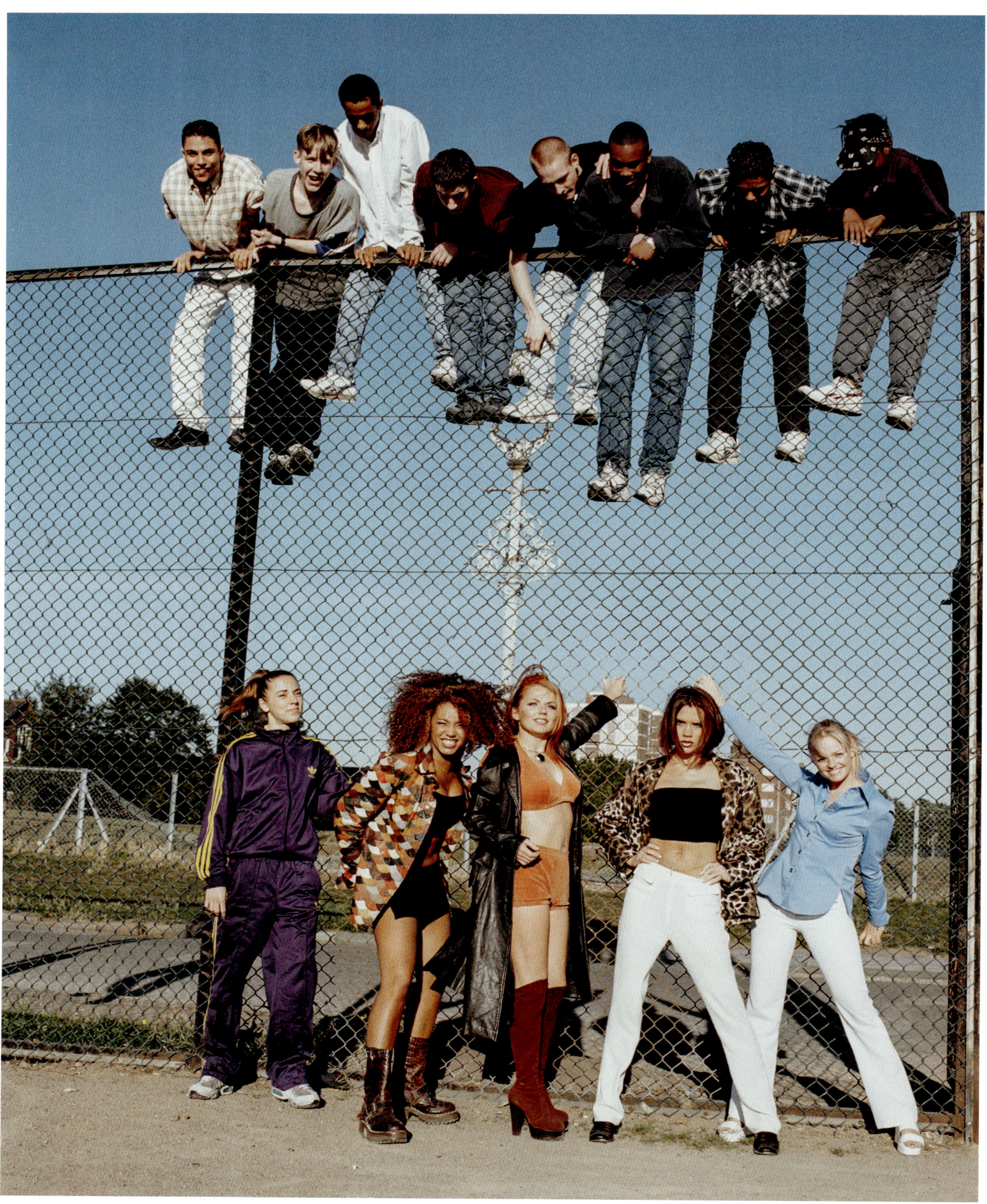

SPICE GIRLS

By Andreas Bleckmann
November 1996

The Face commissioned me to photograph the Spice Girls.
It was early days for the group, and no-one imagined what
a global phenomenon they would become. While we were
setting up in Shoreditch Park, a group of kids playing football
climbed the fence to escape an angry dog. The timing was
perfect, no one was hurt and I got the shot.
Andreas Bleckmann

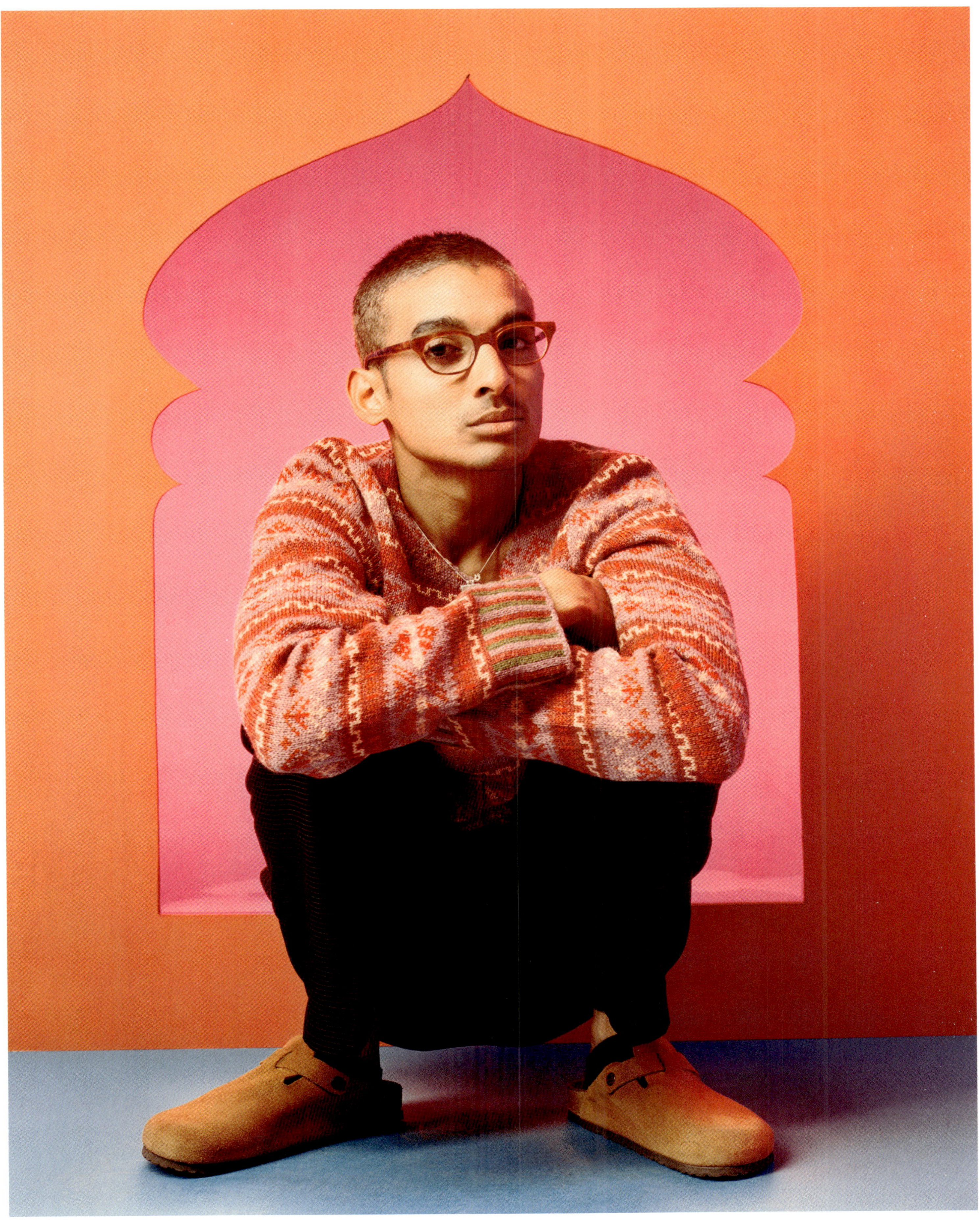

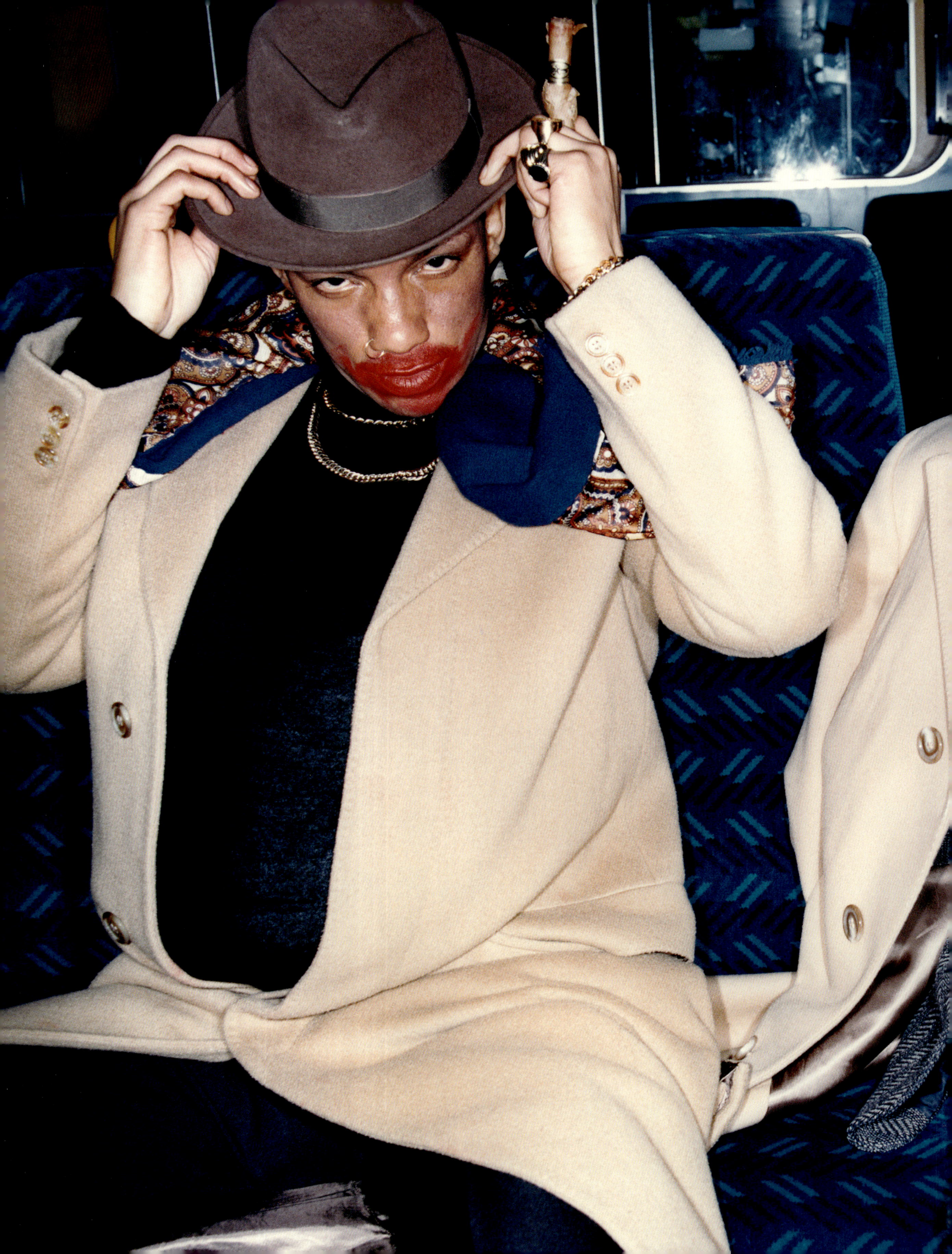

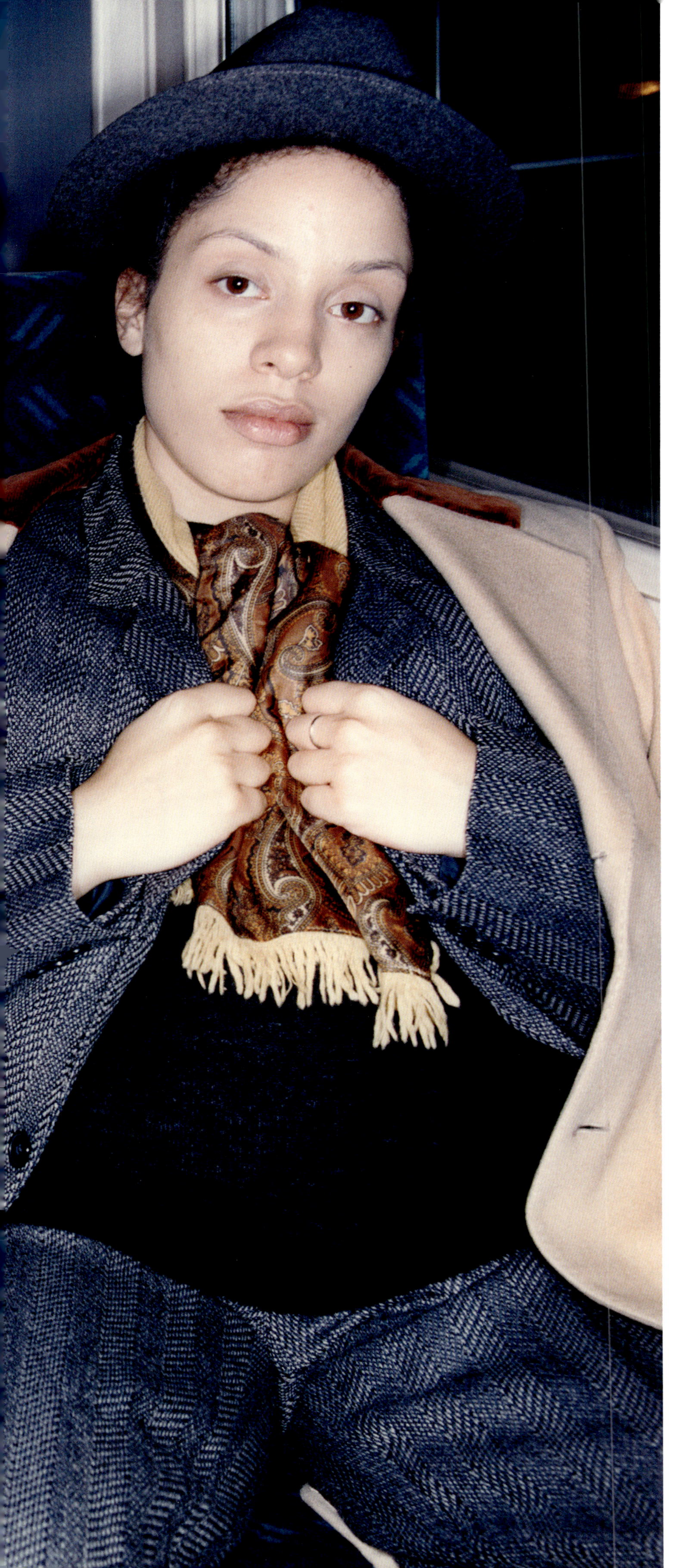

TRICKY AND
MARTINA TOPLEY-BIRD
By Mark Alesky
Styled by Greg Fay
and Justin Laurie
February 1995

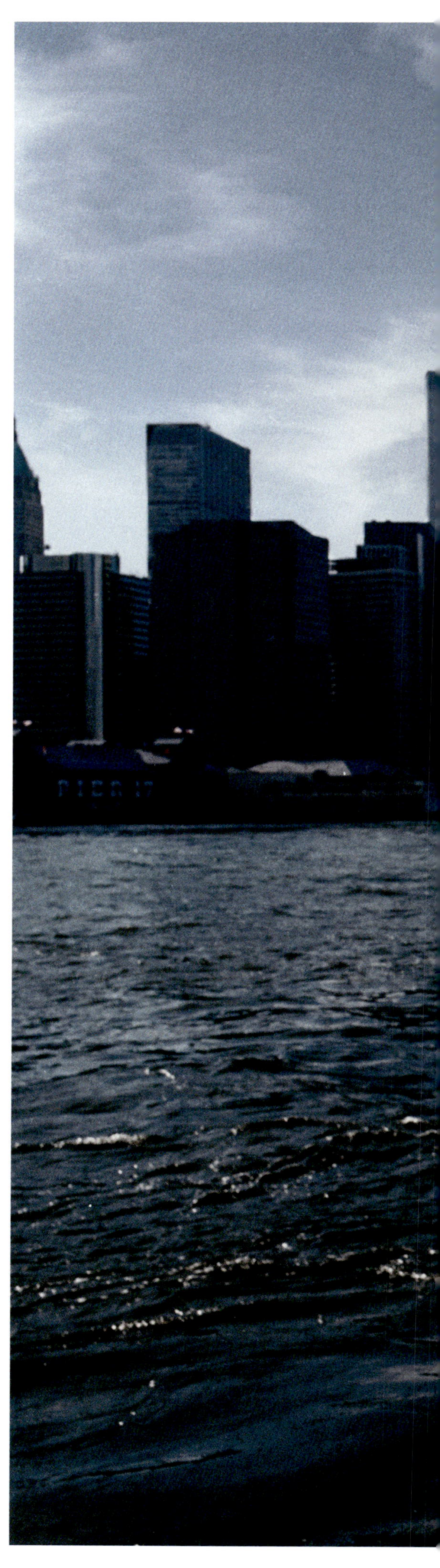

JAY-Z
By Franck Sauvaire
November 1997

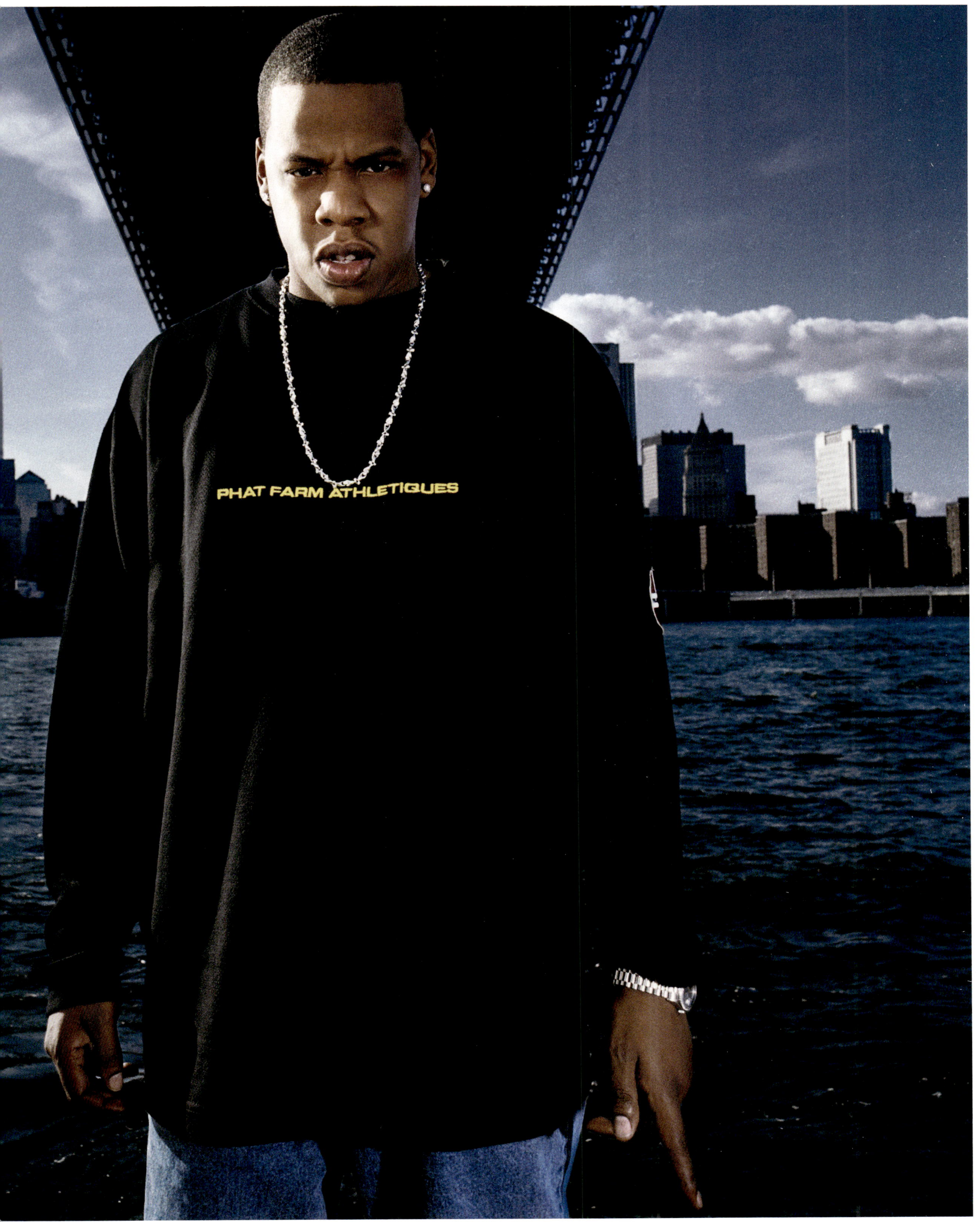
PHAT FARM ATHLETIQUES

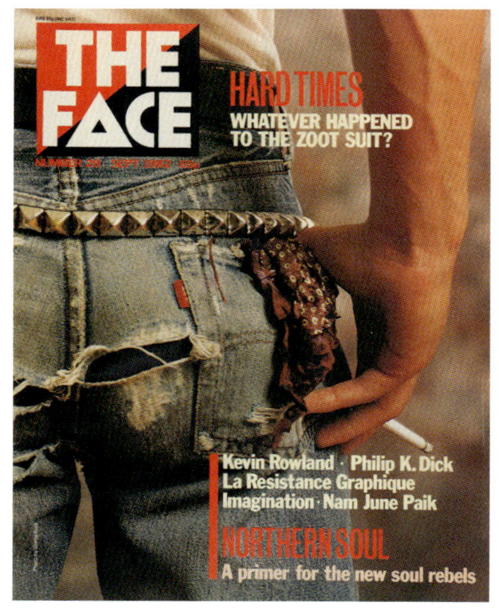

WRITING STYLE:
THE NEW JOURNALISM OF THE FACE

EKOW ESHUN

In 1973, *The New Journalism*, an anthology of ground-breaking newspaper and magazine writing edited by Tom Wolfe, announced the ascent of a stylistically adventurous generation of writers, such as Hunter S. Thompson and Joan Didion. In place of the dryly objective approach taken by others before them, these figures sought to document the swirling culture and society of the Sixties and Seventies with all the urgency, subjectivity and creative adventurousness that the era demanded. Or, as Wolfe put it, 'The hell with it … let chaos reign … louder music, more wine … All the old traditions are exhausted and no new one is yet established. All bets are off! The odds are cancelled! It's anybody's ballgame'.[1] New Journalism marked a period in American letters when the magazine was at its zenith and titles like *Esquire* and *The New Yorker* wielded enormous influence.

It's perhaps little surprise, then, that echoes of New Journalism can be found in the bravura prose style and commitment to speaking of the times characteristic of *The Face* during the Eighties and Nineties. This was another great magazine era when *The Face*, alongside other independently published style magazines like *i-D* and *Dazed & Confused*, spoke with thrilling dynamism and artistry; when story after story captured a scene or a subculture, understanding it both as a short-lived trend but also as a common feeling, a shared belief by a group of devotees in something they deemed precious and beautiful, and therefore something worth devoting time and skill to documenting. Here was Robert Elms on 'Hard Times' in September 1982: 'There is no such thing as a "generation gap" anymore; how can you rebel against the generation of Coltrane or Brando or MacInnes? What we have is a heritage that you can draw succour and inspiration from, and there's those who do and those who don't. That's the only gap.'[2] Here was David Toop on 'Electro: The Beat that Won't Be Beaten' in May 1984: 'The current phase of electro … is like black metal music for the Eighties, a hard-edged, ugly, beautiful trance as desperate and stimulating as New York itself.'[3] And Miranda Sawyer on 'Tribal Gathering' in August 1996: 'At 4am the normal world seemed very very far away … It was out there, somewhere, but far beyond our ken.'[4]

CONTENT AS STYLE

The irony of a title like *The Face* is that, despite the quality of its writing, only a few journalists on the magazine such as Dylan Jones, Julie Burchill and Tony Parsons achieved widespread recognition. For the most part they were overshadowed by the photographers, models and stylists that came to fame through its pages, such as Corinne Day, Kate Moss and Ray Petri. Yet, the worth of the magazine was in its devotion to ideas as much as to imagery; to philosophy and politics as much as to fashion and music. In part, this was a reflection of the times. For a decade or so, beginning in the early Eighties, pop culture in Britain was typified by a bracing sense of intellectual ambition. This was the era when a nightclub could be named after a Situationist International slogan (The

Haçienda), a band titled in homage to the writings of Italian Marxist theorist Antonio Gramsci (Scritti Politti) and a record label named for a poem by Italian Futurist Filippo Tommaso Marinetti, 'Zang Tumb Tumb' (ZTT).

The Face maintained a similarly cerebral approach in its writing. Cover stories on Madonna, Nirvana or Prince were searching rather than adulatory. Inside you might find an interview with an author of speculative fiction, like J.G. Ballard, or an influential theorist of Postmodernism, such as Jean Baudrillard. The magazine could be empathic in tone, as with its reporting on the AIDS crisis or the Somali Civil War; it was also strikingly prescient. 'We could live in a grim, cold Fortress Europe shuttered from outside influences, and allowing "foreigners" in only as guest workers on short contracts … Or we can opt for an exciting, dynamic mix of cultures and races working together,'[5] wrote Sheryl Garratt, the magazine's Editor in May 1992, addressing questions of identity and nationhood that remain very much alive in Britain today, more than three decades later.

In an essay about *The Face* in 1988, the sociologist Dick Hebdige was sharply critical of its heterogeneous editorial approach. To elide fashion imagery and war commentary was to create a magazine stripped of moral consequence. '*The Face* is hyper-conformist: more commercial than the commercial, more banal than the banal. [It has] flattened everything to the glossy world of the image and presented its style as content.'[6]

But that's not how I remember it. I was a teenage reader of *The Face* when Hebdige was savaging it. From the drab suburban London where I grew up, the magazine didn't seem guilty of flattening anything. Rather, it offered the thrilling vision of a cosmopolitan society where ambition, imagination and an acute aesthetic sensibility might turn you into another of the self-made stars celebrated on its cover, from Leigh Bowery and Sade to Blur and Björk.

My heroes were never the cover stars though but rather the writers I followed avidly, and whose ranks I eventually joined. I worked at *The Face* during the Nineties, first as a freelancer and then as Assistant Editor. To write for the magazine, along with my fellow contributors and editors, was to participate in a dizzying exercise that involved the blurring of art and life. It was to conjure the world anew on our own terms each month, with all the audacity and imagination that we could summon to the task. ∎

Ekow Eshun is a writer, curator and broadcaster.

2000

2004

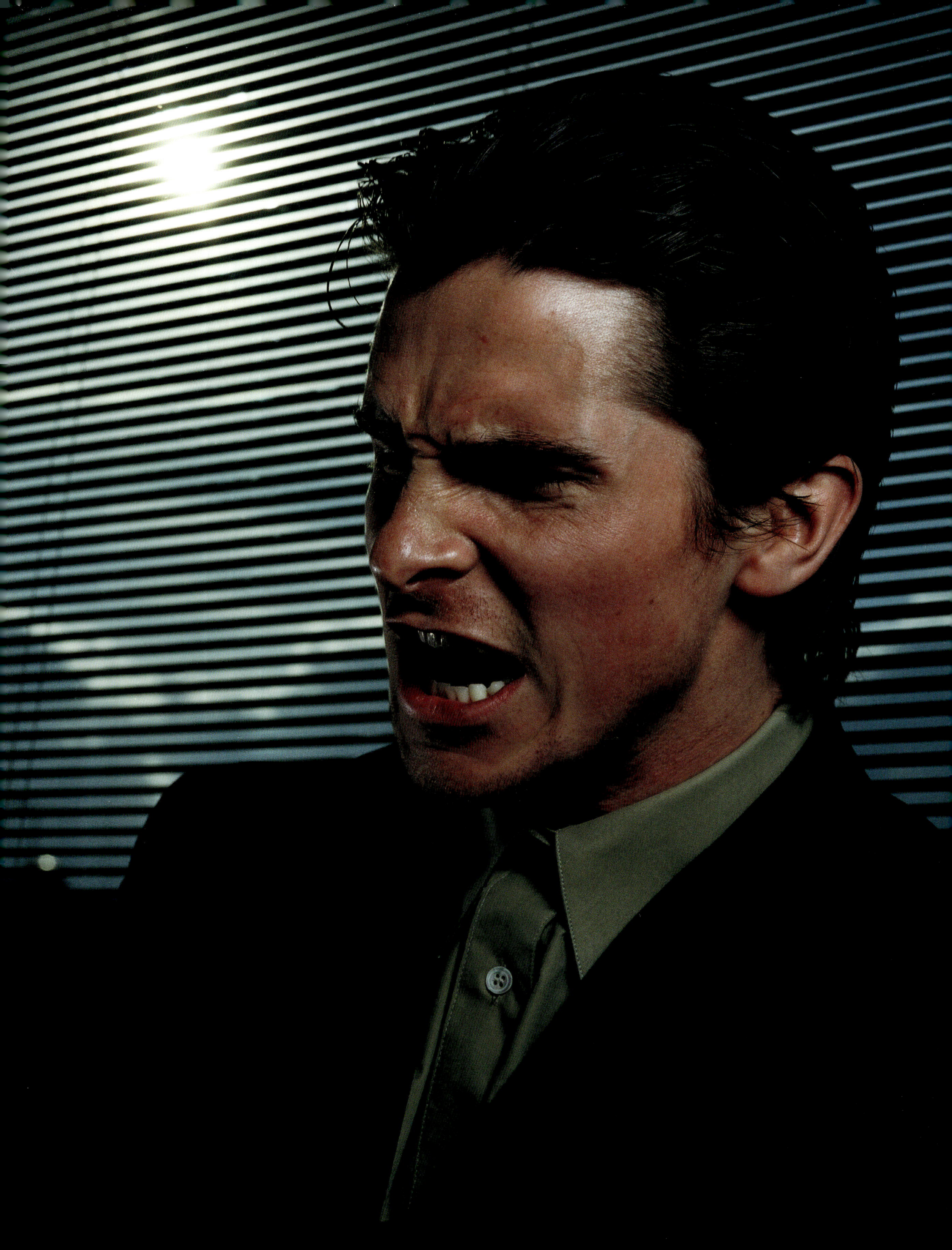

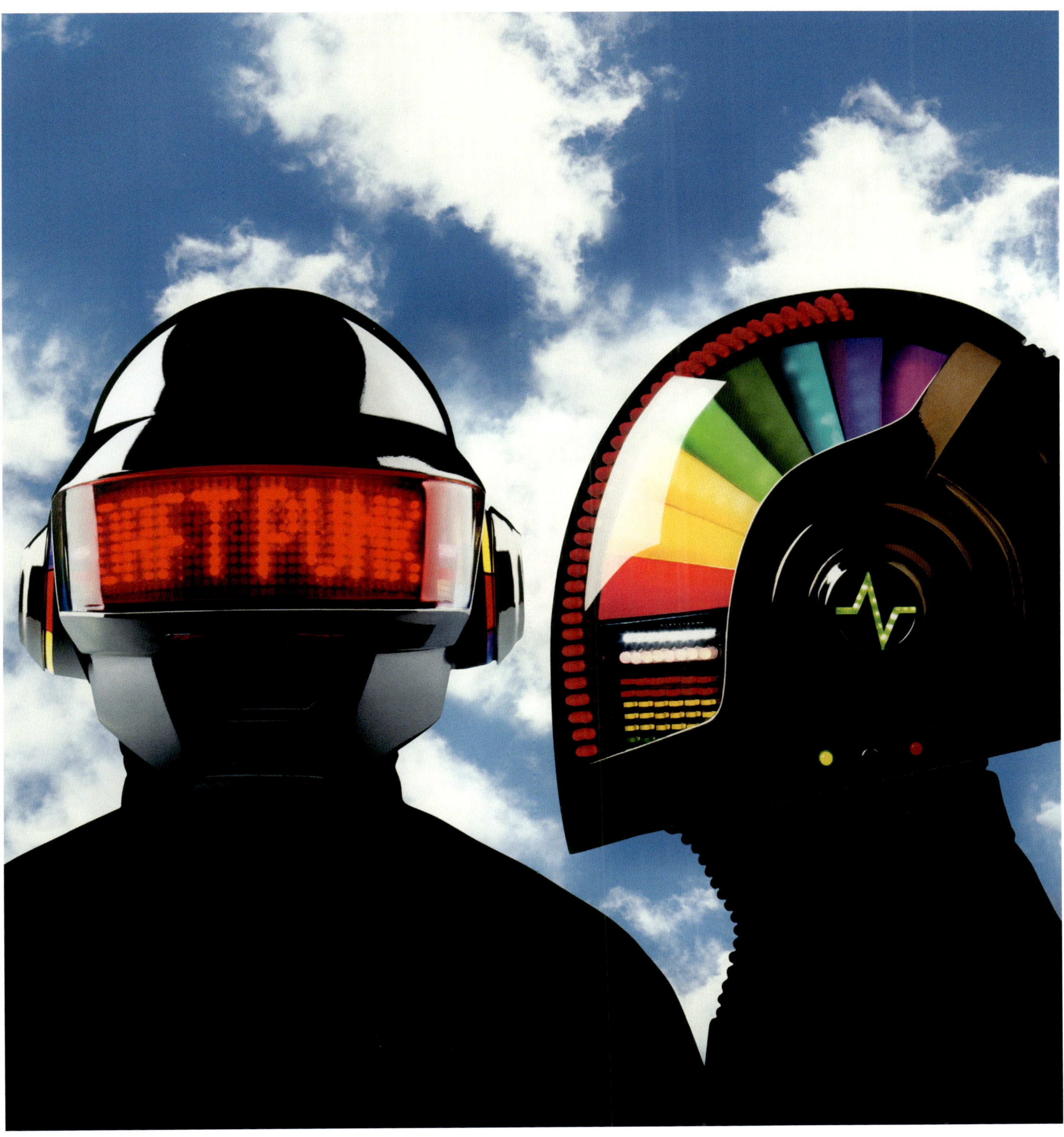

CHRISTIAN BALE

By James Dimmock
Styled by Allan Kennedy
April 2000

DAFT PUNK

By Toby McFarlan Pond
February 2C01

It was one of the greatest moments of my life to shoot a cover for *The Face*, a magazine I used to religiously go and order from the newsagent in Barton-on-Sea back in the mid-Eighties. *The Face* in 1984 was the only way to find out what was going on in a world that actually meant something to me at age 16. It meant a lot and it still does.
Toby Mcfarlan Pond

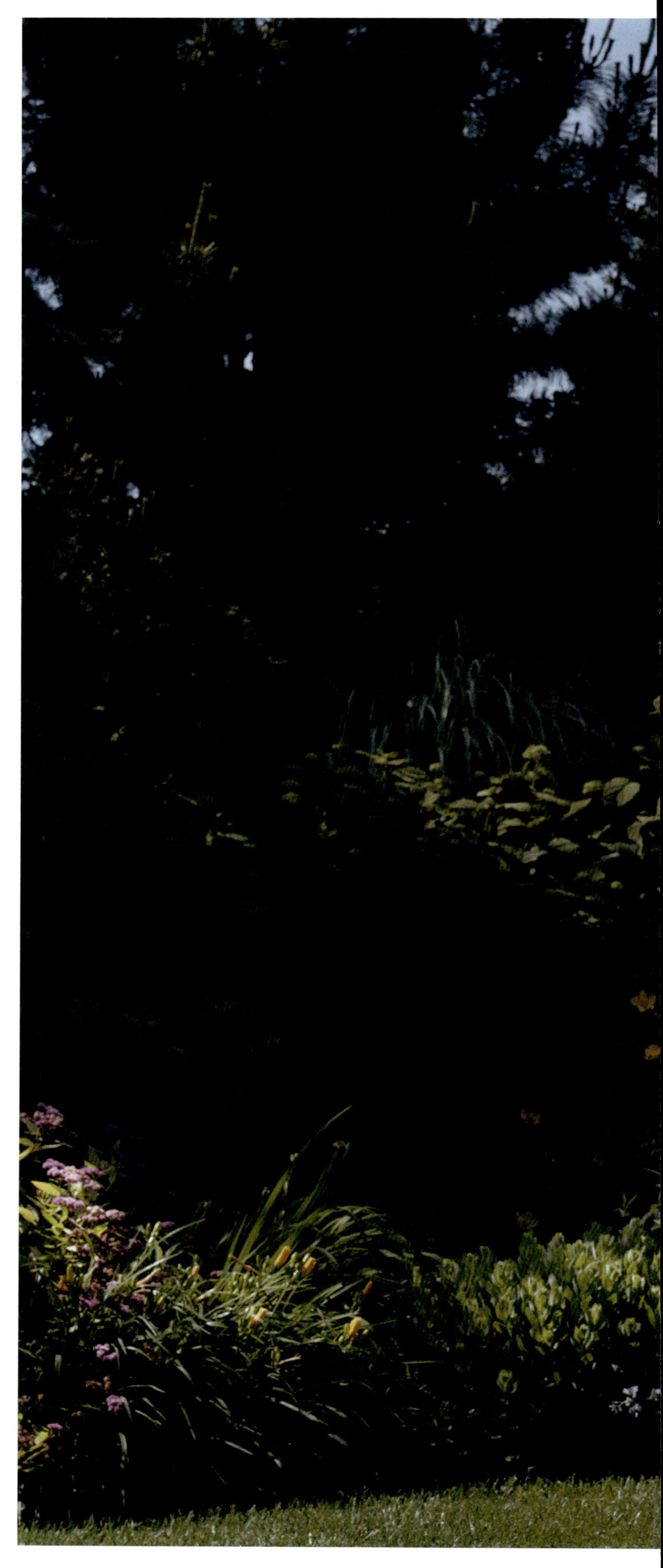

MCQUEEN ON THE GREEN
By Steven Klein
Styled by Katie Grand
June 2003

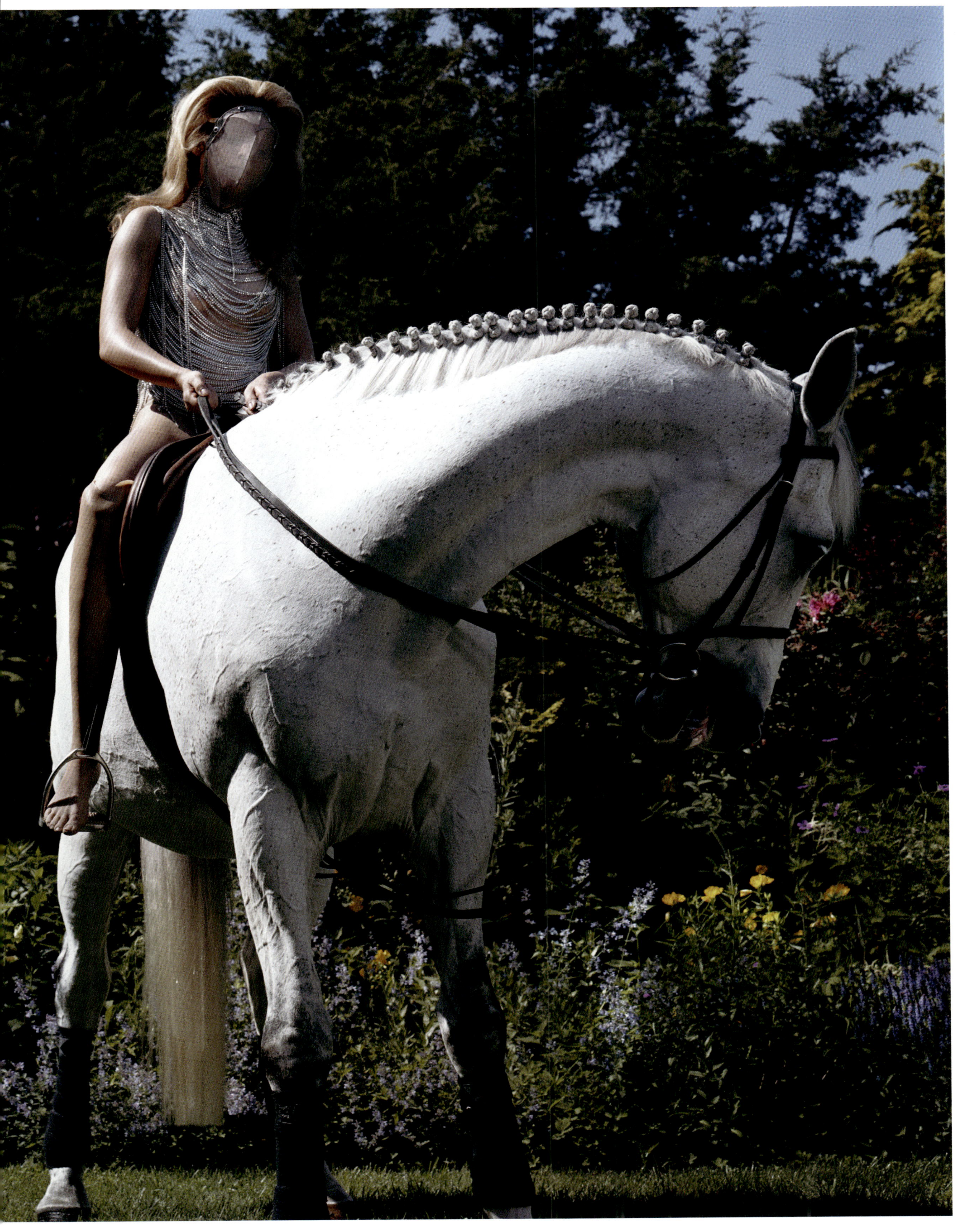

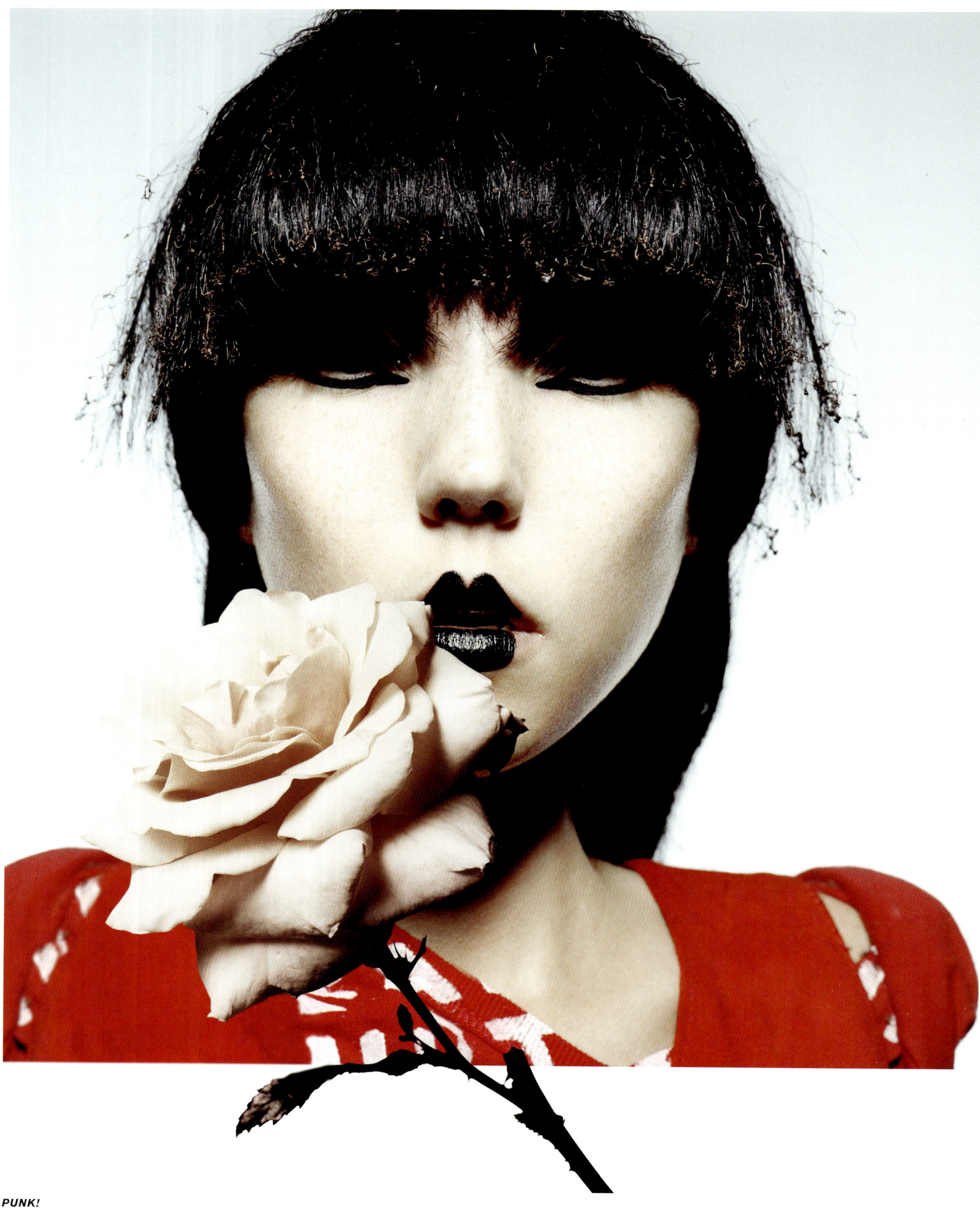

PUNK!
By Mert & Marcus
Styled by Katie Grand
September 2000

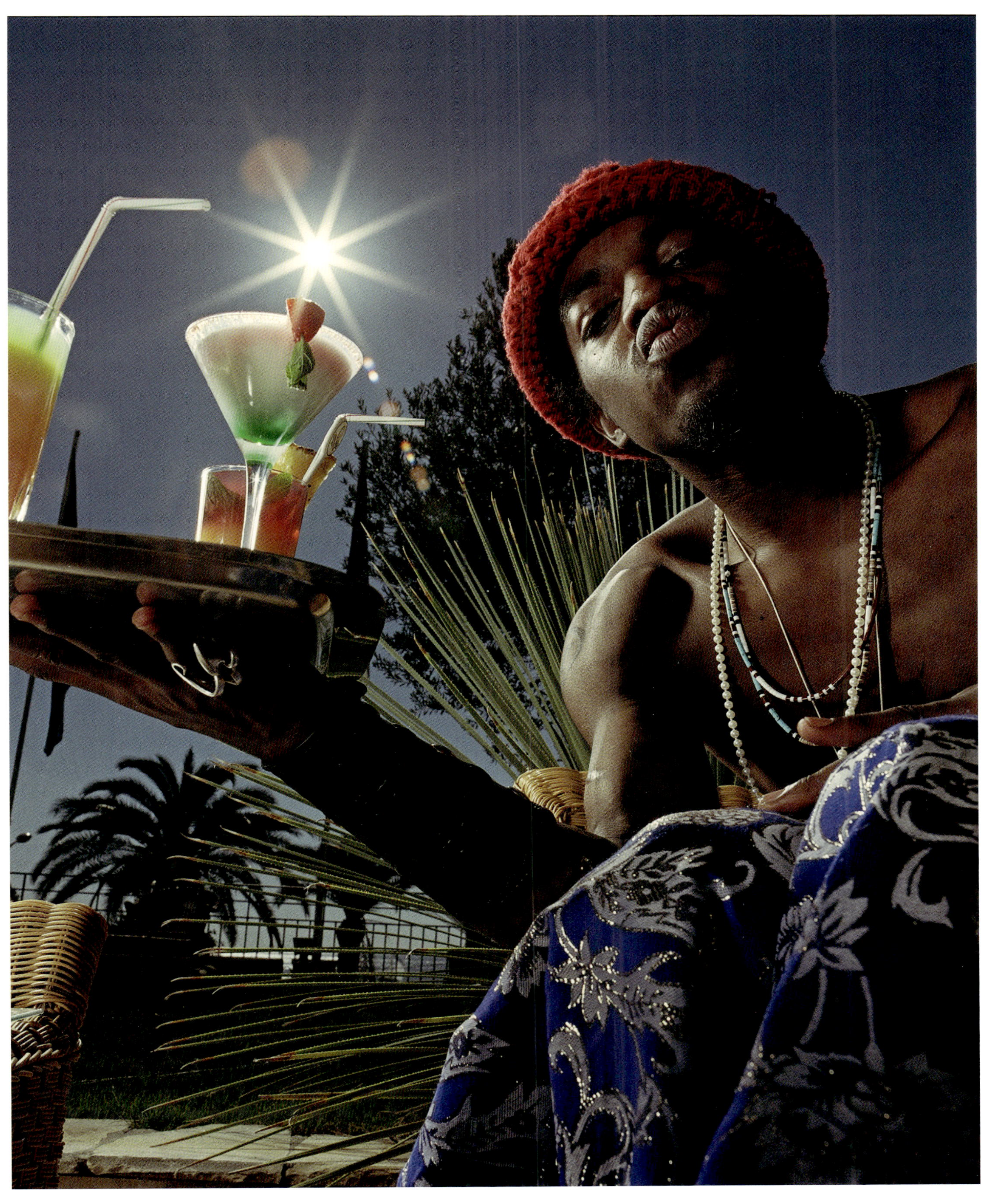

ANDRÉ 3000
By James Dimmock
December 2000

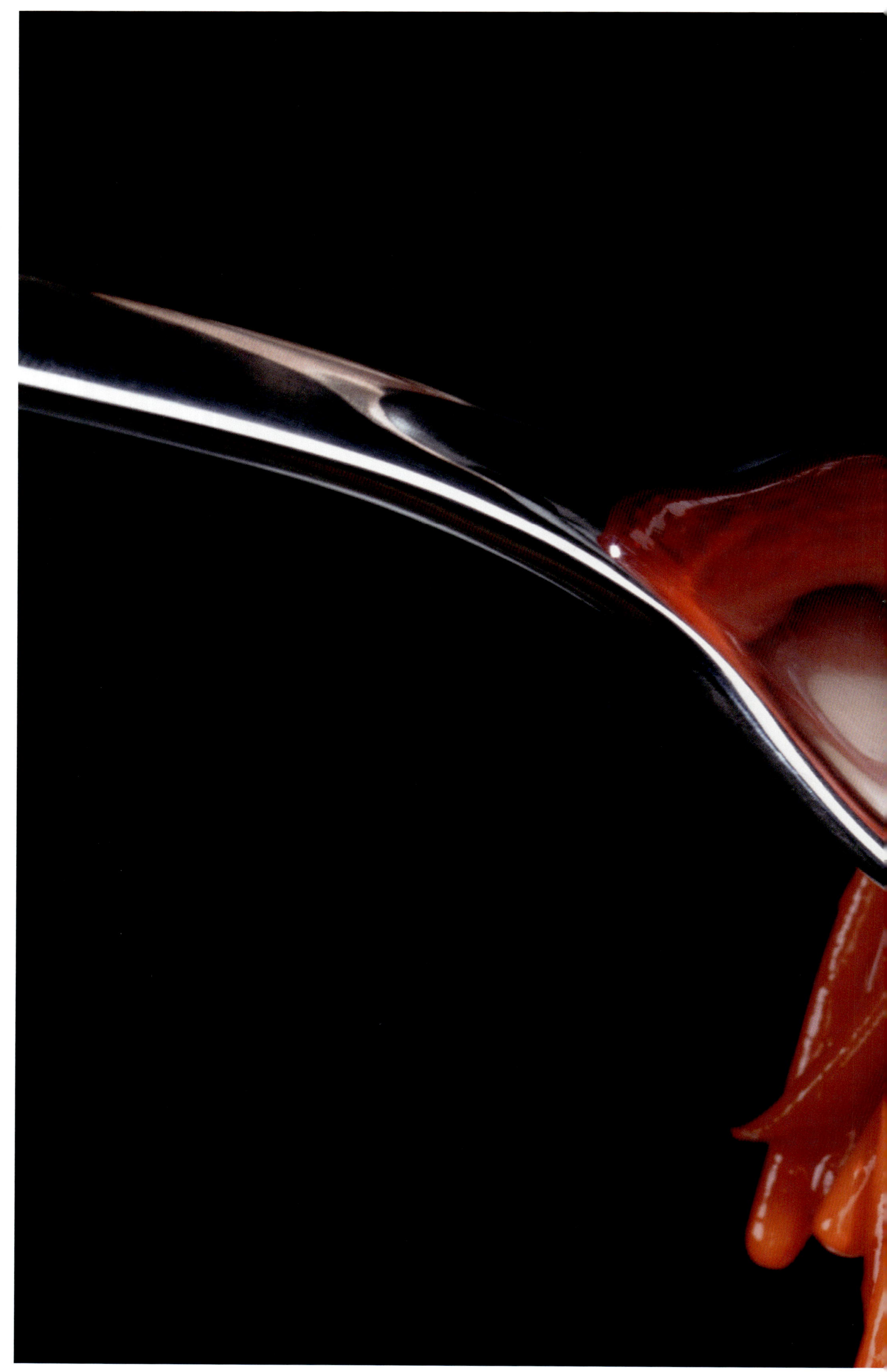

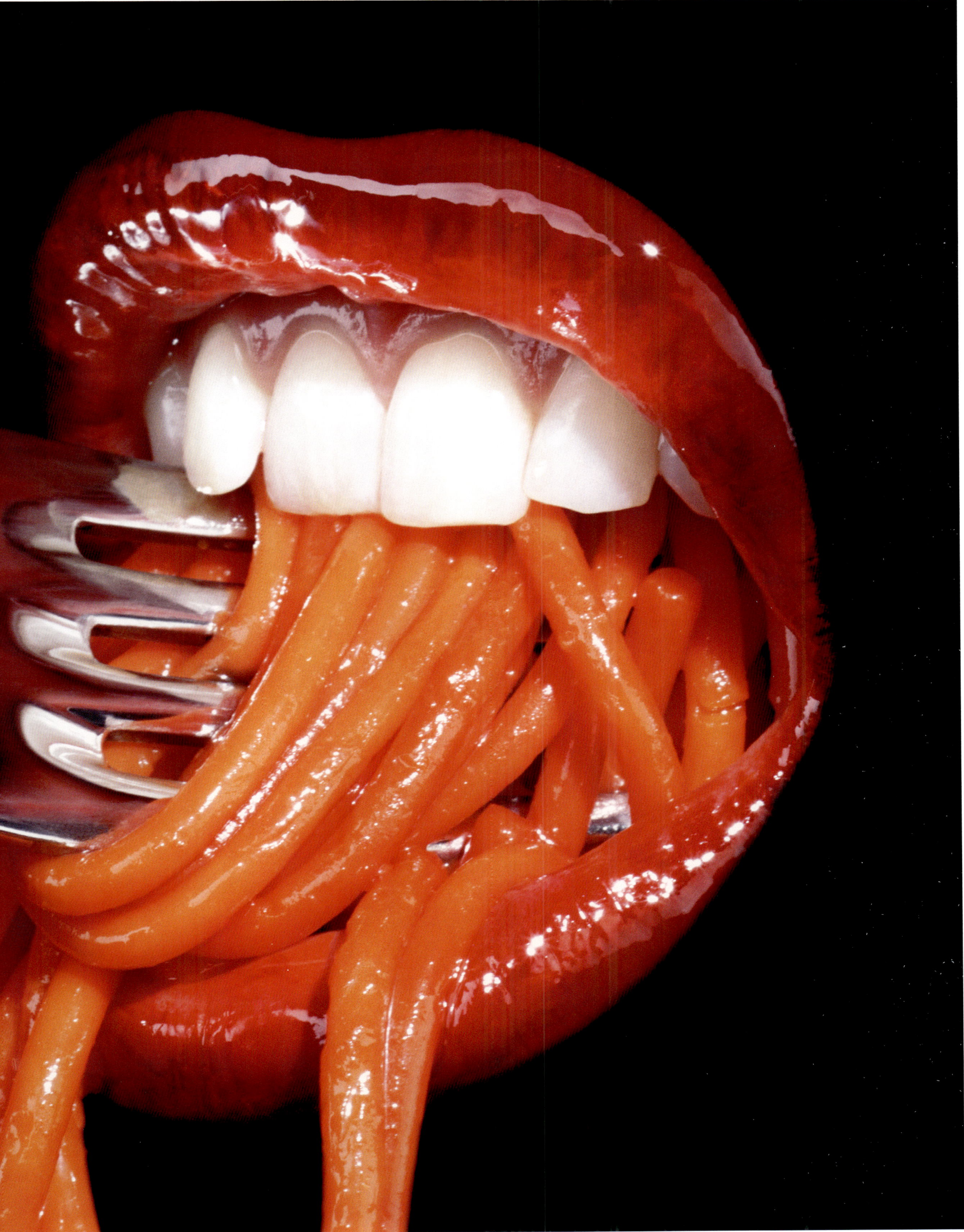

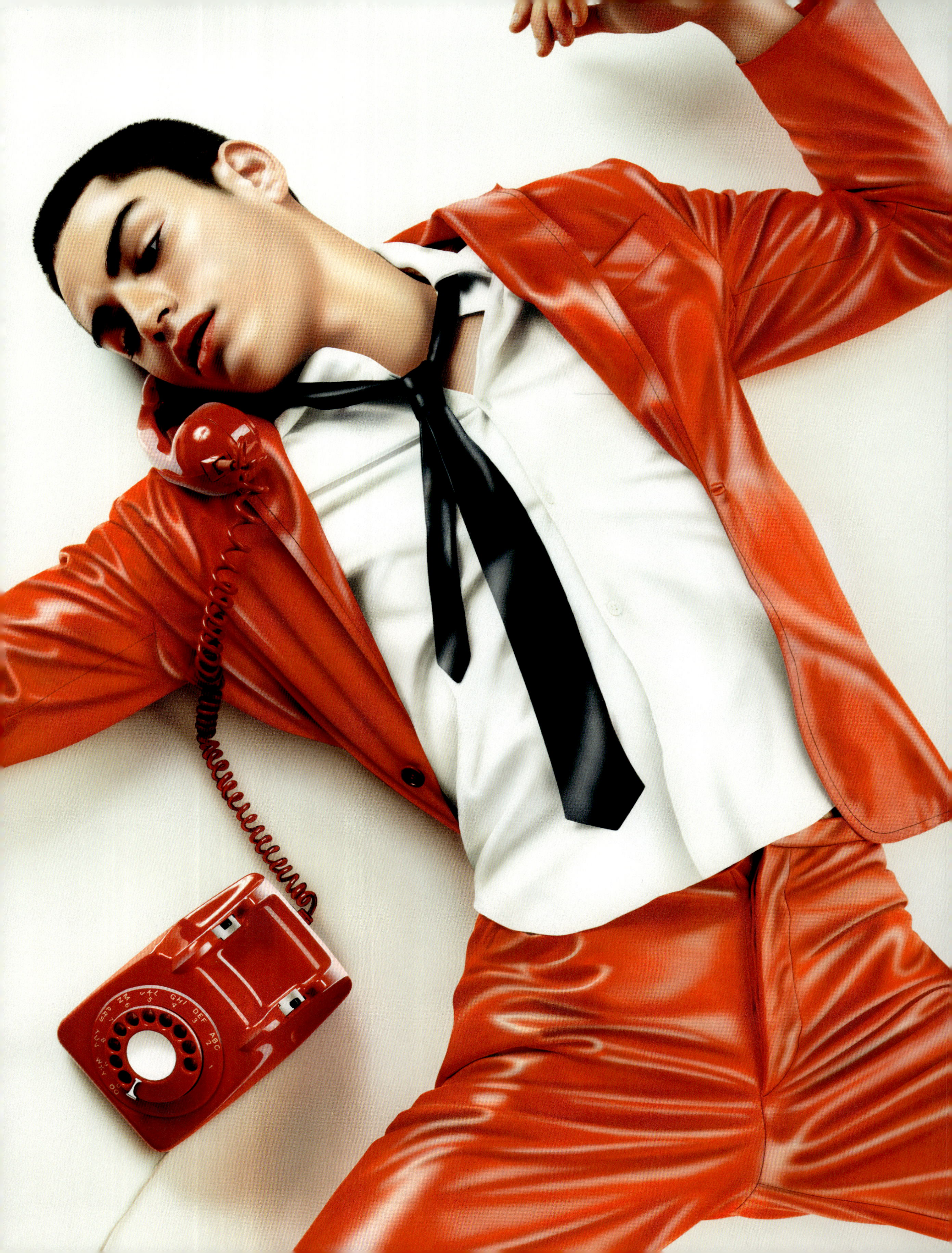

Sølve was always so creative and inspiring to work with, using different techniques that were really new ... we'd work the fashion around the concept, always thinking of the image, rather than just documenting clothes. When I saw these spray-painted images – a collaboration with the airbrush artist, George – I was blown away.
Simon Robins

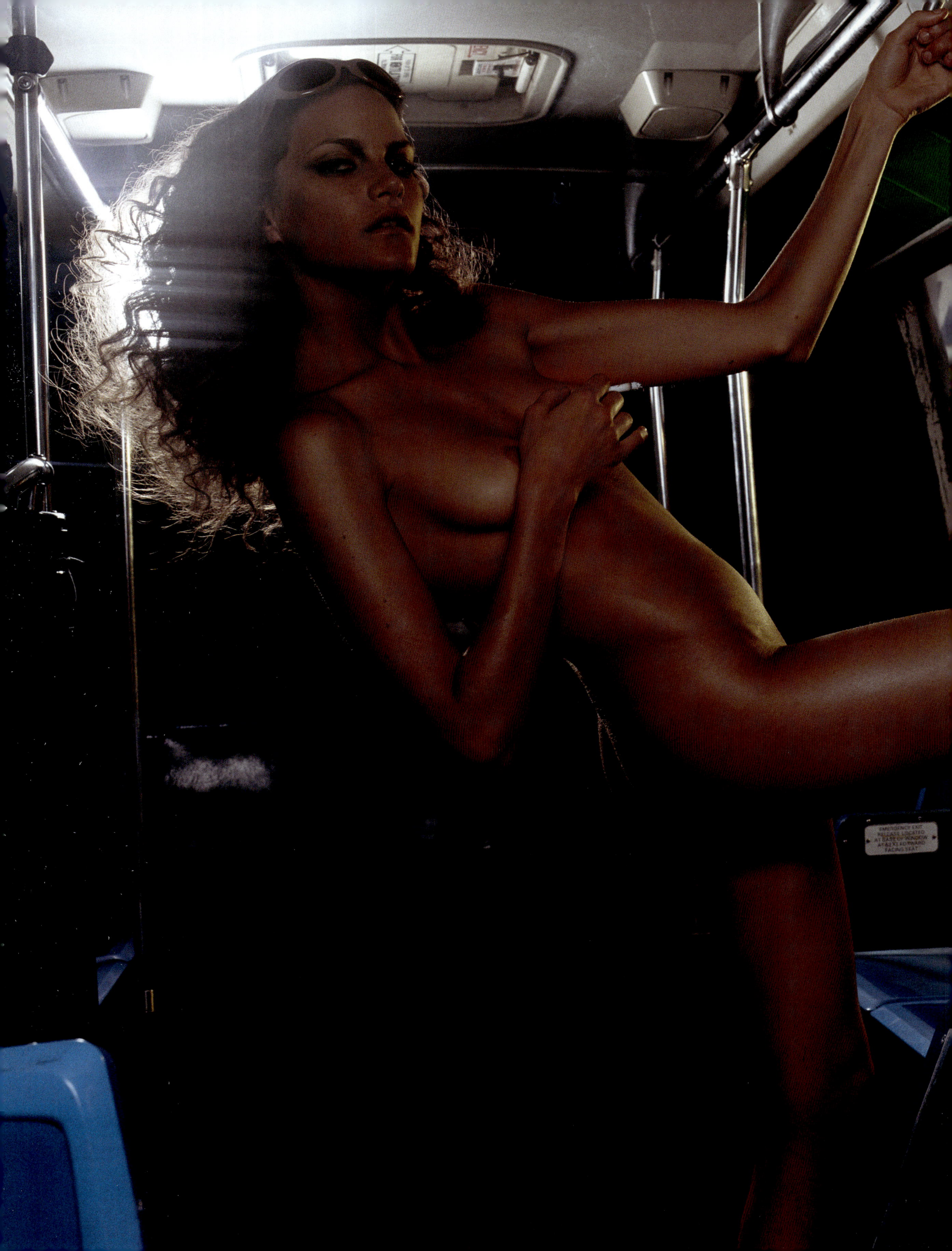

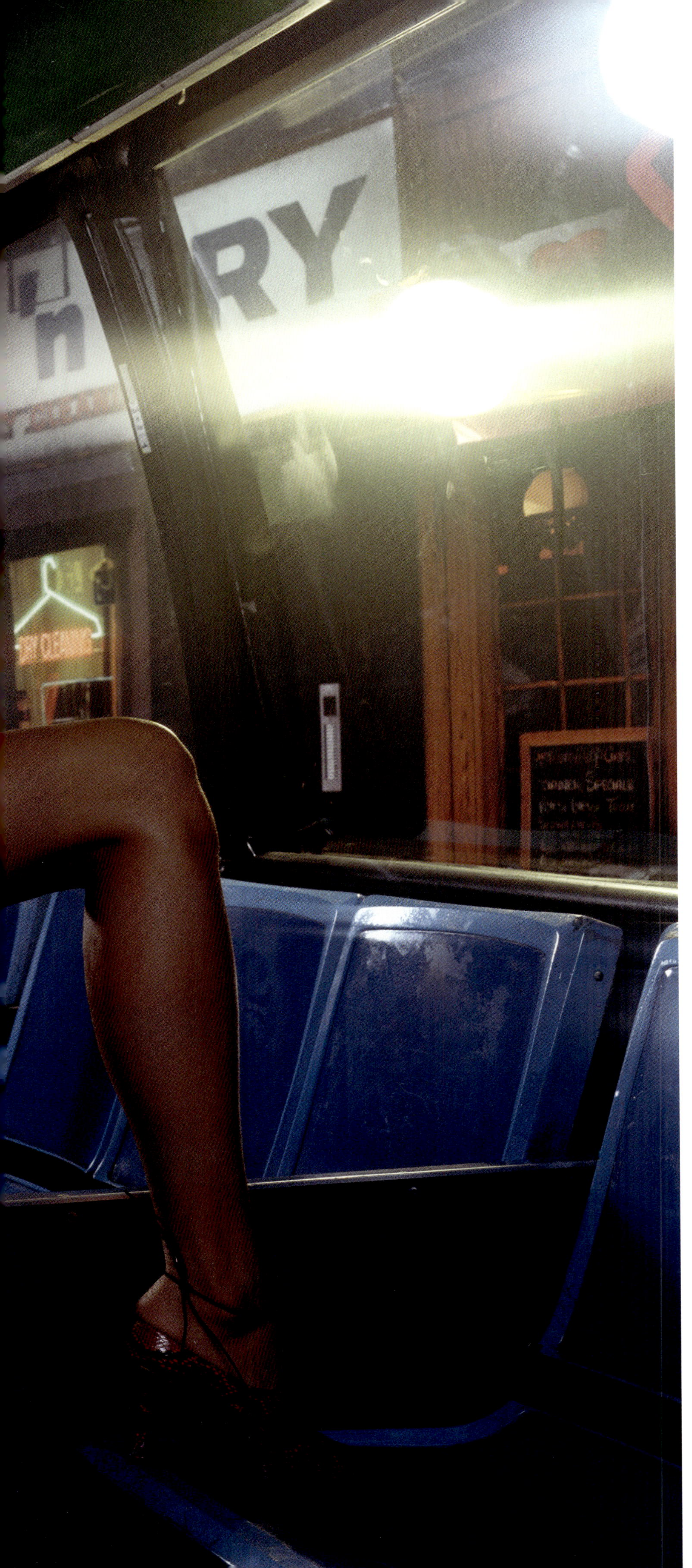

**AND ALL MY CLOTHES
FELL OFF...**
By Vincent Peters
May 2000

The Face had an art school
atmosphere, providing the grounds
to experiment. I was young and
lucky to start with these conditions,
to be pushed into an original,
provocative style. It wasn't about
selling clothes. You were looking
beyond fashion, which brought a
much bigger range and interesting
dialogue to everyone's work.
Vincent Peters

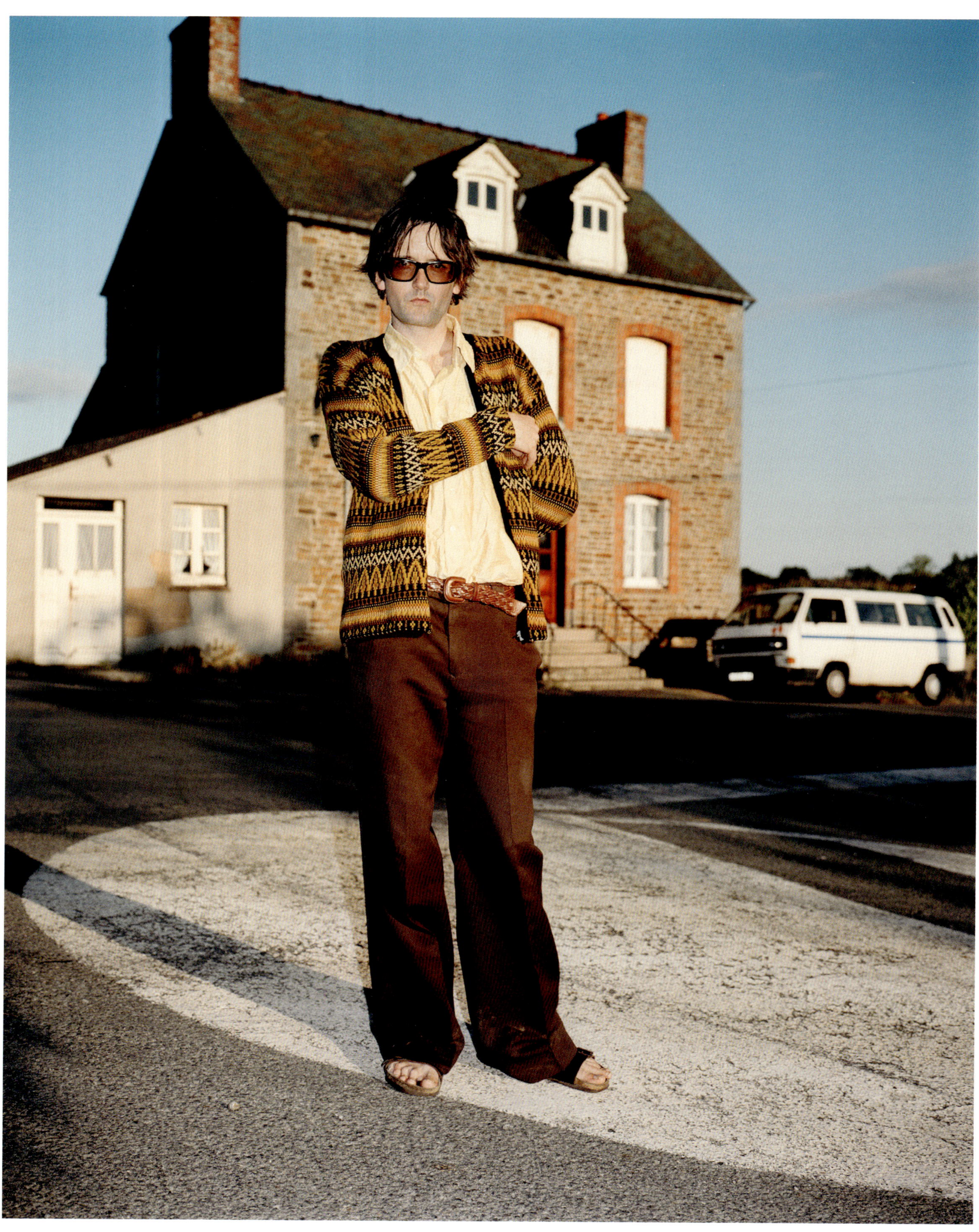

JARVIS COCKER
By Frederike Helwig
October 2001

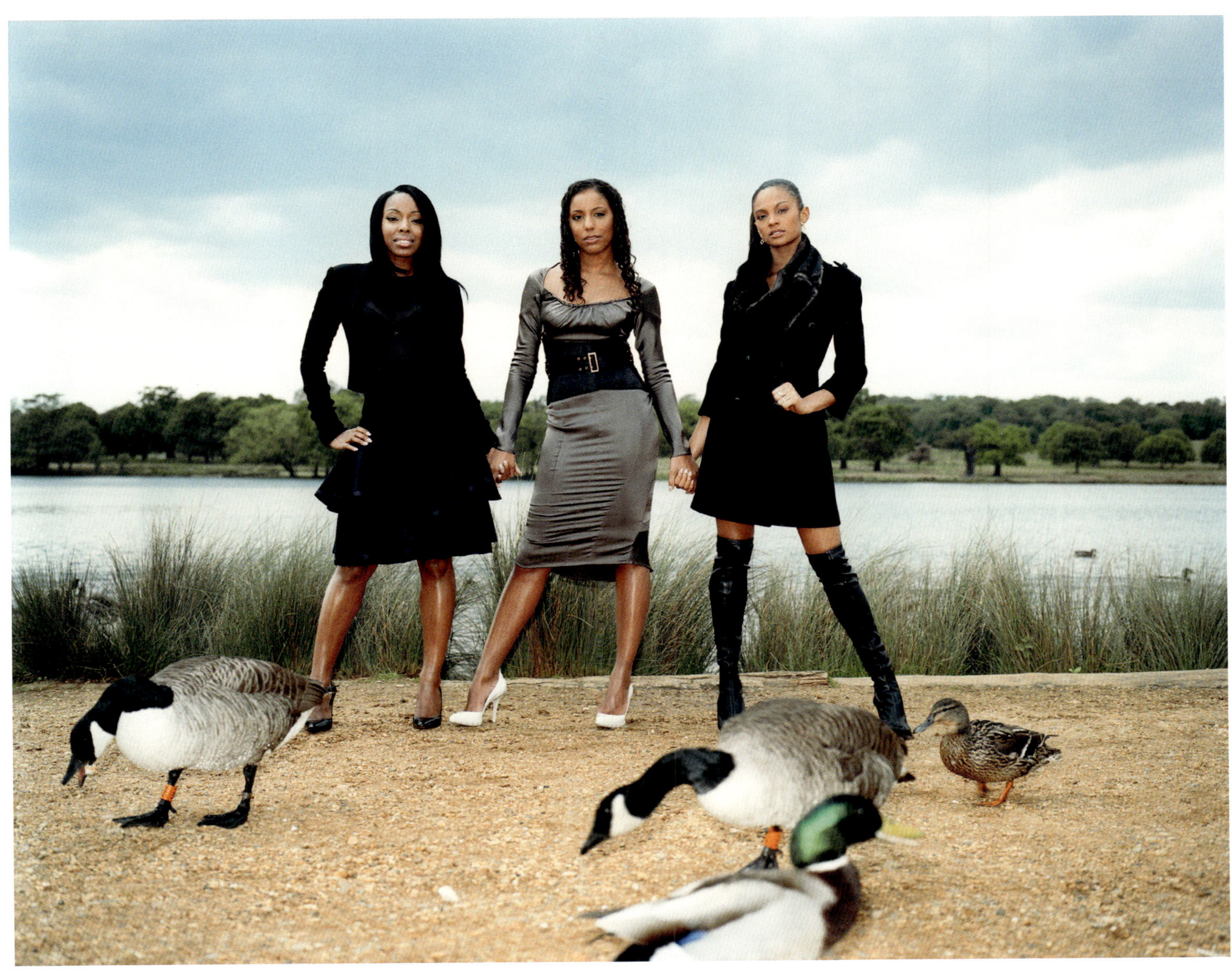

MIS-TEEQ
By Frederike Helwig
Styled by Karina Givargisoff
July 2003

Following left
**SAY HELLO, NEW-WAVE
GOODBYE**
By Sølve Sundsbø
Styled by Simon Robins
September 2000

Following right
PHOEBE PHILO
By Vincent Peters
Styled by Andrew Davis
September 2002

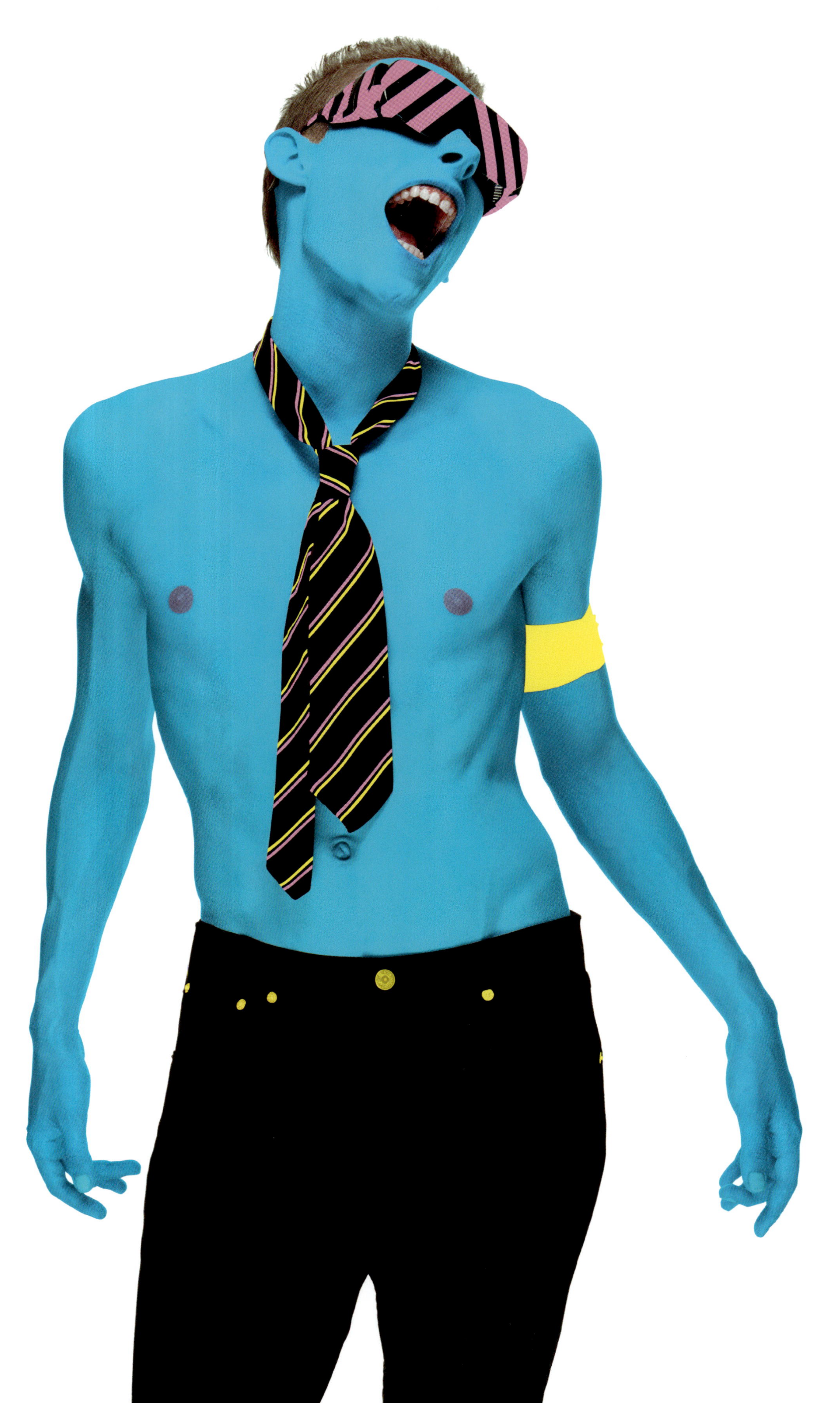

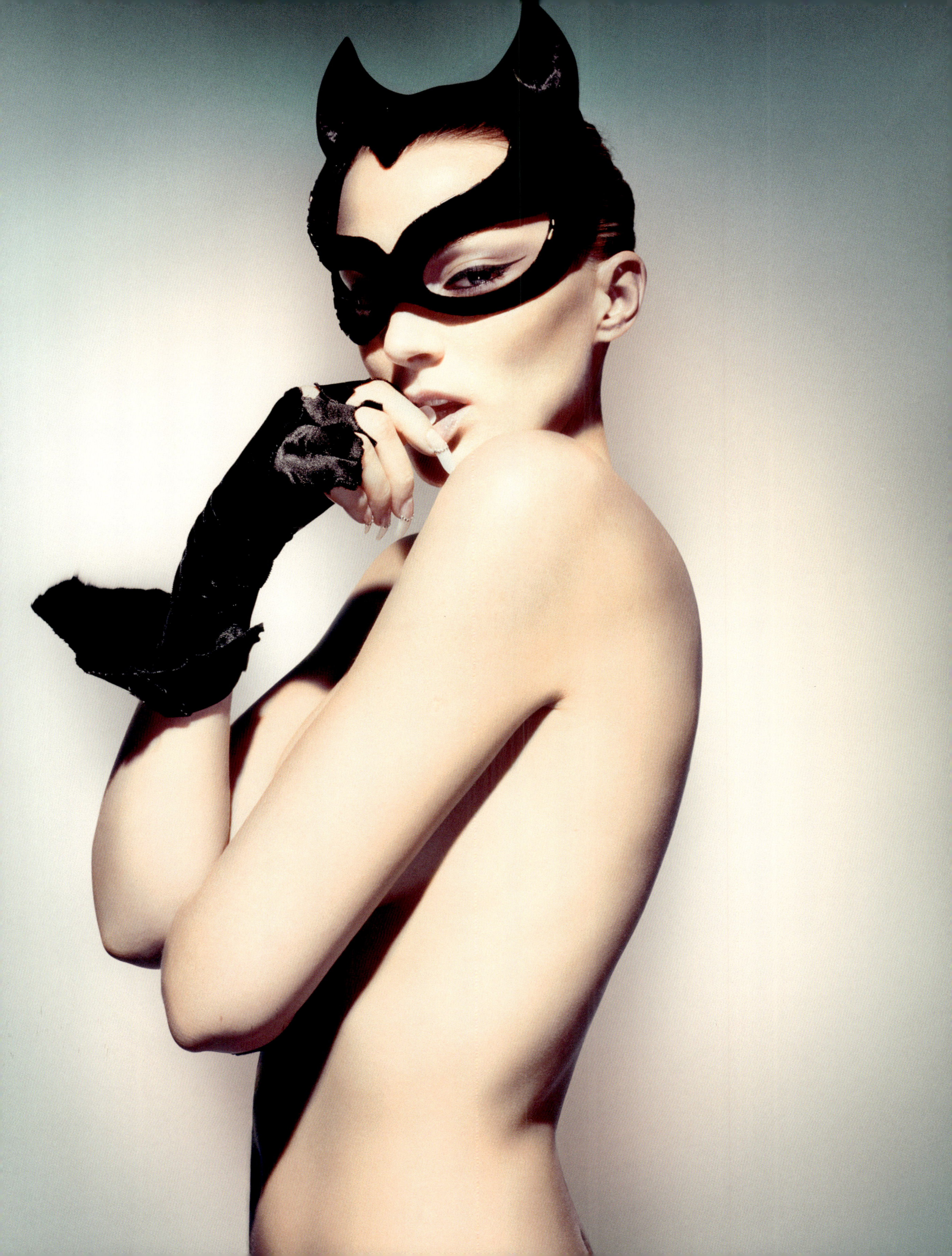

Taking a portrait of someone who is 'famous' brings with it a temporary power switch. When I am photographing, I can feel the power shifting from the person to me. With this shift comes an element of responsibility: to be kind, to be truthful, not to be cruel. But it is also possible to let the door creak open for something more than 'depicting an image' to seep through and manifest itself onto the celluloid.

FREDERIKE HELWIG, PHOTOGRAPHER

RYAN GOSLING
By Frederike Helwig
December 2001

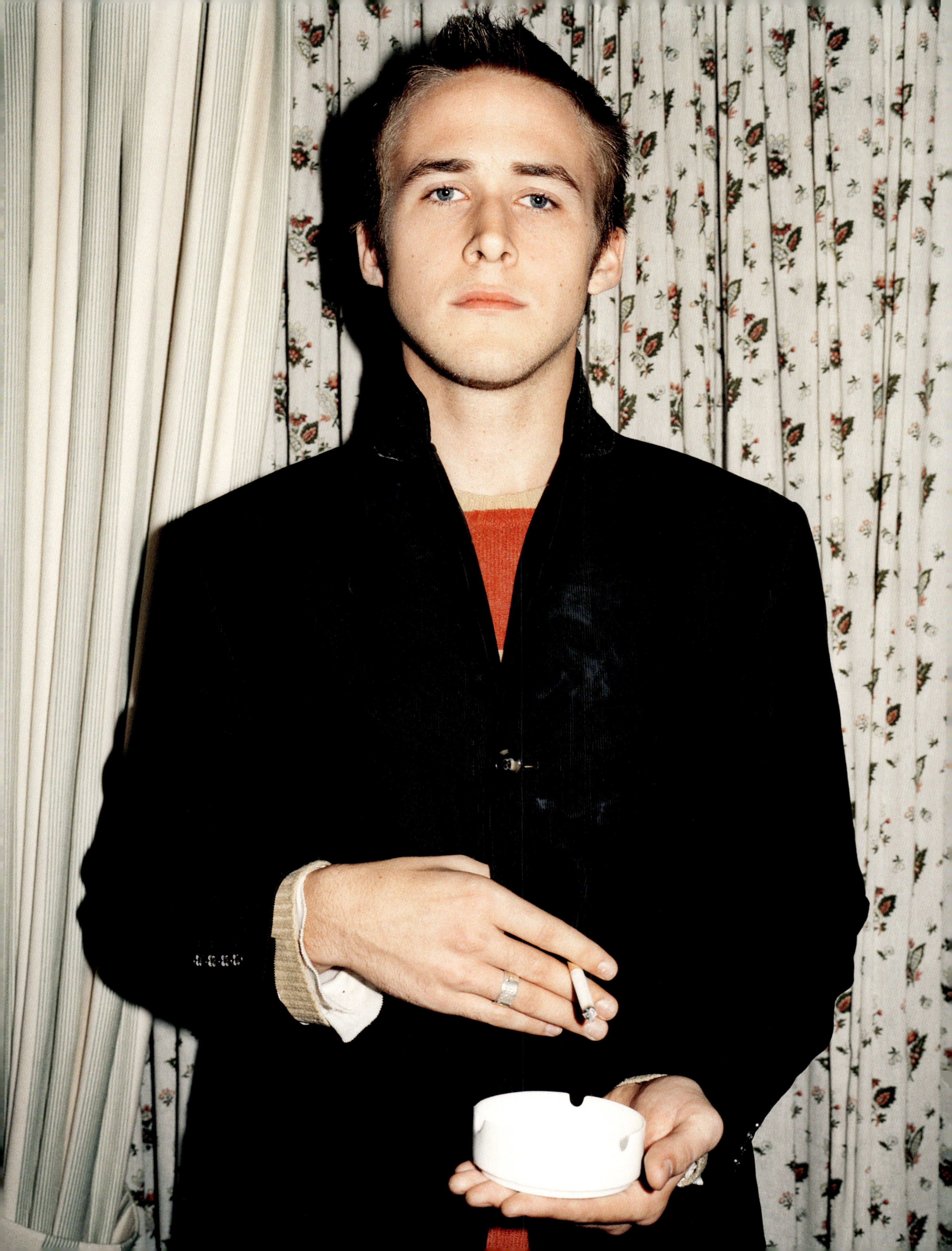

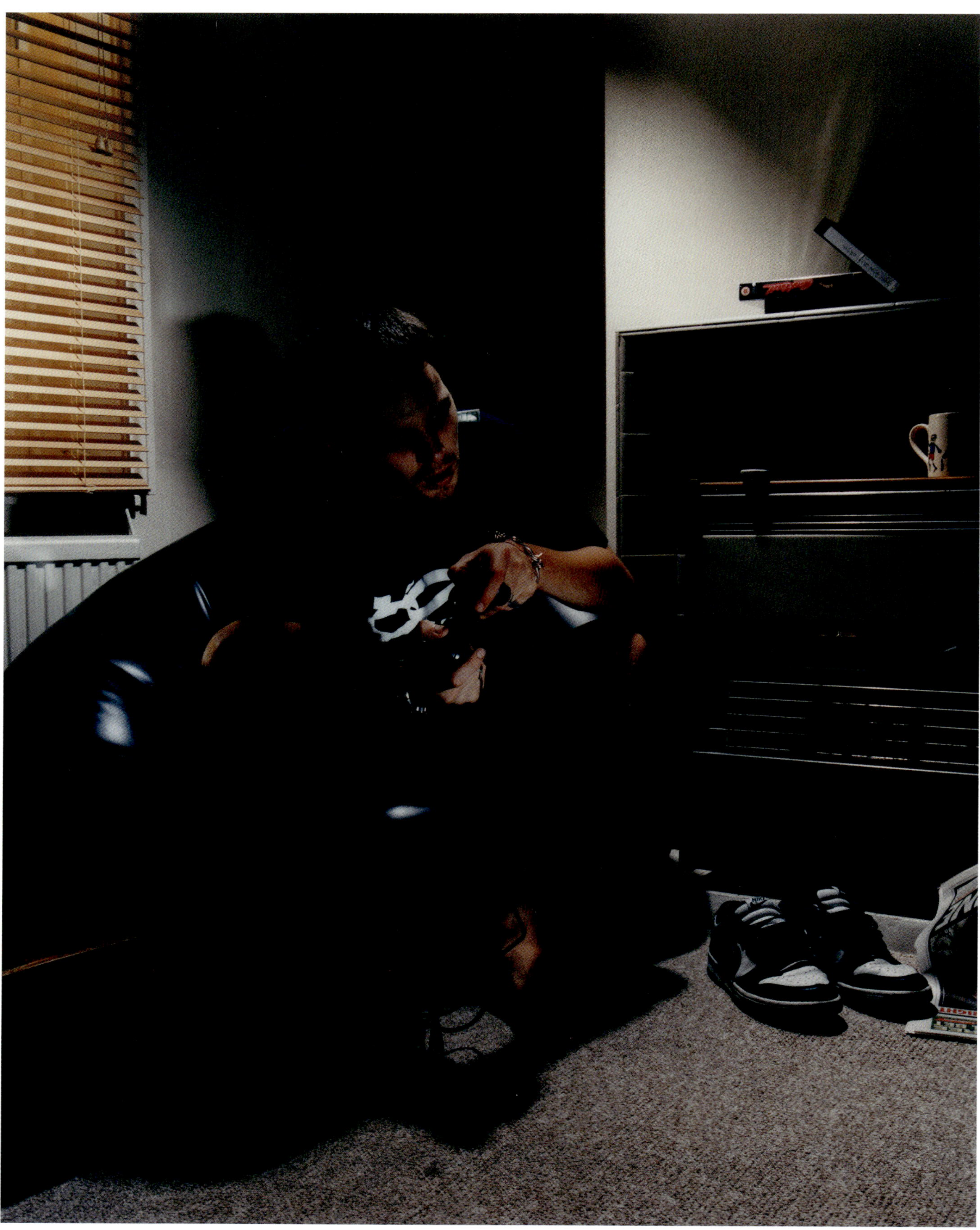

MIKE SKINNER
By Ewen Spencer
February 2004

HARD, HARDER, HARDEST
By Sølve Sundsbø
Styled by Katie Grand
May 2001

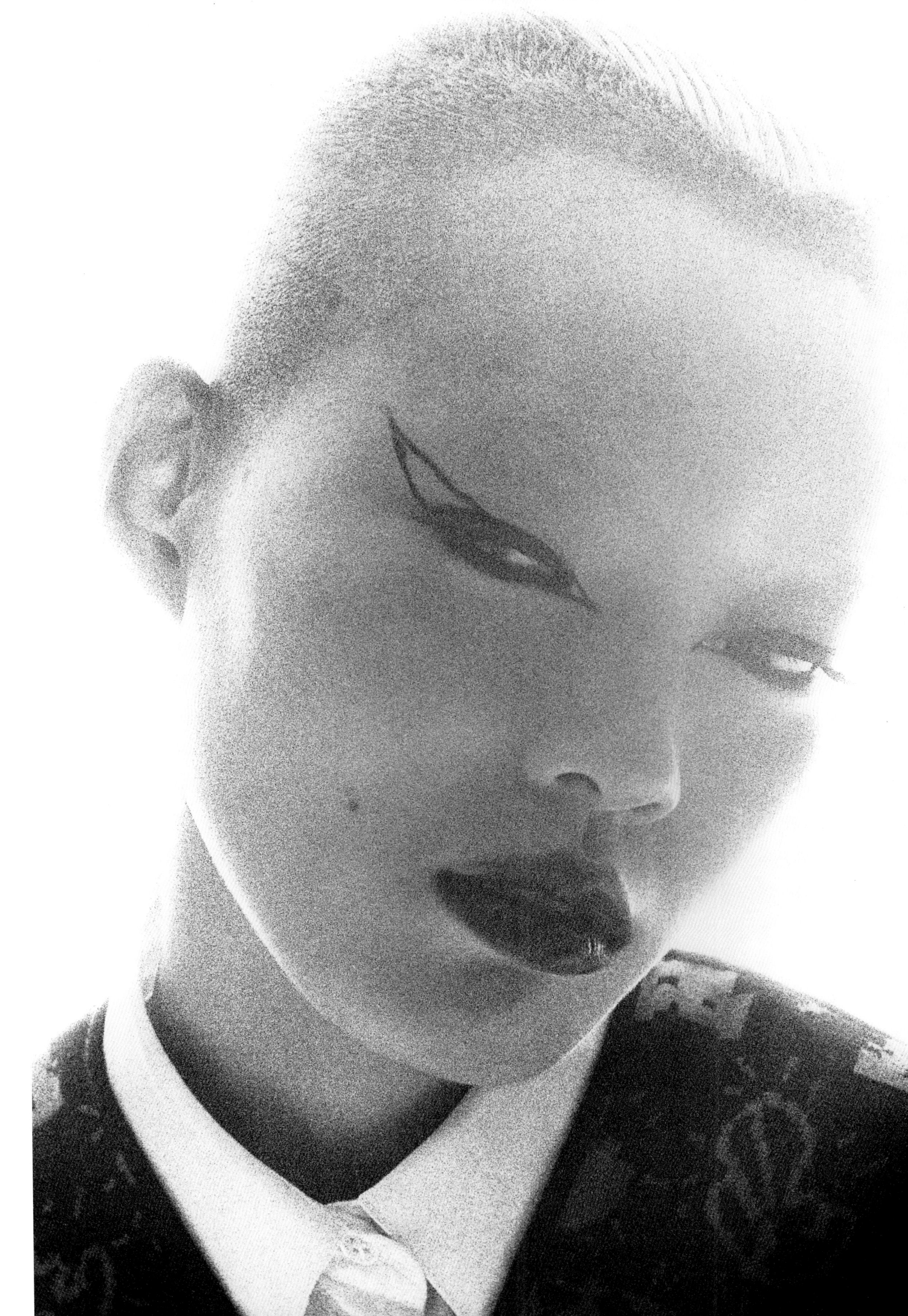

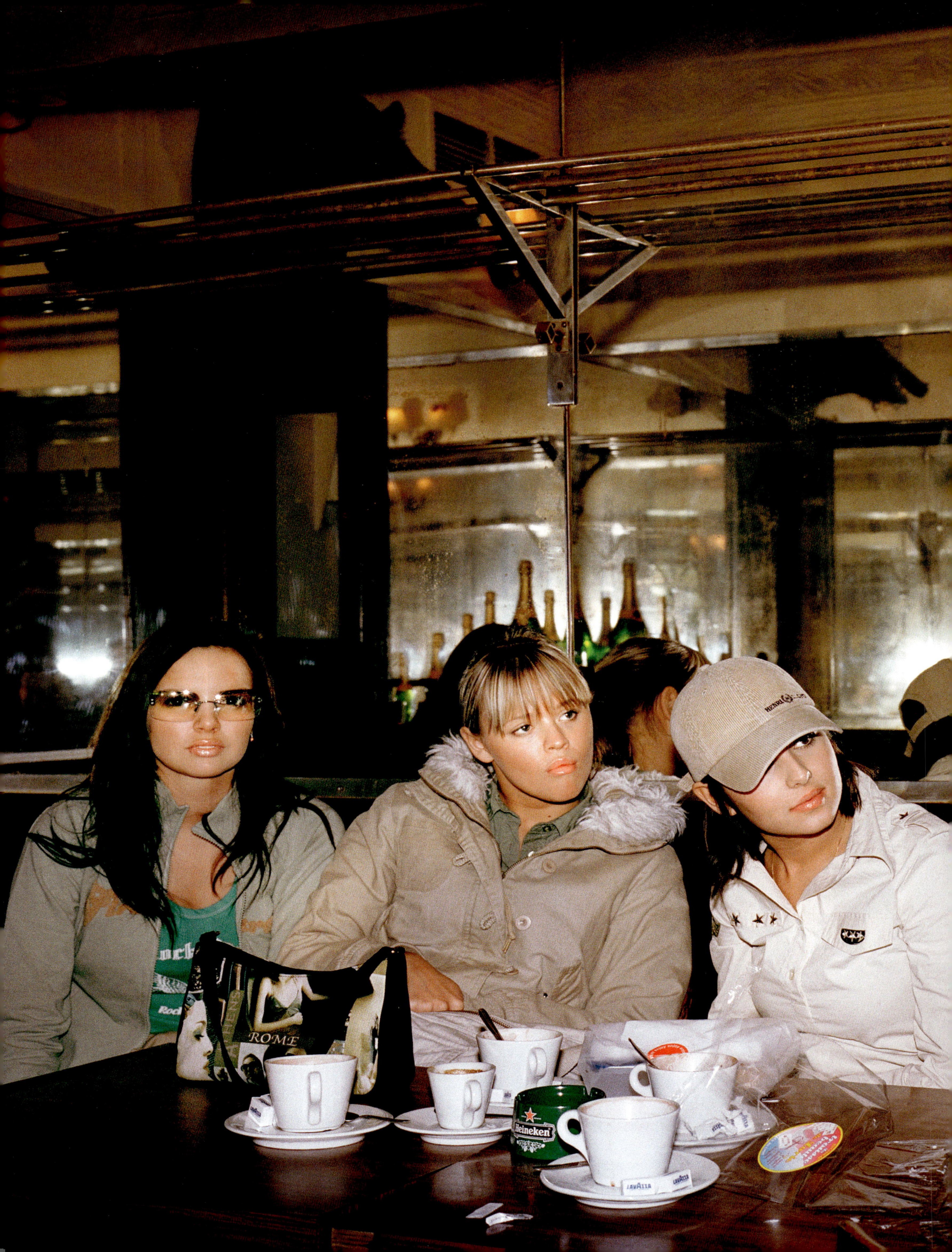

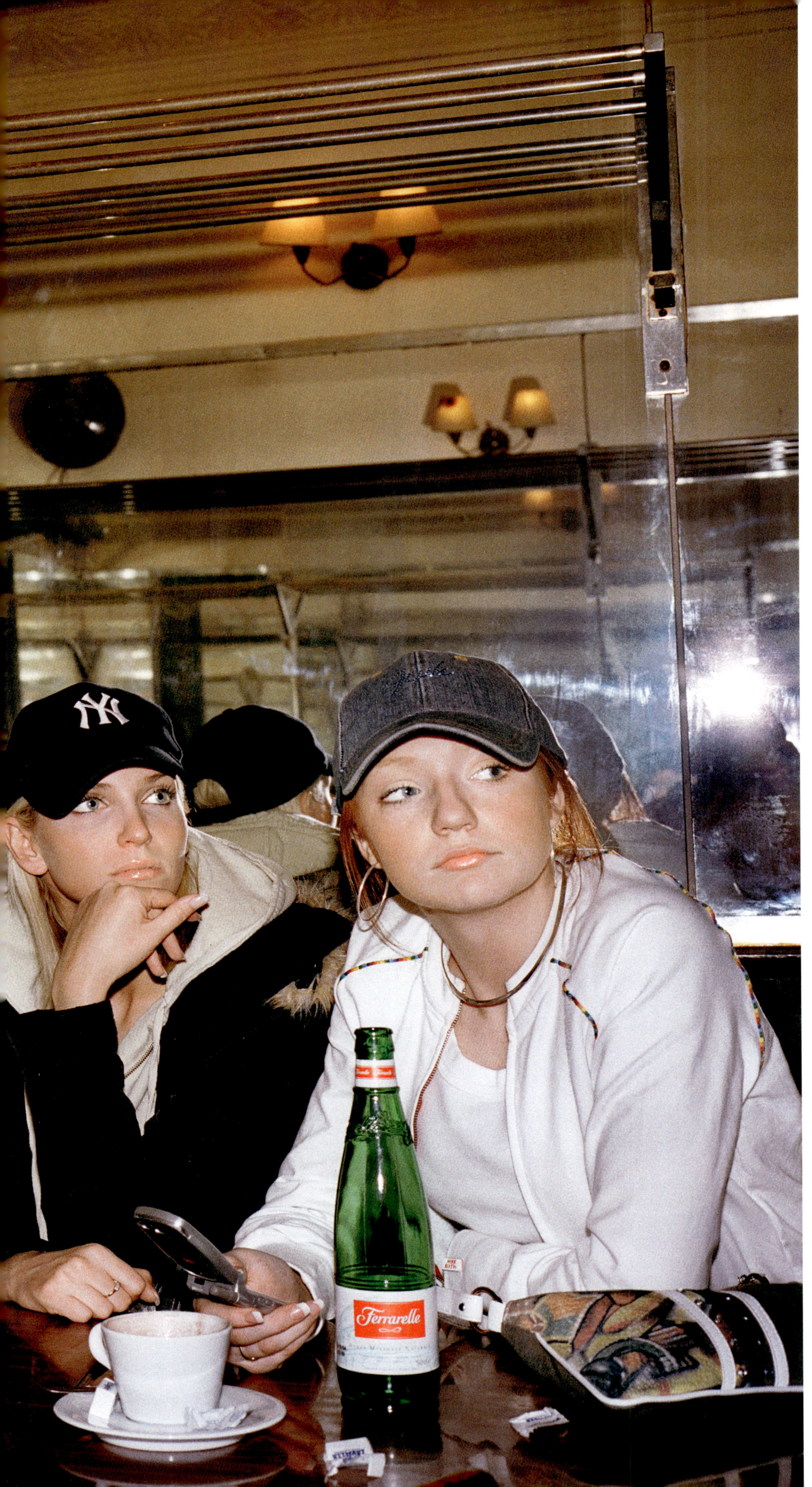

GIRLS ALOUD
By Neil Massey
June 2003

In spring 2003 I joined Girls Aloud in Paris while they were doing a promotional tour for their new single 'Sound Of The Underground'. It was a reportage feature for *The Face*. There was a lot of hanging around between interviews and jingles for French radio stations. The feature ended up capturing that mundane part of the music business. It was the early days of Girls Aloud and I remember they were a group of normal girls, who had been thrust into the limelight.
Neil Massey

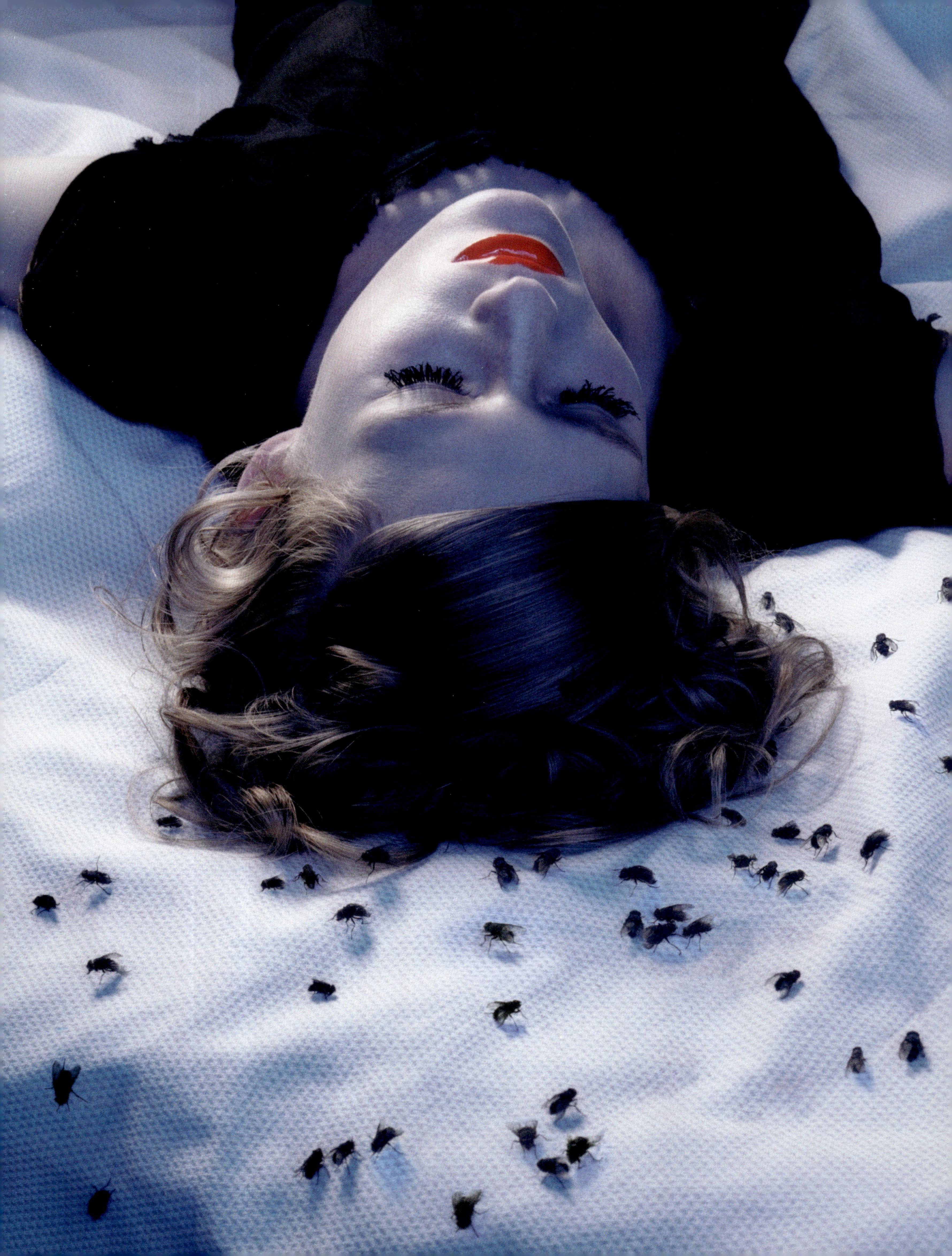

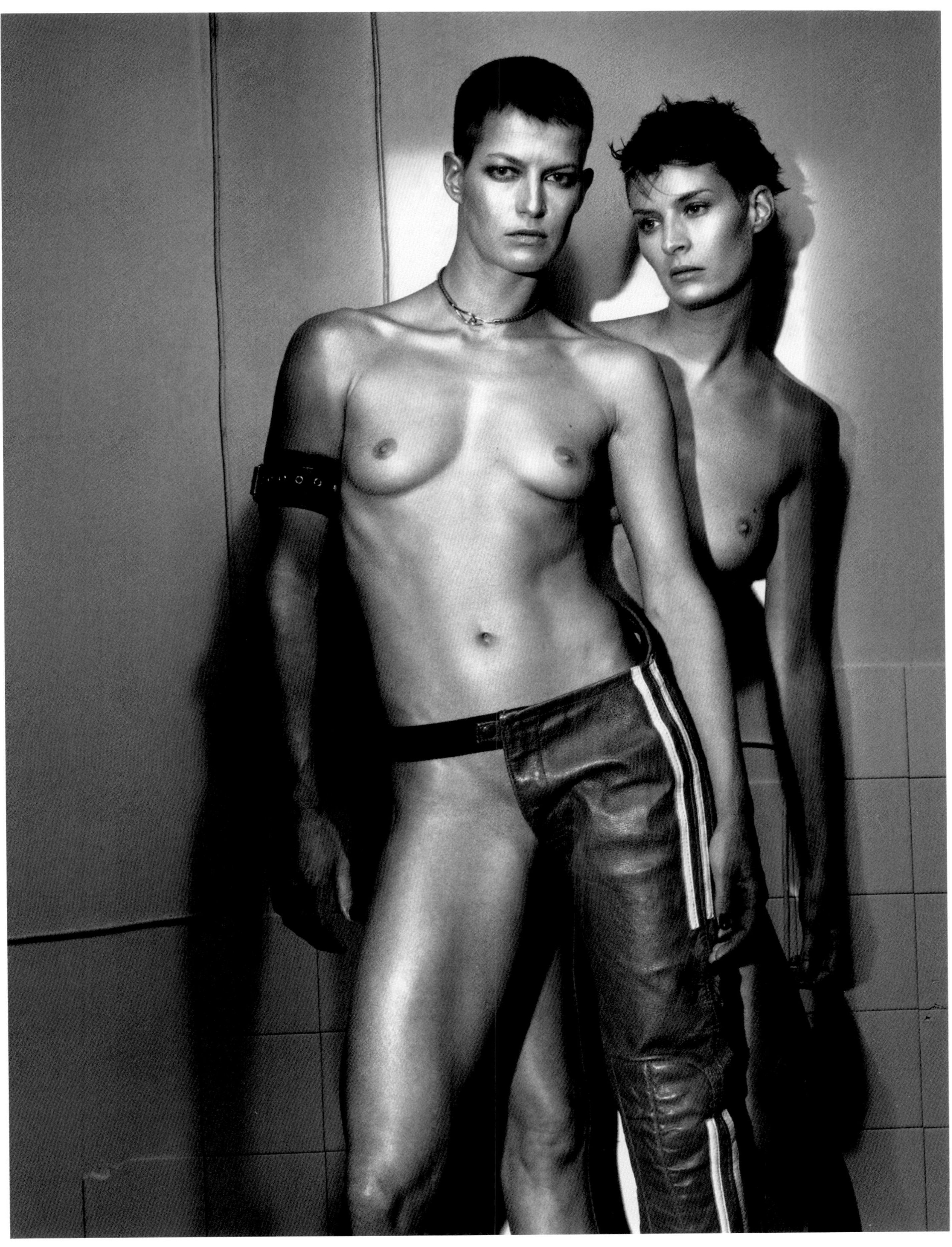

SLEEPING BEAUTY
By Miles Aldridge
September 2000

GRRRR BOW WOW WOOF
By Vincent Peters
Styled by Heathermary Jackson
June 2001

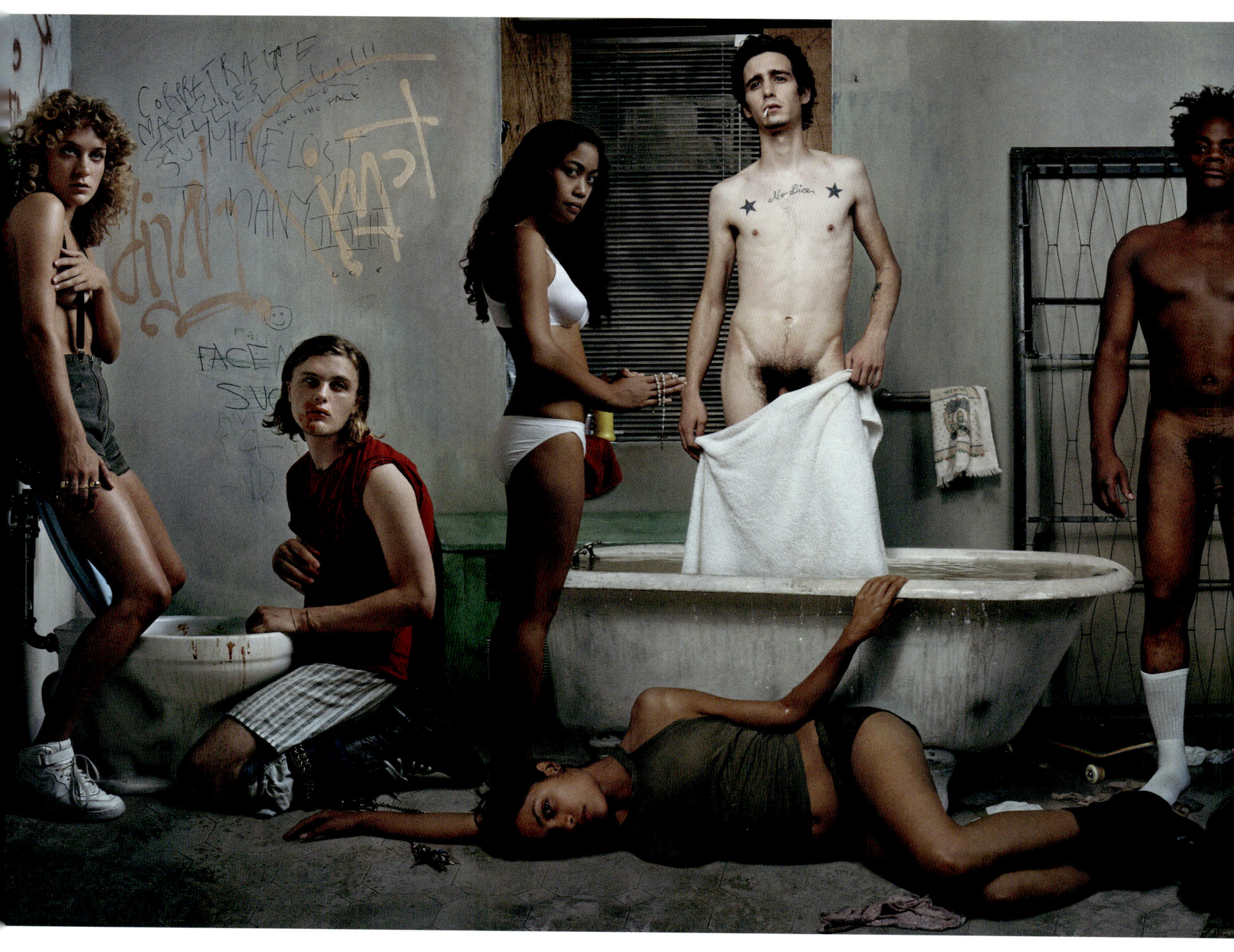

LARRY CLARK'S KIDS
By Steven Klein
Styled by Heathermary Jackson
October 2002

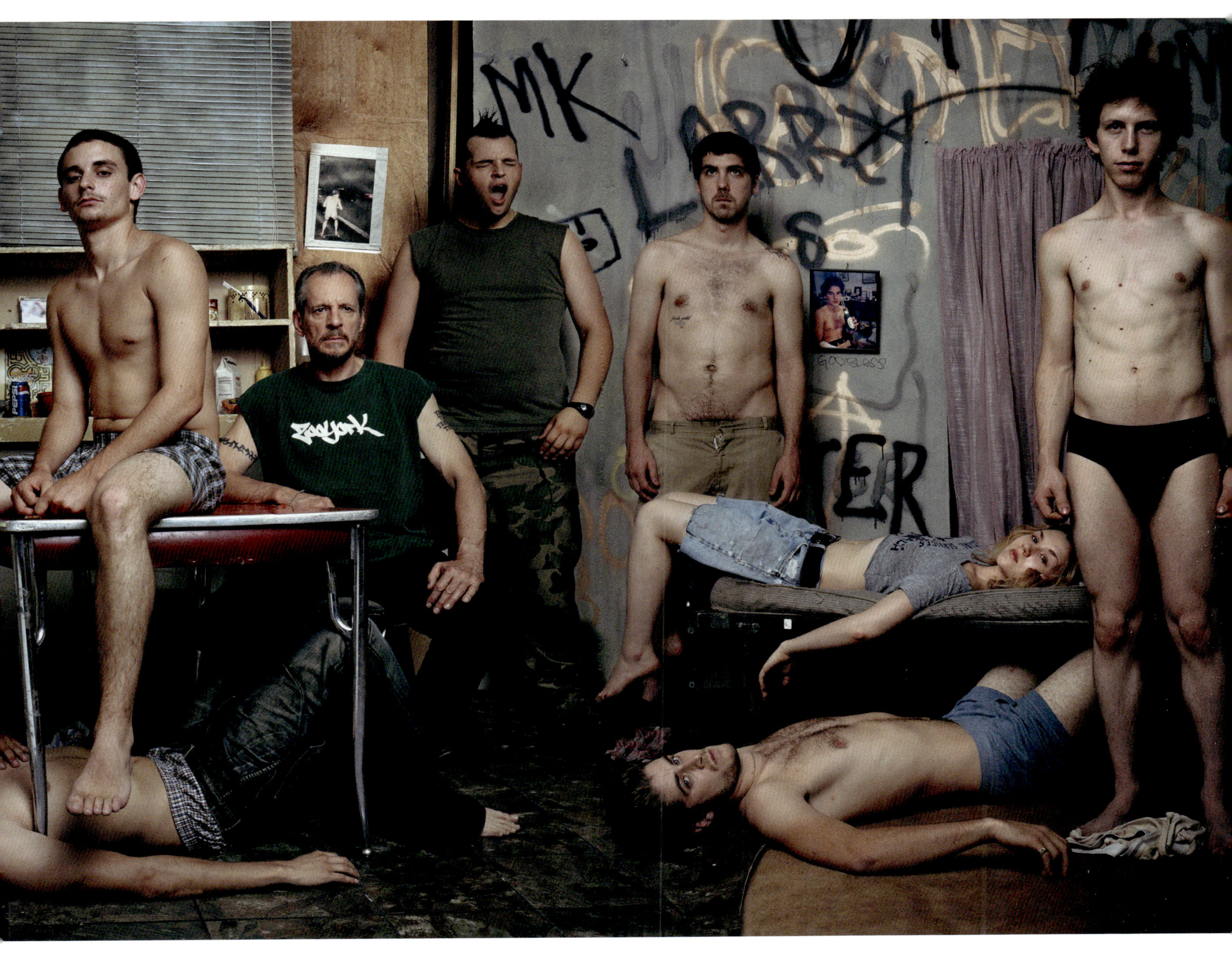

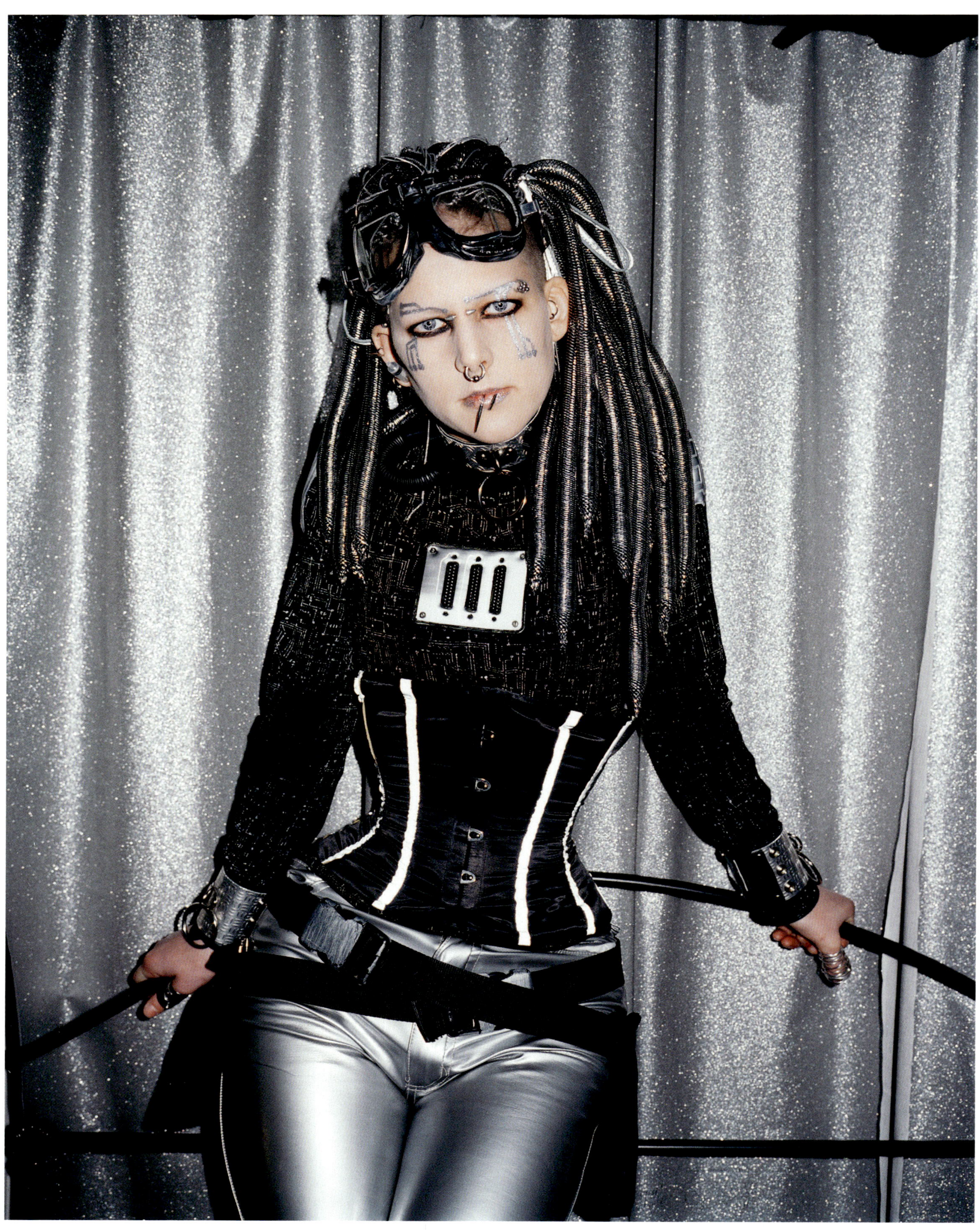

TRIBAL 4 EVER
By Frederike Helwig
Styled by Andrew Davis
February 2002

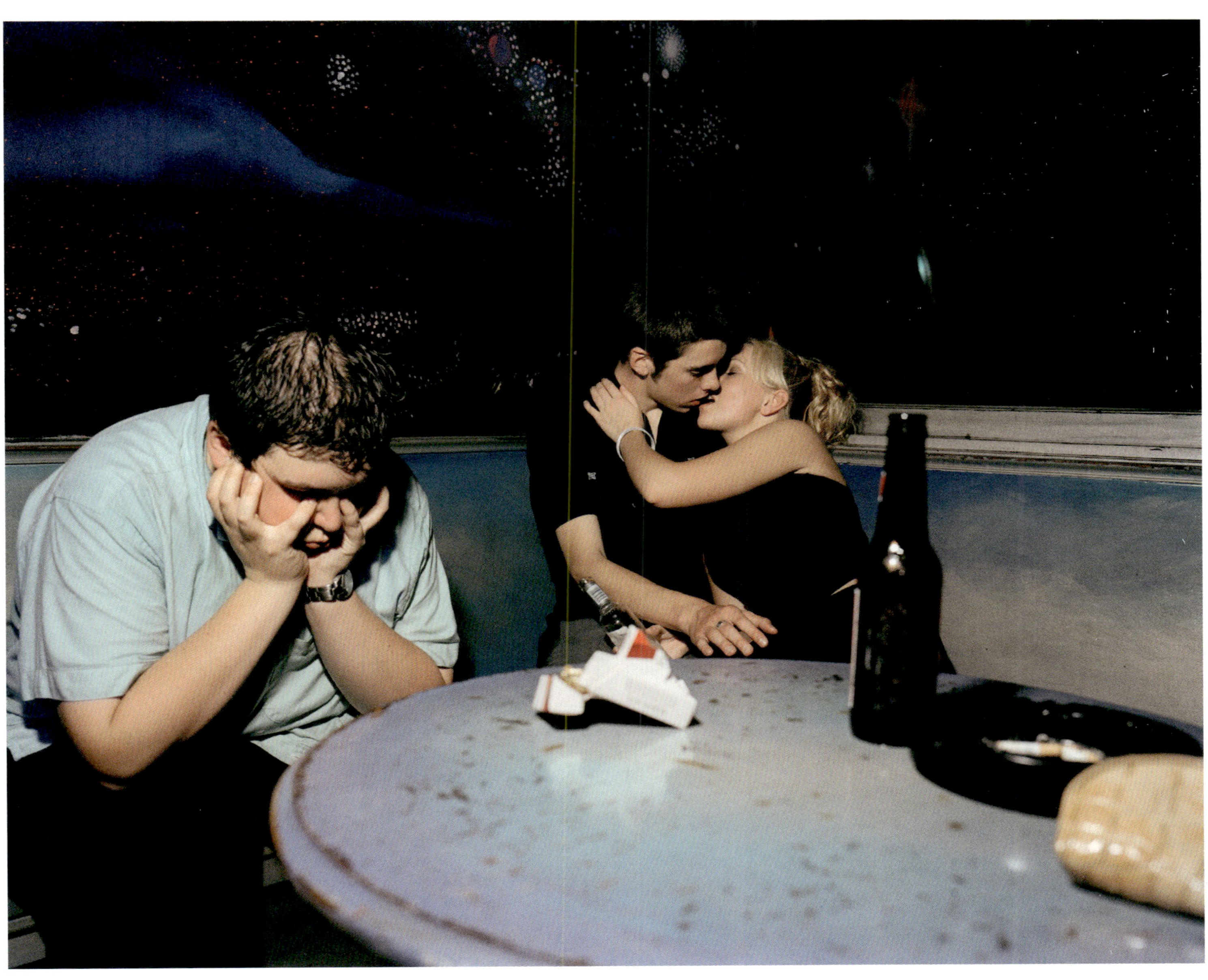

HOW'S YOUR EVENING SO FAR?
By Ewen Spencer
November 2000

Following pages
DISCARDED/REGARDED
By Miles Aldridge
Styled by Anthony Unwin
February 2003

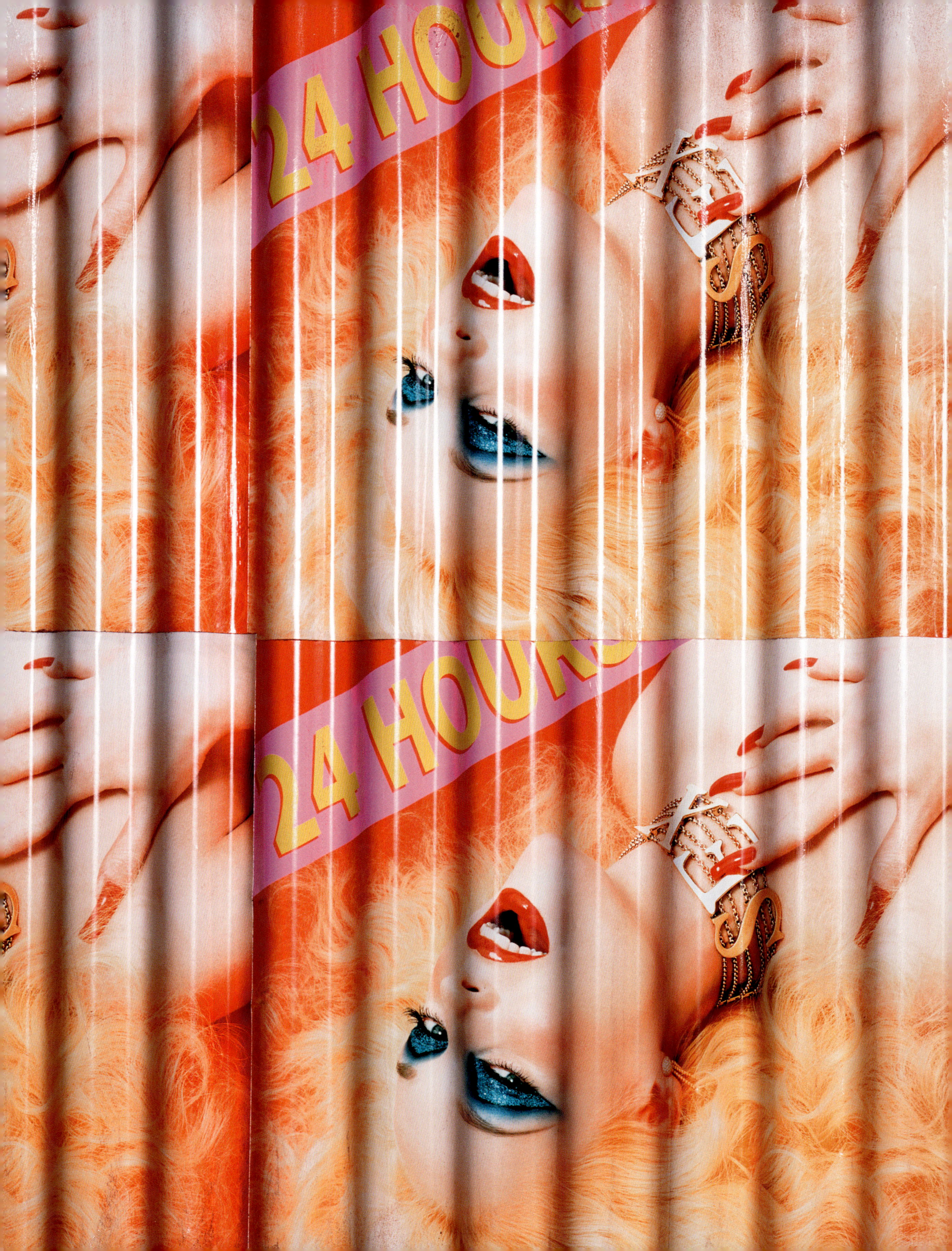
24 HOURS
24 HOURS

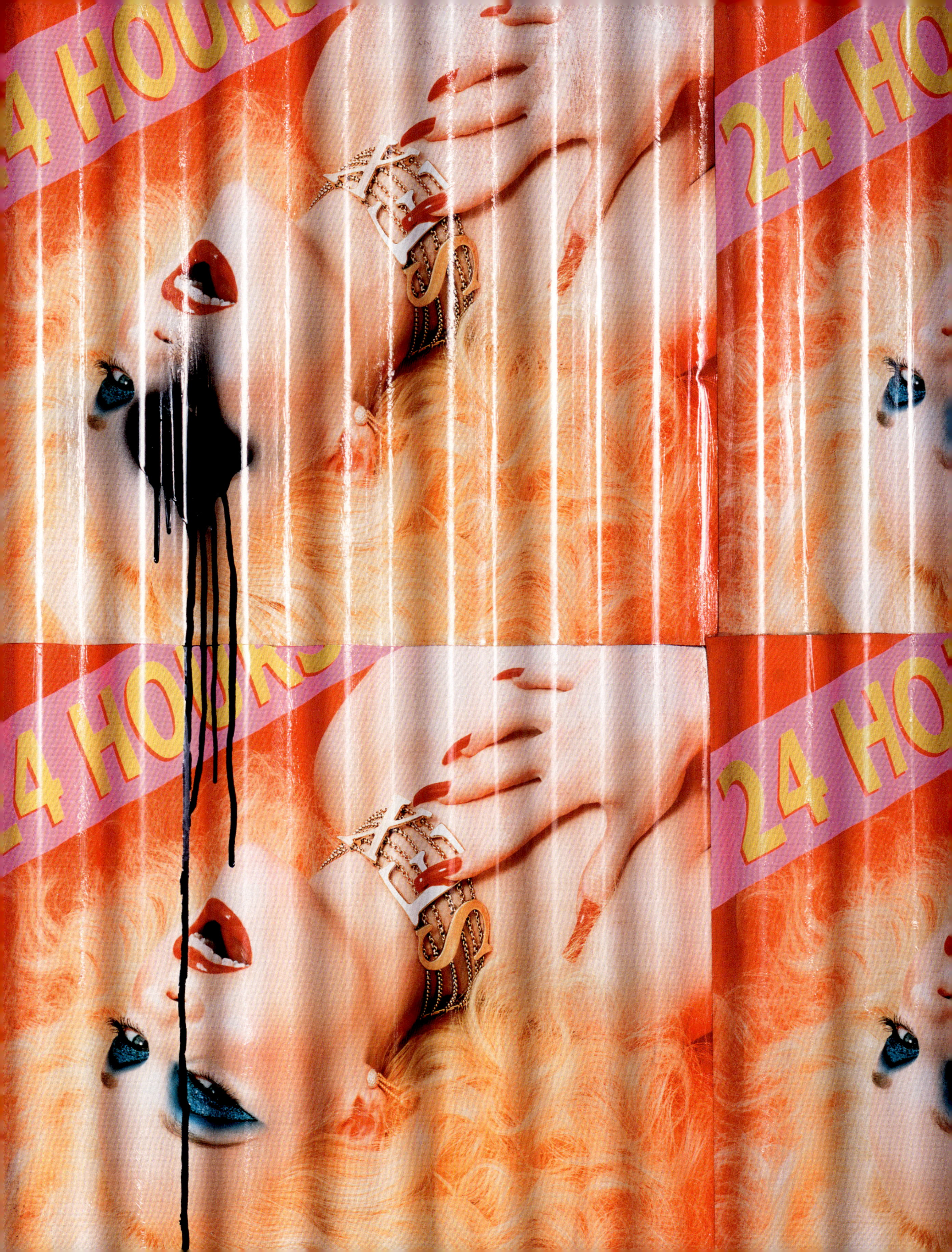

24 HOURS
24 HO
24 HOURS
24 HO

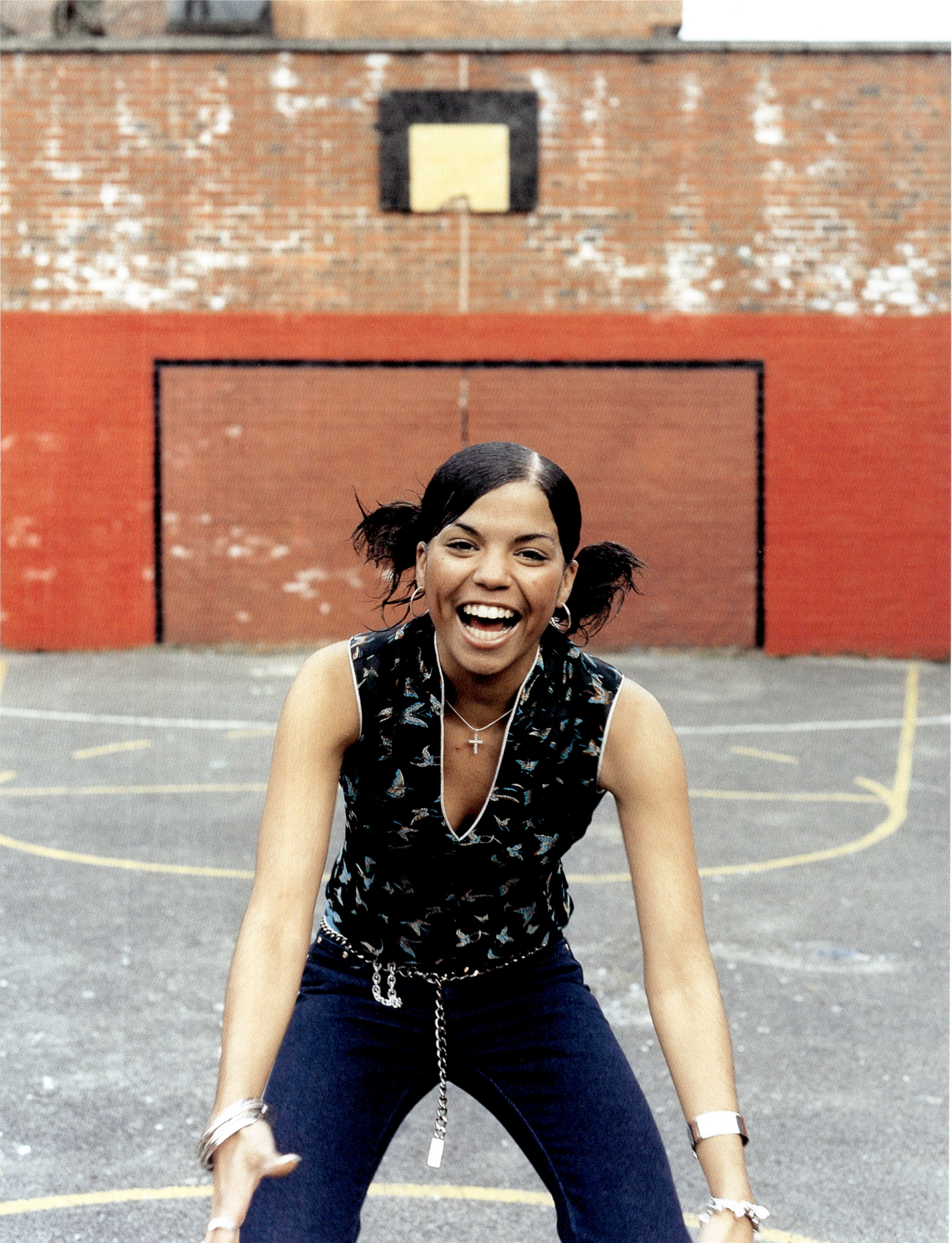

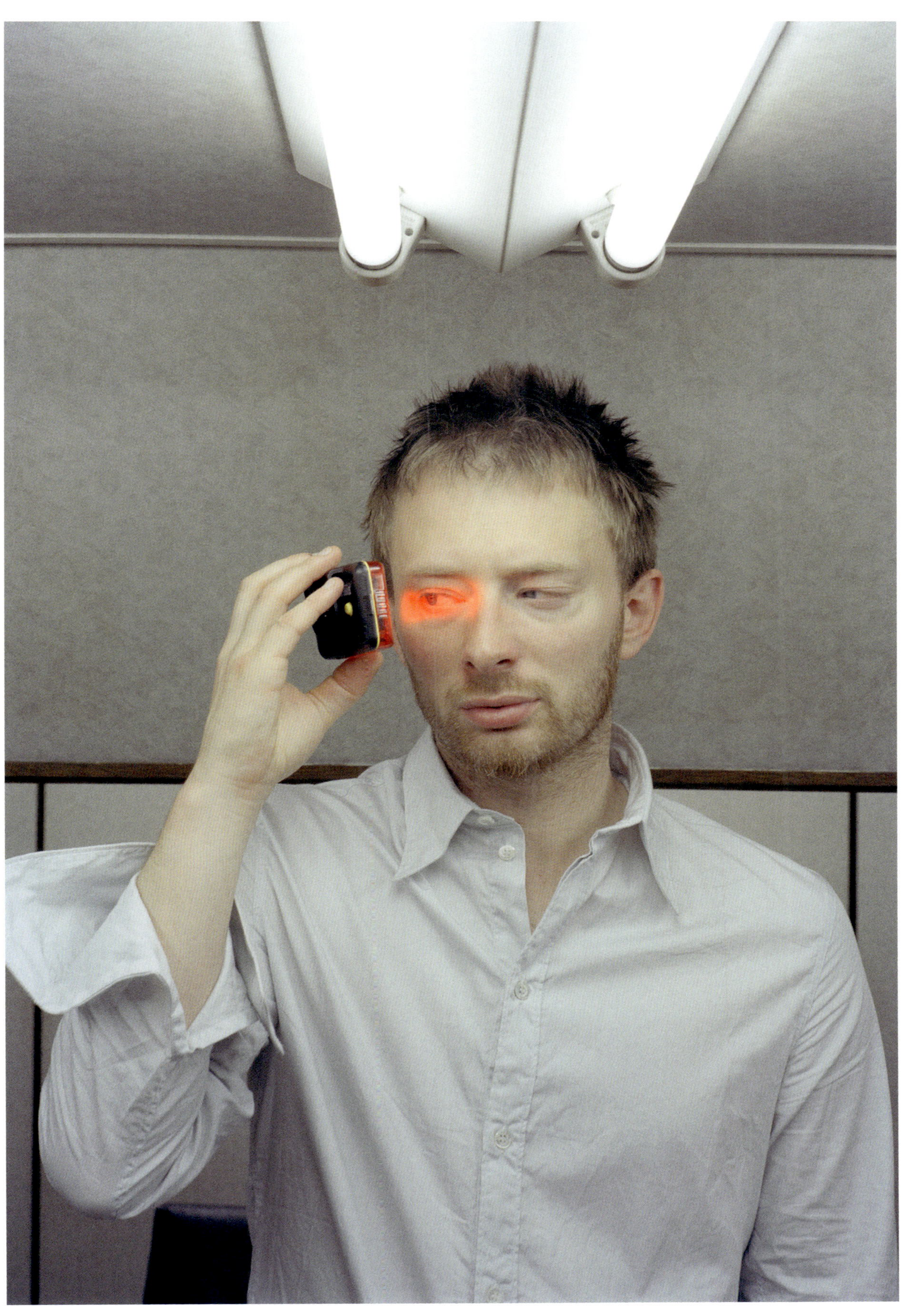

MS. DYNAMITE
By Gemma Booth
May 2001

THOM YORKE
By Jason Evans
January 2002

I worked with Radiohead over a six-year period and there was an understanding that we would work within a framework that suited them and their lives, which often defined the kinds of pictures we made. So I would work quickly and improvise during their downtime. It was very loose and relaxed, and we responded to the environments we found ourselves in. A reader wrote in to say that my Radiohead portraits were the most pretentious thing they'd ever seen in a magazine.
Jason Evans

DAVID BECKHAM
By Vincent Peters
Styled by Simon Robins
July 2001

If you were shooting a celebrity you'd always think, how can I change them? What character can I make them into, or how can I make them interesting? David always looked very put together and clean, so we wanted to make him look rough and dirty. I had lots of worn dirty clothes, and we were spraying him with coffee and soy sauce in a dingy studio in Manchester.
Simon Robins

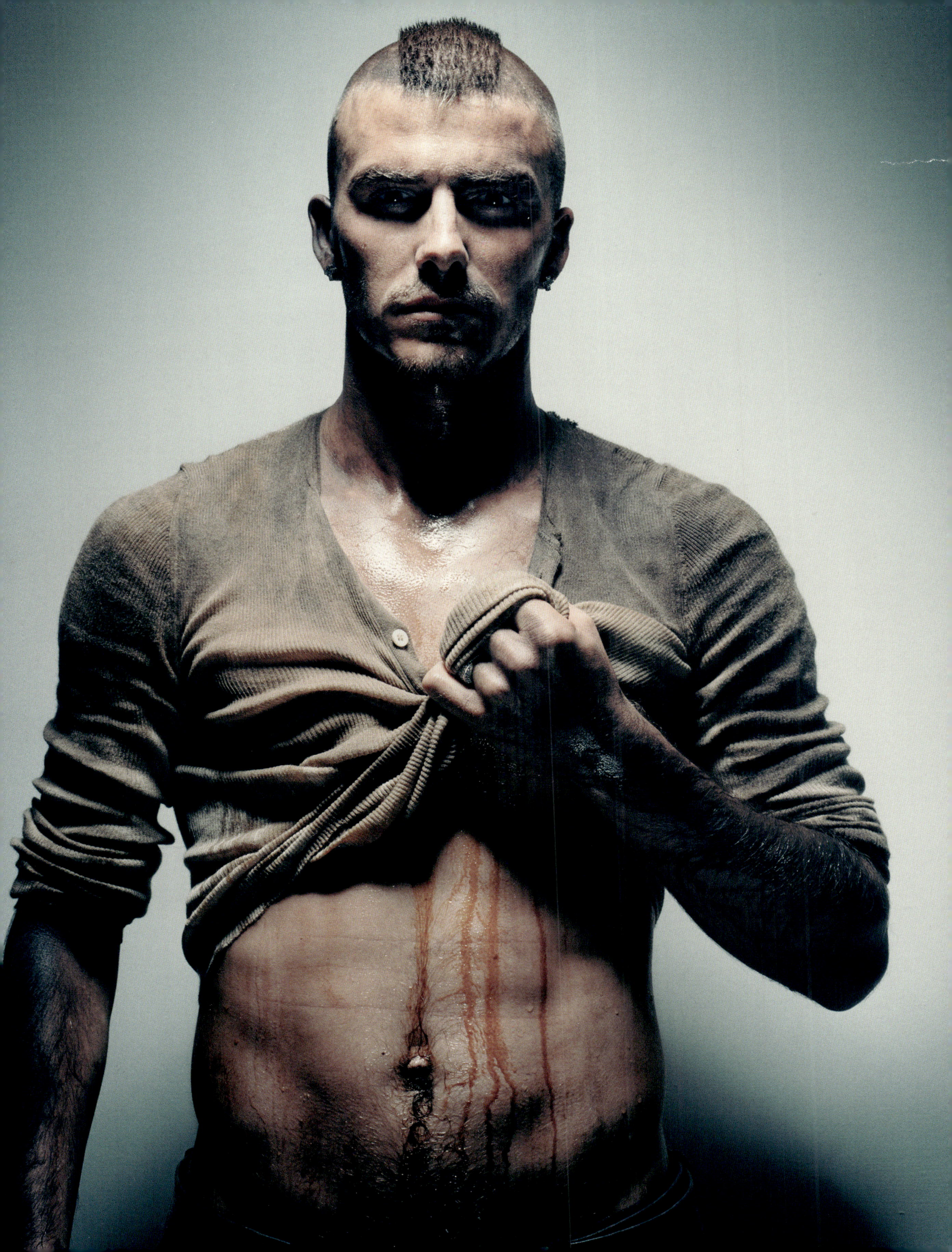

CULTURE IRL

A NEW ERA FOR THE FACE

MATTHEW WHITEHOUSE

It's a funny thing relaunching a heritage magazine title. How do you make what you do feel relevant for a new generation, without completely tarnishing the legacy of one of the most revered publications of all time, one that readers from Newcastle to New York have clutched to their hearts for over 40 years?

I suppose one thing we have going for us is that *The Face* was always about being young and alive right now. And since our relaunch in 2019, after a 15-year gap, we've tried to capture that as much as possible: looking less at the past (or even, to be honest, the future), and more at what's going on at precisely this moment. Facing outwards, not inwards. Reflecting the world and the people living in it.

That's what we look for in our photography. Of course, we want it to be cool and sexy and elevated and chic. But we want it to say something about the times we live in, too; honing in on ostensibly small stories and using them to communicate big ideas. In the end, we don't want *The Face* to be just another trendy magazine, covering things you're used to seeing in the pages of other trendy magazines. We want to photograph what young people are actually interested in: the places they actually go, the clothes they actually wear, the things they actually, really, genuinely care about. *The Face* should be a moment in time. A container of ideas. Something to grasp. Something to hold. Youth culture in its most potent form.

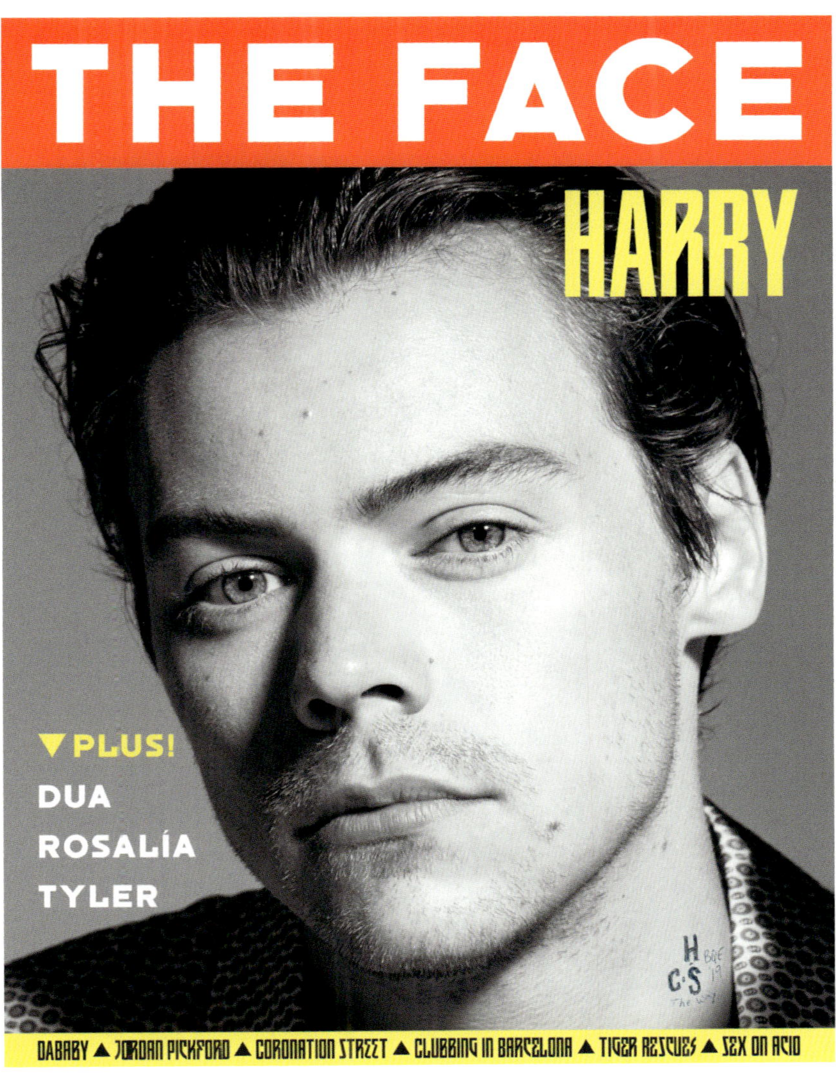

Of course, there have been obstacles along the way in this new life of the magazine; not least a global pandemic that forced half of the planet into lockdown six months after the release of our first issue. It certainly gave us pause, not least because we had to ask for the first time in the magazine's history: what is *The Face* if the kids aren't going out, dressing up, and enjoying themselves anymore?

I began to find my own answers on the day in January 2021 when we photographed Manchester record label, NQ, for the cover. Eight miles from its East Manchester headquarters, in the quiet suburbs of Didsbury and Northenden, a major incident was declared as Storm Christoph raged and more than 2,000 homes had to be evacuated after the river Mersey broke its banks during the peak of the pandemic's second wave. Thankfully, families were safe as defences held, just centimetres from flooding. But it felt a formidable piece of symbolism for what we wanted to capture with the new *Face*: a feeling that life, too, endures, always promising to rise and overflow.

Since then, we've tried to find life wherever we can. We have predominantly focused on stories from within our own shores, documenting rap groups in Belfast, cosmic scallies in Liverpool, and Lime bike hackers in London. But we haven't lost our curiosity for life elsewhere, too: from the drill and amapiano scenes of Accra and Johannesburg, to the banlieues of Paris and the bomb shelters of Ukraine. Not to mention the borderless world of the internet: inarguably the biggest culture shift to have happened while *The Face* was out of print, and a land buzzing with tribes and subcultures and joy, despite what the old fogeys will tell you. It's all life, whether IRL or not.

Our job, ultimately, remains as it always was: to be excited. To be so excited by a story that you manage to convince the best photographers, stylists and writers in the world to work on it. Then for them to create something so brilliant that the reader thinks it's the most exciting thing they've ever seen, too. I see what we do as a kind of folk art, in that sense: selecting ideas, evolving them, passing them on for someone else to do the same.

In that way, I hope we retain much of the spirit of the original *Face*. We certainly take seriously our role as guardians of this magic thing of which people have cherished memories. And we remain forever grateful to our founder Nick Logan, and all the people who set us on this journey. At the same time, I hope that if I pick up a new copy of *The Face* in 30 years, I might think it's a load of rubbish that was better in my day. If I do, I reckon whoever's making it will be doing a good job.

So, from Newcastle to New York, long may *The Face* continue. No matter where the culture shifts to next. ∎

Matthew Whitehouse is Editor-in-Chief of *The Face* magazine.

ENDNOTES

IMAGES WITH ATTITUDE:
PHOTOGRAPHY IN THE FACE

[1] Nilgin Yusuf in Sheila Rock, *80s Sound and Vision* (Frances Lincoln, London, 2022), p.9

[2] Neville Brody in Marcus Fairs, *Dezeen Book of Interviews* (Dezeen Limited, London, 2014), p.46

[3] Nick Logan, 'The Face's Greatest Hits', *The Guardian*, 4 December 2011

[4] Nick Logan's pitch letter for *The Face*, reproduced in Paul Gorman, *The Story of The Face: The Magazine that Changed Culture* (Thames & Hudson, London, 2017), p.21

[5] Chalkie Davies in Gorman, *The Story of The Face*, p.20

[6] Gorman, *The Story of The Face*, p.19

[7] Nick Logan, 'The Face's Greatest Hits', *The Guardian*, 4 December 2011

[8] Author interview with Sheila Rock, February 2024

[9] Author interview with Chalkie Davies, March 2024

[10] Neville Brody in Ben Beaumont-Thomas and Laura Snoad, 'How We Made The Face', *The Guardian*, 11 July 2017

[11] Neville Brody in Alex Needham, Ellie Violet Bramley and Morwenna Ferrier, '"It was Madness. It was Brilliant": the Irrepressible Spirit of The Face, by the People who Made it', *The Guardian*, 4 April 2019

[12] Author interview with Sheila Rock, February 2024

[13] Nick Knight in in Needham, Bramley and Ferrier, '"It was Madness. It was Brilliant"', *The Guardian*

[14] Robert Elms, 'Hard Times', *The Face*, September 1982, p.14

[15] Robert Elms in Gorman, *The Story of The Face*, p.73

[16] Nick Logan, 'Myths and Legends', in Mitzi Lorenz (ed.), *Buffalo: Ray Petri* (Westzone, London, 2000), p.147

[17] Ibid.

[18] Fraser McAlpine, '1960s Mod Slang We Should Use Today', *Modernist Society*, 2 February 2021, https://modernistsociety. blogspot.com/2021/02/1960s-mod-slang-we-should-use-today-by. html [Accessed 1 October 2024]

[19] Nick Logan interview, *Test Pressing*, 15 April 2012, https://www. testpressing.org/magazine/interviewnick-loganpublisher-editorthe-facesmash-hits [Accessed 1 October 2024]

[20] Robert Elms, 'The Cult with No Name', *The Face*, November 1980, p.26

[21] Author interview with Chalkie Davies, February 2024

[22] Nick Logan in Gorman, *The Story of The Face*, pp.62–3

[23] David Brittain in Craig McLean, 'At 50, The Photographers' Gallery Reflects on its Legacy – and The Face', *The Face*, 13 August 2021, https://theface.com/culture/ photographers-gallery-london-exhibition-light-years-felix-howard-buffalo-the-face-magazine-art-exhibition [Accessed 1 October 2024]

[24] Nick Logan, 'Myths and Legends', in Lorenz, *Buffalo*, p.147

[25] 'Style Shows a Leg!', *The Face*, May 1984, p.27

[26] Ray Petri in Dylan Jones, 'Buffalo Soldier', in Lorenz, *Buffalo*, p.157

[27] Nick Logan, 'Myths and Legends', in Lorenz, *Buffalo*, p.147

[28] Ray Petri, *The Face*, May 1985, p.44

[29] Neneh Cherry in Paul Rambali, 'A Walk on the Style Side', in Lorenz, *Buffalo*, p.175

[30] Nick Logan and Dylan Jones, 'Ray Petri', *The Face*, October 1989, p.10

[31] Nick Logan, 'Myths and Legends', in Lorenz, *Buffalo*, p.147

[32] Author interview with Robin Derrick, July 2024

[33] Author interview with Phil Bicker, July 2024

[34] Arthur House, 'Acid Reign', *Spectator*, 12 August 2017

[35] Sheryl Garratt in Needham, Bramley and Ferrier, '"It was Madness. It was Brilliant"', *The Guardian*

[36] David Sims in Charlotte Cotton, *Imperfect Beauty: The Making of Contemporary Fashion Photographs* (Victoria and Albert Museum, London, 2000), p.60

[37] Phil Bicker in Cotton, *Imperfect Beauty*, p.92

[38] 'About-Turn', *The Face*, March 1990, p.104

[39] Simon Foxton in Jason Evans, *W'happen* (Shoreditch Biennale, London, 1998), n.p.

[40] Nigel Shafran in Cotton, *Imperfect Beauty*, p.72

[41] David Sims in Cotton, *Imperfect Beauty*, p.60

[42] David Sims in Kari Molvar, 'Guido Palau and David Sims on What Changed Fashion Photography', *The New York Times*, 23 September 2014

[43] Anna Cockburn in Cotton, *Imperfect Beauty*, p.65

[44] Author interview with Phil Bicker, July 2024

[45] Phil Bicker, '*i-D*, *Jill*, and *The Face*: Fashion's Maverick Magazines', *Aperture*, Fall 2014, No. 216, p.109

[46] Corinne Day in Cotton, *Imperfect Beauty*, p.85

[47] Rosemary Ferguson in Needham, Bramley and Ferrier, '"It was Madness. It was Brilliant"', *The Guardian*

[48] Glenn O'Brien in Corinne Day, *May the Circle Remain Unbroken* (Mörel, London, 2014), n.p.

[49] Jon Savage, *England's Dreaming: The Sex Pistols and Punk Rock* (Faber & Faber, London, 1991)

[50] 'England's Dreaming', *The Face*, August 1993, p.104

[51] Amy Raphael in Gorman, *The Story of The Face*, p.342

[52] John Major, 'Speech to Conservative Group for Europe', 22 April 1993, *John Major Archive*, https://johnmajorarchive.org. uk/1993/04/22/mr-majors-speech-to-conservative-group-for-europe-22-april-1993/ [Accessed 1 October 2024]

[53] Cotton, *Imperfect Beauty*, p.7

[54] Author interview with Lee Swillingham, September 2024

[55] Stuart Spalding in Gorman, *The Story of The Face*, p.253

[56] Author interview with Lee Swillingham, April 2024

[57] Inez van Lamsweerde in Cotton, *Imperfect Beauty*, p.134

[58] Ibid.

[59] Lee Swillingham in Lauren Lipton, 'Seeking Stardom of Their Own', *The New York Times*, 31 December 2013

60 Jean Baudrillard, *Simulacra and Simulation*, (University of Michigan Press, Ann Arbor, 1994), p.1

61 Ekow Eshun, 'Norbert Schoerner', *European Photography*, October 2001, p.44

62 Andrea Giacobbe in *Dazed and Confused*, Dec/Jan 2000, cited in Kathryn Flett 'Altered Images', *Observer Magazine*, 28 May 2000

63 Sheryl Garratt in Gorman, *The Story of The Face*, p.257

64 Jim White, 'Changing the "Face" of the Nineties', *Independent*, 2 October 1995

65 Author interview with Elaine Constantine, March 2024

66 Wolfgang Tillmans, 'Fashion Stories', 2015, *Between Bridges*, https://www.betweenbridges.net/archive/berlin-keithstrasse/fashion-stories [Accessed 1 October 2024]

FEARLESS MODERNITY:
PORTRAITS OF MUSICIANS

1 Paul Gorman, *The Story of The Face: The Magazine that Changed Culture* (Thames and Hudson, London, 2017), p.21

2 David Toop, 'Electro. The Beat that Won't Be Beaten', *The Face*, May 1984, https://theface.com/archive/electro [Accessed 1 October 2024]

3 Gorman, *The Story of The Face*, p.234

4 Dick Hebdige 'Rap and Hip-Hop: The New York Connection' in Murray Forman and Mark Anthony Neal, *That's The Joint! The Hip Hop Studies Reader* (Routledge, Abingdon, 2004), p.230

WRITING STYLE:
THE NEW JOURNALISM OF THE FACE

1 Tom Wolfe, *The New Journalism* (Harper & Row, New York, 1973), p.35

2 Robert Elms, 'Hard Times', *The Face*, September 1982, https://theface.com/archive/hard-times [Accessed 1 October 2024]

3 David Toop, 'Electro: The Beat that Won't Be Beaten', *The Face*, May 1984, https://theface.com/archive/electro [Accessed 9 May 2024]

4 Miranda Sawyer, 'Tribal Gathering', *The Face*, August 1996, https://theface.com/archive/tribal-gathering [Accessed 1 October 2024]

5 Sheryl Garratt, 'Love Sees No Colour: Introduction', *The Face*, May 1992, p.41

6 Dick Hebdige, *Hiding in the Light: On Images and Things*, (Routledge, London, 1988), p.155

Dates given in captions in this book refer to the month and year in which the image or a variant of it was published in *The Face*.

The image titles in this book indicate the name of the sitter, the title of the fashion story as printed in the magazine, or the title given by the photographer.

Block quotes and extended captions have been taken from interviews with photographers, stylists, art directors and editors, conducted in 2024, except:
p.11, *The Face*, May 1980, p.3
p.16, Corinne Day in Charlotte Cotton, *Imperfect Beauty: The Making of Contemporary Fashion Photographs* (Victoria and Albert Museum, London, 2000), p.84
p.95, Sheila Rock, *80s Sound and Vision*, (Frances Lincoln, London, 2022), p.90

The following images are variants of those originally published:
p.13 (*Men's Where?*); p.36; p.44; p.45; pp.50–1; p.57; p.65; pp.66–7; p.74; p.75; p.92; pp.232–3.

MAGAZINE CREDITS

Behind the images in this book were talented models and creative teams, including hair and make-up artists, set designers and production assistants, as well as those working in image post-production. They were not always credited in *The Face* and it has not always been possible to identify them, but those that could be located are listed below, including those who were credited in the magazine by first-name only. Models listed here are those not credited in picture captions.

MODELS

Jon Abrahams, Azzedine Alaïa, AJ, A-Jay, Alex, Akure, Audrey Anderson, Andre, Mike Apaletegui, Alex Arts, Sarah Atkinson, Justine Baker, Emma Balfour, Tyson Ballou, Lee Barrett, Charlie Beat Nut, Zoe Bedeaux, Lara Belmont, Susie Bick, Judy Blame, Lyla Blue, Martin Boothe, Elise Brazier, Sue Brooks, Victoria Brown, James Bullard, James Bunster, Sarah Campbell, Jonathan Chick, Christopher, Larry Clark, Lisa Collins, Philippa Cooper, Culver, Daita, David, Lisa Davies, Rosario Dawson, Zaki Dee, Debbie Deitering, Laura Delicata, Devron, Tom Dixon, Donald, Claire Durkin, Juliet Elliott, Karen Elson, David Epstein, Esther, Rosemary Ferguson, Janet Fischgrund, Leo Fitzpatrick, Antonis Fragakis, Daniel Franzese, Jeffrey Fulvimari, Camillo Gallardo, Jean Paul Gaultier, Glen, Zaldy Goco, Lauren Gott, Bridget Hall, Carly Hanger, Carmen Hawk, Felchley B. Hawkes, Helene, Herbie, Mike Hill, Hilda from Kentish Town, Felix Howard, Claudia Huidobro, Harold Hunter, Count Indigo, Kae Lee Iwakawa, James, Jesse, Stephen Jasso, Jennifer Jones, Rufus Jordan, Nick Joseph, Nick Kamen, Adam Kavanagh, Kelly, Kevin, Leon, Tiffany Limos, Petra Lindblad, Matt Lloyd, Frédérique Lorca, Steve Machin, Keith Martin, Marcella, Nikki Mawhood, Maxwell, Clinton McKenzie, Alexander McQueen, Steve McQueen, Thomas Mead, Rachel Miner, Miyabe, Michelle Moraal, Kate Moss, Thierry Mugler, Aimee Mullins, Muraki, Sarah Murray, Nassim, Natasha, Nigel, Noah, Carsten Norgaard, Erin O'Connor, Orlando, Paul, Lorraine Pascale, Percy aka Medusa, Michael Pitt, Terry Preece, Tim Probert, James Ransone, Lisa Ratliffe, Missy Rayder, Rei, Leon Reid, Remy, Rev, Claire Ringrose, Robert, Matt Rose, Roy, Ryan, Sabrina, Michael Sanders, Chloë Sevigny, Aaron Sharif, Martine Sitbon, Tiara Smith Carey, Sonja, Sophie, Stepanek, Sara Stockbridge, Zonna Stokkink, Sunniva Stordahl, David Thomson, Laurence Treil, Tyler, Tom, Martin Unsworth, Kym Van Der Veeke, Eugenie Vincent, Vivienne Westwood, Marie-Sophie Wilson, Emma Woollard, and the Montparnasse Synagogue Trampoline Section.

MAKE-UP / HAIR / GROOMING

Aaren, Alan, Allessandro, Ray Allington, Jonathan Antin, Philippe Balagan, Barnabé, Regine Bedot, Michael Boadi, Mark Borthwick, James Brown, Adam Bryant, Sam Bryant, Lisa Butler, Kenny Campbell, Oribe Canales, Linda Cantello, Jo Carsberg, Jane Cohen, Jacqueline Colligan, Louise Constad, Christine Corbel, Noni Creme, Dina, Eddie D'is, Hina Dohi, Sharon Doswett, Charlie Duffy, Thomas Dunkin, Lisa Eastwood, Malcolm Edwards, Eugene, Ellis Faas, William Faulkner, Maria Louise Featherstone, Bernadette Francis, Sally Francomb, Val Garland, Gavin, Renee Gelston, Alice Ghendrih, Giovanni, David Grainger, Peter Gray, Charlie Green, Paul Gobel, Anne Guiomar, Cim Hahoney, Jonny Hallam, Jackie Hamilton-Smith, Rachael Howarth, Rick Haylor, Hiromi, Yoshi Hirose, Drew Jarrett, Jim, Tyler Johnston, Nicola Joss, Miranda Joyce, Julian, Julien, Yanni K, Karim, Diane Kendal, Paul Kennington, Lena Koro, Kinuko, Dalila Kummer, Stephan Lancien, Shiralee Law, Julian Lebas, James Lebon, Jacqui Lefton, Cathy Lomax, Marc Lopez, Lance Lowe, Stéphane Marais, Margot, Michelle Marsh, Tracy Martin, J Maskrey, Thelma Matthews, Sam McKnight, Kim Menzies-Foster, Sharon Miller, Gina Monaci, Kay Montano, Neil Moodie, Luigi Murenu, Maria Olsson, Dick Page, Guido Palau, Dennie Pasion, Jimmy Paul, Tom Pecheux, Paul Percival, Orlando Peter, Petros Petrohilos, Lucia Pieroni, Gordon Pindar, Bob Recine, Sarah Reygate, Sebastian Richard, Jeanette Rivera, Romain, Perrine Rougemont, Kevin Ryan, Jimo Salako, Raphael Salley, Samantha, Johnnie Sapong, Satoshi, Peter Savic, Electra Sawbridge, Peter Smith, Eugene Souleiman, Laurie Starrett, Debbie Stone, Michelle Sultan, Marc Thompson, Tish, Topolino, Francisco Valera, Matthias Van Hoof, Matthew Wade, Ward, Ashley Ward, Ellie Wakamatsu, Carla White, Paul Yacomine, Virginia Young, Nick Zieglar.

ASSISTANTS

Alex, Katherine Alexander, Kayo Ando, David Appleby, Jewel Arthur, Lindsay Baker, Daphne Balatsos, Jodi Barnes, Stefan Bartlett, John Bennett, Michael Bergan, Philip Berryman, Betty, Stella Brandt, David Burton, Alain Cagneau Palfroix, Karen Cannon, Beatrice Carle, Carlos, Alex Cayley, Sebastien Clivaz, Coco, Jon Compson, Ken Copsey, Jackie Cunnington, Steven Dance, Dickie Dawson, Emma Day, Giles Deacon, Chris Dennehy, Paul Derick, Jodokus Driessen, Shelley Durkan, John Eastmond, Gemma Edhouse-Smith, Sharon Elphick, John Fenn, Michael Fischer, Fred, Benjamin Galopin, Tanya Gill, Giovanna, Martha Gold, Seth Goldfarb, Annette Graham, Mickey Hayes, Clyde Haygood, Lucy Helton, Chris Henderson, Thomas Heydon, Anthony Hill, David Hughes, Heathermary Jackson, Caroline Jameson, JD, Joe, Nic Jottkandt, Julie, Louise Kay, Jason Kelvin, Devra Kinery, Rosalie Knox, Veronica Leone, Allison Luongo, Thomas Hayden, Jake Langbehn, Lankton, Leona, Dan Liu, Kate Malkin, Bertrand Marignac, Nick Maroudias, Martine, Davina Mashru, Steve Matthews, Mika, Mikolai, Stephane Milon, Monica, Nino Munoz, Brian O'Halragham, Brian O'Holloran, Linda Ohrstrom, Nick Otley, Daniela Paudice, Christophe Perrucon, Louise Pope, Stephen Poskitt, Pascal Preti, Beth Pugh, Jean Ravailler, Christophe Rihet, Simon Robins, Nunu Roney, Vanessa Rubio, Anne Saint Seer, Gabriel Sanchez, Wayne Shires, Katia Sisto, James Sleaford, John Spencer, Christoph Steiber, Dan Stevens, Sylvia, Tammara, David Thomas, Shazzy Thomas, Tobias Toyberg, Nicola Thysen, Jonas Unger, Anthony

Unwin, Lona Vigi, Kat Vinegrad, Eliot Waters, Caroline Watson, Ralph Wenig, Michelle Williams, Rodney Williams, Steven Zeigler.

PRODUCTION / COORDINATION / SETS
Anita, Paula Artioli, Katy Baggott, Zoe Bedeaux, Lee Beurs, Martin Bourne, Julie Brown, Simon Costin, Jeb Darge, Renaud Deschamps, Niki Duku, Paul Elliman, Kate Ellis, James Grant, Lucy Helton, Rob Holmes, Morgan Kennedy, Kirsten Kish, Sarah Lawrence, Camilla Lowther, Claire Mizés, David Morgan, Daniel McKay, Luc Pointereau, Mark Pritchard, Gabriel Rey, Gerard Santos, Marco Santucci, Amie Server, Kim Sion, Siovakni, Rowina Smith, Andrea Stanley, Stevie Stewart, Beverley Streeter, Tom Swayne, Kristen Vallon, Marla W., Andy Ward.

POST-PRODUCTION / PRINTING
Nadira Aourir, Richard Baker, Dean Baker, BDI Colour Lab, Bureau Jasper Bode, Mark Boyle, Leon Chew, Colour Solutions, Contour Colour, Dai Nippon, Brian Dowling, Mike Fiveash, Steve Jackson, Janvier, George Lewis, LTI, Magdalena, Dan Maloney, Kim Mannes-Abbott, Bob Martin, Metro Imaging, George Miller, Leanne Priestly, Arash Radpour, Dan Richardson, Steve Seal, Sixty Eight Degrees, Karin Spijker, Studio Yannick Morisot, Rob Taylor, David Wayman.

PICTURE CREDITS

The National Portrait Gallery would like to thank the copyright holders for granting permission to reproduce works illustrated in this book. Every effort has been made to contact the holders of copyright material, and any omissions will be corrected in future editions if the publisher is notified in writing.

DIRECTOR'S ACKNOWLEDGEMENTS

Victoria Siddall

As well as thanking the exhibition's curators, Sabina Jaskot-Gill, Norbert Schoerner and Lee Swillingham, I wish to extend my thanks to all those within the Gallery and outside it who have made *The Face Magazine: Culture Shift* possible.

Thanks to those colleagues who have supported this exhibition from its inception: Rosie Wilson, Director of Programmes, Partnerships and Collections; Anna Starling, Director of Commercial and Operations; Denise Vogelsang, Director of Audiences, Communications and Development; Sarah Hilliam, Director of Development; and Liz Smith, Director of Learning, Engagement and Access. Thanks also to our former Chief Curator Alison Smith for her support. I am immensely grateful to the Curatorial and Exhibitions teams for their outstanding curatorial and organisational work: Eloise Stewart, Head of Exhibitions; Ruby Rees-Sheridan, Assistant Curator, Photography; Tash Powell and Sophie Clark, Exhibitions Managers; Imo Jeffes, Exhibitions Officer; and Callum Brunton, Exhibitions Assistant. I am grateful to all those in the Gallery's Communications, Learning, Retail, Development and International teams for ensuring that this work reaches the widest possible audience, in particular Poppy Andrews, Head of Communications; Saoirse Walsh, Senior Marketing Manager; Helen Whiteoak, Head of Programmes and Engagement; Ed Simpson, Buying and Product Development Manager; and Grainne McCarthy, Corporate Development Manager. To Jude Simmonds, Jahnavi Inniss and Natalia de Wilde, whose design has brought these works to life; to Oliver Tratt, Exhibition Build Project Manager; and to the entire Art Handling team: thank you.

My thanks go to Kara Green, Senior Publishing Manager; Laura Cherry, Project Editor; Priti Kothary, Production Manager; Katie Anderson, Picture Researcher; and Jemma Jacobs, Publishing Assistant, without whose dedication and expertise this publication would not have been possible. For the design of this book, I am grateful to Lee Swillingham, Stuart Spalding and Fiona Firminger at Suburbia. Particular thanks go to our dedicated Digital team: Isabelle Reynolds-Logue, Digitisation Manager and Ines Alves, Digitisation Officer; and to Gloss NYC for retouching support on this project.

The voices of numerous individuals beyond the Gallery have helped bring this work to life. The support of the current team at *The Face* magazine, especially Jerry Perkins, CEO of Wasted Talent; Dan Flower, Global Managing Director at *The Face*, Leo Robins, Creative Strategy Director at *The Face*, and Matthew Whitehouse, Editor-in-Chief of *The Face*, has been invaluable. I extend my heartfelt thanks to Neville Brody, Elaine Constantine, Jill Furmanovsky, Ekow Eshun, Sabina Jaskot-Gill, Nick Logan, Glen Luchford, Jamie Morgan, Pete Paphides, Sheila Rock, Nancy Rohde, Norbert Schoerner, Stéphane Sednaoui, Lee Swillingham and Matthew Whitehouse for their insightful contributions to the book. Finally, I offer my thanks again to the photographers for their generosity in contributing their images and stories. ■

CURATORS' ACKNOWLEDGEMENTS

Sabina Jaskot-Gill, Norbert Schoerner and Lee Swillingham

Bringing together photography from 25 years of *The Face* magazine has required collaboration and cooperation on a large scale, resulting in the most comprehensive survey of the magazine's photographic imagery to date. It has been a great pleasure to work closely as a curatorial team to bring this exhibition and publication to life. The process has created a unique opportunity to celebrate the magazine and its contributors, and has brought many members of *The Face* family back together again. The enthusiasm from all parties involved is testament to the overwhelming admiration felt for the magazine and its remarkable history.

Firstly, we would like to thank *The Face*'s founder, Nick Logan. It was vital for us to seek his approval before we began to develop this exhibition, and we have endeavoured to stay authentic to the ethos he set out for the magazine; a publication which has radically shaped our visual culture over the 45 years since it launched.

We are delighted to have collaborated with the current team at *The Face*, in particular Jerry Perkins, Dan Flower, Leo Robins and Matthew Whitehouse, who are continuing Logan's vision for a disruptive, creative and inclusive magazine.

We are very grateful to all the magazine's photographers for their generosity in supporting this exhibition, and for taking the time to speak with us about their work. It has been a huge endeavour to find many of the original negatives, transparencies and prints, many of which had previously only had a life within the pages of the magazine. We are incredibly grateful to photographers and their teams for all the work that has gone into searching their archives and locating the images.

Thanks are due to the following photographers, agents, representatives and studios: John Akehurst, Miles Aldridge, Mert Alas and Marcus Piggott, Mark Alesky, Brian Anderson (Inez & Vinoodh), Gabriela Antunes (Mario Testino), Sarah Appelhans (Derek Ridgers), Brian Aris, Peter Ashworth, Antoinette Aurell, Susie Babchick, Enrique Badulescu, Janette Beckman, Andy Bettles, Bruno Biagi (Jean Paul Gaultier), Andreas Bleckmann, Adrian Boot, Gemma Booth, Victor Boullet, Stefanie Breslin (Art Partner), Julian Broad, Lucas Bullens and Tom Moran (Norbert Schoerner), Johnny Byrne and Ghretta Hynd (David LaChapelle), Gemma Cammidge (Elaine Constantine/Industry Art), Jake Chessum, Donald Christie, Liz Collins, Gracey Connelly (Craig McDean), Elaine Constantine, Andree Cooke (Marcus Tomlinson), Anton Corbijn, Samuel Coviello (Miles Aldridge), Richard Croft, Kevin Cummins, Chalkie Davies, Ella Davies (Bridgeman Images), Kevin Davies, Eve Dawoud (David Sims), Corinne Day, James Dimmock, Paul Donahue, Paula Ekenger (Sølve Sundsbø), Sean Ellis, Robert Erdmann, Jason Evans, Simon Fowler, Jill Furmanovsky, David Gamble, Jean Paul Gaultier, Andrea Giacobbe, Anthony Gordon, Jean-Paul Goude, Melissa Green (Jill Furmanovsky), Filipine Guyonnaud (Ellen von Unwerth), Frederike Helwig, Anna Hill-Szaszy (Corinne Day Estate), Martina Hoogland Ivanow, Toyin Ibidapo, Lee Jenkins, Liz Johnson Artur, Steven Klein, Charlotte Knight (Nick Knight/Show Studio), Nick Knight, Bettina Komenda,

David LaChapelle, Inez van Lamsweerde and Vinoodh Matadin, Sandra Laye (Mike Laye), Glen Luchford, Andrew Macpherson, Neil Massey, EJ McCabe, Chris McCoy (Steven Klein), Craig McDean, Toby Mcfarlan Pond, Josselin Merazguia and Sally Waterman (Juergen Teller), Donald Milne, Felix Mondino (Jean Baptiste Mondino/ICONOCL \ST IMAGE), Jean Baptiste Mondino, Eddie Monsoon, Jamie Morgan, Riyo Nemeth (Stéphane Sednaoui), Isabelle Nicolas (Jean Baptiste Mondino/ICONOCL \ST IMAGE), Ewelina Nietupska (Robert Erdmann), Niccolò Pacilli (Mert & Marcus), Cindy Palmano, Vincent Peters, Steven Pranica, Anja Sophie Prilhofer (Vincent Peters), Steve Pyke, Bettina Rheims, Dean Rhys-Morgan (Tony Viramontes), Derek Ridgers, Peter Robathan, Sheila Rock, Luis Sanchis, Carole Sandrin (Bettina Rheims/Institut pour la photographie), Franck Sauvaire, John Scarisbrick, Norbert Schoerner, Collier Schorr, Stéphane Sednaoui, Nigel Shafran, David Sims, Graham Smith, Pennie Smith, Ewen Spencer, Carol Starr, Aki Sukita (Masayoshi Sukita), Masayoshi Sukita, Sølve Sundsbø, Juergen Teller, Yaël Temminck (Anton Corbijn), Mario Testino, Christian Thompson, Marcus Tomlinson, Anthony Tran (Trunk Archive), Max Vadukul, Tony Viramontes, Ellen von Unwerth, Aaron Watson (Albert and Norman Watson), Albert Watson, Norman Watson and Aleksandra Zagozda (Glen Luchford).

Credit must also go to *The Face*'s former Art Directors – Neville Brody, Robin Derrick, Phil Bicker, Boris Bencic, Lee Swillingham, Craig Tilford and Graham Rounthwaite – who each shaped the magazine's approach to design and photography, and who believed in and supported the careers of the photographers and stylists featured.

Many of these contributors took the time to speak with us about about their experiences at the magazine, providing unique insights into the making of the images. In particular, we would like to thank the following Fashion Editors and stylists: Caroline Baker, Polly Banks, Malcolm Beckford, Giannie Couji, Greg Fay, Kathryn Flett, Katie Grand, Adam Howe, Cathy Kasterine, Justin Laurie, Mitzi Lorenz, Alister Mackie, Seta Niland, Simon Robins, Nancy Rohde, Charlotte Stockdale and Melanie Ward. We are grateful to writer and editor Jo-Ann Furniss for sharing her knowledge of the Buffalo movement and the history of *The Face*.

We are especially grateful to private lenders of artworks, Mitzi Lorenz and Nancy Rohde.

Special thanks to Magnus Andersson, Raja Sethuraman and Ali Zilahy at Gloss Studio, and their colleagues Jacqueline Bernal, Janine Crowley, Ron LeGates and Allan Ng, for undertaking the meticulous retouching of lost images, allowing photographers' work to be represented in the exhibition and the catalogue.

We would also like to extend our thanks to all those who we aren't able to credit individually, in particular the talented creative teams behind each shoot – make-up artists, hairdressers, assistants and shoot coordinators – as well as those who re-touched, post-produced and printed these photographs. Every one of these individuals represents a vital part of the success of the final image.

We would like to thank the National Portrait Gallery for commissioning this exhibition, particularly former Director, Dr Nicholas Cullinan OBE, and former Executive Director of Programmes and Partnerships, Sarah Tinsley. We are grateful to the current Gallery team for their continued support, including Director, Victoria Siddall, as well as Rosie Wilson, Director of Programmes, Partnerships and Collections, and Eloise Stewart, Head of Exhibitions.

We are incredibly grateful to colleagues across departments at the National Portrait Gallery who have worked tirelessly to bring this very complex project to fruition. Thank you to Tash Powell, Exhibitions Manager; Sophie Clark, Exhibitions Manager; Ruby Rees-Sheridan, Assistant Curator, Photography; Imo Jeffes, Exhibitions Officer and Callum Brunton, Exhibitions Assistant, for all the dedicated work they have put into this exhibition and publication. Thanks also to the Gallery's Paper Conservation Manager, Emmanuelle Largeteau, and Digitisation team, Isabelle Reynolds-Logue and Ines Alves, for preparing images for the catalogue, and to the curators in the Photographs department – Georgia Atienza, Mariama Attah and Clare Freestone – for their continued support. We are incredibly grateful to Jude Simmons, Head of Design, as well as Jahnavi Inniss and Natalia de Wilde, for their creative exhibition design.

Norbert Schoerner would like to extend a special thanks to Juanita Boxill for her thoughtful advice and intuitive support. Sabina Jaskot-Gill would like to thank Freyja and James Campbell for all their encouragement. Lee Swillingham would like to thank the following people for their support and encouragement during the early years at Wagadon: Boris Bencic, Phil Bicker, Robin Derrick, Sheryl Garratt, Patrick Glover, Dylan Jones, Nick Logan, Rod Sopp, Stuart Spalding, Ian Swift and Kelly Worts. Special thanks go to Kathy Swillingham.

For the project management and production of the book, we are hugely grateful to Laura Cherry, Project Editor; Katie Anderson, Picture Researcher; Jemma Jacobs, Publishing Assistant; Priti Kothary, Production Manager, as well as Kara Green, Senior Publishing Manager, and Anna Starling, Director of Commercial and Operations. Thanks to Fiona Firminger and Stuart Spalding at Suburbia for design, to Rosalind Furness and Mark Hooper for copy-editing, and to Anjali Bulley for proofreading.

Finally, we owe a big thank you to Magdalene Keaney and Robin Muir for introducing the three of us, which sparked the idea to develop this project. ■

Published in Great Britain
by National Portrait Gallery Publications
National Portrait Gallery
St Martin's Place
London WC2H 0HE

Published to accompany the exhibition:
The Face Magazine: Culture Shift

National Portrait Gallery, London
20 February – 18 May 2025

This exhibition has been made possible as a result of the Government Indemnity Scheme. The National Portrait Gallery, London, would like to thank HM Government for providing indemnity and the Department for Culture, Media and Sport and Arts Council England for arranging the indemnity.

Every purchase supports the National Portrait Gallery, London. For a complete catalogue of current publications, please visit our website at www.npg.org.uk/publications

Text pp.8–21 by Sabina Jaskot-Gill
Text pp.28–9 by Pete Paphides
Text pp.78–83 by Jamie Morgan. Edited from the upcoming memoir by Jamie Morgan, from the chapter 'Spirit of Buffalo'.
Text pp.240–1 by Ekow Eshun
Text pp.278–9 by Matthew Whitehouse

ISBN 978-1-85514-584-9 (hardback)
ISBN 978-1-85514-589-4 (paperback)

A catalogue record for this book is available from the British Library

10 9 8 7 6 5 4 3 2 1

Director of Commercial and Operations: Anna Starling
Senior Publishing Manager: Kara Green
Project Editor: Laura Cherry
Picture Research: Katie Anderson
Production Manager: Priti Kothary
Copy-editors: Rosalind Furness and Mark Hooper
Proofreading: Anjali Bulley
Art Direction and Design: Suburbia

Printed and bound in Belgium by Graphius
Reproduction by Dexter Premedia

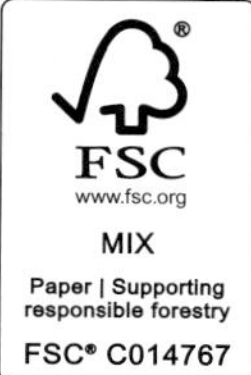

This publication is printed on FSC certified paper and has been manufactured using 100% vegetable oil-based inks and solvent-free adhesives.

Front cover:
Face Off, by David Sims, 1998.
© David Sims – Art Partner/Trunk Archive.